OCEANS APART

The Journal Of A Seaman

by

Michael John Kenn A.B.

DEDICATION

For my late mother who suggested that
I write this in the first place.

ACKNOWLEDGEMENTS

Many thanks to my daughter Dawn for her most considerable help with the English language and proofreading. Also to my son David and his partner Sally not only for their help finding my publisher, but also for their invaluable help with their IT skills.

Many thanks too to Rachael Holtom who first convinced me I could do it and to Dennis Marriott and Ben Davies for their expertise with the photographs. Heartfelt thanks go to the late Geoff Rock for his valuable help and advice; he will be sorely missed.

Most importantly many special thanks to Margaret, my wife, without whose help, patience and understanding this could not have been done.

The days of my youth
Have long since gone by
But the memories flood back
With a smile, or a sigh.
They speed through my mind
Like birds in full flight
And they are all just like ships
That passed in the night.

Some memories I have
Are like dreams in my sleep
And I know forever
Those dreams I will keep.
They are all just like stars
That are shining so bright
But they are still just like ships
That passed in the night.

I go back to the years
When I first went to sea
And I was so young
So happy, so free.
I thought that this life
For me was just right
Now those years are like ships
That passed in the night.

My first trip was a nightmare
I did nothing but throw up
But it taught me the speed
That I had to grow up.
The ship tossed and rolled
Against the wave's might
With no help from the other ships
That passed in the night.

But those years on the ships
I soon learned to adore
So many new places
For me to explore.
There were big shoals of dolphins
What a wonderful sight
Now they too are like ships
That passed in the night.

In the lands that I visited
I saw more and more
Of man's different cultures
On a far distant shore.
But no matter how hard
Or desperate their plight
We were stuck on a ship
That passed in the night.

Any place in the world
Was our port of call
In a country so great
Or ever so small.
No matter if black
No matter if white
We were still just a ship
That passed in the night.

Each ship that we joined
We would soon make new friends
Never to see them again
When that voyage ends.
It was somehow accepted
That it was so right
That we all remained ships
That passed in the night.

But the best days of all
Especially for me
Were the days that we spent
Out there on the sea.
The hours spent alone
Looking out for a light
So we could stay clear of that ship
That passed in the night.

Now I'll always remember
My nautical friends
And the adventures we shared
Whatever life sends.
No truer words
Can pass through my lips
I loved all those nights
That passed on the ships.

PREFACE

I awoke with a start at the sudden shrill ringing of my alarm clock. As I reached out to turn it off, my eyes focused on the faint green luminous fingers, which told me that it was six o'clock, and with that came the sudden realisation that the day I had been waiting almost twelve months for had finally arrived: November 23rd 1953.

I enjoyed an extremely happy childhood but I hated school, and I was so glad that I had to leave at the age of fifteen in the July of 1951. There were no, or very few, further education opportunities in those days so I could not have stayed on even if I had wanted to. I hadn't a clue what I wanted to do, or be. I regularly looked through the situations vacant in the local papers, but nothing seemed to spark my fancy so I ended up dossing around for about a month. I'm sure that I was beginning to get on my parents' nerves.

Then one night my father asked me if I would like to have a go at painting and decorating. The decorator who was repainting the houses on which my father, a carpenter, was working was looking for a boy to learn the trade. With no other prospects in the pipeline I said, "OK" and started on the following Monday.

It was a very small firm, just the boss himself, two men and another boy who had been with them for about twelve months. I seemed to fit in quite well, and I liked the work. They each found the time to show me and teach me how to do things properly. I had been secretly dreading the idea of ending up working in a factory; having to go to the same place and do the same thing day in and day out. Painting and decorating was much better than that I thought, and I quite enjoyed it for over a year.

By then, for reasons I could never explain, I began to feel restless. Although I enjoyed my work, my family, my home, my friends and social life, I felt that I wanted and needed more. The only time I had ever been away from Walsall, apart from a few day trips squashed up with my brother in the sidecar of my dad's old motorbike, was a two-week holiday in Rhyl when I was about ten.

Around four years later I started to develop a longing to travel, to see the world. At first that seemed to be an impossible dream, but it lived with me and wouldn't go away. Indeed with each passing day, the desire grew stronger and stronger; eventually it almost mounted to an obsession. I knew that when I was eighteen, I would be called up for my National Service: compulsory conscription which, at that time applied to all young men with only a few exceptions like coal miners. All eighteen-year-old youths were required to enlist for a two-year period in one of the armed forces. Perhaps there would be a chance of going abroad then I thought, but that was two years away and I really felt that I couldn't wait for such a length of time.

Some months after I had started work, my firm set on another man who had been in the Royal Marine Commandos during the Second World War, and he regaled us with many tales of his exploits. That fed my travel lust and sparked my imagination. So my disappointment was bitter when I told my parents that I wanted to volunteer to join the Marine Commandos and they both strongly objected, steadfastly refusing to give me their blessing.

It wasn't until many years later that I found out that my paternal grandfather, who incidentally I had never met, had also been a Marine Commando and was mentioned in despatches; perhaps my call of the sea came from him. Apparently he had been a very hard, austere kind of man and my mother had never got on well with him. Perhaps that was part of her steadfast objection to my wishes to enlist.

Over the next few weeks, I became very quiet and sullen, but I tried to overcome my disappointment. In the weeks that followed I felt low, unhappy and despondent and got through each day on automatic pilot. I kept racking my brain to think of some way that I could solve my urge to travel. We had very little money, and I had none to save to pay for a trip abroad. I was at a total loss as to how I could remedy the situation.

Suddenly one day, right out of the blue, my father came to my rescue yet again. He sat down with me one evening and started to tell me about the years that he had spent living in Torquay as a boy, and how he used to go down to the seafront to watch the coming and goings of the ships. He had wondered quite often, what life was like for the crew; where they had come from; where they were bound. And he tried to imagine what it would be like to sail on one.

He asked if the idea of joining the Merchant Navy appealed to me. If so, he had talked it over with my mother, and although she would rather I didn't join, she wouldn't stand in my way. A whole weight was lifted from my shoulders. It sounded exactly what I had been looking for.

The very next day I went to the little Labour Exchange Office in Bloxwich and explained to them what I wished to do. They seemed a little bemused at first and said that they had never received a request for the Merchant Navy before, but they asked me to come back again in a couple of days; meanwhile, they would see what they could sort out.

It was with bated breath two days later when I walked up to the counter. I thought that they were going to tell me that I had no chance; therefore I was ecstatic when I was handed a piece of paper with an address to which I had to apply. I posted it off the very next day, but I heard nothing for over a month. Practically every day my workmates asked me if I had heard anything, and I began to think that I never would. My mother consoled me by reassuring me that it would take a little time, but deep down I think that she was pleased, hoping that I would not be accepted.

Finally, an envelope came through the door. I ripped it open eagerly. The letter said that they were accepting boys from the school leaving age of fifteen onwards, up to the limit of seventeen and three months. They had also enclosed a form with a long list of health and medical questions for my GP to answer after a thorough examination. I was to return it as soon as possible and await acceptance or refusal. This I did post-haste, and then I waited, waited and waited.

Every night I came home from work hoping that there would be a letter for me, but there was nothing. My seventeenth birthday came and went so by the time the seventeen and three months deadline had arrived, I was sure that I had been rejected. I was expecting to receive my call up papers for National Service at any time, and I was bitterly disappointed.

A brown envelope came for me in the first week of November. I thought that it was my call up papers, but on opening it I read that if I still wished to join the Merchant Navy as a deck boy, I would have to report to the Merchant Navy Sea Training School at Gravesend, Kent, on Monday 23rd November, no later than 4.30pm. I was elated. Over the moon. I simply could not wait for the following two weeks to pass.

I continued to work until the evening of Friday 20th in a kind of daze. I did my work automatically and at the end of the shift the boss had put an extra week and a half's money in my pay packet: three pounds, saying that he was sure it would come in handy for me. I was really grateful to him for that.

My cases had been packed the night before, and I was anxious and ready to leave by 7.30am. Once I said my goodbyes to my parents, I walked up to the main road in Leamore with my cases where I caught the bus to Walsall.

At the railway station I bought my ticket to Gravesend and I caught the train to Birmingham where I had to change trains and platforms. It was hard work having to lug my cases from platform to platform, but I finally settled down on the train to London. As it slowly steamed out of New Street Station, I felt that at last I was finally embarking on my journey into the unknown.

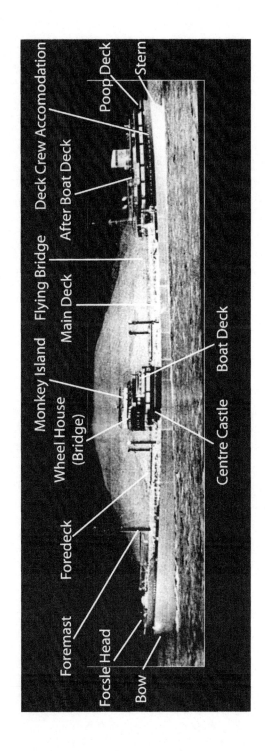

CHAPTER ONE
GRAVESEND
(Of a Late Arrival, Cold Water and Frozen Feet).

I sat staring through the window of the train watching the countryside roll by. It was the first time in my life that I had travelled anywhere on my own. As I watched the fields, the farms and the woods pass by, I couldn't help wondering if I had done the right thing and what I was letting myself in for, but by then it was too late.

As we passed through some of the towns, I noticed quite a few large, empty gaps amongst the buildings, which were obviously bombsites. It was eight years since the end of World War II and most of the rubble had been cleared away, but there was little sign of any actual new building work going on.

Four hours after leaving Birmingham I arrived at Euston Station, which brought me to the stage of the journey that I had been dreading. Not only had my train been late, I also had to tackle the underground to get to Liverpool Street Station. All my fears, as it turned out, had been unfounded. It was so simple. All I had to do was follow the right coloured arrows on to the platform for the right train. Within minutes I was sitting in the train with my cases in front of me, and was swiftly whisked away.

The train's progress could be followed by the maps on the walls of the carriage and I was ready and waiting for the doors to hiss open on our arrival at Liverpool Street. At the top of the steps to the station proper, I showed my ticket to the man on the turnstile and was told that my connecting train for Gravesend had gone over half an hour previously, and I would have to wait another hour or so for the next.

Feeling tired and travel weary, it was four o'clock when I stepped out of Gravesend station into the town. I had only half an hour left before my arrival deadline so I had to hurry. As I left the station, I asked the way to the Sea Training School and was pointed in the right direction. The school was at the other end of town. After I had trudged along with my cases, I was almost on my knees when at long last I finally arrived. It was exactly 4.30pm as I walked in through the gate.

Inside the gate, two boys stood on guard in dark navy blue uniforms, which consisted of trousers, jacket and beret. They ushered me into a small office where I had to present all my letters and forms to the purser. I also had to pay five pounds as a down payment on my uniform and all other items of clothing that I was about to receive.

I was then told that I would have to pay fifteen shillings a week (75p in today's money) out of my one pound dole allowance for the ten weeks duration of the training course. The dole money was my only form of income. The Purser then sized me up with his eyes and handed me my uniform in packages that contained the size that he had decided I was.

The gate into the complex, which completely blocked any views from the street, opened up into a massive oblong courtyard that stretched down almost to the banks of the River Thames, but the access through to the river itself appeared to be blocked off. On the right of the courtyard there was a building accommodating many classrooms, which took up the whole of that side; at the far end a door led to a large, well-equipped gymnasium.

I was shown into the gym by one of the boys from the gate who had accompanied me down the courtyard. The new influx of boys and a couple of training officers were waiting inside. The new boys had arrived at intervals throughout the day from all over the UK and Ireland yet I, travelling only from the Midlands, was the last to arrive.

On the left hand side of the courtyard, just inside the entrance gates, was a wall with open access at each end. I was not amused to find that there was a row of toilet cubicles backing on to the wall from the inside. On the opposite wall was a row of deep sinks; the taps of which only ever emitted icy cold water for the whole of the ten-week course. There was a roof overhead, but the wide-open access at each end left it at the mercy of the elements, and in late November, all through December and most of January, it was anything but ideal.

Everything was kept perfectly clean including the cold, bare, concrete floor. The rest of the left side of the courtyard was taken up by a very large, formidable looking building with double entrance doors opposite the gym. One of the officers gave a welcoming speech. Then he told the boys who were to be trained as stewards to go with the other officer. Two thirds of the gym emptied. Those trainee stewards were to embark upon a six-week course as opposed to our ten-week one. The remaining officer then told us about the programme that faced us.

In the first four weeks of tuition we would learn about a ship's equipment. We would have to memorise the name of every rivet and, he added with a smirk, every nut and bolt too. But that wasn't all; we would also need to recognise every mark on the lead line that was used for depth measurements in rivers etc. and how to convey the information to the bridge. In the old days the crews thought that that was the easiest job on the ship as she was approaching her docking berth, and the sailors used to rush to be first to get the job; hence the saying, "swinging the lead."

We would learn how to stream the log used for gauging a ship's speed, how to read it and retrieve it again, how to steer the ship and to read the compass down to every quarter point and how to respond to every order given. We were to be taught how to lower lifeboats safely and the rudiments of manning and sailing them; we would also have to know where all the equipment was stowed, its purpose and its use. Also, we needed to know where all the food and water was stored and how to ration it. That, he informed us, was only a small percentage of the things that we had to learn, and we would have our first examination after four weeks.

All of that was spoken, it seemed to me, with hardly a breath taken, and by the time he asked us if we had any questions, our heads were spinning, and we met his query with a stunned silence. "Right then," he continued, "that will take us up till Christmas when you can go home for a few days. When you return we will start on the practical stuff and for four weeks you will be learning about all the different types of ropes, how to splice them in different ways, what each individual splice is for and wire splicing too."

3

We had to acquaint ourselves with the numerous different knots and their uses. We needed to know the mechanics of both the metal and wooden pulley blocks and how to assemble them and take them apart for greasing and maintenance. Also we had to learn how to thread the ropes (reeve them) through the blocks and tackles and how to sew canvas covers. In addition, weather permitting, we needed to learn how to handle the school's cutter (a ship's boat used for carrying stores). All this had to be mastered over the following weeks.

That was a brief outline of some of the things we would learn during those four weeks he informed us once again, and then there would be another exam. "Any questions now?" he asked. Still there was a wall of stunned silence. I could imagine the view from where he stood: A group of vacant faces, staring eyes and open mouths. Suddenly a voice asked, "What happens if we fail the exams?" He paused for a moment and said, "You will be expected to reach a certain percentage in your results, and if you are under that then I'm afraid you are on your way home." I heard some muttering from my schoolmates.

"There is one more thing," he said, "I am sure that most of you have come from nice, warm, comfortable homes," he paused, looking at us quizzically, then he continued, "Well you will find things a little different here. It's a tough job in the Merchant Navy and you have got to be able to take it. If you change your mind at any point during the course, you are completely free to pack your bags and go."

With that understood he called out our names and split us up into three classes. I was placed in class S with ten other boys. Each class was identified as either Red Watch, White Watch or Blue Watch. I was in Blue. It was explained that one watch would be required to perform duties in the evening, while shore leave would be granted to the other two watches. A rota system would apply so that each watch had two nights out of three able to do as they wished. But those of us who went ashore had to be back before ten o'clock; any later and we would be disciplined. Everyone was then issued with a pass, which would enable us to leave and enter the school.

Finally satisfied that everyone understood the rules, he took us across the courtyard and through the imposing double doors on the opposite side. Inside was a small square entrance hall, and on the left was another set of double doors that opened out into a big room, which I found to be the dining room.

We lugged our cases through the entrance foyer to another set of doors into a big square hall. Around the sides of the hall were three balconies, one above the other. These contained the sleeping accommodation. It reminded me very much of the prisons I had seen in some of the old movies, and the rumour soon spread that it had once been one, but later I learned that it never had been a prison of any kind.

There was a wide, wooden step-way to each balcony, and the first two balconies accommodated the stewards' quarters. The prospective deck hands were allocated to the very top one. Once there we were separated into our respective watches with each group taken to a different section and allocated a 'cabin.' These were little cubicles, about six to eight foot square, with a bunk on the left, a chair and a chest of drawers. There was no door, just a curtain to pull across.

I unpacked my suitcases and stowed them underneath my bunk. Then I heard a whistle calling us to tea and a welcome meal. The mess was also very basic and austere, quite large and square with rows of tables and a self-service counter. The food was nothing to write home about, but I always managed to digest enough to keep the hunger pains at bay. When I had finished my meal, I returned to my cabin and sat down to write a letter home to let my parents know that I had arrived safely and I was OK. It had been a long day. I was shattered and an early night was called for.

At seven o'clock the next morning, I awoke to a shrill blast of a whistle and along with all the other boys I had to run the whole length of the courtyard to the washrooms, stripped to the waist with a towel around my shoulder. The wind was icy and the water was one degree away from freezing, but it certainly woke us up. Once dressed we went to breakfast then to the classrooms to start the daily lessons. That became the pattern for the next few weeks. There were different officers to teach the different subjects, each one knowledgeable in their own subject.

Another rumour spread amongst the boys that most of the officers had served their time in the Royal Navy. This created a little disquiet amongst a few; they thought that a lot of the instruction might differ considerably from the Merchant Navy custom. Where those rumours originated from has always baffled me. I had no knowledge of the officers' private lives, but doubted that those rumours were true. The lessons really captured my interest. Twice a week we had a diversion from the classroom by having exercises and workouts in the gym, which I enjoyed.

It didn't seem as if any close friendships between individuals were formed, but we all formed into loose, limited groups for nights out in the town. We had very little money left from our allotment, and on our nights off we would pair off in groups of three or four to stroll through Gravesend.

There was not much to do. Window-shopping or an occasional visit to a cinema or, if we were not in uniform, we could go for a pint in our favourite pub. The uniform would have been the giveaway that we were under age. One or two of the pubs refused to serve us even so, but it was not long before we found the pubs that made us welcome. Always at the back of our minds, was the need to be back at the school before ten o'clock.

On the duty nights we were allocated various chores. Two of us would be on duty at the gate checking all the passes; others would be polishing, cleaning toilets, sweeping the courtyard, tidying the classrooms, and buffing and polishing the wooden floors in the main building. Those jobs too were rotated, and soon it all became routine. Every night we had to turn in between 10.30pm and 10.45pm with lights out at 11.00pm.

The first Sunday morning after breakfast we were assembled in the courtyard in full uniform and lined up in a double column. We were then marched into the town to church for morning service. I hated marching through the town under the stares and mimicking of some of the local inhabitants, mainly kids, so I was grateful to actually get into the church away from it. Every Sunday throughout my training the whole school was marched there. I was so glad that I hadn't joined the Royal Marines where I imagined marching would almost be a way of life.

* * *

I had been there for about a week when one night, about fifteen minutes after lights out, I was awakened from my slumber by giggling

6

and subdued whispering. Someone was skylarking. The curtain to my cubicle was yanked back and a voice said, "Come on, we are going to raid Red and White watches on the opposite end of the balcony." "Piss off, I'm not getting out of bed for anyone," I said. How wrong I was.

They disappeared and I soon heard the noises of battle taking place. There were thumps, bangs, shouts and screams of laughter coming from over the other side. Suddenly the lights flashed on, and an angry voice from below shouted, "What the hell's going on?" Instantly I heard the thunder of bare feet on wooden floors stampeding towards me, and then silence as they each scurried into their little holes.

The next thing I knew was a voice outside saying, "Right you lot." My curtain was ripped aside and the clothes snatched from my bed. "OUT, OUT, the lot of you, OUT," the Duty Officer shouted angrily. "It wasn't me," I said, "I never got out of bed." "Don't give me that crap," he snapped, "It's the whole of this section, you were seen." Something in the tone of his voice told me that it would be better if I said no more for I thought the more I protested my innocence, the worse it would be for me. By then another officer had arrived and together they turfed us all out, herded us down the steps and out into the courtyard where we were made to stand in line, side by side, and told that there was not to be so much as a whimper out of us.

It was 11.30pm in early December and I could see the concrete reflecting the shine from the lights where ice patches had formed. We stood there in silence, some of us in pyjamas, others like me in just their underpants, all of us barefooted. We were told, in no uncertain manner, that any disturbances after lights out were definitely not going to be tolerated.

For half an hour we were kept there slowly solidifying with the cold; our feet gradually turned blue and began to stick to the icy concrete as we stood shivering in the near arctic conditions. We were returned to our beds at midnight and there were never any more disturbances at night after that.

The next couple of weeks went by quite smoothly and soon we found ourselves sitting the fourth week examinations. That following weekend, after being lined up again in the courtyard, the exam results were reported. Much to my amazement, my name was amongst the top half dozen.

The officers hoped that our initial and successful examination results would continue, and to those of us who reached a pass mark of 80% an arm badge of crossed anchors would be awarded along with a late pass to allow us to stay out until 10.30pm. It would also be recorded in our personal discharge book for future reference. Those who failed to achieve 80% but attained 75% would be awarded a merit star and a late pass until 10.15pm. Finally, from Monday we would be starting on the practical work.

I found the few weeks till Christmas fascinating as I learned about the ropes, knots, splices and learned how to handle all the tools and ship's equipment. The enjoyment of that was tempered with the dislike of all the menial tasks we had to perform. We quickly learnt however, to take the good with the bad.

The last weekend before we broke up, the officers, their wives and girlfriends had organised a Christmas dance. It had been advertised widely locally and apparently a lot of girls had bought tickets. Dancing was not my scene but I looked forward to having a good time and a good laugh. Come the day, I found that I had been posted on gate duty for the evening. Luck of the draw I supposed, but at least I got to check all of the girls' tickets.

On the following Thursday we broke up for the Christmas holiday. There were no hold-ups or hitches with the trains and my parents were really pleased to see me. The whole family, including uncles, aunts and cousins, were invited to the Christmas Day party at my grandparents; it was an annual event and my mother asked me to wear my uniform. I was far from keen, but I did so to please her. Everyone congratulated me on my smart turnout. Being a seventeen year old at the time, I could have done without that, but the rest of my leave was very enjoyable.

I was due back at school on the following Monday, and after an uneventful journey, I arrived in Gravesend in time for dinner. On the following day a new influx of boys arrived; among them was a boy from Wolverhampton, and by coincidence his name was Michael too. As I was further into the course and taking different classes we didn't mix a lot, but we did pass the time of day when our paths crossed. I was to get to know him quite well a few weeks later.

Following a further week of lessons, we were again tested to see if the tuition was successful and if anything had been absorbed. Two of my coursemates from the other watches had failed to return following the Christmas break, and it wasn't long before a couple more decided that they had had enough and also left, much to our surprise.

One morning we were all given life jackets, and instead of the usual classroom instructions we were marched to the river along a pathway, which ran along the side of the building. This is where the majority of us received our first lessons in manning a real boat, a thirty-foot cutter that we attempted to row up and down the Thames.

The cutter was like an overgrown rowing boat, and very heavy to handle. Our first attempts were laughable, but we soon got the hang of it as we learned to work as a team. Then rowing up and down the Thames became an exhilarating experience for us; we felt that we were becoming sailors at last. Although the wind was slight, it was biting, and despite our exertions we were all frozen. Irrespective of the cold, we all enjoyed the experience very much.

Shortly afterwards a bout of 'Idiotitis' broke out amongst my coursemates. One day as we waited in the courtyard to be called to our evening meal, one or two of the lads decided that chasing each other and ripping the back pockets off each other's uniform trousers was great fun. This was considered by most of their peer group to be hilarious and was greeted with guffaws of laughter and much merriment.

Soon everyone joined in with what I considered a stupid game. Over the next few days it spread like wildfire till there was a large group trying to see how many back pockets they could capture; some of the lads literally had their trousers ripped apart at the seams.

I couldn't believe it; the uniforms were costing money, which for me was in desperately short supply, and all for what I thought was a mindless game. Amazingly not one of the officers appeared to have picked up on what was happening. Gradually, it petered out, mainly because there weren't any pockets left, except mine. It was a total mystery to me why no one had spotted that mine was still intact and no attempt had been made on it.

A couple of days after the 'game' had died out, I thought that I had escaped when suddenly, while on a break in the courtyard, I heard a surprised voice say, "Look, there's a pocket." I turned cold, knowing full well that it was mine. I swung round with my back to the wall, while the whole gang crowded around me. They stood in a semi-circle staring at me. I stared back at them.

My head was in a spin and it was as though I was standing in a foggy distance hearing my own voice cooly and quietly saying, "OK you'll get my pocket, but I guarantee I'll get at least one of you." I remember pointing and saying with a bravery I certainly didn't feel, "It might be you, or you, or you," aiming my finger at each individual as I spoke. I just couldn't believe that it was me speaking.

For a moment there was a kind of surprised silence. Then to my astonishment, they began to back off. Perhaps, for the very first time, it had got through to them that it wasn't a big joke to everyone. I was in a cold sweat and shaking at the knees. My cubical was the best place to cool off and steady my nerves. After I had stopped shaking I knew that once my pocket had been spotted, the rest of the group wouldn't rest until they had ripped it off, and prudence kicked in so I unpicked the stitches myself with a small pair of scissors and the game was over.

The weeks zoomed by and as the first day of our final exams approached, we all became very apprehensive. The instructor first made each one of us show our skills with all the knots and splices, then examined them himself to see if they were correct. We also had to explain to him what all the individual knots were used for and the names of different types of ropes. In fact, each one of us had to demonstrate to him that we had taken in all that we had been taught over the last few weeks.

There was even a big blackboard with the drawing of a compass down to the quarter points, and we each took turns to answer immediately what the different points were that he indicated with a ruler. We spent two days on all the practical things before going on to a written exam the next day, which contained dozens of questions on seamanship.

The weather that day was terrible: it was blowing a full gale. Our concentration on the exam papers was suddenly interrupted by a ship hooting madly. It had broken free from its moorings in the river. We all dashed to the windows to watch, fascinated as the ship drifted helplessly, broadside on, down the river towards two other ships, which were tied up to buoys a short distance abreast of each other. Suddenly we heard the rattle of anchor chains being released; fortunately the anchor held and pulled the ship's bows towards upstream again, and the drifting ship miraculously came to a standstill between the two buoyed ships.

After that exciting spectacle, going back to our desks to concentrate on the exam paper was not easy. Yet again I asked myself what I was letting myself in for and whether I would ever experience near misses like that or maybe even tragic accidents, but those thoughts never once shattered my resolve to carry on.

With the exams out of the way a release of tension and change of scene was needed. So that weekend, along with three of my coursemates, we decided that we would venture farther afield. We caught the ferry across the Thames to Tilbury on the opposite bank to Gravesend. From there we caught a bus to Grays. We found Grays to be a small town much like any other, and we spent the evening looking around and having a couple of pints in the local pubs.

Unfortunately our timing on the return journey was misjudged. The ferry was delayed and we arrived back at the school half an hour late. We immediately had our ten o'clock passes taken away, and as a punishment we were confined to barracks for a week and given the job of cleaning the toilets every night.

The following day we received the exam results. Two members of the group had achieved the necessary level to be awarded the cherished crossed anchor badges along with the extended late pass till 10.30pm. I was amazed to learn, on hearing my name called out, that not only had I been awarded the merit star, but also that I was the only one. I kept silent about my confinement to barracks when I was handed my extended leave pass till 10.15pm so despite being confined to barracks, I was able to sneak out occasionally. I thought of it as being my reward for having been made to stand freezing in the courtyard as punishment for a crime of which I was totally innocent.

The following week, after I had completed the week of not quite so strict confinement, I was called to the office to have my original pass returned. The officer's face was a picture I shall never forget when he reached out his hand to me and I said that I didn't want the pass. "Why not?" he asked incredulously, "Because I already have one," I said, and produced my extended late pass. "How long have you had that?" he asked "A week" I said, "and have you been using it?" he queried. I gave him my best "What do you think?" look, stayed silent and smiled. He burst into laughter and told me to get out of his sight.

11

The remaining days were taken up with cleaning, and a lot of time was spent in the gym exercising. Our final day at the school arrived at last: Friday 29ᵗʰ January 1954. After having packed and checked our gear, we had nothing to do until we collected our personal documents, which were necessary for our future employment. The mystery that was never explained to us was why we had to hang around until 5.00pm before the documents, which consisted of an identity card, a union card and a discharge book, were issued.

The discharge book was effectively to be an ongoing record of my career. Every ship I served on would be recorded as well as details such as where and when I signed on and signed off and a report on my abilities and conduct. It was explained that there were only three possible reports on ability and conduct: a 'DR' (decline to report), which in effect could get you put in front of a committee who had the power to severely tick you off or even kick you out, a 'Good' report, which was almost as bad and was not considered to be of any merit, and a 'VG' (very good), which was considered the acceptable standard. This was the report we were expected to maintain. The discharge book also served as a passport with photograph if for any reason I had to leave a ship abroad. I was pleased to find that the award of my merit star had indeed been recorded in the official document.

The method of employing seamen was through the Shipping Federation Offices, generally known throughout the industry as the 'Pool.' Each seaman was registered with the Pool at the port nearest to his home. I had fully expected to be registered with the London office. I was surprised when I found that Liverpool was nearer, and I had to report there on the following morning. I was wished good luck as I collected my rail ticket and, along with a Scot and two Londoners, I said goodbye to Gravesend and headed for London to catch a train.

The Scot and I had time to kill as we waited for our trains, and having deposited our luggage at the station we headed into the city with the two London lads as our guides. It was the first time in my life that I had had the chance to walk the streets of our capital and I stared in awe at some of the buildings and squares.

After a good meal in a nice restaurant we decided that the theatre was our next port of call. Billy Cotton was appearing at the London Hippodrome and we managed to get cheap seats. We enjoyed the early acts and were looking forward to seeing the old Maestro, but we suddenly realised that if we hung on for his appearance, we would miss our trains. As it was we were fortunate to have the London lads with us who knew their way around; otherwise, we would never have made it to the station in time.

Having reclaimed our luggage we finally arrived at Euston where Jock caught his train for Scotland. The two Londoners said goodbye and headed for their homes, and I finally found the correct platform for the train to Liverpool. There, waiting for the train, was another lad from the training school, but who had not been in my watch. Together we caught the midnight train and finally arrived at Liverpool Lime Street at 5.00am. It was far too early for the Pool office to be open so I snatched a few hours sleep in the waiting room.

When I awoke it was daylight, and having been told earlier by my travelling companion how to get to the shipping office, I found it without any difficulty. It was very similar to a Labour Exchange, dealing specifically with seamen and shipping. It was a busy place with four or five men behind the counter dealing with the queue of men waiting. Eventually my turn came and I explained who I was to the clerk. He pointed me in the direction of an adjacent office where, he explained, the railway vouchers were issued, which he would authorize.

On my return to the counter, he made the voucher valid for Walsall and told me to go home where I should stay until I was sent for. I was soon back at Lime Street Station and on a train heading for home.

CHAPTER TWO
THE OAKHILL

(Of Coal Dust, a Long, Long Journey and Chocolate Biscuits).

I spent the rest of the week enjoying my unexpected leave in the comfort of my home. My enjoyment was short-lived for on Friday 5th February I received a letter instructing me to report to the Pool on Monday 8th. It was with a great deal of apprehension that I caught the bus to Wolverhampton, where the travel voucher that I had received was valid from. Obviously someone in the Liverpool office had sussed out that it was cheaper for them to have me travel from Walsall to Wolverhampton at my own expense rather than them pay for it. However, this meant that I had to carry my luggage from the High Level station in Wolverhampton to the Low Level station from where the Liverpool train departed.

It was midday when I arrived at Lime Street, and I went straight to the Pool with my luggage. The office was packed to the doors and it took two hours before I got to the counter. Once there I was told to report again the following morning, and that I could get a room for the night at the Gordon Smith's Seamen's Home.

I had passed a building on my way to the Pool office bearing the name Gordon Smith's so that was where I headed. On asking for a room the individual at the desk condescendingly sneered, "You can't come in here, this accommodation is for officers only." He pointed with an outstretched arm as he said, "Your place is across the road."

Opposite was a big building, over which hung a massive Gordon Smith's sign; how I had missed seeing it I will never know, but at least I knew then where my place was. Once inside I found that for six shillings (30p), I could book a room with breakfast and for an extra one shilling and three pence, they served tea or dinner.

The key to the room was attached to an oblong block of cast iron. Two would have made good weight-lifting equipment. I went up to my room, which proved to be very basic with plain painted walls, a bed, a chest of drawers and a small wardrobe.

I then had the afternoon to myself so I decided to explore the city. Before doing so, I made sure that I deposited the cast iron key at the foyer. No way was I lugging that around with me, which I supposed was the thinking behind it.

As I came from a relatively small Midlands town, I was soon lost and alone within the sprawl of the large city of Liverpool. I wandered around for about two hours before I found my way back to Gordon Smith's. My hunger directed me to the restaurant where for my one shilling and three pence, I had a substantial and filling meal.

By then it was early evening, and I was at a loss as to how I could spend the time. Then I remembered that I had passed a picture house called the Tatler during my afternoon walk, and no matter what was showing I decided that was where I would spend my evening, come what may. All I wanted was to spend the next three hours or so in a comfortable seat to rest my legs after all the walking I had done that afternoon. So without even checking the program, I settled into my seat. A cartoon was being shown, which was followed by another, then another and another. These were followed by a newsreel after which I expected the film to be screened. But no, it was another cartoon.

I realised then that all of the cartoons were repeated; the whole performance lasted for about an hour. The Tatler was a news theatre only, with cartoons that filled in the spaces between the news screenings. That was a new experience for me. I wasn't aware that such places existed. Certainly there was nothing like it in Walsall. I still had time to kill and after I had stuck it out for three repeats, I decided that was enough. And so off I went to bed.

It wasn't so busy at the Pool the next morning, but I still had to queue for about an hour before I got to the counter where I was directed to the office next door. "Mr Kenn, Deck Boy?" the chap behind the desk queried, "Yes," I replied. He then said, "Your ship is the 'SS *Oakhill*,' but first you must be medically examined. He pointed towards a door, "Go through there to see the doctor."

The doctor gave me a thorough examination and an eye test; he then gave me a form to take back to the counter. "Right," said the man after glancing at the form. "The '*Oakhill*'. She is in the Huskison Dock. To sign on you must go to the Cornhill offices tomorrow morning," then he gave me directions on how to get there.

I made my way back to Gordon Smith's to rebook my room for another night and then, following the Pool Clerk's instructions, I went for a walk to see if I could find Cornhill so that I would know where to go the next morning. It didn't take long and I found that it was a big imposing office building with large double doors at the entrance. I was then at a loose end for the rest of the day.

I was alone in a strange city and at a loss as to know what to do. I decided to explore and familiarise myself with more of Liverpool; then I returned to Smith's for my dinner and later for tea. I took note that time during my wanderings of the locations of several cinemas and one specialised in showing horror films. I felt like I needed a good laugh, that being the effect that those types of films have on me, and "The Blob" showing that night was my evening's pleasure.

The double doors at the Cornhill office the next morning opened up into a large square room where the majority of the crew were waiting to sign on. I soon made friends with Jim, a JOS (Junior Ordinary Seaman) and Richard, who like me was a deck boy. We had to wait until midday before the Captain arrived to sign us on.

We signed what is known as the ship's articles. They committed each individual for a period of two years service aboard the ship; it bound you to the ship for those two years unless she returned to a port in the United Kingdom when you could be paid off. If the ship was bound for foreign climes without returning to the UK, you were required to remain in service for those two years.

However, if after two years it was known that the ship was homeward bound, the contract could be extended to accommodate the homeward voyage. The contract was not even handed though for the company could pay the crew off at any time for any reason and anywhere in the world. The articles also contained details concerning a list of food available and the rations for each member of the crew. Pages and pages of rules and regulations, which I later found to be common to all British seafarers.

After signing the articles I was required to provide my documents: ID card, discharge book and medical records, and told to report to the ship for duty at seven o'clock the following morning.

My newfound friend Richard was also booked into Gordon Smith's and along with Jim, we made our way back to renew our booking for a further night. Richard and I booked an early morning call for 5.30am. The three of us then took advantage of the one and threepenny dinner in Smith's dining room.

During the meal Jim explained that he lived in nearby Wallasey across the other side of the Mersey. Perhaps we may like to visit his home where his mother would make us all very welcome, he suggested. That sounded good to us. So from the Pier Head we caught the ferry crossing the river Mersey, and on to Jim's home, where we spent a very pleasant afternoon with Jim's mother who gave us tea.

Later, thanking Jim's mother for her kind hospitality, Richard and I made our way back across the Mersey and as we approached the Pier Head, the Liver Birds on the top of the Liver building stood out prominently against the city backdrop. We also had a good view of the overhead railway, which ran the full length of the dockland area.

I was curious to see my first ship and could not wait until the morning so I suggested to Richard that we catch the overhead to Huskison dock to go and look at the 'SS Oakhill.' He thought that was a good idea so we climbed the steps up to the platform and we were soon speeding along the tracks.

That unique means of transport was so convenient for it stopped at each and every dock along the way. As we approached the Huskison dock, we decided to see if we could go aboard to take a sneak preview of our new home. When the train stopped at Huskison, we got off and walked down into the dock itself. Without challenge or hindrance we walked up to the 'Oakhill.'

I was later told that she was an old Empire Boat. They had been built during the war, of necessity, and were prefabricated in factories throughout the UK; finally assembled at shipyards up and down the country. The concept of prefabrication evolved during the Atlantic battles, when the German U-boats were sinking our merchant ships faster than we could build them. If they managed to survive only one journey and provide scarce raw material or food for war-torn Britain, they would have served their purpose. Many had survived the war itself, and for many years after they earned good money for the British economy.

Apprehensively we climbed the gangway and I set foot for the first time on my first seagoing ship. Still unchallenged, and in curious anticipation, we wandered aft to seek the seamen's accommodation. Through a side door we could see toilets and shower rooms on either side of the corridor. I later learned that the toilets on the port side were for the deckhands use, and those on the starboard side were for the engine room crew, firemen and greasers.

In the middle of the corridor was a ladder, which led down to a square. Both the deckhands' accommodation and the engine-room crew's cabins, like the toilets and shower-rooms above, were on opposite sides of the square. The cabins were quite small, about ten foot square, with a double set of bunks, one above the other either side, set against the bulkheads. Provided also was a small chest of drawers, one drawer for each occupant, a chair, and a locker each. They were very crowded for four people.

We wandered about curiously inspecting our future home and found the galley with the cook still busily finishing his day's work. He welcomed us aboard in a very friendly manner and before long we were tucking into an impromptu meal of egg on toast followed by a big mug of tea, which promised well for the future. A lesson I learned on that occasion stood me in good stead: always keep well in with the cook. It was our last night ashore and rather than return immediately to Gordon Smith's, Richard and I decided to spend it at the cinema.

After an early breakfast the following morning, we caught the overhead train again, with our luggage, to Huskison dock and the 'Oakhill.' There were fourteen members of the deck crew including us boys, and they were divided into three watches: the twelve to four, the four to eight and the eight to twelve, with three of the men in each watch. The remainder of the crew were employed throughout the day from 7.00am till 5.00pm with breaks for meals. The accepted practice

19

of deciding who served on which watch was left to the crew and was decided by cutting a pack of playing cards.

Richard and I as deck boys were not involved in that procedure. We were to be the 'peggies' on a week about basis. "What's a peggy?" I enquired. "A peggy is the one who looks after the seamen," I was told. "The dogsbody who cleans the mess, wakes up the men to go on watch and to make sure food and drink was at hand at meal times and breaks." I was to take the first week.

A typical day in the life of a peggy meant being called at 6.30am with the rest of the dayworkers to clear and clean the mess created by the night watches. The peggy had to wash the crockery and provide tea for the dayworkers before their seven o'clock start. The next duty was to similarly clean and clear the Petty Officers' (POs) mess. It was then to wake the eight to twelve watch, make fresh tea and lay the places at the mess table.

After ensuring that the watch were up and about, it was to the galley to collect their breakfast. Then back to the PO's mess to perform the same duty. At eight o'clock the day crew would arrive for their breakfast from working on deck for an hour. The peggy bought this from the galley in kits (round containers which fitted one on top of another on a U shaped handle that made them easier to carry). They were placed on the table and the sailors helped themselves. I was amazed to find that curry and rice were included in the choice for breakfast every morning; I found the curry smelt absolutely revolting, reminiscent of a neglected sewer, and most mornings it finished up in the 'gash bucket.' That smell stayed with me and put me off curry forever.

With breakfast over, all the crockery and cutlery had to be washed and the kits returned to the galley. Plates and mugs were piled high, and I had never seen so much washing up. Once that was completed, it was the same chore in the PO's mess. The wooden table and benches in the mess also had to be scrubbed after each meal and kept spotless.

The ship had previously carried a cargo of coal, and the crew had been busy cleaning the coal dust from the holds. From the state of the table and benches following each meal, I suspected that the majority of the dust was on the crew's overalls.

Come mid morning I had to make tea for the crew as they took a break for a smoke and a welcome 'cuppa,' and once again the tables had to be scrubbed clean of the coal dust before it was time to prepare for the twelve to four watch and dinner for the rest of the crew. And so it went on throughout the day, providing food and drink at afternoon tea break (Smoko) and tea at five o'clock, after which the crockery and tables had to be washed again then safely stacked away for the night.

In between times I was required to clean the washbasins and WCs, and to keep the alleyways clean and tidy. The galley provided a cold meat salad for the night watches, which I had to fetch and lay out in the mess. My last task of the day was to empty the gash bucket over the side. I soon learned that it wasn't wise to empty the bucket on the weather side.

Peggy duty wasn't improved by the attitude of some ABs (Able Seamen) who seemed to enjoy finding fault if there was half a chance. Thankfully my peggy duty was to be only every other week, or so I thought, and we would be rid of the coal dust by my next stint so I hoped there would at least be less scrubbing of the tables by then.

The engine-room staff, the firemen and greasers were Arabs of various nationalities, and the segregation was almost complete. They kept themselves very much to themselves. I found them to be pleasant people and always passed the time of day with them. They were always ready with a cheery smile and a hello for me whenever our paths crossed; however, I was not insensitive to the attitude displayed to them by some of the ABs.

My curiosity about my allotted job was cut short as the crew were called to standby, and the order was given to single up. That meant letting go of all the mooring lines except one, and the wire spring at each end of the ship. Then towlines were passed from two tugs that would aid our passage out into the river.

My pulse quickened as I realised that I was about to begin my first excursion into what was for me, the ultimate great unknown. I was fascinated with the mechanics of casting off and the means of taking the ship from its moorings. As each rope was slackened, the shore gang released them from the bollards. An AB threw a couple of turns around the drum of the winch and hauled aboard the remaining ropes. As the ropes came aboard, I helped to coil them on the deck.

With the tugs taking the strain we moved slowly clear of the mooring and out into the Mersey. With a hiss and a shudder, the ship's engines came to life; it was as if a hibernating animal had suddenly sprung back into life. The tugs helped and guided the ship through the buoyed channel, while the deck crew rewound the wire spring onto its reel and covered it with canvas to protect it from the elements. On reaching the river bar, the limit of the Mersey and the entrance to the sea, we let go the tugs and steamed under our own power into the Irish Sea heading north. Our orders were to go north about around the top of Scotland then across the North Sea to a port called Emden in Germany.

* * *

The weather that day was quite calm and very cold, but after I had been exposed to the freezing elements for ten weeks at Gravesend I felt acclimatized. I was still relieved to be sent below into the rope locker with two ABs to coil the ropes down and stow them away for safety while we were out in the open sea. They were passed down to us by the others through a little hatch, which we battened down once we were finished.

The rest of the men then went out on to the decks to make sure everything else was secured ready for the open sea. I, being the Peggy for the first week, went into our mess to start on my duties to get the tables and everything set for dinner.

As we rounded the north coast of Scotland three days later, Richard slipped and fell while working down an empty hatch and broke his arm in two places. Immediately the Skipper changed course for the nearest port, which was Wick on the north east coast of Scotland.

It transpired that the harbour master of Wick at that time happened to be the Skipper's brother and, via the ship to shore radio, it was arranged for a boat to be dispatched to collect the invalid. When we arrived Richard was lowered into the boat, which soon sped towards the shore, and that was my last sight of my new friend. I never saw him again.

We were well out into the North Sea when at three o'clock the following morning I was roughly shaken from my bunk by an angry AB. "Get to the mess and empty the gash bucket," he spat at me, "Jesus! Couldn't you have done it?" I queried. "Oh no, you will do it now and you won't forget it in future," he snapped; he was right, I didn't.

Over the next few days, I was on a steep learning curve both in terms of keeping control of my temper and not venting my frustration. With Richard gone, all I had to look forward to for the rest of the voyage was permanent peggying and there would be no opportunity for me to work on deck.

I felt depressed at the thought of washing up and cleaning all day, every day for the rest of the trip; it was the last thing I had wanted to happen, but there was nothing for it except to put my head down and get on with it. Then, halfway across the North Sea, we ran into bad weather.

The ship pitched and rolled violently from side to side; I went from a state of queasiness to full-blown nausea, and I experienced my first bout of seasickness. Never before had I felt so ill, I couldn't eat or sleep and my stomach performed contortions beyond description. Death, I thought, would have been a welcome relief.

I caught sight of my reflection in the mirror and could have been mistaken for the Grim Reaper. I thought that I was dying, but it was only through the help of some of my shipmates, who insisted that I must drink something to have something in my stomach to fetch up, that my condition began to improve.

The speed of the ship was reduced considerably by the gale, which lasted for four days. It was not until the early hours of Wednesday 17th February that we found calmer seas; only then did I begin to feel somewhat better, and I thought I could try to catch up with my sleep.

I could have sworn my slumber had lasted less than five minutes when I was roughly shaken awake again, "I've emptied the sodding gash bucket," I slurred, slowly regaining consciousness. My shipmate laughed, "We are now off the German coast and we shall be arriving in port shortly. German time is an hour in front of British time so you have an hour less sleep," he said. I reluctantly crawled out of my bunk to start my day's work.

On deck, the coast of Germany was a pleasant and welcome sight after my first experience of the cruel sea. Shortly after midday two tugs passed lines aboard and busied themselves pushing and shoving us into the mooring. I had finally arrived at my first foreign port: Emden, West Germany. The working day finished at five o'clock for everyone except the Peggy. My day's work was not completed until all my chores were finished in both the messes, and the decks were clean and tidy.

A little while later while I sat quietly at the table enjoying a well-earned cigarette, I was surprised to be asked by an officer "How much do you want?" He immediately comprehended the vacant look on my face and explained that all seamen were granted an advance of pay (a sub) in foreign ports at the Skipper's discretion.

I thought two pounds would be enough for a trip ashore. Shortly afterwards the Skipper paid all of the crew their subs in German Marks. It was of course all recorded and then deducted from our final pay at the end of the trip. The previous few days had left me totally exhausted so I decided that there would be no shore leave for me that night. All I needed was bed and I slept like a log.

With the ship in port, the crew performed only day duties, which allowed everyone to eat together. It made the peggying much easier, not having to cater for three different watches. The following evening, along with Jim and an SOS (Senior Ordinary Seaman) Alf, I stepped on foreign soil for the first time. Everything including the houses, roads and office blocks appeared to be brand new and everywhere was spotlessly clean. The difference was stark compared to the bombsites back in England.

We sampled the delights of good German beer in a brand new bar and enjoyed ourselves until the early hours. It would have been about 3.00am as we made our way back to the dock; we passed an elderly local man and we wished him goodnight. The sound of English voices stopped him in his tracks, and he stared at us for a moment or two then turned on his heels and hurried away without a word. That malevolent stare has stuck with me ever since.

It became very cold during the night, and the biting east wind brought snow so we awoke to a white new world. The snow was thick and the dock was treacherously icy. For once I was pleased that my duties were in the warm comfort of the mess. The cargo of coal being taken aboard however was far from welcome, and I didn't relish the prospect of having to continue to scrub the tables clean of coal dust two or three times a day.

The coal being loaded into the holds created little or no dust to begin with, but as it reached towards the top of the holds with the cranes spewing the coal into them from a height, the clouds of coal dust became thicker and thicker. As each load was dropped, the dust swirled everywhere and got into everything including the deckhand's clothes; once more my white, scrubbed tables were black with the hateful stuff again.

We spent a week loading the cargo at Emden and at long last, on the morning of the 24th February, we cast off bound for Trieste in Northern Italy. The cargo was secured, the hatches were battened down and the derricks were lowered and secured for sea (The derricks, for non-seafarers, were long, pole like booms, mainly two to a hatch but sometimes more, which could be lifted up like a crane to any height and swung from side to side. They were used for loading and discharging ships' cargos).

The prospect of sailing again had been worrying me; I feared that I might be prone to seasickness again. As the day of our departure approached, my apprehension rose, but fortunately the gods of the Sea took pity on me and I was never seasick again.

Having stowed away the ropes and once clear of the harbour, the deck crew hosed the ship from bow to stern. What a relief it was to be free from the dreaded coal dust again.

Our passage through the notorious rolling seas of the Bay of Biscay was as expected until we sighted the coast of Northern Spain where we were welcomed by a calm sea and sunny skies. Then the weather became noticeably warmer, and it was a delightful day as we sailed into the Bay of Gibraltar. I was extremely impressed with the vista of the Rock, which stood so high and imposing, rising vertically from the sea.

I was transported back to my history lessons at school and I imagined that very little had changed from those days in 1805 when the few surviving ships from the battle of Trafalgar had limped in for repairs and food supplies before embarking on their victorious journey home; Nelson himself having been killed in battle.

Two tugs came out to meet us and fussily nudged and pushed us until we came alongside a tanker moored in the bay. A pipeline was then passed between the two ships and connected to our manifold. Soon fresh water was being pumped through to replenish our depleted tanks. Within two hours, with the water tanks full again, we sailed through the Straits of Gibraltar into the Mediterranean.

It was with a calm sea and wonderfully warm, sunny weather that I gained my first experience of the Mediterranean. Life had certainly taken a turn for the better and, despite my constant daily chores, I began to enjoy myself.

We rounded the toe of Italy, and sailed in continuous beautiful weather into the Adriatic, with Italy to port and the then Yugoslavia to starboard, arriving finally in Trieste. Without delay we sailed into the port and immediately went alongside.

The deck crew had been busily preparing the derricks, topping them and finally made them secure. Once all the mooring lines were secure, the hatches were opened and the beams taken out in preparation for the discharging of the cargo. Dockers, one gang to each hatch, came onboard to unload the coal. The method of unloading was more than a little primitive. Large baskets were lowered into the holds and were filled by the shovelling dockers then emptied ashore. I thought that there must be a more efficient method of discharge, but at least it kept the dust down to a bare minimum.

I enjoyed Trieste, which was a pleasant airy city in the Italian style. Alf, Jim and I would go ashore of an evening to explore the city with its fine architecture and Roman remains. Strolling in the warm balmy climate was a novel experience and something I had long dreamed of, and it had at last become a reality. Eventually my longing to travel and my yearning to see different places and cultures had begun to be satisfied.

Occasionally we dropped into a bar for a can of beer or sat at pavement tables. That was a novel experience for me, having lived in Walsall all my life, I had never seen tables and chairs actually in the street before; then I realised that I had not yet experienced the slightest twinge of homesickness.

The Skipper would not advance us a second sub from our pay to continue to go ashore each night. He insisted that money would be needed for the final pay off on the completion of the voyage.

Whilst in port the watches were cancelled and the working day for everyone was 7.00am till 5.00pm Monday to Saturday, with Sunday as the only day of rest apart from two hours of compulsory unpaid overtime required to clean the accommodation.

A member of the crew, when ashore one evening, met his brother who he hadn't seen for four years as he was in the army and stationed in Trieste. His brother invited him to bring us, his shipmates, to the

NAAFI, the army's canteen. I'm not sure if it was the beer they served, but along with Jim and Alf we decided that we'd had enough after a couple. Almost next to the NAAFI was the army cinema. The prospect of seeing a British film was irresistible and, for little or nothing, we spent the rest of the evening watching the showing of Blowing Wild. The title is all I can recall of that epic.

The weather continued to be warm and sunny and one afternoon as I stood on the poop deck for a blow of fresh air, I noticed a local fisherman on the quayside. He baited his hook with a hunk of bread and cast it out into the dock. As the bread floated in the dock, I wondered what fish he was angling for.

To my amazement, a seagull swooped down and took the bait. The bird screeched and flew from side to side but to no avail; he was hooked. The fisherman reeled in the screeching bird, which was desperately trying to free itself. He unhooked it, tied its legs together and put it into a bag. I have often wondered if catching the bird was accidental or deliberate, and what eventually happened to the poor creature.

Finally, the cargo of coal was discharged. The method of unloading the coal, albeit archaic, was extremely effective. We said our goodbyes to Trieste as we sailed down the Adriatic to our next port of call, Sirna, a tiny island off Greece.

Sirna was a delight. Pink, green, blue and white painted houses peered out of the greenery and shrubbery of the surrounding hills, basking in the warm sunshine. Two ships were tied by their sterns to mooring buoys. One was a Greek tanker, the other a sister ship of ours the 'Fir Hill.' We were to tie up between them and we edged slowly astern in an attempt to get into place.

The docking pilot had boarded earlier and the helmsman was supposed to react precisely to his orders. Someone was obviously making a dreadful mess of it, for every time an attempt was made to go astern between the two ships, we veered off towards either one or the other. Our antics attracted a large audience. The local inhabitants had gathered on the quayside, obviously enjoying the performance. The crew of the Greek tanker were also casting a critical eye at the farcical display of seamanship.

Up on the bridge, I suspect it was thought that greater steerage would be achieved if we approached the buoys with a little more speed astern. The Greek crew obviously didn't agree with that tactic for, as they saw our stern approaching quickly towards them, they scattered like the wind.

Our engines were quickly slammed back into full speed ahead which helped to slow the drift towards the Greek ship. Finally, we came to a stop within two feet of its bow. I am sure that even the crowds of locals were as relieved as we were when we finally got a line to the buoy and made fast. The whole attempt to tie up to those buoys took an unbelievable five hours.

It was on the poop deck the following morning, as I was enjoying a cup of tea in the warm sunshine before commencing my chores, that I saw a most amusing sight. Coming along the quay was one of the tallest guys I had ever seen riding on one of the smallest donkeys. If he had stood up the donkey would simply have walked out from between his legs.

Tied up to the moorings with no cargo to unload and only domestic chores to perform, the crew enjoyed the marvellous climate: warm and sunny. At home in England folk would be freezing.

As the days passed, rumour became rife. No one had any information; we had been told nothing concerning our future prospects, nor given a destination, or told why we should be tied up between two ships off a tiny Greek island. One suggestion that was met with wholesale horror and condemnation was that we could remain tied up there for months waiting for the company to come to a decision.

After three days of silence from the company and rumour from the crew, we were told that the ship was to be handed over to the Greeks and the whole crew was to be paid off. Two days later, the word went round that we were leaving. By mid afternoon, with our gear packed and lodged in the customhouse, we awaited the midnight ferry to Piraeus on the Greek mainland.

The Arab firemen and greasers were anything but happy. In effect, they had lost their home. Arabs tended to stay with a ship signing on again and again after each trip and many of them had been with the 'Oakhill' for a considerable period of time. They kept themselves apart, huddled in a small group. It was as if they had been evicted. I felt sorry for them.

* * *

28

At midnight, the crew stood at the landing stage awaiting the arrival of the ferry. I did not know what to expect and it came as a surprise to find the ferry was much larger than I had anticipated. There appeared to be no one disembarking and as we reached the head of the gangway, a man who introduced himself as the agent of our shipping firm, The Counties Management Shipping Company, met us. He said he was to accompany us to Piraeus and that he would be catering to our needs.

As we emerged on to the open deck, I had never seen so many people in such a confined space. The whole of the deck space was a seething crowd of people who were jostling and pushing each other in an attempt to claim a little personal space. It was reminiscent of a sell out football derby, like the Kop at Anfield used to be. Our ABs were up in arms and after much pushing and shoving, they found the agent and demanded that he provided us with adequate sleeping accommodation. Off he went to see what he could do.

The reappearance of the sheepish agent half an hour later told its own tale. All the cabins were fully occupied and our beds that night would have to be beneath the stars. My fellow Able Seamen were not a happy crew. In the meantime, it didn't stop us setting sail for Piraeus near Athens, under a beautiful starlight sky.

Conditions gradually became worse as everyone attempted to settle down for the night. Having retrieved our suitcases from the custom house before boarding, we then used them as pillows and joined the wriggling pushing mass of bodies trying to make a sleeping space on the deck. The ship's decks were literally covered with a blanket of bodies. People of every nationality: Greek, Turks, French, German, Spanish, Arabs and us all spent the night in bed together. Who said the races don't mix?

I awoke, not to the roar of the Minataur, Ulysses or Cyclops, but to the snores of the League of Nations. The sun rose over an azure blue Aegean sea and, despite my discomfort, the scene was idyllic. However, it was with stiff and weary limbs that we struggled ashore in Piraeus having endured the frustrations of that Greek ferryboat.

Six o'clock in the morning, after a fretful journey, does not provide a frame of mind geared to enjoy or appreciate the splendour of ancient Athens. Neither did the cafe to which the agent directed us to for breakfast. It was typical of all Greek and Mediterranean cafes. Tables and chairs occupied the footpath and even the first few feet of the road.

As we sat, we anticipated a substantial meal to quell the pangs of hunger. We hadn't eaten since the previous afternoon but our anticipation turned to disgust as the waiter served the breakfast. It consisted of one bread roll each, very similar to the American doughnut, even down to the hole in the centre, which was accompanied by a small glass of water.

The crew were dumbfounded and soon gave way to choice, basic English expressions as opinions were voiced by some of the ABs on the contents of that Greek breakfast. In the midst of the protest, the agent and the Captain arrived. It was our first sight of the Captain since we had left the '*Oakhill*,' and it was generally agreed that we then knew who had occupied some of the cabins aboard the ferry.

"Have you been given anything to eat?" enquired the Skipper, "Yes, bread and water; we may as well be in jail," Mac, one of the ABs, replied with relish. "Let's see if we can do better than that then," said the agent and we all trooped after him in Pied Piper fashion. I'm still not sure who paid for the bread and water or indeed if anyone did.

Eventually, we arrived outside a large, appointed restaurant. It was obvious that the agent had used the place before so why he hadn't directed us there in the first place I will never know and, having sat us all down, he asked what we would like for our breakfast. Some enterprising individual shouted "Egg and chips," which was followed by a chorus of assent from the rest of the crew.

Egg and chips never tasted better, and to finish it off Jim, Alf and I asked the agent if coffee would be served. We were told that the adjoining cafe would serve coffee but we would have to pay for it. Having been told how much it would cost we pooled all of our loose change (all our worldly wealth) and decided that it would just about cover the cost. Seated outside at one of the pavement tables was pleasant after our night's ordeal and we savoured the prospect of a good cup of coffee.

The waiter arrived with the coffee cups, the smallest I had ever seen. You could hardly see them between thumb and forefinger then, to add insult to injury, he poured a brown sticky substance into the "thimbles," which tasted vile and was not drinkable. It was with disgust and dismay that we left the cafe and left the offending liquid, which had taken all our money, unfinished. So much for my first and last experience of Greek coffee.

The crew reassembled and was then escorted by the agent to the British Consulate Office where we were left to kick our heels until two o'clock in the afternoon when the Skipper reappeared accompanied by the Fourth Engineer.

Our Skipper then proceeded to issue the final pay off slip, which indicated the total monies due to each member of the crew, which was to be paid on our arrival in London. Each crewmember was then given around forty thousand Greek Drachmas, which turned out to be worth the equivalent of approximately ten shillings to cover any incidental travel expenses.

We were informed that the journey home had all been arranged and the Skipper gave us into the charge of the Fourth Engineer who he said, had the necessary travel documents and would accompany us. Needless to say, the Skipper and his fellow officers were to travel, we learnt, in a more luxurious mode. I never saw them again.

Accommodation for the night had been reserved for the crew in a hotel, and after we had deposited our gear there Jim, Alf and I made our way back to the restaurant where we had enjoyed that long awaited breakfast. We actually sat at the same table that we had previously occupied and saw, coming towards us, the same waiter who had served us the first time; as he recognised us he stopped in his tracks and without a word turned sharply on his heels and disappeared.

Our initial suspicion was that we were not welcome but within minutes, he returned with three plates heaped with egg and chips. I suppose it could be put down to telepathy or maybe he thought egg and chips was our national dish. Or maybe he was just taking the micky, but we enjoyed it just as much the second time round.

The hotel rooms were basic: they contained two single beds, which proved to be quite comfortable. The only complaint was the pillow, which was rock hard, but even that was an improvement to the previous night when my pillow had been my suitcase.

Breakfast the following morning consisted of a couple of bread buns and 'something' totally unknown to us and alien to our palates. If that was the typical Greek breakfast, I couldn't recommend it. At around 10.30am the agent arrived and, after we had collected our suitcases, we walked to the docks.

At the docks a Greek liner, the '*Koluxotronis*,' awaited us bound for the South Italian port of Brindisi. The accommodation was good with individual comfortable cabins. The agent, after seeing us securely aboard, assured us that our documents and travel arrangements were valid and in order for the remainder of our journey home before he bade us farewell. It was mid afternoon when we finally set sail, and I lay in my cabin revelling in what was sheer luxury compared to the experience aboard the Greek ferry, blissfully unaware of what was to follow.

My thoughts were disturbed by the call for the early evening meal and as we took our place in the dining room, wonder of wonders, we were to be waited upon. That was a special treat for me after all those weeks of peggying. Our waiter placed a row of knives, forks and six small plates before each person. Upon one plate he placed two olives, on another a spoonful of rice and so on with small portions of an unknown food until each plate contained something. The lot heaped together on one plate would not have made a decent meal. "God," I thought, "don't these people eat?"

The weather was wonderful with warm sunny skies and a delightful sea breeze to keep us comfortable. The '*Koluxotronis*' regularly sailed between Piraeus and Brindisi, calling at several small islands en route where passengers were collected and delivered. The islands were extremely beautiful and picturesque. Seemingly still from a bygone age, with a placid and slow life style that did not wish to join the rat race of my world. The houses and small cottages were whitewashed and basked in the warm Aegean sun.

One island I shall always remember, but whose name I never did know, was very striking. An old large fortress was in ruins upon a hill, and the locals had built a small community within the shell of the castle. As the passengers disembarked, the view from the anchorage enchanted me and to this day, the magic and memory of that place still enthrals me. I was glued to the rail as we sailed into the blue starlight night, trying to catch a last glimpse of the island's beauty.

It was mid morning the following day when I walked out on to the deck to glimpse a high cliff range on the coastline ahead of us. As the coast got closer I naturally expected that there would be another port of call hidden somewhere amongst the cliffs.

Our bows remained heading directly towards them and the high cliffs became ominously close; surely a change of course would be ordered soon for nowhere was there any sign of other shipping or habitation along the cliffs. Suddenly with our bows heading towards a collision, or so it seemed, a break in the cliffs appeared.

The ship slowed and passed its nose into a very small channel with massive cliffs rising vertically on both sides, with only a few yards leeway on either side of the ship. The whole incident was stunningly breathtaking as we slowly moved along the channel, which was as straight as a die.

Later, as we passed through the Gulf and out into the Ionian Sea, I was told that we had sailed through the world famous Corinth Canal.

Built in the seventeenth century, its length of four miles

took about four hundred miles off the original sea route to Italy; thereby saving many hours of tedious sailing around the coast. The lights of Brindisi winked and beckoned us in the dark when we finally docked there at about ten o'clock that night.

Custom officers the world over are a suspicious lot, but none it seemed to us more so than those of Brindisi on that particular night. Most of us were thoroughly searched especially our Arab shipmates who were carrying their own food, which was of great interest and suspicion to the customs.

On producing the crew's documents, the Fourth Engineer was given a great deal of hassle and the immigration officials were determined to justify their existence. Finally, after a great deal of arm waving and much unintelligible Italian argument amongst the immigration officials, we were allowed ashore. Our brief spell of luxury had come to a sudden end I realised as we lugged our gear from the docks to the railway station.

* * *

Midnight had come and gone as the Fourth Engineer produced the tickets for the onward journey. On reflection, with the long delay imposed upon us by the customs, it came as no surprise to find that the train we should have caught had long since departed. The next train we learned would leave at six o'clock that morning.

We had over five long dreary hours to wait with nowhere to sleep. Our dismay turned to anger as a pompous railway official ordered us out of the station. We were put out onto the street. It transpired, or so we were informed, that Italian railway regulations forbade entry into the stations until just before departure. So, as we tried to find some comfort sitting on our suitcases in the street, our misery was compounded as it started to rain.

It was the Fourth Engineer I felt sorry for; a young lad really, only twenty or twenty one years old, he was saddled with the task and responsibility of getting a motley bunch of penniless seamen back to England. He decided that it was not good enough to be pushed out into the street to spend the night in the rain so he disappeared, to return shortly afterwards accompanied by a policeman.

We watched the spectacle of the pompous upstart of a rail official being read the riot act. After much gesticulation and at one point the policeman waving a very authoritative finger, we were allowed back under cover into the station.

The marble floors of public buildings in the Mediterranean serve their purpose in the summer; they keep the buildings cool. In cold damp weather however, they fill you with foreboding. A platform was made of the bags and suitcases on which we tried to sleep insulated, we hoped, from the freezing marble. Needless to say, I couldn't sleep.

My clothes dampened by the rain didn't help the situation. I had to stretch my limbs constantly to maintain the blood circulation, and after five hours of doing that the sound of the train arriving at the station could not have been more welcome.

Never had a night been so long and dreary, and never was a Fourth Engineer greeted with such disbelief and rancour as when he told us that the rail official had rejected our tickets stating that they were valid only for the train that we should have caught the night before. More money was needed if we were to continue on our journey.

A whip round left us all abjectly penniless, or would it be liraless. For the few coins I still possessed amounted to about three pence. However, the total amount that the official was offered appeared to satisfy him, and we were finally allowed to board the train.

It was good at last to be on the train in comparative comfort. My clothes had dried, and in the warmth of the carriage I began to enjoy watching the Italian countryside roll by. The lack of sleep soon took its toll and one after another we nodded off, only to be awakened after a short while by the ticket collector.

Arguments conducted in Italian and English with the participants not understanding a word of each other can be hilarious if you are not involved, and arguments there were for it soon became obvious that the validity of our tickets was for the second time being strongly disputed. Once again more money was being demanded. It soon became even more apparent that the guy was threatening to throw us all off the train at the next station.

My heart went out to the Fourth Engineer who once again found himself, through no fault of his own, to be in the hot seat. He pleaded, he cajoled and he begged, and finally he charmed the ticket collector to allow us to stay aboard until we reached Rome. With much gesticulation and shrugging of shoulders, the ticket collector departed along the corridor chorusing in Italian what I supposed were his opinions on the legitimacy of English seamen.

The Fourth Engineer had successfully argued that Rome would be the best place to find a British Consulate Office where he hoped that financial help would be forthcoming to pay the man. Hopefully extra money could also be obtained to sustain our journey homeward.

We reached Rome, the eternal city, after seven long hungry hours. The beauty of the countryside was little consolation and did nothing to quell the pangs of hunger, which grew in our empty bellies. On arrival at the Rome station, we all spilled from the train onto the platform. The Fourth Engineer disappeared to seek the aid of the British Consulate whilst we languished in despair as prisoners on the platform. None of us were allowed through the exit.

It seemed ironic to me that in Brindisi, Italy, according to the railway official, we were not allowed onto the station before the train arrived, but in Rome, Italy, we were not allowed off the station, and we waited and waited.

Speculation amongst us became rife, with many expressing the opinion that the Fourth Engineer had had enough and was by then on his way home by another route. And who could blame him? What idiot would wish to be saddled with a crew of penniless seamen stranded in Italy? It is to his eternal credit that he returned yet again after another seven long frustrating hours with the magnificent sum of twenty pounds to finance the rest of the journey. It was nearly 8.00pm when he reappeared.

The vast majority of the twenty pounds he had to pay out yet again to update the tickets. What little change remained was shared between us all which added just a few more pennies to our empty pockets. It still didn't amount to enough for something to eat, but after seven hours incarcerated in Rome central station a change of scene was called for so I, along with Jim, Paddy and another AB decided to see a little of the famous city.

The train for Paris was not due to leave for two hours and the Vatican beckoned. Someone suggested that the trams were the cheapest and best form of travel into the city, and after a rickety but pleasant ride we found ourselves at St Peters. Unfortunately, St Peters was locked and barred but the square was so impressive with its magnificent architecture and its aura of history, one could imagine the Pope giving his blessing to us sailors so far away from home.

The returning tram deposited us at the station with just minutes to spare and as we settled into our seats, it was with relief and a feeling of satisfaction that at least we had seen the Vatican square. We were once again about to continue on our way home via Paris at ten o'clock of the evening. It had been twenty-eight hours since we had eaten tea on the '*Koluxotronis*,' which had been our last meal.

Sleep proved elusive as we sped northward through the night passing through the sparsely populated Italian landscape as the hunger pains became more persistent. It was a relief that dawn allowed views of the pretty countryside, but it did little to distract the attention from our bellies.

I must have dozed off for I awoke to the definite smell of food. At first I thought that I was dreaming, but No! There in the corridor of the compartment was an attendant selling hot dogs from a tray. With us not being able to buy even one, the wafting aroma from his tray amounted to torture.

It was then forty hours since we had eaten. As he departed, advertising his wares along the corridor, the smell of hot sausages still tantalised my nostrils and taste buds, the hunger pangs returned but lessened somewhat as we began a torturous climb through the mountains.

As the train struggled slowly up inclines and passes, I was glued to the windows, stunned by the magnificent vista of snow-clad mountains, glaciers and gullies. Scenery I had only dreamt about completely captivated my thoughts and attention even to the extent of forgetting my hunger, but not for long. My dreams were rudely interrupted by the return of the sausage man and the hunger pains returned worse than ever.

No scenery in the world could block out my need for food and the smell of those sausages. Two ABs from the adjoining compartment were obviously in similar throes of hunger; they came into the corridor and attempted to cajole the sausage vender to sell them a hot dog for what little lira they possessed.

"No, No, I want more money" he kept repeating, till it developed into a slanging match and while one AB gesticulated madly, imitating the distraught sausage man and distracting his attention, the other

AB discretely nicked a couple of sausages from the tray; that to me, highlighted the things that man will do when he is hungry.

My fascination with the wonderful wintery mountain scene was abruptly broken by a rumbustious spasm in my long neglected gut. I dashed along the corridor to find the loo. That was my first encounter with continental railway toilets. There was just a round hole in the floor of the cubicle through which I could see the rail track fast receding. Previous occupants had not been too particular and, not to paint too bright a picture, it was critical where one placed one's feet. It was not a pleasant experience and it did nothing for my complaining stomach.

As I retraced my steps along the corridor, I bumped into one of the Arabs. He had obviously seen me as I had dashed past his compartment towards the loo and was waiting in the corridor for me to return. He smiled and said, "Hello." Smiling back, "How are you doing?" I asked. He did not reply but silently reached under his jumper and produced a large packet of biscuits. "For you, but you must not give to any ABs" he said. It was manna from heaven! As welcome as an oasis in the dessert.

"Hide them" he said, as he slid them under my jumper. He had realised how desperately hungry I must be. His generosity overwhelmed me and for a moment I was speechless, not only for his kindness but for his thought and consideration for a seventeen year old boy and a fellow human being. I wondered if my own nationality shipmates would have been so considerate if they had food. I thanked him profusely, but he brushed my thanks aside and repeated his request for me not to give to any ABs.

I pushed the biscuits under my jumper around to my side to hide their bulk with my arm in order to keep them from the view of the ABs in our carriage, and I returned to my seat. With great difficulty, I restrained my desire for a few minutes to get at what was to be the first food that had passed my lips for two days, and I pondered on how to eat them away from prying eyes. As hungry as I was, I certainly didn't want to eat them in the loo compartment.

"Let's stretch our legs," I said to Jim after a little while, and we walked in the opposite direction to the toilets. Unexpectedly we came upon a carriage that was empty, and I ushered Jim into it to sit down. "I thought you wanted to stretch your legs" he said.

The expression on Jim's face was one of disbelief as I produced the packet of biscuits. Only on opening the packet did we find a bonus: they were chocolate biscuits. "Where did they come from?" he queried amazed. "Ask no questions" I replied as we wolfed them down. I thought it was the most wonderful meal of my life and I have loved chocolate biscuits ever since. Jim was just a few months older than me and also an ordinary seaman, not an AB, so I felt that I had not broken my pledge to my generous Arab by sharing them with him.

Exactly twenty-four hours after leaving Rome, we ran into the Gare de Lyon Paris. It was 10.00pm, and the train to Dieppe was not due to leave until 6.00am. The Parisian railway officials were much more considerate than their Italian counterparts, and we were allowed to sleep in the second class waiting room.

On the stroke of 6.00am the Dieppe bound express left the station. As it pulled away smoothly and without any hassle I reflected, with a little disappointment, that my first visit to Paris had consisted of sleeping in a railway waiting room.

The journey was fast and uneventful in comparison to the previous ones and two hours later, on the stroke of 8.00am, we pulled into Dieppe docks. A short walk then found us on the quay and boarding the cross channel ferry, the 'SS Worthing.'

Within an hour we were Blighty bound, and within a further two and a half hours the ferry had tied up at Newhaven. I felt a great sense of relief when I set foot back on English soil, but still there was no food. Customs officials were as cooperative and helpful as usual for it was more than one and a half hours before we took our seats on the London train.

The Fourth Engineer had advised the company office of our estimated time of arrival, and had arranged for the company representative to meet the train. It was six o'clock early evening when we finally arrived at Waterloo to find that there was no company rep.

Yet again tempers within the group started to get a little edgy, and my stomach began to complain again. Another hour went by and still no representative had appeared. The Fourth Engineer once again rang the company office thinking that it would be a fruitless task given the time of day. He was somewhat surprised to find that someone was still on duty, and he was informed that a representative had indeed left the office three hours previously to meet the train.

We next heard the station announcer asking over the tannoy system if any representatives from the Counties Management Shipping Company were anywhere on the station then they should report to the Station Master's Office. Shortly after, as if by magic, they appeared. They had awaited our arrival at the wrong platform. We were then informed that they proposed to pay each man ten pounds, and the remainder of our money would be forwarded by post to our homes. That went down like a lead balloon and created quite a rumpus. I was not too disturbed though as I reckoned I had very little more than that to come anyway in accrued wages.

Eventually my shipmates realised that it was a 'fait accompli' so the money and the discharge documents were issued to everyone, and we all dispersed to go our separate ways with little or no goodbyes. Jim, Alf and I decided that our stomachs could not endure starvation any longer and quelled the pangs of hunger in a nearby cafe. I said my goodbyes to my two friends and took the underground to Euston and before too long, I was comfortably on my way to Birmingham where I arrived at New Street at three o'clock in the morning.

I never understood why the taxi driver was reluctant to take me to my home; it would have only taken an extra few minutes, but he would only agree to take me to Walsall, which meant that I had to walk the last three miles or so.

Walsall in the early hours of the morning is not to be recommended. It was like a ghost town, not a soul was to be seen as I paid off the surly taxi driver and began to walk. Halfway home a policeman appeared from nowhere. His torch wandered all over me as he asked who I was and what had I got in my cases.

"This," I thought, "was great. It had taken almost a week to travel home from Greece and now a couple of miles from home I'm to be arrested on suspicion," but after examining my discharge papers, the policeman's attitude changed, and he let me go on my way. I still wonder that maybe he thought that I had been looting Woolworths.

I was tired and worn out by the time I arrived home, and I was literally on my knees. Given that the company granted one day paid leave for every month in their employ plus one day for every Sunday spent at sea, I was due for nine days at home.

And so ended my first adventure at sea. I had seen a lot. I had learned a lot and I knew what it was like to feel real hunger. I never thought that seamen could be left to fend for themselves as we had been on our overland journey from Greece. But I was young and I had come to no harm.

What is a little hunger when I had seen such wondrous sights and places that I had never in my wildest dreams expected to see. Despite all the hardships and hunger, ironically it had whetted my appetite.

CHAPTER THREE
SAN VELINO

(Of Meeting a School Mate, Mosquito Repellent and a Jellyfish).

Food, food, food. The privacy of my own room. A comfortable bed that maintained an even keel and no one to shake me awake at unearthly hours. That was the bliss in which I wallowed for nine glorious days. My mother's good, wholesome, home fare, plentiful and tasty, pushed my recent experiences into the realms of a bad dream.

I spared my mother the nightmares and the bad bits as I related to her my experiences and described the places that I had visited; she then seemed more at ease with my new job and not quite so worried. It was at her suggestion that I decided to keep a log of all my travels, and I resolved to keep the journal on a daily basis as much as possible.

I allotted a monthly allowance of money to my mother, which she banked for me as she did not expect me to make a contribution to the family budget when I was away at sea. My allowance was put away for me with the intention that it would provide a nest egg for me.

My time on leave was spent looking up my old mates, and I spent the evenings visiting old haunts and renewing old acquaintances. I found it extremely amusing to hear their repeated questions; "How long are you home for?" and "When do you go back?" I'm sure my friends were genuinely interested and not only interested in how soon they would be seeing the back of me again.

The days flew by and then one morning, the letter came that recalled me back to Liverpool. I was due to report to the Pool on the 14th April

1954; it was with a returning sense of excitement that I packed my bags on the night of the 13th. I said my goodbyes, and as the bus took me to Wolverhampton for the Liverpool train, I wondered again where I was bound that time, and what awaited me.

After the ticket collector at the gate had clipped my ticket, I turned onto the platform and came face to face with the Wolverhampton lad, Mick, who had been those few weeks behind me at the training school. He had completed his training, and he too was off to Liverpool to join his first ship. We got on well together, and as the journey progressed, he continually questioned me about my first trip and hung on to every word as I related the details of my first encounter with the world of the sea.

I enjoyed having his company on the journey, and on our arrival at Lime Street station I led him to the Pool office and showed him the ropes. After all, I was an old hand. The office was virtually empty and the clerk directed me to the Union Office and then turned his attention to Mick.

After I had paid my dues and with my membership card duly stamped, the clerk then pointed me in the direction of the doctor. It had only been a few weeks since my last medical and as I presented myself in the surgery, I saw Mick coming out. I asked him to wait for me before he returned to the counter.

Despite my recent medical, I had another thorough going over before I was given the all clear to report once again to the Pool clerks. As the clerk busied himself with official looking documents at the counter, I asked him if Mick and I could both sign on the same ship. "I don't see why not" he cheerfully responded, "Yes, the 'San Velino' of the Eagle Oil and Shipping Company. She is a tanker, signing on tomorrow morning aboard ship. She's docked in Birkenhead," and as he returned our documents to us, he explained how to get there.

As we left the office, I was chatting excitedly to Mick when someone bumped into me in the doorway. "My god! Don't tell me you've come back for more?" It was an AB from the 'Oakhill.' "You're a glutton for punishment" he joked as we laughed with each other. He was probably right, maybe I was a glutton for punishment, but looking back it had all been one big adventure for a naive, inexperienced, seventeen year old Midlands lad.

"All the local lads from the '*Oakhill*' had lodged a complaint on their return to Liverpool" he told me, and suggested that I should go round to the Union Office as there may be something for me. "I have only just had my book stamped this morning," I said. "Well go back and tell them that you were on the '*Oakhill*,' you might get a pleasant surprise" he called as he disappeared into the office.

Mick tagged along and we made our way once again to confront the union official. "You again," he said as I walked in, "what is it this time?" He listened to my tale then disappeared into a back room and returned with an envelope addressed to me. It contained seven pound ten shillings (£7.50). "I was rich. I had struck gold" I thought as I thanked him. Mick and I then made our way back to Gordon Smith's to book a room. With our gear safely stored in our rooms, it was time for a meal.

The afternoon was spent with me acquainting Mick with the delights of Liverpool, what few delights I knew about from my first brief encounter of the city. After an early tea we spent the last night ashore at the cinema, not the Tatler I hasten to add as one visit there was enough for me.

At seven thirty the following morning we made sure that we would not join the '*San Velino*' hungry and, like the condemned men, we ate a hearty breakfast at Smith's. Then we paid our bills and lugged our gear a short distance to the nearest bus stop. "Do you stop at the Pier head?" I asked the conductor as a bus pulled up. "There will be a bloody big splash if we don't," he replied. That instantly turned the bus into roars of laughter. A wonderful example of the famous Scouse humour, and although we were on the receiving end of the conductor's wit, we both joined in with the laughter.

Was that a good omen? Was it going to be a happy trip this time? I pondered as we made the short ferry trip across the Mersey. We caught a glimpse of our ship docked at Birkenhead as we approached the landing jetty, and eventually we could make out the company emblem: an enormous black eagle mounted on the top of an equally big 'O' emblazoned on the buff coloured funnel.

EAGLE OIL & SHIPPING Co.
Britain

It was very impressive, and so it should be for I learnt that prior to the war the company had quite a number of tankers, but come the peace the once large fleet had been reduced by the activities of the U-boats to just three ships. The '*San Velino,*' built in 1944, had survived the remainder of the war along with only two other sister ships; she had seen war service and was then employed contracted to the main oil producing companies, BP and Shell.

Mick and I stood at the top of the gangway to view the layout of our first tanker. There was nothing for'ard really but the foredeck and fo'c's'le head with all the accommodation amidships and aft. Watertight steel doors led from the after deck into the crew's quarters. A long alleyway inside those doors on both the port and starboard sides housed the crew's cabins with the stewards' to starboard and the deck crew's to port. Between them lay the engine room going down into the bowels of the ship.

The second story deck above accommodated the petty officers, the firemen and greasers. The deck above that housed the engineers, and at the very top was the galley with a door on each side, which led out on to the poop deck (the poop deck being the deck farthest aft of the ship.) The officers' accommodation was amidships.

Mick and I found an empty cabin where we stowed our gear and went to join the rest of the crew who had gathered in another cabin for a getting to know you session. As we introduced ourselves to one group, a young fellow detached himself from another group saying, "Hi! I'm from West Bromwich, I recognise your accents." Andy was a Junior Ordinary Seaman, and on first impression seemed a pleasant, amiable shipmate, which indeed he turned out to be.

We soon found the whereabouts of the mess, showers and toilets and came to grips with the layout of the ship. The accommodation proved to be a great improvement to that of the '*Oakhill.*' The cabins were larger and twin berth with plenty of cupboard space and a bench settee along one bulkhead.

The unpacking of our gear was interrupted by a call to amidships for the crew to sign articles. That formality took place in the officers' recreation room (I looked in vain for the crew's recreation room. It did not exist). It was there we met most of the ship's officers for the first time.

It was the duty of the Second Steward on the ship to issue bed linen etc. Two pillows, two sheets, two pillowslips, two blankets, one counterpane and one bath towel for each man, which all carried the striking company emblem. One pillowslip, one sheet and the towel were changed every week, and the practice of top and tailing was the order of the day, which meant that only the sheet and pillow slip we had lain on for the week would be changed, and the sheet used to cover us would go to the bottom and rotate in that way. That practice, I came to find, was common throughout the merchant service, at least to us the deck crew. As we settled in, it was time to change into working clothes and stow away our shore going clothes. Mick was for claiming the bottom bunk but that was not on. I pulled seniority.

The Bosun was a giant. A Scot from Stirling. Six foot six and twenty stone. He was massive and I resolved there and then that if there was to be any trouble, I would make sure that I was on his side.

Peggying was to be both Mick's and my role. A week about, and because I had done it before I was told to take the first week to share the job with him to show him the ropes. It was much easier for that one week with two of us doing it. The size of that Scottish giant precluded any argument from me. He called us to turn to at about eleven o'clock, and together Mick and I drew rations for the crew. A week's supply of condensed sweetened milk, one tin supposedly to last a week for each man, as well as tea, sugar, bread, butter and other sundries. Soon it was time to prepare both the PO's and crew's mess for the lunchtime meal. The meals had to be fetched from the galley. There were three flights of steps to negotiate, and I eventually became quite expert at carrying six plates or dishes at a time speedily, without spilling an item or a drop.

As the Bosun had said, once Mick had learnt the peggying ropes, we would rotate on a weekly basis: one peggying, one on deck. I wondered where I had heard that before. Then as soon as we had washed up the lunch dishes, stowed everything away and cleared the mess deck, we were called to stations. Again I was positioned aft on the poop deck to help to coil the ropes as they came in from the quay.

It was not, as I had first thought, time to commence our journey into the open sea for in a very short time we were tying up again at Ellesmere Port for bunkering (taking on fuel, oil and water). That operation took about two hours, after which we cast off and sailed slowly along the Manchester Ship Canal to take on our cargo at Stanlow.

Mick and I were initially busy preparing the messes for the afternoon tea, while the rest of the crew hung around the deck on standby. The only person of the deck crew other than us purposefully engaged at that time was the helmsman.

Immediately after tea, everyone was called to stations again, and the peggying duty had to wait till the deck duties were completed. The ship was equipped with a derrick both to starboard and to port, just aft of the centre castle, and they were tightly secured whilst the ship was under way. On tying up at Stanlow the starboard derrick was swung and positioned to hoist the pipeline aboard through which the cargo of petrol was pumped into the ship after the manifold had been connected.

It was not until late the following afternoon that the 'San Velino' slipped its moorings and slowly began her passage to the open sea. In case there was any sudden need for the ropes, they were not stowed away immediately, and it was not until we reached the relatively wider reaches of the Mersey that they were. I marvelled that ships of such magnitude were able to navigate the ship canal; it was so narrow in parts. Rabbits playing in the fields were easily visible from the deck.

Only a few miles from the sea, my mind dwelt momentarily on the responsibility of the helmsman. Maybe soon I would have to share that same responsibility, I mused. The prospect of me steering a ship through those places did create a certain tension in my stomach along with a few tremors of apprehension, especially at the lock, through which the ship canal was joined to the Mersey.

It was a fine April day, mild and pleasant to work outdoors. The ropes were finally stowed away, and we headed into the open sea. As we passed over the river bar and left the buoys swinging in the swell, I began to enjoy myself, and I looked forward to my first journey across the Atlantic to Curacao in the Dutch West Indies.

The weather continued fair as we lost sight of the tip of Southern Ireland, which was to be the last landfall for three weeks. It was shortly after breakfast the following morning that my peggying chores were interrupted. All of the crew were mustered aft where, for the first time, we met the Captain.

The introductory meeting, whilst being quite pleasant and amiable, was the Skipper's opportunity to state his game rules. Everyone was responsible for the cleanliness and tidiness of their individual cabins, and there was a collective responsibility for the continuous cleanliness of our shared accommodation. Cleanliness was what he expected and to ensure that it was what he got, in addition to his weekly inspection on Sundays, he would make unannounced spot checks during the week.

* * *

I quickly began to settle into the routine of the new ship. The galley was an integral part of the after living accommodation, as opposed to the 'Oakhill's' galley, which was amidships. This meant that there were no further journeys half way along the ship to collect the food. Significantly, it meant there were no kits to wash as the food could be carried to the mess already on plates, but the greatest improvement for me was the absence of coal dust. No constant scrubbing or wiping the furniture.

The Formica topped tables had never seen a scrubbing brush and needed only a thorough wash and wipe. Life was much easier, but on my first week of peggying alone, I remembered Richard on the 'Oakhill' who had got injured and had left me the single permanent Peggy. I was so pleased to see Mick present himself at meal times each day, all in one piece, with no broken bones.

A very popular song constantly being broadcast at that time was 'Bimbo.' Mick was forever to be heard singing it, all day long and all over the ship. In a very short time he acquired the title as his nickname, and he became known as Bimbo for the rest of the voyage.

That first week peggying seemed like a lifetime and, while I enjoyed the comfort of the new ship and the new experience of journeying in the vast ocean, I could not wait to start my deck duty. On my first morning I joined the rest of the deck crew who were 'sugeeing.' That was the task of washing away the salt spray from the bulkheads (walls) and deckheads (ceilings) prior to repainting them. A copious amount of soda water was used, which was finally washed off with clean fresh water applied with balls of cotton waste.

I took part in that exercise until the Bosun took me under his wing, and I began my apprenticeship under his supervision. I followed him into the centre castle where I was put to work. The centre castle is the area at main deck level underneath the midship housing. I was to spend the week with him cleaning and tidying lockers, greasing wires, overhauling blocks and tackle and many other common place duties that were so new to me. The Bosun, that hulk of a man, was kindly and patient, and I thoroughly enjoyed my first week of deck duty under his guidance.

Unlike the 'Oakhill,' which had been a dry ship (no alcohol allowed at all, at least to the crew below decks), on the 'San Velino' the Chief Steward would open the 'Bond' every Saturday evening following tea. That was for the crew to buy beer and cigarettes. Each member of the crew was allowed four cans of beer and two hundred cigarettes could be purchased for ten shillings. Bimbo and I were underage, and we were not allowed the beer, only soft drinks. Smoking was allowed inside the accommodation, but as we were sitting virtually on a tinderbox on the oil tankers, it was permitted outside only aft of the funnel.

Life was much more pleasant on the 'San Velino' as the journey continued through the vast ocean with only the sea, sky and gulls for company. The weather became warmer, and I was happy. Perhaps it was that happy introduction into tankers that coloured my future preference for that type of vessel.

It was hot, very hot, with the sun blazing down from a cloudless blue sky as we sailed through the Caribbean, and it was three weeks to the day as we tied up at Bullen Bay in Curacao, a small island off the North coast of Venezuela. On first impression Curacao Island seemed to me to be a massive oil refinery, nothing but oil storage tanks and miles of connecting pipes.

The first evening in port, subs were distributed to the crew. Bimbo and I were restricted to the grand sum of two pounds. Our more mature colleagues had vanished. I later found out they went to Campa Legre to make use of the pleasures on offer there, which were booze and women. The place was more fondly nicknamed Happy Valley. We were told it was not for the likes of us kids, and as Bimbo and I talked to the Bosun he suggested that we stay clear, and that Willemstad was for us much more worth a visit. We caught the local bus from outside the dock, and we were pleasantly surprised to find that all public transport was free throughout the island.

Willemstad proved to be a gem. Set on a narrow inlet from the sea, the town stood each side of the inlet, which then widened out into a large natural harbour in which were moored many tankers. The inlet was spanned by a pontoon bridge, which swung open to allow the passage of shipping and then shut to allow traffic to pass between the separated sections of the town. The entrance to the harbour was guarded by an ancient castle. Rumour had it that Henry Morgan, the notorious pirate who I believe later became governor of Australia for a while, had used the well concealed haven as one of his bases to slip out into the Caribbean to plunder the Spanish Main.

I mused about what stories that old building could have told as it witnessed those pirate ships returning to the safe, secluded anchorage with their holds loaded to the gunnels with Spanish gold, or anyone else's gold for that matter; Henry Morgan, prior to winning the royal favour, was not particular who he raped and pillaged.

The town of Willemstad had a wonderful atmosphere. The whole place buzzed with a happy-go-lucky air and had a wonderful ambience. Its people were happy, smiling and enjoying the balmy evening air. The West Indian atmosphere was a new world to me with its strange smells and pungent aromas of evening cooking. I was amazed and dumbstruck.

Bimbo, Andy and I found our way to the seamen's home and headed straight to the bar where I indulged in my first rum and coke. Never have I found one since with that wonderful authentic taste so perhaps the happy atmosphere and ambience of the place was also an integral part of the experience. I have since reverted to just the rum itself.

Part of the cargo was discharged, and as we sailed on the morning of the 16th May, I cast a wistful eye back at Curacao, my first experience of the Caribbean. We had caught the tide bound for Havana, Cuba. I was given the task of painting the deck rails, a much more cheerful task than house painting at home for the weather was fantastic: hot but not uncomfortable. With a calm sea and cool breeze, working on deck was idyllic.

On the Tuesday I was distracted by what appeared to be two fountains of water spouting from the sea some distance to starboard. I was puzzled at first until I saw two humps lift above the waves. That was my first sight of whales. Possibly they were aware of our presence and kept their distance, but it was disappointing for I would have welcomed a closer look at those monsters of the deep.

Thursday 20th May found us anchored in Havana Bay with the city as a backdrop. Its skyscrapers framed by the surrounding hills made for a pretty and inviting picture. I looked forward to the prospect of exploring the capital of Cuba. Our stay anchored in the bay was short-lived as the Pilot arrived to guide us to the inner anchorage, where the remainder of the cargo was to be discharged. It took three days to completely fulfil that task, and the crew were allowed shore leave following the day's work aboard.

I enjoyed pre-Castro Havana, and I explored its modern waterfront, which was in contrast to the old Spanish quarter. Once again I was taken with the happy, carefree atmosphere of the Caribbean island with happy, smiling people. I particularly enjoyed the pretty, nubile young girls who decorated every bar, and whose services we knew could be available, but not on a deck boy's pay.

It was Sunday evening the 23rd May as the sun was setting in a calm, deep, blue sea when we said our goodbyes to Havana and began the cruise back to Curacao. It was Trojan work cleaning the tanks in preparation for the next cargo to be taken aboard when we reached our destination.

The ABs disappeared into the tanks with large hoses to clean them from top to bottom. That activity also helped to clear the toxic fumes from the tanks and all of their crevices. Finally the resulting shale and rust had to be bucketed out by hand, a fearsome task with the men breathing in the fumes, which remained trapped within the shale. Each man was given a tot of rum to knock straight back as he emerged from the tank after a days work; that was, I heard, to help to neutralize any gasses within the stomach.

Two days later on Tuesday evening, we came to a halt. All engines stopped. I later learnt that an engine valve had to be replaced. In the pleasant, calm conditions it was the most opportune time to affect the repair. It really was a pleasant, warm and balmy evening, and as my friends and I lounged about on the poop deck after work, I spotted a large fish swimming in circles off the stern. It was about six to eight feet long with a long tapered snout. "A marlin" someone remarked. It was a very handsome creature streamlined to perfection. He was soon joined by two sharks of the same size that were also attracted for some reason to the stern.

Shark fishing was an expensive tourist sport, but it wasn't costly for us. We decided to cut the expense. An improvised tackle was made, and a heaving line was threaded through a block and tackle, which was then tied on to an awning spar, and a meat hook was lashed to the end of the line. The galley provided the bait, a meaty bone, which was then tied on to the hook. The line was then lowered to the surface of the water and held there. The marlin immediately began to show an interest. Three or four times it came within six or seven feet and warily turned away discarding it, and finally he disappeared.

The sharks were far more persistent though and continually milled around, circling and edging nearer and nearer. Eventually, in turn, they both came to the bait slowly and gently nudged it with their nose, only to turn away. All the frantic encouragement from the crew in flowery language did little to entice the sharks, and perhaps the colourful basic English caused them to disappear too.

Minutes passed without any sighting, and it was thought that they too had smelt a rat when one surfaced about thirty or forty feet away; it turned and headed back toward the baited hook at speed. The breathless crew stood aghast as a few feet from the bait, the shark rolled over, and belly up, with a born killer's expertise, he took the bait, hook and all. It was then all hands to the heaving line, and a muted cheer went up as we felt the hook bite into solid flesh.

The shark thrashed and lashed but to no avail, at least until he was way out of the water and level with the ship's rail. At this point he wriggled frantically, he slipped the hook and fell back in with a splash. Disappointment was felt all round, but the diversion had whetted the appetite, and some of the crew continued to rebait the hook with more cut-off's from the galley, endeavouring to entice more sharks. Later in the evening a small shark, about five feet long, was brought aboard. One of the crew was anxious to obtain the shark's teeth to make a necklace but judged that that one wasn't big enough so it went back over the side unharmed.

Our return journey to Curacao provided no further distraction, and we arrived on Friday 28th May where we proceeded immediately to the loading mooring. It was amusing to wave to the smiling people who waited on both sides, on foot or in their cars, to cross the pontoon bridge on the completion of our passage into the harbour.

Immediately opposite us at our mooring lay the deep-sea tug 'Turmoil.' Two years previously I recalled being enthralled, along with the rest of Britain, as I watched on TV the endeavours of the 'Turmoil' trying to tow the ill-fated freighter 'Flying Enterprise,' off the Scilly Isles into safe waters. The cargo of the 'Flying Enterprise' had shifted, which had caused the vessel to list heavily, and despite the 'Turmoil's' crew successfully securing towropes, they parted due to the tremendous storms. The crew were taken off but Captain Carlson, if I remember correctly, remained with his ship. In spite of repeated efforts and renewed towropes, the attempted tow into Falmouth finally failed and, after taking off the Captain, the 'Flying Enterprise' succumbed to the treacherous waters and weather off the Cornish coast and sank.

No sooner were we alongside than a further cargo of petroleum was pumped aboard. With the day's chores completed, I couldn't get ashore quick enough. That tiny island with its balmy climate and warm sun-shiny, happy-go-lucky inhabitants was like a wonderland to this teenager from the Black Country.

Willemstad with its welcoming bars and the seamen's home that always made everyone welcome was a place I could have settled for a while. Most of my mature shipmates spent the majority of their time in Campa Legre.

In effect, Campa Legre was a purpose built brothel. Curacao, with its massive trade in oil, attracted ships from all over the world and all nationalities. In the bars and cafes of the town, the local girls and some immigrants had plied their trade. The place became notorious, and the wives and daughters of the oil refinery employees were being accosted on the streets by the visiting seafarers. Trouble was endemic, and the locals had called upon the authorities to clear up the town.

Campa Legre was the practical and common sense solution, built at a distance from the town, regulated and overseen by a responsible authority. The bar girls, a euphemism for prostitutes, were medically examined on a regular basis and the seafarers knew exactly the situation and what they were about. There was no more trouble for the local female inhabitants, and a happy workable solution was achieved.

The happy days in Willemstad ended on Monday 31st May as we shifted ship around the coast to Bullen Bay to top up the tanks in preparation for the next voyage. I had been too engrossed in my new experiences of the moment to wonder much about where my next port of call would be, but I soon found out as on the 1st June we let go our mooring lines and were bound for Houston, Texas. I then wondered what awaited me in the deep south of the USA.

* * *

I was becoming more experienced and more adept at tying up and letting go under the watchful eye of the Second Mate, who's job it was to oversee the operations of the after gang which I was in. The more times I helped, the more confident I became to take on other deck jobs such as heaving in the ropes on the drum end of the winch; occasionally I was allowed to drive the winch itself. I became adept at using stoppers and making fast around the 'bits,' with both the ropes and the wire spring. I also gained experience in topping and lowering the derricks to allow the pipelines to be lifted aboard. The peggying had become routine and boring, alternating with Bimbo whilst at sea.

On deck I had never been happier; I turned my hand to any of the many jobs that needed to be completed. It was with eager anticipation that I revelled in my new world of clean sea air, clear sky and sea.

It remained hot but not uncomfortable as we voyaged across the Caribbean.

The weather remained glorious throughout the seven-day journey, which I could not help contrasting with the indifferent summers of my childhood at home in England. My euphoria was sadly destroyed at my first sight of the land of plenty. It was nowhere near my expectations as we sailed into Galveston Bay.

Houston hove into sight but remained a distant mass as we proceeded to our berth fifteen miles beyond. I took stock of my surroundings once the mooring routine was completed. The upper reaches of Galveston Bay did not fit my idea of the country I had envisaged. It certainly didn't live up to the pictures conjured up by the cinema and TV. Not a cowboy or a gangster in sight, nor a single skyscraper.

My first impression was of being surrounded by one huge swamp, which was confirmed when later that evening the Chief Steward issued everyone with mosquito repellent. His advice (translated into respectable English) was to apply it liberally all over, but after one sniff of the lotion I thought, "No way was I going to smother myself in that evil smelling goo." It is strange to relate that, while all my mates had taken the steward's advice, the following morning they had all suffered from the mosquito's urgent attention and were covered in bites. I had remained untouched.

I was not surprised that no one went ashore in such an unwelcoming spot and after discharging part of the cargo we sailed out on Wednesday 9th June bound for I knew not where. Perhaps because Bimbo and I were the junior members of the crew, discussion as to our destination didn't reach us, but more likely was the fact that I was so involved in the new life and strange places, it didn't matter for wherever we were bound would be a new and different experience for me.

We steamed our way across the Caribbean in weather that I revelled in and continued to head into the Atlantic. I still had no clear knowledge as to where we were bound but there was a vague notion that Gibraltar and the Mediterranean would be our next destination.

My work on deck, still under the guidance and watchful eye of the Scottish giant, was mainly removing rust from the rails, bulwarks and the decks with a chipping hammer, then applying a couple of coats of red lead paint and finally undercoat and a gloss finish. My earlier experience as a painter and decorator stood me in good stead and my proficiency met with the Bosun's approval. I was to find that the task of attacking the rusting process on ships was a continuing battle and was one of the main occupations of deckhands whilst at sea.

We were six days out on the afternoon of the 15ᵗʰ June when the engines failed. The ship drifted aimlessly. I wondered if it was a common occurrence and found as time went on that it certainly was, especially on the ships in which I sailed. My reverie was immediately forgotten as the cry went up, "Shark ahoy," and the fishing began. Meat hooks and scraps of waste meat were hurriedly commandeered from the galley, and within minutes three good size sharks were hauled aboard and the teeth acquired for making gruesome necklaces. The remains were cut up and returned to the deep where the rest of the school had no qualms about cannibalism.

The engines finally came back in action only to fail again the following midday. Within minutes of the ship coming to a halt, six or seven sharks surrounded us. I don't know whether it was the noise and vibrations minus the engine noise that attracted the fish, but attracted they were. Once again fishing was the order of the day and three more were hooked in no time at all. Whatever the fault that was plaguing the engine, it was proving to be elusive for the engine-room staff as we drifted to a halt for the third time the following morning.

I never found out the reason for the engine failure, neither did I hear the Captain's reaction, but there were some pretty grim faces among the engine-room staff. We only caught one shark that time but it was a monster: eight foot from snout to the tip of his tail.

It was late evening before we started up again and to the engineers' credit, it appeared that they had found a more long lasting cure. It was lucky for us that the engines had been repaired and were in good order for after sighting the Azores on Thursday 24ᵗʰ June, we ran into a gale. It was my first Atlantic gale and I was amazed that the vessel could perform such contortions and yet still right itself.

I was astonished that she could wallow in the trough of a wave with seas approaching higher than the ship itself. I was further astounded by the apparent unconcern of my shipmates who seemed to take it all in their stride. What further amazed me was that I didn't feel seasick. Not a twinge and other than a sense of apprehension, I was not averse to the roller coaster ride for which I didn't have to pay.

The weather provided further diversions and proved that peggying could be fun. Food on plates at one end of the table would suddenly slide and congregate at the opposite end. It was quite an accomplishment to finish a meal from one's own plate during stormy weather as we had to hold our plates with one hand and eat with the other.

I don't know whether it was my relief at not being seasick, or my apprehensive enjoyment of the storm, but I slept like a log that night to waken next morning to a beautiful sunny day. The storm had blown itself out and I felt great. My euphoria was short-lived however, for the gremlins struck again, and once more there was a worried look on the Chief Engineer's face as we glided to a halt.

It was the 29th June, and as we drifted aimlessly an old tall ship appeared over the horizon, all sails aloft; it looked magnificent in full sail. No engine trouble there. "Where was she bound? Wherever did she come from? What would it be like to sail on one of them?" Those were questions I asked myself as she soon disappeared from view.

Our troubles were shortly over and soon, with the engineer looking somewhat more benign, we sailed on towards Gibraltar and the Mediterranean. It was during the following night that we passed through the Gibraltar straits so on that occasion I failed to get a glimpse of the Rock, one of the last bastions of the British Empire.

The weather improved appreciably; it became hot and sunny with calm placid seas. The change in climate on leaving the Atlantic and entering the Mediterranean amazed me as it was not a gradual change but quite distinct and sudden. As the Bosun said, "It's two overcoats warmer when you pass through the straits into the Mediterranean."

My thoughts returned to the sailing ship that we had encountered, and what life would be like aboard her when they ran into a gale. She was most likely a training ship for youngsters whose aspirations were for a life at sea. There were myriads of lines, hawsers, guys and halyards onboard tall ships like her, each for a specific purpose so newcomers had to quickly gain a working knowledge of their uses. This gave birth to the phrase 'Learning the ropes.'

My idle thoughts were brought to a sudden end with a cry of command from the Bosun. His bark was far worse than his bite for at heart he was a gentle giant, always keeping an unobtrusive eye on me. Painting the funnel was the immediate task. Taking advantage of the improved weather, my Scottish mentor thought that it was time I extended my experience.

Permanent steel blocks were arranged at intervals around the rim of the funnel, which facilitated the gantlines (ropes) by passing them through the blocks, which were then tied to the bosun's chairs. An AB climbed the ladder inside the funnel to pass a line down, to which the Bosun and I attached the gantlines. The AB then pulled them up and one by one passed them through the blocks. He attached twelve gantlines all told around the funnel, accomplishing it in the shimmering heat and fumes from the engine. What lungs; what staying power he had.

Under the guidance of the Bosun, I attached a bosun's chair to each gantline, and as he checked my work I was quite pleased not to have forgotten my instructions from the training school. Pots, paints and brushes were then brought to the base of the funnel.

It was then breakfast time. Afterwards three men from both the four to eight and the twelve to four watches were called for overtime duties. Two men from the eight to twelve were called as the third man of the watch was doing his stint on the wheel. Together with the three men on daywork they made up eleven of the chairs. I was a little puzzled as to who was going to occupy the twelfth and last chair, and was totally shocked but secretly proud when the Bosun said to me, "Come on, let's have you in the chair."

Once I was in he heaved on the line, and with one hand he lifted me a couple of feet from the deck. I marvelled at his colossal strength for he held me there with no apparent effort, while he made sure that I was able to fasten myself in properly and using the correct slipknot so that I would be able to lower myself when necessary. Once again my initial training stood me in good stead, and when he was satisfied that I would be safe, he hauled me effortlessly to the top of the funnel.

The lofty perch gave me a wonderful view of the ship from a totally different angle, but my heart was in my mouth as I gazed down to that giant who was still observing my demeanour. Satisfying himself that I was not too terrified, he attached the paint pot and brush to the line for me to haul up and make secure on my seat.

Painting the top of the funnel was the trickiest part for there was little play in the gantline attached to the rim blocks. In turn, your partners on either side of you had to chuck you their rope so they could pull you as near as possible towards them to enable you to paint as much of the space between you as possible (Rollers, especially the ones with an elongated handle, which were just beginning to appear in the shops, would have made it so much easier).

You would then repeat the manoeuvre, pulling your partners towards you till they could reach to where you had painted, and once that was completed, we lowered ourselves a little to continue painting down the funnel. With each lowering, the longer line from the blocks would allow for a greater swing, which enabled easier traverse across the spaces between you and your partners.

With both the exhaust fumes swirling around and the hot sun, the heat was intense, and I could feel the hot steel of the funnel singeing my legs through my jeans. Despite the discomfort, I enjoyed my newfound experience of painting the funnel in a bosun's chair. Who would be a peggy when they could be aloft doing a real seaman's job?

The weather continued hot, and Malta came into view on the 3rd July,. We were unable to berth immediately so we anchored in the bay until Monday 5th. The journey from America had taken almost a month and on looking back over my recent experiences, I had come a long way, not only in distance but also in growing up and learning.

As I looked across the bay to the George Cross Island basking in the heat of the day, I thought of the tales that piece of rock could tell. Valletta harbour with its grand barrage during the war when constantly under siege by the enemy bombers; The large grey buildings of Valletta beckoned and I longed to go ashore.

We moved into the harbour on the 5th and no sooner had we got alongside and made fast, what appeared to me to be half the traders of Malta came up the gangway. Those people, commonly known as 'bumboats,' invaded the ships with their wares. Within minutes our mess had been transformed into a Maltese bazaar.

Silk tablecloths, shirts, clothes and a myriad of souvenirs from music boxes, sandalwood ornaments, trinkets and jewellery were on display. Assured by the eager traders of its authenticity, the jewellery looked like gold and I was tempted to buy but wise heads warned me off and anyway, I had other plans for what little money that I possessed. It was late that evening before we were able to rid ourselves of our persistent vendors but I had enjoyed the traders eagerness and friendly good humour, especially after I had just spent a month at sea.

Unfortunately, as we only discharged just part of the cargo, it did not allow the time to go ashore so there was little opportunity for me to explore Valletta. It was a disappointment, but I consoled myself with the belief that it would probably not be the last time I would tie up in Valletta harbour, and hopefully next time I would have the time to explore.

The following morning found us bound for Naples, and come the 7th July there on the horizon, standing high out of the sea, stood Stromboli with its wisp of smoke curling gently into the sky from its volcanic rim.

That was the first of many sights of mystery and beauty for me as within a few hours, we slipped between the mainland of Italy and the Isle of Capri into the Bay of Naples.

"See Naples and die" they say, but who would want to die there? It is surely one of the most beautiful places in the world with Mount Vesuvius standing watch ominously above it, scanning the whole scene. Resting at the foot of the mountain were the ancient remains of Pompeii, and its history of the eruption that had savaged and destroyed the village.

My nostalgia for school history was interrupted by the arrival of the Pilot who very quickly had us safely berthed and tied up alongside the quay. That time there was an opportunity to explore the new port and that evening, along with my two contemporaries, we sampled the delights of the bustling city in the bright Italian sunshine.

A man approached us in the street and opened his jacket to reveal dozens of watches pinned to the inner lining. He enquired if we would like to buy one. His price we worked out was about one pound ten shillings (£1.50). I picked one out that I liked and handed him the money. Subsequently it turned out to be a very good watch and I had it for years.

Yet again our stay in the delightful city was short-lived for our lines were cast off early Friday 9th July, and the Pilot guided us through the buoy marked channel out into the bay where his boat picked him up. Then we headed for Piraeus in Greece.

It was not the glory or the majesty of Greece that I remembered when given our destination, but only the pangs of hunger that flooded back in my memory on that epic trek home across Europe from Piraeus on my previous trip.

The voyage there was uneventful and I continued with my duties, both on deck and peggying. I still felt the eyes of the Bosun upon me, but he only spoke to me to instruct me in a new task. I was quite pleased with myself, and I basked a little in his approval.

It was late on the Sunday evening when all our lines were finally secured, and the Skipper had signalled finished with engines. As I finished my deck duties I looked around the harbour for sight of the 'Koluxotronis' but to no avail.

* * *

During breakfast the next morning, a Steward arrived with the news that the Skipper had organised a conducted sightseeing tour of Athens for those who wanted to go. The sting in the tail was that the cost would be deducted from our wages at the end of our voyage. The prospect of a half-day holiday was a great incentive, and the majority of the crew decided not to look a gift horse in the mouth. Immediately after dinner we changed our gear and joined the half a dozen taxis waiting on the quay.

As the convoy of taxis made its way into the city, our route took us past a certain café, and I had thoughts of stopping the cab and taking everyone in for a plate of egg and chips. First we were taken to the Acropolis where the guide gave us a tour and a potted history of the ancient remains. It was like being on holiday as we vied with the other tourists and all the beautiful Greek girls to hear what the guide was saying.

Next we went on to Socrates' Grotto with quotes from his wisdom. Then a short tour of the city took in the Parliament, the Royal Palace, and last but not least, we went to the Olympic Stadium: the source of the modern Olympic games and traditions. It was early evening when we finally arrived back onboard. It had been one of the best afternoons I had spent since I had begun my seafaring ways.

Tuesday 13th July was my birthday and was marked by our departure from ancient Athens; we were bound for Marseilles. Within two days, as I busied myself peggying, we approached the foot of Italy. One of the ABs, Tommy, asked me if I had an empty pickle jar. There were several at hand in one of the cupboards, why they were being kept I had no idea, and I wondered what the AB was going to store in a jar. "It's for posting a letter home," he replied to my query. Whereupon he put the letter and a handful of cigarettes into the jar, made it watertight, and then he threw it overboard. "The fishermen will pick it up and for the fags they will post it on for me," he explained. Sure enough, later in the trip, he received a letter from home in response to the pickle jar post.

As we sailed closer to the foot of Italy, I could see what appeared to be land beyond the mainland, and I suddenly realised that it must be Sicily. Within a few hours we had moved into the Straits of Messina, between Italy and Sicily. Once again the scenery was awesome, and I could only marvel at such breathtaking beauty, especially as the sun began to set behind the mountains of Sicily.

The weekly opening of the bond was the moment that I had been looking forward to since my birthday: my 18th birthday. The Steward said, "I'll have to check with the Skipper" when I said to him that I wanted beer, and that I was finished with 'pop.' Having got the OK from the Captain, I was handed my four cans. "Under no circumstances are you to give any to Bimbo or else" I was told in no uncertain terms.

As I took them back to the cabin, I thanked god that keelhauling (a punishment for errant sailors in long, bygone days) had gone out of fashion as I felt from the tone in his voice that it would have been my punishment for disobedience. Keelhauling was done by passing a rope beneath the ship; the culprit was then tied to it and lowered down one side, pulled under the ship and up the other side. Even so, Bimbo did enjoy sharing them with me.

It was early in the day on the 17th July that I spotted another sailing ship. In the stiff breeze with all sails flying, she was a magnificent sight. Maybe it was an optical illusion, but as she scampered along on the opposite tack to us, her speed seemed much faster than ours.

During the day, I caught tantalising glimpses of the Cote d'Azur, the so-called rich man's playground in the South of France. It is not only for the rich to enjoy any more as these days, thousands of ordinary British and Continental people swarm to the area for their holidays, and many actually buy homes there.

With the weather fair and delightfully warm, as it had been throughout most of the voyage, we found a berth quickly in Marseilles harbour late that afternoon. Tying up alongside, poor Bimbo was still within the Bosun's sight as he was in the 'for'ard' gang on the fo'c's'le head.

In the early evening I helped Bimbo finish his peggying chores; we quickly changed into our shore going gear to explore a little bit of the important French port. Even with very few French francs between us, we still managed to sample the local brew, but as Bimbo said, "he preferred his bevies to be English."

The rest of the cargo was eventually discharged on Monday 19th July, and we sailed empty (light ship) to Lake Berre, a few miles along the coast from Marseille. It should have taken only two or three hours to complete that short trip but yet again the engines failed. The ship seemed destined to be plagued continually with engine failure. Once again, the engine-room crew went around cursing the engines and all the extra work that they entailed. The fault was not rectified until the following morning, and we then made our approach to the lake.

Sailing past Port de Bouc, we entered a very narrow channel, which was the entrance to the lake, and I suspect that a fervent prayer went up, not only from me, but also from the rest of the ship's compliment that the gods smiled on our engines while we passed through.

Passing the village of Martigues at the far end of the channel, we finally arrived in Lake Berre itself, albeit a day late. Our berth for taking on the fresh cargo was at the distant end of the lake, and within minutes of having made fast, the derricks were swung over the side hoisting the pipes aboard. Once they were bolted to our manifold petrol began to be pumped into the ship's tanks. What little work had then to be undertaken was not arduous, and following the evening meal, Bimbo and I decided to go ashore, if only to stretch our legs once again on terra firma. There was little to interest us in the village and our knowledge of the French language didn't come up to engaging the locals in conversations; in fact it was none existent.

It took two days and two nights to load our maximum capacity of cargo and, once the pipes were ashore, we limped into the lake where we anchored to await the arrival of a gang of engineers to undertake specialist repairs to the suspect engines.

The sun blazed out of a cloudless sky, and in our exposed position it became red-hot during the morning. The lake, although shimmering in the mid morning sun, became very inviting and several of my shipmates, myself included, decided that the most cool place during lunchtime would be in it. All of us who had braved the waters of the lake thoroughly enjoyed ourselves; we wallowed away like walruses in the cool and refreshing water. After a while, I decided that I had had enough and, doing my impression of Johnny Weismuller (Tarzan), I swam back to the ship.

Concentrating on my crawl stroke, my arm came over and landed on a large jellyfish that I hadn't seen. I felt the sting instantly, and it scared the crap out of me. Not knowing what had caused the sudden pain, I spun away from it and sank below the surface at the same moment. It was not until I resurfaced that I saw the jellyfish floating away from me.

At olympic speed, I swam to the gangway and hauled myself aboard. My arm was already red, swollen and stinging as I presented myself before the Chief Steward. He found some antiseptic cream from the medical cabinet and asked, "What kind of jellyfish was it?" "What sort of stupid question is that?" I thought, "A bloody slimy floppy one," I retorted indignantly.

With a shrug of his shoulder he mischievously said, "You are dead within two hours of being stung by certain types of them." "Thanks a lot," I shouted as I retreated to my cabin. It was the longest two hours of my life, I could not drag my eyes from the clock and needless to say, I was very relieved when those two hours had passed, and I was very wary of where I swam after that painful encounter.

We said goodbye to the local engine repair gang on Saturday 24th July, and weighing anchor we made our way back along the channel to anchor for the night off Port de Bouc. I awoke to the sound of the engines running at full speed. We must have left the anchorage off Port de Bouc very early since when I came on deck at 6.30am, there was no land in sight, and I learnt that we were heading back to Greece and Piraeus.

Five days later and with no engine failure that time, we finally tied up in Piraeus at exactly the same berth we had occupied on our previous visit. It was Friday 30th July. There was no organised conducted tour on that occasion, but the bar at the entrance to the dock looked inviting so we contented ourselves with the friendly company and the cheap lager.

Once again only a parcel of the petrol was discharged, and we headed out to sea on 1st August bound for Beirut in Lebanon. Another country, another port, another new experience I thought as we arrived four days later. However, I was to be disappointed for our berth was tied up to two buoys, half a mile from the shore. Having made fast, dockers arrived to raise the pipeline from the seabed to discharge the rest of the cargo.

It seemed as though the pipeline had been just connected to the manifold when pumping began and the 'bumboats' arrived alongside. Why oh why, was it during my spell of peggying that the bumboat men always came aboard? Within minutes of their arrival, the mess was transported again into an 'Aladdin's cave' filled with cheap colourful trinkets, and a myriad collection of goods for sale.

I was especially taken with the clothes on offer, and I selected two shirts that took my eye. To my surprise, they shunned the coins of the realm and even the local currency but readily accepted two bars of soap in full payment. Obviously soap was in short supply or it was a very saleable commodity.

It took two days to complete the total discharge of our cargo, and we sailed on Friday 6th August, light ship. I had completed my tour of duty peggying on the Saturday and we headed back across the Mediterranean to Port de Bouc.

I had looked forward to my spell of deck duty, but my Sunday morning slumber was disturbed by a flurry of activity. The Chief Cook, the earliest riser of the crew apart from those on watch duties, had come to the galley to prepare breakfast only to find that the gas burners from the stoves were missing.

The Skipper immediately called all hands for a minute search of the ship but to no avail; they were never found. The general consensus was that some misbegotten idiot had thrown them over the side but for what reason remained a mystery. If the culprit had been discovered, he would have fared badly at the hands of his shipmates for cold food and sandwiches were the order of the day until the engineers had fashioned new burners out of spare parts.

Approaching the toe of Italy on Wednesday 11th August we encountered the Royal Navy on manoeuvres, possibly fresh out of a base in Malta. I counted at least eight or nine destroyers and corvettes scurrying hither and thither at some rate of knots. It was estimated that some of the destroyers were doing at least twenty-five knots. They made a brave picture as they came past and before long, they had disappeared from sight.

When we arrived off Port de Bouc on Friday 13th August I was determined not to tempt fate, and I never went swimming there again no matter how inviting the cool waters of the lake appeared. The swelling and soreness in my arm had only lasted for a couple of days, but the memory of that jellyfish lingered on.

Without delay we passed through the channel to anchor off Martigues. On our previous visit to the lake I had hoped to get the opportunity to visit Martigues, but there had been very little time. This time after having asked the Skipper for a sub, Andy, Bimbo and I were soon into our shore-going gear and down the gangway, where a small boat was waiting to ferry us ashore.

The town was small but pleasant, typical of the French coastal resorts, and I compared the setting to what I had been used to in the summer at home as we sat outside a small bar, supping French beer in the evening sunlight. It was so different from Bloxwich High Street.

We crossed the lake on Saturday night and berthed alongside the petrol storage tanks. Soon after we made fast, the oil pipe was aboard and attached to the manifold with the ship's tanks being replenished for a further voyage. It did strike me that our role was similar to that of a ferryboat carrying petrol instead of people to different ports around the Mediterranean.

Sunday in port was our day of rest. After completing the breakfast duties the three of us were free for the day. It was far too nice a day to stay aboard and, although we knew there was little to see or do in the tiny village, the prospect of dry land was appealing.

It must have been a local holiday or fiesta for a travelling fair had set up camp in the village. Complete with hoopla, swing boats and the usual fairground rides, it made for a change and was a welcome interlude, which we greatly enjoyed.

Fully laden once again, we set forth early on the morning of the 16th August. Given the number of times we entered and left the various ports of call, I had become as proficient as any of the older deckhands at handling the lines and mastering the techniques of what at times could be a complicated process. And, due to my youth and fitness, I was probably much more nimble about the deck, which was a big plus, especially in rough weather.

And so back into the Mediterranean we sailed destined for Italy and Spezia, another name to conjure with. I was not to be disappointed for on arrival the next day, I was enchanted. Spezia was a gem, breathtaking in its setting. Jutting out into the entrance to the harbour was a strip of land, on which cannons were placed every few yards. Off it lay the wreck of an old ship, which defied reckless navigation. Edging our way gingerly between the wreck and the shore, we let go the anchor in the middle of the harbour, where again a small boat had been made available to ferry everyone to and from the quayside.

I liked Spezia immediately. I could have lived there. With its long wide road, which ran along the shore and its wide walkways lined with what I suspected were orange trees. The town had a happy and welcoming atmosphere, with the people busy but cheerful, talking loudly and gesticulating at one another constantly.

A further attraction was the many wine bars where free tasting was an added temptation. After sampling the free offers in several of the bars, we were all a little sozzled and at no cost. Not a lira had changed hands.

On Thursday we moored the ship alongside to discharge a parcel of cargo. That took little time and after only three or four hours, we were casting off and on our way south.

Stromboli had become a familiar sight away on the port beam. On our way to the Straits of Messina I decided to try my luck with the pickle jar post. As we wended our way through the Straits, I threw the pickle jar, containing a letter home and cigarettes, over the side for the fishermen.

Once around the foot of Italy, we headed eastwards destined for Istanbul and the delights of the Dardanelles, which is the gateway to Asia. Turkey and the Dardanelles rekindled vague memories of my school history lessons when the Turks waged a disastrous campaign against us in the First World War that had ended in carnage.

Tuesday 24th August brought us to the Dardanelles where, stood prominent on the hillside, was the monument erected in the memory of the thousands of troops from both sides who had lost their lives in that campaign. Two fortresses guarded the entrance through which all vessels proceeded. It would be a daunting task for any unwelcome guest to attempt to sail past that stronghold for guns could be brought to bear on either side.

We passed through safely into the Sea of Marmara, across which we headed. I was asleep in my bunk in the very early hours of Wednesday morning when we let go the anchor to await a berth in Istanbul: my first Asian city.

* * *

When I walked out on deck at 6.30 that morning, my first glimpse of the city across the water stopped me in my tracks. It was as if we had sailed through some sort of time warp during the night. I stood transfixed and stared at the vista before me. There in the bright sun was a scene of light morning mists rising from the ground, folding themselves around some of the buildings as though trying to protect them from the sun, but the silhouettes of the buildings could still be seen through the thinness of the mists.

Rising through above the mists, the brightly coloured domes of the mosques shone brightly in the clear morning sunlight. It was like a scene from the Arabian nights or a scene from a Disney fantasia. The heat from the sun got warmer by the second and swiftly evaporated the mists, which in turn created a heat haze that caused the mosques and minarets to shimmer, and the calls to the faithful to come to prayer echoed around the bay. I gazed at the scene staring in wonderment until I was rudely reminded that my presence was required by one of the ABs who was waiting for his breakfast. "Don't you know it's breakfast time?" he snarled in not so polite language.

The breakfast suddenly became a hurried affair for the word was passed that the Pilot was on his way. As soon as he was aboard the anchor was weighed for us to quickly tie up alongside one of the many jetties to discharge more of our cargo.

On Friday 27th August, a small water tender wished to come alongside the jetty, but our ropes were stretched across where she needed to berth. She couldn't sail under them so we had to loosen our ropes down into the water, in a deep U shape, so that she could sail over them. No sooner had she done so, a strong sudden gust of wind sprang up from nowhere, which caused us to drift away from the jetty because of the slackness in the ropes. We sprang into action immediately to heave our ropes tightly on the drum ends of the windlass and slowly pulled the ship back alongside. Unfortunately one of our ropes had caught across the wooden structure of the crane on the jetty that was used for lifting the pipeline aboard the ships, and we heard the sharp cracking of timber as some of the stanchions snapped.

The next day, Saturday 28th August, we returned through the Sea of Marmara back through the Dardanells and south to follow the coast around down to Iskenderun on the Turkish mainland, just above Cyprus. We arrived there the following Tuesday. Yet again, there was no delay into our berth for us to discharge the remainder of our cargo.

We sailed towards Berre for replenishments two days later on Thursday 2nd September. In the early evening on the following Sunday, a giant hawk landed on the top of our mainmast; he was obviously tired out and in need of a good rest to recuperate. What actual species he or she was I have no idea, but it was a really massive bird, the biggest I had ever seen.

One of the lads noticed that a large sack of potatoes had been left outside the galley for the Cook, and as we were always on the lookout for unusual diversions from routine life, he opened it up and started to throw spuds at the bird. Of course, when we saw him doing that, nearly everyone else began to have a go, laughing and joking all the while. No one got anywhere near to the bird; it just sat there, high on his perch, looking down at us without the slightest concern, but the deck below was soon littered with spuds.

That night Rusty, an SOS, went up to do his stint of lookout on the fo'c's'le head with blankets wrapped around himself and a saucepan over his head. "That hawk is not going to swoop down on me," he said. Sometimes I wondered what sort of nutters I was sailing with, but a good sense of humour was essential for the job as a merchant seaman, and the bird had flown by daybreak.

The Cook went berserk that morning on seeing the fate of his sack of spuds. He immediately reported it to the Skipper, who ordered us all to go around the decks to collect them up and to return them to the galley. Whereupon he ordered that those particular spuds were to be kept separate and dished up to the sailors' mess only, until they had all been used. That was met with much laughter amongst the deck crew.

The following day I went to empty the gash bucket and as I looked down into the crystal clear waters, I saw a giant turtle surrounded by a shoal of small, multicoloured fish, which appeared to be attending to all his needs, while he seemed to be oblivious to his brightly flashing technicoloured entourage. Again, I thought how incredible it was, and how lucky I was to be given the opportunity to see those wonders of nature in the flesh and in their own natural environment.

Wednesday 8th September saw us back in Berre where once more the whole process started again. Fully laden on Saturday 11th, we sailed for a return visit to Spezia where we arrived the following day. Again the three of us, Bimbo, Andy and myself patronized more of those wine bars with their free samples; we deliberately missed out the places that we had visited previously, in the fear that our faces would be remembered and once again we became quite pleasantly happy.

Two days is all that we had in that pleasant place for we sailed on Tuesday 14th September and headed south, once again through the Messina Strait and on to Piraeus, arriving there on Saturday. I had begun to think that Piraeus was my second home because of the amount of times I had called there since my travels began, and I did not bother to go ashore on that occasion.

Having sailed on the Monday, our next port of call was Volos in Greece. On Tuesday morning, in warm sunshine, I was sent up on to the fo'c's'le head to paint the rails. We were following the coastline around about three miles offshore. As I looked ahead to the horizon over our bow, the sea appeared to have changed colour from a beautiful blue to a murky brown. I puzzled upon it for a while, but as we gradually got closer the whole surface of brown, as far as the eye could see, was bubbling strangely like a sauce simmering in a giant pan.

Our bows headed swiftly towards its rim and suddenly entered its brown murkiness. I couldn't believe my eyes, it was one vast mass of jellyfish, billions of them. They had round yellowish domes in the centre of their mainly brown rims. As I looked down directly on to them from over the rails, it appeared for all the world as though we were sailing through a vast sea of fried eggs that had gone rotten. It was a spectacle I have never seen the likes of before or since. I was profoundly grateful that I was on the fo'c's'le head and not aft where no doubt the mass slaughter of the unlucky ones that were being churned up by our propeller could be witnessed.

We anchored in the beautiful bay at Volos; most of the coastline around us was high, green and hilly, perhaps even mountainous. A guy in a rowing boat came out to us to ask if anyone wished to go ashore; therefore that evening the three of us decided to go. While he rowed us ashore, we spoke to him about those jellyfish. He must have had some local knowledge of them as in excellent English he told us that they were harmless, but after my encounter with what was, in all likelihood, the only one living in the vast expanse of Lake Berre, I wasn't so sure.

Once ashore we strolled leisurely along the dusty road, with the intention of going into the town, which was quite some distance away. The hills and mountains were all around us. Suddenly Andy stopped, looked up at the highest peak and said, "I wonder what the view is like from up there?" "Well let's find out" we chorused.

Off we set, first through a wooded area and then we continued through thick bracken until we reached a brook. The other two jumped it easily, but I slipped and fell in. I was soaked from the knees down, and both Bimbo and Andy could hardly stand through laughing, but we carried on. It seemed to take ages, but we gradually ascended until we finally reached the summit. I was totally dried out by then, and it had just begun to get dusk, but we still got a most spectacular view. I for one thought that the climb had been well worth it.

When we looked down to our right, we could see the green hilly coastline worming its way along for miles. To our left, beyond the hills in the distance, we could just make out the shapes of the buildings of the town that we had originally been heading for. Slowly, more and more lights began twinkling in the oncoming dusk. Right behind us were more mountains, as far as the eye could see, while right below us was the harbour, and in the middle of the bay we could see our ship at anchor. She was the only one there, and from the height of our vantage point she looked lonely. To us she seemed no bigger than the rowing boat that had brought us ashore.

It was very dark when we started our descent, and it was very difficult to see where we were going. On more than one occasion, one or another of us almost disappeared over a steep drop. We had obviously climbed down by a different route, and our teenage minds hadn't even considered the possible dangers. Luckily when we reached the bottom almost an hour and a half later, we were all still in one piece.

We found ourselves in another wood and didn't have a clue where we were so we just ambled around aimlessly. Fortunately we stumbled on to a little pathway, which before long brought us out onto the road again. By then, we were too tired to go all the way to town so we headed back to the ship. The man was there waiting to row us back out to the ship. We didn't know if he was paid by the company to transport us or not, but we each gave him a few drachmas anyway, which he seemed quite happy about. It had been a very tiring little expedition, but all three of us had enjoyed it.

After Volos, Istanbul was again the place for the remaining parcel of that particular cargo so we sailed on Wednesday 22nd September; we went through the Dardanelles on Thursday and then back across the Sea of Marmara to arrive early Friday morning. We moored up to exactly the same jetty as previously, and the first thing I noticed was that the wooden crane was no longer there; it seemed that we must have broken it beyond repair thereby forcing every ship since to use their own derricks to hoist their pipelines aboard.

It rained all day on Saturday 25th September. Unbelievably I suddenly realized that it was the first rain that we had seen since we had left England over five months earlier. It still poured down heavily later that night when we had to turn to on stations to let go. We were to return yet again to Berre.

All the ferrying from port to port, with little time spent at sea and even less ashore had by then begun to take its toll on some of the crew. It had started to become monotonous. Being on a very confined, mobile, steel island and living so closely together in cramped quarters, tempers sometimes seemed to be on an ever shortening fuse.

Each Sunday, as if by ritual, our dinner was roast chicken; the sailors' mess always had the leg, the breast always went to the officers. It was as though the breast was the upper class meat for the upper class officers and the legs were fit only for us lower life. One particular Sunday, I had just started on my week's stint of peggying when I placed a dinner in front of one of the ABs. He took one look at it and banged his fist on the table top and shouted for me to go and tell the Cook that he wanted some breast.

As bidden I went up to the galley and told the Cook that some of the ABs were complaining that they wanted some breast. He turned sharply on me and shouted, "A chicken has only got two tits." "It's only got two legs as well," I retorted, and I turned on my heels as he chased me out of the galley and halfway down the flight of stairs, waving his spatula at me threateningly. I was too quick for him so he gave up and returned to his job. Never once did we get any chicken breast. Oh the joys of being a peggy.

When the opportunity arose in wide open sea, the Skipper allowed Bimbo and I to do a ten to fifteen minute stint at the helm. This was under supervision of the AB who we temporarily relieved, and it helped us to gain experience in steering the ship.

We didn't get a chance to do it on that particular trip back to Berre however, as we ran into bad weather and heavy seas for most of the way. We arrived and anchored in the lake on Friday 1st October and slipped alongside the jetty the next day. Yet again it didn't take long to pump a whole cargo of petrol back into us. Hardly anyone bothered to go ashore there any more after so many visits.

On the Sunday night we sailed back through the channel and anchored off Port de Bouc to wait for our clearance papers. As soon as they arrived we weighed anchor, or perhaps to be more correct I should

74

say we weighed chain. Much to everyone's amazement, there was no anchor attached to the end of the chain! It must have unshackled itself in the depths from its chain, but how will always remain a complete mystery to me. Nonetheless, not wasting any time, we sailed anyway and followed the coast along until we arrived in Vado in Italy on Monday 4th October.

While they were discharging their parcel of cargo, we had to rig up our big derrick, the 'Jumbo', with our heavy lifting gear. It was situated up for'ard adjacent to the foremast. Then we had to raise it to the required height and swing it out over the port rails. Once in position we lowered the runner wire. Next, we had to rig a paint stage over the bow so that two men could go down to shackle the block on the end of the runner on to the anchor chain.

Once they were back onboard, we lowered both the anchor chain and the runner shackled to it down to the seabed. Then as the ship's carpenter (who was always in charge of the windlass when the anchor was to be used) slowly gave slack to the cable, we heaved up on the 'Jumbo.' This brought the end of the cable up out of the water. Once it was high enough, we swung it inboard so that the end link was adjacent to where our spare anchor was chained down, making sure that the cable itself was secured so that it could not slide back into the sea. The next task was to release the spare anchor. That in itself posed another problem.

The spare anchor had sat chained in its position on the deck for the last ten years or so, exposed to all the elements, with rust and coats of paint that defied a normal release. Chisels and hammers were called for and following deft blows to strategic spots, the rust and paint finally gave up its hold on the reluctant anchor.

With much sweat and lots of very basic English, the shackling of the anchor to the chain was completed. At which point it was knocking off time. The moment of truth came the next day: would the derrick hold the weight? We all wondered as we raised the newly shackled anchor clear of the deck and rails. Fearful eyes were cast upon the derrick as it gently swung probably its heaviest load ever over the side. Many sighs and expressions of relief accompanied its passage as it was gently lowered to the bottom of the sea. All that remained then was to heave the anchor up on the windlass as normal.

The whole operation was extremely delicate. I asked the Bosun why the anchor had to be lowered to the seabed first. "Why couldn't we have heaved it along the side of the ship towards the bows?" He told me that the weight would be so great, it could bring the whole derrick crashing down. I was to remember that later.

All that remained to do then was for two ABs to go over the side again on the paint stage to unshackle the runner block, and then we secured the 'Jumbo' back into its place. The lads were well satisfied with a job well done, but it had taken two full days to complete the whole task.

In the hot sun, the work had been hard and strength sapping, and a new scene and recreation beckoned so, in the welcome cool of the early evening, other shipmates and I headed ashore. There was absolutely nothing in Vado itself, so a couple of us took a short bus ride into Savona, a small neighbouring town, with its welcoming bars and willing young ladies. Being a hot blooded healthy young eighteen-year old male, who had in effect lived for the last few months aboard ship in a world without women, I found myself in a dingy, sleazy room where one of those willing ladies began my education on the delightful journey into manhood, and I lost my curiosity.

* * *

On Wednesday 6th October we sailed on the way to Egypt, Port Said and the entrance to the Suez Canal. After three uneventful days we anchored amongst the many vessels of different nationalities that were awaiting passage through the canal. The anchor had hardly touched the water when the ubiquitous 'bumboats' surrounded the ship. The enthusiastic, enterprising Arabs appeared to sell and stock almost anything: souvenirs, toys, clothes etc. One of the more persistent Arabs, a man who called himself 'George Robey,' was hard to shake off. Haggling and bargaining was not only the order of the day, it appeared to be the accepted custom.

George Robey was soon onboard vending an amazing stock of shirts, jewellery and watches. Everywhere you turned someone tried to sell their ware to a mostly disinterested crew, the majority of which had seen it all many times before. But to me it was all new and fascinating.

Eventually the decks were cleared of the persistent hawkers, and for a little while it was pleasantly quiet until we were interrupted by the arrival of more Arabs. That gang were official, and with a specific task in hand. I looked with disbelief as they hoisted two small rowing boats aboard. My curiosity was deduced by that Scots accent.

The Bosun had noticed my puzzlement and explained that the boats were necessary in case any ship suffered engine failure during passage through the canal or for any other emergency for that matter. The boats would enable a rope to be passed from ship to shore for the ship to be tied up safe. Throughout most of the length of the canal, bollards were situated at regular intervals on each side for that purpose. A ship out of control in the confines of the canal would create havoc and bring all traffic to a standstill.

Another small boat came under our bow that carried a large searchlight. Therefore our next task was to heave it onboard and fasten it on to our bow so that the beam of light would flood forward and light up the whole of the canal ahead. Once again, my Scots mentor explained that it was necessary to enable the Pilot to plot our passage and keep a clear view of the ship ahead in the convoy during the hours of darkness.

In the early hours of the following morning, we were called to stations as one by one the waiting ships began to enter the canal. Up until then I had not realised that the canal operated under a one-way system. Neither had I known that the canal was wide enough only to allow safe passage in one direction. Consequently convoys formed to allow the maximum number of ships to pass through at one time. When our turn arrived, we edged our way into the canal. We were not the last in line, but we were towards the back of the line, and there were approximately three ships' lengths between each vessel. Once we had passed the lights of Port Said and into the canal proper, I went to bed.

As I walked out on deck in the early morning sunlight, on either side of the ship all I could see was desert: miles of sand without any sign of vegetation. The weather had become increasingly hot, sticky and stifling without a breath of air, and the slowness of our progress did not raise the usual breeze that we mostly got at sea. There was no escape from the stifling conditions and there was little consolation when we arrived at the Bitter Lakes around midday.

I had first heard about the Bitter Lakes in my geography lessons at school, and I was surprised to find them so vast for I had imagined them to be long but very narrow. It was a relief to escape from the claustrophobic atmosphere of the canal itself into the expanse and space of the lakes. I was at first a little perplexed as to the reason for us to be riding at anchor along with the rest of the convoy. It soon became apparent though when, from the south of the lake, another line of ships hove into view. We had been waiting for the northern bound convoy to clear the southern section of the canal. In its design, the Bitter Lakes had become a conveniently placed area to allow the passage of ships that were headed in opposite directions.

Port Suez situated at the southern end of the canal was our destination, and we arrived there at 5.30pm. After we had turned to starboard we dropped anchor to wait for a berth. The sun shone relentlessly as we later went alongside to discharge the rest of the cargo.

The discharge was completed on Sunday 17th October and we anchored off the entrance to the canal to make the northbound passage. Such was the effect of the temperature and the stifling climate that no one had been ashore while we were tied up in Port Suez. At times it was dangerous to touch the ship's metalwork; it was so hot, that strange as it may sound, it was wise to wear gloves when working out on deck.

As we waited for the arrival of other ships to make up a convoy, it gave me time to reflect on the basic history of the canal, what little I knew. Considering it was constructed in the mid nineteenth century and opened in 1869, it was a fantastic memorial to its builder, the Frenchman 'de Lessops.' On its completion the canal realised the dreams of the merchant traders: to connect the Mediterranean and the Red Sea. This enabled ships to reach India and the Far East without having to go round Africa and the Cape of Good Hope, cutting the passage time by weeks rather than days.

In hindsight, it is a shame that a man of such vision did not anticipate the future development of modern ships and the eventual size of those built today. Otherwise, perhaps the canal would have been built twice as wide and even deeper, to allow for the passage of both North and Southbound ships within its confines. But how much more sand would have had to be shovelled by the natives who had worked in that pitiless climate?

In the late evening we joined the northbound convoy and took position about third or fourth in line. The passage through was uneventful, although a southbound convoy was entering the Bitter Lakes, just as we had done, and was waiting for us to get clear of the southern section. There was no delay on that occasion and we sailed on into the northern section. The claustrophobic atmosphere could not be dispelled and I marvelled at the desolate, uninhabited desert all around as far as the eye could see.

It was with little regret that we waved goodbye to Port Said, and as we reached the open sea it was as if we had been enclosed in a sauna for days and were then back in the fresh air. But I was swiftly finding out that relief is very often tempered with disappointment. The word was passed around that our destination was, yet again, Berre.

On that occasion only a part cargo was taken onboard, and after only arriving on Sunday 24th October, we were bound for the northern Italian port of Genoa by Tuesday 26th. It was a short voyage, and we arrived in the bay of Genoa the following day only to have to ride anchor for a while to wait for a berth.

As we were guided into port we learnt from the Pilot that a brand new berth was to be opened that day, and we would be the very first occupants. To mark the occasion an official ceremony with all the civic dignitaries attending had been arranged. The press and an army of photographers were waiting for our arrival. With much flashing of cameras we tied up alongside.

Once the pipe was hoisted aboard and connected to the manifold, with much pomp and ceremony the Mayor opened the valve to release the first cargo of petrol. Speeches were made, and although I didn't understand the words, the meaning was universally international and could have been understood if delivered in any language.

We were quite disappointed that there was no opportunity to scan the local news sheet the next day to see if there were any photographs because in the early hours of the morning we set sail bound for Greece. Once again to Piraeus, and we arrived after an uneventful voyage on Tuesday 2nd November.

By that time we had been away from home for over six and a half months, and the crew were getting really restless, fed up with the continuous shuttle around the Mediterranean, to-ing and fro-ing from one port to another. The general feeling was that if they had wished or wanted a job on a coaster, they could have easily found one around the English coast with the opportunity to see home and family more often.

On reflection it would have been better for the crew's moral if the Skipper had arranged an organised tour of Athens during that period of the tour of duty rather than at the beginning. But to be fair, he could not have known that we would return all those months later, and I for one was grateful that the Skipper had taken the trouble to organise it at all otherwise I may have never seen those sights.

As we approached our berth, a misjudgment on the bridge created a diversion. Only rapid evasive action prevented the ship's bows coming into contact with a German vessel moored in an adjacent berth. Where were the cameras then? I imagined that a lot of flowery English was bandied about on the bridge, especially as we had to move to a different berth the following day. Why couldn't we have just anchored overnight?

The weather gradually changed. Thursday evening, it clouded over and a breeze got up, usually a sure sign of rain. By morning a full storm was blowing and after the heat of the Suez Canal and the Red Sea it felt quite cold.

While we prepared to let go, a tug arrived to assist us and struck into the accommodation ladder before it had been hoisted and secured. Fortunately it caused no damage. Finally, with the ladder secured, we started to let go. Because the strong winds would have blown us away from the quayside, the tug settled against the hull to hold the ship steadfast against the quay, which aided the task of casting off. Ropes were then secured to the tugs at bow and stern, and they then began to tow the ship clear of the quay.

Due to the conditions and severity of the storm, the towrope to the for'ard tug parted. Fortunately we had travelled a sufficient distance from the quay to enable the tug to take a position between the quay and the ship to continue to push us out while the stern tug guided us backwards into the open sea, where both tugs then left us to our own devises.

Sailing at a safe distance offshore, we followed the coastline and, as we progressed along the coast, the storm diminished. Finally we arrived off Salonica in northern Greece on Saturday 6th November in beautiful spring-like weather. From Salonica where we had discharged the last of the cargo we sailed empty to where else but bloody Berre.

The passage in delightful weather was uneventful. Throughout the journey the main task of the deck crew was to clean out the tanks when empty. As mentioned before, the ABs descended into the tanks equipped with a high power hose, but due to the heat and conditions each man was allowed only a limited time in the tanks, and the residue and slurry was pumped into a holding tank on completion.

Under the instruction of the Bosun, I was given the task of removing the tops of a dozen or more fifty-gallon oil drums. It was done the hard way. Equipped with hammer and chisel, the giant Bosun took the top off the first one, and then he told me to do the rest.

With the job completed under the guidance of my mentor, the oil drums were then lashed to the outside of the rails. Once each tank was hosed down and the residue slurry and oil pumped into the holding tank, they were then virtually gas free; the sailors then had to go down to the bottom to shovel all the loose rust and gunk into buckets, which I then had to hoist up and tip into the oil drums. We were not allowed to dump the waste over the side, especially not into the waters of the Mediterranean since it is virtually a landlocked sea with minimal tide to disperse such contaminating garbage. Berthed safely in Berre, the oil drums were taken from the ship, the slurry was pumped ashore and the process of loading began again.

During the three-day stay that we had in Berre, the weather changed, and we let go again early morning at six o'clock on 16th November bound for Spezia. It was bitterly cold. We did not know it then, but that was to be the last we saw of Berre. As we berthed in Spezia the following evening, I received a letter from home in reply to the one that I had sent by the pickle jar post almost three months earlier. There was no such thing as email in those days but we did have 'sea' mail it seemed. Later Bimbo and I made our rounds of the wine bars again, but that time we were recognised and the free drinks were not forthcoming. We had to pay.

Tied up alongside opposite us in Spezia was the charred and burnt out hulk of a ship, which we later learnt was the luxury cruise liner the '*Empress of Canada.*' She had been towed to Spezia on route to the breakers yard after she had succumbed to flames in Liverpool docks; a sad sight indeed for all sailors.

Once we had discharged part of the cargo we let go on the 18th November, and the keel hit and bounced off the bottom as we left harbour, and the ship almost ran up the beach. Again, we were pulled to safety to continue our passage to Piraeus.

As we passed through the Messina Straits four days later, I recalled that the following day, November 23rd, was the first anniversary of my arrival at the Gravesend training school. Was it an occasion to celebrate? On balance, I decided that it was, and on the evening of the 23rd, Andy, Bimbo and I sampled the delights of the Piraeus dockside bars and the local beer and wine. So much had happened in just one year.

On our departure on November 25th we headed for Istanbul; the journey took two days. I was still enthralled with the charming scenery of the Dardanelles, the coastline of the Marmara Sea and the skyline of Istanbul. The magic had not yet worn off.

* * *

As previously stated, tying up, weighing anchor, casting off and all the procedures of entering and leaving port had all long since become routine. They were however much more preferable to my peggying duties, which became more and more tedious and boring. It was with some relief that I went to stations on our departure heading for Spezia again, having discharged part cargo in Istanbul. I couldn't understand why we had to return to Spezia so soon to discharge further petrol, especially petrol that we already had in our tanks on our previous visit; maybe storage space ashore had been in short supply.

As we crossed the Sea of Marmara one night, I was awakened by what I thought was a loud explosion, only to realise that mother nature was venting her spite upon us. A violent thunderstorm raged across the waters, and it died out at daybreak in time for my peggying duties to begin again.

The journey back to Spezia passed without further event and in pleasant weather. On our arrival we found no sign of the '*Empress of Canada.*' Obviously she had commenced on her final unhappy voyage to the salvage yard. That evening I went ashore to exchange the few lira I still had left from the last visit into a few glasses of wine.

On leaving Spezia we anchored off Genoa on the 6th December. We knew that we would not get the same reception as on our last visit. No brass band welcomed our arrival at the small jetty we had christened. That time was just for bunkering, and on the completion of that operation, we had to shift ship the next day to a different jetty.

Along with the cargo of petrol we took aboard thirty-six fifty-gallon drums of motor oil. They were lashed on deck to the stanchions of the 'flying bridge.' This was an elevated walkway on all tankers, which ran along the centre of the main deck from the after housing to the centre housing and again from the forward end of the centre housing right up to the fo'c's'le head, virtually for almost the whole length of the ship.

I had been told that real violent storms were an unusual occurrence in the Mediterranean, and that was to be one of those unusual occasions for on the 12th December we hit the worst storm I had experienced so far as we headed for Beirut. Gale force winds, mountainous seas and waves crashed over the decks, which caused the old '*San Velino*' to be tossed around like a corkscrew.

Sleep was impossible, and during the night two of the lashed oil drums broke loose and could be heard rolling and crashing about the deck. Eventually they went over the side and took three sections of the guardrails with them. Such were the conditions out on the open deck that nothing could be done to stop them or repair the damaged rail until the storm had abated and hands could be brought out to secure ropes along the damaged section of the rail.

We rode out the storm and it was with thanks that we found safe anchorage off Beirut. After we had made fast to the buoys, the operation of lifting the pipeline from the seabed began, and we started once again to discharge part cargo. I looked across the mile or so expanse of water between us at the skyline of Beirut, and I took in the mainly creamy looking squarish buildings of the town itself. Perhaps unfairly from that distance, I felt it looked plain, hot and dusty. I did not know that shells would ravage many of those buildings in years to come. Nonetheless the guys who made up the bumboats seemed happy and friendly to me, and I bought two more silk shirts.

The amount of petrol discharged must have been slight for early the following morning we set loose from the buoys and were on our way to Port Said again. We arrived at midday on the 18th December. The scene at Port Said was the same as on the previous visit; a galaxy of ships was waiting for a passage through the canal and we had to weave our way through them to tie up in Port Said harbour. Once secure and tied up the bumboats again along with the boat gang. We also lifted the searchlight and made it fast over our bow again.

Shortly after midnight we inched our way into the convoy to commence the slow tedious five-knot meander towards the Bitter Lakes, the first port of call on the south bound voyage if the place we went to could be called a port. On entering the Lakes we broke away from the convoy to tie up at a rickety, possibly unsafe jetty, which looked as though it may once have been used by Noah for his Ark.

It was the time when there were problems between the British and Egyption governments, and President Nasser wanted to take control of the canal. The British army were in preparation of pulling out of Suez after having been involved in some skirmishes, and they required a replenishment of their petrol tanks. We found out then where the fifty-gallon drums were destined, minus of course the two which lay somewhere on the seabed.

That evening an army launch hove alongside, manned by two soldiers who invited all and sundry to the army's canteen, the NAAFI. It turned out to be a raucous evening with soldiers and sailors enjoying each other's company. In fact, we got along famously, and to everyone's satisfaction a lot of beer was consumed.

The festivities of the previous evening were evident amongst the revellers as we let go the following morning to await the passing of the northbound convoy. Nonetheless, once the southern section of the canal below the Bitter Lakes was clear, we joined the convoy to begin the tortuous journey towards the Red Sea.

On arrival there, having rid the ship of the searchlight, we set course for Port Sudan. With new scenes and a change from constantly plying our trade in the Mediterranean, what lifting of our spirits there was soon dampened as we experienced the changed climate. We had thought that it had been unbearably hot in the Medi., but it was quite autumnal compared to the heat of the Red Sea.

The change was dramatic. It was striking hot, the sun was blazing relentlessly and the steel of the ship reflected the heat back upwards. There was no refuge, no respite, and the heat from the engine-room spiralled up into the cabins and turned them into veritable saunas. The two air blowers we had were aimed directly onto our bunks, aided also by a small fan. Wind shoots (half rounded tins devised to put into the port holes to catch any breeze and direct it into the cabin) were fitted. It was all to no avail, and at night we lay on top of our bunks on sheets that were soaked in our own sweat.

With no air conditioning and no let up from the heat, there was little or no sleep. Cold showers were our only salvation. As soon as we left that haven of coolness, the pouring sweat returned. To add to our discomfort, word was passed around for us to curtail showering as water was not in plentiful supply. Despite the torrid conditions and the lack of sleep, eight hours work a day still had to be performed.

Conditions did not improve as we tied up in Port Sudan on Thursday 23rd December. If anything it was worse for with the ship tied up, what little breath of air there was obtained by the motion of the ship was gone. Salt tablets were issued to everyone with explicit instructions that one must be taken religiously each and every day to help to replace the body salts lost through the rivers of sweat that constantly left our bodies.

It was approaching Christmas, my thoughts and no doubt those of my shipmates were of home, England and wonderfully cold weather. Our minds were momentarily relieved of our misery by the news that our next destination was to be Aden in the South Yemen where we were to pick up a cargo for the Isle of Grain, England and home.

The attitude of the crew was magically transformed, and the cheers must have echoed around Port Sudan probably causing consternation amongst the natives who most likely wondered what us infidels were about. With the cargo discharged, we cast off bound for Aden on Christmas Eve, cherishing the best possible Christmas present.

Except for those on watches, the deck crew were excused from duty on Christmas Day, all except the Peggy (my turn of course). Other than it being the hottest Christmas I had ever spent, the day was much the same as any other. We were however, given the privilege of purchasing two extra cans of beer, and in addition we had chicken for dinner but still no breast, even at Christmas.

Upon our arrival in Aden the day after Boxing Day, we went straight in and began to take aboard our cargo for home immediately. The usual colourful array of bumboat vendors arrived alongside, but on that occasion they did not invade the quarters. They set up their stalls in the starboard alleyway, displaying their wares as in the bazaars or a local market. Little was sold and few were tempted; everyone's thoughts were on home.

During a routine inspection a small crack was discovered in the hull. Loading had to cease immediately, and the ship was moved out to anchor in the bay while a metal plate was welded over the crack. Once the inspectors were satisfied that the fault had been rectified, we returned to the original berth to recommence the loading, and it was New Year's Eve when we gratefully and unbelievably started the long but welcome journey home.

The heat remained intense as we made the passage up through the Red Sea. Matters were not improved by an engine failure on the morning of the 3rd January 1955. Evidently faulty valves were diagnosed as the problem, and they had to be changed before we could continue on our way.

Before long, as we drifted in the blazing hot sun, someone called "Shark Ahoy" and the grizzly monsters were spotted swimming lazily round the stern. Meat hooks and heaving lines were produced like magic, and a call went to the Cook for any waste meat available. It passed through my mind to ask the Cook for some spare chicken breasts, but I recalled my early maxim, "If you want to eat well, don't upset the Cook" and on reflection, it may well have caused a mutiny had he given us some.

Shark fishing was then in full swing, and it was not long before three had been successfully hooked and landed. No one was looking for souvenirs that time so they were all returned to the sea, no doubt scared but unharmed. It was the only diversion and sport of any description we had enjoyed for many a day. I pitied the engineers toiling away in the engine-room, it was bad enough on deck, but it must have been hell down there.

Eventually the engines sprang back to life and we made way, slowly at first, but we gathered speed as the engines gained confidence. We said goodbye to the sharks and bemoaned the stifling heat as we tried to find shelter from the pitiless sun.

There were dozens of ships anchored or manoeuvring for position when we reached Port Suez on Thursday 6th January. The ship-to-shore radio informed us that the congestion at the southern end of the canal was due to a vessel that had collided with a swing bridge in the southern sector of the Suez.

With care and stealth, the helmsman wended his way through the maze of anchored vessels to hopefully gain a beneficial position in the convoy when traffic recommenced. We dropped anchor in as good a position as possible and the helmsman must be applauded for the Captains of other ships must have been cursing our initiative and cheek. Many more ships arrived to join the others jockeying for position until a veritable armada stood at the southern end of the canal awaiting clearance.

Shortly after breakfast on the 8th January a loud explosion was heard and on deck I could see a column of smoke and flames about a mile or so away to starboard, which died away almost immediately. I later heard that two Greek tankers, the 'Olympic Honour' and the 'Olympic Thunder,' probably jockeying for position, had got a little too close to each other and collided. Rather aptly I thought, the explosion had occurred on the 'Olympic Thunder.' We never found out if there were any injuries or what the scale of damage was for within half an hour of the explosion we had weighed anchor and taken our position near the head of the convoy.

Both ends of the canal then must have been kept open and priority given to an extra large northern bound convoy to clear the backlog assembled off Port Suez. Our passage through both sections was without stoppage or incident. Thankful to be rid of the extreme heat and sun, it was a pleasure to be back in the Mediterranean well before midnight.

It was a further bonus not having to tie up and discharge cargo every two or three days. Life became less hectic and more pleasant as we made our way towards Gibraltar. I got the distinct impression that the ship knew it was on the way home; everything seemed to run more smoothly, and I found my peggying duties less distasteful, as did Bimbo.

Once we had passed through the straits of Gibraltar on Saturday 16th January the weather took a distinct change. It became cold and we felt it. It may have been due to the extreme heat that we had endured only a week previously, but the change was very noticeable.

The Bay of Biscay lived up to its reputation with the seas choppy at first, and then they developed into a heavy swell and mini-storm. Those conditions I could tolerate for I began to anticipate a landfall, and looking at the northern horizon I knew full well that we were still miles from the Channel. Then on the morning of the 24th January there was a dark smudge on the horizon. It wasn't until hours later when the White Cliffs of Dover hove into view, that I dared to say to myself "Yes, that's England, we're home." It felt great. But I didn't know then that there would be times in the future that I would be looking at those cliffs with a heavy heart.

The Pilot came aboard on the morning of the 25th to navigate our course up the Thames Estuary to our berth at the Isle of Grain. And it was bloody cold. When we were tied up and all secure, the crew expected to be paid off. We were disappointed for following the discharge of the cargo, we found that the ship's final destination was Sunderland on the northeast coast. It was made very clear to all and sundry that the ship's articles stated categorically that the crew's discharge would be at the ultimate port of call in the UK.

After two more days of frustrating tedium, we headed down the Thames into the North Sea. As we swung hard to starboard, the Pilot's cutter scurried back towards the Thames, while we headed north to what we hoped would be the last port of call.

Such was the congestion in the Port of Sunderland that the berth allotted to us was doubled up alongside an already tied up ship. Fenders had to be hung over the side as we gently eased alongside the moored vessel. Once everything was secure, tied up and shipshape, we showered, packed our gear and changed into our shore going gear. Topcoats were worn by those who had them for the northeast of Britain can be very cold.

The Customs required a manifesto of everything that we had purchased or acquired whilst in foreign countries. Then for some unknown reason, nothing happened for the next few hours, and tempers became frayed as we hung about. It was with some sense of relief when the goodies we had accumulated were taken to the officers' saloon for customs inspection. My goods were given clearance and I was finally and gratefully paid off at five o'clock in the afternoon.

Andy, Bimbo and I took a taxi from the quayside to the railway station, and before too long we had settled into the welcome warmth of a Birmingham bound carriage. We had been away from home for nine and a half months, and the six weeks leave we were due seemed an eternity, which I for one was determined to enjoy. As I pondered the past months at sea and the next six weeks, it suddenly struck me like a hammer. I hadn't said goodbye to the Bosun. Perhaps, maybe, we would meet again. I hoped so for he was a kindly man.

CHAPTER FOUR
THE MARTAGON

(Of a Little Tow, a Big Tow and a Wet Engineer).

I had grown up somewhat over the past twelve months, and I had come to realise that nothing in life stood still. I was certainly not the inexperienced youth that had graduated from Gravesend. That was apparent to my parents and while they had altered little, other people had changed greatly. I had girded half of the northern hemisphere, seen new countries and strange, different people with what to me were strange, different customs and alternative ways of life. I myself had grown to view the world with a different perspective. Friends with whom I had enjoyed a social relationship had either moved away or had got entangled with girlfriends, which consequently left little time to spend with someone like me who was at home for only a limited period.

On the way home from Sunderland, Andy, Bimbo and I had arranged to have a night out together in our respective hometowns. They were boozy sessions in each of our favourite pubs. We had always got on well together and those occasions proved to be happy and enjoyable.

After so long at sea, the days and weeks flew by as though two different clocks applied, one at sea and one on leave. Bimbo and I had hoped that we would ship out together again and so it came to pass. We arranged to meet at Wolverhampton station and travel to Liverpool together for our next berth. Once again we obtained rooms at Gordon Smith's where we stowed our gear and reported to the Pool. "Come back tomorrow," instructed the clerk, and on doing so we got the same response.

Both Bimbo and I felt more than a little miffed at being called back only to kick our heels around Liverpool for two days when we could have kicked our heels in the comfort of our homes. As we went into dinner that second day, we bumped into Andy and sat at his table. He told us that he had also been recalled two days earlier and said that he was sailing that very evening. He had signed a contract with the Blue Funnel Line to work exclusively for them. That was a firm with a sound reputation as good employers and whose ships were known to be as good as most and better than many.

After much reminiscing later that afternoon, we helped Andy to take his luggage onboard. His ship was in good order. Everything spic and span, newly painted and clean as a new pin. The cabins, although not spacious, were twin berth with a carpet and oak polished furniture. Decidedly more upmarket than what I had known to date. We wished him luck and expressed the hope that someday we would all get together again. Mick and I then headed back to Gordon Smith's. Our paths never did cross again.

It seemed common in the Merchant Navy that on joining a ship, both friends and enemies were made, and with the voyage completed it would be a rare occurrence to meet either one again, although it did happen from time to time. In the early days it was a little unsettling to lose people who, in a short space of time, had become good friends and who, in different circumstances, could have been good friends for life. However that was the nature of the job, with us all sailing off into the world in different directions; in time it became the accepted thing. Again I wondered if I would ever meet up with the Scottish giant, the Bosun from the 'San Velino,' but sadly it was not to be.

When we reported to the Pool on the Wednesday morning, the clerk had our discharge books at hand. "You have got more than enough sea service time in to be classed as a JOS (Junior Ordinary Seaman) he said to me. It carried with it a rise in pay, not much, but still it was an increase. Then on looking at Bimbo's record, he decided to overlook the fact that he was a couple of weeks short of qualifying and regraded him too. That was typical of my luck I thought; I had to do over my time to qualify, but he had qualified in less. Even so, I was still pleased for him. "Report again tomorrow and I'll have a ship for you" was the good news from the clerk, but a rider was added, "Don't forget to have your union cards brought up to date," he warned.

We survived the routine medical check the following morning and acquired the necessary documentation; we were then dispatched to the Bidston docks and the '*SS Martagon*.'

It took little time to collect our belongings and pay our dues at Smith's, and it was not far to the overhead railway where we took a short journey to the Bidston dock. On our approach, we sighted the '*Martagon*' sitting it seemed waiting for our arrival. My heart sank, even from that distance the rust bucket she was, was evident. Things became even worse for as we signed on, we learned that no deck boy had been signed, and Mick and I were to share week about the peggying chores once more. I did wonder then if I would have escaped the peggying duties if he not been given early promotion and was still a deck boy. Then to rub salt into our wounds, the cabin accommodation compared to the Blue Funnel Line was a slum with nothing more than the bare essentials.

We had barely two days to acclimatize and meet our newfound shipmates for it was early on Saturday 19th March when we moved out into the Mersey. For the first time I found myself in the for'ard gang at stations and consequently on the fo'c's'le head as the Pilot safely brought us to the Mersey bar towards the open sea. As the Pilot's cutter hurried home to his Mersey base, I could feel the cold sea air in my bones.

The Irish Sea in March, with a high wind prevailing, can be inhospitable and bloody cold. Maybe my exposure to the heat of the Red Sea just a few weeks earlier didn't help so I was glad to find myself in the warmth of the mess once all the deck duties were done, and I looked forward to the prospect of a little more warmth at our destination, which was Casablanca in Morocco.

My deck stints were cold and uneventful. As we sailed southward out into the English Channel then on through the Bay of Biscay, the temperature improved. The Bay of Biscay, notorious for its bad weather conditions, was not too bad on that occasion but it was not all that good either; the sea was still quite heavy but at least the days got warmer.

During the relatively calm spells the main task was the rigging and topping of the derricks. All eighteen had to be swung upright and the runner wires hooked into an eye bolt on deck, which were then pulled tight by the winch and held by the guy ropes. The starboard ones pulled to port and the port ones to starboard. This made them relatively secure while still at sea even though they were topped.

The heavy seas that we encountered through the bay had prevented virtually all work on the open deck, but plenty of work was found for us cleaning bulkheads in the shelter of the housing. Slowly the weather improved with our progress southward. Indeed, it improved enough for the deck crew to embark on the task of attempting to camouflage the rust with gallons and gallons of paint, but to no avail. Despite the frantic expectation of the Bosun, it would take more than a lick of paint to disguise the true condition of the '*Martagon*.' At that time there were a number of companies under the loose heading of London / Greek; the '*Oakhill*' had been one and the '*Martagon*' was another.

We were however bound for Morocco, and eventually we berthed and tied up in Casablanca on Friday 25th March. The work then commenced for all the deckhands to uncover the holds of the ship in readiness to accept the cargo of iron ore. First we removed the tarpaulin hatch covers by knocking out the wedges and batons, then we folded them out of the way, either to the for'ard end of the hatch or to the after end that revealed the heavy hatchboards. Each board was about six-foot long, about fourteen inches wide by three inches thick and very heavy. We had to stack each and every one on deck out of the way. Then we used the derricks to remove the supporting beams to make way for the conveyor belts positioned over the open holds before we were ready to load the cargo of iron ore.

As the loading process began, the dust started to fly, but it wasn't as bad as the coal dust had been on the '*Oakhill*.' As one hold became full, the ship had to be repositioned as it was necessary to line up the conveyor belt to the other holds. The procedure for moving such a short distance was for the for'ard mooring ropes to be slackened away and the after lines to be heaved on by the winches; thereby pulling the ship aft. The procedure was reversed to move the ship for'ard.

Hardly had the process commenced the first time when the cry went up, "Man overboard." To our horror, the Third Engineer had fallen between the ship and the quay. Fortunately the thick fenders that stopped the ship from scraping against the quay wall prevented him from being crushed to death. A Jacob's ladder suspended from the deck rail was hurriedly lowered, and a very relieved and soggy Third

Engineer ascended eagerly. He was a lucky man. There was a saying that only fools sat on ship's rails, which is what he had been doing. The crew then extended that to only fools and engineers sit on ship's rails.

As each hold was filled, the beams and the hatchboards were replaced and covered with the tarpaulins before being battened down and secured. Finally the derricks were lowered and made fast.

My deck duties gave me the Sunday off, and as we sailed from Casablanca in the early hours of Sunday 27th March I revelled in the beautiful spring weather. The sun was hot, the sea calm and the ship was gently gliding through the water. At such times and in such conditions it felt so good to be alive and cruising along on a deep blue placid sea.

* * *

While Bimbo was peggying in the afternoon, I decided to go to the bridge to ask the officer of the watch if I could take a spell on the wheel as I had done on the 'San Velino.' The Skipper, who happened to be in the wheelhouse at the time, gave me a quizzical look, and although there were several ships close at hand he said, "Yes it's time you got your hand in." The AB helmsman was quite happy to be relieved and left me under the watchful eye of the Skipper and the Third Mate. Me! Steering a ship again. All my fantasies were realised (well, not all of them!), and after a cautious, anxious half an hour I was well into it.

For some strange reason it hadn't sunk into my head on my few short stints at the helm on the 'San Velino,' that with the feeling of euphoria came the realisation that all the painful study of learning and remembering the cardinal and quarter points of the compass at Gravesend were all in vain. They were never actually used for the degrees from one to three hundred and sixty were recorded on the outer circle of the compass so that numbers did all the steering and course setting. Also by that time there was a gyrocompass with numbers only on most ships

The Skipper and the Third Mate stood apart on the bridge chatting and gazing ahead through the wheelhouse windows when suddenly we began to veer sharply to port. Immediately I swung the wheel hard to starboard to counter the turn, but nothing happened. "I've broken it," I thought, as I heard the frantic cry of the Skipper, "Hard to starboard, hard to starboard," "I already am," I screamed back. He pushed me out of the way and took the wheel. "THERE," I thought, as he wrestled to go to starboard and failed. "Whistle," he called to the Third Mate who promptly gave warning blasts on the ship's whistle to alert the ships close by of our predicament.

"Hold the wheel," the Skipper ordered me, a little more calmly as he realised that it wasn't my fault, and he rang to stop engines on the ship's telegraph. We narrowly missed two nearby ships as we completed a full circle before we finally came to a halt.

The wheel was tested by turning it fully both ways. Nothing seemed amiss; there was no obstruction. Then the Skipper ordered "Dead slow ahead" on the telegraph. That resulted in a loud clanging and banging which came from aft. Stop engines, he telegraphed, and immediately summoned the Chief Engineer to the bridge, suspecting that there may be trouble in the engine room. Once assured that there was no trouble in that department, both he and the Engineer assumed that something must have struck the propeller and the rudder.

On our departure from Casablanca, our orders had been to sail northwards and wait for further instruction, but as we had broken down with a fault that no one onboard could do anything about, we needed assistance and a call went out requesting a tug to tow us into port.

We wallowed in a calm sea until 6.30am the next morning Monday 28th March waiting for the arrival of the tug, and we thanked God for the calm weather. When it arrived the tug was able to come directly under our bow in the placid sea, and a line was lowered to heave aboard their tow spring. That was made fast around the bits exactly as when we entered port.

A very slow tedious tow then began and it took over a day to complete the sixty-mile journey into Lisbon, Portugal. It was late on the afternoon of Wednesday 30th March before we finally dropped anchor in the harbour. The tow had been uneventful, but interesting too for the mind boggles at the possibilities of mishap and danger, especially if the weather had cut up rough.

Early the next day a diver went down to inspect the propeller and the rudder for damage. His inspection was quite lengthy, and it was a while before he resurfaced and reported to the Skipper. Evidently the rudder stem had cracked which had caused the rudder to drop a little and foul the propeller; hence the clanging and banging. His verdict was that the whole lot would have to be removed and replaced.

I presumed that the Skipper had taken advice from the company's head office for some little time later the diver descended again with an oxyacetylene torch. Later we learned that the repair was not to be executed there in Lisbon, and we would have to await the arrival of a deep-sea tug to undertake the tow back to the UK.

On Friday 1st April a massive floating crane arrived alongside. No one dared make reference to the significance of the date, but fools we certainly felt as the crane finally completed the diver's work by slowly, very slowly hoisting the rudder out of the depths onto the after deck where it was chained down and secured.

The floating crane also helped us to disconnect the anchor from the cable; what for at that moment in time, I didn't know. They lowered the anchor onto our deck where that too was chained down. I thought that we were fast becoming a ship that carried its own parts as a cargo, but the separation of the anchor from the cable was a much simpler operation with the shore crane than it had been with the derrick on the 'San Velino.'

Our days were taken up chipping away at the rust warily, in case our chipping hammers broke something else. We had been with the ship a very short time and consequently we had little money in the ship, but both Mick and I drew what we could, determined to enjoy the nightlife of Lisbon. The bars were welcoming and cheap, and the Portuguese girls were lovely and friendly.

It was on the 3rd April that an American warship, one of the biggest I had ever seen, came in and anchored in the bay. That night, the bar where Mick and I had become regulars was invaded by the American Navy. Everything I had been told about American servicemen's behaviour in ports proved to be true. They were loud, brash and had money to burn. They swaggered into the bar in their immaculate white uniforms, intent on impressing the girls and imposing themselves despite the fact that the majority of the girls seemed to hold a little contempt for them. At least the girls who were drinking with us resisted their advances saying "We like English boys better." Never one to look a gift horse in the mouth, I didn't resist the opportunity to embark on a little further education on the road to manhood with a beautiful Portuguese girl.

During the first few days after we had joined the ship, I had tried to keep the nickname of Bimbo going but the song wasn't played much on the radio any more and he had stopped singing it all the while so it didn't catch on with the new crew. We were back to being the two Micks.

We had five delightful days in Lisbon, interrupted only by the arrival of the deep-sea tug on the 5th April. Aptly named '*The Englishman*' she had come to our rescue. It was the following day before clearance was given for the tow to commence. That was when I found out why the anchor had been separated from its cable; the tug's towline was connected to the anchor-less cable, using a short tow at first until we had cleared the harbour. On reaching the open sea more of the anchor cable was lowered. It was still attached to the tow spring and the tug slacked away; thereby lengthening the tow. That continued until the distance between the towing and the towed was several hundred yards.

The tow became submerged to a U shape, and as the tug got under way the anchor cable was lifted, and the weight forced the '*Martagon*' forward. Before long we were progressing at a steady eight knots. The gods of the sea shone on us for it was April, a month that had produced many a storm in the past, but even the Bay of Biscay decided not to hinder our passage, and the weather remained relatively calm.

It was strange to sail without the noise of the engine, listening to the wind in the rigging, the waves lapping at the hull and the groans and creaks of the old rust bucket. That must have been what sailors through the centuries had heard under sail, just the wind and the waves before those rather pleasant sounds were deadened by the steam turbines.

However, given the romantic nostalgia of my flights of fancy, it was with some sense of relief on Thursday 14th April, eight long days later that we came up the Irish Sea into the Clyde and tied up just a few miles downstream from Glasgow.

On the following afternoon, the crew were paid off. Mick and I shared a taxi to the railway station with two others. Their train to Liverpool was quite imminent so we wished them good luck and parted ways. We found that there would be a wait of three hours for a train to Birmingham.

That created no problem as Mick and I adjourned to a good old Scottish pub nearby. After a couple of pints of good 'bevvies' I could have sung, "I belong to Glasgow," but it was to the train and home we went and arrived on the morning of Saturday 16th April 1955.

CHAPTER FIVE

THE KINGSBURY

(Of a Favour Done, a Short Trip and a Skeleton Crew).

My short stay at home was a welcome change to the restrictive life aboard ship. In particular, I appreciated the availability of unlimited amounts of tea, sugar and fresh milk in comparison to the rationing that we had at sea. That was a further lesson for me not to take the simple ordinary things in life for granted, and it made me realise that those things are only valued when they are not available.

It had become routine for Mick and I to meet on Wolverhampton station to catch the train back to Liverpool and the Pool office. It was Friday 22nd April. We both felt the need to experience something other than rust buckets like the '*Martagon*' and we decided to try to follow Andy's example and go for a contract with a well established reputable line. Like Andy, we tried the Blue Funnel Line Offices, but unfortunately they had no vacancies at that time so we returned to the Pool.

We presented ourselves at the counter early on the Saturday morning, and the clerk greeted us enthusiastically, "You two are just what I am looking for. The '*Kingsbury,*' a Holder Brothers vessel, needs a crew for the short run down to Avonmouth. It's a nice little job for a couple of days," he enthused. "Two days work is no good to us," both Mick and I retorted, but he was obviously desperate. He promised us that if we did it for him, he would view it as a personal favour to him, and he would return the favour when we reported back but we would have to make sure that we reported to him and no one else. "I will look after you," he said.

With the promise of a better tomorrow and the realisation that two days would not hurt us, we agreed to take it on. There was no need for a medical for what was in effect just a cruise down the Irish Sea. "You have no time to hang about because she sails this afternoon" was then the urgent message from the clerk as he tried to hurry us on. And so to Smith's we went, to check out and make haste to the docks.

The '*Kingsbury*' was an impressive, clean-cut cargo ship and we cleared the Mersey Bar later that afternoon after we had signed on and changed into our working gear. We didn't bother to unpack entirely as it seemed pointless to do so. Our main task was to help with the tying up and casting off, but on the way down we were put to work doing a little cleaning and tidying up. Thankfully there was no peggying. Everyone drew their own meals from the galley and washed their own dirty crockery.

For the short trip down only a skeleton crew was required, which meant that it was hard work at stations, and although we had to work closely together we really got to know no one in such a short space of time. The trip went without a hitch and we hove to off Avonmouth later that evening, but we were unable to go alongside until the next morning, Monday 25th April. Once we were tied up the job was done and shortly afterwards the crew was paid off.

We had to repack our working clothes unwashed as there was no time for dhobying, but we showered, changed and went ashore then took a taxi into Bristol. We travelled under the Clifton suspension bridge on the way to Temple Meads station. I thought the bridge was quite impressive.

Both of us found Bristol to be a pleasant city in which to kill a couple of hours for that was the amount of time we had before our train back to Liverpool departed. Once we had booked our cases into the left luggage office, we enjoyed a stroll around the city streets in the pleasant spring sunshine.

The travel vouchers that we had been given were exchanged for our train tickets back at the station, and we boarded the train and settled down to a comfortable journey back to Liverpool arriving late in the evening. As we booked back into Smith's, I reflected on the past two days and hoped that the Pool would want another favour from me one day. Cruising down the Irish Sea then along the Bristol Channel plus a comfortable train journey was not, I thought, a bad way to earn a living after all.

CHAPTER SIX

THE LLANDAFF / ONE

(Of a Favour Returned, a Randy Monkey and a Drunken Parrot).

It was a pleasant and lazy breakfast the following morning with both Mick and I full of anticipation about reminding the Pool Clerk of his promise to return the favour. The office was crowded so Mick and I hung back until our man was free. "Yes, I've got something for you," he said as he recognised us. While he shuffled his papers, another clerk came beside him and said to us, "I've got just the job for you two on a London / Greek." Our stomachs sank at the prospect. "Oh No! Not another one of those rust buckets" I thought, but we were rescued by the first clerk who kept his promise and quickly claimed us for the job he had in mind for us. "Thank God for that!" I thought, but we still did not know what he had got lined up for us.

Since our visit to the office when we had been allotted the '*Martagon*' it had been arranged that a union representative would be in attendance in the Pool itself at all times so that saved us a separate journey to the

Union Office. With the documentation completed and our union cards stamped up to date we were told to report back to the Pool with our gear the following evening, where a coach would be available to take us and the rest of the crew to the ship. We were told that The '*Llandaff*' was a tanker owned by Radcliffs of Cardiff and was berthed in Eastham dock.

As we did not have to report until the evening of the next day, it gave us most of that day free so Mick and I decided to spend it sightseeing in Chester. The weather continued sunny and warm, and Chester was at its best. As I had lived all my life in the Black Country with its grimy sooty buildings, Chester and its sun baked walls was like a fairyland, nestling in the bend of the River Dee. Below its ancient walls and the river was the racecourse where the Chester cup had been contested for over a hundred years. I was surprised for I had imagined, never having been to one, that racecourses would cover vast parcels of land. I had not realised that they could be as compact as that one was.

The day flew by and soon we had to hurry to get back to the Pool in time for the coach. We were the last to arrive, and no sooner were we aboard the coach and settled into our seats than there was another first experience for Mick and I as we headed off through the Mersey Tunnel.

The '*Llandaff*' was indeed in the Eastham dock. Almost brand new, just two years old and sparkling clean. It had a white superstructure, light grey hull and red painted decks with not a spot of rust anywhere. A giant spray of three feathers adorned the funnel, appropriately I thought, as the Prince of Wales insignia was the three feathers. "All that glitters is not gold" as the old adage says, but it did not hold on this occasion for the accommodation was equally welcoming. With a large sailors' mess and an even larger recreation room equipped with many fans and blowers. The cherry on the cake however was the crew's accommodation. Each member had his own single berth cabin that contained a bunk along the bulkhead opposite a comfortable sofa bench, a small wardrobe and a chest of drawers with a pullout leaf to write on.

Everything was light and airy with patterned Formica bulkheads. Five star accommodation indeed, at least in comparison to my previous ships. The clerk at the Pool had really come good with his promise, but at the end of the day each silver lining does have a cloud. I was glorying in my newfound luxury only to find out that nothing was perfect. Yet again no deck boy had been signed on and the peggying, once again a week about, fell to Mick and I.

We sailed on Sunday 30th April bound for Mamonal in Columbia. That was welcome news to me as I had a hankering for the wide-open spaces of the Atlantic. Spotless as the '*Llandaff*' was, it soon became obvious that it was the intent of the owners that she would remain so. The washing down and repainting started at the fo'c's'le head, and continued each day along the whole length of the ship to the poop deck at the stern.

The whole of the deck crew were on overtime, the eight to twelve watch worked on into the afternoon until 5.00pm. The twelve to four watch were called to work from 9.00am to 12 noon before going on watch. The four to eight watch worked both mornings and afternoons. The dayworkers did not escape either for they were employed in the evenings on overtime until 9.00pm having started their day at 7.00am, and when our peggying was finished after tea both Mick and I were expected to turn to on deck each evening. Refusal to do so from anyone could end in disciplinary action of some sort such as being fined or logged a day's pay since once articles were signed, you were effectively on call twenty-four hours a day, seven days a week for the duration of the voyage. I for one was mostly glad of any overtime that came my way.

Whether it was the new and clean environment and the opportunity to play darts, cards and dominoes in the recreation room in what little spare time we had, I began to enjoy the voyage, despite my disappointment at having to do half of the peggying again. I enjoyed the vastness of the ocean; with the weather warm and sunny, and the sea smooth and calm, I could put up with the routines and the painting. But still there were only six cans of beer allowed a week. Mick got his also after he had reached his eighteenth birthday. On reflection, that was the first ship I had felt truly comfortable on, but at that tender age I hadn't fully realised it.

The weather improved as we continued into the voyage. It was hotter, but with the improved accommodation it was not unpleasant. The busy days passed quickly and we finally arrived in Columbia on Sunday 15th May. Mamonal was my first encounter with the jungle proper. The port consisted of one jetty, which could accommodate only one ship at a time, and the inlet was surrounded by dense, green jungle.

As soon as we had made fast alongside a dozen or so natives, clad only in loincloths, appeared out of the jungle in very shallow dugout canoes. They tied their canoes to anything that they could find and clambered aboard. They were the Columbian equivalent of the Arabian and Mediterranean bumboats, eager to proffer their wares, which in that case consisted mainly of carved figurines, fresh fruit and live birds and animals.

A parrot was bought by one of the crew for his mother. "She has always wanted a parrot" he explained. Another lad bought a monkey for his girlfriend only to find out later, to everyone's glee, that the animal started to continually play with himself. "I can't give him to my girlfriend if he's always doing that" he cried in anguish as he desperately tried to reclaim his cash, but without success. It was too late; he was stuck with it. "With a sex drive like that she will probably prefer him to you." He was ribbed unmercifully. I never found out if it was due to his own inadequacy or embarrassmen, that he wanted to be rid of it, and I wasn't sure if he could have got it through the customs anyway. I had grave doubts about the parrot too, but the small monkey soon became very popular amongst the crew and was instantly named 'Wanker.'

The next day we sailed and arrived at Willemstad, Curacao two days later. As we passed through the narrow entrance with the pontoon bridge, I was pleased to be back there once again. Although we were still peggying, neither Mick or I felt that we were boys any more and we were earning a little bit more money so that evening we decided to try our luck in Campa Legre, only to be disappointed. There were sailors of all nations packed at the bar, and after we had fought our way to the bar for only one drink, we decided to return to the comparative peace and quiet of the town for a few civilised drinks.

That was the only evening we spent ashore for it was at two o'clock on the Friday morning that we cast off bound for Venezuela. It was just a few hours' sail to Cardon, where the pilot boat scurried out to meet us and the Pilot took us along the coast to our destination, a place called Maracaibo. Dawn was breaking as we nosed into the Maracaibo Lake. Wisps of mist rose up from the water, masking the forest of oil derricks that pumped oil from beneath the vast bed of the lake. Everything seemed so still with the dark shapes of the derricks that appeared out of the mist, like the dead trees of an eerie forest in a Disney film or alternatively, with a little imagination, they could be mistaken for the masts of the galleons of old, shrouded in the mist.

Memories of long forgotten pirate stories came flooding back yet again and I felt sure that Maracaibo would have been one of Bluebeard's haunts. It was certainly secluded enough to give cover to those who did not wish to be found and, with the narrow entrance to the natural deep harbour, it could easily have been defended, especially in those days.

The early morning sun burnt off the mist as we eventually tied up to a buoy in the middle of the lake. No one went ashore because there was nowhere to go. The oil pipeline was quickly connected to the manifold, and the required amount of crude oil had been received aboard by the early hours of Sunday 22nd May. No sooner had the oil pipeline been disconnected than the Pilot was aboard to take the ship on the two-hour journey back to Cardon where no berth was immediately available so we swung at anchor until late that afternoon.

The Docking Pilot came aboard to take us alongside and we had started to prepare for the oil pipeline to come onboard to top up the cargo of crude immediately. Suddenly the order came to hold everything. It transpired that the Pilot had brought alongside the wrong ship. There was nothing for it then but to let go and return to our original anchorage. We got alongside again later, took on the additional cargo and finally cast off, fully laden, bound for Rotterdam in the Netherlands.

* * *

The return journey across the Atlantic took on the same pattern as the outward voyage. Everyone, including Mick and I, was on overtime busily painting the ship. It reminded me of the history of the Forth Bridge. Once the bridge had been painted, the painters returned across the Forth to begin all over again. We did the same; once we had finished all the way along the ship to the poop deck, we started again from the bow.

With the excellent weather, the good conditions and being kept extremely busy, the time passed quickly and pleasantly. It was a happy ship and it seemed like no time at all before there, on the horizon, someone said, "That's Cornwall."

We sailed on through the English Channel and when we passed the White Cliffs of Dover it did not evoke the same emotion as the last time I had sighted them because we were not heading for home. The thought of journeying on past them to Rotterdam was wistful to say the least, not knowing at the time where we would be heading after discharging the cargo in Rotterdam. I had little time to ponder the immediate future though for early on Wednesday 9th June, we were called to stations to tie up, deep in the vast dockland of Holland's premier port.

The docks covered a great area, but once ashore and clear of them, I found the city itself to be clean and pleasant. Similar to Emden, my very first port of call on the 'Oakhill,' most of the buildings seemed brand new; I believe the Luftwaffe had raised the City of Rotterdam to the ground in the early months of 1940 prior to the German army driving through Holland and Belgium to do battle with the British Expeditionary Force at Dunkirk.

I liked Holland and its happy and friendly people, its quaint bars, which although expensive, made us feel very welcome. We also had something to celebrate for shortly after tying up, the news was passed that our next destination was to be Falmouth.

Friday 11th June came, and the ship was empty. We headed back home to arrive off Falmouth the following day. Although I had enjoyed the six weeks or so aboard the 'Llandaff,' I did get a little frustrated not being able to get ashore as we swung at anchor off Falmouth until the Monday morning.

Once alongside the long ritual of paying off began. The ship, though spotless, was bound for the dry dock in Falmouth harbour, and the shore gangs came onboard to clean out the tanks to make them gas free. It was said that the work in dry dock would take about ten days, and they would need to re-sign a new crew.

If anyone wished to return, we were told this was the time to give our names stating our intention. Several crewmembers accepted the offer and although I was only a few weeks short of eighteen months service, which would qualify me as a Senior Ordinary Seaman, I thought nothing ventured, nothing gained, and I decided to ask the Captain if I could re-sign as an SOS. To my delight, after a studied glance, he said that I could. Mick also decided that he would come back too. We were paid off. Customs cleared us, and poor 'Wanker' was arrested. He lay contentedly in the Customs Officer's arms looking up lovingly into his eyes as he was taken into custody, showing in his own demonstrative way exactly what he thought of the arresting officer who was carrying him ashore.

There was unfortunately a major snag. We had landed in the middle of a rail strike. How and when were we to get home was the question on everyone's lips. Then to our relief, we learned that the company, Radcliffs, had laid on a coach to take us to Liverpool. Our relief was rudely dashed on the realisation that Mick and I would still have to get back to the Midlands from Liverpool. Not everyone was happy about it but eventually, after one or two moans from the selfish amongst us about detours being time consuming, it was agreed that we would be dropped off on the way in Wolverhampton, and we boarded the coach.

The general hubbub of chatter and banter died down about an hour after we left Falmouth in the early evening. People started to doze off, knowing that they had a long journey to face. A shrill squealing and squawking raucously disturbed our slumbers: it was the bloody parrot that most of us had forgotten about.

Annoyance was overtaken by hilarity on this sudden realisation, and the question on everyone's lips was how had our shipmate got it past customs? "Ah," he said, "Therein lies a tale." Avidly, we all listened as he related to us his story. Apparently, he had mixed a little rum with water and fed it to the bird, which had greedily drunk it only to become 'Pie Eyed' and fall asleep. He then hid it during the customs inspection and stuffed it inside his shirt before he boarded the coach. "Give it some more rum now then and shut the bloody thing up" was the humorous advice he then received.

Motorways were none existent in 1955 and the A38 was narrow and tortuous so it took us twelve tiring hours overnight before we arrived in Wolverhampton at 5.30am on Tuesday morning. Mick and I waved the lads goodbye as they continued on their way to Liverpool. It was too early for the local buses to start, but Mick knew of a cafe which would be open, and after a welcome cup of tea we caught our respective buses home with ten whole days leave to look forward too.

Once home my mother showed me a clipping that she had cut out and saved from a newspaper. It was headed, "Ships in collision. Beached in the Elbe: The British steamer, The '*Martagon*' (7,086 gross tons) is to be surveyed at Hamburg following a collision in the river Elbe on Friday with the German steamer 'Moselstein' (6,968 gross tons). Both vessels sustained damage and the 'Martagon' was reported to have been beached with damage on the port side forward of number one hold.

Managers of the 'Martagon,' Kaye, Son and Co. Ltd said in London on Saturday that they were still awaiting details of the damage, but the 'Martagon' would be docked and inspected by their surveyors. Reports from Hamburg said that both vessels were interlocked for some time and, after hours of difficult salvage work, they were separated; the German vessel later proceeded to Hamburg under her own power. No casualties were reported on either vessel."

Unfortunately, that clipping has been lost in the passage of time.

CHAPTER SEVEN
LLANDAFF / TWO

(Of Nasty Black Rocks, a Great White Shark and a Sad Goodbye).

Being recalled after only eight days of my furlough instead of the ten days of my entitlement would normally have gone a little against the grain with me. Fortunately, as I was secure in the knowledge that I was to return to the '*Llandaff*,' and its comparative comfort, rather than being at the whim of the Pool Clerk for my next berth, the pain was eased a little. I realised there was a lot to be said to have the foreknowledge of some of what I was about to let myself in for, instead of heading off into the totally unknown.

On my arrival home I had spent a couple of days acclimatising to my mother's cooking (which was not difficult) and recovering from the long coach journey home before I started to look for company. Few of my school friends seemed to be around any more. They had moved on; naturally they were getting on with their own lives. Only Norman and his sister Mavis remained. We would meet in the local club and I didn't need any encouragement to satisfy their curiosity about my travels. They thought it all sounded very glorious and exciting, so I was loath to disillusion them.

I had arranged to meet Mick for a drink in Wolverhampton one day, and as I waited in the bus queue on my way to meet him, I couldn't take my eyes off a lovely girl who was also waiting for the bus at the front of the queue. I realised that she was aware of me looking at her for as she boarded the bus, she gave me a little smile and blushed. She climbed the stairs to the upper deck and I chose a seat that gave me a good vantage point to see everyone who got on or off. My destination was the terminus and I watched at each stop to see if she left the bus. As luck would have it, she was also bound for the terminus and she gave me another shy smile as she stepped off the bus in front of me and started to walk in the same direction towards Mick's house. I followed a short distance behind.

Mick stood waiting for me outside his home, and I noticed that she spoke to him as she walked on by. "Who's that girl?" were my first words to him when I got there. "Oh, that's Sylvia, she lives farther along the street," he replied. As she reached her gate, she turned once again and smiled. "I think she's gorgeous" I said. "When you get a chance, would you ask her if she would write to me?" I asked tentatively. "Sure," he said, "and by the way, I've been seeing a girl while I've been at home so I could be doing a bit of writing myself."

Those eight days fled by, and thankfully, the train strike was over when Mick and I met at Wolverhampton station to catch the train. It was what they then called an express train, the 'Cornishman,' which actually started from Wolverhampton so there was never any seating problem; it went straight through to Penzance and stopped at only the major stations on the way.

I had to lug my gear from the high level to the low level, which was a chore I always hated. I had to go down through an old concrete staircase that had a twist and a turn until I emerged on to the lower platform. Once onboard the train, we settled down, and I began to enjoy the countryside through which we travelled.

On our arrival at Truro we had to change trains and board a small train on a single track to take us down to Falmouth. The whole journey could take anything up to eight to ten hours, which was a little less than the time that the coach journey home had been, and we arrived late on the evening of Wednesday 23rd June.

The 'Llandaff' lay still in the dry dock, and as I unpacked my gear in my cabin, Mick came to give me Sylvia's address. "I forgot to tell you," he said, "Sylvia says that she would like you to write to her first, and if you do so, she will reply." "Fancy forgetting to tell me that," I chided more than a little amazed. We had just spent all day together on the train journey down, and only then had he thought to tell me.

The work on the ship had not been completed, and the dockyard gangs were all over the place; their equipment and materials were strewn in the alleyways and on the decks, but we eventually found the First Mate and signed articles.

I was a Senior Ordinary Seaman. "At long, long last," I thought, "my peggying days are over." Not so for Mick though, he was hoping that a deck boy would be signed on to take that chore away from him. The majority of the crew had still to arrive and there was little or no work for us to do. When we docked eight days earlier in Falmouth, I had hoped to have the opportunity on some future occasion to explore the town further; I then had at least two or three days to wander around at will.

I lost my heart to Falmouth during those days. I fell in love with the place and even to this day, it's one of my favourite places. Its narrow Cornish streets and alleyways, and the steps that rose from the quay then continued above the town to the small homes of fishermen and dockers enthralled me. For me it was a far cry from the traffic and hassle and frustrations of Liverpool city life.

The quaysides were busy and bustling as the ferries arrived and left for St Mawes, Truro and other Cornish havens. The main street was fascinating with its welcoming pubs where I could sit and listen to the locals in conversation with their Cornish accent, complete with its 'handsomes' and 'me dears.' I particularly liked the pubs where the front entrance was at street level, where you could come out from the rear on to the Custom House Quay; I would sit and watch the hired shark fishing boats come in with their catch. I loved it.

I wandered along towards Pendennis Rise and Castle Drive where I could look down upon the '*Llandaff*' in dry dock, then on to the cliff top walks to Swan Pool beach and beyond. There were quiet and secluded coves in contrast to the friendly hustle and bustle of Falmouth town itself, but all were equally delightful.

I was told that Falmouth was known amongst seafaring folk as England's Tanker Hospital, and invariably the bay would have several tankers awaiting berth. There was always something of interest going on to take the eye. To my delight I found that Maracaibo and the Caribbean were not the only haunts of the buccaneers and pirates. For the Killigrew family had lived in Falmouth; one of their ancestors was an enthusiastic and active pirate who had spent several years in the Tower for his brigandry.

113

Their family home 'Arwennak,' which has its roots in the 13th century still stands today on the main street between the docks and the town, not far from the dock gates. Its great hall was burnt down during the Civil War when it held out for the King, but its wings escaped the carnage. Unfortunately it is not open to the public but there are information plaques there, which give anyone who is interested a potted history. The Killigrews can also boast of their association with Pendennis Castle, prominent on the headland, for they were the first captains of the castle until they took to piracy.

The following days saw more and more of the crew arrive to sign on, but it was not until the Thursday that we eventually turned to. We could easily have had our full ten days leave at home after all. Mick was over the moon for although no deck boy had been signed on, a first trip steward had been engaged and assigned to be our mess boy so, given no accidents, he would not be peggying either.

Was that a new trend? Was the job to be allotted to a steward's boy in the future? I began to ask myself. Were Mick and I amongst the last of the peggies? As it turned out, we were. Why oh why could it not have happened two years earlier? But as it will be seen, it was not going to be all roses and violets for Mick.

Another body appeared onboard in the guise of the new Bosun. Mick and he just did not gel. For some unfathomable reason the new Bosun took an instant dislike to him. Obviously a personality clash, and there was little that Mick could do about it other than to grin and bear it as the hassles the Bosun gave him were far too subtle to make any complaints about, but it took away much of Mick's enjoyment of his job.

From the first day's work, and for the following week, our tasks amounted to general jobs like taking inventories, tidying stores, greasing and overhauling lifting tackle, making fast and securing ready for sea. The dockyard gangs worked alongside us as they completed the repairs. A new coat of paint had also been given to the hull and red boot topping paint applied to the bottom and below the waterline. The '*Llandaff*' shone and gleamed.

On Wednesday 7th July the sluices were opened to allow water into the dock, and eventually there was a shudder and a slight movement of the ship so we knew we were once again afloat. The '*Llandaff*' became buoyant and when the water level was equal, the dock gates were opened. Awaiting us was a tug, to which we soon made fast and began to make our exit, stern first, into Falmouth Bay. Once we had cleared the dock a further tug took a line from our bow, and together both tugs towed us to a safe distance before they cast off and left us to our own devices.

Engine and manoeuvring trials then had to be completed before we could proceed, and for the next two or three hours, we wended and turned at varying speeds around the bay before the Skipper was satisfied. I had been so caught up and fascinated with exploring the port that our destination was still unknown to me but on sailing, Tripoli in the Lebanon was where we were headed.

This was to be the first time that I became a member of the watch. I had drawn the eight to twelve watch, and it was well into the afternoon before we were stood down with several hours of overtime already clocked up. There was to be another first for me that evening for I was to be the 'farmer.' A farmer's duty entailed being standby in either our mess or our recreation room to assist the officer of the watch. Between 8.00pm and 9.00pm I had to listen out for the blast of the officer's whistle, which was the Third Mate who was always in charge of the eight to twelve.

If the whistle blew, I would have to go to the bridge to answer his needs. At nine o'clock I had to take up position on the fo'c's'le head to relieve the lookout. Any light ahead between the port beam and the starboard beam had to be reported to the bridge by ringing the ships bell, one single ring for every light which appeared on the starboard side, two successive rings for every light that appeared on the port side and three if they were dead ahead.

I had learned the pattern of the watches at sea from having to cater to them from all my previous peggying duties, and the pattern usually covered all eventualities. The farmer's spell on lookout in the eight to twelve was from 9.00pm to 11.00pm, and the last hour of the watch would be on standby in the mess once more to listen out for the whistle.

At 11.30pm he would make some tea and call the three men on the twelve to four so that they could have a drink before going on watch at midnight. He also had to go amidships to call the Second Mate, who was in charge of the midnight watch. The duties of the three men in the watches rotated; the farmer at night was first helmsman next morning, and second helmsman that night, then farmer again next morning. It was a constant merry-go-round.

The watches themselves also changed every two to three months or so, by changing backwards four hours; the eight to twelve men became the four to eight, and the twelve to four men became the eight to twelve, and the four to eight men became the twelve to four.

All that seemed very complicated, but it worked very smoothly, and it gave the men in each watch a fair share of the time in each watch. It also played havoc with our body clocks especially as we had to absorb the regular hourly or even more regular half hourly changes as we passed through the time zones as well. A kind of sailor's jet lag I suppose, but it relieved the boredom.

We picked up the painting of the ship where we had finished on approaching Falmouth on the previous trip, and as the work progressed towards the stern, everything was painted. Overtime became a way of life throughout the trip, and a paintbrush was my closest companion.

Painting in the unusually calm Bay of Biscay, with its blue skies and seas to match, was a different kettle of fish to house painting and, as the '*Llandaff*,' swathed its way towards Gibraltar, my birthday came and went, unnoticed and uncelebrated. The weather continued to grace our passage with a distinct increase in the temperature as we passed through the Straits and on into the Medi.

The atmosphere between Mick and the new Bosun appeared to be slowly worsening. For no apparent reason other than I suppose that simple clash of personalities, the Bosun really had an attitude towards him, and Mick began to make matters worse by retaliating, snapping back and giving him cheek. I couldn't see how he could just sit and take it in silence. The Bosun was constantly giving him the most rubbish, dirtiest jobs, and always criticizing and running him down, but there was never anything tangible for Mick to complain to the Skipper or Mate about without making himself look foolish or petty.

It was Sunday morning 18th July when we tied up to two buoys about a mile off Tripoli. The pipeline was very quickly connected to the manifold and all was secure. No one went ashore nor was anyone encouraged so to do for, as everything went like clockwork, we disconnected the pipeline a little after midnight. By one o'clock, we had cast off and were heading west towards Gibraltar and the Atlantic bound for Philidelphia.

* * *

Since we left Falmouth, the sun had shone and the seas were duck pond calm through the Medi., and continued to be so across the Atlantic. The period was uneventful but pleasant, and we made good time in what can only be described as wonderful cruising weather.

America came into view on the 3rd August. Perhaps the stories of the Yanks being on the ball were true. For once we didn't have to hove to and await the arrival of the Pilot because while we were still quite a way out his cutter came scuttling alongside for him to board to take us up beyond the city of Philidelphia, along the Delaware, to finally moor us up about twelve miles away from the city itself.

I would have dearly liked to accompany my shipmates who were soon into their going ashore gear. I had been looking forward to experiencing some of those large American cities, but I had decided that on rejoining the '*Llandaff*' I would make a hefty allotment to my parents to build up a healthy bank balance for me. So I judged that the meagre amount I could draw at that moment, after only a little more than a month into the trip would not even pay for my fare into the city. I consoled myself with the notion that there would hopefully be many other future opportunities.

The main job while we were in port was to repaint the funnel; it followed the same pattern as my first experience on the '*San Velino.*' However, there was a difference. Whilst the sun shone, it did not blaze down, and the ship was tied up so there was no swinging and swaying with the motion of the ship and no choking fumes from the engine. And as I had mastered the control of the bosun's chair by then, I found the work quite enjoyable.

During the midday break, I was pleasantly surprised to receive a package of mail that had caught up with us. Birthday cards from home, only three weeks late, but they were welcome nevertheless. I had penned my first letter to Sylvia before we had sailed from Falmouth, and I was delighted to receive a reply. That was the start of a regular feature and was something I had been really looking forward to.

Although we were about the same distance from the city that we had been from Houston on the '*San Velino*,' there were no swamplands there, and no ghastly smelling gunk to protect us from mosquitoes. After tea, although we had little or no money between us, Mick and I decided to go ashore just to stretch our legs in the local area.

Once through the dock gate we entered a field that had a small wooden built stand, which at a guess would seat up to about a hundred people. We surmised that it was a place where the locals would gather to watch a game of baseball or something; perhaps there was a school close by. Once across the field, we entered into the streets of the suburbs.

As aforesaid, we had no cash for transport into the city so we meandered through the streets admiring, what to us were, the palatial American houses, with neatly manicured open plan gardens. We walked around until it began to get dark at which point we decided to return to the ship.

Lights to the houses were being turned on and curtains were being drawn as we passed, with the exception of one. The lights were on but the curtains were not drawn. A woman of about forty was sat on a large comfortable looking armchair facing the window. Both her feet and legs were placed apart upon the cushion that she was sitting on. Her skirt was very short and she wore no underwear. It looked like it was quite a deliberate attempt to show herself to any passerby.

"Did you see that?" Mick asked incredulously with his eyes bulging as he turned towards me once we had gone past. "See what?" I asked, pretending innocence. "The woman in that window," he said as he pointed back over his shoulder, "What about her?" I replied nonchalantly. "Didn't you see her? She was exposing herself," he said incredulously. "Oh," I said with a grin, "I hadn't realised, I thought that she had got a pet hedgehog." Our teenage laughter could then be heard echoing through the streets all the way back to the ship.

As soon as the funnel was completed the following morning the Pilot came onboard, and soon we headed back down past Philadelphia and out into the Atlantic bound for Mamonal in Columbia once again. It was Saturday 6th August as we headed south when the word went around that there was a hurricane in our path. The order was given to reduce our speed to about eight knots in the hope that the hurricane would have moved on before we reached the area where it raged.

The early evening brought evidence of the hurricane's destructive power. Over the horizon came a cargo ship that was listing heavily to starboard, limping along at a much reduced speed. The usual niceties were exchanged by Aldis lamp and we offered assistance. "Thank you, but we think we'll be able to make it safely back to port" was the cheery answer.

The storm had moved on out of our path by the time we reached the area ahead of us where it had raged, but the aftermath was evident by the remaining mountainous seas, which were spectacular and awe inspiring. As we headed south, the waves gradually subsided, and when I did my stint at the wheel that night, I was amazed at the night sky. The night was cloudless, and with no light or auburn glow it was as if you could reach out to touch the stars.

I had never seen such a clear and distinct display. And with little to occupy my attention other than steering on the correct bearing, my thoughts could marvel at the beauty of the night, and where we were heading; we were cruising inside the notorious Bermuda Triangle. That phenomenon is an area in which stories are told amongst seafarers and others of strange incidents, unexplained disappearances, strange happenings and crazy compass gyrations. It had not yet in 1955 received much of the sensational publicity that was to create interest and speculation in later years especially by the media of television. To a young immature youth that was like manna from heaven, and I revelled in the mysteries of such stories. There were however, no strange happenings nor did anything else untoward happen during my watch.

Of course, the slowing of the ship to avoid the hurricane lengthened the duration of the journey, and it was not until early on Wednesday 10th August that we arrived off Mamonal. Once again we were the only vessel on the scene so we were able to tie up alongside without delay. As if by magic, the bumboat people appeared and swarmed all through the ship again, but on that occasion no monkeys or parrots were purchased. We had learned our lesson.

It took less than twenty-four hours to take aboard the fresh cargo, and at four o'clock in the morning we slipped out bound for Curacao.

By chance a few days later, as we approached our destination, I was at the wheel and with the knowledge of just how narrow that channel was, my heart was in my mouth as I nosed the ship into it. I hoped my apprehension and caution was not apparent to the other occupants of the bridge and by instantly obeying the directions of the Pilot, it was with huge relief that we finally tied up without mishap, not withstanding a degree of self satisfaction and pride in having done my job well.

With a sense of well-being a couple of hours later, I climbed into my bunk to sleep a sleep well earned. Later Mick and I took another stroll ashore to stretch our legs and of course to find a welcoming bar to enjoy the solace of a couple of rum and cokes.

On Sunday 14th August our slumber was rudely interrupted to cast off, we found ourselves slipping through the channel in a brilliant dawn, bound once again for the Mediterranean. As we headed into the Atlantic the routines of the ship at sea took over, with the continuous painting interspersed with meals, and more painting interspersed with sleep and watches.

My early enthusiasm for painting the ship had palled a little and I began to wish for anything to break the monotony, tentatively I wished for engine failure for a short while and the opportunity to indulge in a spot of shark fishing. Whether it was down to the original craftsmen or the efficiency of the engines I don't know, but the '*Llandaff*' ploughed relentlessly on.

It was on Friday 26ᵗʰ August that we arrived at Gibraltar, and the, by then, familiar sight of the Rock, which rose steeply from the water was still a magnificent view. Coincidentally, the tanker in the bay which we tied up to was the same one from which the '*Oakhill*' had taken bunkers. That time however, the roles were reversed and we delivered part of our cargo into her. Our stay was short-lived however, only long enough to deliver the needed amount of fuel into the old tanker, and eight hours after we had tied up, we cast off heading for Greece and the port of Piraeus yet again. It seemed as though I was destined, no matter in which ship I sailed, to end up in Piraeus sooner or later. Again the berth was the same as that of the '*San Velino*,' but a little distant from the ferry terminus where we had been dropped after we had spent the night under the stars sleeping on the deck of that old Greek Island ferryboat.

Such was the demand for oil in the industrialised democracies that tankers that sailed under whatever flag were bound for the same destinations time and time again. Momentarily I pondered as to whether we were to be constantly destined to tie up at the same ports repeatedly throughout the civilised and sometimes not so civilised world, irrespective of what ship or company we worked for.

Piraeus was becoming almost like a second home to me, and I was getting to know the place. The magnanimity of the different Skipper did not stretch to a sightseeing tour, and I doubt if I would have taken up the offer if he had. Mick and I did however wander ashore to the nearest bar a couple of times for a change of scene.

All but two thousand tons of the cargo was discharged, and three days later we sailed for Salonica to complete the discharge of that which remained. Salonica, in Northern Greece, was once again a place that I had previously visited, but this visitation was to be even shorter than the last. We arrived on Sunday morning, and once the two thousand tons had been discharged we were on our way again, southwards down the Aegean Sea by 5.30pm of the same afternoon, 4ᵗʰ September.

Just over two days of pleasant sailing brought us off Port Said. With my two watchmates I turned to at 8.00pm, and at 11.30pm on Tuesday 6ᵗʰ we anchored amongst a fleet of ships awaiting passage through the canal. A full watch had been completed by the time we had secured the ship and stood down. After a drink of tea and a shower, I was soon between the sheets only to be called to stations almost at once. It was 1.00am. Slowly we eased our way inside the breakwater to finally tie up to a buoy. It was to be a night of all nights. Twenty minutes after we had tied up, we were called to let go and shift ship alongside the quay for bunkering. It was gone six o'clock when we finally secured the ship.

Meanwhile, the dockers had mounted the searchlight for'ard and brought aboard their boats. To add to the mayhem, the bumboats and their merchandise swarmed all over. Eventually I managed to get to my cabin to flop down on my settee exhausted, only to be awakened an hour later for breakfast, before starting my eight o'clock watch.

As my watchmates and I walked out on deck, a barge laden with forty or more fifty-gallon drums of oil came alongside. They, with the aid of the derrick, had to be hoisted aboard and rolled across the deck to be lashed to the stanchions of the flying bridge just as on the '*San Velino*.' As one barge was emptied and sailed away, another loaded with provisions took its place. Bags of spuds, cabbages and tons of fruit, the latter presumably destined only for the officers as none ever reached the lower decks. In addition, sides of beef and lamb were loaded for the forthcoming trip.

Once the provisions had been hoisted aboard, the stowage and storage was taken over by the stewards. All departments were supposed to take a hand in the loading of the provisions but invariably it fell to the deckhands and stewards alone. For the whole period of the watch we were so engaged, and the last barge was emptied only minutes before we were stood down for the midday meal; even that was foreshortened by being called to let go within twenty minutes. By one o'clock we had taken up our position in the convoy and slowly edged into the Suez Canal.

I was utterly shattered. Along with my watchmates, I had been on the go more or less for sixteen hours. I crawled into the shower and just about made it to my bunk. I cannot recall my head hitting the pillow. I went out like a light only to be called six hours later to stand my next watch. Bleary eyed and still only half awake, I was shaken to full consciousness in the sudden stark realisation that I was the first helmsman.

What a time to find oneself, for the first time, at the wheel in the narrow confines of the canal. They were anxious moments for me for I still felt tired from the exertions of the previous couple of days. However, with the aid of the searchlight, I fixed the bow of the ship onto the centre of the stern of the proceeding ship and, with the Pilot correcting if necessary, I was soon able to relax a little. Nevertheless, I was not sorry to welcome my relief two hours later.

I had showered and taken breakfast as we emerged from the southern exit of the canal. It was Thursday 8th September and I took the eight o'clock watch as we headed into the Red Sea. The 'Llandaff' was a comparatively modern vessel but no match for the Norwegian and German ships of similar tonnage. They left us standing but to be fair, we overtook some ships too, and not all of them were rowing boats.

The Red Sea lived up to its reputation; it was scorching. There was no respite from the heat, and I came to learn to endure the reality of being roasted alive. In the recreation room, air blowers were in plentiful supply, but to get near to one came to be a struggle as they were in such great demand. Despite the stifling and unbearable conditions, an eight-hour shift still had to be worked, plus overtime. I learnt that the practice on other European ships in those conditions was that the vast majority of the unimportant work was performed in the early mornings, before the heat became too intense, and in the evenings when the heat of the day had diminished somewhat.

It appeared that it was beyond the reasoning of the officers of the British Merchant Marine to organise the working day for the benefit of the common British sailor, and as the old song 'Mad Dogs and Englishmen go out in the Midday Sun' shows, others had obviously experienced this British tradition.

Upon our arrival at the southern reaches of the Red Sea, we passed through the appropriately called Hell's Gates at midday on Sunday 11th September. We went about our work dripping with sweat and took a cold shower in our off duty periods, which only brought a temporary relief. Sleep was a dismal doze in a pool of sweat. No one actually enjoyed a full night's sleep, and the temperature continued well above a hundred degrees Fahrenheit.

The flickering lights of Aden hove into view at around midnight, and as we lost sight of them, I noticed the temperature had dropped to the mid nineties. We were in the Gulf of Aden and were heading toward the open spaces of the Arabian Sea. But I was still sweating.

The following afternoon as the crew finished their tea, all talk and chatter stopped as had the engines. The constant throb of the engines is part and pattern of life aboard ship, and you get to not notice them after a while so the sudden halting and the silence that follows when they unexpectedly stop is a strange experience. It transpired that the fans and boilers had failed. We were approximately twenty miles from the Yemen coast; everyone thought at first that it was a minor fault and two hours would see us on our way. But the fault as it turned out was more serious than that. The engineers and the firemen worked like Trojans throughout the night to rectify the failure. Labouring in the depths of the engine room must have been hell as the temperature must surely have been in excess of a hundred and ten degrees down there.

Dawn found us drifting in with the tide towards the coastline, and offshore the towering, jagged black rocks we could see quite distinctly were only ten miles away. That sounds a long way but it is surprising how quickly a ship drifting on the tide can eat up those miles. Those rocks looked very menacing and threatening indeed. With the change of tide, we would drift out once again to sea but each incoming tide brought us ever closer and closer to those ragged, inhospitable rocks and shoreline.

The attempted repair work continued in the engine room but with no reports of a successful completion. Watches were still kept and, though the helmsman's duty was unnecessary while we just drifted, he still had to take his watch on the wing of the bridge, which fundamentally meant that during that time we had two men on lookout, one on the wing of the bridge and one on the fo'c's'le head.

As I took the morning eight o'clock watch, the tide was taking us out to sea again, but the ragged jagged coast was that much nearer. The Third Mate offered the welcome news that according to the pilot book, the natives locally were anything but friendly. Apparently, it stated that a few years previously the locals had boarded a ship in a similar situation. All moveable equipment and goods had been taken, the officers were held to ransom, and some of the crew were never seen again. "Thanks," I thought, "that was just the thing you need to know to cheer you up."

The adage 'be careful what you wish for,' turned out to be true on that occasion because as we were returning back across the Atlantic, I had wished for a breakdown to allow us to break the monotony with a bit of shark fishing. Now we had actually broken down and found ourselves in different circumstances, I then wished for the exact opposite so prayers were being offered for a speedy repair.

We drifted throughout the following day and night and kept an ever watchful eye on the coast before the word came that the work was done. However, because the boilers had failed, there was no steam power to restart the engine. It was decided that dunnage (wood), which was stowed in the forepeak (a compartment below decks up in the bow) would be burnt in the boilers in an attempt to raise sufficient steam pressure to start them up. All the dunnage then had to be bundled and brought up from the forepeak and brought aft where it was chopped up to make kindling before it was taken down into the engine room to be burnt. The work in the forepeak hold was hot and dirty. With little movement of air, the heat made it more difficult to breathe and with the added fear of a rock coming through the side at any moment, we were quite apprehensive.

The surface rocks were by then very close, but the possibility of there being hidden, submerged rocks that we couldn't see was foremost in our minds, especially while we were so far below decks. 'For those in peril on the sea,' came to mind as we sweated and cursed our luck. "All ships should be fitted with kick-starts," I said to Mick, who didn't appear to enjoy my humour. We worked on and on for hours on that hot, dirty, back breaking job, but the whole exercise proved in the end to be a fiasco. We still couldn't get enough steam. It was a complete failure so there was nothing else to do but to call for help.

At about four o'clock in the early morning, a distress message was transmitted. A request for a tug from Aden was made, along with a call for any nearby ship to come to our aid. Shortly after that, a message was received stating that a British ship would come to our assistance. There was nothing else to do then but sit and wait, and the British ship hove into sight approximately four hours later.

She proved to be an old troop ship, the 'Captain Hobson,' packed with British troops who were returning home from the Far East. There was much cheering, jeering and waving as she came as close to us as she possibly could. A lifeboat was lowered and a line was passed from her stern to our bow. That was used to haul a mooring rope aboard to be made fast around our bits, and once it was secured the tow began. Not a moment to soon; by then there was only a very short distance between those dangerous rocks and us. We were towed out to sea for about forty miles where the 'Captain Hobson' cast us adrift again to await the arrival of the tug. Thanks and good wishes were exchanged as we watched her disappear over the horizon bound for England and home. They would surely be eating their roast beef and yorkshire pudding long before the crew of the 'Llandaff.'

A further twenty-four hours went by before the aptly named tug the 'Protector' arrived from Aden. That tow from the old 'Captain Hobson' was a lifesaver for surely we would have been upon the rocks within the twenty-four hours before the tug could have reached us. Fenders were slung over the side by the dozen as she gently slipped alongside to make fast. A smallish pipeline was passed and connected to the manifold, and the process of transferring steam began. It proved to be a tedious operation, which lasted until nine o'clock in the evening before it was estimated that we had sufficient steam to start the engine. Then the 'Protector' let go. She stood off us for some little time to ensure our well-being as the 'Llandaff' slowly came back to life and, with many "Thank Christ" epitaphs, we finally got under way signalling our thanks to the 'Protector' who in return signalled their best wishes to us and soon disappeared bound back to her home port of Aden.

After four days adrift, it felt good to be the masters of our own destiny again, and with purpose we started on our way. Our original orders had detailed us to proceed to Mena-al-Ahmadi in Kuwait, to pick up a cargo of crude oil, which was to be delivered to Geelong, Victoria, Australia, but due to the unforeseen delay, that schedule had to be revised. We still headed towards the Persian Gulf, but with our final destination unknown. Maybe some of the crew thought that we too, like the British soldiers, could be enjoying a Sunday roast before too long, but that was not to be.

Life returned to normal rotating watches, and Mick was still at loggerheads with the Bosun. A couple of days later, it was my trick at the wheel, and we were on a northeasterly course a hundred or so miles from the nearest land. It seemed that we were the only living souls within our perimeter, and it was difficult to maintain a constant attention to the job in hand. So what if we did wander a point or two off course occasionally, that was easily rectified; that was what I was there for.

As the novelty of the importance and responsibility for being in charge of the steering diminished, that too became routine and commonplace. So as I stood at the wheel my mind would sometimes wander and meander over the future, and what it held. On this occasion, I was suddenly alerted from my reverie by an indistinguishable object more or less straight ahead of us. I drew the attention of the Mate to it and as we got closer, it eventually materialized as a very small Arab type Dhow, with the smallest sail imaginable. What further amazed us was that it was a very small boat, but it still carried six black guys clad only in the flimsiest of loincloths.

With much beckoning and waving of arms, their distress was apparent to all. The officer of the watch, to his eternal credit, signalled "Stop engines." As we wallowed to a halt in a slight swell four of the men manned two extremely small canoes that they had in tow and they came alongside. They refused our offer to pick them up, but by using internationally recognisable hand signals, they asked for food and water.

Such is the bond of all seafarers that, despite their wretched condition, plenty of bread and water was lowered over the side by the stewards to be eagerly accepted by them. Then to our astonishment, not only were bread and water lowered down to them but fresh fruit, apples, bananas and oranges. Delicacies that us deck members of the crew never saw. Delicacies that we could only dream of. Just what was it in the system during those years that declared that such items of food were to be denied us? That question baffles me to this day.

What were those men doing so far from land in such a flimsy craft? The general opinion was that they were fishermen, perhaps blown out to sea for they were equipped, as far as could be seen, only with spears. There was evidence that kills had been made for one of the canoes had blood red water sloshing around their feet. As we got under way again with much grateful waving of hands, the revised orders for our next port of call came. We were to take on crude oil at Fao, Iraq in the Persian Gulf.

When we crossed the Tropic of Cancer into the Gulf of Oman the temperature rose, and the humid conditions became almost unbearable. As we pressed on into the Gulf, the thermometer rose even higher to a hundred and twenty degrees and still, like mad dogs, we painted ship in the midday sun.

Clad only in a pair of shorts and flip-flops, I was painting the bulkheads of the after starboard alleyway. It took approximately two minutes to paint each fleet of bulkhead (the space between two vertical rows of rivet heads) with a roller, and as I looked back along the alleyway, a pool of sweat marked each spot I had stood to apply the paint. The 'Llandaff' was a floating Turkish bath.

I was enthralled by the clarity and cleanliness of the sea. It was possible to see deep into the water, and it was as calm as a millpond. With the water being crystal clear, it was as if we were sailing through a vast aquarium. Far into the depths we could see thousands of multicoloured fish, small and large, with the occasional ominous fleeting shadow of the grey torpedo shape of a cruising shark. Like a marine concord there was the giant manta ray, which majestically flapped its wings, totally indifferent to the world around it. Not so majestic, to me at least, were the dozens of sea snakes, distinctive with black and yellow banding. Only eighteen inches or so long, but very venomous. Those animals were to be avoided.

We spent two days in Fao, quickly accepting a cargo of crude oil. On the second day we pulled out into the open sea to await bunkering. It was Thursday 22nd September when a BP tanker gently nosed towards our anchorage, and nearly all hands lowered fenders over the side for her to snuggle up beside us.

The bunkering took only two or three hours, and was finished well before early evening. We had changed watches I was in the four to eight. I was at the wheel heading south towards the Gulf of Oman. It was during that watch I learnt that our next port of call was to be my first experience of the Far East. We were headed for Balikpapan on the island of Borneo.

Conditions gradually improved, and it became less humid as we headed on a southerly course through the Straits of Hormuz, ever southward through the Gulf of Oman, into the Arabian Sea, and on then into the vast expanses of the Indian Ocean. I began to enjoy the evening watches for, while sleep was difficult during the day, dozing in a pool of sweat could hardly be called sleep, but once in the cooler atmosphere, the nights were magical.

We sailed around the southern tip of India and Ceylon (now Sri Lanka) then eastwards across the Bay of Bengal. One moonless night it was as black as coal, but the stars shone like miniature beacons. That was the farthest south I had been so far. Once across the bay, we turned southwards again, down through the Strait of Malacca between Malaysia and Indonesia, on beyond Singapore and into the Java Sea. We crossed the Equator then steered eastwards to Borneo.

As we headed farther south, the constellations changed. It was the old early mariners who had called for a star to steer by, but the North Star, their chosen eternal signpost, was missing in the southern hemisphere. It was there that I caught my first glimpse of the Southern Cross, low down on the southern horizon.

We arrived at Balikpapan on Saturday 8th October. For once we berthed without delay, and within minutes the manifold was connected and the cargo was pumped ashore. We had been at sea for sixteen days, and the majority of the hands couldn't wait to get their feet on dry land. Mick was ashore like a shot, mainly I suspect to get away from the Bosun who was still subtly making his life a misery every chance he got. The tension between them was constant and no one ever knew why.

Uncharacteristically I did not go ashore that night. For some unfathomable reason I didn't fancy it and I stayed onboard what was almost a deserted ship. That in one way felt a little eerie after all the activity, hustle and bustle that goes on normally onboard ship, but on the other hand the peace and quiet was something to treasure.

The whole cargo was disposed of by the following Tuesday, and we caught the evening tide bound for Miri in Sarawak, which is the northern part of the island. We arrived on Thursday 13th October, and for the first time since I had been a seaman, a shore gang came onboard to tie up ship.

Across the harbour from our berth, the tops of two masts could be seen sticking out of the water. Apparently it was the wreck of a Japanese ship, which had been attacked and sunk at the end of World War II; it had lain there ever since as a grim reminder of that terrible period.

* * *

By Friday morning we had taken on another cargo of crude oil. I could never fathom the logic of bringing crude oil to one side of the island, and taking a cargo of crude from the other. To me a layman, the economics of the operation defied explanation, but such is the way of the world; sometimes there are no obvious explanations.

Once the shore gang had taken the pipeline ashore and cast off, we sailed that Friday morning bound for Singapore for minor engine repairs and to take on more stores. The bay of Singapore was crowded with other ships on our arrival on Monday 17th October, but eventually we found what was considered a suitable anchorage.

Later that day as the tide receded, to everyone's amazement the ship didn't follow the tide. We were moored on an uncharted sandbank with our hull exposed almost as much as when we were in dry dock. The Skipper was livid, and after much checking and rechecking of the charts, he and a red-faced Mate went ashore to tell the local Harbour Master what he thought of the charts, and the competence of the pilots. You can bet the air was blue with typical basic nautical English.

With so much of the hull exposed, the Chief Mate couldn't resist the attempt to take advantage of our dilemma. He resorted to the old maxim of 'if it's exposed, paint it.' So sharp at seven o'clock the following morning, the Bosun turned the hands too. "Right lads, stages over the side, and let's paint the hull; we will never have a better opportunity." One of the older ABs shouted back, "No way! Nobody's going over the side here." "We'll see about that," retorted the Bosun as he turned on his heels. Within minutes, he was back with the Chief Mate in tow. "What's the problem? And why are you refusing to obey orders?" "I'll show you why," said the objecting AB.

It was customary when in port or at anchor to lash a fifty-gallon drum to the outside of the rail to put the gash and rubbish in, which would later be dumped. The AB walked to the drum, took out two empty beer cans and hurled them over the side. Almost immediately six very large sharks broke the surface of the very shallow sandy coloured water. "If anyone goes over there, they will have their 'f***ing' legs ripped off," he told them. It seemed so obvious then that the Chief Mate turned to the Bosun and said, "Find them something else to do." Thank God for an old sea dog with prior knowledge and experience.

Later that day, when the minor engine repairs had been completed, we upped anchor and the "Full ahead" order was given. The ship didn't budge. So the Mate rang full astern on the telegraph, but still not a tremor of movement. We were well and truly stuck. It was found that there would be a high tide the following morning so it was decided to wait until then and call for the help and assistance of two tugs to get us off the sandbank.

The tugs arrived in the early morning and made fast, one off the bow and one off the stern. With the tide at its height, the "Full ahead" order was given and the tug at the bow took the strain, but to no avail. We did not move an inch. With the Skipper raving about the inaccuracy of the charts, the incompetence of the bloody port officials and the inadequacy of the bloody tugs, things were a little hairy on the bridge. It was then decided to let go the for'ard tug and bring it to the stern. We then had one tug on the starboard quarter and one on the port quarter, with their sterns towards us. With their combined power pulling at full steam ahead, we put our engines at full astern to see if it would make any difference trying to pull us out in exactly the opposite direction to which we had slid on to the sandbank.

Nothing happened for what seemed like a lifetime, then suddenly we began to slip slowly backwards and sank gradually into deeper water until we finally became fully buoyant. Once afloat we let go the anchor, and an inspection was made to ensure that no damage had occurred whilst she had been aground. The Skipper satisfied himself that there was no damage. Later that evening, Wednesday 19th October we finally and thankfully said our farewells to Singapore.

We cleared the Malacca Straits by Friday 21st then sailed across the Bay of Bengal and the Arabian Sea. Throughout that great expanse, only two ships were sighted, and those were in the far distance. We kept well clear of the Southern Yemen coast and those ragged rocks as we slipped past Aden into the Red Sea on Monday 31st October.

Three days later I was on my way along the foredeck to the fo'c's'le head because I had been detailed by the Bosun to carry out some small task. The sea was as calm as could be, hardly a ripple anywhere, when for some inexplicable reason, the bows dipped sharply and sent a wall of water over the port rails. It hit me like a tank and had sufficient force to send me somersaulting; it washed me back along the deck towards the centre castle. Thankfully, I missed all of the pipes and valves as I was washed along between the tank tops.

When the water hit the bulkhead of the centre castle, it bounced back and in doing so, it stopped my forward progress and spun me around, and I knocked my head against the last of the tank tops. As I struggled to my feet like a drowned rat, the Mate hung his head out of the wheelhouse window and shouted down to see if I was hurt. "Not really," I said, and I went aft to change my dripping shorts then I carried on with my work. The knock I took wasn't too hard, but I had a sore head for a couple of days.

Port Suez hove into view early the next morning, Friday 4th November. We anchored and took on fresh water from a barge, then awaited the northbound convoy taking on the customary searchlight and boats at the same time. We entered the canal at nine o'clock that evening. I was the farmer of the watch, and with my head still sore from my watery escapade I was glad not to be at the wheel. At eight o'clock Saturday morning we stopped only long enough to get rid of the Pilot, searchlight and boats, then we were on our way into the Medi.

Although still damned hot in comparison to England, the cooler weather experienced in the Medi. made life so much more comfortable. It was such a pleasant change not to be constantly sticking to yourself and sweating continually. Everyone seemed to be happier and more content.

We pressed on ever westward, and made good time. We slipped through the Strait of Gibraltar on Friday 11th November. As I have said before, the change in the temperature and the weather as you leave the Medi and hit the Atlantic is nearly always evident. But it was more so that time for it was November, and it was freezing as we met the seas of the Bay of Biscay. No doubt, we felt it more so after being so recently in the Tropics and the heat of the Red Sea. I supposed that the ability of the British to endure all types of climates, extreme heat or extreme cold, could explain the fact why they are such good sailors and soldiers.

It had been five long months since we had last seen England, and we wanted to cheer as we sailed up the Channel and saw that essentially English sight of the White Cliffs. From the moment we had left Singapore, all the crew had at least been hoping and praying that the orders would be changed, and we would make port in Britain, but no such luck. On the evening of Tuesday 15th November we hove to off Rotterdam, Holland.

The Pilot came aboard the next morning to take us up the River Mass to Pernis. Rotterdam had one of the biggest dock areas I have ever seen. That night everyone except the duty watch went ashore, after last touching dry land almost a month previously. We had a great time in the many different bars with the very friendly Dutch folk, many of whom could speak excellent English. We were alongside for three days and were kept busy lugging and stowing away the Christmas stores.

The Chief Steward, the Pumpman, the Second Engineer, the Chief Cook along with the Second Cook and an EDH (Efficient Deck Hand) went ashore with various complaints to visit the local doctor. All of them were paid off and sent home for treatment, much to Mick's dismay that he hadn't tried it. He was by then desperate enough to try almost anything to get away from the Bosun.

Most of the replacements were shipped out from England with the exception of the two cooks. They were recruited in Holland. They were both Dutch, and made a big improvement to our daily fare; everyone began to look forward to their meals.

On Saturday 19th November we left Pernis bound for Baniyas in Syria. The White Cliffs didn't receive the same joyful acclaim that time, and the depression of watching them disappear into the distance could be measured as we huddled into our heavy weather gear to keep the chilling winds out. But sailors are ever hopeful that the next port would be our last before we headed back to a British port, and it could have been worse for Syria was not the Far East or even the Red Sea. We had come to terms with our lot, and the deepest depression had lifted as we passed under the Rock back into the Medi. and the improved weather.

In the crisp clear winter air, the snow capped mountains of Southern Spain could clearly be seen on the port bow. What is now known to all as the Costa del Sol was then nothing more than a series of small fishing villages being developed into the now vastly popular resorts of Torremolinos and Marbella. Other than the major port of Malaga, there was little life along that coast at that time.

As we plied further eastward, we saw more of the Spanish southern coast. The Costa Blanca was indeed the appropriate name for that coastline, which shimmered white in the winter sun. The coastline must have been at least forty to fifty miles away but such was the quality of the light and the cleanliness of the air, it was easily distinguishable. No wonder the most famous painters from all over Europe, including our own Turner, loved the translucency of the light in that part of the world.

My musing and marvelling at the beauty of the Mediterranean was brought up with a jolt. Our worst fears were confirmed when the word was passed that our orders had been changed, and we were bound once again for Fao.

Morale sank to a new low as we headed for Suez and the canal. To add to our misery on Friday 25th November we ran into rough weather. The ship, being empty, had little ballast, and it pitched and rolled violently from side to side. Sleep was impossible.

Overtime in plenty was to be had, and the work kept our minds occupied, but there were few smiling faces when we arrived off Port Said on 30th November. I was by then an old hand at the wheel going through the canal; my early fears had vanished with experience even as we negotiated the narrowest sections.

We had cleared the canal and were well out into the Red Sea by the next morning when, as the temperatures soared, it was decided that it was time to clean the tanks. Unlike the 'San Velino' where the deckhands had took the hoses into the tanks and washed them down manually, the more modern butterworth system was available on the 'Llandaff.'

The butterworth system consisted of a hose connected to one of the many water valves on the underside of the flying bridge and was fitted at the other end with a sprinkler, very similar to a garden hose sprinkler but much larger and heavier. We had to lower them into the tank with water pressure applied and maintained for varying periods at different levels of the tank. It was gradually lowered till it reached the bottom with the water being pumped out into a holding tank. The process helped to create an almost gas free situation.

The system took away the need for an AB to direct the operation from inside the tank itself, but the resultant rust and gunk still had to be cleared manually. For that we were required to don thick rubber protective suits to go down to shovel the accumulated rust and gunk into containers. These were hoisted out of the tanks and put into empty oil drums as on the 'San Velino.'

Given the stifling temperature down in the bowels of the tanks and those rubber suits it was hot. Through my life I have had various concepts of hell, but that I am sure was the nearest I ever want to be. However, the butterworth system considerably reduced the amount of time that the deckhands had to spend in those contaminated areas.

Nevertheless the accumulated rust still had to be removed, and as it was shovelled into the containers, the residual gas within the piles of rust escaped and was inhaled. The effect of the gas was immediately apparent when your stint was completed; when you emerged from the tank and hit the fresh air, it felt as if you had been on the booze all day.

With the day's work finished the routine was, as on the 'San Velino,' to line up for the Bosun so he could issue each man with a tot of rum to be taken neat and knocked straight back to kill the effects of the gas in the stomach. The main result of which as far as I was concerned was to wheedle me on to the delights of that seafarers tipple, and it has remained my favourite beverage to this day.

* * *

On Sunday evening 4th December, the lights of Aden twinkled on the port beam as we left the Red Sea. Fortunately there was no engine failure on that occasion, nor were there any natives in small boats to delay our arrival, and we kept well clear of that unwelcoming coastline. It took a further week for us to reach Fao, where we arrived on Sunday 11th December.

We loaded a cargo of crude oil the following morning when for some inexplicable reason the Pumpman made a miscalculation, and one of the tanks overflowed. The black oil flooded the deck and power hoses had to be used to wash the decks down. Not a pleasant job, and a situation that didn't improve the Bosun's temper. However it was necessary, not in the least to rid the ship of the heavy stench of oil.

I thought I may be getting acclimatized as it didn't seem quite so hot on that occasion, but it was still far too hot for comfort, especially in December. With the loading completed we let go and anchored in the river to await the tide. The Pilot came aboard about eight o'clock that evening, and with a pleasant cooling breeze after the heat of the day, we cleared the river bar, waved goodbye to the Pilot's cutter and hove to awaiting our bunkering. It was the afternoon of 13th December when a tanker, the '*British Prestige*' slipped alongside, and it took four hours to supply our bunkers before we got under way bound once more for Borneo.

The heat became less intense as we retraced our passage, with few sightings of other vessels. Christmas was spent in the Straits of Malacca with the usual chicken leg dinner and the few cans of beer that we were allowed. Other than that it seemed just a normal day.

Over the previous weeks the crew, by and large, had saved and stashed some of their rations of beer in anticipation of the Christmas festivities. There was no splicing the main brace, but those off duty did attempt to enter into a party spirit (unintended pun: apart from the single tot of rum given as we emerged from the tanks, no spirits were ever sold to those below officer status, only our weekly allowance of beer was received, even at Christmas). As with all people so it is with seafarers, one's thoughts and memories take you back home. Nothing could be more different than a bleak December in Bloxwich or the Malacca Straits. Perhaps the possibility that after Balikpapan we could be heading home was the reason for a slightly better atmosphere, for even Mick managed a smile, though out of sight of the Bosun.

Another five uneventful days brought us to Balikpapan and without delay or hitch we tied up at the same berth as before. The discharging of the cargo began at once with everything normal and routine. Nothing seemed to be amiss until all of the hands were redirected from their duties and those off duty called to work. Our task was to rig steam pipes to pressurise the tanks. Evidently during our passage from Fao, the temperature of the tanks had been held incorrectly; consequently there was an excess of gas in the tanks. The steam would, we were told, neutralise and expel the gas; thereby combating an extremely lethal situation. "Christ," I thought, "one spark and we could have been in the epicentre of an atom bomb." Thankfully the corrective action proved to be successful, and the cargo was got rid of with many muttered prayers of thanks.

On Monday 2nd January 1956 we were called early to stations to let go and hove to in the harbour. Due to the excessive gas that had accumulated on the voyage from Fao, it was considered prudent to butterworth the tanks yet again. All twenty-seven of them. The work progressed throughout that day and night, and was finally completed late on Tuesday morning only for all hands to be called to stations to tie up again within the harbour. It took the shore inspection team until late that evening before they were satisfied that the gas levels within the tanks were acceptable, and we were able to accept a further cargo of crude oil.

As I have remarked previously, the economic logic of oil transportation beggars rational thought. For the last time we had delivered a cargo of crude oil to Balikpapan, it was our lot to take on a cargo of crude oil from the other side of the island. This time however, having delivered a cargo of crude oil to Balikpapan we now took onboard a further cargo of crude oil from the very same jetty where we had just discharged one. The only thing that made any sense to me was that the cargo we had brought from the Gulf was directly from the wells, and the cargo we were loading had been refined ready for use, but that was just a theory of mine, which was never confirmed.

Wednesday morning brought a change; for once, we worked on dry land. Equipped with paint rollers (which ships by that time carried), fastened to the end of long bamboo canes, we began to paint the ship's hull from the quayside. Meanwhile the tanks were accepting our further cargo, and word had it that we were bound for Sambor, a small island just off Singapore. From there we were destined to return to Miri to pick up a cargo for, delight of all delights, Shell Haven, England. The cheers and frolicking that went on around the ship when the news was spread was something to behold. So was the look of relief on Mick's face.

As we sailed that evening Wednesday 4th January, I could sense the change of mood. We were going home. Sambor, in the early morning of Sunday 8th January, had a different air as I strolled ashore I thought that it was time to buy presents. There was a series of magnificent stores and shops in Sambor, whose wares unfortunately were out of the reach of my pocket. There were however bargains to be had in the smaller stores of which I took advantage.

Leaving Sambor we approached Singapore harbour the next day, Monday. We then heard that minor repairs were to be done yet again. I am sure that it was in everyone's mind, "keep away from that bloody sandbank." Certainly, the course we took indicated that that was the intention on the bridge. Boilers had to be cleaned and minor engineering checks made.

One of the engineers had to be paid off. During the repair work he had managed to break his thumb, and after a visit to the local doctor, he was on his way home. As we waved what we hoped would be our last goodbyes for the trip to Singapore, it was found that one of the shore leave ABs was missing.

We arrived at Miri on Friday 13th January and as we took note of the date, toes as well as fingers were crossed as we hoped against hope that it was not a bad omen. We went alongside at once. There in the next berth was the sister tanker to the '*Llandaff*,' the '*Llanishen*.' She was the only other ship which belonged to Radcliffs at that time. She was an older ship than the '*Llandaff*' and indeed she looked it. When we talked to some of her crew, we found that she was bound for Rotterdam and then on to dry dock. I didn't find out how long she had been away from home, but the mention of dry dock gave the crew an air of certainty about their eventual home coming, especially as we on the '*Llandaff*' had done just that from Rotterdam on our previous voyage. We waved goodbye to her on the Saturday and followed ourselves on the Sunday.

Whilst we had been in Singapore, Mick had asked permission to see a doctor on some pretext or other. It is fair to say that he had been feeling low and out of sorts for some time, but on hearing that we were homeward bound, the doctor had declined to pay him off.

We sailed from Miri and we were soon off Singapore on the 17th January. I was surprised to note that we had slowed almost to a standstill only to see a launch pull alongside to deliver the wayward AB who had gone missing. A Jacob's ladder was slung over the rail, and the shamefaced miscreant was taken to the bridge to face the music from the Skipper.

The next day the valves had to be cleaned. After we stopped engines, it was not long before a shark appeared swimming around the stern. It was by far the biggest shark that most of the crew had ever seen, a veritable monster: a great white. It was at least fifteen foot long from snout to tail, and my suggestion that we should take a swim to cool off went down like a lead balloon. No one suggested that we should try to catch him.

Our delay was short-lived, and our trip back across the Bay of Bengal was lonely and monotonous with no sign of life, no other ships or birds, just mile after mile of uninhabited sea. The only respite was at night and my ever-eternal wonderment of the sky at sunrise and sunset each day in all its resplendent, glorious colours.

Despite the increase in temperature and the added discomfort that created, it was a relief in a way to enter the Red Sea and be amongst other shipping again. The monotony of the routine had been softened by the prospect of being homeward bound. Our steps were lightened too as we arrived off Suez on 1st February. We were getting ever nearer and nearer to a home port, and we were certainly not prepared psychologically for the news that the sister ship 'Llanishen' was to deliver her cargo to Shell Haven (near Portsmouth), and we were bound for Rotterdam. The original orders for the two ships had been completely reversed.

Our passage through the canal was zombie-like. Everyone reacted in varying degrees, but to everyone from the officers down, it was a bitter pill to swallow, and all our duties were performed automatically. One could understand how and why in the years of sail under the harsh conditions of yesteryear, mutinies were fermented. Not that it ever reached that pitch, but there was great resentment. The cleanliness and comfort of the 'Llandaff' did not enter into the equation at that time. Mick was devastated.

There was little that could be done about the situation. Articles had been signed which entitled the owners to require our services for at least two years foreign service and no one had twisted anyone's arm to sign on as most of us had returned to the ship voluntarily. It was however in most people's nature to hanker after one's family and the comforts of home. We just had to put our heads down and get on with it.

A seafarer's life in the fifties, if no longer harsh, was certainly spartan, and the thought of home and family is what kept the spirit alive and well. I finally came to terms with the news, rode the punches of disappointment and learned not to worry about that which I could not change or alter, although my philosophical approach did little to ease my pangs of wistfulness as we once again looked longingly to our port side at the White Cliffs of Dover.

Tuesday 14th February brought us to Rotterdam where we anchored in the approaches to await the service of a Pilot to take us up to Pernis. As I took my place at the wheel the next morning I reflected upon the changing conditions a sailor experiences, just two short weeks previously we had been wallowing in intense heat, now we were carving our way through sheets of ice to at last tie up and discharge our cargo of crude oil. Pernis was no substitute for us homesick seamen, but spending time in the Dutch port with its friendly bars and happy welcoming people, although it was not home, was a consolation of sorts.

Mick, probably recalling the luck of other members of the crew on our previous visit who had been paid off sick, asked again to be allowed ashore to visit the doctor. Whether the Dutch doctor was more sympathetic than his far eastern colleague I don't know, but he agreed that Mick should be paid off. What a change came over him. It was as if he had earned a reprieve from a life sentence, and he had been freed from the Bosun's attitude and bad temper towards him.

In that respect I was happy for him, but we had been shipmates and friends both at sea and ashore for two years, and we had done a lot of growing up together. I was extremely sorry to see him go. It was a sad goodbye. Mick had put me in contact with Sylvia, she and I were by then regular correspondents, and on future home leaves when I would visit her, I also called on numerous occasions at Mick's home, only to find that he was always away at sea.

Orders were received on the 18th February that we were bound for Gibraltar and as soon as we were fully discharged we moved to a loading berth to take on a fresh cargo and sailed on Sunday afternoon. Mick was not replaced, and after I'd had him as a constant companion for two years, I missed his friendship. It felt strange to be sailing without him.

As we came down the North Sea and into the English Channel, the lights of Dover twinkled invitingly. In the dusk, I could just make out the White Cliffs that signified home to so many sailors. There was one little consolation at least, Mick was home and feeling much happier I hoped.

The Bay of Biscay was kindly to us by not behaving as its usual boisterous self, though it was bitterly cold. I was at the wheel as we entered Gibraltar harbour on Friday 24th February and, under the Pilot's instructions, I gently took her alongside one of the old Shell tankers, which were permanently anchored in the bay. Another successful manoeuvre to add to my experience. The tanker took part of our cargo then we shifted ship a few hours later to go alongside another tanker anchored in the bay, which took all the rest except for four thousand tons.

Mail was awaiting me in Gibraltar with the news that my brother Roy had been called for a Board of Trade examination and he would forward the result on to me. I had previously advised Roy, who was an apprenticed engineer to Rubery Owen, a large Midland industrial firm at that time, that he should apply to the Shipping Federation since he too expressed an interest in a seafarer's life.

In good warmer weather we headed east to Malta and Valletta where we arrived on the 28th February. I remembered that I had called there just once on the old '*San Velino*,' which then seemed a lifetime away. The remaining four thousand tons of crude oil was soon discharged so once again I did not get ashore. In no time we were sailing light ship due east, heading for the Suez. Dawn on 3rd March saw us tied up, stern to, on a buoy in the bay where we took on water.

Our midday meal was interrupted to let go to take our place in the southbound convoy. At four o'clock that afternoon I had a new experience in the canal. The convoy was shepherded into what can only be described as a layby, a waterway crescent arcing off from the main canal in a long semicircle. Each ship tied up one by one with little space between stern and bow to allow the passage of the north bound convoy. Then I saw what the small rowing boats were for. Our mooring ropes were taken ashore and secured to the bollards on the canal side so that we could heave ourselves alongside and tie up.

They had allowed the northbound convoy into our section of the canal before allowing us to get clear into the Bitter Lakes. It appeared to me that the northbound convoys had the right of way and, not wishing a long delay themselves in the Bitter Lakes to await our clearance, they continued on, and so it was that the southbound convoy had to use the layby. It took four hours for the northbound convoy to clear our position. Then one by one we let go and continued on our way where we in turn had no further delay in the Bitter Lakes.

Shorts and flip-flops were the order of the day for both work and leisure as we felt the full force of the Red Sea heat on our journey down. Invariably we always seemed to pass Aden at night, and we always hoped that the next time we saw those twinkling lights we would be heading home for a well-earned leave.

It was a century ago, or so it then seemed, since we had broken down and were towed clear of those rocks yet it was in reality only a matter of months. On and round into the Persian Gulf we sailed, that time to the northernmost point to the entrance of the Shatt-al-Arab waterway, where the Pilot came aboard and stayed with us for the forty mile river trip to the oil terminal of Bandar Mashur.

If white desert sand and nothing else as far as the eye could see is your scene then Bandar Mashur is the place for you. It consisted of two big storage tanks, four jetties, a narrow road that ran into the desert as straight as a die for ever, a cluster of small huts and, of course, the sand. It was bloody hot. That was Bandar Mashur. The nightlife, well the legions of the dead could have livened it up.

Thankfully the loading was quick and uneventful and once given clearance, the Pilot was back onboard. We said a not so wistful goodbye to the place on Friday 16th March. The Pilot's cutter was awaiting him as we cleared the bar and once we had found deeper water, we anchored to enable further minor engine repairs to take place.

I had received mail in Bandar Mashur amongst which was a letter from Roy explaining that he had failed the Board of Trade examination because marine technology was totally different to industrial engineering, which his apprenticeship had equipped him for. Their suggestion was that he would need to take a specialist Marine Engineering course should he still wish to join. I replied to him suggesting that he could still apply to the individual shipping companies, several addresses of which our mother would have of my previous employers.

The heat is to be expected and has to be accepted in the Gulf, what we did not expect was a sand storm. It soon blew itself out it left the ship caked in sand. So out came the power hoses, and the ship was hosed from stem to stern, which was a job to be enjoyed in those steamy sticky conditions.

It was received with some sense of disbelief and a great deal of cynicism when we were told that we were to bring that cargo home to Eastham. There was little cheering or frolicking that time, more the doleful comment from the cynics that, "Ten to one we will finish up in Rotterdam."

The Red Sea was greeted with silence from the company. We came through the Suez with silence from the company. We crossed the Medi.

in disbelieving silence from the company and while some of us younger crew members believed that that time we really were homeward bound, those old heads who had seen it all before sage-like muttered "We will believe it when we are sailing up the Mersey."

The passage through the Medi. was halted a couple of times, but the stoppages were of little consequence for only minor repairs. The rock hove into view on Wednesday 4th April and, as on every occasion, I felt a change in the weather. The Bay of Biscay tried to be unfriendly but failed, and for the next five nail-biting days, our toes, our fingers, and everything else we could cross was crossed, until we finally sailed over the Mersey bar and docked at Eastham on Monday 9th April.

There was a wonderful feeling of euphoria amongst the crew as we tied the ship up to English soil on a lovely mild April day safe in the knowledge that they could not then send us abroad again. Several of us made our way into Liverpool to try the local brew, which tasted strange after nine and a half months, but we soon got our taste back. It was a great feeling to be home, and such a relief after never knowing if the orders were to be changed again at the last minute.

The 'Llandaff' was finally pumped dry on Wednesday 11th April. We cast off, cleared the Mersey bar and anchored in order to butterworth the tanks for the last time. It took three tedious, frustrating, never ending days to complete the butterworthing. The process was meticulous; those tanks had to be totally gas free before the ship could go into dry dock again.

I was beginning to look beyond my seven weeks leave, which had been uppermost in my mind since the Red Sea, and it was time to prepare for my Lifeboat and Efficient Deck Hand exam. It was necessary for me to obtain a Steering Certificate and as we made our way down the Irish Sea, I asked permission to see the Skipper. To obtain the certificate I had to have spent a minimum of twenty-five hours at the helm, and I certainly had done well in excess of that. Nevertheless I was still pleasantly surprised and a little bit chuffed when the Captain, without hesitation, willingly and quite affably stamped, signed and presented me with the official qualification.

It was April Sunday 15th and Falmouth never looked lovelier as we anchored in the bay on that morning. Who was it that said "Oh to be in England now that spring is here? Never were those words so true. It was fantastically beautiful, now that I knew we were home. We came alongside to tie up at two o'clock the next afternoon. By 4.30pm we were paid off; we made our way to the station for our journey home and seven weeks leave. I had no specific plans on how to spend my time for those seven weeks other than to see my friends. I looked forward to meeting up with Sylvia and I sorely missed Mick's company on the homeward journey.

CHAPTER EIGHT
THE HARTISMERE
(Of a Mad Skipper, a Dispute and a Smuggler).

Good news awaited my homecoming; Roy, undaunted by his unsuccessful application to the Mercantile Marine through the Shipping Federation, had taken my advice and persisted with his intent by writing directly to some of the companies.

He had finally been accepted, interviewed and tested successfully by Radcliffs of Cardiff of all companies, and was to report to Falmouth where he was to join the '*Llandaff.*' I simply couldn't believe the strange coincidence of it all. I hadn't really held out much hope for him to be honest. So not only was I surprised, I was also happy for him.

He would join and be in a different world to the one that I knew. He would be a Junior Officer, which was an automatic rank for all engineers of any grade or experience; he would enjoy all the frills and comforts that accompany the status of an officer. He would have his own cabin, cleaned on a daily basis by a steward, he would eat in the comfort of the wardroom with tables laid on spotlessly clean tablecloths, he would have the best of food and fresh fruit, definitely no peggying to do and he would enjoy all the trimmings common to the officer class.

I was not jealous at all, far from it, for I was exactly where I wanted to be, but the class system that existed between officers and crew always bewildered me. Obviously they deserved and had earned some of the benefits and perks that came with their ranks, but why was the gap so great?

In the realms of fantasy, I pondered the prospect of the two of us being shipmates. The scenario of two brothers on the same ship with just fourteen months age difference, brought up in the same family surroundings with the same values yet we would be worlds apart. It all seemed to me in many ways to make a mockery of the so-called class system.

It is strange how things work out. Little did I know then that while I was bemoaning my cruel luck as I had wistfully watched the White Cliffs of Dover recede into the distance, that the extra excursion down to the Gulf would allow me to celebrate Roy's 21st birthday with the rest of my family. His birthday occurred during the third week of my leave, and preparations for a super celebration were well in hand.

Fate cannot be denied for it seemed as if I was destined not to drink my brother's health face to face after all as a couple of days before the event, he was called to report to the 'Llandaff.' My family was not one to allow that small detail to interfere with the prospect of a good party, and Roy's health was drunk many times despite his absence and my hazy recollection.

It was not long before we learnt from his first letter that he was bound for Fao. That message had come from Malta where they had put into for minor repairs and whilst there, the ship had been fined five hundred pounds for making excessive smoke while anchored out in the harbour.

Meanwhile I had been picking up my previous social life, what was left of it. A lot of my time was spent with Sylvia, which was very pleasant and went really well, even the dreaded first introduction to her parents. We had many happy outings and evenings together, and it was with a certain misgiving that I received the summons to report back to the Pool on June 6th.

It was mid afternoon when I booked a room at Gordon Smith's, and after I had stowed my gear I renewed my acquaintance with Liverpool, which was after all my home port. I found little to keep my interest in the city centre, and hunger hurried my steps back in the direction of Gordon Smith's dining room. It was busy with hungry seafarers making the most of the simple but adequate fare. No one that I knew appeared on the scene.

To kill time I found an empty table, and while I enjoyed the food I decided that it would be the cinema and an early night for me. By half past ten I was back in my room, such was the quality of the film that I recall nothing whatsoever about it.

I was half undressed when there was a sharp knock on my door. To my amazement and wonder on opening it, there stood Mick. He had been in the dining room and caught sight of me as I came through the entrance and had tried to attract my attention but I had disappeared along the corridors. He had been given my room number on request at the foyer. It was great to see him again and for a moment, I harboured the hope that we could team up again but sadly, that was not to be. We sat quite late reminiscing and comparing experiences since his departure from the 'Llandaff.'

Mick was reluctant to leave but he had an early morning call. He had joined a passenger liner called the 'Newfoundland,' which was on a regular run between Liverpool and Canada. I wished him luck as he returned to his own room. Sadly, our paths never crossed again.

I was early at the Pool office that following morning expecting a thorough medical because having re-signed on the 'Llandaff' for a second trip, I hadn't seen a doctor for over twelve months. "Is there anything you want me to check, or is there anything I should know about?" he queried. "I don't think so," I replied, "OK, that will do," he said, and within less than five minutes I was back at the counter handing my last two payslips from the 'Llandaff' to the union rep.

The union dues were paid automatically from my wages, which were recorded on the payslips, so each week for the last fourteen months was duly stamped up in my union book. However every month or six weeks or so, there was also a compulsory political levy to pay so I still had a fair amount of cash to hand over before I became eligible to be offered further employment. I must confess that compulsory political levy did not sit well with me.

I was offered three ships from which to chose by the clerk and the one that most captured my interest was the 'Hartismere' because she provided a six month running agreement, plying cargos of iron ore between Newfoundland and the UK funnily enough. The agreement allowed for the contract to be extended for as long as one liked, but one could request to pay off every three weeks or so whenever the ship returned to a home port. The prospect of another long '*Llandaff*' experience had for the moment lost its attraction, so to me the short-term agreement sounded just fine.

The '*Hartismere*' lay in Kings Dock Number Two and, considering the cargo that she regularly carried, her dusty appearance could be accepted for other than that she appeared to be in good nick. After I had spent a good half an hour taking a look at my new home, I walked up to Cornhill to sign on articles.

Most of the crew were in the office already signing on, the majority of whom were Scousers who were laughing and joking in the inimical manner that characterizes the Liverpudlian. I was immediately attracted to their happy, easygoing attitude and secretly hoped that the officers and the Bosun would be of a similar make up.

On being told to be onboard by seven o'clock the following morning, I had the rest of the day to myself. Back at Gordon Smith's I bumped into Paddy who had sailed with me on the first trip of the '*Llandaff*.' We sat chatting in the dining room and as I related the nine-month saga of the '*Llandaff's*' last trip with all its many mishaps and near calamities, his expression became more and more incredulous. "Bloody glad I didn't sign on," he uttered in his heavy Irish brogue.

I booked an early morning call and at 5.30am I was awake with my gear packed so after an early breakfast I arrived at Kings Dock Number Two in good time. Probably the only thing that I missed from the '*Llandaff*' was the privacy of a single cabin for the '*Hartismere*' afforded only dual accommodation. I found a cabin and met the guy with whom I was to share. His name was Jimmy. He hailed from Birkenhead, but that was near enough for me to think of him as a Scouse. It was akin to me hailing from Walsall but known to everyone else outside as a Brummy. He was an amiable and a pleasant guy with whom to have to share a cabin and we got on well. Neither of us bothered to unpack there and then, except to just extract our working gear. The rest of the day was spent hosing down and generally cleaning up.

It was about dinnertime the next day when we let go and moved out to the river bar where we sailed up and down to test the engines. Something seemed to be untoward and not to the satisfaction of the engineers so we anchored until the early evening. Repairs were finally affected and we weighed anchor and came back into the Mersey proper, through a lock into one of the Birkenhead basins where we tied up alongside.

Sundays were always traditionally a day of rest whilst in port unless overtime was called for or the crew called to stations. Many of the crew, being local Scousers, looked forward to spending the day either in the pub or with their families or girlfriends. So it needs no imagination to visualise their attitude when word was passed down from the Skipper that we would cast off at about ten o'clock that night, and there would be no shore leave. That was like waving a red rag to a bull to those Scousers.

The language that greeted the Skipper's dictate is not printable and was very basic, followed by a mass exodus from the ship. Perhaps there was an element of comradeship that directed my steps in the wake of my shipmates as I didn't fancy spending all day twiddling my thumbs aboard ship all on my own; I caught the ferry to New Brighton where being a Sunday in early June the place was dead. Nothing was open and there was hardly a soul about. Perhaps it was always that way, I didn't know. It certainly wasn't Blackpool, but it was much better than a lifeless ship on a Sunday.

Most of us were back aboard by nine o'clock to learn that we were to assemble in our mess where the Skipper and a couple of officers awaited us. To say that he was not pleased was an understatement. He was livid. "Everyone is to be logged a day's pay," he stormed, "And fined a further day's pay for disobeying orders." His anger was impressive, but when it was reported to him that two ABs were still missing he went berserk. His temper was something to behold; he screamed and shouted that the crew would have to pay for the cost incurred by the delay and the cost of the two tugs that were standing by to take us back into the Mersey.

As he stormed out he was followed by five of the lads, who had rushed to pick up their gear from their cabins and headed for the gangway. He almost had another fit when he saw them at the head of the gangway. "NO, NO, NO," he screamed. "Put your bags down lads, I was too hasty, I didn't mean it, I only meant it for those two who are still missing," he pleaded. Reluctantly and with much misgiving, the mutinous five turned around and peace reigned for a short while. Following that pantomime, most of the crew had decided there and then that the short three-week trip would be the only one they would be making with that nutter.

It was not until the early hours that the two absentees came aboard. When they heard of the happenings, and the retribution that the Skipper had threatened upon them, they retorted, "That's what he thinks," and they took their gear and headed amidships towards the gangway. They must have been seen as they came aboard for the gangway had mysteriously been taken inboard, in an attempt to forestall any further escapes I assume. About they turned, coming back through our accommodation and out on to the Poop Deck where a large steel pontoon had been positioned directly below our stern. The two men got a rope and lowered their luggage down onto the pontoon, and then they both rapidly shimmied down the rope to make their escape.

As they struggled up the quayside wall by a vertical ladder, they were spotted by the Skipper who shouted, cajoled and threatened them to come back, but all to no avail. They were not sailing with that madman, and they emphasised their decision by giving him the honoured two-finger salute. I did wonder what would happen to them on their next appearance at the Pool Office and what excuse they would make but I wished them good luck.

Albeit with a deficient ship's compliment, the Skipper would delay no longer and we headed out into the Irish Sea, and the tugs sailed back to their berth on reaching the river bar. The ship to shore radio must have been busy for as a new watery day dawned we anchored off Hollyhead to await replacements for the two absentees.

It was late in the day, about ten o'clock, when a launch headed towards us and two men clambered aboard. Hardly had their feet touched the deck when the officers hauled up the accommodation ladder and we were on our way. There was no escape then for our two new shipmates.

The vision of the officers hauling up the accommodation ladder was met with much humour from the deck crew who's job it was. "One thing less for us to do," they joked. At least it had solved the previous mystery of how it had been hauled up in the first place. It was not a self-stowing gangway after all, much to our disappointment.

Once on the move we were told to make the accommodation ladder secure for sea. Life settled in to the normal routine as we saw the last landfall, the southwest coast of Ireland, disappear in the mists and fog of the North Atlantic.

As the voyage progressed and new friendships and acquaintances were made, one of my new shipmates provided a talking point. Evidently, he had been a regular aboard the '*Hartismere*' and had completed several trips. What no one could fathom out was what on earth could be the attraction with such a volatile Skipper. The guy was a bit of a loner and never volunteered the reason for his loyalty. The consensus was that there had to be a reason for him to stay on the ship, but no one could come up with a logical explanation.

The North Atlantic proved to be extremely unfriendly: bitter cold, fog and drizzle throughout the trip. Four days out from Newfoundland on Saturday 16th June, we learned that there were icebergs ahead on our present course. Evasive action was immediately taken as we steered a course thirty-seven degrees further south to skirt around them.

The night watch was cold and eerie and the fog swirled as I stood on lookout in the bows with the ship's whistle blasting every few minutes. My job was not only to stare out into the mist in the vain hope of spotting the lights of other ships, but to listen out for an echo of the whistle, which I was told would bounce back off an iceberg should there be one. I had visions in my head of the '*Titanic*' disaster. They did not help my unease, nor did the thought of the icy North Atlantic waters. I constantly kept awake and alert for if anything did crop up in front of us I thought I would be the first one to cop it.

The decision to change course proved to be a wise one; fortunately we saw nothing until the coastline of Newfoundland suddenly appeared and the mist cleared. As we followed the coast at a distance of about three miles, there on the starboard bow was my first sighting of an iceberg, and shortly afterwards two others appeared. According to the Bosun they were quite small ones, though they didn't look all that small to me. The thirty or forty foot that sailed majestically above the surface reminded me of the old adage about the tip of the iceberg and that there was probably twice as much ice below the waterline that we couldn't see. That all added up to a lot of ice according to my reckoning.

As we closed upon the land mass the weather improved to become much warmer and considering that it was June, it was as though we had come through a full cycle of seasons since leaving Birkenhead. It was late as we sailed amongst a group of small islands off the coast of Newfoundland to anchor off our destination, Wabana in Conception Bay.

Wednesday 20th June was spent in preparation for taking aboard the iron ore. First we topped the derricks and stripped the five hatches of their three sets of tarpaulins, then we stacked the hatch-boards well out of harm's way and finally we secured the derricks. It doesn't take long to describe the task but it was late in the afternoon before it was completed and we went alongside.

We made fast to a large, long wooden jetty situated at the foot of a sheer cliff face at least two hundred feet high by my estimation. Attached to the jetty was a crane like structure connected to a conveyer belt that reached to the top of the cliff. The whole of the cliff face was a solid mass of iron ore, which ranged for over half a mile. It looked as though the whole island was made of iron ore to me.

Opencast sites could be seen in some parts of the cliff face and how far the seam went inland was hard to fathom. There were steps up to the top, about five hundred of them, also a lift for easy access. I was not keen on climbing all those steps and even less keen on the rickety looking lift so while some of the crew went ashore, I declined on that occasion. In any case I had not got a lot of money in the ship so I couldn't really afford it.

The ship had been positioned with the number three hatch immediately below the conveyor belt, which once it was lowered into the hold, soon began to spew the ore in at a terrific rate. Once the hold was full the conveyor was removed. We then shifted ship so that the conveyor belt could be lowered into number two hold to be filled.

To ensure that the ship remained on an even keel as much as possible, number four hold was next followed by number five and finally number one. We had to shift ship on each occasion. We were also kept busy covering and battening down each hatch as it was finished. Then we headed back out into the open sea. As the Pilot jumped aboard his cutter with a cheery wave of the hand, we headed out into the Atlantic towards home. It was Thursday 21st June and the moon sailed across a clouded sky as I took my lookout position in the bow on the first watch. The sea thankfully was calm; the weather too was also calm and clear with not an iceberg to be seen.

The return trip was much more pleasant and the sun did its utmost to aid our passage and relieve the routine. We each kept a personal record of the hours of overtime that we had worked so when we were one day out from the UK the First Mate asked for all of our overtime slips. It was routine as they were needed to make up our accounts of wages so nothing of significance was made of it.

Saturday 30th June saw us sailing up the Bristol Channel beyond Cardiff and on up to Newport, Monmouthshire. Once having made fast and secure the Mate returned to everyone their overtime slips. Uproar broke out. Eight hours overtime had been deducted from everyone's claim and the Mate swore blind that we hadn't worked them, which was totally untrue. Immediately the union rep was sent for to argue what we all saw as an attempt to claw back from the crew some of the expense incurred by the delays at the start of the voyage. In effect, as we saw it, the Skipper had as good as logged us all a day's pay like he had threatened to do in the beginning.

The general opinion was that all the trouble could have been averted if the Skipper had not tried to stop Scousers from going ashore on a Sunday; an official day off in their hometown, especially as they were not required to work until stations later that night. The arguments between the Skipper and the union rep raged on well into the afternoon, which caused even more delays. The new crew could not be signed on until we had been signed off. Consequently no work could go ahead to prepare for the next voyage.

In the midst of all the argument I decided that I would take a shower in preparation for the long trip back to Liverpool. Clad only in a towel I made my way towards the bathroom when I bumped into a customs officer. We had only been away for a short time yet they were still aboard searching. He walked ahead of me in the corridor and turned into the bathroom. "Surely he's not going for a shower," I thought.

As I turned into the bathroom, the loner who had been on the 'Hartismere' for several trips was squatting washing his gear in two buckets. As he stood viewing that domestic scene the customs officer said to him, "Every time we come aboard, you are doing your dhobying. Come on, empty those buckets." Reluctantly he did as he was bid and as he emptied the soapy water and his clothes out onto the deck, they were followed by a metallic clink as several tins of tobacco fell out too.

With a broad smile, the official confiscated the tobacco and took him off for further questioning, no doubt proud that his theory had proved to be correct and the smuggler was apprehended. I stepped into one of the shower cubicles more than a little amused that I had been the one privy to stumbling on to the answer to the little mystery that had been surrounding him.

Still the arguments raged with the crew refusing to sign off. It was a stalemate. Finally it was resolved by the union rep advising us to sign off under protest and the union would continue to pursue the case with the company. He collected our names and home addresses and stated that he would be in touch as soon as the problem had been sorted, but I for one never heard any more about my lost eight hours. Once we had signed off and been paid we spent a few hours in Newport until we caught the Liverpool train, vowing to steer well clear of that Skipper in the future.

Jimmy and his parents allowed me to leave my gear at his home in Birkenhead before I caught the train to spend the rest of the weekend at home.

Chapter Nine

The Albemarle

(Of a Happy-Go-Lucky Guy, a Foxy Lady
and an Attempted Robbery).

The weekend gave me little time to do anything extraordinary
except to spend a few hours with Sylvia and my mother's cooking too
had lost none of its appeal, but Monday 2nd July found me back at Lime
Street Station with Jimmy waiting for me at the previously arranged
rendezvous.

At the Pool office we both presented our steering tickets and once we had completed the application form for the Lifeboat and EDH school, we were told to report to the Salthouse dock the following morning. The school turned out to be a small prefabricated building where we met up with a dozen or so other hopefuls. The Lifeboat certificate was an essential qualification in obtaining the Efficient Deck Hand certificate; without it, you were not able to enter the EDH course.

So the next four days entailed intensive instructions on the million and one things that we had to know about lifeboats. Of course at sea we had lifeboat drill once a week (fire drill too) but they mainly touched on how to lower the boats safely so that each one of us knew exactly what to do. In some respects it was a refresher course to the Gravesend Sea Training School, which by then seemed like a lifetime ago. I relearned a great deal, especially concerning the equipment and its usage.

It was not all lecture and demonstrations, there was practical work done too. On the side of the dock was an actual lifeboat that nestled snugly in its davits. The practicalities came to the fore when we lowered it into the water and safely freed it from its blocks.

As at Gravesend we memorised the name and use of every single item and where it was stored. Our knowledge had to be extensive, even down to how the supplies should be rationed out if we ever found ourselves cast adrift. The instruction also included the rigging of the sail and going out into the dock itself. As we tacked back and forth across the dock we learned what to do and how to cope in stormy weather. I found the four days to be very enjoyable and handling the boat under sail was good fun.

I stayed with Jimmy at his parents' house and we took the ferry from Birkenhead across to the Pier Head in Liverpool every morning, and then on to the Salthouse Dock. We finished a little early on the Friday afternoon and I was soon back at Lime Street and on the train for another weekend at home.

It was exam time on the Monday morning and as the results were read out, my pleasure at being successful was dampened somewhat by Jimmy's failure. He along with another couple of lads would have to try again at a later date.

Previously Jimmy and I had talked of applying for a berth with the Athel Tanker Company after obtaining our EDH certificate because the company had a good reputation. Jimmy's failure of the Lifeboat exam was a big set back to our plans but he said if he could delay signing on a ship for a week while I took my EDH we could still go for it.

Early that afternoon we presented ourselves at the Pool office where with some little pride, I handed over my Lifeboat Certificate and asked for the application form to continue for my EDH. The clerk handed one to me, which I duly filled in. On hearing of Jimmy's failure the clerk said, "I've got a ship for you, it sails tomorrow." "Oh no you have not!" said Jimmy, "I'm off to get my teeth seen to."

The following morning I started my course, which like the lifeboat course was more or less a refresher. We were reinstructed in the art of splicing ropes and wires, making strops (rope slings for loading and discharging cargoes) and had to demonstrate our familiarity with the many knots and their uses, which I had first been taught at Gravesend. Most of the other instruction I was also familiar with given that since I had finished peggying I had been performing them as part of my every day duties.

Although I found the course comparatively easy, I still dreaded the forthcoming exam. As stated previously, I had been staying at Jimmy's home and since his failure of the lifeboat course he was not allowed to continue the training so I travelled into Liverpool every morning alone, which became a little irksome. That was why I made my excuses and thanked Jimmy's mother for her kindness and friendly hospitality and I slipped a little money (as much as I could possibly afford) into her hand for my board. She seemed happy with it and then I left to book a room at Gordon Smith's. Friday teatime saw me once again at Lime Street heading home to spend my twentieth birthday with my family.

On my return to the school on Monday and Tuesday our time was given up mainly to revision and on Wednesday morning we sat the exam. To everyone's delight there were no failures. With congratulations ringing in our ears, we were told to pick up our EDH certificates from the Cornhill office on the Friday, and the money that we were entitled to for attending the course would be waiting for us at the Pool office.

It was still only lunchtime and as I suddenly found I had the afternoon free, I decided to pay Jimmy a visit to find out if he was still keen to apply to the Athel Tanker company. If so, we could go together. Unfortunately he was not at home so I left a message with his mother that I would call back again later that evening.

My ready cash was by then running extremely low so to the Pool I went to collect the money that was due to me. The clerk said that although he knew that I had been told to pick up my certificate on Friday, he wanted me to go to pick it up there and then and to bring it back to him. He would then pay me my dues. My intuition then clicked in which made me feel that there was something strange going on. "He is messing me about," I thought suspiciously. But there was little I could do as I needed the money to square my bills at Smith's. As I trudged my way up to the Cornhill offices I bemoaned my fate but cheered up somewhat when the clerk handed over my EDH certificate without question. It was good at last to have hold of it; not only did it entitle me to a higher rate of pay, but after four years of actual sea service I would automatically become a qualified Able Seaman.

It was a different me who walked, not trudged back to the Pool to collect my money. My euphoria then took another blow when the clerk said I could not be given my money until I had a new ship. That was the moment it finally sank into my brain that those people, armed with the knowledge that without a job, money would sooner or later run dry, and make one desperate to accept anything that they had on offer. They had the power to manoeuvre and manipulate the situation to suit their own ends, and it seemed that they wouldn't hesitate to do so.

With my back against a wall, I was offered the choice of three jobs: one was a standby on the 'Albemarle.' "What does being a standby specifically entail?" I queried. "The ship's compliment has already been allocated, but an EDH or AB was needed to be onboard ready to sign on if someone defaulted or failed to return from leave," he told me. "If however the full crew did attend, then I would have to return to the Pool for another job," he added.

A small light opened up at the end of the tunnel, with the prospect of me not being needed I would still be able to go with Jimmy to the Athel Line as we had planned, so I accepted. I was told that the 'Albemarle' was lying in the Sandon Basin, and I was to report aboard her the next morning, Thursday July 19th. I was finally paid my money: the princely sum of five-pounds fifteen shillings. In these days of decimal coinage £5.75 doesn't sound a lot and looking back it wasn't a great deal then, even if it was just a little short of a week's wages. But I was young without anyone to support other than myself, also my food and lodgings were free while on ship's articles so that amount did stretch a fair way.

I caught the ferry across the Mersey and made my way to Jimmy's to explain all that had happened and that I had been given little or no choice at all about most of it. I told him that if I was not required on the 'Albemarle,' I would meet him next morning to go to the Athel Line, but if I didn't turn up he would know that I had sailed. I lugged my gear aboard the 'Albemarle' in the Sandon Basin the next morning. Although I was early, the returning crew were already signing on in the officers' recreation room.

The 'Albemarle' was a fine looking cargo boat. Small and compact, only three hundred and sixty feet long, clean and tidy, with only four hatches, she was a very similar build to the Blue Funnel Boat in which Andy had sailed. She also had a small amount of accommodation amidships for paying passengers, in fact there were already two people onboard destined for Bermuda.

The ship belonged to the Pacific Steam and Navigation Company (PSNC). The Second Mate appeared to be in charge of the signing on, so I told him that I was the standby. He told me that one man had not yet turned up and he would know if I would be needed in about an hour's time, so I went on a tour of inspection aft to the crew's quarters. The cabins were tiny but neat and clean, as everything about the ship appeared to be, and I sat talking to some of the crew who were settling in.

In one way as I found the 'Albemarle' to be such a neat, clean and tidy looking little ship, I felt that I would like to sail in her, and half an hour later the decision was made for me. I was sent for and as he pushed the articles towards me, the Second Mate said, "Sign here, we are waiting no longer." Mentally I said sorry to Jimmy as I signed. I had mixed feelings as I put pen to paper. On the one hand I had guilty feelings about letting Jimmy down, and I hoped that he would understand, but on the other hand I felt that I had been given very little choice about most of it.

I found an empty bunk, and with little or no time to change into my working gear we let go outward bound for the West Indies. Unlike the last trip across the Atlantic on the 'Hartismere,' that one was much smoother and warmer as we headed into summer climes.

At that time in the mid fifties, there were many ex-Royal Navy and other ex-service men who found it difficult to settle back into civilian life on the completion of their national service, and many applied to the shipping federation for work in the Merchant Service.

Britain boasted the largest Merchant Navy fleet in the world at that time and consequently, there was always need for crews to man the ships. To train and equip those men with the necessary skills would have taken much time and effort, not to mention cost. So to overcome the problem, a new grade was created, a Deck Hand Uncertificated DHU.

That created much bitterness amongst some of the old hands the EDHs and the Abs, who had taken years and passed exams to achieve their ratings because the DHUs, including those from the Royal Navy, had little or no experience of the workings of cargo boats or tankers, but their pay was only a few pounds less a month.

It was a bone of contention with some that their training and experience seemingly counted for so little, however the AB's wrath and anguish was not aimed at the DHUs themselves, but more at the ship owners and the union for accepting the situation. They believed that the gap in the wages should be made a little wider by giving them, the Abs, a rise in pay. One such DHU onboard the 'Albemarle,' was Kenny with whom I struck up an immediate friendship. He was a happy-go-lucky fellow with an infectious sense of fun. No one was allowed to be miserable around Kenny.

The weather had stayed calm with good, warm, sunny spells and we passed the Azores on Tuesday night 24th July. We sailed once again into the Bermuda Triangle and arrived off Bermuda on Sunday 29th July. I had just started my stint at the helm when the Pilot's cutter scuttled alongside and soon he was giving me the headings to steer.

Following the coastline we rounded a headland into a narrow channel. The greenery of the island set in an azure blue sea in brilliant sunshine made a breathtaking picture. My enjoyment of the scenery was disturbed by the Pilot querying the heading, "Two thirty-eight degrees," I told him. He looked puzzled and came to check the compass himself. "Something is wrong here," he said. "On this course we should be on two twenty-six degrees." Was this another unexplained Bermuda Triangle mystery? I thought. "God! I hope we don't disappear from the face of the earth." "Forget the compass," the Pilot said, "just follow my instructions."

From then on he directed me to point the bow towards this house on the coastline or that tree or any prominent landmark that stood in the direct heading that we needed to go. Up small creeks and through narrow channels we navigated in that way, onwards between the islands to finally berth in a delightful small harbour. The harbour must have been yet another perfect hidey-hole for the Jolly Roger brigade; it was completely hidden from the open sea. What tales it could no doubt have told of times gone by.

That evening Kenny and I went ashore sightseeing. We took a rickety old tram like bus for the short ride into town and we sat there somewhat bemused by the stares that our fellow passengers were giving us. It wasn't until we arrived that we saw the notice in the bus directing black people only to the seats that we had occupied. There were no black people on the bus, just all whites sitting at the front staring at us, but not saying a word. Both Kenny and I agreed that we would not have moved if they had told us to. It was my first experience of a colour bar and racial segregation on any public transport.

We wandered around at will for it was a pleasant town, but we soon became somewhat disillusioned when we saw the prices of everything. Even a glass of beer was beyond our pockets. So we bought nothing and ambled slowly back to the ship.

It took until Wednesday 1st August to unload part of our cargo, which included many, varied items. Posh brand new cars came out of the holds, wire netting, washing powder, shoes, clothes, toothpaste, soap and, would you believe it, a consignment of raincoats. But I supposed that it must rain sometimes on that beautiful island; hence the lush greenery and vegetation. It was there we said goodbye to our passengers of whom I had seen little throughout the voyage.

* * *

We sailed late on Wednesday afternoon and I was thankful that it was not my turn at the wheel that time as we passed back through the narrow channels and creeks. Whilst the gyrocompass had been repaired while we lay in Bermuda, it still needed only a slight error in the steering to put the ship in jeopardy. We were bound for Nassau in the Bahamas. We arrived on Friday 3rd August and we unloaded a further parcel of cargo, much the same as we had discharged in Bermuda, but on that occasion it included two beautiful speedboats.

Kenny and I ventured ashore and to our dismay we found that the prices corresponded to those in the Bermudas. No wonder those places were known as millionaire's playgrounds. There was little drinking done by us in Nassau. Though a lovely island we were not sorry to see the Bahamas disappear over the horizon as we headed for Cuba and Havana the following morning.

What remained of the cargo was discharged in Havana on Monday 6th August and as I had been there a couple of years previously, that night I introduced Kenny to a couple of the bars that I had frequented. The comparison with Nassau and Bermuda was amazing, not only could we afford a drink, we could indulge all night, and we did. Come the morning, with sore heads, Kenny and I were not over enthusiastic at the task set us by the Bosun: painting the hull of the ship.

Stages were lowered over the port bow and once on the stage Kenny and I sat lazily painting away in brilliant sunshine. Slowly our heads cleared. It was hot, but very pleasantly so and by the time our one hour lunch break came, we were both desperate for the hair of the dog so we decided to forsake the food and slipped ashore for another couple of glasses of the local brew.

We were thirsty and a ten-minute walk found us sitting in our favourite bar, its ice-cold beer to us was as near to paradise as one could get at that moment. And so it proved to be. As we sat on stools against the bar, still in our paint stained working gear, we were enjoying our last cool beer before returning to paint more of the ship, when a very attractive young lady appeared on the scene. She ignored the locals as she entered through the door; she walked straight over to us and put her arms around our waists as she sidled between us. Smiling sweetly, she said, "Hi boys," and slowly but deliberately ran a hand up each of our thighs. "You buy me a drink?" she queried. "If you keep that up we will buy you the bar," we thought. What could two defenceless guys do? We didn't buy her one: we bought her four.

She spoke perfect English, and we answered all of her queries. The conversation ranged over our voyage. Where we had been and where we were bound ,and she appeared to be genuinely interested but throughout, her hands busily roamed free. Neither Kenny nor I raised any objection, especially when her searching fingers found our zips for her to explore further. Another round was ordered quickly, and our response to her query if we liked Havana was a very positive "yes" and getting better by the second as her hands became extremely personal.

Kenny was on her right and she, being mostly right handed, had to leave him from time to time to pick up her glass so I thought he had drawn the short straw and I found it extremely amusing when he asked her if she would like a straw. I on the other hand, to coin a phrase, was quite happy to find that in some things she was extremely ambidextrous. Her administrations continued for quite a while, but after her fourth drink she smiled sweetly and said, "Must go now," and wishing us "Good luck," she disappeared as quickly as she had arrived.

Neither one of us could budge off our stools until the 'excitement' had worn down. It was far to late for us to be bothered with painting the ship any more so a few more ice-cold beers was what we needed to cool things down.

As we left the bar a couple of hours later, we noticed a shipmate ahead of us down the street also making his way back to the ship. He was the nightwatchman whilst we were in port so he had every right to be ashore, unlike us. From his gait, it was obvious that he had visited several bars, or just one for a long session. In an attempt to catch up with him, our steps quickened only to see him disappear from sight. Arms had appeared from a doorway, grabbed him around the neck and pulled him inside.

Breaking into a run we barged into the house where two women were holding him pinned down on the floor while a third was taking his wallet. In the ensuing melee his wallet flew across the floor. We grabbed our legless shipmate and his wallet and dragged him back into the street accompanied by screams of abuse from the frustrated females.

Once back on the ship we left him collapsed on his bunk hoping that he would have slept it off come the time for him to commence his nightwatchman duty. The following morning as we related the saga to him, he was very vague in his recollection of the incident.

Bright and early that morning and feeling no worse for the previous days excitement, I was confronted by the Mate. "Where were you yesterday afternoon?" He said in a tone that defied contradiction. I was somewhat taken aback as he had approached me from behind unseen and I stammered, "I went ashore for the dinner break and never got back." "I know bloody well you didn't get back," he shouted and stormed off to find out where Kenny was.

Later that morning Kenny who still didn't have a care in the world, told me his side of it. He laughingly told me about being shaken awake and there before him was a dazzling white suited figure with a uniform and cap, screaming at him. He realised it was the Mate once he became a little more conscious.

"Are you going to get up or are you going to lie there all day?" "OK" said Kenny, "I'll get up now," to which the Mate retorted, "You should be out on deck working now and incidentally where were you yesterday afternoon?" Kenny, still half awake said, "I took the afternoon off." "So you normally take an afternoon off when you feel like it do you?" retorted the Mate angrily. Kenny, by then wide-awake, just shrugged his shoulders and said, "Yes, sometimes." At which point the Mate realised he wouldn't get any rise out of Kenny and stormed off not well pleased.

Laughingly Kenny said to me, "If the Skipper fines us, we'll tell him the real reason why we were late back. That will look good in the ship's log," but nothing transpired over the next few days, and I thought our transgression had been either overlooked or forgotten.

Friday 10th August dawned bright and tranquil, warm and pleasant and it created a feeling of contentment and well-being within me as we set sail in the sunshine bound for Falmouth. Not my beloved Cornish one, but the Jamaican one.

During the voyage the four holds had to be cleaned and prepared to take aboard a cargo of sugar. The cargo of varied merchandise we had transported to Cuba, Bermuda and the Bahamas had required a significant amount of 'dunnage,' used for packing the cargo securely. That and the waste it created had to be cleared away and the holds swept clean. It was hard work given the hot conditions, but nothing compared with cleaning the holds after a cargo of coal as the crew on the '*Oakhill*' had done.

Once we had cleared the holds they had to be lined with rolls of brown paper from top to bottom to protect the sugar from contamination. It was our second day out as Kenny and I went about our work in the hold when the Bosun's head appeared over the hatch shouting down, "You two, the Skipper's room, right away."

Apprehensively we knocked on the Skipper's door and sheepishly answered his summons to come in. He was sitting at his desk checking what appeared to be official looking documents; we hadn't covered half the distance towards him when he looked up and without any preamble he said, "You were absent without leave on the afternoon of Tuesday 7th August," it was more as a statement than a query. "Yes," we both replied, as we stopped in our tracks. "Logged half a day's pay, now get back to your work," he snapped. The real reason for our absence never did get recorded in the logbook, which I still think is a great shame. But before we did get back down the hold, we skived off aft for a crafty smoke.

The sun still shone on us when we arrived in Falmouth. It was a golden day, Monday 13th August. We anchored in the bay and watched a gang of Jamaican labourers come aboard to load the sugar. It was brought to the ship in large barges loaded to the gunnels with sacks piled high. The two Jamaicans rowing the barges were sweating profusely such was the weight of sugar being conveyed in them.

All the derricks were swung out over the barges and the sacks were loaded about ten to each load into the rope stops that we had spent a couple of days making. Then they were lifted, swung inboard and landed onto two hatch-boards placed over the hold to be slit open with a knife, which allowed the sugar to cascade down into the hatch. Down below a gang of men busily shovelled it into the corners and maintained a level surface as more and more sugar came aboard.

It took three days to load all the sugar available from that supply and with the hatches secured we sailed for another Jamaican port, Boden, to take on another part cargo of sugar. On that occasion we were moored alongside the jetty, which made for much easier loading.

The holds were by then half full and as a load was being swung over, a bag came adrift from the strop and fell into the hold. It hit an unfortunate Jamaican docker who was working below on the back of his head. There was much screaming and shouting as they eventually lifted the unconscious body out of the hold to lay him on a hatch-board and four of his mates lugged him ashore. As they ran along the jetty he was bounced up and down on the board, which I thought could risk causing more damage than the initial injury.

Later that evening, with my day's work done, I sat on the poop deck watching the many fish in the harbour. There were lots of garfish about eighteen inches long with long slender bodies. I had been previously told that they were extremely difficult to catch, as their long snouts were all sharp teeth and bone. Borrowing a line, I baited the hook with a piece of bacon rind and lowered it down to the water.

I allowed it to float on the surface and drift slowly out on the current towards the area where the garfish were milling around. One fish eventually was attracted to it and really took the bait. I could clearly see him and allowed him to chew on the bacon rind for quite a while as I resisted the urge to strike, eventually he began to swim away still taking the bait and as the line tightened, I knew that I had him. A few of the onlookers said that they had never seen a garfish landed before, which pleased me no end. He was about sixteen inches long and I unhooked him, taking great care to stay away from all those teeth, and returned him back to the water where he swam back towards his mates unharmed.

It was a balmy evening with the sun yet to set as the Jamaican dockers finished their loading. They came from the hold with their bodies caked with sugar. As we leaned over the rail we watched as they went down the gangway on to the jetty where they dropped their shorts and took the most effective means of removing the sticky mess from their bodies by plunging into the harbour.

Tales have always been told about the size of the Afro-Caribbean male wedding tackle and believe me, in that particular instance, it was true. It was agreed amongst those of my shipmates observing the scene of male nakedness that not one of us came anywhere near to matching their stature, not even when in a certain Havana bar being somewhat encouraged. All we could do was look upon the scene with envy in our hearts.

We caught the tide to make the four-hour journey along the coast to Kingston where we anchored in the bay, to go in alongside the following morning. Kenny and I ventured ashore that evening and wandered around aimlessly. We were not taken with Kingston for some unknown reason, and after a couple of beers we came back early to the ship; thereby avoiding any trouble with the Mate and Skipper that time.

The loading began again the next morning, but once again it was only a part load and still did not fill the holds completely. It baffled me why only comparative small amounts of sugar were being taken aboard at each port. It created lots of hard work for us uncovering the hatches and recovering them on each occasion. Surely it would be much more cost efficient to have those small loads transported to one place and delivered into the ship in one operation. Nevertheless, who was I to query the wisdom of the powers that be?

Once again we sailed on the Sunday for Montego Bay still with an incomplete cargo. As soon as we anchored in the bay, it was not long before the hatches were uncovered and the derricks swung out to receive what was to be a last delivery of sugar. That time a single man sculled the barges out to us from the stern of the barge. They made sculling look so simple and easy with an apparent effortless rhythm stemming from years of application.

Finally with the holds full, the hatches battened down and the derricks stowed we caught the tide bound for home. It took us fifteen glorious days of trouble free cruising from 21st August till the 5th September before we moored up in the Huskison Dock.

It was Saturday evening and with everything stowed and secure, we were free to leave the ship, but told that we wouldn't be paid off until Monday morning at Cornhill. Immediately I asked to see the Skipper to explain that I lived in the Midlands, and I was loathe to travel home only to have to return on Monday, neither did I wish to hang around Liverpool for the weekend.

He soon solved my problem by introducing me to a practice which I had no previous knowledge. I found I could pay off by completing a form, which could be presented to the company officials at the paying off table authorising them to forward my money due plus my documents to my home address. It was known as paying off Board of Trade.

There was however a snag. Because of the lateness of the hour, I would not be able to obtain a train voucher until the following morning. I said my goodbyes to Kenny and the rest of my shipmates as they vanished ashore then I resigned myself to a night alone onboard the ship. It was bright and early when I awoke and finally got the train voucher and was on my way to Lime Street and the train home.

CHAPTER TEN

THE GRANFORD

(Of a Dry Bathroom, Goulash and Cream
Crackers and another Big Tow).

I had become more than a little familiar with the Lime Street to
Wolverhampton train journey, even down to some of the out of the way,
lesser known stations. Travel must have been a part of me; in the blood
for I never tired of looking at the passing scenery in all of its seasons.

I also felt more than a little miffed that I had to wait overnight for my travel voucher, but I was glad to arrive home early on the following afternoon. It was Saturday and on a leave of short duration Saturday night down the club beckoned so I had no time to waste.

Disappointment awaited my homecoming too for my brother Roy had been home on leave from a longish trip, and I had missed him by two days; it was welcome news that he was doing well but, despite the fact that I had just missed him, it was good to be home to see my parents and younger brother Barry again.

My documents, payslip and money order did not arrive on the Monday, just a note which informed me that they had been delivered to the Walsall Main Post Office, which meant a trip down town for me to pick them up. I was due to report back to the Pool on Thursday 10th September and I thought that if I reported a day late on the Friday I may be able to wrangle another weekend at home. The Pool was closed when I finally arrived back in Liverpool late on Friday afternoon due to delays on the journey. After I had booked a room at Smith's for the night, I asked for a seven o'clock call and after breakfast I reported to the Pool as soon as it opened. The doctor was a formality and my examination was over in minutes. The clerk at the office immediately offered me a standby on a Cunard ship.

That extra weekend at home loomed large in my mind, "I don't want it," I said, "But it belongs to the Cunard company," he replied incredulously, as though he was offering me the crown jewels. He was amazed that one so young would pass up the opportunity of working for such a famous company, but as will be seen, I would come to regret it. "It's only a standby and if the ship is that good, there won't be a job on it for me," I ventured. "OK let's have a look at what else we have got," he said as he paused to look at his ledger. "There is the 'Granford,' he said. "When is she signing on?" I asked. "Midday on Monday at Cornhill," he replied. My ruse had worked I thought. Lime Street here I come. Once I had collected the forms, I was out of the Pool in a flash and on my way home within the hour.

Saturday night was spent at a personal beer appreciation party in the club. I needed a moral lift for the previous week Sylvia and I had broken up. She had found someone else. I felt hurt, disappointed and downhearted, but I was never around, being away at sea for long periods of time, and at the end of the day letters were a poor substitute. I can't remember much about that weekend other than that I saw old friends and acquaintances (mostly acquaintances by then), but the greatest consolation was my mother's cooking which was just as appetising as ever.

I returned back to Liverpool in good time on the Monday morning feeling sad and melancholy so, despite the fact that I had more than enough spare time, I decided to break my own resolves and did not even bother to go to take a preliminary look at the '*Granford.*' I hung about killing a couple of hours before I made my way to Cornhill, only to find once there that most of the crew had already signed and gone aboard.

I asked the Skipper (who stood at the height of five foot nothing) where we were bound. He said, "Firstly to the United States, then we will return to Rotterdam where she will be in dry dock for three weeks after that back to the States, with the strong possibility of returning to England from there." He also suggested that it was possible that before entering the dry dock in Rotterdam, there could be a cargo for the UK instead, but I thought that was just a sweetener.

"Come what may it will only be a shortish trip," I thought and that was quite acceptable to me on that occasion. So after I had signed articles, I was told to report aboard immediately. My gear had been stowed at Gordon Smith's over the weekend so once I had collected it, I went off to the overhead railway.

I always enjoyed that noisy, clanking form of transport, peculiar to Liverpool that allowed you to look down and scan the docklands. I was fascinated at the wonderful inspection platform it offered as the different docks slithered by, and the opportunity to see the many vessels of all nationalities harboured there. As we approached the Huskison dock, I could still see the '*Albemarle*' moored up there.

The sight of another ship interrupted my reverie; the corner of a wharf building hid its bows. She was rusted all over and smothered in a thick layer of coal dust. The white paint on the fore part of the bridge had weathered and cracked open and the coal dust, which had settled in the cracks gave a wonderful crazy paving effect.

I smiled to myself as I recalled my past experiences thinking, "Who in their right mind would want to sail on that?" As we rounded the end of the wharf, the bow came into view and there, in big white letters as if proud of the fact was spelt the name '*Granford*.' The grin froze on my face as a sense of déjà vu overtook me. Memories of the '*Oakhill*' flooded back.

Like the '*Oakhill*' she was an old Empire boat and like the '*Oakhill*' owned by a Greek company based in London, the Goulandris Brothers. My desire for an extra weekend had landed me on another London / Greek, the very ones I had vowed to myself to try and avoid like the plague. Déjà vu indeed. Little did I know then that conditions and events were to be repeated in some ways and in others they were to be even worse. That berth was going to be anything but uneventful.

I had no one but myself to blame I reflected philosophically, I greatly regretted that I had not gone to take a look before I had signed; therefore I felt committed and I resolved to serve my time onboard her with as good a heart as possible. The conditions were by far the worst I had yet experienced.

Scouser Vince, an AB with whom I was to share a cabin, had taken the better of the two bunks. And who could blame him for while his was solid and against the outside bulkhead below the portholes, my bunk was stood along the left hand bulkhead on entering, and the door opened on to it so that it doubled as a doorstop; it had a nasty habit of collapsing whenever the cabin door slammed on to it. I solved that problem by binding some wire that I found on deck around the broken parts.

What laughingly constituted locker space amounted to two small drawers and a tin locker, each painted in a hideous bright blue. I thought that was sparse to say the least, but the toilet accommodation and ablutions had to be seen to be believed. There was one shower for fourteen men to share, a big sink in which to do our 'Dhobying' and three small hand basins minus their plugs. It soon became apparent why there were no plugs; they were unnecessary because there were no taps. But why would you need taps when there was no water supply? So, it did not matter that there was only one shower for fourteen men because no one could use it anyway. I just stood and stared in total disbelief and amazement.

As on all other ships we were supplied with a galvanised bucket each, but unlike on other ships it became one of our most treasured possessions. For on the starboard side of the deck, outside our accommodation against the bulkhead was a handpump from which, after some effort, came cold water. Each one of us had to fill our buckets when required and carry them to the bathroom where we could enjoy the delights of a cold body wash from the bucket.

Alternatively, we achieved the luxury of a hot body wash by taking our bucket of cold water to pour into the steam geyser in the mess. That heated the water to far too high a temperature; so we would refill only half a bucket and then take it back to the pump to cool it down to obtain the required temperature. We would then take the bucket from the pump and leave it in the bathroom while we made a quick dash down to our cabins to undress and only then, clad in a towel, would we return to the bathroom for a wonderful warm or warmish wash down.

Occasionally all those exertions were to no avail for it was not unknown for some disgusting swine to have waited until you had dashed off to get undressed and in your absence help himself to your water. The solution to that was to revert to getting undressed first and then go through the whole rigmarole with just our towels around our waist so that at no time were our buckets left unattended.

Right from the start the trouble and friction that those conditions created augured badly for a happy forthcoming voyage, and it came as no surprise when two of the lads said that they'd had enough. They went ashore and came back a little later with sick notes, which gave the Skipper no alternative but to pay them off.

The Pool then had to be approached for two replacements that came onboard on the Thursday morning as we were about to sail. I instantly recognised one of the replacements as someone from my part of the world before I even clapped eyes on him; I heard him talking. The accent was unmistakable so it came as no shock to learn that he came from the Midlands, but it was quite a surprise to find that he lived within half a mile of my parents' home.

We had three days in which to clean up the ship before we sailed on Thursday 20th September, and none of us had any enthusiasm for the job as we turned to each morning. A feeling of doleful melancholy pervaded throughout the ship and no one did any more work than was necessary.

Upon sailing, we encountered heavy weather immediately. The old rust bucket was flat out at ten knots, but for the next four days the gales strength, winds and the heavy seas knocked us back and we hardly achieved seven or eight knots. The continuous pounding had one advantage though: it washed away the coal dust and the old tub looked almost respectable, that was more than could be said about the food. That was worse than atrocious. It was vile and virtually uneatable. Even worse most of it was not recognizable and certainly looked nothing like anything I had ever seen on a plate before.

Breakfast each day consisted of a round thing with a yellowish blob in the centre of it, very reminiscent of just one of that vast mass of jellyfish we had ploughed through on the old 'San Velino.' There was also a black burnt tube like object and a strip of red and white substance. I was told that it was bacon, egg and sausage but the only way they could have possibly come to that conclusion was if they had seen the food before the Cook got hold of it.

Cook? Now there's a laugh. Dinner each day was a collection of alien objects on a plate, and tea every single day was a large bowl of a dark brown liquid with lumps of unknown substances floating around in it, from which we had to help ourselves. And to top it all, it tasted vile. Day after day after day it would appear on our table at teatime. Thank God I wasn't still a peggy. Hungarian Goulash we were told was its title; it could have been Australian Crocodile stew, or Dung Beetle soup, for we would have known no different. Morale was at rock bottom, complaint after complaint was made to both the Skipper and the Chief Steward or whatever officer could be found. They incidentally never had any complaint about their meals.

Finally one day improvements were promised for the following night but the goulash, from which any self-respecting Hungarian would disassociate themselves, appeared yet again. Two of the lads immediately stormed off amidships to search for the Steward to remind him of his promise. They were rewarded with the news that it actually was different. It was no longer Hungarian Goulash because potatoes had been added which meant that it had been changed into a Lancashire Hot Pot. We could only conclude that somehow his fevered brain and two small spuds had miraculously transformed it. How he had the nerve to claim that it was Lancashire Hot Pot to a crew of mainly Scousers, I will never know.

The only item on the menu recognisable as food was the bread so at every meal, I would select that which looked least likely to kill me and I made a sandwich with it. At least then my stomach felt that it had a little something in it. I existed throughout those weeks, which were to turn into months on the great British standby: sandwiches.

The storm abated, the seas became less violent and the days more pleasant weather wise and we had more time to enjoy the turn in the weather for there was little or no overtime. Rumour had it that all the money saved by not affording overtime was being spent on our lavish diet. Well, cryptic humour like that was all that kept us sane. Our off duty periods allowed for much idle chatter and speculation that concerned the parentage of the Chief Steward, the Skipper and the money-grabbing owners.

Seventeen long days it took us to cross the North Atlantic, and we arrived off Newport News, Virginia on Sunday 7th October to take on another cargo of coal. We found anchorage amongst many ships of varied nationalities that were waiting to load.

For three long weary days we remained at anchor in the bay before going alongside on the Wednesday evening. It was the fastest and easiest tie up I had experienced so far. It was also my first experience of automation for having removed the hatches that covered the holds, the crew's only task was to batten down hatches again once the coal had been loaded.

The ship was tied up to two wire hawsers attached to an automatic winch on the quay amidships so shifting ship was simplicity itself. For instance, if the ship needed to be moved forward, the winch would heave up on the stern wire to pull the ship along while at the same time slackening the bow wire and vice-versa. That positioned the ship's hold adjacent to a gantry-lifting device. Along the quay was an inclined twin rail track along which a coal wagon would appear. This was lifted by a gantry and turned upside down, depositing its contents into a chute, which lead to the hold.

A man with a remote control box in his hand stood on deck operating a swivel on the end of the chute that enabled the coal to be deposited to all corners of the hold. That meant that the man controlling the chute loaded the ship, and the coal was levelled in the hold without anyone having to put a foot into it.

Once it had spilt its load into the chute the wagon was automatically righted and returned to the track where it rolled down the incline picking up speed so that its own momentum took it half way up a ramp at the end before it began to roll back down and changed tracks to roll back to its loading bay. The process was so efficient and fast that we were kept busy working throughout the night battening down the hatches, lowering the derricks and securing for sea, therefore we had no chance to sample the Virginian hospitality. The whole load was completed in time to catch the morning tide.

* * *

The weather on our return across the Atlantic seemed to dog our presence with one consolation: the following seas speeded our progress. Never was a ship's crew so unanimous in its prayers and hopes to dock in a British port before the ship entered into the dry dock in Rotterdam. Fate however had other ideas in store for us, and many days were to pass before we would see any part of Europe so all our prayers and hopes were dashed.

As we progressed, the storm with mountainous waves that crashed over the poop deck made it extremely dangerous to venture out on deck. To do so was to literally take your life into your own hands with a definite prospect of being knocked down by the colossal waves. To fetch water from the pump to bathe was a tricky operation indeed. We had to judge the moment very carefully and stand in the doorway to scrutinize the motion of the waves, then wait for the ship to start rising from a trough. While she rose and rode the crest of the wave, we had to dash out to the pump to collect some water and get back inside before another wave came crashing over.

That was the way of life, dodging waves whenever duty called. But despite the weather, or perhaps because of it, the old tub moved along at a healthy twelve knots on a steady course of 066 degrees with the aid of the following seas. It was Wednesday 17th October when for no apparent reason, we were knocked off course. Unbelievably yet again it was during my trick at the wheel. The engines were running smoothly and the wheel felt OK but the ship would just not respond. I tried first hard over to starboard, then hard over to port, but nothing happened.

Ships will automatically turn to head into the weather when they lose steerage and at the point where we became broadside onto the seas, a huge wave lifted us on its slope and we listed drastically to starboard. For a split second I thought that we were about to capsize, and if we had been light or partly loaded we may well have done so.

The wave reached its peak and the ship slid down into its trough and righted itself again. Immediately, a further wave came over the port side and crashed right through the galley and out the other side; it put out the stove and polluted itself by taking our goulash with it. Those were hairy moments and being a lot older and I hope a lot wiser now, I see those moments as being much more thwart with danger than my young inexperienced mind appreciated at the time.

Eventually the ships bows headed into the oncoming seas, and while we were still being pounded with waves that crashed over the decks, there was much less prospect of us turning turtle. The down side to all of that, apart from living our lives twenty-four hours a day on what can only be likened to a bouncy castle, was of course that we were then heading in a westerly direction back towards North America and Canada.

All of the crew were at a loss to know what was wrong with the steering gear, but the officers did not appear unduly perturbed, the Skipper especially shot down anyone's and everyone's views that there may be something wrong, however seriously. "It's the storm," he insisted, stating that we would regain our steerage once it had abated a little.

The mishap to the galley stove created much speculation about our evening meal. Anything would be better than the goulash was the general collective opinion. It was soon commonly known that the officers were to be served a lavish salad with all the trimmings. With our goulash poisoning the fish, what would we be served in its place? We were all on tenterhooks to know what delicacy would appear before us.

Wild and weird suggestions were tossed about but no one in their wildest dreams got anywhere near to the reality. Uproar broke out as the mess boy arrived and placed a packet of cream crackers on the table, not a packet each but one packet between fourteen hands. Given the situation mere words could not describe the scene that followed; never have I heard so many different words to describe the Chief Steward's birth status.

That time I drew the short straw to go to complain and as I confronted the Chief Steward he screamed at me. "What do you expect in such foul weather with the galley washed out?" "More than one packet of cream crackers for fourteen men," I remonstrated. "Oh hang on then," he said and disappeared for a few moments only to return with another packet of cream crackers. Words failed me. I turned on my heels clutching my precious prize. "You simply cannot reason with a moron," was my only consolation as I munched on my cream cracker sandwich.

Still the Skipper insisted that there was nothing wrong, despite the inescapable fact that we were travelling without steerage in the opposite direction to what was intended. The engines were maintained on full speed ahead and still, despite its total futility, we had to stand our watch at the wheel.

What or who finally convinced the Skipper that all was not as it should be is not known, but having at last discussed the situation with the Chief Engineer they did a thorough inspection throughout all of the steering system. It was not long before we learned the facts. We had lost the rudder.

For me history had repeated itself, but instead of the stem cracking to make it lean into the propeller as on the 'Martagon,' that time we had lost the lot completely. It had simply disappeared into the depths and for over twelve hours that fountain of knowledge, the man who literally held our lives in his hands, the Skipper, had employed us in mountainous seas by attempting to steer a ship with no rudder. I had very little time or respect for him. I also felt it prudent not to mention to anyone that a similar thing had happened to me while at the helm of a previous ship as I had in my mind what had happened to Jonah.

Without the rudder even the Skipper finally realised that as the sea was taking us hither and thither completely at its mercy; there was only one course of action left open. Radio messages were dispatched and very shortly we heard that a deep-sea tug was to be sent to come to our assistance from Halifax, Nova Scotia, one thousand miles away. Contact was also established with the sister ship 'Caspania,' one of the company's fleet which was currently in the North Atlantic.

There was nothing further to be done then but to ride out the storm and hope that assistance would arrive before any further misfortune overtook us. Little did we know that it would be a further four full days before the help we urgently required would be at hand, and what happened to the sister ship, '*Caspania*' was anyone's guess. She never showed.

The weather, along with the reappearance of the goulash for tea, continued to be lousy, and I began to think that the crackers would be more preferable, which taste wise they actually were. The only consolation was that by heading into the weather at the whim and mercy of the sea, the engines still functioned and they took us very slowly in a zigzag course in the general direction that we then wished to go.

It was anything but comfortable as the seas swung us through one hundred degrees, fifty to port and fifty to starboard but there was nothing to be done to halt the continuous yawing. Still, life went on as normal as possible with each of us doing our eight hours a day duties with no shower, no sleep, no comfort, no food (hardly), no overtime and the feeling that no one gave a toss about our welfare.

On the morning of Sunday 21st October the pride of the British maritime fleet the '*Queen Elizabeth*' appeared on the horizon and rapidly approached, I was not aware if she knew of our plight, but she came within a couple of cables and was gone over the horizon in a matter of minutes. I never knew the exact position where the '*Titanic*' had foundered, but the closeness which the '*Queen Elizabeth*' had come to us, suggested that we were on that main shipping route hoping to be towed into Nova Scotia. Could the rusting hulk of that great vessel be resting on the seabed immediately below us or close by? Fortunately we did not sight any icebergs.

It was in the evening, just after dark the next day that our engines suddenly stopped. We all assumed the worst, that we had broken down and were then completely at the mercy of the elements. The storm had abated somewhat, though the wind remained strong and a large heavy swell was running, but the main savagery of the storm had gone for which we gave thanks.

We walked out on deck and scanned the horizon to the west, seeking salvation. There ahead of us were dozens of little lights scattered across the water like sparkling diamonds. It was a large fleet of small fishing vessels. We hadn't broken down; the Skipper had stopped the engines as it was far too dangerous to go through them with no steerage.

As the Skipper and Mate pondered the new problem, there nosing its way through the fishing fleet came the deep-sea tug '*Foundation Frances.*' She had found us at last. As she circled around us, all hands were called to stations for'ard, and as the tug approached to within fifty yards or so, a loud speaker blared. "We are going to shoot you a line, watch your heads," was the message. There was a mad dash to find cover behind hatches, bulkheads and housing followed by what sounded like a gunshot.

There soaring towards us was a brilliant red flare, arcing over our bows to land in the sea on the opposite side depositing a thin line across our foredeck. We quickly gathered it in, threaded it through our panama lead, around the bits and took it to the drum end of the windlass. As we heaved in the line, it seemed to go on forever and it gradually got thicker until eventually, the thick rope gave way to a wire hawser, which was attached to the towing spring. It was back breaking work as we constantly coiled the ropes and wires on the deck; there was no let-up until the towing spring had been made fast.

Once again I found myself undertow, and in some ways it reminded me of my younger days when we were constantly being towed all around the Midlands in my dad's old bangers. We were at that point eight hundred miles from the mainland having miraculously edged two hundred miles nearer in our five days without steerage.

The weather did not improve further and due to the heavy sea we made slow progress towards Nova Scotia. At times we were down to only two or three knots. When we were about six hundred miles from Halifax, those of us who had portable radios began to pick up the local news bulletins. Everyone was agog when someone picked up a news flash that our plight was big news on the Atlantic seaboard. I first picked up the station on the Tuesday to hear that we had been reported drifting aimlessly and rudderless and the tug, '*Foundation Frances*,' had been sent out to search for us. Obviously they had not at that point received the news that we had been found and taken in tow.

It was a couple of days later when it was reported that a successful tow was in progress but due to the high winds and heavy seas progress was painfully slow. Henceforth we were the prime topic on the newscast and it was quite exciting to know that despite our problems, or rather because of them, we were the centre of attention.

Everyone tuned into Halifax radio and no one moved away from that wavelength for they knew more about our progress than we did. What they did not know about or report upon was the food and the conditions, both of which remained abysmal for us.

The days passed slowly in accord with our progress with little to do other than complain amongst ourselves about conditions, food, the weather and of course the Chief Steward, the officers and especially the Skipper, who's bad temper and behaviour never improved.

The weather began to improve though after a couple of days so as the wind dropped and the seas became more calm, our speed increased to five or six knots. On the Saturday, Halifax radio reported that we were making steady progress and were due to dock on Monday afternoon. It was nice of them to tell us. We suddenly realised, given the media coverage, that we were becoming seafaring celebrities in the local community; our plight had attracted much attention. It was a big joke when someone ventured the possibility of us being reported on the BBC World Service. Stranger things have happened, but in reality I don't suppose that we ever were.

We finally arrived as predicted on Monday afternoon in Halifax. As we proceeded up the approaches, the welcome was something to behold. Tied up were ships of all nationalities and warships moored along the naval quay. Ship's whistles and sirens gave us a raucous welcome; it was a heart-rending moment to see all of our seafaring brothers welcoming us to a safe landfall.

Lying at anchor midstream was a very large aircraft carrier. Its compliment lined the flight deck, immaculate in their white uniforms, saluting our safe return. And from the bridge, an Aldis lamp blinked its coded good wishes. Our safe arrival and the welcome we received from those seafarers of all nations was an occasion I will always remember.

A smaller docking tug came alongside which carried the Pilot and once he was safely aboard, it made fast to our stern. Two more tugs then came alongside, one to port and one to starboard and sandwiched us like mother hens. I was detailed to standby on the wing of the bridge. From one of the tugs, two reporters came aboard and shouted up the ladder. "Are you the Captain?" The Skipper eyed them with some annoyance and said, "Yes, who the hell are you and what are you doing on my ship?" "We are the press, can we talk to you?" "No, I'm too busy," he snapped. "So," I thought, "It wasn't just us, he was like that with everyone." Undaunted the reporters disappeared aft to get their story from the crew.

Within moments the reporters were forgotten as the line to the tug astern snapped and a new one had to be secured post-haste. The 'Foundation Frances,' our saviour and companion then let go; in some ways it was like severing the umbilical cord as we both waved our farewells as she veered off into Halifax harbour.

I could not believe that they would put us into dry dock still fully laden with our cargo of Virginian coal, but that is exactly what they did. The docking tugs slowly but purposefully edged us into the dry dock. Once the dock gates closed, the water began to drain away to finally reveal that we were indeed rudderless, as most of the crew had guessed about twelve hours before our quick-witted Skipper had come to that obvious conclusion.

The newscast to which we had avidly tuned during the long, tedious days of the tow had alerted us to the knowledge that we were newsworthy, but no one in their wildest dreams envisaged such a homecoming. Not only had the navy and our seafaring brothers given us a hero's welcome, but crowds of local people had gathered to watch our arrival too. I wondered and pondered what type of reception would we have been afforded if we had performed some heroic or praiseworthy deed instead of just losing the rudder.

The media was out in force, reporters and photographers from local dailies jostled with the TV crews and radio reporters. No doubt our safe arrival was probably the biggest thing to happen in Halifax for quite a while. I was not too put out when the Mate gave me the news of my next duty for I was to be the nightwatchman. There was little to watch in the dry dock, the main responsibility was to wake members of the crew for their specific duties and the overtime the job entailed came in handy.

Before I sought my bunk the next morning, I went ashore to gather copies of the early editions of the newspapers, both for myself and for some of the lads. The front page was taken up with a large picture of the 'Granford' entering port with the headline in big bold letters reading "TUG 'FRANCES' TOWS 'GRANFORD' INTO PORT" and just below that it read, "Hard-Luck Vessel Is Towed 800 Miles." The article then went on to read:

"A week long tow from mid-Atlantic ended this morning when the tug '*Foundation Frances*' slid into Halifax Harbour with the disabled freighter '*Granford*.' This marked the second time in seven months that the '*Granford*' put into Halifax with trouble aboard. [That was news to us]. The 7,000-ton freighter ran into trouble just over a week ago when she lost her rudder in heavy seas at a position in the Atlantic 800 miles from Halifax. She was on her way to Rotterdam from Newport News, Virginia, loaded with 8,000 tons of coal. Last Easter was her last call at this port when she put in with boiler trouble.

The ship is a familiar caller at Halifax and was better known under her former name '*Empire Haldane*.' She is presently owned by Goulandris Brothers and is registered out of London, England. Her Skipper Captain H.G. Garrett of London, would not make himself available to reporters this morning and denied the bridge to them stating that he was too busy. Deckhands however were co-operative, and from them the full story of the ship's long tow was gathered. The '*Granford*' first ran into trouble on October 10th in 'very heavy' seas. As she steamed along her rudder came loose, leaving her adrift in seas that washed her decks. Although the crew suffered no hardship during the incident one crewmember described the slow tow as very monotonous. The combination of stormy weather and heavy seas limited the speed of the tow to two, three and four knots, depending on the winds. When last reported Sunday the '*Frances*' and the '*Granford*' were approximately 80 miles from Halifax indicating that the last leg was somewhat calmer allowing faster progress.

The '*Granford*' was warped into the Halifax Shipyard floating dock immediately on arrival where she will be fitted with a new rudder. It is not known how long the work will take until surveyors have had opportunity to appraise the full extent of damage." It was the usual press hype but it went down well with the lads.

* * *

My slumbers during the days were constantly disturbed by the noise of the work that was being carried out by the shipwright and marine repair specialists. For not only was a new rudder being fitted, but the ship's hull was also being repainted. The noise of the electric chipping hammers was incessant, which made sleep impossible. There was no point in lying awake amidst all that hustle and bustle and so I took further strolls ashore. As I walked along the quay and out into town, numerous people stopped me to enquire if I was from the '*Granford.*' They were very kind, extremely well informed and sympathetic about our rescue, stating that it must have been a rough time for us.

I could never fathom how the local folk instantly recognised me and other members of the ship's company for we carried no insignia. It must have been our clothes and manner of dress and of course, once entering into conversation, our accents gave the game away. I'm not sure if it was the importance or the notoriety, but the kindness of the Halifax folk did a lot for our self-esteem.

The ship teemed with workers during the day and it was not unusual for some casual sightseers to venture up the gangway. The link that the locals had with Britain still appeared to be a strong factor, and they liked to yarn about the 'Old Country.' The casual visits of the locals who came aboard had its lighter moments and at times were great fun with lots of laughter banter and joking, but there were other not quite so funny moments too. One day, I was in my bunk desperately trying get some sleep before I went on night watch when the incident occurred. It was during the midday meal when some idiot found his way into our mess. He claimed to be an escapologist and challenged the assembled crew to bind him and secure him, and within moments, he bragged, "I will be free."

With great enthusiasm I was told later, my shipmates found some sail twine, which is very thin and extremely strong. With his hands behind his back they circled both his thumbs three or four times, then circled it between his thumbs a couple of times and fastened it tight; thereby putting a strangle hold like a figure of eight around each thumb. His distortions and manipulations to free himself had been something to behold. Eventually with much mirth and ribald advice, my shipmates offered to free him, but he refused so they left him to struggle on alone. After a couple of hours some of the more kind-hearted of the crew went back to rescue our brave escapee, to find him weeping and almost hysterical, pleading to be set free. Needless to say, the Great Houdini was seen no more.

It took eleven days to complete a full repair and it was during the evening of Friday 9th November that we watched the waters fill the dry dock until we eventually achieved buoyancy. With a brand new rudder and chipped and painted bottom we slipped from the dry dock into the bay to await the bunkering barge.

At two o'clock the following morning, I was at the helm as we commenced our long delayed and eventful journey back to Europe and Rotterdam. We were then told that the dry-docking after Rotterdam was no longer an option as we had already spent eleven days in a dry dock in Halifax. We had already been away for almost two months without a single cargo being delivered and we knew full well the economics of the situation and the attitude that the owners would probably adopt; there was much speculation then about how long it would be before we made a UK port. That shortish trip for which we had all signed on began to look extremely remote.

Though the weather throughout the passage was not good, it was nothing compared to both our outward journey and our first attempted return. The seas, although heavy on the present occasion, created us no problems; the only frustration was those White Cliffs again as they slipped past when we made our way through the Straits of Dover.

On Friday 22nd November we arrived in Rotterdam and still no further orders had been received. Beyond the main port we tied up at a coal jetty and were met with a succession of small coasters that came alongside us to be filled with our cargo of coal by the giant dockside grabs. It was at that point we realised that we knew nothing of the economics of the situation after all. Once loaded, those coasters were to bring the coal to the UK, and the economics of that defied all rational logic, while at the same time fuelled our fears that we ourselves would be away for a long time.

With the cargo discharged, our fears were realised. Tuesday morning found us a couple of miles further up the river at Bolnes in a repair dock for a major overhaul. Workers of all skills and descriptions invaded the ship. More rust and paint from around the hull was chipped away, damaged plates were removed, replaced and repainted. The bilges were flushed and cleaned, the masts stays were renewed and wonder of wonders ventilators were fitted. Up until that point, we had seen the owners as money-grabbers, but at long last money seemed to be no object; they even fitted taps to our sinks and an electric pump was installed to pump water through to our bathroom, shower and toilets. It was an innovation to have not only taps, but water as well; we were at a loss as to know how to cope.

During that period obviously there was major disruption for us and for a couple of days instead of bucketing water from the pump to flush our toilets we had to fasten our buckets to a rope and scoop it from the harbour. Our steam supply was also cut off as pipes were renewed, so our washing water had to be heated on the galley stove and whilst the galley stove itself was being repaired, there was no hot or cold water for us at all. It was of course, beyond any possibility for our officers to allow a temporary sharing of their washing facilities. No doubt their thinking bordered upon fear of contamination by the lower order and us lesser mortals.

The refit was expensive and life was, of necessity, chaotic. Much of the work was welcome and would improve our lives and living standards immensely, reading lamps were even fitted above our bunks, but I think in a better-ordered company, the crew may well have been paid off during the period of such an extensive refit. I can't begin to relate how stressful that period was for us as we still had to perform jobs around the decks for eight hours a day amongst the absolute mayhem and chaos. Most evenings I went ashore with one or another shipmate, taking the bus at the dock gate to travel through the tunnel into Rotterdam. Even the certainty of goulash for tea couldn't keep me aboard.

One incident during the refit made a big difference to our future well-being. The Chief Steward was caught red-handed selling ship's supplies. He was sacked on the spot. And wonder of wonders the Cook went sick with an infected foot and he too was paid off. Two of the main architects of our misery had disappeared off the face of the earth within two days.

It was with bated breath that we awaited the arrival of their replacements. The following day the new Chief Steward of Asian origin arrived followed the next day by the Cook, a cockney. That evening the new Cook presented us with his first meal, a good old-fashioned British fry-up. For a few moments, we all sat looking at it in stunned silence. It actually looked like a fry-up. The way we wolfed down that meal was something to behold, stifling all the cheers, which had they been heard would have reverberated across the river to Rotterdam itself. Later, the Cook related to us the very first conversation he'd had with the new Chief Steward. "You and me are good friends," the Steward had said, "We must conserve rations and save money for the company." "You can get stuffed," had been the Cook's admirable response.

Slowly, amongst all the chaos, came improvements that changed life aboard immensely. Smiles came back to faces and waistlines visibly expanded and during the following three weeks of the completion of the refit, life became tolerable. Mealtimes, though by no means Ritz-like, became something to relish for us, rather than the guessing game that had been our lot. But the ultimate pleasure of all was 'NO MORE GOULASH.' That thought, that feeling alone was almost orgasmic.

Towards the end of the refit, I applied for a five-pound sub, only to be refused by the Skipper. "Your allotment, due shortly to your parents, exceeds your earnings," he growled, "You can have a pound, but don't die in the meantime, else it will have to come out of my pocket." I told him to stick it. The fact that I had a fair amount of overtime money in the ship didn't seem to enter into his calculations.

After we had spent almost a month in Rotterdam we departed for Flushing for bunkering on the morning of 17th December. We tied up to an old hulk and took on fuel oil and water in readiness for the next voyage across the North Atlantic. It was close to midnight when we slipped our moorings and headed out into the buoyed channel.

The weather changed rapidly and soon we were engulfed in swirling fog with visibility down to a few yards, which made the buoys invisible. We had to anchor until the fog finally cleared at about midday. The forecast was not good. Conditions in the English Channel were atrocious, sufficient to delay the departure of the 'Queen Elizabeth' from Southampton. That made little or no impression on our Skipper, it appeared, as our engines sprang to life and we started on our way. The only consolation being that there was no heart-rending sighting of those White Cliffs of Dover as we battled through the storm.

As I turned to the next morning with the eight to twelve watch, I was detailed to go with the carpenter into the number two hold. Apparently, there was a storage tank between number two hold and number one, which had inexplicably filled with water. How was a total mystery. There was no means of pumping it out so the solution was for me to go with the carpenter to help him drill a hole through the steel at the bottom of the tank to allow it to run into the bilges to be pumped away.

Travelling light left the ship high in the water and while there were at that moment no waves breaking over us, there was still plenty of spray. To cut down to the minimum the amount of spray that would find its way down the hatch we removed only enough of the hatch tarpaulin to expose just the one hatch board by the ladder so that we could climb down into the hold. The bilges at the bottom had been cleaned in Rotterdam and after we had taken off some of the bilge boards on the port side, the carpenter climbed in to drill his hole. Once that was done successfully we covered up the bilges again and left the water flowing freely along them, then we climbed back out of the hold, battened up, and orders were given from the bridge to the engine room to keep the bilge pumps on until the tank was dry.

Later in the afternoon, the seas began to get more angry, which caused the ship to start to roll violently again from port to starboard and loud booming noises could be heard coming from the bowels of the ship. We uncovered the hatch once more and we could see that the bottom of the hatch was awash with water. It had forced its way beneath the 'ceiling boards' (Large three inch thick planks laid out at the bottom of the hatch to protect the steel bottom from damage by the coal or ore or whatever when being dropped from a great height into the holds). The water had ripped them from their bedding and each roll of the ship was slamming them against the inside of the ship's hull. Obviously, the bilge pumps had not been working and it was subsequently found that someone in the engine room had switched them off. The water still draining from the tank had then overflowed the bilges, cascaded out into the hold itself and caused all the damage.

Those long heavy planks swirling about at the bottom of the hold were a lethal danger to life and limb to anyone who ventured down there, but also a vast threat to damaging the ship's hull as they swirled and banged against it like battering rams at great speed, first one side, then the other each time the ship rolled. There was no choice; something had to be done. All deckhands were called out and we went down into the 'tween decks' (a shelf like deck half way down around the hold). The Bosun and an AB climbed down and stood on the ladder just above the swirling water, while we lowered a line down.

Occasionally, the ship would level out for a few moments, which brought the boards to a standstill. The Bosun and the AB would then steal those moments to jump out knee deep into the icy cold water and secure the line around a board for us to haul up by hand. They then had to quickly jump up on to the ladder again out of the way of the swirling planks as the ship began to roll again.

It was a long, hard, slow, dangerous task, especially for the two men at the bottom; if any of those boards had hit them at speed as they swooshed from side to side they could have been crippled for life, but one by one we hauled them to safety and lay them on the deck to dry. The Skipper in his usual thoughtful wisdom declared that the task came under the heading of 'safety of the ship' so no overtime was paid.

The bilge pumps had been restarted, but the water level in the hold remained the same. Someone peered over the side and saw that there was no water coming from the bilge pump outlet. It was again confirmed that the pumps were working, so the logical answer then was that the bilge filters were clogged up, which prevented the flow.

The prospect of cleaning those was daunting. The water, once it had escaped into the hatch and dislodged the ceiling boards, had picked up all the coal dust that lay in-between, beneath and all around them and with each swoosh on the roll, had carried it into the bilges.

With the ceiling boards out of the way, each one of us took it in turns for a few minutes to kneel and reach down into the bilges up to our shoulders to grab a handful of the soggy mess from around the filter and put it into a bucket. Each time the ship rolled the icy, filthy, coal dust filled water would gather speed and depth and roll right over our backs and completely submerge us as we were crouched over the bilges; we had to be extremely careful not to swallow any of it. It really was icy cold, black sludge and the state we were in defied imagination. Each time the filter was cleared, it allowed only a few litres of water through before it became clogged again. It was a long, hard, icy cold, back breaking, heart-rending job.

After only a few minutes one became frozen and exhausted. We had to be relieved at that point and we emerged covered in a black gunge clinging to both skin and clothing. How we thanked our lucky stars that our shower had been made functional; the hot water made us feel almost human again. It was a miracle no one suffered hypothermia. Had we been denied the benefit of the hot shower and had we still been using our buckets I'm sure that the possibility of that would have been very real. Still we toiled in the freezing hold and with Christmas looming very close, not one of us was in the festive spirit, but the water level in the hold gradually receded.

* * *

Christmas Day brought a welcome respite from that awesome task, and the Skipper allowed us to to purchase six small cans of beer for the festivities. There actually was a smidgen of humanity left in the man after all I thought. I did wonder if the state of my wage balance in the ship would stand such an expense, but I knew that if I sarcastically asked the Skipper if I could afford it, I would end up with nothing so I stayed silent.

Though we welcomed the short rest and the beer, Christmas was still less than festive and, given the fact that the hold still had to be finished and the weather was getting even worse, there was little to celebrate. Also the knowledge that our family and friends all those miles away would be enjoying a traditional Christmas didn't help. Wherever I was in this wide and wonderful world, home was the only place to be for Christmas and that didn't happen all that often.

Boxing Day, the traditional day in my book for recovery, presented us with the task of draining the last of the excess water from the hold; that left a layer of black sludge which had to be shovelled and bucketed out. Thankfully we did not have to work in icy cold water anymore; it had all gone. The work remained hard and tedious, but our efforts and the energy we used at least helped to keep us warm for empty holds in an icy sea are cold places.

Our final task, once the hold was dry, was to replace the ceiling boards, which proved to be a problem. Due to the shape of the hold the ceiling boards were of different lengths so matching the boards to their proper place was the equivalent of a giant jigsaw puzzle, and the pieces of the jigsaw were not lightweight. Surprisingly it took three days to replace them in their correct positions and get them bedded properly.

The weather continued to be rough, but at least we had solved the problem of the bilges, or so we thought. Our satisfaction was rudely and cruelly dashed when the carpenter reported water in the number one hatch. "Christ! More news like that," I thought sarcastically, "And I could get depressed." Thankfully the amount of water proved to be much less than was the case in number two hold, but there was still enough to lift the ceiling boards. They were lying in the shallow water and dragging along the bottom of the hold, not swilling and banging about as previously.

When number two hatch had been flooded, the water must have swilled forward along the bilges when the bows dipped violently as we rode the heavy seas, carrying the coal sludge with it along the bilges into the for'ard hold. This in turn clogged up that particular filter and trapped the water in there too. We were able to stack the boards square within the hold and that time it was not necessary to stand knee deep in water to clear the suction pipes. However, we still had to reach down into the bilge water up to our armpits to clear the filter and the water had not got any warmer.

Returning the boards back into their correct position did not present such a problem given our previous experience, and the whole exercise was completed in two days. Nevertheless, everyone was pleased to get the hatch boards back and the tarpaulins in place for within hours of completion, as the forecast had predicted, the weather, already wicked, got worse.

The seas became mountainous and the 'Granford,' being light, pitched and rolled continuously and, unless you could hold on to something solid, both life and limb were in danger. She would continuously ride up an extra large swell and would literally appear to stop for a slight moment at its peak then, just like the big dipper at Blackpool, she would jump and jerk into a downward spiral. Then as the bow pitched into the trough, the stern would come clear of the water and cause the propellers to race in thin air with the engines screaming and the whole of our stern accommodation would shake and rattle which made it feel and sound as if we were inside a road drill.

It was frightening to say the least, to see the elements combining in an attempt to destroy us. Time and time again we were blown off course and to regain the heading took some considerable time and effort. Thank God we'd just had a new rudder fitted and we prayed that we didn't lose it again.

Luckily our course kept us heading into the oncoming seas, which slightly lessened the pitching and the tossing of the ship but the waves would hit the bows with a clap like thunder. The combined noises of the whirl of the screw in thin air, the waves hitting the bows and the screams of protest from the engines all added to the apprehension of the moment.

Due to the impact of the sea we only made at times headway of only one or two knots. The knowledge that but for a quirk of fate we would still be faced with goulash was at least one consolation. I was always amazed that in such conditions the new Cook could produce good but wholesome food, when our original Cook on all occasions produced rubbish.

Throughout the journey there was little respite from those giant seas, which pounded us first from starboard then to port. We had finished the eight to midnight watch one night and Vince and I had just turned in when the ship was blown off course to starboard. We were suddenly and viciously startled out of our attempts at slumber. Our cabins were on the port side and a giant wave hit our bulkhead with a loud bang. It smashed the portholes open, broke the quarter inch glass and flooded into the cabin.

Vince, who had chosen the bunk along the outer bulkhead, was almost washed out of his bunk and his bedding was saturated. I didn't escape entirely as the remaining splash soaked my head and shoulders and my pillow was drenched, such was the force of the water. Similar damage had occurred in other cabins along the port side. Next door, it had actually sheared the light bulb in the centre of the 'deckhead' (ceiling) from its socket.

We all swore and cursed our luck. The language alone during our unexpected early hours mopping up operations was so hot it could have almost turned the water into steam. Sleep was virtually impossible under such conditions. What sleep we did get was from sheer exhaustion and, long before we sighted the Americas, the crew resembled living Zombies and we performed our duties like programmed robots; we sometimes even fell asleep over our meals.

Twenty-eight days after casting off at Bolnes we thankfully sighted the Virginian coastline. We were eight days overdue and had only two days fuel left. We finally entered the calmer waters sheltered by the coast to dock with thanks to whatever God it was that had brought us safely into Norfolk Harbour. It was Monday 14th January 1957.

I was at the helm when the Pilot came aboard to take us alongside. Talking to the Skipper he enquired about the trip and the atrocious weather we had been subjected to. The 'Doric Star,' he informed the Skipper, had radioed her estimated time of arrival as January 3rd, but since that message there had been no sight or sound of her. If she had sunk, such had been the ferocity of the weather that eleven days on, little hope of any survivors being found was held.

Loading began immediately we had made port not, as in Newport News, with their super modern new technology, but with more time-consuming giant grabs. The lack of technology, was compensated for by allowing a grab at each individual hatch to load simultaneously. At nine o'clock of the evening we were battening down the hatches and preparing to face the unwelcoming cold Atlantic once again. It began to snow as we made fast that morning and the temperature dropped down to fifteen Fahrenheit below freezing. Ice covered the ship and the decks were treacherous.

While we were being loaded a repair gang came onboard to make repairs to the damage caused by the heavy seas. It was a blessing to have the portholes of our cabin refitted for, while temporary covers had been fitted, they were not draught proof or watertight, and our cabin had been like an icebox.

With everything battened down, the call to stations brought all hands to let go only to find that the after docking winch was inoperable. On inspection, the Engineer concluded that it had frozen up so a small fire was built beneath it. Within minutes with much hissing of melting ice everything freed itself so with the aid of tugs we made anchorage in the bay. It was not until the following afternoon that we learnt of our next destination. A destination not welcomed for only a homeport would have been acceptable to us, and it was a heavy-hearted crew that made to sea. We were bound for Italy.

North or South? Tyrrhenian, Ionion or Adriatic? We did not know. Just Italy. That was all we needed to know, our lord and masters it seemed had decided. But to be fair and given the reputation of the owners, perhaps Italy was all that the Skipper knew. The only consolation was the knowledge that we were hopefully to escape from the freezing conditions. Also the weather had improved somewhat. Still rough, but nowhere as severe as the outward journey had been, and although it was a bonus that the swell was running with us, the fact that we had been in the same position before was still fresh in our minds.

As we headed southward we encountered the Gulf Stream; it became warmer, and finally calm and sunny. Nothing went right however. If it wasn't the weather, it was the engines. Four days out the engines failed and we were adrift for three hours. Once more our engineers sweated over their reluctant charges. We were not over concerned though as we enjoyed the improved weather, but we would have been had we known what the elements were preparing for us. When we resumed our course, the skies darkened and the temperature began to descend. Early the next morning another storm hit us. Mountainous waves again broke over us and being fully laden, we were low in the water, which caused us to be continually awash.

On leaving Norfolk the watches had rotated and I was then part of the twelve to four. As we relieved the morning watch who came off duty soaked, we found that a hand line had been rigged along the port side, from the after housing to the midship housing. Without that essential aid it would have been foolhardy to attempt to move along the deck, any more than was absolutely necessary. We used to say that in adverse conditions it was one hand for the company and one hand for yourself.

Jack, the first wheelman on our watch that day, went out to relieve the eight to twelve wheelman who came into the mess where Vince and I were awaiting our orders. He told us that a gigantic wave had washed along the boat deck amidships and dislodged the box that contained the gangway gear. It was adrift on the boat deck. Vince and I, he informed us, were to go out and secure it before it caused any damage or was washed away.

Cursing our luck and the weather, Vince and I waited in the doorway until we were in the trough of a wave, and as the ship began to rise on the next wave we frantically dashed amidships and up the ladder to the boat deck. The box had fortunately become jammed between a ladder and an awning stanchion. Though it seemed secure as an added precaution we decided to lash it to the stanchion with a rope from the box. We then noticed that a block and tackle had somehow escaped from the box and had been washed down on to the starboard side of the main deck.

The block had become entangled around the railings but the rope tail had dropped into the sea and was trailing alongside and far astern into our wake. If that rope wrapped itself around the ship's propeller we would be in colossal trouble in such conditions we both agreed.

"Stay and finish lashing the box," Vince said to me, "And I'll go to see what I can do." He was literally taking his life in his hands as he fought his way down to the main deck rail. It was just as if the gods above were looking after him for by some miracle the waves which had been continuously and incessantly breaking over the exact spot where he was working, stopped doing so as he recovered the blocks and pulled the rope back inboard. He knew however that a wave of magnitude could come over at any second and sweep him away. He did it simply because it was his job.

He must have struggled for five or six minutes, pulling in the rope against the forward motion of the ship. I made to assist him, but he waved me to stay where I was as he struggled back to the boat deck before the waves broke over us again. I really believed a guardian angel must have been watching over him for if a wave such as the one that dislodged the box in the first place had hit us whilst he was recovering the block and tackle, he would have been a goner. Such acts are not recorded, nor do they become known to the owners, neither are they rewarded.

Once he stowed the recovered gear in the box, we made a mad dash back aft to the cabin to change our sodden clothes, as the spray was continuous even while we were on a higher deck. Dry once again, we climbed the ladder to sit in our mess to await further orders.

The Bosun appeared on the scene at about 1.30pm and detailed us to remove all the contents from the box, carry them aft and lash them down on the deck above our housing where it was sheltered. I simply couldn't believe him. I told him that the box was jammed tightly between the ladder and the stanchion as well as being lashed to them with rope. "That box is going nowhere," I said incredulously. I then asked him if he had noticed the conditions and the size of the waves that were crashing over the decks. "Don't be so bloody sarcastic," was his snappy response. "The Mate has ordered it to be done, I am only carrying out his orders." Vince was due to relieve the Wheelman at two o'clock and didn't want to get wet again so it was down to the Bosun and me.

The recovery of the block and tackle from the rails had been hairy for Vince, but I bet he was happy to be on the wheel rather than what I was about to embark upon. The Bosun jumped out of the doorway and up the ladder immediately to his right on to the deck above our housing. At the same time he told me to run along the deck past the galley housing, on up to the boat deck and start to bring the contents of the box back down to him while he stayed there in the comparative safety of the housing.

"Well, maybe one day I might be able to pull rank," I thought. Perhaps it was the pay back for my sarcasm, but then I remembered that he had gone down the hold amongst those swirling boards after all. Within seconds I was soaked to the skin once again. It had started to rain and with the decks almost constantly awash with the various sized waves that were thundering across, I was constantly trying to run in knee-deep water. At times it washed up to my thighs and filled my wellington boots. I could hardly move, in desperation I kicked my boots off and put them in the box where I felt certain they would be safe and I carried on in my stocking feet.

I could not believe that they would risk a man's life and limbs on what to me seemed a totally unnecessary task. If there ever was an occasion for the one hand for the company and one for yourself theory to come into operation that was it. So I carried the stanchions, block and tackle and similar equipment under one arm and hung on to the lifeline with the other, I made numerous journeys back and forth and handed the gear, little by little, up to the Bosun. The rain by then was absolutely belting down and I couldn't help having a little inner feeling, a tiny glow of satisfaction that because of the rain the Bosun was getting wet too.

I had half emptied the box and was bending into its recess when a heavy wave washed over the boat deck it came towards me at great speed. I jumped into the box like a flash, thinking that it was the best place to be and indeed it proved to be so. The water rose almost up to the brim of the box before it receded, but the box never budged, which only added weight to my belief that I was being put at risk for nothing.

Surely the gear was safe enough where it was inside the jammed box until the seas calmed a little, rather than risk life and limb to remove it especially as it still got wet from the rain on top of our housing.

Jack, our watch mate, came to give me a hand once Vince had relieved him at the wheel. Laden with block and tackle and stanchions we had climbed down to the well deck when the ship rolled sharply to starboard, and as we looked across we could see the ship's rail descending swiftly downward while at the same time a wave was rising upwards at great speed. We knew instantly that it was going to be a big one as we both dived for cover behind the galley bulkhead. A solid wall of water, fifteen foot high, shot right across the ship between the galley and the midship housing. The galley bulkhead sheltered us from all its force, but the water came swilling around the corner as the ship rose from the trough of the wave.

Jack jumped for the galley bulkhead ladder and made three or four rungs up it, which left me unable to climb to evade the rising swirling water. I was able only to hang on to the ladder while the water swooshed around my thighs. Then as the ship rolled to port a fountain of water poured from the galley roof; it missed Jack altogether and cascaded over right down the back of my neck.

Jack hung on to the ladder desperately not for fear of the water, but because he was laughing uproariously at my plight. Nevertheless, we made a good team and it was not long before the task was completed, and we changed into yet another set of dry clothing. We had little commendation from the Bosun or anyone else. There had been some scary moments during that escapade, but it was all part of the job. A job that I had taken expecting little thanks, and I very rarely got any.

* * *

At midnight I was first man at the wheel, and during my off watch period there had been little or no sleep. I was tired, but there was no fear of dozing off for the weather was relentlessly trying to wash us away. Suddenly as I was desperately trying to keep the ship on an even course I could have forgiven myself for thinking I had succumbed to fatigue. I was immersed in a murky green surrounding. I couldn't believe that a wave had actually broken over the 'Monkey Island,' the highest deck on the ship immediately above the wheelhouse.

197

It was fortunate that the massive wave had come athwart ships from starboard to port; if it had hit us head on, it would have probably smashed through the windows of the wheelhouse. It was also fortunate that the wheelhouse doors were closed because it would have washed all the way through. Damage was still inflicted though as it carried away the wind dodger and a lifebelt from the wing of the bridge. The attempt to keep on course was a continuous battle until in the creeping grey dawn, the storm finally relented and blew itself out so the seas became less ferocious. As the wind died away, a sense of satisfaction pervaded the atmosphere; yet again, we had survived.

Two days out from Gibraltar, clad only in shorts we began to enjoy the dramatic improvement in the conditions. It was then that we finally learnt of our destination: Venice, Italy. Firstly we were to take on supplies and we put in to Ceuta in Spanish Morocco. Ceuta is immediately across the straits opposite Gibraltar and it was on Sunday 3rd February that we tied up for bunkering. The approach to the harbour at Ceuta was quite tricky, the entrance was narrow with difficult tides and currents, and there was a heavy swell running.

To counter those difficulties, the harbour had to be entered at speed, while at the same time we had to execute a sharp turn to starboard as we entered through the breakwater. The manoeuvres were tricky and not without anxious moments, but once successfully achieved, we completed the bunkering and within a few hours we were back in the Medi. bound for Venice.

The Mediterranean lived up to its reputation: warm, sunny weather and a sea as calm as the proverbial millpond. To go about one's duties dry, warm and not having to cling to a lifeline changed the whole atmosphere. Even the Bosun and the officers seemed almost human.

Engine problems remained however, and the powers that be considered that the shorter course via the Messina Straits was a risk not worth taking so it was decided to take the longer route around Sicily. Those fears as it turned out were unfounded, and progress was unhindered as we enjoyed a normal or perhaps for us an abnormal passage revelling at last in a stable ship and good weather.

It was on the 11th February that we ran into a mist and visibility gradually deteriorated until it was like pea soup. We anchored off the approaches into Venice to wait for an improvement in conditions, but the fog persisted. The fo'c's'le head was manned throughout the night where the ship's bell was rung at short intervals; there was also a man on the poop deck with a gong. The rest of us stripped the hatches ready for unloading.

The next morning a large American export ship came across our bows within yards of colliding with us. Shortly after that an old Italian tramp steamer, loomed out of the fog, heading straight for us. She spotted us and slammed her engines into full astern. We could only stand and pray that the manoeuvre would halt their forward motion before she hit us broadside on.

All we could do was stand and watch her open-mouthed as her bows loomed ever closer; we were helpless to do anything and it was an eerie experience. Her bows seemed to get bigger and higher by the second as they approached us in the swirling fog, but finally our prayers were answered for literally inches away from contact, she stopped, and very, very slowly began to reverse away. We could have reached out and touched her, she was so close. How relieved we were to see her skirt around our stern and disappear again into the mist. Had she been travelling just the slightest bit faster in the fog we would not have avoided a collision.

Incidents galore appeared to be the order of the day on that trip, but somehow we seemed to overcome them. My thoughts could only wonder as to what else the voyage held in store for us, but I could not allow my thoughts to dwell along those lines for very long.

The fog persisted for a few more hours and with those two near misses staying fresh in our minds, vigilance was paramount. When the fog finally cleared sufficiently to complete the last few miles we proceeded to the mooring berth. I had the wheel as we sailed in. It was a tricky passage through a narrow channel then onwards, past the city and I got an excellent view of the famous St. Mark's Square. Beyond this I could see a funfair with its gaudy painted swings and bumper cars. Much of the journey was narrow and the helm demanded constant attention; it did not allow me to study the beauty of the place. Onwards we went beyond the city to our discharge point and we tied up way out in the wilds and began to discharge the cargo immediately.

Within hours a gang of Italian engineers came aboard to overhaul the engines and the noise they made combined with the noise of the grabs, which was accompanied by their hammering and what I took to be the cursing of the Italian engineers was deafening. I was reluctant to apply for a sub as the cost of the transport into Venice itself would probably cost more than the Skipper would allow me.

We had been there for four days when Alan, an Efficient Deck Hand, suggested to me that a trip to the cinema would relieve the boredom. A cinema close to the dock gates was showing an American Western with an Italian sound track. The proverbial line between the hero and the crook in many of those westerns at that time was, "This town isn't big enough for both of us." It didn't sound quite the same in Italian, but the message and plot were easy to follow and I desperately needed a change of scenery so I was glad I had sold a couple of bars of soap for the entrance fee.

Early that Saturday morning the call to stations was somewhat surprising as the engineers were still attacking the engines with gusto. We needed to shift ship to a different berth and all hands were soon busy taking lines from the tugs that had arrived to tow us to the new berth. We completed the discharge of the cargo late on Sunday 17th February whilst the engine repairs were still being undertaken. With little to do and unable to face a refusal of a sub from the Captain time dragged. Not so much for my shipmates however for they frequented the local hostelries nightly.

When the banging and cursing ceased, I concluded that the engine repairs were complete for the word came down that departure would be at about eight o'clock on Thursday morning, 21st February. The crew were on seven o'clock shake and were called to stations shortly after breakfast. As I entered the mess, lying on one of the benches lay Bill who, like Kenny on the 'Albemarle,' was a DHU. His face and shirt was caked with dry blood from a nasty cut over his eye. I shook him awake, but he remained half dazed, and anything but well, he accepted my advice to go amidships to get it fixed. At that moment, the Mate appeared on the scene and took him amidships to get some first aid.

He was back amongst us in no time and, on call to stations, he was not excused from work. He had no recollection how he had collected his injury; only that along with Alan he had visited one or two bars. Alan was still adrift and was to stay so for we were ordered to cast off by the Skipper without it seemed any further thought for his well-being or welfare.

It came to light later that the Skipper had indeed notified the authorities of his absence but that was all. Obviously to him only engine trouble had the right to delay the ship. The welfare and well-being of the crew came well down the priority of his consideration. What had happened to Alan remains a mystery; he was ashore with Bill who could not remember anything with his head injury, it was a worry that something might have happened to him too, but we sailed and he was never seen or heard of by us again.

Southerly into the Adriatic in beautiful weather we sailed, bound for Bone Harbour (now Annaba) in Algeria near to the borders of Tunisia. Our main task during the four-day voyage was to clear the residue of coal dust from the hatches. It was dirty, dusty and it was hard to understand the need to get it as clean as was demanded since the next cargo was to be iron ore.

On Monday 25th February we stood off Bone Harbour and anchored to wait for our berth at the loading stage. Almost immediately an official looking launch approached, which was soon to be identified as a French army launch. A French officer came onboard and demanded that there be no radio communication with other ships or shore installations. It transpired that a large contingent of the French Foreign Legion was having trouble with Algerian rebels (or were they freedom fighters?) Apparently a guerilla force was attempting to sabotage the railway line that carried the ore down from the mountains to the port.

That French officer informed us that the mines in the distant mountains were ideal country for guerilla activity and the Foreign Legion were policing the line with difficulty. Empty trucks preceded the trains from the mines down the tracks, both as decoys and to ensure that there were no explosive devices on the lines.

Despite all the talk of hostilities we carried on with our cleaning of the hatches. The anchor was weighed on Wednesday evening and as we passed through the harbour entrance, the tugs took over to push and pull us into position and we tied up alongside the iron-ore loading quay.

They could only load one ship at a time and we waited our turn while the ship astern of us was loaded. That took until Friday evening when all hands were called to shift ship into the position that she had vacated. The hatches were uncovered and we started to prepare for

201

the loading; however, to our amazement, the conveyors were moved forward to the ship, which had just come in to take the berth that we had just left. Unbelievable.

We were left kicking our heels until Saturday 2nd March before our loading began. No explanation was given for the queue jumping and due to the local hostilities, we were confined to the ship. All shore leave was cancelled. So with time being heavy, deck cricket was the order of the day. A bat was fashioned from dunnage and a ball made up from canvas filled with sand; this afforded us much fun in our off duty periods, without undue regards for the rules. The manufacture of canvas balls took on a matter of some importance as budding England players hit sixes into the harbour.

The fact that shore leave was curtailed may well have been a blessing for us for news soon spread through the ship that a local cinema had been bombed with four dead and many casualties. Our frustration was lifted somewhat as we cast off early Monday morning, and entered a calm and peaceful Mediterranean bound once more for Rotterdam.

It remained calm, warm and peaceful as we traversed the whole length of the Medi., but once again the phenomenal change in the temperature as we passed through the Straits of Gibraltar into the Atlantic hurried me out of shorts and into a thick pullover and jeans. And as we progressed northward through the Bay of Biscay a distinct wintery flavour reminded us that March at home could be a wicked month.

One night well into the Bay and with my stint at the wheel completed, I was enjoying a well-earned cup of tea on my hour's standby when I was summoned to the bridge by the blasts of the Mate's whistle. At the same time I heard the engines splutter into silence, we were drifting once more in the darkness and the Mate ordered me to rig the 'Out of Command lights' up on the foremast. They consisted of two red lights mounted vertically about six feet apart and are the international signal warning other shipping that the ship is stationary or as the name suggests out of command, and that they should stay well clear.

As I plugged the head into the socket I cursed my luck for some idiot had replaced one of the red bulbs with a blue one. I then had to lower the rig and dash back up for'ard to find a replacement bulb. Once fixed the rig had to be hoisted back up. Many curses and blasphemies escaped my lips about the time wasted. The second I had finished securing it, the engines came back to life whereby it all had to be stowed away again. I had just enough time to gulp down a quick cup of tea before I resumed my watch on lookout.

Without further incident other than March living up to its reputation we arrived at Rotterdam on Wednesday 13th. Barges were soon alongside into which the ore was soon disappeared. During the night the ship in the next berth moved out and we were called to stations to shift ship for no apparent reason. We were unloading into barges on the outboard side and even if we had to unload ashore, the cranes on the quay were mobile and could move up and down at will. It was always a source of puzzlement about which I pondered many times, on the many occasions that sort of thing happened, there seemed to be no logical explanation why our manpower, labour, sweat and tears were used to move the ship in preference to someone ashore just pressing a few buttons.

The unloading continued throughout the night and was finally completed late on the following evening. The expectation of the crew was for a quiet night before possibly sailing the following morning but that was not to be. We were called to stations to shift ship yet again to tie up to buoys in the river.

The majority of the deck crew, deprived of shore leave since we had left Venice, had taken advantage of the opportunity to reacquaint themselves with dry land and had not yet returned, so the Second Cook, the Stewards and some of the Arabian Firemen were dragooned into helping to let go and tie up to the river buoys. One can imagine the shock of the shore leave members of the crew on their return to find the ship missing, especially to those who had not drunk too much.

Later that evening launches began to arrive with the merrymakers grumbling and bewailing the fact that some no good bastards had shifted the ship. Despite my doubts and forebodings, the Skipper allowed me a sub and along with Barry, another DHU, I went ashore. It was Saturday afternoon and in the true tradition of British sailors we headed for the nearest bar. We were determined to take a weekend break and that bloody ship wasn't going to see us until Sunday night. The guy in charge of the launch pointed us in the direction of the bus into town and the many friendly bars with good Dutch beer. We booked into a small hotel, cheap but clean and comfortable and after a few more beers we went up to our rooms and to bed for an excellent night's sleep in peace and quiet.

After so long living in spartan conditions the clean sheets, the clean smell, no noise and a satisfactory belly full of beer was as near to paradise I had been for many a month. It was so good to spend a night away from the ship. I slept like a log and was somewhat surprised to awake in strange but clean comfortable surroundings. You don't miss the normally accepted things in life until you haven't got them.

Sunday was spent with us both enjoying the sights and exploring the busy cosmopolitan port, which was fast becoming one of the largest in Europe, interspersed of course with many rest periods in those friendly bars. It was late when we took the launch back out into the river and climbed up the accommodation ladder, broke but happy.

On our return to the ship on Sunday evening, I had not noticed that yet again they had shifted ship. That time they were given no choice. Apparently on the Sunday afternoon, the ship had come adrift having broken free from its moorings, and it drifted down stream at the whim of the current. Panic stations ensued and the anchor was lowered with much haste. I was told that as the anchor had taken hold, the ship began to swing and a passing coaster had to take drastic evasive action in order to avoid a collision. Immediately my mind flew back to the examination day at Gravesend Training School where we had witnessed a similar incident through the classroom window.

Tugs had immediately come to the 'Granford's' aid and with much huffing and puffing, they brought the situation under control. With the tugs holding her midstream, the anchor had been hoisted only to find that it had become entangled with another anchor, which had obviously been lost from another vessel in the past. With a double anchor hanging from our starboard bow, the tugs had then manoeuvred the ship to another buoy a little further downstream and held her until they were safely tied up. Then they had lowered both of the starboard anchors and our port one too as an extra precaution. Once again with most of the deck crew ashore, including stewards, the firemen and me were called into service again. The main question from us deckhands then was why didn't they pay us off and send us home? They seemed to be able to manage quite well without us.

Another incident happened during our night ashore that saddened me. As mentioned previously the 'Granford' was an Empire boat, an exact replica of the 'Oakhill' and as on the 'Oakhill,' we lived in the well of the after accommodation. Deck crew to port, and the Arab firemen and greasers to starboard. I again had throughout the voyage been friendly and pleasant with those guys and they with me. I would never forget the kindness that one of their compatriots had shown me on a certain train with the life saving packet of biscuits. Again, certain members of our deck crew held views of animosity towards them. At the forward end of the well was a small storage room that was never used so the firemen and greasers had converted it into their prayer room.

A small group of our ABs returned in the early hours well under the influence of alcohol and decided that they the Arabs had no right to the room. They broke into it, threw out and scattered all their belongings. I was amazed that a riot had not broken out. But without a word that morning the Arabs silently picked up their prayer mats and items, mended what was broken, replaced what was missing and returned it to the prayer room. At first I was bewildered at their reaction or lack of it, but on reflection I realized that perhaps their silence was their victory, by proving that my so-called shipmates had achieved absolutely nothing.

* * *

It's an old adage that bad news spreads like wildfire. The news the next morning that we were bound for Cuba was a real blow to our hopes of sighting a British port in the immediate to near future. But the additional news that the cargo was to be sugar we thought was a bad joke.

As it turned out it was no joke at all. The 'Granford' had been shipping coal and iron ore for years and, while the holds had to be kept in reasonable condition, all the crooks and crannies missed in the cleaning were not considered too detrimental. But to carry sugar the whole inside of the five holds, which was the vast majority of the inside hull of the ship had to be given the equivalent of a drastic spring clean. The task called for a specialist gang to carry out the necessary cleansing. Soon Dutch was the dominant tongue heard throughout the ship as they prepared the hatches for the new cargo. "Thank God we haven't got to do it," we thought.

Steel cleats or hooks were welded in rows about eighteen inches above each other and about six foot apart all the way up the bulkheads of the holds and wooden battens (spar ceilings) were placed into them to protect the sides of the ship and to protect the forthcoming bags of sugar from the cold steel plates.

Along with the piles of coal dust and ore that was being dumped on them, the decks were littered with dunnage from the cargo, hatch boards, beams, ceiling boards, wires and guys were strewn all around. Amidst that pandemonium more engine repairs were being carried out and bunkering commenced. To add to the turmoil the oil tank overflowed and the black gold flowed out onto the decks and in accordance with sod's law began to mix in with the piles of coal and iron ore dust. The chaos was added to by the arrival of the victuals, which despite the state of the decks, had to be carried aboard and stowed away.

Later that day the news quickly spread, right out of the blue, that the Skipper and the Mate were to be relieved. "There is a God after all," was the main consensus of us all throughout the ship. We did not wave them goodbye. Few if any of the crew missed them, and we awaited their replacements with interest.

Whether it was of any significance we never knew, but the next day the Chief Steward, the Second Steward, the Second Engineer and the Cook all paid off with various ailments and notes from the doctor ashore. The Cook who had rescued us from the grips of the dreaded goulash was the only one we were sorry to see go. As their replacements arrived, the atmosphere aboard improved. The first to arrive were two ABs who were flown out from London. Their arrival brought the deck department back up to full strength.

The Chief Steward and Chief Cook followed soon after. The Chief Steward immediately made more most welcome improvements like relaxing the strict rationing that had been imposed upon us. From then onwards, we could all have as many cups of tea a day that we wanted and sugar and milk them to our individual tastes. Such small luxuries but they were extremely appreciated.

It was the third Chief Steward and the third Cook that we had had since the beginning of our voyage and the new Cook proved to be the best so far. We began to really look forward to our meals, and rarely were we disappointed; maybe we were easily pleased after those first months of garbage that we had become used to.

I think the spirit and atmosphere in a ship stems essentially from the attitude of the officers and especially the Captain, for he sets the tune. And from the moment the new Skipper set foot aboard, the ship became far happier and the men more contented. He was as different as chalk and cheese to his predecessor. Where the relieved Skipper had been short, rotund, full of his own self-importance and virtually unapproachable, the new guy was tall and imposing, yet very approachable and courteous in manner. For once the deckhands were treated like human beings, not scum who were not worthy of any consideration. While he still maintained that air of authority the new Skipper ran the ship with a thought to decency, courteousness, and discipline was kept by fairness and understanding.

The day before we sailed, a German AB and a Dutch AB came aboard together looking for a berth. After the Skipper told them that the ship's compliment was complete, they came back aft for a chat. Over a cup of tea, they told us of their unsuccessful bid for a berth where upon immediately two of our ABs asked them to go back with them to see the Skipper. Later our two mates were seen busily packing their gear. They were leaving us. It transpired that our quick thinking opportunists had approached the Skipper with the proposition that they be paid off and they would pay their own fares back to the UK. As there were two replacements immediately available the Skipper readily agreed and the deed was done on the spot.

Was it a sign of things to come we thought? No one would have dared to approach the previous Skipper with such a novel suggestion. Their departure left only seven of the original fourteen members of the deck crew who had signed on in Liverpool. Many of the crew including the newer ones, mentally kicked themselves for not having thought of that ruse, especially faced with the prospect of at least two to three more months minimum aboard the 'Granford.'

The stay in Rotterdam amounted to eight days in all and on Thursday 21st March we made ready to depart. The buoy to which we were tied up had disappeared below the water level due to the weight of the ship pulling on it in the current. A mooring rope had to be passed down from the starboard side, over the foredeck and hatches down to the tug. Once the rope was made fast the tug then took the strain, gradually edging the ship closer to the buoy which eventually broke back through to the surface. With the buoy clear, the men in a launch then let go our ropes from it.

Our port anchor came up with no trouble, but on hoisting our starboard anchor we still had a problem; the other anchor that we had gained from the deep was still attached. They were lowered on to the deck of the tug where after feverish activity for an hour or so by the tugs crew, the anchor refused to come unstuck. They probably wanted it for salvage.

The delay finally became too much for the Skipper so he had the entwined anchors lifted from the tug and he told the tug to stand clear. He then sent the anchors crashing down to the bottom and proceeded to bounce them up and down off the river bed, which after a couple of attempts did the trick and separated them.

Once we had cleared Rotterdam we were told that despite the fact that the Dutch gangs had cleaned the holds we would be working down them on our journey across the Atlantic to pick up what they had missed in anticipation of the sugar cargo.

The weather had improved along with conditions aboard. Also the bond was opened up for the crew and everything that was available in it was for sale. For the first time there was an unlimited supply of cigarettes and soft drinks etc. The only restriction being a maximum of ten cans of beer per person per week. Only small concessions, but given the changed approach from the officers it became a different world, and for once there were smiles and cheery banter.

As the southern coast of England became a smudge on the horizon, I couldn't resist a last wistful glance back towards Land's End not knowing how long it was to be before we were home again. The weather turned windy and choppy, and the cleaning work continued. The shore gang in Rotterdam had performed a Herculean task, but the Skipper wanted the holds spotless, every last speck of coal and iron ore dust was to be found and cleared.

Spar ceiling boards and bulkheads were brushed from top to bottom then hosed and washed. In hatches three, four and five the ceiling boards were ripped up, hoisted to the decks, hosed down and cleaned with long handled scrubbers. The ceiling boards in hatches one and two (as they had been done previously in the voyage with the floods) were not touched again, and at long last there was loads of overtime to be had.

So the hard back breaking work continued until three days out of Cuba, but there was a difference. The new Skipper led by example; he was, along with the Mate, down the holds with the crew, jacket off and getting as filthy as the rest of us. The bilges were once again cleaned out and the bottoms swept and swept. Wet sawdust was sprinkled everywhere and swept again to pick up any residue of iron ore or coal remaining.

Finally great bails of brown paper were produced and laid on the bottoms, held in place by the dunnage, and finally all five holds looked fit enough to accept a cargo of sugar. Due, I must say, to the insistence of the Captain who had earned respect from some of his crew, but not all; for some insisted that his place was on the bridge, not meddling in matters not becoming his station. It takes all kinds, but I know the type of skipper with whom I preferred to sail.

With the watches having been changed again on leaving Rotterdam I was then on the four to eight. On 21st March I was first wheel, about to relieve the helmsman at 4.00am when I found that the engines were on slow ahead. It transpired that a securing pin in the steering gear had become dislodged and for the previous two hours, the ship had been virtually drifting and unable to steer. As I took the wheel, the engineers reported that the fault had been rectified and the Skipper rang for full speed ahead as I pulled her round back on course.

The weather gradually improved further and as the Azores receded on the port side, we stripped to shorts and tropical gear. Work in the holds continued for seventeen days and once completed, we embarked upon work on the overhauling of the ship's lifting gear.

In the years of shipping ore and coal, which had been loaded by various means such as cranes and grabs all essentially shore equipment, the ship's gear had not been used for ages, and consequently it had deteriorated and was in a sorry state of repair.

Loading sugar was a different task and our derricks would be needed so everything had to be in full good working order before we reached Cuba. New guys and runners for the derricks had to be made up. Shackles had to be found and we had to make forty rope strops for loading the bags of sugar. We also had to find time to splice new eyes in the mooring ropes and wires that had been snapped during the escapades in Rotterdam.

The engine-room staff were recruited to overhaul the winches, not one of which was faultless. It must be said however, that most of the engineers enjoyed the opportunity of working out in the sunshine for a change. So for a further three days there was not an idle hand aboard the ship and few if any moans. Such was the demand for endeavour that within those twenty days from leaving Rotterdam, I worked in excess of one hundred and twenty hours overtime.

It was warm and sunny when we tied up in Sagua La Grande in Cuba on Wednesday 10th April. The crew were tired, but mostly happier than they had been for many a long day. We were safe in the knowledge that the work in the immediate future would be much less hectic as loading the sugar was the responsibility of the stevedores and the native gangs.

As I leaned over the rail, a line of wagons came rolling along the jetty, and were positioned adjacent to the derricks. Two guys stood on top of the wagons, which were loaded with our cargo. The derricks lowered the strops, which could accommodate four bags of sugar; these then were winched up and lowered into the hold. A guy stood at each hatch signalling to the drivers of the winches as the sugar was lowered, while a gang was busy stowing the bags in a safe and orderly fashion in the hold.

To begin with the first bags were used to make a square tower platform in the centre of the hold to the height of a man, onto which each load was then lowered. Once released from the strop it was made simple for each sack to be rolled onto a stevedores shoulder and stacked uniformly throughout the holds.

After a couple of days the normal ritual of a crew in port began: painting the ship. The stages were rigged over the bow and as we began the irksome task I was reminded of how history manages to repeat itself. On another Caribbean Island, Jamaica, where an accident in the hold of the 'Albemarle' had occurred when one of the stevedores was injured whilst loading sugar. Once again, there were screams from the hold and much frantic panic on deck. Yet again a sack of sugar had fallen from the strop in mid-air and down onto one of the gang in the hold. That time it broke the poor guy's leg.

The method of removing him from the hatch on that occasion however, was much more humane and quicker for a straight jacket and stretcher was found so the guy was soon hospital bound in a more comfortable position, not being bounced up and down along the quay on a hatch board. Lightning never strikes twice they say, not to some folk maybe, but I appeared to be a conductor so I wouldn't bet on it.

As Barry and I lowered ourselves closer to the surface of the water on our stage I looked down and I saw a silver fish about eighteen inches long arc out of the water. In a flash, it was followed by the massive head of a hammerhead shark rising after it, literally within inches of our feet before it sank back into the depths. "JESUS CHRIST!" I screamed and scrambled up the rope ladder with Barry hot on my heels, our hearts were pounding ten to the dozen. Only when we were safe on deck did the realisation come that we had probably found an instant cure for constipation. From then on we only painted the ship halfway down and kept our feet well clear of the surface of the water.

The Skipper gave us all a half-day off: half the crew was to take Thursday afternoon, and the remaining half to take the Friday afternoon. Barry and I decided to take the half-day due to us on the Friday, with the intent of making a long weekend of it in the local town. We had walked about three or four hundred yards when the heavens opened up. That gave us the excuse to find shelter in the nearest bar, which was as far as we got on that particular trip ashore and the long weekend was deferred.

Day after day the sugar kept coming in what appeared to be a never-ending supply with loading a monotonous regularity. Barry and I took to going ashore every night, we took a taxi into the nearby town of Sagua. Evidently the Captain remembered being young himself once for he obviously understood the call of youth, and there was no trouble or hesitation in handing out our frequent requests for subs.

Sagua was a small and friendly town, well equipped with bars that catered for the needs of us seafarers as well as the natives. On the third night ashore Barry and I sat in a small bar enjoying the local tipple of rum and coke and appreciating the reasonable price of that thirst quenching nectar, when from nowhere a young black guy came and stood between us at the bar. He spoke to us as if he had known us all his life; he introduced himself to us as Chocolate. He would, he said, be our guide and show us the delights of Sagua.

He was extremely jovial; his English was perfect, always laughing and continuously cracking jokes. It was a real change for us to see a genuine happy, smiling face so we welcomed his company. He pointed out to us the places of interest in the town and where the value for money was to be had and where it was not so. For the price of a couple of beers he was himself we thought, "good value for money," but nowhere near the value of the girl that Kenny and I had met in the bar in Havana just around the coast.

Following the amount of work we had put in during the voyage, we were entitled to a good laugh. Every night wherever in town we were, he would materialize as if from nowhere and at the end of the evening he would disappear likewise. One minute nothing, the next there was Chocolate.

Easter was upon us and Good Friday was a holiday. That evening we wandered into the town square, which housed the church and in front of the church were rows of permanent chairs. The square was crowded with young folk aimlessly milling around. We took a seat and paused to wait and see what was about to happen.

Suddenly all the girls began to walk around the square in an anti-clockwise direction while the boys moved in the opposite direction. "That's how they meet to start their courtship," explained the voice of Chocolate who had yet again suddenly appeared from nowhere behind us. "An old, very old tradition. If a boy sees a girl he fancies then on the next time around, he will single her out and stop to talk. If the feeling is mutual, that's the start of a courtship."

"God!" exclaimed Barry, "I fancy them all." "Yes," said Chocolate, "The women of Sagua are noted for their beauty." In mutual agreement, we pondered our chances. Chocolate laughed and shook his head knowingly. "You are here today and gone tomorrow, these girls are looking for a more permanent relationship," he said. Perhaps he knew something that we did not for, come the morrow, 20th April, we were to leave. After the delays in loading because of rain showers, holidays and winch failures, we finally cast off from the mainly sunny, happy Sagua without a chance to wish Chocolate farewell.

* * *

Once everything was secured for sea we meandered along the coast to arrive at Tarafe on the following afternoon. Tarafe was a tiny port and it was Sunday. Nothing appeared to be moving as we tied up to an almost deserted jetty. Alongside the jetty were a small collection of derelict huts and a railway line. The only semblance of civilisation on the edge of the jungle was a lone taxi patiently waiting for the prospect of customers from the ship.

I had enjoyed the stay in Sagua and I was keen to sample further hospitality of those happy Cubans so Barry and I made use of the taxi to get to the nearby town of Nuevitas, where we had decided to spend the evening. With another sub in our back pockets, we endured the bouncy, bumpy ride until we emerged from the jungle onto a more decent road.

The comparison between Nuevitas and Sagua was amazing. Whereas the folk of Sagua were welcoming and friendly, the 'Nuevitans' were surly and would not even give you a second look, let alone a smile or kindly word. Chocolate would have been a welcome immigrant maybe he could have taught the locals how to smile.

Only a few bags of sugar were added to the cargo already in the holds and by the following evening we had sailed and were tied up at Passtilo, a further short distance along the coast. I was undecided whether to stay onboard but my mind was made up for me by Barry's insistence that the place could not be as bad as Nuevitas. Along with Frank the Dutchman, and Hans the German, Barry and I took a taxi into town. The only similarity with Nuevitas was the jungle and the road.

Every so often I glimpsed through the trees a railway track that I felt sure was the same track that served the jetty and it came out on the outskirts of the town. The next night I decided to prove my theory and foregoing the taxi, the four of us followed the track from the jetty. Within a few minutes walk, we came across a stationary dockers train, which was used to bring the sugar down to the jetty. The engine driver indicated with a friendly wave that we would be welcome to a ride into town. There wasn't quite enough room on the footplate for five of us so, as Frank and Barry were the first to jump up, Hans and I were relegated to the flat truck directly behind the engine. Slowly we began to chug towards the town where we were dropped off.

It was anything but comfortable, but it was as quick as the taxi and much cheaper for the engine driver would not accept anything for his kindness. It was a small town, and after we walked around to acquaint ourselves with the place we came across a small, quiet bar where a smiling welcome soon serviced us with iced rum and cokes.

Hans, Frank, Barry and I all stood our rounds, which did not take long as they went down very well. Hans and I decided to seek pastures new while Frank and Barry were quite happy to stay put. It was arranged that we would meet up with them again at the same bar later.

We didn't have far to search for our next watering hole as there were many bars beckoning with their welcoming lights and we visited a number of them. Finally we ended up in one where, along with the rum and cokes, a couple of pretty young ladies came and we were soon on our way to take a long awaited refresher course and a further lesson in love.

Both Hans and I arrived back in the bar more or less simultaneously, having passed the test. After a farewell drink with the girls we made our way back to pick up our shipmates. Obviously the rum and cokes had been flowing like water over Niagra and they were both well on the way to happy land. We decided to join them for one for the road. They were too well established, too comfortable and too drunk to want to move anywhere and our urgent requests for them to return to the ship fell on deaf ears. We paid for our drinks and in the absence of the train, Hans and I took a taxi back to the ship and to our beds.

My immediate concern the next morning was the state of my head so it was a little time before I realised that Barry and Frank were still ashore. That was not anything to worry about for it was quite a common occurrence amongst seafarers in port and they were grown men.

Dinnertime passed and as Hans and I were painting the bow from the stages, it was remarked that they were still absent. "The Skipper wants you two in his cabin right away," said the Bosun, as his head and shoulders appeared over the rail above us. Yet another feeling of déjà vu swept through me.

Wondering what misdemeanour we had committed, we were no wiser when the Skipper asked. "What's your story about last night?" Noting our bemused looks, he said. "You were with Barry and Frank weren't you?" "Well yes, but not all of the time and we left them in

214

a bar," I offered. "Well they are both in gaol," he retorted. We were both dumbstruck for a second. "Why?" I asked. "The owner of the bar presented them with a bill for nine dollars which they refused to pay and he claims that you both also walked away without paying on your first visit, so the police have been told."

We then gave the Skipper our version of the events, insisting our bills had been met as we ordered each round, there was nothing ever put on the slate or tabs. "It was hardly plausible that the bar would have served us further drinks without payment on our return if we had not settled our bill in the first place," I suggested. "The fact remains they are still in gaol with a bail of a hundred dollars on each of them," the Skipper said. Then he paused a little before he said, "The agent and I will have to see what we can do, now get back to work," he said, and we could hear him tutting as we walked out through his door.

That day a German ship, the 'Levante' arrived and moored opposite. Having finished work and taken our evening meal, Hans asked if I would accompany him to the German ship where he could get the latest news from his compatriots and chatter a little in his native tongue. Leaving the 'Granford' and boarding the 'Levante' was like stepping out onto a different planet. She was spotlessly clean: her paintwork gleamed. Steel cranes operated by the press of a button replaced the derricks, while the hatch covers were also electrically operated, it was most impressive and yet I was to be even more impressed. Hans struck up a conversation with an AB who invited us both to his cabin. I was flabbergasted. The difference between that accommodation and the 'Granford's' was like a five-star hotel and a tuppenny doss house. Luxury was the first word to spring to mind.

Each cabin was single berth. Carpets, a large comfortable bunk, an enormous soft settee, a spacious wardrobe, a chest of drawers and a table with four chairs accompanied the privacy. Each cabin had its own shower and washbasin I was also told to my amazement, that in the near future wives would be able to accompany their seafaring husbands. "Why was England still in the grip of the Middle Ages?" I thought.

I sat around the table with my shipmate Hans and our German host, chatting away; they broke into English occasionally to include me in the conversation. A bottle of brandy was produced and while brandy isn't my favourite tipple, it would have been ungracious to refuse.

When the bottle was finished, the AB left the cabin and soon returned with another. Noting my surprise, he explained that they were allowed unlimited supplies of anything they wanted around the clock. The words "Britania rules the waves" had a very hollow ring to them when I recalled all those totally dry ships in which I had sailed, including the first months on the present one. Such thoughts were soon forgotten though as I sipped the brandy and finally passed out on the settee.

Barry and Frank appeared in court the next morning and returned aboard at midday. Everyone was agog to hear their story. A mini-saga indeed. It transpired following Hans and my departure from the bar that the owner had presented them with a bill for nine dollars that they refused to accept. They argued that they had paid in the British tradition up front, as the drinks were served. Within seconds, the police had arrived and without any recourse, they were bundled into the police car and taken to gaol.

It appeared to be too great a coincidence that the police were on hand so quick; suspicion and prearrangement seemed obvious. Frank reckoned that it was the funniest gaol he had ever seen. Obviously, I pondered with amusement, "Just how many had he been in?" but I kept my own council. They had entered through a large heavy wooden door that closed with a resounding clunk and they found themselves in a large courtyard, enclosed by a high, very high wall. Small cells were let into the walls, all unlocked with open doors. Only one of the cells appeared to be occupied so they selected one each and dossed down on a rickety old bunk.

They woke the next morning with a raging thirst and shouted for the guard. "We need a drink," they called, as the dreary eyed, scruffy policeman came through the gate. "Go and get your own," he muttered, pointing across the square to a cafe. "And be back here at nine o'clock" was his strict instruction. There was nowhere to escape to and amongst the locals they stood out like a sore thumb so they did as they were bid.

A small park opposite the gaol was used as an exercise yard, and accompanied by a gun totting guard they strolled round and round. Once back in the gaol Frank asked the guard why he wore the gun, "We are not going anywhere," he said. The guard immediately put aside the gun and locked it away in an office drawer. Their only other fellow prisoner they found was a guy doing three months for hitting someone over the head with a bottle.

They got thirsty again later and bemoaned the lack of refreshment; their fellow inmate offered to fetch some coke from the cafe. Unbelievably they watched as the three month convicted intern just strolled through the gate to return shortly with half a dozen cans. They were sitting on the veranda drinking coke with the guard, when the Skipper turned up. "What the hell is going on?" "What is this place, a gaol or the Ritz?" he asked.

While they waited to appear in court another guy turned up. At first they thought he was another ne'er-do-well, but it was the briefcase that was the give away. "I am to represent you in court," he said and shoved some English pound notes (now obsolete) and Dutch guilders into their respective hands; he suggested that should the bar owner demand money they should offer it to him in the respective currency. "That might create a good impression," he said "and could well influence the judges finding, and the bar owner himself would be reluctant to accept it for losing value in its exchange."

It was however all to no avail. They were both fined the equivalent of twenty-two pounds each, which the Skipper arranged payment of. "You will be twenty-two pounds short in your pay at the end of the trip," he informed them. The agent then told them, rather belatedly, of other cases that had been brought by the same bar owner and other seamen having fared in similar fashion. It was obvious that a racket and scam was in operation. Unfortunately due to seamen not being locals and spending little time in port, appeals were non-existent and the bar tender and company were on a nice little earner. Suggestions in the vein that memos should be issued to all incoming ships crews warning them of the trap in that particular bar were, I suspect, totally unheeded.

When they reported to the Skipper on their return to the ship, the two miscreants burst into laughter and the Skipper joined in. Looking back in retrospect, they could see a funny side to it; they were lighter in pocket, but no harm was done. I still think luck was with Hans and I that night; there but for the grace of God go I (my turn was to come in later years). Had we still got our first Skipper, I strongly suspected that he would have left them there to rot.

The following day with a cargo of eighty one thousand bags of sugar, each one weighing two hundred and fifty pounds, all hatches were battened down and we said our farewells to sunny and eventful Cuba. For seventeen days we had tasted the delights of the island that I hoped to see again some day as I had on previous occasions. Next time I would be aware and much wiser.

* * *

It was good to be at sea again. The weather favoured us: blue cloudless skies with a warm westerly to temper the heat. I should have known that the jinx I seemed to carry with me would soon raise its ugly head once again to take away the pleasant atmosphere and my feeling of well-being. It was my stint at the wheel late on Sunday when the ship veered to starboard. To bring her back to the required heading, I gave her a little port helm, then a little more and finally hard over. All to no avail. The steering mechanism had once again failed. "Oh no! It can't be me again." I bewailed my luck as we swung around in a large circle. Fortunately we were well out to sea and in no danger of running aground and there were no other ships around. On that occasion however, the fault was not a catastrophe, and the engine-room staff soon had it sorted: the pin had dislodged itself again.

It was during my next stint at the wheel whilst in conversation with the new Mate that I related to him what had befell us in Venice in the fog and those very near misses. He had been researching the history of the 'Granford' by reading up the old logbooks and there had been numerous incidents. Built during the war, the 'Granford' (then the 'Empire Haldane') had survived the conflict without a scratch and up until three years previously she had been incident free. Then off the coast of Portugal she had collided with a Spanish vessel that sank but left the 'Granford' hardly damaged.

Twelve months on, along with another ship during a gale she had been driven on to a rocky coastline. The other ship sank but the 'Granford' had got away with it, to have new plates welded to her bottom in New York. Also there was the loss of the rudder and the tow from mid-Atlantic as already related.

During the rest of the voyage, there were several breakdowns, nothing serious and the delays were not of great duration. Yes, the old

'*Granford*' was a rogue, but she seemed to have a charmed life and kept getting away with it and in comparison to previous trips, that one back across the Atlantic for us was a good voyage.

Our orders were to first discharge part cargo in Rotterdam and to deliver the rest to Hamburg, Germany. Rumour became rife that the ship's company would be paid off in Hamburg, but I had long since learned not to totally believe in rumours of that sort until they finally happened. Sometimes they did. Sometimes they didn't but as that dark smudge appeared on the horizon, hopes of home and good English grub loomed large.

That dark smudge of the Lizard, just south of Falmouth had appeared after sixteen days at sea and soon those White Cliffs of Dover were there too, which brought that lump to your throat when your destination was Europe and not England. We then received news of a dock strike in Rotterdam and we were to be rerouted to Germany, Emden, my very first port of call on the '*Oakhill.*' Was it really only just over three years previously?

We arrived on Wednesday 15th May. The river Ems was in full flood as I relieved Jack at the wheel while we awaited the departure of a ship from the lock into the basin. With the help of a tug at each end, I took her into the lock where we made fast with just one rope fore and aft. Expecting the lock gates to close I was surprised to see a small French coaster nosing its way into the lock with us. There was ample space to accommodate both vessels but the '*Granford*' decided once again to spoil the party.

Whether it was the turbulence from the coaster's propeller that caused the '*Granford*' to sway, which in turn caused the after rope to snap I don't know, but with the rope gone she began to swing across the lock. The French coaster was in imminent danger of being crushed against the lock wall. The tug to our stern spotted the danger, sped quickly forward and just managed to get her nose up against our port quarter to shove the '*Granford*' back away from the coaster. Quickly another rope was passed ashore and secured then the lock gates were closed with water entering to lift both vessels up to the basin level.

It took twenty minutes to flood the lock and open the gates. The French coaster scurried off under its own steam glad to be out of reach of the '*Granford*' and her tricks. The tugs saw us safely to our mooring and before we were fully tied up, the barges were alongside awaiting discharge of the sugar.

Using the ship's derricks the stevedores loaded nine bags of sugar into each individual strop then landed them on to scales on the deck where a tally was kept before they were lifted again and lowered into the barges. We had arrived on Wednesday and by early Sunday morning, three thousand tons had been discharged.

On the Saturday night, I decided to renew my acquaintance with Emden and its German beer. Emden was much the same, the beer was just as good and after two or three 'Steins,' I was back aboard.

With the hatches battened down, we entered the lock bound for Hamburg on Sunday morning the 19th With no further mishaps Hamburg hove into view early on Monday morning where thank God that time the rumour proved true; it was confirmed that we were to be paid off. The 'Granford' would in future be sailing under the Liberian flag and was to be renamed the 'Vulcan.' The sense of relief amongst the crew, especially those who like me had been with her from the start in Liverpool, was plainly visible for all to see. The prospect of home and leave defied description, but readily understood as we headed for the nearest bar to celebrate. The celebrations were somewhat muted though as the cost of Hamburg beer was extortionate and, while late night carousing was the plan, most of us were back onboard and safely tucked up well before midnight.

Packing our gear the next morning Tuesday 21st May took no time at all, but the wait for the launch was an eternity. Each minute was like an hour. We were like kids waiting for Christmas and it wasn't until 5.30pm that it eventually turned up. Cases and kitbags were stowed in the middle of the launch and were sat on by those who couldn't find a seat.

As we sped across the harbour towards the landing stage no one looked back towards the 'Granford' except me, I couldn't resist that last look, rogue that she was. She had kept us safe over the past eight months in sometimes wicked conditions and I thanked her for that.

A human chain was formed at the landing stage to pass the luggage on to a waiting lorry and a bus awaited the crew to carry us to the railway station. Aboard the bus the Third Mate doled out the railway tickets and ten German marks each for expenses. Once at the station, we were told which platform the train would depart from at three minutes past midnight and that our luggage would be waiting for us on the platform. Till that time we were free to wander at will. Hans, once his wages had been paid to him in German marks, he said his goodbyes and departed for his home, wherever in Germany that was. He was the lucky one; he was already on his home soil.

Barry, Frank and I decided to take a look at Hamburg. I recalled reading somewhere that Hamburg was one of the most bombed cities in Europe, but there was little sign of the devastation then. Leaving one of the main thoroughfares we turned into a side street. A short way along which we passed a doorway covered with what appeared to be a thick curtain. From inside the house came the sound of voices, soft music and laughter. There were no visible signs to distinguish it from any of the other houses, no hoardings or neon lights so Barry and I walked on by. Frank however, stepped back to peak around the curtain and immediately disappeared into the house. "What the hell is he doing?" both Barry and I thought as we retraced our steps to take a peak ourselves around the curtain and we too went straight in.

Frank was already seated at a table talking to a beautiful topless blonde waitress. Like a flash we were at his side admiring the view. It was quite a large room full of customers, mainly men as you would imagine with half a dozen gorgeous topless waitresses plying their wares around the tables. Our eyes were everywhere.

Ten marks, the equivalent of about a pound sterling then, didn't buy a lot of beer, but it bought us two steins, and we made them last until we had to hurry back to the station where the train was already at the platform. We picked up our gear from the platform and found a carriage that was reserved in our name. We were fortunate not to be late for, in the tradition of German efficiency, the train left right on the dot of three minutes past midnight.

We reached the German / Dutch border bedraggled and sleepy, and the wait for the train to start again didn't help. It soon became obvious what was causing the delay as customs officials meticulously checked passports and baggage.

Frank left us at Rotterdam. It had worked out well for both him and Hans. We still had a sea crossing to make and then another two train journeys. The ferry was due to sail from the Hook of Holland and it had arrived there at ten o'clock on Wednesday morning and it was due to sail at twelve midday.

Once more, we passed through customs and boarded the handsome Dutch ferry the '*Princess Beatrix.*'

I had no German marks left but those who had wasted very little time changing them for English money. The after deck provided a splendid platform for observing the loading of cars as they were lifted from the quay and lowered into the ferry's hold. That passed the time until twelve midday. Dutch precision also had to be admired; on the stroke of twelve, she cast off and we were once again in the English Channel.

I felt sorry for some of the school children aboard; the sea was choppy and they began to look a little green. They were soon hanging over the side. I wondered if I had looked that green when I had experienced my one and only bout of seasickness on my maiden voyage.

The short trip across passed quickly enough, and at 6.40pm we passed through customs at Harwich to board the boat train on its return trip to Liverpool Street Station. The Third Mate had contacted the company office and was told that a company representative would await our arrival in London.

It was good to be back on English soil but with no money, no food and nothing to drink, I looked forward eagerly to meeting the guy from the company despite the fact that I had lived through it all before. He took us along to a waiting room where he handed everyone ten pounds and a voucher for the train journey home. I remembered my return home from my first trip on the '*Oakhill*' and being handed ten pounds on the station, I wondered if the ten-pound handout was the policy of all shipping companies when their crews returned from a foreign pay off or was it peculiar to just the London / Greeks.

There were not many goodbyes as we hurried to our various London stations for the final leg of our journey home. Brian led the way to the underground and I closely followed. Strange to say, despite the fact that we lived within half a mile of each other, we hadn't mated up much during the trip to go ashore or anything. It was just one of those strange anomalies I suppose.

We caught the first train to Wolverhampton from Euston and arrived finally at 3.30am. Wolverhampton was deserted, not a taxi to be seen. Brian said he knew a taxi driver from Willenhall he could ring. The operator put him through, but he got no reply, so he asked the operator to connect him to a taxi rank. It rang and rang, eventually it was answered, "Christ!" he said, "It's a copper."

The policeman explained that the bell had been ringing outside the taxi rank for quite some time. Could he get us a taxi to take us to Walsall? Brian asked. "I'll see what I can do," he replied and hung up. He was as good as his word for shortly after a taxi rolled up and I was in bed by 4.30am and past caring.

It was late afternoon when I surfaced; hungry and eager to taste again my mother's cooking. On Friday morning two money orders landed on the doormat and as I cashed them at the local Post Office, I was determined that that would be my very last association with the Goulandris Brothers.

CHAPTER ELEVEN
THE NACELLA

(Of Avoiding a Whale, Little and Large, and a Chance Meeting).

June outperformed its reputation for 'Flaming,' and one hot summer's day followed another for virtually the whole of the five weeks that I was on leave. I wallowed in home luxuries, looked up old friends and renewed old acquaintances. My mate Norman had been conscripted for his period of National Service and was serving with the Brigade of Guards. Mavis had married and her husband Alan invited me to join them for a drink at a local club. Alan was welcoming and companionable, we soon became firm friends and I spent many happy evenings with them.

Time flies when you are enjoying yourself, so goes the old adage, and I was well into the fifth week of my leave before I suddenly realised that I was due back at the Pool on the following Monday. It was 1st July when I changed trains in Crewe to catch the express to Lime Street, and it was early in the evening when I went to book into Gordon Smith's to be told that they could only offer me a bed in Sefton House as all of their accommodation was occupied. Sefton House turned out to be the place opposite Smith's that I had once been turned away from. "Officers only" I clearly recalled the snooty clerk saying.

Over breakfast I learnt that a new Pool office had been built beneath the overhead railway. That was a most welcome rearrangement as far as I was concerned, and I thought that whoever had planned the move must have had the welfare of the seamen in mind; access to any of the docks was only a matter of climbing the steps outside the Pool door up onto the overhead railway platform.

From Sefton House it was but a short walk to the new Pool offices, which were a great improvement. I sorted out the new layout and headed for the door marked "Established men only." When I handed over my discharge book to the clerk, he reminded me that my two-year contract had expired and asked me if I wished to renew it. It was optional and signing it made me duty bound to return to the Pool over those two years the moment my leave expired. As I saw it, my only benefit was that they would pay me for each day on my return if they didn't find me a berth. As that had never happened so far, I decided not to re-sign at that time.

Another part of my thinking was that perhaps because of that small payment, they could pressure me into taking anything that they were having difficulties in finding a crew for. Also last but not least I thought I could possibly add a little to my leaves by pinching a day or two occasionally as was my want.

"Go into that waiting room," said the clerk as he pointed towards a pair of swing doors. I was not aware that an electric lock operated by the clerk behind the counter opened the swing doors, and I flattened my nose against them as they refused to open. I got the distinct impression that the clerk had pulled that trick many times and from the expression on his face, he still found it to be a big joke.

Through the doors was a small office. I sat myself down alongside the only other guy who was also waiting to be allotted a berth. He was big, older than me and he was Irish. So, I was not surprised when he introduced himself to me as Paddy. He seemed friendly and amiable and more than ready to swop ship talk as we waited.

We exchanged experiences of the different ships, companies and countries that we had visited. After a pleasant fifteen minutes of chat, we were called to the adjoining room where another clerk was allocating berths. Paddy was immediately offered a Shell Tanker and on being told that it would be a short trip, he accepted and left to take a medical.

As he glanced at my documents, the clerk asked if I wanted a transfer to another port. "There are ships a plenty around the country looking for crews," he said. "No" was my immediate response. I was not about to transfer to somewhere else with no knowledge of what I would be getting into. "How about the '*Empress of Scotland*?'" he then asked.

Again, I thought a passenger liner was not for me. I had heard many stories of the conditions and discipline aboard those floating palaces. My expectation was that everyone was to be dressed in uniform, which would have to be bought out of one's own pocket and there would be twice as many men walking around in gold braid as there were doing the actual work. Whether those stories were true or false, I didn't feel the inclination to find out so I turned that down too.

"Well that leaves the tanker" the clerk said, which caused me to wonder why he hadn't offered it to me in the first place. "OK, I'll take that. Where is she?" I asked. "It's the 'Nacella' and she is in the Alexandra dock. They are signing on this afternoon so get off to the doctor now" was his parting shot. Paddy was still waiting on the doctor when I walked into the room and, on hearing that I had accepted the tanker, we agreed to go to sign on together. The examination by the doctor was cursory and brief. He listened to my breathing, asked me to say, "Aaaarg," then asked me if I was feeling well or was there anything that he should check on? "Yes and no" I replied respectively. "Good," he answered, "But I see you haven't had an X-ray for two years, so I suppose you had better get one now."

It took only minutes before I was back with Paddy and we returned to the main counter to collect our documentation. "Three pounds twelve shillings political levy" demanded the union official. I was not well pleased. We made our way up the steps to the overhead railway only to find that the system had been closed. A notice on the entrance informed all and sundry that dismantling would start immediately. I was struck speechless, amazed. The convenience to us of having our new Pool office built right beneath the overhead railway was very short-lived indeed. The cheap, convenient means of transport that served the whole of the port of Liverpool was to be scrapped. I thought that was unbelievable as we humped our gear to the nearest bus stop cursing the stupidity of the local authority in ridding itself of an asset which would never be replaced.

The 'Nacella' was almost an exact replica of the 'San Velino' and had recently been moved into Alexandra for a refit in the dry dock. The company colours gleamed on the newly painted funnel with its bright yellow shell emblazoned upon it. She looked positively new. Carpenters, electricians and workmen of all trades swarmed all over her and as we ploughed and picked our way aft through all of their rubble, we passed the officers' smoke room where other crew members were signing on. Paddy went to go in. "Hang on" I said, with the memory of the '*Granford's*' accommodation still fresh in my mind; "let's go down to take a look at our living quarters first." "Good idea," Paddy said.

A cleaner had just finished and was about to leave as we arrived there. Thankfully, on inspection the accommodation seemed decent and comfortable. There were three cabins with two berths in each for ABs and a fourth cabin for four ordinary seamen.

Deck boys seemed to me to be a dying breed as I hadn't seen one signed on a ship for ages, and the peggying had become the responsibility of a young steward, who at least had been trained in some catering skills. How I wished when I looked back at my two years doing the peggying that a young steward had been available to do it then. Having said that, it had been an excellent experience and discipline for life.

An AB lay on a bunk in one of the cabins. He had sailed with her the previous trip and he told us that it was a decent ship with plenty of overtime. That was all we needed to know so we said, "we will see you later" as we dumped our gear into an empty cabin. The signing on only took a few minutes and a further few minutes later, we were safely sampling the local brew in the pub by the dock gate.

Breakfast wasn't bad and afterwards we started to load the ship's stores. It was Wednesday 3rd July and our immediate task over the next few days was to load twelve months supply. Every morning lorries deposited stores on the dockside and we were all hard at it; we lugged the lot up the gangway into our storage rooms until Saturday afternoon. The comfort of the dock gate pub was enjoyed by most of my new shipmates on Saturday night in accordance with the British tradition. Although that night a lot of beer was shifted, no one had to be carried back aboard.

As we lounged against the rail enjoying the morning sun, we wondered how to spend a free Sunday when the Bosun appeared. There was to be a series of engine trials he explained. The engines were to be turned slowly whilst the ship was still tied up so that the engineers could examine something. It would require some of the crew to remain onboard as standby in case of mishap and the possibility that the mooring ropes could snap.

As usual there were a large proportion of locals amongst us so it surprised me a little when each one chose to stay onboard for the overtime rather than go ashore. This was the opposite to the 'Hartismere' when we had been ordered to stay onboard on a Sunday with no overtime pay by that mad Captain; an action which had created mayhem.

That alternative course of action was a much better system of keeping the men onboard. It proved to be the easiest overtime of my seagoing life to date as, try as they might, the engines refused to start anyway. We stood down in the late afternoon and the Bosun remarked that a further attempt would be made in the morning.

The engineers must have spent most of the night overhauling the engines for immediately after breakfast the next day, we heard the sound of their steady beat. The belated trials were successfully completed and with the final tidying up done we made ready for sea in the hope of an early departure the next morning.

And so it was on the morning of Tuesday 9th July as we headed down the Mersey, the word was passed that we were bound for the Americas. We were told to head towards Key West until further orders were received. Under the guidance of the river Pilot, we proceeded very slowly, and we hadn't reached the river bar when at four o'clock, being the first wheelman on the four to eight watch, I commenced my stint at the wheel. I relieved the twelve to four man and under the instruction of the chatty Scouse Pilot, it was five o'clock when finally outside the bar, our engines were stopped to allow the Pilot off. We waved him farewell as his cutter headed back towards port.

As the Mate then telegraphed for slow ahead, the engine room requested a five-minute delay to rectify some minor defect. Subsequently, that so called five minutes meant that I spent the next hour of my steering stint propped up against the wheel doing nothing and it was a further hour after I was relieved before we got under way again.

Whoever had overhauled the ship's engines could not be recommended for the Queen's award for industry as they proved to be a constant source of doubt and unreliability. Over the following four days, as we headed into the Atlantic, we had the signal to "stop engines" for two to three hours each day in succession as adjustments and repairs were undertaken. Not once during those periods of stoppages was there any hint of danger, but a stationary ship without power in mid-Atlantic must always be considered a potential hazard. After those four days the initial problems appeared to have been rectified; we sailed serenely on, in increasingly good weather, still on a westerly heading.

As the days passed, the weather got warmer and it was pleasant to be painting out on deck in the sunshine, but then it got hot and we were glad of the ship's movement as there was little or no breeze, only that which was created by the ship's forward motion.

* * *

Two days out from Key West the new orders were radioed to us. It was to be Curacao and that was confirmed by a change of course to a southerly heading. By that time it came as no surprise the next morning when the sound of the engines died. Again there was no apparent danger as there were no other ships in sight, and there were many worse places than the Caribbean to have an engine problem, but even so the watches were kept on constant alert. It took eight hours to cure the fault but the delay created no problems for the crew as we basked in the Caribbean sun. "Would I ever sail in a ship which was problem free, with fail-safe engines?" I pondered. However, I also reflected on the benefits in faulty engines, especially when they failed in such pleasant conditions; sometimes it made life much more interesting.

Surprisingly, the shark population decided to ignore us that time; we did not spot a single one. Those eight enjoyable hours (at least enjoyable to us on deck) were productive as they cleared the faulty engine, which then gave us no more trouble and we to tied up in Curacao on Saturday 27th July. Bullen Bay, according to our instructions, was to be our first port of call, but it was decided to put into Willemstad first to launch another attack on the bugs that plagued the engine.

It was lucky that one of my favourite landfalls in the Caribbean was Curacao, given the number of times that I had found myself tied up there. Unfortunately on that occasion, I didn't get ashore as the repairs took little more than four hours, then we were on our way around the coast to cover the short distance to Bullen Bay. Our stay there too was quite short, just long enough to load a couple of tanks before we started on our way to Puerta La Cruz, Venezuala on Sunday evening.

The heat became oppressive and I welcomed my two-hour stint on the wheel in the early hours of the morning because by that time it had cooled a little. The cooler temperature did not last for long, and as we arrived at Puerta La Cruz early on Tuesday 30th July our cabins had become like bakers' ovens. I lay there in a pool of sweat expecting to be called to stations, but then I felt the engine vibrations as the ship was put into reverse, which meant that we were anchoring in the bay. I turned over and tried to get back to sleep in a dry part of my bunk.

It was daylight when we were called to stations, and we tied up to take on another part cargo. The transfer of the oil from shore to ship was uneventful and by late afternoon we were anchored back again in the bay. We swung at anchor for three days and, as the sharks appeared, I had visions of baited hooks and a sign upon the cabin door "Gone Fishing," but the Bosun had other ideas. We did at first try to tempt the circling sharks but they were too wise to fall for our lure. The Bosun interrupted our sporting pastime by detailing Paddy and I to brushes and paint. The masts were to be the first job and they took all of the three days that we lay at anchor. The mainmast was relatively easy; it was the usual bosun's chair job where you hoisted yourself up to the top and progressively painted down the mast. By that time I was pretty competent at manoeuvring the bosun's chair, and in some respect it had its attractions. The foremast however was a different kettle of fish. Being a table mast it produced several problems.

As its name implies, it was shaped similarly to a table with two vast posts rising upwards from the deck: one halfway in from the port side to the flying bridge, the other half way in from the starboard side to the flying bridge with a bridge that spanned between the two, across the top. Whilst the stanchions on both the inside and outside of the bridge proved to be no problem, the underside was damned awkward. We had to rig stages over and secure them for us to clamber over so we could sit on them and hang on like circus performers as we struggled to paint the underside. "Why us?" Paddy and I asked ourselves as we sat there in mid-air and looked down at some of our shipmates who sat on the deck lazily painting the rails. It was hard work, time consuming and, on reflection, it was damned dangerous as we had no safety nets, but to the Bosun's satisfaction, we had the job completed before we weighed anchor and proceeded back past our original berth to a remote creek which was miles from anywhere.

The rest of the cargo was pumped aboard with a minimum delay to enable us to catch the evening tide. With five different grades of oil onboard, we cleared Puerta La Cruz bound for West Africa, glad to be rid of the energy sapping heat as we welcomed the breezy salt tainted air.

My doubts concerning the reliability of the engine were well and truly confirmed when three days out the silence from the engine was deafening. The muttering and curses emanating from the engine room, queried not only the competence of the people who had supposedly overhauled the engines, but also their parentage. It was six hours before we heard the engines hiss and spit into life again.

The weather was settled but hot, and it could have been difficult had we been in a spate of rough weather. But from then onwards we ran into a cooler period, interspaced with heavy showers and sunny spells; April type weather in August, which lasted for several days.

I had relieved the twelve to four wheelman on Saturday 10th August and everything was routine with no perceived problems. Nothing could be more peaceful as I checked the heading on the compass. It was then I thought I caught a flashing glimpse of a flying fish ahead in the corner of my eye. As I gazed more intently, I saw that it was not a flying fish but a spout of water, which gave a silvery flash as the sun reflected upon it. It was a whale blowing and basking immediately in our path. I yelled to the Second Mate who was in the chart room behind me. "Hey Sec. there's a whale immediately ahead of us." Without any undue haste he ambled out towards the wheelhouse window to suddenly scream as he quickly realised how close to the monster we were; "Starboard! Starboard! Hard to Starboard!" he yelled.

In my excitement at seeing that wonderful creature so close, it hadn't registered that he had no intention of shifting. And, in the grand order of rights and territory, he had more rights to be there than the man-contrived contraption that was invading his privacy. The evasive action brought him within six feet of the port beam. He still lay there blowing and studiously ignoring our very existence. He was indeed a monster and in the aftermath of the excitement of seeing a whale at such close quarters, the reality suddenly struck me. If we had hit him at twelve knots, it would have not only probably killed him, but running into tons of flesh and bone could well have damaged the bows and possibly perhaps even holed the vessel.

Five uneventful days of wet, miserable weather followed before we anchored off Freetown, Sierra Leone. Early the next morning we were called to stand by fore and aft to tie up. Oilskins were the order of the day as the rain bucketed down. It was the heaviest rain I had ever experienced and limited visibility to just a few yards. The fo'c's'le head was my station, which afforded no shelter from the torrential downpour. The oilskins offered little or no protection; the rain cascaded from our heads down our necks inside the so-called protective clothing and soaked us within seconds. I stood there like the proverbial drowned rat, unable to see farther than a few feet and I pondered my need to be there at all. Thank God the Pilot knew his job. Whilst I and my shipmates could not see a thing other than a solid wall of water cascading down, the Pilot must have known his patch like the back of his hand. He finally eased us slowly but surely alongside our allotted berth.

The ropes had become stiff and hard due to the soaking, and it was with much difficulty and cursing that we finally got two of them made fast. Luck was with me as the wire spring was secured. I had managed to put on a chain stopper before the wire was taken from the drum end of the winch to prevent it going slack. My shipmates on the other hand had only managed to get two figure of eight turns around the bits and when the ship moved forward, the wire jerked and slid a little around the bits, and the stopper jammed. I immediately dropped the end of the stopper to go to the aid of my mates to put a couple more turns around the bits but before we could do so the stopper snapped which caused the wire to screech out around the bits. Sparks and smoke flew everywhere before it had slackened enough to stop.

When I inspected the chain stopper later, I found that the steel links had embedded themselves into each other and it was as stiff as a poker. I dread to imagine what could have happened to my hands if I hadn't dropped it just split seconds before.

It took three long, wet, dreary hours to safely come alongside and secure the ship, and as we walked aft, every single one of the crew was literally soaked to the skin. I soon learnt that it was customary to issue anti-malaria tablets to the ship's company when visiting the coast of West Africa. So when the Second Mate doled out the supply of pills, my comment that a waterproofing pill would be more appropriate went down like a lead balloon.

Saturday was taken up with the discharge of most of the cargo and the rain slowly abated. Sunday dawned bright, sunny and hot, and as we cast off I once again admired the skill and knowledge of the Pilot as he brought us out to the open sea where his cutter scuttled back to Freetown with him onboard. We headed southwards then westward bound for Lagos, Nigeria.

It was four days later that we hove to as we awaited the arrival of the Pilot to conduct us safely into the port of Lagos. The small amount of oil that remained took little or no time to discharge, but it was not until the following morning that we were ready to depart.

It had been some little while since my feet had trodden on firm ground and, along with a group of shipmates that night, we decided to savour the delights of Lagos. A nearby bar was found to be accommodating and the beer, although nondescript, was cold and thirst quenching.

We had finished breakfast the next morning when we were called to stations to cast off when the word went around that one of our number was still missing. He was a young ordinary seaman, a bit of a loner, who had gone ashore the previous evening alone, not with the crowd. He had been anything but happy for most of the voyage so far, and the consensus was that he had jumped ship so it came as no surprise when we sailed without him that afternoon Friday 23rd August.

The received orders were that we were to head back across the Atlantic to the West Indies, namely Trinidad. Fate however was to take a hand and the next couple of days or so were to prove to be eventful. Watches had been changed and I was in the eight to twelve watch. That same Friday night at midnight as I was making my way to the wheelhouse, there came a graunching and grinding sound from the direction of the engine room that could only signal engine failure. As I took the wheel, the familiar words to the question "Am I a jinx?" again echoed around my brain, but mercifully, the problem was rectified within thirty minutes or so. Slow ahead came the signal over the telegraph from the engine room, followed by full ahead as I brought her round back on course.

All the repairs and the spirit of well-being were however short-lived. At four-thirty in the early hours of that same Saturday morning the engines were silenced yet again and we drifted aimlessly for the next twelve hours, in little danger, for we were well out into the Atlantic in a calm and placid sea. The arrival on the bridge of the Chief Engineer was an ominous sign for it transpired that the engine could only be patched up enough to deliver the ship back to Lagos at a much reduced speed. To proceed across the Atlantic was, in his opinion, definitely the wrong thing to do.

The Skipper took heed, and early Sunday morning found us hove to awaiting the Lagos Pilot, who finally arrived about five hours later. "It's Sunday today, so I am only taking you in beyond the breakwater this morning," he said. "We will moor you up properly tomorrow." "I didn't realise you were that religious," the Captain said, "I'm not," the Pilot replied, "But I'm not missing my Sunday lunch for you lot," he joked.

We anchored in the river just beyond the entrance and turned to at six o'clock the next morning to rig the gangway over the side awaiting the Pilot. When he arrived we sailed quietly to a mooring on a row of buoys. We tied up with three wires for'ard and three wires aft in the middle of a line of ships in the centre of the river.

* * *

The Mate designated me to be the nightwatchman from 7.00pm to 7.00am. "That would be a doddle, moored in the middle of the vast river," I thought as I climbed into my bunk to grab a couple of hours sleep, and as always the overtime that the job entailed would be most welcome too.

I surfaced at about 6.30pm and made my way to the mess to scrounge something to eat, I bumped into the guy who the crew had decided had jumped ship. The local police had picked him up virtually as soon as the Skipper had reported him missing. They had held him in custody, and were on the point of discharging him to a ship bound for England when news reached them of our return to Lagos.

If he had been returned home, his discharge book would have been stamped VNC (Voyage Not Completed) and possibly a tribunal would have interviewed him to decide his future. The worst scenario from which would be the possibility of being blackballed, never to sail again. In the event the Skipper logged him five days pay plus all the expenses he had incurred whilst he was ashore as an extra punishment.

He was sad and miserable before, but he was even sadder because he had been returned to the ship, and as it turned out his return was not welcomed by us his shipmates either; the next day he went down with the Asian Flu that was raging up the West Coast of Africa at that time. Soon it raged through the ship like a torrent. The crew dropped like flies as they succumbed to the virus. Officers, engineers, stewards and ABs alike were all confined to their bunks as the shore doctor insisted when he was hastily summoned aboard to deal with the epidemic.

I was one of the few not afflicted, not even a sniffle, and I was detailed to administer the pills prescribed by the medic every four hours during the night. As I pursued that duty by waking them in the early hours, I was not the most welcome visitor to my reluctant patients, all seventeen of them.

The Bosun one morning, determined to carry out the day's duties with a much depleted crew, collapsed in a heap as he tried to rise from his bunk. His legs had given way and he lay writhing in agony on the deck of his cabin complaining of a searing back pain. It looked to all purposes as though he was paralysed from the waist down. Rightly or wrongly we lifted him back into his bunk as gently as possible with an urgent request for the doctor to return.

After the doctor had administered painkilling tablets, the poor guy still writhed in agony. Finally, the doctor diagnosed a slipped disc and stated that he would have to be paid off as quickly as possible. It was my job then to keep an eye on him throughout the night to ensure painkillers were delivered every four hours along with all my other flu patients.

It was a weary old me that turned in at seven o'clock on Wednesday 28th only to be rudely awakened by the Third Mate after what seemed like a very short sleep; just two hours in fact. "The Chief Mate wants to see you in his cabin, and the police are with him," was the type of message that jolts you out of dreamland.

A curt "come in" was the response to my knock on the Mate's door and I entered to find him seated at his desk along with two black police officers. "During the night, the paint locker in the fo'c's'le head has been broken into and four hundred and thirty pounds worth of paint and other materials have gone missing," he told me gravely. It was a moment or two before I realised the implication of the tone in his voice, but it soon became glaringly apparent as the two civilian police began to question me. Had I seen or heard anything suspicious during my watch? "Absolutely nothing at all," I replied. "Strange," said the Mate, "For it must have taken whoever it was that hacksawed through the lock at least half an hour, which isn't a noiseless task and the carriage of all the paint and other gear must have added a substantial amount of time on to that."

I then felt sure that at the back of his mind, he suspected that I had either been asleep while on duty or I had had a hand in it. "Fat chance," I thought, "with all my nursing duties dishing out pills throughout the night." "Sorry Chief," I said, sticking to my own little private policy of not calling the officers 'Sir,' but I insisted that I never saw or heard a thing.

I spent a fruitless half an hour undergoing the third degree and I was glad to climb back into my bunk, but not to sleep as I lay worrying about the incident. Perhaps it was just as well I couldn't sleep for within the hour I was called back to the Chief Mate's cabin to face further questioning by plain clothes CID officers. Evidently photographs and fingerprints had been taken at the scene of the crime and the questioning took the same line as before. I hadn't liked the look of the previous two coppers, but that couple, it seemed to me, were downright sinister, and my apprehension was more than heightened when they said I should accompany them ashore for further questioning.

My glance at the Chief questioned the legality of the proposition and I thought, "I need some protection here, or at least have someone to accompany me," but he just nodded and said, "I suppose you had better get changed and go with them." I showered and changed into my shore gear and, as I waited for them at the head of the gangway, some of the lads appeared with the Bosun who was strapped to a stretcher ready to be taken ashore. As the stretcher was manoeuvred down the companionway into the waiting launch, it was obvious that the Bosun was in great pain as he was tilted first one way then another, and it was a relief when he was finally laid down on a bench on the launch. I followed him down and chatted to him in an attempt to take his mind off the pain.

We did not have long to wait before we were joined by the Captain who was accompanying the Bosun to the hospital and the two CID officers who were going to take me to only God knew where. The launch was quickly taken to the dockside where the Bosun and the Skipper were put ashore. I said my goodbyes to the Bosun and wished him well and a speedy recovery. The launch then sped off along the river to another jetty where a police jeep awaited our arrival.

I was ushered into the rear of the jeep and the CID men followed in a police car. Throughout what to me seemed to be a never-ending journey through the city, my imagination ran riot. I had visions of rubber truncheons and spotlights, beatings up and all the tortures reminiscent of the gangster movies of my childhood of which I had seen hundreds. Perhaps I was to be taken into the jungle and fed to the lions or the crocodiles, or locked into some filthy dungeon with the key thrown away.

My two escorts seemed by appearance to be capable of anything, but I came to the conclusion that I had read too many cops and robbers books of late. After what seemed an age, we turned off the road into a compound where I was escorted into a square yellow brick building. Inside a dingy small room that was reminiscent of a badly distempered air raid shelter were a couple of rickety old tables. Behind one of which sat a cop busying himself answering the telephones that cluttered up his desk. A couple of equally rickety chairs stood in front of the tables and there was a wooden bench along one wall. That comprised the sum total of the furnished room.

My two awesome escorts told me to sit down and then disappeared, they kept me in a state of apprehension for a further twenty minutes. The longer the wait lasted, the more nervous I got, and it was with some relief when one of the policemen reappeared, equipped with pen and paper. Once again they wanted a detailed report of my activities during the night. As I sat and recounted the night's saga yet again, he sat staring unblinking without once taking his eyes off me and, as I ended my account of the night's happenings he continued to stare. Perhaps, I thought, he is some kind of hypnotist, but if so he was badly out of practice.

He then took a large form from the desk drawer and began to ask me details of my origin and he proceeded to fill in the form, my date of birth, nationality, place of birth, home address, religion etc, etc. Virtually every answer had to be spelt out to him as he laboriously attempted to complete the form. It was a tedious task and when he came to my home address, he threw down his pen in frustration as he attempted to write Hollemeadow Avenue.

He then took another form from the table drawer and threw it towards me. "Here, you fill it in," he said as he stormed from the room. The form itself was quite straightforward until I reached the question, "Name of Tribe." I was at a loss so the space had to remain blank and I completed the rest of the form.

As I sat staring around the room he returned, checked the form and then he pushed it back across the table towards me and said, "Now write your account of the night's events," then he left again as suddenly as he had appeared.

My statement read, "On the night of August 27th I reported to the Chief Mate at 7.00pm to receive my orders as nightwatchman. I was instructed to rig a cluster light above the gangway. Unable to find the lights I reported to the Mate that the Bosun would have the keys to the locker where the equipment was stored and as he was ill, I was reluctant to disturb him.

The Mate told me not to bother and to leave it for the time being, but to switch on the deck floodlights. Previously, I had reported failure of the foremast lighting, which left the fore part of the ship in darkness, and the fault had still to be rectified. As I reported that to the Mate, the Skipper appeared, his main concern seemed to be the possibility of natives in canoes trying to smuggle beer aboard. If I spotted them he said, I was to inform the duty officer immediately." "Sure," I thought, but only after, I had secured a few cans for myself. The latter of course was not put in writing on the report.

"It would have been about ten o'clock when, having made my second tour of inspection, I made a pot of tea and took a cup to the Bosun. He was awake, and he asked me if I would pack his gear for him for the next day he was to be paid off sick. By midnight I was on my rounds in my dual role as angel of mercy administering pills and potions to the sick. A further tour of inspection had found nothing untoward and along with the Fireman nightwatchman I went to the galley to cook supper.

For the rest of my watch I patrolled regularly and woke my patients at their allotted times to dish out their pills and make them hot drinks. At 6.30am everyone was awakened who had needed to be, and at seven o'clock I completed my watch then climbed thankfully into my bunk. The first indication I had of the robbery was being woken and told to report to the Mate's cabin. I had seen nothing, nor heard anything suspicious during the total period of my watch." I signed the statement and handed it back to my silent and sinister inquisitor.

He took what seemed an interminable time reading it, then turned away saying as if on an after thought, "OK, you can go now." "Hang on a minute," I said, "You brought me here so I need a lift back." I wasn't sure how he would take that, but maybe he was glad to see the back of me for, unceremoniously, I was shortly ushered outside to another waiting jeep. The driver was ordered to take me back to the jetty where we had landed.

The journey was completed in silence without a single word being exchanged between the driver and I, not even when I was deposited at the dock. As I strolled along the jetty, there was little sign of activity and no launches readily available. A black guy was lounging against the door of a shed so I asked him how I could get back to the 'Nacella,' out there on the buoys. "Yo betta see de Harbow Masta," he said in his wonderful drawl and pointed to a building on the far side of the dock road. Upon climbing the stairs on the outside of the building, I found myself in 'De Harbow Masta's office,' where he sat talking to another well-dressed individual.

He asked what he could do for me and I told him that I had been brought ashore from the 'Nacella' and was looking for a launch to take me back aboard. "You are in luck, this is your ship's agent," he said, nodding to the other guy, "He will fix you up." The agent looked and said quite friendly, "My car is in the street. It's a black Ford; if you wait there, I'll give you a lift. I won't be five minutes." He was true to his word and ushered me into the back seat, "Friday," he called to his driver, "Stop at the Elder Dempster jetty."

In a matter of minutes the car pulled up at the jetty to which the Bosun had been brought, and pointing to a small green hut the agent said, "In that hut you will find a Scotsman, he will fix you up." He was away in a flash and I trundled over to the hut where I was greeted by a genial Scot whose Glasgow accent was still as marked as the day he left. "Sure, sure," he responded as I related my tale of woe. "I'll have you back aboard in no time."

He opened the door and yelled some incomprehensible name and a black guy appeared from nowhere. 'Nacella' the Scot barked at him, and with a grin as big as Christmas the guy chatted away, and led me to a bright blue spick and span launch. As I sat and admired the tidy cleanliness of the boat, the Skipper appeared and sat alongside me. He was returning from the hospital where he had overseen the admission of the Bosun. He was not over reassuring concerning the Bosun's condition, "He'll be alright" was his dismissive answer to my enquiry

"How did it go with the police?" he queried, "No rubber truncheons or anything?" I think that was a small attempt at humour, but if so it totally failed on me, as it showed that the possibility, however remote, had entered his mind too, and he had still allowed me to go ashore with them alone without an escort. It left a slightly nasty taste in my mouth. "It must have taken quite some time to get away with all that stuff" he muttered, half to himself as I related the procedure at the local cop shop. "There was a hint of suspicion in his voice too" I thought. I had told my story so many times in one day that I was fed up with it and, as there was no more to be said, the rest of the short trip back to the ship was spent in silence.

* * *

There had been little or no sleep for me over the twenty-four hours, and I fully expected the Mate to excuse me of my nightwatchman duties so I was amazed when he came to my cabin that evening to explain that from then on, there would be a security firm coming aboard at night to maintain the watch. Two guards were to be employed throughout the night to watch over the ship, and my main duty as nightwatchman was to watch over them. That eased the situation a little for me, considering the suspicion that I felt I had endured throughout the day. It felt better knowing that they still trusted me to do the job. I was very tired and felt sorry for myself as I started my watch that night. The feeling only lasted for a short while though until the arrival of the shore watchmen.

The sight of them would enliven any occasion. One was a giant of a man, six-foot-four and about twenty stone. Very reminiscent in build of the Bosun on the old 'San Velino.' His companion struggled to reach five-foot and weighed about eight stone wringing wet. The long and the short of it raised a smile at the very sight of them. 'Tiny' instantly became my nickname for the giant, and 'Colossus' was my name for his diminutive mate. From the very first moment we met, I got along with them famously and every night as they commenced their tour of duty, they presented me with a large bag of peanuts.

From then onwards the nights passed peacefully and without incident as they patrolled the decks which released more time for me to go about my own duties, not least of all administering drugs to the flu ridden crew. During that time word came that the Bosun had indeed slipped a disc and a longish stay in hospital was therefore necessary. On recovery, he would be shipped back home on one of the ships that traded between Lagos and England on a regular basis.

With my newfound friends, Tiny and Colossus, I sat one night taking a tea break. The conversation turned to conditions in Nigeria and local customs. "Any man can marry as many women as he wants," Tiny said, "As long as he can afford to keep them. I have two wives," he added as a matter of fact. "And what does your first wife think about it when you take on a second wife?" I inquired. "She no like, no woman like, but they get used to it, you make them like." How? I didn't need to ask as I thought that Tiny would have no problem enforcing his wishes on his women or anyone else for that matter with muscles like the Alps and hands like tennis rackets, but Colossus on the other hand may have met with a few problems.

Paddy was full of woe. The Mate had offered him the Bosun's job, and Paddy being the happy-go-lucky guy that he was, seemed reluctant to shoulder the responsibility of the promotion. "I'm happy as I am," he confided to me. "I'm no good at ordering guys about." Next day he was once again summoned to the Mate's cabin. That time the Skipper was there too and he said he thought that Paddy would make an admirable Bosun, just the bloke to run the crew.

The pressure they put him under to take the job was too much even for Paddy and shortly afterwards I helped him move his gear into the Bosun's cabin. "I'm no good with a pen," he moaned, "I won't be able to keep a record of the bloke's overtime." It was simple I assured him as it was only a matter of following it up in the overtime ledger as the Bosun had done previously, and I would be at hand to help if he needed it. So for a short while, not only was I the nightwatchman and Florence Nightingale but also the Bosun's Clerk.

The engine lay scattered around the engine room in a million pieces and although the engineers and the contractors worked hard, I wondered if it would ever be reassembled. On Friday 30th August when I presented myself at the Mate's cabin to receive my orders for the watch, I was told that all hands were to muster at 6.30am ready to sail at daybreak, but during the night unexpected engine complications arose, which were to delay our departure for a further twenty-four hours. "You have got at least one more night watch to do" said the Mate as he countermanded his previous order to call everyone to stations at 6.30am.

It was hot but the nights remained incident free and peaceful. My new mates, Colossus and Tiny were prompt and regular; they arrived every evening on the dot, along with my big bag of peanuts. We were just one of numerous ships of all nationalities moored in a single file down the centre of the river. Some were loading cargoes, some were discharging cargoes and others like us were there for repairs.

At three o'clock on Sunday morning, as I sat enjoying a cup of tea, Colossus appeared in the mess doorway beckoning frantically. I followed him all along the flying bridge to the fo'c's'le head when he whispered to me. "Six men have arrived in a canoe and four of them had shinned up the anchor cable of the Danish ship immediately ahead of us. They had passed a tarpaulin down to two other men who had remained in the canoe that they had tied to the anchor cable.

We both then began to shout over our bow in an attempt to attract the attention of someone on the Danish ship. The four robbers onboard immediately clambered back down the anchor cable like greased lightening and they paddled away into the darkness. It was a pound to a penny that those men were the same gang who had helped themselves from our paint locker. I looked over the bows but all was quiet and in total darkness, nothing further stirred. "Where is Tiny?" I enquired of Colossus. "Patrolling aft" his little face grinned up at me.

Back in the mess after I had made sure everything was secure on the 'Nacella,' I busied myself for a little while bringing my travel log up to date when at about 4.30am both Tiny and Colossus came calling frantically. "Massa, Massa, come quick, they are back again." Those two were prone to a laugh and a joke and I thought that maybe they were pulling my leg but no, they insisted. So keeping our heads down I followed them up to the bows again. The robbers had probably gone away the first time and then decided that there was little or nothing we could do to stop them from where we were and had opted to return for more booty.

In the meantime someone aboard the Danish ship had switched on their forward floodlights, but even that did not seem to concern them for as we peered over our bow, we could clearly see the villains calmly and unconcernedly lowering paint, ropes, tarpaulins and anything else that came to hand into the canoe moored to the anchor chain below.

I told my companions both to remain there and keep quiet and I dashed back amidships to waken the Mate. He was out of his bunk like a flash and within seconds, he was in the wheelhouse. In an attempt to attract attention from the shore, the Mate switched on the Aldis lamp. He focused at first on the Harbour Master's office, signalling but to no avail and in desperation, he turned the lamp on to the Danish vessel hoping to stir up some interest there. He did, but not much, the robbers just stopped for a moment and looked straight at us into the light then casually carried on with their looting. No one else on the Danish ship noticed our call.

A launch left the shore and momentarily we thought help was at hand as it headed our way only to turn midstream and head off up the river. Even the possible approach of a launch did little to disturb the robber gang, so in desperation at the lack of assistance, the Mate on the bridge and I with my two companions on the fo'c's'le head began to shout at the top of our lungs.

It was only when Tiny and Colossus poked there heads over the bow that the cheeky miscreants took notice. They probably thought that we might be able to recognise them and give their descriptions for they were working under the full glow of the floodlights and they decided to abandon ship. Even then not in any great hurry, they calmly shimmied down the anchor chain, climbed into the overloaded canoe and disappeared into the night.

On reflection, in some ways I was glad that I had not disturbed their nocturnal activities on the 'Nacella.' If they were the same gang who had looted us, by their appearance and coolness, they might not have been averse to a bit of physical violence. I could well have found myself lying at the bottom of the river feeding the fish. Through all of the commotion and hullabaloo, no one had stirred; there were no police, no help from the shore and no sign of crew life whatsoever from the Danish ship.

Gallant efforts in the engine room had reassembled the many pieces of machinery that had cluttered the decks down there and the word was passed that all hands were to be at stations at 6.30am. My job then as nightwatchman was to call everyone at 5.30. Tiny and Colossus bade their farewells and in some ways I was sorry to see them go. I had enjoyed their company and I missed the peanuts. I think that they had a certain regard for me too for the friendly way that they had been treated.

The Pilot came onboard at six o'clock and, even though I had been on duty throughout the night, I was told to do a stint at the helm. It was 6.30 when the Captain gave the order to cast off and the tug took a line onboard. The wires were winched aboard as the tug pushed and pulled, and turned us within the confines of the buoyed shipping channel to head downstream towards the open sea.

Under the direction of the Pilot I took her down the channel at dead slow ahead and we left the tug to return upstream. As we came up to the harbour entrance, just short of the breakwater, without warning the engine room telegraph rang on the bridge "Stop engines." As we were going so slow it took but a few moments to lose steerage, the tide began to swing us around and the breakwater wall loomed dangerously near.

Engine failure was most of the time not a pleasant experience, but to happen as we approached the harbour entrance was, to say the least, damned awkward. As we swung with the tide, we spanned the harbour entrance and completely blocked the whole entrance to the port for a short period. Finally we had turned full circle and our bows headed back towards where we had come from.

The word came up from the engine room that it would take about twenty minutes to right the defect so with the breakwater wall looming ominously close, the Skipper ordered the for'ard gang to drop anchor. We swung on the anchor for just seven minutes when again without word or warning, the telegraph rang full ahead and the engines started. Both the Captain and the Pilot jumped to the telegraph to reverse the order but too late, we were slowly under way dragging the anchor chain under the ship. The anchor chain rattled out over the 'Gypsy' on the windlass. Though the chippy attempted to brake the flow of chain, all that created was sparks and clouds of smoke.

Before the forward motion had ceased, almost the whole of what anchor chain we had was dragged off the windlass and it took half an hour to recover it. The Skipper was livid and I guessed that someone down in the engine room could look forward to a severe telling off.

As soon as we recovered the anchor, we moved slowly up river again until we could attempt to turn seawards again. It was like trying to do a three point turn in a car on a narrow street, and the Pilot was using caution as the buoyed channel was quite narrow he was worried in case we ran aground. I was knackered, having to keep turning the wheel hard over one way and then the other repeatedly.

Then, on the advice of the Pilot, it was decided to seek the assistance of a tug. So once our bow was headed in the correct direction again, we lay in the channel for what seemed an eternity to await the reappearance of the tug and I was grateful for the rest.

My stay in Lagos was memorable: I had been given the third degree by the local police, I had been sick nurse to half the crew, I had witnessed a shipboard robbery, I had become the new Bosun's Clerk and whilst at the helm we had almost hit the breakwater wall and nearly ran aground. However, every cloud has a silver lining, with Paddy becoming the Bosun he moved out and I then had a cabin to myself, what luxury! Getting back to sea and a routine was peaceful and certainly less stressful. I was not sorry to say goodbye to Nigeria. As the coastline fell away, I was relieved at the helm having done all the hard bits, and I was asleep before my head hit the pillow.

I awoke feeling extremely hungry and was secretly pleased with the meal the Cook had prepared, but I couldn't tell him, he would only get big headed. Fresh orders had arrived and so we headed west, bound for Trinidad in the Caribbean.

* * *

The weather deteriorated and we ran into a squally showery spell. It was cooler too, which gave a welcome albeit short respite from the sticky heat of the African coast. We were five days out when there on the starboard bow was another whale. We didn't get so close to it that time, but he too was a monster, and it was a pleasure to see the hulk of its massive body rising and falling as he rode the waves, blowing and snorting regardless of anything or anybody. It must have been twenty minutes or so before I lost sight of him.

On the Monday and Tuesday, 9th and 10th September, it just bucketed down endlessly. Then, just as the showers had turned into a forty-eight hour continuous downpour, it stopped to give a period of brilliant sunshine. On the 12th our trusty, or should I say rusty engines, failed again so the improved weather was welcome. For eight hours we drifted aimlessly with not even a shark to relieve the tedium.

A further delay of nine hours occurred the following day. The Skipper, not being a happy man, was giving the impression that he was speaking to no one, least of all to those fatherless misbegotten wretches in the engine room. The most popular pastime during those couple of days was dodge the Captain, everyone kept out of his way if it was at all possible.

Our enforced immobility however had its compensation, at least for me for suddenly out of nowhere, there came a vast shoal of dolphins. There must have been five or six hundred of them and to my delight they cavorted, leaped and splashed around the ship. They put on what can only be described as a 'Water Ballet' as they had fun.

To my amusement they would stage mock fights and headbutt each other and chase each other in speedy swerving races, leaping and turning in a display that would put circus acrobats to shame. Jumping straight upwards from the water they would drop tail first back in. Others would turn complete somersaults to splash in headfirst. The gyratons often would be performed by two, three or more dolphins in perfect symmetry, as though following the perfect choreography for a spectacular show. It was obvious to anyone with a scrap of grey matter that those intelligent, delightful creatures could communicate with each other and were also having the time of their lives. I was enthralled with their magical display, which must have lasted for a half an hour or so, and it was with a great sense of disappointment as they began to move away to finally disappear into the distance.

Still the sharks remained absent and maybe the presence of such a large school of dolphins in the area had something to do with it as I had been told that sharks were afraid of dolphins because they the dolphins would attack them by ramming them and headbutt them to death. I can't vouch for the truth of that story but those I saw were doing exactly that in a playful way with each other as though practising so that could possibly lend a little credence to it.

I suspected our orders to go to Trinidad were just to have us heading in the right general direction for we soon had our orders changed to go to Cardon, Venezuela. As our heading altered slightly to a couple of degrees north of due west, so the showery weather was left astern. It became hot, increasingly so, to what can only be described as torrid. Ropes from the rope locker were hauled up onto the deck to be coiled in preparation for arrival in Cardon the next day.

The sun had drenched us over the past two or three days, and the ship was nothing more than a floating barbecue. The steel deck plates were so hot it was impossible to remain standing in one spot for more than a few seconds; the heat seared through the soles of our shoes. The sweat poured from every pore and we hopped about like cats on a hot tin roof as we attempted to coil the ropes. Once the for'ard ones were stacked to the Bosun's satisfaction, a dark thunderous cloud came over the horizon, and with eager anticipation of a much needed cooling shower we could see rain streaming down as it approached, only to veer off to starboard shedding not a single drop on us.

We cursed our misfortune then headed aft to perform the same task with the after ropes. Sod's law prevailed for having performed our cat's dance at both ends of the ship, another shower came over the horizon and that time it caught up with us. So there was a God after all! We cheered like mad, stripped off and stood naked on the poop deck and showered in the cold, lifesaving liquid downpour from heaven. We forgot all about the cursing that had taken place a few days previously during the two days of incessant rain.

What great and wonderful wisdom it was that had decided I would, more often than not, be at the wheel either entering or leaving port I do not know, but we arrived off Cardon on the morning of Wednesday 18th September where I relieved the helmsman. For some reason I have yet to fathom, the sight of the Pilot's cutter always excited me a little. Probably a new face after seeing the same people day after day or the prospect of a new country, town or new experience. Who knows?

All went well as I followed the Pilot's instructions until we approached the jetty. The Pilot ordered, "Stop engines," and we still had steerage as we moved slowly forward towards our berth. The final manoeuvre to bring her alongside, "Hard to port" was the Pilot's order. I thrust the helm over to its limit but needing a little more steerage, the Pilot ordered the Third Mate to ring "Slow ahead." The combustion hiss from the engine was plain for all to hear, and was followed by a second and a third, but no engine came throbbing into life. Picking up the phone the Third Mate, anxious to avoid any blame, rang the engine room and was greeted with the not exactly startling news that, "They won't bloody start!" "We already bloody know that," he shouted back.

It was time once again to start playing dodge the Skipper, "Tell them to hurry up and get it fixed," he bellowed, "Or there is going to be some damage done." Whether the damage referred to the jetty, the ship or the engineers was arguable, but at that stage it was an open question.

Once again I stood just holding the wheel, "Why, oh why, does it always happen to me?" I pondered. The Bosun and the for'ard gang managed to get a line ashore as the bow swung towards the jetty and the dockers dragged it and placed the eye over the bollard. Operating the windlass, slowly the bow came around and as we came under some semblance of control, just as on leaving Lagos, yet again without warning, the engines came to life. For the second time there was a mad dive for the telegraph to stop engines. Again the Captain was fuming. "How many 'f***ing' times do I have to tell them never to start the engines without warning me first?" he stormed.

The extra bit of forward motion those few revs had given us stretched the for'ard mooring rope that they had managed to get ashore to its limit. It was singing with the tension, wringing the droplets of seawater from its very depths, but it held and the Pilot showed his great relief as we finally slid into place and called for "finished with engines." Tying up was effortless after the previous hectic twenty minutes, and it was a relief for me to get off the bridge and away from the Skipper's foul mood. But who could blame him.

An inspector came aboard and after a while he reported that water had entered into the tank bottoms so they would have to be dried, cleaned out and pass a further examination before a further cargo would be allowed into them. Eighteen of the twenty tanks were found to be in need of attention so mops and buckets were the order of the day.

Working like Trojans in a stifling confined space it seemed as if we sweated as much liquid as we mopped up. Having completed six tanks to the Mate's satisfaction, I led the way down the ladder into the seventh tank, and as I walked towards the far corner, I walked into a solid barrier of gas. Choking as I turned to warn my mates, I ushered them frantically back up the ladder out on to the deck and welcome fresh air. With a lung full of gas, I found it difficult to climb the ladder and it was with sheer will power that I made it to the top.

Being the last man out I breathlessly explained to the Mate and the Pumpman that there was a large pocket of gas down there, far too much to work safely. "There can't be gas down there, we have steamed it and tested it," the Pumpman insisted, but he didn't stand by his own conviction though as his reaction to my suggestion that he go down himself to find out was to mumble that they would steam it again.

It was past midnight when dirty, sticky, weary and half cut from the noxious fumes we finally completed the task. A tot of neat rum was issued to each man to help kill the gasses collected in our stomachs. As I had walked into that wall of gas and taken in a lung full I half-heartedly, like Oliver Twist, asked if I could have a second glass; the two short sharp words I received in reply made the refusal crystal clear.

With the fumes and the rum it was a somewhat bemused crowd who showered before they turned in, only to be awakened by Paddy the Bosun who required us back on duty as the inspector had found two tanks not to his satisfaction. The air was blue and my old mate Paddy nearly had a mutiny on his hands as we refused to return to work. Eventually Paddy, after much cajoling and the application of Irish charm, managed to persuade four blokes to go back. I was, along with the rest of my rebellious mates, expected to be hauled over the coals and logged by the Skipper the following morning. To his eternal credit and his understanding, Paddy hadn't put us on report.

After the previous nights heroic efforts, a fresh cargo was soon pumped into our newly cleaned tanks and late in the afternoon of the 19th September we cast off bound for Curacao.

The short passage to Curacao saw us passing through the narrow channel to Willemstad and we tied up without a hitch. That time I wasn't at the helm and the docking was faultless, which was further proof to me that I was jinxed for things only went wrong when I was at the wheel.

Johnny, one of the crew, suggested a run ashore would not go amiss for other than my enforced visit to the police station in Lagos it was the first time my feet had touched dry land since we had left Liverpool. Having got a sub we headed for the seamen's club. Inside was the usual collection of international motley crews who were sampling the cool, local nectar. Four or five of our crew had been there for some little while by the look of them, and so we joined them to wash the taste of oil from our throats.

The atmosphere was good with much merry chatter coming from all corners of the bar. On a stool against the bar sat a bearded guy who was gazing intently at me. He stood up and made his way towards me, "What the hell does this geezer want?" I thought to myself somewhat apprehensively. "How are you doing Mick?" he queried. It took a few split seconds for me to realise that it was my brother Roy who I hadn't seen since he had joined the Merchant Navy two years before, and that magnificent bushy beard was an effective disguise. I couldn't believe it! We eagerly shook hands and marvelled at the fact that either one of us could literally have been anywhere in the world and yet we had bumped into each other on a tiny island off the coast of Venezuela. Needless to say we celebrated in the bar long into the night.

He was signed on with the London Overseas Shipping Company. Johnny and I finished up staying the night with him aboard his ship, the 'London Loyalty,' a tanker. We talked well into the early hours, comparing notes and conditions. He, as before stated, being an engineer was officer status and he was amazed to learn how us deckhands were rationed on basic items like soap and matches and most other things too; one bar of soap per fortnight and two boxes of matches per week.

As we left the ship the next morning, Roy gave me a large bag full of soap and matches. The bag unfortunately gave way as we made our way to the gangway and scattered the contents over the deck. Roy, in a frantic endeavour to hide them from his shipmates' sight, picked them up off the deck and stuffed them down the front of my shirt. Unfortunately my shirt was not tucked into my pants, so they just fell through on to the deck again.

Finally Johnny and I, both looking pregnant, managed to get ashore with our ill-gotten gains and for some reason we couldn't stop laughing. They were however a very welcome addition to our paltry rations over the next few weeks. It was nine o'clock when we climbed our gangway to be greeted with the news that we would be casting off at midday.

* * *

With the engine set at slow ahead, the little steerage we had aided the tug to pull our bow around to starboard, which reversed our position and pointed our head towards the narrow passage and out to sea. For some unknown reason the tug came full astern, right across our bow. We gave him an almighty clout broadside on and put a large dent in his side. Fortunately we were going slow ahead for if we had been full speed ahead we may well have cut him in two or perhaps even turned him over. Luckily no one was hurt, the only injury being to the Tug Master's pride. Strangely I wasn't at the helm when that mishap occurred, perhaps I was escaping from the grip of the jinx after all, but more likely it had more to do with the crappy ships that I sailed in.

251

After a brief inspection it was found that we ourselves had suffered no damage and shortly afterwards we arrived off Bullen Bay, just up the coast. The three loading berths were occupied so we drifted until one of the occupants decided to leave. At about 5.00pm the '*London Loyalty*' came out of Willemstad and, as she cleared the horizon, I wondered when Roy and I would meet up again. It was to be hoped it would be in similar circumstances for we had spent a great evening and night together.

It was while we drifted off Bullen Bay that we heard of a tragic mishap on the Shell Tanker whose berth we were to take when she left. The unconfirmed report told of three men being gassed in the pumproom. Evidently the Pumpman had gone down into the pumproom and had failed to reappear, a second man went in after him and he didn't return either then, when a third man didn't come out, one of the crew equipped with a gas mask went down and found them all dead. The gas had taken them in a matter of seconds, which starkly brought home to me how lucky I had been only a few days previously when I had walked into that wall of gas down the tank.

The Shell Tanker eventually came out and within minutes we were alongside with the pipes connected to the manifold to complete the loading of the cargo, which continued throughout the night. This enabled us to cast off at midday on Sunday 22nd September bound for a place where I had always wished to visit, Rio de Janeiro in Brazil.

It was by then a joke aboard the '*Nacella*' that we had the most clapped out engines in the whole of the Merchant Navy. At two o'clock on the Monday morning we adopted our usual stance and drifted. It was no joke really for the engineers who toiled and cursed and cursed and toiled but failed to rectify or maintain an engine that should have been renewed years ago.

We drifted throughout the whole of Monday and the order of the day for us deckhands was to paint ship. Shoals of fish came to inspect us and one shoal looked like giant dolphins. They were about fifteen feet long and their torpedo shaped bodies gave them the appearance of having no heads. As they came closer, we could see that they blew waterspouts, so it was an educated guess that they were bottle-nosed Pilot whales. As they had appeared suddenly out of nowhere, their departure was just as swift; there one minute, gone the next. Maybe their sudden departure was explained by the appearance of a large shark. He was obviously hungry for he attacked the garbage that was floating around with relish.

Soon a tail block was fastened to the awning spar with a heaving line threaded through and a meat hook attached. From the galley a lump of gristle was to be the bait that was then lowered to lie on the surface. Suspiciously the shark eyed it and circled ever closer and closer. Having scented the gristle, hunger overcame his suspicion. He snatched at it and he was hooked. It took five of us to heave on the line to raise him up above the rail. He must have then thought that that was enough and rejecting our obvious hospitality he gave a mighty jerk and he actually straightened the meat hook, and with a resounding splash was off like a flash without a goodbye or thank you.

Shark fishing and the excitement that came with it was our only relief from the boredom of just drifting around so often. After our evening meal a repeat performance occurred and once again the shark got away. Not to be discouraged a further hook was baited, more in hope than anything else for there was no sign of any more sharks around. It was assumed that as it darkened the likelihood of attracting further fish would be less and so was our concentration. Suddenly while no one was looking, the line tightened and on the hook was a five-foot long shark. He was heaved up and landed on the deck where he lashed and squirmed until a line was secured around his tail, and he was hauled up to hang head down from the awning spar.

I hurried to my cabin for my camera. Photographs were the only proof of our prize and I was disappointed to find on my return that my gory shipmates had returned to their savagery and were already cutting him up for souvenirs. The fins and the tail were evidently prize possessions, and one guy had taken the teeth to polish up for a necklace. I didn't want any pictures of that carnage so I returned my camera to my cabin. The remaining unwanted bits were then thrown back over the side to feed his waiting relatives.

For twenty-seven hours the engines were out of command before they could be repaired. Unbelievably they failed again on the Thursday night for another four hours and yet again the following Monday for another all day drift. We appeared to be drifting aimlessly towards our destination, making a little progress in fits and starts. The only consolation was the prospect of taking on Mr Shark in our free time.

The first one to be enticed on that Monday straightened the hook again and departed in some haste. A second one cleverly nibbled at the bait, took it without taking the hook and departed with it totally ignoring the verbal abuse and seaman like obscenities that followed him. I wanted to catch up with my writing and I occupied myself in my cabin for a couple of hours. When I arrived back on the poop deck later, I found the bloodthirsty lot hacking another five-foot long shark to pieces to add to their souvenirs.

As we finished the evening meal, the engines came to life with an ironic cheer from the deckhands. The weather had become warm and sunny with the sea as calm as a millpond, hardly a ripple, but as we headed south for Rio the temperature started to drop.

It was just after dark when we arrived off Rio on the evening of Tuesday 8th October. The news was that the Pilot would not be coming aboard to take us in until daybreak so there was nothing for it but to steam slow ahead around the bay all night.

Surprise! Surprise! I started my stint on the wheel as the Pilot boat came alongside, and it fell to me to take her in. With fingers crossed I uttered a little prayer to the patron saint of engines as I took the heading from the Pilot. In some ways I was lucky, for the wheelhouse is a good vantage point on a ship and as we sailed into Rio that morning, it was absolutely beautiful and the scenery was breathtaking. Sugar Loaf Mountain loomed in front of us with the wires of cable cars clearly visible in the early morning clearness. I imagined the views from the top must be stunning.

The skyscrapers that made up the main architecture of the city were dwarfed by the backdrop of the mountains and there, on the highest peak, was the famous statue of Christ with arms outstretched. It stood about thirty metres high, but from our position so far below it looked to be small in perspective.

Night-time however, was the best time to view it for it was lit up in the dark. With no other light in its near vicinity, the single illumination made it appear from below for all the world as if Christ was standing in his heaven, looking protectively down over everyone. It truly was an awe-inspiring sight and I was totally entranced with the magnificent natural beauty of the surroundings.

I was too entranced. For a quizzical disapproving glance from the Pilot suddenly made me realize that I was a degree or two off course and my attention to my steering could have been better so I had to tear my eyes away from the scenery and concentrate on the compass before we ourselves became a part of that scenery. We navigated the entrance to the harbour to proceed up river some way before the Pilot signalled stop engines to anchor midstream.

As soon as we were anchored and I was walking back aft, I was amazed to find that it was seven o'clock and I had been at the helm for three hours. More than a little bemused as to why I had not been relieved by my watchmate after my allotted two hour stint, I found that, the crew had been put on standby and he, being a young ordinary seaman, had not been allowed to come and relieve me at the helm. No one had bothered to tell me. But, thanks to the beauty of my surroundings, three hours had never passed so quickly.

Having fetched a welcome cuppa from the mess, I stretched my legs along the poop deck to relieve the stiffness in my legs after such a lengthy spell of steering. As I leaned over the rail, I looked down into the clear water and saw four ray fish put on a spectacular display as they glided gently along. They had about a three-foot wingspan each and gave the impression of four spacecraft or UFO's majestically flying through the water.

We had been at anchor for an hour when another Pilot came aboard to conduct us to our berth at Governor's Island. The discharge of a small parcel of cargo began almost at once, and was completed in the early hours of Thursday 10th October, which allowed us to catch the morning tide. Such was the communication between the upper deck and the lower deck that very often it was only by chance that we would be aware of the next port of call. On that occasion all I knew was we were travelling south and it wasn't until the following day it became generally known that we were headed for Rio Grande do Sul. As we progressed south we kept the coastline within sight for virtually all of the journey and the weather deteriorated. It became windy and showery which gave a little respite from the previous sweltering conditions.

Two days out I saw my second giant manta ray. We passed the enormous specimen very close on the starboard quarter and I stared at it spellbound, watching the tips of its massive wings slapping the sea as it rode with such grace and style on the crest of the waves. It was a magnificent creature with its dark triangular body spread like a blanket across the surface of the water as if guarding it from any possible harm, like a mother hen protecting her chicks.

We hove to off Rio Grande do Sul on Sunday 13th October to await the arrival of the Pilot. He didn't keep us waiting long and, although the sea around us was calm, there was a patch of rough water just off the harbour entrance. The Pilot first headed our bows towards it then at the last minute cleverly skirted around it and the second we were beyond it he ordered the helmsman hard to starboard and we swung sharply and entered safely into the harbour.

He explained that the reason for the shoal of water cutting up rough was because of submerged rocks just below the surface. The helmsman told that information to us when he finally came back to the mess once we had anchored about a mile up stream. Thank God our engines hadn't failed, I thought. Yet again, I hadn't touched the wheel heading in to a harbour and once again, everything had run smoothly.

* * *

Claps of thunder and streaks of lightning awoke me with a start in the early hours of Monday morning. It was the most spectacular display I had ever witnessed before or since. All the fireworks experts in the world would be hard put to match such a wonderful display. I knelt on my bunk to see what was going on and as I peered through the porthole it was reminiscent of Dante's Inferno. Sheet lightning lit the sky from an icy black to a red glow as flashes from afar died away. Fork lightning was sizzling down from high, seemingly to lightly touch the sea and surrounding hillsides with the tips of its fingers before it vanished to make room for the next one.

All that while simultaneously long, thin, white streaks flashed across the sky horizontally, accompanied by the drumbeats of thunder as it rolled away in the distance. All of what was happening in the sky was doubled by the reflection being mirrored upside down in the calm placid water, which made the whole scene even more spectacular.

I knelt at the porthole enraptured by the brilliant natural display, which would outshine anything that man could muster. The thought did however occur to me that amidst all of that spectacular display, I was sitting on a virtual powder keg; namely on a steel vessel loaded with thousands of tons of high-octane aviation fuel; sparks were to be avoided at all costs, as we could be blown into the next galaxy. The storm continued unabated for over half an hour and then it stopped as quickly as it had started. I had knelt glued to my viewpoint, a little scared to crawl back into my bunk until it was all over.

The Pilot returned aboard early the next day to see us alongside. The quay was very long, lined with ships of all nationalities and sizes. A space existed amidst the line of vessels and with accomplished skill, the Pilot manoeuvred us in without any undue haste, fuss or bother. Again only part cargo was to be discharged, most of which was done throughout the night. That normally would have allowed us to slip ashore for an hour or two in the evening but our berth was too far from anything or anywhere of interest so the chance passed us by and we were on our way back to Rio de Janeiro on the morning tide.

On two occasions during the passage up, the engines lived up to their reputation and each time we drifted for about an hour and a half. The unsettled weather we had experienced on the outward journey persisted on the return trip until we neared Rio.

Arriving on the afternoon of 19th October, we sailed without a Pilot into the harbour and anchored for about half an hour until the Pilot came to take charge and bring us alongside. The berth we had been allocated that time was, to everyone's delight, much nearer to the city, and virtually everyone put in for a large sub.

Washed, scrubbed and changed I went ashore with the three ordinary seamen and though I was still friendly with Paddy, he then tended to associate with the other petty officers i.e. the Chippy and the Pumpman since his elevation from the rank and file.

The dock road extended for about a mile before we walked into the outskirts of the town. There were lots of smiling people out and about in the warm, balmy, early evening, which gave a friendly atmosphere to the place. As we walked on into the town itself we explored the streets and alleyways and stumbled upon a large souvenir shop, little knowing what our accidental find would lead to and what pleasure was in store.

Over the door of the shop hung the sign 'Danny and Frank's Souvenirs.' Inside it was a veritable Aladdin's Cave with a multitude of articles ideal for souvenirs and presents. Other members of our crew who had also stumbled on to the place were already buying goods to take home to family, friends and girlfriends. There was such an array, you were spoilt for choice. Amongst the many presents I purchased were four ornamental trays made of a highly polished wood and inlaid in their centres were beautiful pictures assembled entirely out of multicoloured butterfly wings.

Every member of the crew present was laden down with parcels of all different shapes and sizes. I had spent most of my sub and, in one respect, I was glad for I couldn't carry another parcel. "Danny and Frank have done well out of the crew of the '*Nacella*,'" I thought.

When everyone had either spent up or had purchased enough, we headed back towards the entrance of the shop. As we reached the door however, the shop's owner Frank made himself known to us. He thanked us for our custom and offered to run us back to the ship to save carrying our purchases. I was never known to look a gift horse in the mouth so we collected not only our own parcels, but also most of them from our other crewmembers and put them into the boot of Frank's luxurious big Packard Sedan, then we piled in ourselves. As we approached the dock gates, Frank offered to wait while we took the presents aboard and said that he would run us back into town. Although we were almost broke, we thought "Why not?" All the parcels were dumped on to Paddy's old bunk in my cabin to be sorted later, and we were back in the Packard in minutes.

By that time it was eight o'clock, and when we arrived back at Frank's 'Emporium' (it was more, much more than just a shop really), he pointed to a bar and suggested that if we would wait in there until he had finished we could go for a drink. We desperately counted what remained of our subs and found that we had got enough left for a couple of beers each.

By half past ten our money had long since run out and we feared that Frank had forgotten about us. Just as we decided to make a move to head back to the ship, a shop assistant appeared and explained that the boss was waiting for us outside the shop. Frank apologised for the delay claiming that he had been very busy and urged us to get into the car, "I will make up for it, we are off to see the sights," he said.

As we drove through the city, which at that hour was still teeming with people who were not yet ready for bed, he pointed out the important buildings and features of interest. Then we headed out along the beach with its promenade lined with luxurious hotels and miles of the golden sands of the magnificent Copacabana.

Onwards we sped almost silently in the luxury of the Packard and headed towards the mountains. In what seemed to us no time at all he stopped the car close behind the statue of Christ. It was a spectacular view standing thirty metres high illuminated and solitary in the sky as though hanging in space.

As we climbed higher into the mountains the engine purred softly like a kitten (I wished we could take it back for the 'Nacella'), we came upon a clearing in the woods. A flat plateau with lots of parked cars and crowds of people, many were sitting at picnic tables eating and drinking. Frank sat us at one of the empty tables and made off towards a large open sided building from which came the smell of wood smoke and exciting cooking with the glow of a vast barbecue. He returned after a few minutes with a massive bone that had juicy meat all around it along with salad, bread rolls and butter, and we attacked it with relish. Then followed an incredible thick, juicy barbecued steak for each of us, the size of which I had never seen before or since. It was so juicy, succulent and tender our mouths were literally watering. It was then washed down with ice-cold ale from a large stone jar.

A feast fit for a king, especially compared to the plain fare we had been fed over the past months. There was far too much for a normal meal but it was so delicious with its strong barbecue flavour it was impossible to resist. For the next few weeks I dreamt about that food. Frank may well have been the happiest of us; he obviously enjoyed the spectacle of the four of us so appreciative of the food.

To say that we walked back to the car is an understatement. I well recall holding my belly; it felt so full as I sank back into the luxury of the Packard's upholstery. We drove on, higher into the mountains, round horseshoe and hairpin bends on the edge of cliffs with the sea far below.

As we climbed higher still, the air became cooler, thinner and fresher. The car, a credit to Packard, took the mountain roads with the ease of an eagle on a thermal upstream. Arriving at a small hostelry, probably the highest pub in Rio, we stopped and got out for a look, but unfortunately, the pub itself was closed. Opposite was a waterfall that cascaded down the mountain with panoramic views on all sides; it was a beautiful spot even at that time of night. I tried to imagine just what it would be like to sit and relax with an ice-cold beer on a warm summer's night in that idyllic spot.

Higher and higher we continued until Frank pulled onto a grass verge. We had reached the summit of the range. Again we stretched our legs. There were picnic tables dotted all around, obviously a popular spot. As we looked down over the edge, the whole vista of the city lights laid spread out at our feet, it was terrific in the darkness from that height but it must be absolutely breathtaking in the daylight.

It took far less time to descend and soon we found ourselves at 2.00am at the dock gates, dog-tired but replete in the knowledge that we'd had one of the most memorable evenings of our lives. Thanking Frank we explained that cash was in very short supply but was there anyway we could repay him for his kindness and hospitality. Smiling he said, "It's been my pleasure. I've enjoyed your company and if you really feel the need to repay me, then please tell all your friends about my shop, that is all I ask." And as quickly as he had appeared in the doorway of his Aladdin's Cave, so he was gone. Next day, Sunday, was one great anticlimax as we pinched ourselves: but it had not been a dream.

When we headed out to sea on the morning of the 21st October, the temperature began to soar into the hundreds, and the next nine days were to be some of the most uncomfortable it was my misfortune to spend. With the heat from the sun and the heat rising from the engines below, the cabins became unbearable.

Attached to the bulkhead in our cabins was the usual small electric fan that was practically useless; it just wafted the hot air around. The blowers, which were meant to provide cool air, blew hot air instead and were better turned off. Sleep was virtually impossible and even the steel bunk rails were too hot to hold for more than a few seconds.

What sleep did come was through exhaustion; when you woke it was in a pool of your own sweat. Half an hour was the average duration of each restless heat laden nap before waking soaked with your tongue sticking to the roof of your mouth. Given that everyone still had to complete eight hours work in the full heat of the sun each day for me the situation could not continue. We burnt during the day and swam in sweat at night. I had a bright idea: hammocks were the answer.

I got a bail of duck canvas and some rope off Paddy and made one. I gave the remainder of the bail to three other shipmates who wished to make one too. Within hours I was the hammock king of the '*Nacella*.' Strung from the awning spars on the boat deck, hammocks were a great improvement and for the first night in a week I had a reasonable night's sleep under the stars.

Strong currents sweep along the South American coast in a northerly direction and aided by the flow, the '*Nacella*' was at times able to achieve fourteen knots: a wonder to behold in that apology for a ship with a clapped out engine. The additional speed also created a bit of a draught that helped the conditions, especially at night.

It had taken sixteen days on the southern trip, but due to favourable currents the return journey took a mere twelve. The weather became contrary and a sudden storm was welcomed as the rain poured down, cooling not only the ship, but the crew as well. Those occasions were the only times I used my cabin for sleeping purposes. The next day following the storm, it returned to the previous high temperatures.

We left Trinidad behind on the port beam, to arrive off Cardon, Venezuela on Sunday afternoon, 3rd November. That particular trip down the South American coast had been remarkable; with the spectacular firework display Mother Nature had provided for us as well as the wonderful experiences in Rio. The engine gave us no trouble on our return northward and I had some wonderful night's sleep out in the fresh air. The only fly in the ointment was the incessant heat of the day.

I took her into the anchorage once again without any mishap. My jinx theory was beginning to be disproved, or was that wishful thinking? Two of the tanks failed inspection and had to be cleaned out but by eight o'clock we were alongside ready to receive part cargo. Only a very small amount came aboard for eight o'clock the following evening saw us tied up and secure in Willemstad. Nowhere could I see the '*London Loyalty*,' but that would have been far too much of a coincidence to meet my brother for a second time had she been there.

Immediately after we had tied up, a large pontoon barge appeared below our bow. Evidently a sister ship of the Shell fleet had lost an anchor along with the whole of her anchor chain so each company ship, on arrival, had to give a section of their anchor chain to her until it had all been replaced.

The Chippy had the responsibility of lowering the anchor onto the pontoon where workmen then unshackled it. Once that was completed, the Chippy slowly let out more chain while the men on the pontoon coiled it up and down their deck in a snakelike fashion until the first shackle appeared which was then undone and our anchor replaced on to the end. Once finished we then heaved our anchor back home and the barge made off with the section of our chain to wherever the other Shell tanker was berthed.

How can a ship lose the whole of its anchor and chain? I wondered, then I recalled the fiasco that we had endured coming out of Lagos when our chain had been dragged beneath the ship and I stopped wondering. Quite easily was the answer. It was all go and at 11.00pm that night, we departed through the pontoon bridge and narrow entrance, which appeared even narrower at night. I was really glad to turn in at three o'clock that morning as we were finally secured at Bullen Bay.

Loading commenced at once and the bulk of the cargo had been pumped aboard, which allowed us to slip our moorings at 8.00pm that evening. Once more fortune placed me at the wheel but for once, that was the best place to be; it was November 5th and as I stood at the helm slipping out of Bullen Bay bound for Rio again, another electric storm was raging. Was Mother Nature aware of the English tradition in celebrating Guy Fawkes Night? Yet again she put on a pretty good show as the storm raged around.

In an electrical storm at sea, the wheelhouse is an exceptional vantage point for you have a fairly panoramic view of the lightning display and unlike those at stations out on deck, you were not getting wet. And while the pyrotechnic display was well worth watching, the rain that teemed down made it a little uncomfortable for those who were out there.

We made quite good headway and we passed Trinidad on the morning of Thursday 7th November. The engine, it must be said, had outperformed itself since we had left Rio, only to revert to its previous norm at 7.00am the next morning.

It took fifteen hours to cure the fault and, while the crew never heard or had even the remotest knowledge of the atmosphere in the officers' quarters, we only had to look at the Skipper's face to judge his state of mind. It's strange how a small number of men can live on the small confined space of a ship and travel into vast expanses of lonely oceans together; one half living totally different lives to the other.

As we drifted a small shark only two feet long appeared around our stern. Bait was not offered because it was so small and we didn't want to frighten it. We wanted its mummy or daddy.

During the next three days the engine failed a further three times for the sum total of twelve to fourteen hours. I began to wonder if having to push against the currents contributed at all towards the engine's failures and it did pose the question of how long the company would accept the continuous stoppages.

I was taking a nap on the Sunday afternoon when during one of the enforced delays, the lads caught a big shark, about seven feet long. They had long since given up on their gruesome need for souvenirs and were then throwing them back alive, but that one they wanted photographs of before they returned him. I was put on a shake for it appeared that I alone had still got film in a camera.

After the stoppage on the Monday night we progressed with the engine performing as it should, going for a whole week before it failed again for a few hours the following Monday. With the weather having improved throughout the week, I had taken to sleeping in my hammock on the boat deck again, taking blankets and sheets as required. I found it exhilarating spending my nights under the stars breathing fresh sea air away from the stuffy cabin.

That idyllic period came to a sudden stop as the weather worsened a few days out of Rio. A heavy swell developed that caused waves to crash over the decks. Being fully loaded she lay low in the water and as the wind strengthened, it also carried an occasional spray up over the boat deck so my preferred bed had to be abandoned in favour of my cabin.

* * *

Rio greeted us with drizzly, cold weather reminiscent of England and a reminder that the holiday brochures tend to ignore the fact that Britain isn't the only country that has bad weather. We went without delay through the harbour entrance only to anchor for a couple of hours to await the convenience of the Pilot. It was 6.00am Friday 22nd November.

The Pilot came at eight o'clock and we hoisted the anchor to sail to our original berth on Governor's Island. "Who was the Governor? And for whom and for what did he govern?" I pondered as we tied up quickly and easily for once. I never did find the answer to those questions.

As the crew settled down to being in port, especially after the heavy seas we had been exposed to, the watches were stopped for the duration of our stay in port so everyone was on daywork except one. Paddy brought orders from the Mate detailing me as nightwatchman again. When I presented myself to the Mate's cabin, I asked for my specific orders for the night. "Just keep your bloody eyes open for thieves," was his brusque reply. "God! That was a lifetime ago," I thought, "He doesn't forget, does he?" but I thought I detected the faintest of little smirks at the corner of his lips. I must have been forgiven, else why trust me with the job again? But it was for only the one night.

We sailed the next morning and got just clear of the entrance to the harbour when once more the curse of the 'Nacella' struck, again we were drifting, not in any danger, but very frustrating for the long-suffering engineers who were still attempting to maintain an engine that should have been in the scrapyard years ago. The cycle of comic farce however continued; the engine was fixed and within an hour and a half we headed southward again to arrive off Santos at six o'clock the next morning where we anchored.

I took the opportunity to grab an hour's sleep and I was surprised when I arose to a late breakfast to discover that we were fog bound. It was as thick as pea soup, visibility was down to a few yards and obviously there was no pilot. The engineers had decided that our enforced stay at the anchorage would be an ideal opportunity to carry out much needed improvements to our very sick engine. Sod's law of course prevailed, and the fog lifted shortly after I had surfaced. Our engine was still in bits as the Pilot arrived. He seemed an amiable character who laughed and joked with the Skipper and Mate on being told the news that he couldn't take us in. "I know the Skipper of a good tug," he said with a smile as he returned to his launch and disappeared towards the shore.

Later, making sure that the engine was back in good order, we sent a message on the ship to shore radio beckoning the Pilot for his services again, and they were certainly needed; the river twisted and turned around a sharp horseshoe bend followed by a T-junction. I was happy to see someone else had the responsibility of taking us through that extremely difficult passage. But the fun was about to begin.

On our arrival at a quay lined with ships of all nations, we proceeded to anchor midstream ahead of a ship already at anchor. I failed to see the need to anchor midstream for within a half hour we upped anchor again to occupy a berth downstream that we had passed on the way up. With the Pilot still onboard and the anchor stowed, the ship swung around, eventually lying athwart-ships across the river just as we had done on leaving Lagos. Then the current took hold and we began to drift downstream broadside on towards the stern of another ship anchored midstream. There was little or no room for manoeuvre, which caused some consternation for those on the bridge. Had we started the engine we could have run aground on the banks of the river, the only solution was to slam the helm hard over, hoping that the momentum from the current would provide steerage.

Slowly, very slowly we began to swing and straighten up and the order was given, "Slow ahead" that brought her head around from the riverbank, but more importantly it brought the stern around to finally miss the other vessel by the minimum of space. Just a matter of two or three feet separated us; many a heart stopped pounding, not least of all the Captain and the Pilot. The possibility of sparks flying as the steel plates rubbed, could have led to horrendous consequences for both ships as we were loaded with thousands of tons of petrol and high flash point octane. With no more ado, and no doubt much wiping of sweaty brows, we finally came alongside in an orderly fashion.

As we had sampled the delights of Rio, we hoped Santos would prove to be as rewarding. There was only one way to find out so we took a sub and walked along the dock road to the town. I was disappointed both with the town itself which sported no elegance or quaintness, and with the local folk who did not display the same vivacity and cheerfulness of their near neighbours. It was with an air of 'Que Sera Sera' that I made my way back to the ship. You can't win them all. I had been ashore, had a drink and got away from the ship for a short while, and perhaps the comparison with Rio was a little unfair.

The ship that was anchored in midstream with which we had almost come to blows had departed. Was that incidental or had they got out of our way while their luck held?

The trip back up to Rio was short and uneventful; we had left Santos on the 26th November. I was at the helm as we anchored for half an hour or so before tying up at the same berth closer to town as the last time. The proximity of the berth to the town allowed those who wished to enjoy once again the happy atmosphere of that carefree city.

Each evening found most of us taking advantage of the friendly bars and enjoying the company of the locals. Unfortunately we felt that Frank's shop should not be revisited for we had bought enough presents already and we didn't want to impose on his good nature again. We had however, kept our part of the bargain for by then the whole crew plus many others we met had heard of Danny and Frank's of Rio.

After we sailed on 30th November I took to slinging my hammock on the boat deck to escape the heat of my cabin once again. Strange to relate, the engine behaved impeccably, just as it had done on the previous trip up from Rio; thus strengthening my notion that the strong flowing currents assisting our passage may cause less strain on them. Either that or it was a coincidence.

Four days out from Trinidad, for that is where we were bound, the showers began again, heavy on at least one occasion during the night and I dragged my wet bedding back to my cabin. It was only a temporary respite for on the 10th December, the temperature soared under a cloudless sky to return to boiler oven conditions.

As I woke from my hammock early the next morning, I caught sight of the coast of Trinidad and we sailed within sight of it for four or five hours. The coastline had become familiar as we had passed it many times during the voyage, but that was the first time we had made port there.

There was a narrow channel between two islands that would shorten the passage by hours and the Captain decided that was to be our course. We passed between massive cliffs resplendent with greenery on either side, it was generally agreed amongst us deckhands that with a dodgy engine like ours it was a bit risky and there was many a sigh of relief as we left the vertical greenery and came out into the open sea. Within two hours we had anchored off a long wooden jetty at Point Fortin and made an easy docking, under the Pilot's guidance, less than an hour later.

Leaving the greenery of that lovely island, which had been a delight to our eyes after the blue of the sky and the sea for so many days was hard, since we were also carrying the memories of a number of ice-cold rum and cokes, which had been a delight to our palates. We slipped back out to sea on Friday 13th December.

Nothing untoward transpired on the short trip to Curacao and, given the favourable currents, I was awakened in my hammock by the sound of the engine slowing at two o'clock on Sunday morning. I recognised the lights of the town and lay half asleep and comfortable. I decided that I was going to stay there until I was called to stations. As the engine stopped, the ship began to swing and a sudden strong gust of wind almost blew me from the hammock but, still unwilling to abandon the comfort of my bed, I pulled the blankets back around me determined to get some more sleep.

It was fate that decided I was to sleep no more in that most comfortable of all beds for a sudden downpour saw me running, with sheets and blankets, for the dryness of my cabin. In my haste I left my hammock hanging there and on my return to it the following night, some misguided idiot had shredded it with a knife and left it in ribbons. No one admitted to the senseless act and I never found out who had done it.

I sat with a couple of the lads chewing the fat with a cup of tea on the poop deck at six o'clock that morning. The topic, which was never far away in any conversation, was how long it was to be before we headed for home. With a 'whoof' it became big game fishing time for lazily swimming immediately beneath us was a large shark.

It took only seconds for the line to be brought to hand and for the Second Cook to scurry to the galley to return with a large piece of bacon rind. I had learnt many of the rudiments of coarse fishing in my youth in the canals and pools around the Midlands and learnt that some species had certain preferences for certain baits but sharks, it seemed, would go for almost anything.

That particular six-foot shark certainly appeared to have a liking for bacon rind for as soon as it touched the water he dived at it. The speed in which he took the bait took us unawares so he wasn't hooked properly and he wriggled off, leaving the bait still there, so we pulled it in to make it more secure on the hook. Having felt the hook we expected him to back off or swim off, but the smell of the bacon rind must have been a far greater temptation to him so it was with much glee for us that he hung around for another go. He was much more wary though as the bait was lowered again to the waters surface, but he gave the impression that he wasn't a quitter.

Other members of the crew gathered around to enjoy the sport, readily observing, "Look, there's another, and another," finally we counted four of them, all with the same bacon rind in mind. Amongst them was a big fellow, at least seven-foot long, and as they all circled the bait it was as if it was the sharks equivalent of musical chairs. When would the music stop? And who would grab the chair?

Slowly the monster began to adopt a more positive attitude and came to within inches of the bait only to turn away. It created lots of frustration amongst the crew and the air was rife with bad language as they continued to circle; finally one cleverly took the bait without taking the hook. What was said then, is not printable. No more bait was available as the galley was busy preparing the first meal of the day.

Once breakfast was over however, the Cook obligingly produced more bacon rind, which appeared to be one of the favourite dishes for a shark, and so we were soon back to the big game hunting. Still they swam around, all four of them were very wary until one threw caution to the wind and took the lot. He didn't get away and was heaved onboard and hung up on the awning spar.

The hook was rebaited with the intent of going for the big one. Suddenly, from about thirty-foot out he turned, stopped and faced the bait. It was new tactics on his part and it became obvious that he was going to go for it. The rail was lined with lads intent and eager to witness the take. Excitement rose and adrenaline rushed as the shark came in at full throttle. At that precise moment, without warning, the propellers began to churn the water. The fish slammed on the breaks to stop just two or three feet from the bait, turned and in a flash he had vanished.

Everyone groaned; it was as though each one of us were captured in a bubble of frustration and anguish as the bubble burst. The frustration turned into laughter with the sound of someone's voice saying "The only time this 'f*****g' ship goes is when you don't want it to."

Entrance into Willemstad was always interesting given its aforementioned narrowness. The pontoon bridge that opened to allow the ship's passage provided a ready assembly, as the local folk gathered on both sides waiting to cross. It was decided to leave the shark that we had caught hanging from the stern to see what reaction it would cause amongst the locals as we passed through.

The pilot launch came out and both the Pilot and the helmsman showed much interest in the prize. With the Pilot safely aboard, the launch came to the stern. The helmsman smiled up at us and pointed to the shark, "Very good to eat," he said. "Would you give him to me?" he asked cheekily.

On reflection we couldn't very well dump the shark in such an enclosed harbour, in fact it may even be illegal. On the other hand, we couldn't leave him hanging there smelling for what may be a couple of days. So we agreed to give it to him and lowered it into his launch . With grinning teeth and many thanks and salutations, he soon disappeared back to his moorings. That night I related the incident to the barman at the seamen's home who roared with laughter. "Shark is a delicacy in these parts," he said, "He will get a very good price for it." "Well at least the shark has done someone some good," I thought.

The loading of our cargo was delayed for another tanker was being loaded at the berth to which we had been assigned. After shifting ship once she had gone, it was four days before our part cargo was onboard so it was a good job we had got rid of that fish. The delay had occurred because the storage tanks ashore were empty.

* * *

Again on Wednesday 18th December it was my trick on the wheel bound for Bullen Bay, but my relief had taken over just as we were about to dock, and I had to go to stations to help to tie up. At four o'clock the next morning we cast off again, heading for Cardon. Little time had been wasted as we just picked up small parcels of cargo. Christmas loomed and speculation on where it would be spent was rife. It was certain that it would be spent somewhere no one wished to be. There was not enough time to get to Rio for that, apart from home would have been the second best place to spend it.

It took just ten hours to get to Cardon only to find that there were no empty berths. The prospect of an early turnaround was thwarted and we swung on the anchor for a day and a half before the Pilot came out to take us in during the early hours of Friday 20th December.

Further delay was caused by a malfunction of the shore installation pumps, which operated at half of their normal pressure. Those delays were soon forgotten though as the crew got an early Christmas present. As had happened to me on a previous occasion, Father Christmas had come early for the news flashed around the ship that we were homeward bound.

The next day, Saturday 21st December, we cast off fully loaded with various types and grades of fuels in separate tanks. There was a new glint in the eyes, a more positive purpose to the step and even the Chief Engineer seemed almost normal. We knew that the crossing at that time of the year would be cold and rough, but that meant nothing; we were going home. And so it proved to be for almost immediately it became cold with heavy winds building the sea into a large heavy swell.

The ship rolled and pitched. We had all seen worse and it wasn't sufficient enough to spoil Christmas day, which was spent quite pleasantly, but with a lack of a sufficient quantity of beer. No one could get enough to get even a little bit squiffy. The only reaction I got from the beer and the combination of sudden coldness was that it made me piddle a lot.

The seas calmed, the wind died away and turned to pleasant sunny weather, but it was still a little chilly considering the temperatures to which we had been accustomed. Time dragged as watch followed watch until 1st January 1958, when the Azores appeared on the horizon.

Almost immediately the weather changed back with cold winds and rain and the seas became mountainous. We battled through a gale for two days then took a more southerly course in an attempt to run out of it. The seas crashed over the decks from what appeared to be a mountain of water. The move southwards worked and eventually, after two more uncomfortable days, the weather calmed and the original course was resumed. Although she was still rolling and pitching it was less angry than it had been in the gale.

I shudder to think what would have become of us if the engines had failed us during those hectic days. Shudder I would even more, if the events of the next few days could have been predicted. For the weather turned extremely bad again on Monday 6th January. I awoke as the ship rolled and pitched more violently than ever before. The engine had failed again, not due to a mechanical defect this time, but a fuel supply blockage. With the yawing and rolling, the collected sludge in the bottom of a fuel tank had been swirled around and had mixed in with the fuel, which in turn blocked the filters and the supply pipes.

No fuel, no steam, no engine, no steerage, nowhere to go. We were left entirely at the mercy of the elements as she drifted all day with the wind angrily howling through the rigging, and the waves crashing across our decks. I wondered if that was what had happened to the '*Llandaff*' but being almost a brand new ship as the '*Llandaff*' was then, there should not have been such a build up of sludge. Our plight was similar, but we were not in danger of coming up on the rocks. Our battle that time was with the sea itself.

A plan of action from the 'think tank' was about to commence and, as it will be seen, it was quite hazardous for certain members of the crew. First the remaining contaminated fuel had to be drained from the tank into the double bottoms to allow the sludge and waste to be cleaned. That was a job for the engine-room staff. Once drained, a large steel plate was unbolted from the side of the tank to allow access. It also allowed many fumes to escape and then three or four men went in with masks on.

Eighty buckets of muck came out before the tank was resealed. But fresh fuel oil could not be transferred from the reserve tank because the pumps were dead and we had no steam pressure to start them. It was estimated that we would need three ton of the stuff to get everything going again. Steam was exactly what we had needed on the '*Llandaff*,' which the tug had supplied to us.

Had we been a tanker carrying crude oil there would have been no alternative but to call for tugs, and I would have had to experience the saga of the '*Granford*' all over again. We however were carrying different kinds and grades of fuel oils, which was the reason for only loading small parcels in different ports. Luckily, in just two of our tanks, there was a fuel oil that would be suitable for our needs.

Halfway along the starboard alleyway aft was a small ventilation pipe, which came up from the recently emptied fuel tank. The problem was the fuel we needed was in two tanks on the fore deck, just in front of the bridge. The question was how to get the three tons out of one for'ard tank into the fuel tank at the rear end of the ship?

That's when the fun started for us, the watch on duty. What other watch could it possibly be but mine? The wheelman was put on standby and sent to keep lookout on the wing of the bridge as he wasn't required to steer; thereby releasing the real lookout to come and assist us. So together with Paddy and the Pumpman, we gathered all the canvas fire hosepipes we could find and put one end down into the small ventilation pipe.

We then rolled them out one by one, and connected them together and took them for'ard along the alleyway. We were not able to run them down along the deck itself, which would have been the shortest route because of the waves that were crashing over. Instead, we had to lead them around the fore part of the after housing, all along the main deck flying bridge, around the midship housing and down to the tank on the foredeck in front of the bridge. Then two planks were lashed together, one above the other, on to the tank rails to form a protection barrier against the heavy seas, which were constantly breaking over the ship to lessen the main force of the waves before they hit us.

We unscrewed the small round cap in the centre of the tank lid and fed the inlet pipe of a small hand pump into it, then connected the end of the hosepipes on to the outlet and lashed the pump into position on the top of the tank immediately above the inlet. Four of us, in icy water up to our waists, battled to hold the pump in position. The planks rigged to the tank rails did their job and broke the full force of the waves that continually crashed against it but the water then swirled around them and hit us first, still quite strongly, before they hit the fore part of the bridge and bounced back to hit us again from behind.

The water was freezing cold as two of us held the pump steady while the other two pumped like madmen. Nothing happened until we remembered that the pump needed to be primed. As the cap was removed from the priming chamber, the sea decided to give us a hand, an extra large wave came over and filled the priming chamber up for us, but at the same time it washed the cap away.

Paddy dashed to the centre castle to return with a wooden plug that was hammered into the aperture. Then, working in atrocious conditions, we started to pump again; pressure at last began to build, then the wooden plug flew out and raw fuel streamed up into my face. My eyes began to burn and fortunately the tears began to flow which washed away most of the oil. Paddy grabbed the floating wooden plug before it got washed over the side and hammered it back in. We continued then with one man holding the pump steady, another held the plug in place by pressing all his weight onto it and two men, one on each side of the rocking handle, pumping up and down like crazy.

Gradually, the canvas hose began to fill and became round; the roundness began to slowly travel along its length at a snail's pace, but that in itself gave us hope and encouragement to carry on. "God! It's working, it's actually working!" We pumped on like we were in a frenzy and swapped around regularly as those pumping became tired.

Remembering that the oil had to travel three quarters of the ship's length, we had no way of knowing at any given moment how far along the pipes the oil had got or even if it was dripping down into the tank at the other end. It was only when we heard a cheer from one of the engineers we realised that it had just begun to reach the tank. It took over another hour and a half of constant pumping with the freezing water rising up and down sometimes over our shoulders as we bent over the pump before we got word that sufficient oil had been transferred.

After putting all the makeshift gear away, we stashed the hosepipes into the centre castle ready to be washed out next day. Our brains as well as our bodies were numb as the four of us like frozen, drowned rats made it back walking like zombies to the warmth of the accommodation where a hot shower and dry clothes transported us back into the human race.

I remembered once previously being swept along the deck by an ice-cold wave, also being soaked and almost washed away by freezing water while moving the gangway gear from a box on the 'Granford,' then being submerged in ice-cold coal dust laden sludge in the 'Granford's' holds and I had then just experienced that. No wonder that in future years I would feel very loath and reluctant to submerge myself into cold water again. It took about another four hours before enough steam was raised to start the engine, and the sound of those much-cursed engines coming back to life was like music to our ears. Our efforts had not been in vain.

The English coast appeared as a dark smudge on the horizon on the morning of Wednesday 8th January and as the weather calmed appreciably it was a pleasant thought that that smudge was Cornwall, where my favourite port of Falmouth lay. On we went past the Scillies and up through the Irish Sea, arriving at the Mersey Bar to anchor along with other vessels awaiting pilotage. No berth was available until Friday, which heightened the frustrations of the crew desperate to get ashore and go home.

During the next twenty-four hours the weather worsened; it blew to a force eight gale. For safety reasons, the anchor came aboard and the ship turned into the oncoming swell, with the engine ticking over to keep the bow into the storm. So we rode it out. Throughout the night it raged, and no pilot was going to risk his life coming out in such bad conditions.

Sunday saw an improvement with the winds abating and the seas less violent that enabled the anchor to be lowered again, but not for long. At eleven o'clock the Pilot came aboard to take us through the buoyed channel into the Mersey. At twelve o'clock the watch changed, giving me once again the doubtful privilege of bringing her into port. With the Liver building to starboard impassively observing everything that goes on, and Birkenhead to port, the scene on a dull January day was anything but impressive, especially after experiencing the magnificence of Rio and the other beautiful landfalls of the Caribbean.

But that was something special. We were coming home and the dismal, dreary, January Mersey somehow carried an almost magical air as Eastham lock came into view. That was when my watchmate came to relieve me at the helm to take us into the lock. That was all he did as we stayed in the lock until after he had been relieved at four o'clock. It was 4.45pm before we finally cleared the lock and entered into the Manchester ship canal.

The MV prefixing the 'Nacella' did not, in my opinion, stand for Motor Vessel, but Monster Vandal. For on passing two vessels moored in the canal the wash from the propeller set them rocking at their moorings and snapped a couple of their ropes. Wherever the 'Nacella' was, there was trouble.

Our destination was Stanlow where the mooring was a square basin off the main run of the canal into which we had to turn. This was difficult to manoeuvre when the basin was empty, but even more so when other vessels were already tied up there. The tugs awaited our arrival, and with lines being quickly and efficiently made fast, they began to turn us to head into the basin. Our stern went aground in the mud, which left us broadside on across the canal, effectively blocking all navigation both ways (We seemed to be in the habit of doing that).

The stern tug came up on to our quarter and with both her engines and ours at full speed ahead, we slipped off the mud moving both forwards and sideways at the same time and we collided with a Swedish tanker already moored alongside. Our bulwarks amidships and the stanchions were buckled badly, but fortunately no damage was inflicted upon our Swedish neighbour (perhaps they were built of stronger stuff) and even more important, there were no sparks. Ropes fore and aft were hurriedly scrambled ashore to secure a safe berth without further ado.

All but two thousand ton was discharged and everyone started to pack their gear when a further load was pumped into us bound for Belfast. There was absolute mayhem amongst the crew with many demanding to be paid off, but as the Mate explained, a quantity of the original cargo remained aboard, and the articles say that not until all the original cargo has been discharged can the crew be paid off unless, of course, it was at the company's discretion.

There was one consolation, the ship could not be taken out to foreign parts again once the discharge was completed, and after the discharge in Belfast we were bound for Falmouth. During that furore a shore gang had come onboard to fit a new cylinder to the engine. So our departure was delayed for the shore gang to finish the work. The Swedish ship left on Tuesday 14th to be replaced by a sister ship of the Shell fleet.

Our departure was then to be at 10.00am on Wednesday, but a thick blanket of fog delayed us again until four o'clock on the Thursday morning. Once the fog had cleared, it was a bright, frosty morning as she moved "slow astern," gently out of the basin, then all hell broke loose. Sparks and flames shot from the new cylinder as the engineers frantically stopped the engines. With little steerage and very little room, she swung around and our stern hit the stern of the other shell tanker. Once again heroic efforts were made to get ropes ashore and eventually we brought her safely alongside.

The collision caused further damage to the rails and stanchions on the boat deck, but again no apparent damage was inflicted upon the other ship. Our troubles were still not completely over for a couple of hours later the wire back spring snapped which then had to be replaced with a temporary rope while the deckhands spliced another eye into the wire spring.

The shore gang reappeared at about eight o'clock to put right whatever had gone wrong with the new cylinder. Soon everything was assumed to be satisfactory so we made another attempt to depart, and that time the entrance to the basin was negotiated without further mishap. One of the departing shore gang was heard to say, "Thank God they have got that bloody thing out at last." "Don't count your chickens," I thought, but we made it back down the canal OK.

We awaited the high tide before we entered the Eastam locks, and at 9.30am we cleared the Mersey bar. It is only a few hours for any ship to cross the Irish Sea to Belfast but the 'Nacella' lived up to her true reputation to the very end. An hour or so later we were drifting around without power for another hour and a half then only to continue at slow speed ahead once the engines were started again.

Whatever demonic forces possessed those engines, they refused to be expelled and still after six months, they played up to the last. We sighted Belfast at two o'clock on the Friday afternoon but it was not until eight o'clock before we went alongside to tie up immediately astern of the 'Empress of Scotland.' Later that night I learned that the 'Empress of Scotland' had been acquired by a German line and her next port of call would be somewhere in Germany for a refit. "What ship would I now be on if I had taken her when I was offered a berth on her?" I wondered.

As we had never called into Belfast before, several of us decided to take a look around the city. Snow had fallen heavily during the day and with a northerly wind blowing, it was bitter cold. After we had visited a couple of local hostelries, we wandered into a local dance hall but not for long. It was not my scene.

Before we had gone ashore the word was passed around that the 'Nacella' was due to make its last scheduled departure with us as her crew later that night. We cast off at midnight; nothing had been done to the engines so it was slow ahead for Falmouth as indeed it was during the whole of the passage down. Whether it was a conscious decision and the Captain refused to take a chance to run the engine at full speed or whether it was because they were in such poor condition they couldn't be run any faster I don't know, but it was slow ahead all the way.

On our way down, a large Esso tanker passed quite close. "I wonder what it would be like on one of those." I spoke my thoughts out loud to no one in particular, but one of the older ABs replied, "You don't want to go there," he said, "they are nothing but Eat, Sleep, Shit and Overtime, that's why they are called ESSO."

Our problems were still not at an end; prior to entering Falmouth dock, the ship had to be rendered gas free. So along with the Bosun and Pumpman, four of us were detailed to form a butterworthing gang, me amongst them. For three days and three nights we worked non-stop, steaming and washing down every single tank. First we put a short length of the heavy hose into the tank to wash the top part, then lowered it towards the middle and finally almost to the bottom. The only rests that were taken were between the drops and that only allowed for short catnaps of twenty to thirty minutes. Midnight on 22nd January saw the task completed and we moved "Slow ahead," to the anchorage.

After I had showered, I literally collapsed on my bunk and to all intent and purpose died. It was the noise of the engine starting that brought me back to consciousness at exactly midday. I had slept the clock around. As the tugs were made fast, the engines were stopped and to no one's surprise, when we attempted to restart them they acted as they had throughout the past six months and flatly refused. So without any hindrance from the by then no doubt notorious '*Nacella*,' the tugs made an exceedingly professional job and brought us safely alongside under their own steam.

Once showered and dressed for shore and with my suitcase packed, I presented myself for pay off. At four o'clock on Thursday 23rd January, the crew of the '*Nacella*' walked through the dock gates to the nearby Falmouth railway station. There were few glances back as most of us were thankful to be saying our final goodbye. The good folk who drove past in their shiny cars were totally unaware of the trials and tribulations encountered by the lads of the Merchant Navy to provide the fuel for their pride and joy.

We rattled along the branch line from Falmouth to pick up the main line at Truro where, after we shook hands all round, I caught the train to Birmingham while the rest of my shipmates were bound for Liverpool. As the train click-clacked through the delightful West Country, I relaxed and recalled the last six months during which I had added more places to my ever expanding list of countries visited throughout the world, and had experienced probably more of life than the vast majority.

I reflected on sailing across the Atlantic, seeing all of its moods, from millpond calm to violent gales; the Caribbean in its sweating heat, in a ship whose engines were reluctant to participate. Meeting my brother Roy in a small bar on a tiny island, and seeing more of Rio in a different way on one night than most tourists would see in the whole of their stay.

I had wondered many times if the engine would stay the course, or if the engineers could work another miracle. Finally, battling against the elements in mid-Atlantic as fuel oil was transferred from a tank on the foredeck to the engine, soaked and freezing. And, with a little shudder, the recollection of the sinister police in Lagos, which in turn had led to meeting Tiny and Colossus; I remembered them with a smile, I wondered what they were doing now. All those thoughts were with me as we rumbled into New Street Station.

CHAPTER TWELVE

THE EMPRESS OF BRITAIN

(Of a Ghost, an Invisible Fire Station and a Self-Styled Plumber).

It was time to review my life. My last two voyages had covered a period of around sixteen months with just six weeks leave in between and they had been full of incident and stress. I was in need of respite and it was time to consider my future. The high seas were not the place for such serious consideration and a more prolonged time at home in a settled environment was called for. Home comforts and the normality of a shore life would, I thought, enable me to view objectively the best course to follow.

It is the little things that are taken for granted in a normal life, such as fresh milk and fruit, hot baths, a bed that remained stationary and certainly not least good food; those were no doubt the unconscious reasons for me not renewing my Pool contract.

After a couple of weeks of contemplation I found work with a local painting and decorating firm and settled back into the routine that I had thought to be a part of my past, never to be revisited. Work was plentiful, decorating the many council developments which were springing up everywhere at that time.

I renewed old acquaintancies. Mavis and Alan took me in tow on their visits to the club, where I soon learned of the monotony of playing Bingo, which had become all the rage whilst I had been away at sea. Fortunately the monotony was relieved by the many small wins I received.

Norman too had completed his National Service with the Brigade of Guards and he would join the three of us at the pop group concerts and entertainment that the club provided at the weekends. Those concerts had become very popular. He had also found work with the same firm that employed me and he made a very agreeable workmate whenever we found ourselves in the same gang.

Normality, routine and pleasant companions made for a satisfying existence while the weeks rolled by effortlessly into months. Almost nine months had elapsed since my home coming when, for some inexplicable reason, the spirit of the wanderlust began once again to disturb my sleep. The thought of foreign shores, cloudless blue skies, warm breezes and the sun glittering on a calm blue sea crept insidiously into my mind as the painting of doors and walls became automatic. I was somewhere else. I had forgotten the horror and danger of the mountainous seas of the North Atlantic and remembered only the dolphins at play and the flying fish that had scurried out of our way.

Nine pleasant and happy months had been my lot but the call of my mistress the sea began to beckon strongly and the prospect of a cold English winter finally hastened my decision to try to renew my contract with the Pool, and my acquaintance with the cruel sea. Never in my wildest fantasy could I envisage the feelings of excitement the Liverpool bound express evoked in me. Such was the call of the sea, and I was responding. It was in the blood and no doubt common to many of our island race that, by and large, I thought, made the best seamen.

Having booked into Gordon Smith's, I made my way to the Pool, and bumped into one of the '*Llandaff*' lads who gave me the bad news that jobs were very few and far between. "No chance," was the prompt response from the clerk to my request to reregister with the Pool. Try again in a few weeks was his advice. I felt extremely disappointed and returned to Smith's where I cancelled my accommodation and headed quickly back to Lime Street Station. There was nothing for it but to go home to sort out my next move.

After a dismal seven days more at home, I came to the decision to explore the possibility of trying elsewhere. Liverpool was not the only port in the land and my love affair with Falmouth and Cornwall was the deciding factor that found me on the Low Level Wolverhampton Station awaiting the 6.00am Cornishman express for Penzance. Twelve hours later I booked a room at Armyn House, the sailor's home adjacent to the Falmouth docks and the Pool office. The Pool was closed but it was not too late for the last house at the local cinema but perhaps because of tiredness through the journey I can't remember a thing about the show.

I presented myself bright and early to the Pool the next morning. The officials proved to be both pleasant and helpful, they most certainly could find me a berth but there were problems. Not being a native of Cornwall I had no permanent address within their catchment area. They could not reregister me until my records had been transferred to them.

"Liverpool," they said, would be contacted with a request for the forwarding of my records but, obviously, that would take time. There was then little for me to do other than await the outcome of the official request and the prospect of getting to know Falmouth a little better was certainly not as foreboding as hanging around Liverpool.

Fortunately the weather was good and I enjoyed the walks along the cliffs and lazing on the beaches and coves. Every day I called at the Pool to be told "No news yet." After five days, the very helpful clerk telephoned the Liverpool office to be informed that, as far as they were concerned, it was necessary for me to reregister as a seaman at Liverpool before my records could be released.

I fumed. Less than two weeks previously the Pool had no jobs and had refused to reregister my application, I then had a sixteen hour train journey to satisfy the whim of some self-important idiot at an expense I could ill afford. I felt sure that they were playing power games.

I arrived at Lime Street at 4.30am on a cold dismal day and caught a few hours sleep in the warm waiting room. It was not a happy person who presented himself at the Pool at nine o'clock, to tell the clerk that I had come to reregister. "Oh no you have not, we are not taking anyone on at the moment," he said. I was in no mood to be reasonable. I was being messed around.

Angrily, I told him how I had been sent up from Falmouth under Liverpool's own instructions to reregister and have my records transferred back to Falmouth. They, Liverpool, did not have to find me work as Falmouth had undertaken to do that. He hastily shuffled me on to another clerk who realised my determination and provided me with a reregistration form.

I took the form to a nearby cafe and filled in the hard to come by document over a cup of tea with a misguided sense of achievement. I was incensed when on accepting the form back the clerk asked me for references, not only for the period that I had been ashore, but from everywhere I had worked since I had left school. I would have to go home and send them in before any further progress could be made I was told.

It was unbelievable. References for the last few months that I had been ashore I reluctantly could understand, but since I had left school? I felt gutted. I would not be their problem, I would be Falmouth's, and yet it seemed to me those Jobsworths were deliberately blocking my reentry.

I was so deflated and disappointed on the train journey home that it was a journey best taken alone for I was seething and quite unapproachable, and then to arrive home to a further unpleasant surprise was the proverbial last straw. Something I had completely forgotten about: there was a request from the Ministry of Defence to join Her Majesty's forces. My National Service papers had arrived.

As I had served in the Merchant Navy, there was an exemption until the age of twenty-six and having broken service still at the age of only twenty-two, the powers that be had caught up with me. National Service was at that time being phased out, but still it seemed that my presence was still required.

Several weeks later a request was received for me to attend a medical centre in Birmingham. In the meantime, I made a desperate effort to obtain references from the firm that I had worked for on leaving school. Luckily he was still in business and he gave me one willingly. So did the firm that I had recently worked for and I sent them off to Liverpool with a little note stating that their own records of me would fill in the gaps and Falmouth would find me a job once I was reinstated. A few days later I received a letter from them stating that my application had been deferred. I'm afraid that my verbal response was that, "Not one of them, had been born in wedlock."

It was also necessary for me to register at the Labour Exchange to maintain my National Insurance stamp payments. "Army here I come" was my thought as the result of the medical arrived on the mat. The A1 pass somehow didn't fill me with the well-being that it was supposed to. I kicked my heels and did all the things that angry impatient people usually do. Too many boozy sessions, long periods of self pity and disillusionment until three weeks before Christmas a brown envelope landed on our front door mat.

My first thought on seeing it was that I would be spending Christmas in a khaki suit and I must admit it was a great relief to find on opening it that it was from Liverpool. The relief went a long way to help calm down my initial reaction which was "They want me now." "The "b*****ds" want me now that they can't find enough men to crew the ships just before Christmas." But it was my chance to reregister and my acceptance was on its way 'post-haste.'

A telegram arrived on 18th December, a Thursday, with the instruction to report to the Pool the following Monday, three days before Christmas. A small queue had formed when I arrived at the Pool, which I was surprised to see, but perhaps we were all strays that had been rounded up.

The clerk inspected my telegram and having looked closely at my files, he pointed me in the direction of the union official who swiftly relieved me of four-pound back dues to cover my eleven months absence. I rejected the option to rejoin, as that would have cost me even more.

Along with all those who, so it seemed, were desirous of deserting their loved ones during the festive period we awaited the medical, which we were told after a couple of hours would not take place till after lunch.

"Back at 2.00pm," was the cheerful call from the receptionist, which was met with the usual flowery language from those of us who had waited so long. Even so, it gave me the opportunity to book in at Smith's and grab a quick meal. By 2.30pm having passed the doctor, to my initial dismay I was allocated a berth on the 'Empress of Britain' which lay in the Gladstone Dock.

As I had only been reinstated that very morning, it would be inadvisable I thought, to start arguing my preferences, and although the dislike I felt for passenger boats persisted I really had little or no choice. A bus dropped me off at the dock gates and there she lay, all twenty four thousand tons of her, and a pretty impressive picture she made. Both the 'Empress of Canada' that had burned out in the Gladstone Dock and the 'Empress of Scotland' in which I could have sailed once came to mind. Had I missed anything? Was my dislike of the thought of working on one of those impressive looking vessels a little unfair? I was about to find out.

As I climbed the companionway at the stern, my feelings were that at least I was back in the service, and it couldn't be any worse than some of my previous experiences. A uniformed figure, later to be identified as the Bosun's Mate, sternly watched my approach, and he queried my business. "To sign on," I replied. "Through that door," he pointed, "Then as far for'ard as you can go, then up the stairs and through the door facing," was his instructions.

I offered my thanks to the kind face and set off along the longest corridor in Christendom. It went on forever with off shoots at regular intervals. Then I needed to make a detour due to a gang of cleaners who were washing the decks. That was a mistake. I was lost in a maze of passageways that all looked alike and, after I had asked for directions on three occasions, I finally found the stairs.

I signed articles in a little room and asked, "Could half monthly allotments home be paid?" Only weekly ones I was told, due to the duration of the voyage being only seventeen days. There is a God after all, I thought, and to be told that we would be docking back in the UK after only seventeen days was a real novelty to me.

My gear was still in the left luggage at Lime Street Station where I had deposited it on arrival so I hailed a taxi back into town first to pick my gear up and then to drop me off at Smith's. I arranged with the driver for him to pick me up at 7.30am the following morning to get back onboard by 8.00am. By then it was teatime, my hunger was real, the food at Smith's that day was edible, but after almost twelve months of my mother's cooking, that's about all it was.

Three Men in a Boat is a book written by a bloke from Walsall, Jerome K. Jerome, and Jimmy Edwards was in the film that was showing at the local Odeon. There have been worse evenings entertainment wise, but I was between the sheets by eleven o'clock.

* * *

Washed, shaved and breakfasted I stood with my gear outside Smith's the next morning and the taxi arrived dead on the stroke of 7.30am to take me to the Gladstone Dock. Once onboard, I found that the deckhand's cabins were situated in the bows at the distant far end of that long corridor; it was there where most of the deck department, my new shipmates were gathered, about thirty men altogether.

Each cabin was shared by four men with two sets of bunks one above the other. The cabins were double banked, those along the side of the ship had portholes but those on the inside had none. They were all still locked and that gave us the opportunity to socialise, to get to know each other as the Bosun's Mate didn't turn up with the keys until ten o'clock.

Occasionally while we stood there talking I glimpsed what to all appearances was a bent, shuffling figure with a bucket in one hand and a wad of cotton waste in the other. Periodically he was there one moment and then just as suddenly he would disappear only to materialize in a different part of that long, long corridor. I caught a closer look at him on one occasion and he was, it seemed to me, a very old man, old enough to have been a cabin boy on the 'Golden Hind.' It transpired that his job was cleaning the bulkheads of the long corridor. That was his sole occupation and during the next three weeks, I only caught sight of him a couple more times. He became known as 'the alleyway ghost.'

Eventually the Bosun's Mate arrived to unlock and allocate the cabins. We all stood in line as they were detailed. I was with John, a Taffy, Sid from Ellesmere Port and Bob from Liverpool, together we all made up the eight to twelve watch and we were allocated one of the inner cabins with no portholes.

"Get into your working gear and report to the promenade deck" were the Bosun's Mate's orders. Where the hell was the promenade deck? I pondered. It could have been on the moon for all I knew so I just followed the crowd.

The ship's company was assembled. Officers faced us as we were made to stand in line in front of the housing. There were almost as many officers as there were crew, all in their pristine uniforms smothered in gold braid. In fact, there was so much gold braid on display it almost hurt your eyes and as there were no passengers onboard at that time; just who were they trying to impress? It was my opinion along with some of my newfound shipmates that it could only be themselves.

An officer stepped forward to give each of us a card on which was the lifeboat and fire drill station to which we were allocated. Other than the distribution of the cards, the reason behind that formal assembly was not easily understandable for there was no ritual address from a senior officer or any other information imparted, but this was the passenger service! And it was completely new to me. It was not a freighter carrying coal, iron ore or consumer goods like I had been used to, it was a liner carrying or about to carry people. Perhaps the smartness and grandeur of the display of gold braid and class was a subtle show for us lesser human forms.

Number 18 and 19 fire hoses on the promenade deck were my designated fire station so once we were dismissed, and as I was already on the promenade deck, I set out to search for them before I returned to my cabin. Odd numbers up to 17 were on the port side and even numbers from 20 upwards were on the starboard side. "Where the hell 18 and 19 were I was at a loss to know, but all would be revealed in good time I assumed.

I stopped searching as the call to stations came to let go. With the for'ard gang to which I had been assigned I helped to coil the mooring ropes as they came in, and we emerged from the dock to anchor in the Mersey. Immediately on dropping the hook, the call came for fire drill.

Taffy and Sid were stationed outside the bosun's cabin as messenger runners if needed and it was to be hoped they never would be needed. Still my fire station hoses eluded me. Rather than appear to be wandering around aimlessly and be an easy target of some self-important junior officer, back I went to join Sid and Taffy at the bosun's cabin. In a short time the Bosun's Mate returned and, on explaining my predicament to him, I was just told to hang on where I was as the fire drill was almost over. Where the Bosun himself was I had no idea. I had only seen him briefly at the for'ard stations as we were letting go.

As on all ships, the boat and fire drills were carried out once a week and during that voyage a further three were carried out, which as far as I was concerned were a waste of time as I never did find my station. Boat drill though was a different matter, the ship's whistle blasted out to call the crew to stations. Lifeboat 8 was my allotted one. The whistle belched out like a bloated cow, which gave a sense of urgency as we all hurried to our positions, but the urgency soon vanished as everyone hung about for ten minutes without instruction or explanation until the order to dismiss came.

A thick fog had come down which reduced visibility to a few yards, nevertheless on the stroke of 11.30am we heaved up anchor to move very slowly down river to tie up at the landing stage.

The number of passengers who came onboard surprised me for they were very thin on the ground. I don't know exactly where the order came from or who issued it, but it became known amongst us that we, the deckhands, were never to be seen talking to any of the passengers. How mind boggling can you get? Perhaps it was just as well that, after seeing them come aboard I at least never set eyes on any of them again. Being in the eight to twelve watch we were relieved soon after we had made fast and I leaned over the rail to watch the passengers embark. I assumed that the trickle of people who had stepped aboard must be the first bunch. But as it turned out it was the sum total, about sixty in all. It was amazing the ship was able to accommodate paying passengers in their hundreds and would not, I thought, be making much profit on this particular run. What would all those stewards have to do? For there was surely more than one for every passenger.

The afternoon was our own but the call for stations fore and aft came at 5.30pm. The fog had cleared and the last of the luggage had been brought aboard as we in the eight to twelve watch froze on the fo'c's'le head. We soon warmed up as we struggled to stow away the hawsers and coil them into the rope locker before we reached the open sea.

There was a significant difference in the work on the passenger liners to that which I had become accustomed to on the freighters and tankers. At eight o'clock on the dot, the deckhands lined up outside the Bosun's cabin where the work detail was issued for the day. All three watches were five strong: myself, my three cabinmates and an ordinary seaman who was the dogsbody that did any odd job while we shared the lookout. The lookout was manned twenty-four hours a day, not as in cargo boats and tankers where they were manned during the hours of darkness only and between dawn and dusk the officer on watch took over the roll. Neither did the Able Seamen perform any steering duties; that job was the responsibility of the Quartermasters.

The lookout duties were soon sorted out amongst ourselves, rotating two-hour stints night and morning. When not on lookout during the day there was paintwork to clean and other jobs to be performed on deck. Every evening the job for those who were not on lookout was to sweep that alleyway from aft to for'ard and once that was done our stint was completed. It became a competition and the eight to twelve watch held the record. Fifteen minutes was never beaten and it was perhaps significant that the 'Alleyway ghost,' never appeared at night; he would have disintegrated in our slipstream.

It was the second night at sea that the cry came along the alleyway, "Cocoa's up." "Cocoa!" Never had that call been heard before on any ship on which I had sailed. Evidently, every night at eight o'clock everyone who wished to took their mug to the galley where in a hatchway was a large steel container of a strange tasting nightcap that we could help ourselves to. Its taste defied description, but it was made more palatable by a liberal dose of sweet condensed milk. If nothing else, it made a change from the interminable cups of tea.

As the coast of Ireland receded into the mists, the temperature dropped and the weather worsened. It would have been a frozen watch on any of my previous voyages on lookout, exposed on the fo'c's'le head or the monkey island. Not so on the 'Empress of Britain.' Lookouts were accommodated in the crow's nest, high up on the main mast. It gave a superb view of the horizon ahead from one beam to the other.

It was quite a route march to get there though, we had to walk back along the alleyway from our cabin in the bows to amidships where there was a spiral staircase to climb; I invariably had to stop half way up on most times to catch my breath. Once at the top there was a doorway which led out on to the Captain's deck, then we had to continue aft onto the navigation deck, through an archway at the back of the housing to finally arrive at the foot of the mast where there was a small door which led into the inside of the mast. Then we had to climb another ladder inside the mast up to a small trap door, which was the entrance to the crow's nest.

There was just sufficient space for the watch and his relief to squeeze past each other. Once the trap door was closed it became part of the deck of the crow's nest, and you became encased in a tiny, cosy little cocoon. Inside was a bosun's chair hooked to the bulkhead, on which you could sit and regain your breath after having climbed the one hundred and fifty steps to get there. Also a little electric heater made the miniature room so warm against the cold outside. The position of any light or ship was reported to the bridge through a press button speaker.

As the seas remained stormy, the roll of the ship became greatly exaggerated in that lofty perch. In my younger days, I would have paid good money for similar experiences at the local fair. My reveries were interrupted with the realisation that it was Christmas Eve and there was nowhere to hang my stocking and no one to come and fill it.

The issue of one bottle of beer distinguished Christmas Day for each member of the lower deck; otherwise it was business as usual with the promise that we would be treated in the passenger lounge to a Christmas lunch on arrival in port.

On that Christmas morning I was accosted by an officer in the alleyway who enquired in a very officious manner, "Why are you not in uniform?" "Here we go," I thought, "Because I haven't got one" was my simple but truthful reply. "Well you had better get to the shop and buy one," he snapped as he turned and went on his way. That was exactly what I had been told in the past would happen if I ever went on a passenger boat.

Without any intention of buying, just out of curiosity, I called in to the shop to enquire what the uniform would cost. It did not take long to calculate that the total of my expected earnings for the trip less the cost of a uniform would leave me in debt of at least five-pounds. "Get stuffed" was my mental response to that nameless model of gold braid.

With much less to do than I was accustomed to, the days dragged and the weather didn't help: it was cold, wet and drizzly, but the stint in the crow's nest once there was a welcome respite. I had been relieved one day, and while I made my way back to my cabin along the alleyway around the corner of one of the offshoots came the uniform fanatic.

"Have you bought a uniform yet?" was his rather stern query, "No and I have no intention of buying one," I replied. If it wasn't his hackles that rose, it was a sudden attack of high blood pressure that made him change colour to an almost crimson red. I don't think he expected to be replied to in that manner. "Why not?" he almost shouted, "because I'm only on this ship for three weeks," I retorted. I think that took the wind out of his sails, and it was a strange look of hurt I saw in his eyes as he muttered "I see" and walked off along the alleyway. Strange to relate, I never set eyes on him again.

It was cold and frosty when the tying up was completed in St John's, Newfoundland, Canada on Monday 29th December. I showered and turned in for a couple of hours when I came off watch at midday, only to be woken up by Taffy suggesting a trip ashore. Together with Sid we caught a bus into the town with the idea of seeing the sights and taking a couple of beers. It was a disappointment though as everywhere appeared to be shut.

It had snowed quite heavily and it was damned freezing. The streets were virtually deserted, but one of the few people we did encounter to engage in conversation said that the cold weather and snow hung around usually for about six months. "There are only two seasons here: winter and summer," he said. "God, and people from Britain actually emigrate to make a life here" was the thought uppermost in my mind.

During the stay in port the watches were dissolved and all hands were on daywork. Every morning we assembled in an orderly line outside the Bosun's cabin where work for the day was allocated. My task one morning was to find the plumber to tell him that the Chief Officer's toilet in his rooms was blocked and needed urgent attention. "Rooms!" I thought, "in the plural," while four of us were stuck in a box with no air.

Through the maze of corridors I wandered, lost because of what I thought were inadequate directions. Eventually I found the plumber's office. The door opened in response to my knock and there stood the smartest, immaculately dressed, gold braided, navy blue uniform in the ship. Slowly he looked me up and down and, whilst I would admit to not being the smartest deckhand on the '*Empress of Britain*,' there were worse.

The expression on his face seemed to pose the question, "What has brought this virus to my door?" Obviously, my appearance pained him and with difficulty he deigned to ask, "Yes?" "Are you the plumber?" I ventured. Apoplexy is something I had only heard about and never seen but that, I am sure, is the nearest I will ever come to witnessing such an event. His eyes bulged, his chest expanded like a balloon at his sudden intake of breath, his face reddened like a tomato, "Plumber!" he exploded, "I am the SANITARY ENGINEER." Without revealing to him the slightest sign of how impressed I was, I looked him straight in the eyes and said, "Well, the Chief Officer's shit house is blocked and he wants you to clear it, right now!" I did not wish to witness his reaction to that, and I turned on my heels to head back for further orders wondering, "Is it me or these guys who are living in Disneyland?"

Christmas dinner was taken on New Year's Eve when all hands went up top to the dining room. It all looked the part; tables laid out as for a passenger feast with menus, paper hats and balloons. The stewards did the serving. That was the first time I had ever been waited upon, except of course for that once on the '*Koluxotronis*' so long ago.

The meal was good and we were each given one small bottle of beer to celebrate, but the atmosphere was spoilt on being told that the cost of any further drinks would be taken from our wages. Not able to stomach the sight of those who could afford to get stoned I, along with the rest of the eight to twelve watch, headed back to our cabin.

Friday 2nd January 1959 saw what I thought must be an unusual occurrence for a passenger liner; we shifted ship from the passenger terminal across to the commercial dock where a consignment of grain was loaded into the empty baggage hold. The weather got worse; heavy snow had fallen overnight and the morning was taken up with all hands snow shifting. There was much hopping and sliding, and once we had got rid of the snow, the decks remained extremely dangerous for ice formed as the temperature steadfastly fell lower and lower.

A welcome change was announced on the afternoon for all the crew who wished to go were invited to the ship's cinema for a double feature that evening. At eight o'clock everyone trooped into what was a carbon copy of any cinema at home only smaller and cosier with a big screen, red curtains and plush comfortable seats. The format was much the same as the program comprising of a couple of cartoons, a newsreel, some totally obscure 'B' movie and a feature film, which in that case was 'The Two Headed Boy' starring Jack Hawkins.

The snow returned and the sub-zero temperature remained so, each morning, the order of the day was snow-shifting again. Very often it was over a foot deep; our misery was offset occasionally with a little merriment as deckhands slid and fortunately fell in soft snow.

Though it was bitterly cold with a penetrating icy wind, our exertions kept us warm up to our breakfast, dinner and 'smoko' breaks when our hands were warmed around steaming mugs of tea. Perhaps the Captain took pity on us for once again the cinema was made available for an afternoons showing of 'I was Monty's Double.'

And still the temperature sank even lower, registering 22 degrees of frost Fahrenheit. Tuesday 6th January was a memorable occasion. Making ready for sea was a routine that by then I never gave a second thought ordinarily, but there was nothing routine in those conditions. Everything was frozen solid. The lowering of the derricks, normally a formality, was a horrendous task and having started after dinner we still hadn't completed them by teatime. Icicles had to be chipped away from the guys and blocks and all moving parts had to be released. Letting go was back breaking too, trying to release the hawsers from around the bits and put to the capstan to be heaved aboard and, back breaking as that was, it was simple compared to stowing the ropes through the small hatch into the rope locker. The coils of ropes which had been standing on the decks had frozen and fused together, we had to use crowbars to force them apart and sledge hammers to bend them to enable us to feed them bit by bit into the little hatch. During that turmoil as we slowly edged out into the estuary, we were hit by a raging blizzard and were well out to sea before the task of stowing all the gear was completed.

Once clear of the land the conditions got even worse. With no shelter on the fo'c's'le head the icy wind stung the exposed skin. That prompted me to cover most of my face with the top of my polo necked jumper, which in turn had an adverse effect for the moisture from my breath froze almost instantly, and the ice built up on the wool and began to chaff my face.

It was with great sighs of relief that after four hours of solid mauling, tugging and dragging frozen ropes over frozen decks, finally the last strand disappeared into the hatch. We were anticipating the warmth of our cabins when the Bosun appeared and ordered us aft as they were still struggling and our help was required.

My arms were about to drop off and I had trouble straightening my back; the prospect of having no break was daunting. The position of the for'ard gang was far more exposed than the after crowd and surely we deserved a break for a smoke, the Bosun's Mate ventured. "OK, but only for ten minutes, anyone who is not back will be logged," was the Bosun's reluctant reply. So we only had time for a quick drag and a very welcome sip of hot tea before we went out again to help the after gang. Most of the crew were almost in tears suffering from the cold as we finally made our way back to our cabins at midnight.

Both crying from the cold and laughing with relief, I was happy to be finished and out of the coldest elements I have ever experienced before or since. Thankfully the twelve to four watch was not mine and I felt for those unfortunates who had to remain on duty for those four hours. I doubt if I could have made the climb up to the crow's nest. Throughout the whole afternoon and evening saga I had worn two pairs of gloves, and as I removed them, tiny white flakes of dead skin peeled from the back of my hands.

Two days out of St John the temperature had recovered to twenty-four degrees Fahrenheit, still eight degrees below freezing, but with the sun making a reappearance everyone thought that summer had arrived. The climate improved as we ploughed uneventfully across the North Atlantic to arrive back in Gladstone dock at midnight on Monday 12th January. It was 11.30am the next morning when they paid us off and at 11.40am. I was in a taxi hightailing it for Lime Street and home.

To say I had received a cold reception back into the Merchant Navy would be an understatement. I had been forced to fight hard to get back in. I had given up my Christmas at home and sailed on a passenger liner, which I had never wanted to do. Most of my fears for doing so had come true, being told to buy a uniform, being told who I could and could not talk to, being looked upon as the lowest of the low by some self-important 'persons'. This was not an environment I wished to live in, but to be fair it hadn't all been bad.

Ironically I had looked forward to missing the cold English winter and had sailed off into much worse and three weeks later I was back in it, but I had finally been reregistered as a seaman again, and could get back into what was for me the real world of the sea. I was looking forward to whatever adventures lay ahead.

CHAPTER THIRTEEN
THE HYALA

(Of a Journey in Fog, a Pilot Sacked and a
Taste of the Cockleshell Heroes).

The sleep inducing click-clack of the wheels lulled me into a state of semi-consciousness after I settled comfortably in my seat as the Birmingham bound express roared through the countryside. I relived the past few weeks in my mind and compared the two different worlds of commercial and passenger services that the Merchant Navy provided and definitely came to the positive conclusion that it was the commercial life for me.

All that gold braid and self-important people tended, at least for me, to be in a world that was not for me and was something I could certainly forgoe without any worries. I decided there and then that my future seagoing life would be amongst the more worldly fraternity, even if it were on the occasional rust bucket.

Not being on contract to the Pool meant that the four days leave that I had could be extended a little, but not to overdo it I caught the early train to Liverpool on Monday 19th January and reported immediately to the Pool where I was told to return after lunch at two o'clock.

Smith's was the first port of call to book a room and then I returned to Lime Street to collect my gear. In the station snack bar I ran into Tony, an AB with whom I had sailed way back on the 'San Velino.' He had given up the sea and currently worked in the docks.

Bearing in mind my recent icy experiences on the Canadian run, more sunny climes beckoned and I thought tankers would probably be my best bet so I enquired of him if there was an office of the Shell Tanker Company in Liverpool. Without ado Tony led me through the city to show me where the Shell Office was. He suggested that if I went to them direct, they would probably require me to sign a contract and perhaps my best immediate bet would be the Pool but, as I had found the location of the office, I could apply at my leisure either then or at any time in the future.

I decided to go back to the Pool where I recognised two ordinary seamen, shipmates from the '*Empress of Britain*.' The clerk directed me to another waiting room. Shortly, my two mates came to join me with the news that they had berths on a Shell tanker, the '*Hyala*.' "Right up my street, that will suit me" I thought as the clerk called me to the counter. "I have one job left on the '*Hyala*,' the clerk told the guy in front of me. "Just my luck," was my immediate reaction only to hear the guy say, "No thanks, I will call back tomorrow."

The clerk then turned to me as he walked out, "There isn't much on, only a standby," he said. "What about the '*Hyala*?' I flashed back, "I didn't think you would want a tanker, that's why it wasn't offered," he replied. "Yes," I thought, "You can't get anyone to accept the standby more like," but I kept my thoughts to myself as he gave me the forms for the '*Hyala*.'

The doctor gave me the OK and I was told to be outside the Pool at one o'clock Wednesday dinnertime when a bus would take us to the ship. As I wandered around the city centre the following day Tuesday, I came across the two guys I had met in the Pool who would be with me on the '*Hyala*.' I told them that I had also got a berth on the '*Hyala*' and they informed me that they had received telegrams to tell them that they were not to meet the bus until Thursday and they had returned to the Pool to ask for another ship. They had been given another Shell Tanker that proved to be a rust bucket. They had refused to sign on her too and they were currently on their way back to the Pool to make yet another request. Their friendship and desire to sail together reminded me in many ways of my early friendship with Mick (Bimbo) and how we had shared many experiences together. As we walked back to the Pool, I wondered where he was now.

It was my intention to find out the details of the pickup for the 'Hyala.' Thursday morning at 9.30 was the fresh instruction. I thought that at least they could have tried Gordon Smith's to let me know, even if they were not sure if I was there or not, but I gave them the benefit of the doubt. In order to make sure then I asked, "If there was any further change could a message be left at Smith's for me?" "Yes, we will let you know," the clerk assured me.

Thursday morning at 9.15am found me with my gear outside the Pool, quite alone, no sign of any other crewmembers; 9.30am came and went, no crew, no bus. Back I went into the Pool to be told that it had been put back once again until one o'clock on Friday. "Thanks a bundle for letting me know," I sarcastically retorted. All the others must have been told for no one else was waiting. There was nothing for it then but to cart my gear back to Smith's to rebook a room with the prospect of yet another wasted day.

It was obvious that they meant business the following day for a gang of guys, with their gear were hanging about. The bus arrived at a quarter past one; it pulled up and the driver disappeared, leaving us to load all of our gear ourselves.

Five past two came and the bus driver had still not returned; that was enough to try even my patience, and the patience of others, to the extent that several guys also disappeared across the road into the Seamen's Mission for a quick cup of tea. No sooner had they gone through the door than the driver reappeared and ushered us all onto the bus and drove off; he took absolutely no notice of all our cries and entreaties that some of the crew were missing. Without a word he just left them behind with all their gear onboard; he just didn't give a damn. It was not as if it was just up the road to one of the Liverpool docks. The 'Hyala' lay at Stanlow, way up the Manchester ship canal.

The driver still ignored our continued protests on behalf of our fellow shipmates and proceeded through the Mersey Tunnel to deliver us safely, but still protesting at the gangway of the 'Hyala' forty-five minutes later. She was a big ship (for those days), about twelve thousand tons and for once the crew's accommodation was decent. She was similar to the 'Llandaff' with single berth cabins. Some were quite spacious, but all had a comfortable bunk, a small mirrored toilet cabinet, chest of drawers which doubled as a writing desk, a built-in wardrobe and a full size bench settee.

It was a veritable palace compared to many of my previous ships and I did love the privacy of a single berth. I chose a smaller cabin further aft where perhaps it would be a little quieter and there was a little less deck space to scrub clean.

The guys who had missed the bus turned up some hours later; it was a good job we hadn't sent their gear back on the bus else they would have been sick about it. We had decided to take it onboard to sort it out with the Skipper if they hadn't appeared before we sailed. After they returned from having a cup of tea to find the bus and their gear gone they had reported their dilemma to the Pool; they were each given two shillings (10p) and told to make their own way to the ship.

The crew were turned to on Saturday morning. A formality really for there was little to do as she wasn't to sail until Monday afternoon. Most of the crew, being local, went home for the weekend, and it needed little persuasion for me to decide to do likewise so the Birmingham express had me back in the club for what could possibly be my last Saturday night at home for some time.

It was a short but enjoyable sojourn for Sunday evening I arrived back at Lime Street to be welcomed by a fog as thick as pea soup. Fortunately the ferries were still running across to Birkenhead, but all other local transport had ground to a halt. A guy at the bus station gave me the glad tidings that the Stanlow, Ellesmere Port service would not be running, at least until sometime on Monday.

I just had to get back and in desperation I asked about taxis. A small shelter across the square masqueraded as a taxi rank and within a short while a car appeared out of the murk. The driver was anything but happy at the prospect of getting to Stanlow for it was by then not only practically nil visibility but icy as well. He looked hard at me and I thought he was going to refuse but instead he said, "OK let's give it a go, but I'm not guaranteeing getting there," he drawled in his strong Scouse accent.

It was a nightmare, we were unable to see a hand in front of our faces, added to which was the unseen hazard of icy roads. Driving at a snail's pace along the new Chester Road we slowed virtually to a standstill to allow a motorist to overtake. He wouldn't; he obviously preferred to tail the taxi.

It was extremely cold and the windscreen iced up. "A little further up the road is a lay-by," the driver said, "I will pull into it and clean the windscreen." Amazingly, despite the lack of visibility, he always appeared to know exactly where we were. The car that had tailed us had to swerve to get back on the main road as he had partly followed us into the lay-by and suddenly realised his mistake.

With the driver's care and the help of the gods, we finally arrived outside the dock gates at Stanlow. By then it was eleven o'clock and the driver looked a little apprehensive when he asked for thirty shillings (one pound fifty) as if he was a little afraid I would think it too much. He was even more surprised when I gave him two pounds. That was a fortune for me, but it was well worth it for without him I would very possibly have had to spent a few very cold and miserable hours in that little shelter, not to mention the strong possibility that I could miss the ship. He had been very kind and considerate and had embarked on a hazardous journey for me that he could easily and understandably have refused, and he still had the return trip to make. I thanked him for getting me back safe in such conditions and wished him safe journey back as he drove away.

As it turned out, I would not have missed the ship because we didn't sail until after dinner on Monday 26th January when the fog had been cleared by a freshening wind. The call to stations went out and with the tugs in close attendance, we let go. By tugging us astern into the mainstream of the canal the tugs managed to turn the ship around. It was all very precise as the length of the 'Hyala' was almost the width of the canal. She was not the 'Nacella' so the turn around was completed without a hitch.

Exactly who was going to man the watches had not yet been sorted, and an AB volunteered to take the first helm as far as the lay-by at the entrance to the lock. Once there the cards were cut in the usual way to choose the nine watchmen, the rest of the crew had to undertake daywork duties. As luck would have it, I drew the twelve to four watch.

We still did not know what time we would clear the lock but it was known that once through, we were to anchor in the Mersey for the night. My two watchmates and I cut the cards again to decide who was to be first wheel, second wheel and farmer, we agreed beforehand that the first wheel would stand the whole four hours anchor watch from twelve midnight to four in the morning to allow the other two to turn in.

Needless to say I drew first wheel; it wasn't worth trying to turn in. Indeed it was impossible to do so as everyone was needed at stations to go through the lock. It was 9.00pm before that happened and, by the time we had finally anchored again, it was almost time for my watch to begin. The watch itself passed without incident but by four o'clock I was dead on my feet and greatly pleased to see my relief.

I slept like a log, being called to stations at 11.30am on Tuesday morning only to tie up again in the Gladstone dock in the berth opposite to where the '*Empress of Britain*' had been. She was no doubt well on the way to sampling the delights of Canada in January again.

Engine repairs were undertaken and to everyone's surprise, it took a further six days to complete the work. Everyone in the deck department was then employed on daywork to wash down, paint and renew the things that had to be renewed.

Most of the crew would go home of an evening and weekend but considering the trouble I had recently experienced with the fog, I was loath to risk another weekend sojourn at that time of the year although I would have loved to have done so. As it turned out it was just as well I had decided not to for at four o'clock on the Monday morning, February 2nd we were called to stations. We sailed back through the lock into the Manchester Ship Canal again and returned to tie up once more at Stanlow to load our cargo.

We had taken on the cargo by the Tuesday evening and at 3.30am on the Wednesday morning, we cast off to sail straight down into the Eastam lock. By that time the ship's crew had been signed on for twelve days and we were still in the Mersey. The trip had certainly been unproductive so far, and must have cost the company plenty. Still there was no word of our destination as we headed north through the Irish Sea other than our immediate port of call was to be Heysham.

We stood off Morecambe at anchor at midday to await the service of a Pilot who once aboard quietly and with a surety of skill edged us alongside a jetty, which was about a half mile long where we tied up. Ten shore men came onboard to help us do that, five at each end of the ship, because no fewer than six five-inch wire hawsers were to come onboard both fore and aft and made fast to buoys.

A thin rope (a messenger) was passed through the lead down to a waiting boat, which scurried across to the buoys where it was attached to a small wire that we then hauled aboard. That in turn was attached to ever increasing heavier wires until eventually, the five-inch wire was hauled inboard to be wrapped around our bits. It was tantamount to wrestling with a giant python, and needed repeating a further five times until everything was tied up and secure. Everyone was completely knackered and the length of that isolated jetty dissuaded any thought of shore leave.

Part cargo was discharged and when we were called to stations at 9.00am on the Thursday morning, it was a pleasant surprise for us that the shore gang had already singled up to one of the five-inch wires fore and aft. Our task was simple as only the tug had to be made fast and let go as we cleared the jetty.

* * *

Once again it was to the north that our bows headed bound for the Clyde and Kilpatrick. While we were in territorial waters the bond could not be opened, consequently everyone was beginning to run out of cigarettes. We asked the Bosun to try to do something about it and so he approached the Skipper who agreed to radio ahead requesting the Pilot to bring along with him forty cigarettes for each man who ordered them. Such consideration and nicety was, to me at least, a new approach in attitude from the officers.

I had been ashore only eleven months but subtle innovations had taken place one of which was, I felt, not to be made to feel like Oliver when a further supply of rations were requested. Extra cans of beer were available and surprise of all surprises, each ship had its own film projector; a worldwide library of films were available, which could be changed at the next port of call. It made life at sea just that tiny bit more full with the means to relax when off duty. That evening with the screen set up in our mess and the projector in the pantry poking through the serving hatch, Jack Hawkins performed for us in 'Man in the Sky.'

We anchored in the beautiful Clyde at 10.30am and true to his word, the Skipper had got the Pilot to bring aboard the long awaited cigarettes. The cost of which was deducted from our wages.

Sunday dawned foggy and the watch were stationed with a man fore and aft. The for'ard watch was positioned on the fo'c's'le head to ring the bell, and the after watch banged on a gong on the poop deck in the hope that other ships in the vicinity would hear them and steer clear. Our watch came on duty at midday and it fell to me to beat the gong on the poop deck. It was with some relief that the fog lifted within twenty minutes and the gong was dispensed with.

At 11.30am on Monday 9th of February tugs were made fast fore and aft to bring us on up the river to a basin almost within the port of Glasgow where the ship could be turned around to allow passage back down to Kilpatrick. It was bitterly cold, but it did not distract from the natural beauty of the Clyde with its snow-covered banks that glistened in the pale wintery sun.

Tying up at Kilpatrick was a back breaking job, manhandling the large heavy shore wires with no shore crew to give a helping hand. The strength of the large wires was essential for the wash from the traffic on the river caused the ship to rock and roll, with the possibility of breaking free if not properly secured. Nevertheless, everyone was glad to see the end of that strenuous task.

As the hands took a well earned break the word was spread that the next port of call was to be Dingle, Liverpool, and from there to Thames Haven in Essex then once again back up to Kilpatrick. That created much unrest amongst the crew, everyone had signed 'Deep Sea' articles and no one wished to stay on the coast for various reasons, not in the least the prospects of those back breaking tie ups every other day or so. The following morning union assistance was called for. The case was put quite strongly that if we had wanted a coasting life, we would have signed on a coaster and not have to toil with the back breaking work of an ocean going vessel.

The Skipper was approached and once again, I was pleasantly surprised with his response. It was reported back to us that enquiries would be made to the head office during our return journey south to find out exactly what the company's plans for us were. But the Skipper had added that, irrespective of whether the plans were for remaining on the coast or deep sea, any crewmember that was dissatisfied could sign off after docking at the Dingle. "I do not want anyone on my ship who is unhappy" were his reported words. Things had changed for that was, as far as my memory went, the first time I had sailed with a Skipper who gave a tuppenny toss whether his men were happy or not, or had I just been unlucky?

Once again the Skipper's word was his bond for as Heysham, Morecome and a little later Blackpool disappeared past our port beam, the word went around that after discharging at the Dingle we were Curacao bound.

My shift was finished as we anchored at the Mersey bar at 4.00am on Thursday 12th. It was my trick at the wheel at one o'clock that afternoon when we upped anchor and I took her up the river past Liverpool and Birkenhead to anchor once again just beyond. We were too deep in the water to proceed further and had to wait for a couple of small tankers to come alongside to load a part of our cargo to lighten us in the water. By midnight sufficient cargo had been got rid of to sail up to Dingle and tie up at 4.00am at the oil jetty to discharge the remaining cargo.

Despite the assurance of foreign waters, some of the crew still took the Skipper by his word and signed off: two ABs and three firemen. Replacements were soon aboard and one of them had sailed with me on the 'Empress of Britain.' I had toyed with the idea of a flying visit home but the fates were in opposition for it was up, off and away at 2.00pm on Saturday afternoon.

Once clear of the land and out into the open sea the ship was put onto automatic pilot that was a further innovation, which came as a surprise as it was another first experience for me. It was commonly known as the Iron Mike. It relegated the wheelman to being a lookout on the wing of the bridge or the monkey island, both places being close at hand if the automation went haywire.

The three of us in each of the watches worked them an hour about in turn, but after one day out, the Bosun let it be known that during the periods that we were clear of land, the Mate was depleting each watch by one man who would be employed on daywork. There was no volunteer from our watch so the time-honoured practice of cutting the cards was once again invoked. My luck with the cards made me sometimes wonder if they were marked and I was the only one unaware of the fact. I was on daywork. Strong, cold winds accompanied us for the first few days and extra clothing was required when out on deck.

We passed the Azores on February 19th which brought the expected change and soon glorious warm, sunny weather prevailed, which was a large part of the reason for my returning to sea and it had the effect of lightening and cheering up the atmosphere.

Friday morning, on being called at 6.30am because daywork hours still started at 7.00am, the Bosun came with the orders that the tanks had to be butterworthed. All through the day we toiled and overtime into the night was worked. I finally collapsed into my bunk at 4.00am Saturday. I slept like a log, but not for long. Three and a half hours later, we were back hard at it as Saturday from 7.00am till midday was part of our working week. That particular Saturday however did not finish at midday as further overtime had to be worked right through till Saturday evening, and all day Sunday. I always liked to work as much overtime as I possibly could as it gave me money in the ship to offset my large allotments home.

Sunday evening brought a little respite for, given the beautiful weather, the projector and the screen were rigged up on the boat deck and in contrast to the 'Empress of Britain' the crew sat in the balmy evening air watching James Stewart in a film called The Far Country. That indeed was the life and still I was surprised at how some things had changed in my eleven months absence.

New orders were received the next day. It was to be Maracaibo not Curacao. Once before way back on the 'Llandaff', Maracaibo had been a port of call of mine, where the oil derricks stuck up out of the Venezuala lakes. It was early afternoon on Thursday 26th February when we let go the anchor off Cardon to wait for the Pilot, and we finally reached the lakes at about 11.30pm where we tied up to the buoys by 2.00am on Friday morning. It was then realised that bunkering should have taken place at Cardon but, as the pipes had by then been lifted from the bed of the lake and were being attached to the manifold, bunkering would have to wait. It was five o'clock that morning before I got my head down. As I had to start my normal duty at 7.00am, it seemed pointless to get into my bunk so I slept on my settee.

The loading was completed by ten o'clock that night and it was close to midnight when everything was stowed and made ready for sea. Those off watch turned in once we had let go so the dayworkers, myself included, had the lion's share to do. The depletion of the watches, especially the twelve to four which I had been taken off, created a problem which then came to light as the twelve to four only comprised of an EDH and an Ordinary Seaman. The Skipper, on realising the set up and the fact that a very narrow channel had to be navigated under the guidance of the Pilot, insisted that I must be brought back into the watch for that night only to replace the Ordinary Seaman and to relieve Frank the EDH at the wheel. He wouldn't risk giving an Ordinary Seaman the responsibility in such conditions. Frank and I took the wheel an hour about.

Since our arrival off Cardon on Thursday morning, I had worked my daywork shift plus the overtime into the early mornings at stations I had only managed to snatch the odd couple of hours sleep here and there. Then instead of being able to turn in like the rest of the dayworkers, I had to stay up until four o'clock to do the watch and be called again at 6.30am for another day's graft, which started with a call to stations at Cardon. "Who the hell needs sleep anyway?" I thought.

No one could have foreseen that having missed the intended bunkering on the inward journey it would result in what became a dangerous situation as we attempted to come alongside at Cardon. Docking there was considered quite straightforward so that time my presence in the watch was not required. As the Pilot directed operations on the bridge I stood on the fo'c's'le head with a heaving line with the express instruction to get it ashore as soon as possible. Once level with the jetty, broadside on, slowly, very slowly we edged closer. While still a fair distance from the jetty, I thought I would give it a whirl. Summoning all my strength, I threw the line and it was a pleasing sight to see the heaving line snake through the air to its full length and be caught by the shore crew on the jetty.

The wire back spring was attached to the line and the shore gang hauled it ashore and placed the eye over the bollard. We then took a couple of turns around the bits then she began to drift aft with the bow of the wire dipping into the water, but we were still no closer to the jetty. The engines were put ahead slowly and the ship moved forward took up the slack and caused the turns around the bits to strain dramatically, giving off puffs of smoke caused by the extra friction.

Forwards and backwards, backwards and forwards we went, and still got no closer to the jetty. My mate and I were sweating, trying desperately to hold the wire in place; it was singing and twanging first under the strain as we moved forward and then limply dipped into the water as we came aft. Suddenly the Pilot decided apparently that we needed more speed, and as we came forward that bit faster we tried to give a little slack on the wire just to ease the tension, but someone was screaming at us from the bridge to hold on.

The inevitable happened: the wire snapped like a whiplash. It whistled alongside the bows and slapped repeatedly against the starboard side like the shots from a tommy gun. It was most fortunate no one was hurt for it would have cut anyone in two had they been standing in its flight path.

In the resulting aftermath of stunned silence came the realisation that the ship had drifted alongside of its own accord despite the efforts of the Pilot. Soon the tying up was completed and the bunkering commenced. The Wheelman on his return to the mess had a tale to tell of the commotion in the wheelhouse for evidently the Skipper had more or less kicked the Pilot off the bridge who in return threatened to make sure that no Pilot would be made available to assist our departure. "I don't f*****g want one if they are all as inefficient as you. I'll take her out myself" was the immediate response from our extremely angry Skipper. And to his eternal credit, that is exactly what he did at 7.30pm that evening.

An auspicious start to our return passage. Was it an omen of things to come? Some pondered, but No! Other than the weather being cooler the trip back across the Atlantic proved to be uneventful which made a nice change for me. How nice it was to settle into a routine for a little while.

As the days passed it got steadily cooler until, upon entering the Bay of Biscay, we needed extra clothes and topcoats. The Pilot came aboard as we approached the Gironde, the French river that flows up to Bordeaux; it is noted for its fierce tidal swim that was much in evidence that Friday night 13th March. I hoped that the date Friday 13th would not be unlucky and that the Pilot would be more skilled at his craft than the last one.

We headed slowly upstream against the fierce current, and if you looked directly downwards over the side the tidal race gave the impression of great speed, but that was brought to reality when you measured our progress against the banks. We were crawling along making possibly only three or four knots. It made me realise the enormity of the task that those brave men the so called 'Cockleshell Heroes' had undertaken by struggling against the current as they paddled their canoes up river to perform deeds of daring by blowing up German ships in Bordeaux harbour during the Second World War.

It was much later that night that an anchorage was found off Pauillac, Bordeaux. Everywhere that the ship docked, it seemed that she had to be tied up with wires; no doubt, in that case it was due to the strong current. The next morning we tied up to buoys then the procedure began, all hands went for'ard to haul in three six-inch wires and made them fast around the bits, that was repeated with all hands aft. We were under the impression then that we had finished, but no such luck; we were detailed once more to go for'ard to make fast two more and finally aft again to take in four more.

The wires were all coated with the slime of the riverbed and everyone was covered from head to toe in an evil smelling gunge. Mud wrestlers could not have been covered more fully so it was straight to the showers for us and we needed to soak our working clothes immediately; the rancid smell was everywhere.

Alone, I took myself ashore, essentially to stretch my legs and feel my feet on dry land. Like many small French ports, there was little to see and I had neither the time nor the inclination to venture into Bordeaux itself.

The discharging seemed to be a long slow process on that occasion for some unknown reason. Although it took the whole weekend there was one consolation, the weather improved and it got warmer. While we did expect a warmer climate in France, albeit on the Atlantic side as opposed to the Mediterranean, it was still March, and England would still be shaking off its winter mantle.

Letting go on the Monday evening was a much more simple task than tying up. The turns were taken off the bits and the wires allowed to just run free out through the leads to lie once again on the river bed to collect more mud and slime. First we had to make sure that their buoys were attached to them ready for the next unfortunate sailors to come along to wrestle with them.

Sailing downstream with the current, we sped along the Gironde towards the open sea. It was quite an experience for we certainly got a move on. "Much faster," I thought, "and it would be like shooting the white water rapids." Once the Pilot was gone we set a northerly course heading for Falmouth and once back on the open sea the temperature dropped to its seasonal coolness.

It was an early start the next morning as the Bosun and I, with another dayworker, began to butterworth the then empty tanks. Starting at 5.00am we worked on through until one o'clock the next morning to complete the work. Having to maul the equipment from tank to tank exposed us to a gale force wind that whipped up an icy spray from the sea to soak us and chill us to the bone.

A hot shower and the comfort of a warm bunk helped to relieve the chill and the thought of no more butterworthing that trip soothed my slumbers. But it was not to be; on our arrival off Falmouth on Wednesday 18th March, the Mate spread the news that there were no berths available.

Falmouth was chock-a-block with shipping and it would be a couple of days before a berth would become vacant. "These two extra days will allow us to butterworth the tanks again," the Mate informed the Bosun. That was met with agonised moans, which were totally ignored as all four of us day workers began again the task, which we thought had been finished.

The fact that four of us were working together did give us the opportunity to work in pairs and rotate in turns which enabled us to take short breaks and cat naps occasionally, but it was five o'clock on Thursday morning before we had finished for the day.

Once again I lay on my settee to snatch a couple of hours kip. It was eight o'clock when breakfast was served, and I worked it out that since Monday I'd had less than fifteen hours sleep, all in little snatches, and still there remained a further thirty hours of cleaning to complete.

We were dead on our feet when the task was finally completed at midday on Friday. A hot shower and bed was the only thought in my befuddled mind and I just 'crashed' solidly for almost twenty hours. It was hard to believe but I didn't surface until eight o'clock breakfast time on Saturday morning.

Breakfast was a rushed affair for at 9.00am we went in and tied up without incident. Our gear was quickly packed with the pay off at midday and once the customs formalities were completed, everyone made for the little station just beyond the dock gates.

The connection to Wolverhampton had gone by the time I reached Truro and I travelled to Taunton with Derek (Lofty) an AB to catch a connection to Bristol where I arrived just after 9.00pm. Once again I was disappointed for the next train to Birmingham wasn't due till 1.05am so I cat napped in the waiting room for its arrival. After which a further frustrating and tiring journey finally got me into Wolverhampton at 4.00am, and a taxi got me home sixteen hours after being paid off.

CHAPTER FOURTEEN
THE CUZCO

(Of yet another Large Coaster, The Royal
Yacht and a Glimpse of School).

A fortnight at home with time spent equally divided between pub, club and bed provided a welcome, much needed rest after the strenuous exertions of the last days of the '*Hyala.*' The strong antipathy shown during the early days aboard the '*Hyala*' to doing coastal work on such a large ocean going vessel, would it seemed make a mockery of my acceptance of a short trip aboard the '*Cuzco.*' A strange name for a British ship I thought as it is the name of a place in Peru.

My association with the '*Cuzco*' came about by the chance meeting with Lofty as I presented my documents to the Pool Clerk. I had got back on Monday 6th April to be greeted with the news that no tanker work was available.

A berth on a cargo boat to the West Coast of Africa was on offer but I refused that in the hope that a tanker would come up in the next day or so. I told the clerk that I would be back again the following day and left the Pool office. Lofty did the same thing and decided to book a room at Smith's where I had already reserved my night's accommodation.

I arranged to meet up with Lofty later and made my way to the office at Cornhill to secure my ABs certificate. I had recorded sufficient time and seagoing service in my discharge book, which elevated me to that coveted position. The charge of one shilling for the certificate would be amply repaid, for the rank of AB immediately guaranteed a rise in my thirty-day monthly wage.

It was at breakfast the next day when I caught up with Lofty, and we were both disappointed when we reported to the Pool. Still no tankers we were told. The rest of the day we spent calling at the various tanker company offices in the city including Shell asking for a job, but to no avail.

Back at the Pool the next morning, there were still no tanker berths, but on offer was a PSNC ship that belonged to the same company who owned the 'Albemarle.' It was the 'Cuzco,' she was signing articles for the home trade and plying around the British coast for a couple of weeks.

Lofty and I agreed to sign on ironically considering the commotion we had kicked up on the 'Hyala,' for coasting on a large ocean going vessel, but needs must. Our reasoning at the time was that the deep-sea tanker situation may well have improved on our return and our ready cash was running low.

So despite our aversion to coastal work on anything other than small coasters, as a stopgap we accepted her. There was no medical required and we were directed to the Alexandra dock. The 'Cuzco' was indeed quite a large ship with six hatches and eighteen derricks. She was in good order with a well looked after air about her. Upon signing articles, everyone was told to report on Friday morning and be prepared to start work at 9.00am. Because cash was getting scarce, it was a relief to get onboard where our accommodation was a part of our wage.

Boat drill was the first exercise we were put to, followed by the lowering of the derricks and everything was made secure for sea. We sailed in the early afternoon down the Mersey and out into the open sea first we headed south and then east up the English Channel. We were bound for London.

Along with Lofty, I had caught the eight to twelve watch, and we were well out into the Irish Sea when I began my stint at the wheel that night. The weather throughout the trip was pleasant, surprisingly mild for April and, without undue incident, we tied up in the river Thames a little above Gravesend on Sunday afternoon, 12th April.

As we progressed up the estuary all the derricks had to be topped. I had just finished making a guy fast when I looked up and there across the water lay the '*Kingsbury*,' anchored off Gravesend against the backdrop of the Sea Training School. Memories of pocket ripping and standing almost naked in the freezing cold courtyard came flooding back. Those days were just a little over five years previously, but they seemed like a whole lifetime away by then.

There was no going ashore because of the shortage of ready cash; London was some distance up the river and it was noted for being expensive. What exactly the cargo was I had no idea but many large boxes that hid their contents were discharged and many more taken onboard during our five day stay. After which we sailed again with hatches battened and derricks secure on Friday 17th April, bound for Hull and the river Humber.

When we reached the North Sea we headed north and while passing Lowestoft, the Royal Yacht heading south slipped between us and the coast, no doubt bound for London and we dipped our flag in salute. As we approached Hull, the derricks once again had to be topped; it was all the constant entering and leaving port and the colossal amount of work involved with the derricks and hatches on freighters that made life on deep-sea tankers more attractive. A further attraction was the time spent at sea where one could settle into a routine and normal quick turn around in ports on the tankers didn't allow wages to be frittered away.

I'd had the wheel for most of the journey along the Humber when Lofty relieved me at ten o'clock to take her through the lock and immediately on to the berth where we tied up. The locality around the docks didn't attract and no one ventured ashore. So at about 4.30pm on Tuesday 21st having discharged and taken a fresh shipment aboard, Hull disappeared behind our stern as a course was set back to Liverpool.

The night was calm with almost a full moon and scarcely a ripple on the water. It was a formality being at the helm as the conditions were such that the ship more or less steered itself. It was a strange and novel experience to be in sight of land for a whole voyage and landmarks that had been but names on the shipping forecast came and went.

The Wednesday morning came up hazy, necessitating a lookout in the bows until the sun burnt the mist off by midday. It remained calm and mild through the Channel and the Irish Sea, and we arrived back in Liverpool in the evening of Thursday 23rd April.

With all the mundane and usual chores completed the next morning, we were paid off on that occasion not onboard, but at the Cornhill office. Then it was cheerio to Lofty and a leisurely dash to Lime Street Station with a further seagoing experience under my belt, but not one that I was determined to repeat too often, if ever again.

CHAPTER FIFTEEN
THE CLYDE CHIVALRY

(Of a Red Sea Tiger, Big Bangs, and a Very Long Walk).

The problems I was having with the Liverpool Pool office eventually came to a head when the suspicion that I was being messed about was finally confirmed. When I reported back on the morning of May 4th, the clerk posed the question to me, "Are you going to sign a Pool contract to become established?" Over the past few weeks I had myself wrestled with the same question many times. However at that moment in time for me, the prospect of being able to steal the odd extra couple of days unpaid leave at home outweighed the benefits of being on contract to them, even if they did pay out a small amount of money whilst awaiting a new berth.

I believed at that time that it curtailed one's freedom for at the end of a leave period one would have to make oneself available for work immediately. You would probably also be expected to take anything that was on offer since it would be in the Pool's interest to ship you out as soon as possible so that they didn't have to pay out so much. I had already decided against it but I pretended to consider signing and then replied, "No, not at this time." "Fine, try again tomorrow" was the apparent couldn't care less attitude of the clerk. "There is nothing doing today."

At breakfast the next day in Smith's, I bumped into Lofty again who was also waiting for a berth and we decided that it would be a waste of time to visit the Pool that day and we would try again on the morrow.

Lofty was offered a standby at once the next morning and with his funds running low he was left with little choice other than to accept. Once again, the clerk offered me the opportunity to sign the contract, which once again I refused. "Still no jobs, try again tomorrow" was his immediate response at which point I really began to smell a rat.

I bade farewell to Lofty and wasted another day wandering around Liverpool. The next morning the response was still "No jobs." By that time I felt certain I was being strung along and that they knew full well I would soon run out of money to pay for my digs and would be obliged to sign up.

When I left the office, I ran into an AB with whom I had shipped out for that couple of days on the '*Kingsbury*.' In an attempt to prove my suspicions I hung around outside for my former shipmate to see how he had fared. Waving his papers, he emerged after half an hour to confirm to me that he had been fixed up. "They offered me the choice of three jobs," he volunteered. "You are established then?" I queried. His immediate answer "Yes" confirmed all of my suspicions.

Perhaps the clerks themselves were under pressure to get as many of us as possible to sign contracts I don't know, but I hated being manipulated like that and I was not about to continue to play in a game I couldn't win with people who obviously were not out to do me any favours.

Only five months previously, whilst the Falmouth Pool had been willing to offer me work, the Liverpool office had blocked and deferred my reregistration as a seaman until a time that it suited them. Those events were still fresh in my mind and the blatant attempt to manipulate me was the last straw. I didn't have to be a resident in any particular catchment area in order to reregister any more I was already back on the seamen's register and I could go where I liked. I collected my gear from Smith's and headed for Lime Street Station mentally saying goodbye to Liverpool. I was determined to try my luck again in Falmouth.

After a fretful weekend at home, I was aboard the Wolverhampton to Penzance express at nine o'clock on the Monday morning. I changed at Truro and arrived in Falmouth in the early evening just in time to book the last bed at Armyn House, the Seamen's Home.

I had an evening to kill and so I satisfied my appetite in the restaurant and went off to the cinema. When I asked for a seat on the balcony I was informed that there was no film that night as they were showing a live stage production and it was five shillings (25p) a ticket.

I was tired from the journey and needed a rest so I took a ticket without even bothering to ask what the show was. With the frame of mind that I was in then, I thought that anything would do to pass away a couple of hours. It came as a shock to find that it was an opera being shown and a comic one at that.

That was my first introduction to opera in any shape or form and it was to my utter amazement I found that I enjoyed the music and could follow the plot and enjoy the comic sequences. From my original doubts to my eventual delight, it proved to be a very enjoyable evening and I felt really nice and relaxed as I made my way back to my room.

There was something about Falmouth that got to me; it made me feel good. It was not only the set up with the railway station, the Shipping Federation offices, the Pool office, the Seamen's Home and the dock gates, not to mention the Admiral Nelson pub all within spitting distance of each other. It was also the welcoming atmosphere; I felt at home there.

After breakfast the next morning I strolled next door to the Pool office; it was small compared to Liverpool and staffed by three young men all cheery, courteous and helpful. I had no idea if they remembered me from my previous attempt, but I explained my situation to them and handed my discharge book and certificates to one of the clerks who said that he was sure they would be able to find me something.

"In that case if my records could be transferred from Liverpool to Falmouth I would in future sail from here" I ventured. "I will ring them immediately" he said with a smile and walked away to the other end of the office. He was soon back still smiling and cheerfully told me that "Everything had been arranged and they could give me a ship straight away."

The medical examination took no time and on my return to the Pool Clerk, I was informed that my berth was on a tanker called the 'Clyde Chivalry,' and she was signing on at the shipping offices on the corner the very next morning.

I had fully expected the next step and was not surprised when the clerk asked if I would sign a contract. Considering that there had been no attempt to deliberately manipulate me given that they had already offered me a job before they asked, I put my signature to the contract without any further thought. Their cheerful helpfulness was in stark contrast to the Liverpool clerk's attitudes, and the fact that it would secure me to the Falmouth Pool were also good reasons for my change of heart.

The rest of the day was mine; the sun shone and the beaches and cliff-top walks beckoned. I lazed around in the May sunshine and enjoyed the contrast of my new surroundings to those of Liverpool. There was no comparison. I took an early evening meal and spent the rest of the night at the second one of the cinemas that Falmouth had way back then, but reflected as I made my way back to Armyn House that the Opera had been better than the film.

The following morning provided a turnabout in the previously agreed arrangement for when I presented myself at the Pool, the clerk asked if I would mind changing ships. Four ABs, all old friends, wished to sail together but only three berths were available aboard the 'Clyde Chivalry.' There was a berth on the 'Hyrcania' that I could have and as

I appreciated all the help that the Pool Clerk had afforded me I agreed to the swap.

Once again I found myself on Castle Drive overlooking the harbour and the docks. The whole of the area was buzzing with active work with ships on almost every berth and all the dry docks were occupied, it was all happening. There in the largest dry dock right below me was another rusty old tub, the '*Hyrcania.*' My heart sank, "I'd done it again!!" my mind wailed. "What had I let myself in for?" "Here we go again!"

The weather changed; a southwesterly brought cloud and drizzle in off the channel as I turned to go for dinner at the seamen's home. It was an afternoon for bed and a book I thought so I stripped off, crawled between the sheets and was soon deeply engrossed in the novel that I had bought earlier.

I was brought sharply back to reality by a sudden rap at my door. I used the door as a shield because I did not wish to provoke embarrassment or envy. I opened it slightly and poked my head around and I was confronted by the Pool Clerk with the news that someone had failed to turn up for the '*Clyde Chivalry*' and the berth was mine if I wanted it. "There is a God after all" was the immediate thought that ran through my mind. "I'll be right with you," I said and turned to hurry into my clothes.

Five minutes later I was in the Pool office only to be completely ignored by the young man who had interrupted my afternoon rest. Then after a few seconds, he turned saying "What can I do for you?" "You have just got me out of bed to sign on the '*Clyde Chivalry*' I said, more than a little bewildered. "Oh yes, I didn't recognise you with your clothes on," he said giggling heartily at his own little witticism. "Only joking," he laughed, "get round to the Shipping Office next door and sign on," he said.

On my return to the Pool after doing his bidding, I collected eight shillings (40p) for a day's Pool pay and then on to the seamen's home to collect my gear and a refund for the lodging that I had booked for that night. It was a short walk through the dock gates to the '*Clyde Chivalry*,' which had belonged to the British Tanker Company when she was named the *British Chivalry*. Suddenly I remembered reading an article about how a number of ships had been stopped by the Japanese during World War Two and their crews were mown down by machine guns one hundred and eighty *British Merchant* seamen in total.

The article also stated that some men were captured and taken aboard a submarine where some were beheaded and others were thrown overboard still alive, tied together with the headless corpses of their shipmates. It almost defies belief that mankind even in times of war could commit such atrocities on their fellow human beings. It also highlights the fact that very little recognition or appreciation is shown to those brave men of the Merchant Navy for the sacrifices they made for their country during those years.

The '*British Chivalry*' had been one of those ships. Could this be that very same ship where those atrocities had taken place? Or was this her replacement? It was a possibility as the '*Clyde Chivalry*' looked quite old. Could that horror have happened to one of her previous crews? I never did find out but it was far more likely that the Japanese had sunk the original one. She was on charter to BP still, and the only visible difference was a change of colour to the funnel and the British part of her name changed to Clyde.

I reported to the Chief Steward and was issued with all the usual bed linen etc. then I went off to find a cabin aft. All the cabins were twin berths several of which remained locked and those that were not locked were occupied.

The locked cabins had been claimed by local guys who, knowing that she was not to sail until the Monday, had gone ashore taking their cabin keys with them. My cabinmate was to be a guy called Titch who had high tailed it up to his home in Newton Abbot with the keys in his pocket, which caused me to bunk down on the settee in one of the occupied ABs cabins until his return.

* * *

A further advantage of Falmouth was that no sooner had the anchor been weighed than you were out into the open sea, no rivers or buoyed channels or locks to negotiate.

On the morning of Monday 18th May, we headed out into a cool and showery English Channel where we learned that we were on our way to the Persian Gulf. We enjoyed the coolness while we could for we knew of the intense heat that we would soon be exposed to. It continued to be cool and blustery through the Bay of Biscay on to the Straits of Gibraltar. As we passed through, the Rock itself was wreathed in mist and hardly visible, the rain became a torrent, but not for long as the Medi. lived up to its reputation, providing a warm sunny day after we cleared the Straits.

It was Thursday 21st May when the familiar jinx struck and the engines stopped, "nothing changes," I thought, but that time the fault whatever it was, was soon rectified. Initially everyone was content as we enjoyed the warm May sunshine, but as we ploughed relentlessly on towards Port Said and the entrance to the canal, the heat increased.

On Wednesday 27th May the Pilot came aboard to take us past the waiting convoy to the head of the queue, to tie up to buoys at the mouth of the canal. Such was the tension between Egypt and Israel at that time, the fact that the '*Clyde Chivalry*' had at sometime or other delivered oil to Haifa in Israel meant it was blacklisted by the Egyptian authorities, and although they were not able to deny passage through the canal, little assistance was given and no provisions in any shape or form could be obtained. Only the minimum safety requirements were afforded. Ironically, the major plus for us was the fact that there were no bumboats.

At eleven o'clock that night we let go to head the convoy through the canal, and arrived to anchor without a hitch in the Bitter Lakes at 7.30am the following morning. I was on daywork duty so there were no worries for me about doing a stint on the wheel.

As we waited for the passage of the northern bound convoy, the Pilot took ill. It was of little comfort for us to realise then that the stifling heat sometimes adversely affected even the natives. It was well into the afternoon before the North bound convoy cleared the lakes and still a replacement Pilot had not come aboard. Was that further delaying tactics due to the blacklisting? He finally arrived in the early evening, by which time we had to tag on to the end of the next convoy that passed through. We had arrived at the entrance of the canal and had become the first ship of one convoy and ended up being the last ship in the next one, which doubled the time it usually took to get through. We were glad to see the searchlight and boats disappear so that we could progress into the Red Sea where we had hoped to catch a breeze to help cool down our cabins but there was none.

Throughout the trip down, the Bosun had kept us busy cleaning and painting the ship, and so it continued in the stinking heat of the Red Sea. A day's work coping with a relentless sun aggravated by uncomfortable hot steel decks was a tiring and strength-sapping ordeal.

One of the ABs, an experienced one at that, had persistently refused to wear any headgear of any type; ignoring all advice he said in a boasting manner, "I'm OK, I'm a Red Sea Tiger."

Our orders were changed after two days into that Red Sea furnace, we were redirected to go to Aden in Yemen so we were to remain in the oven a while longer. We were just a day out from Aden when a Junior Engineer collapsed with heat exhaustion, little wonder I thought, it must have been like hell down in that engine room, but he recovered quite quickly. The following day, June 1st the Red Sea Tiger keeled over on deck with sunstroke. That happened a few hours out of Aden and he was rushed to hospital on our arrival. For the rest of us, a canteen at the end of the jetty beckoned strongly that evening and the cold beers, accompanied by the equally cool air conditioning, made for an extremely welcome interlude.

It was the last we saw of the Red Sea Tiger for his stay in hospital was expected to be for at least two weeks and we were long gone by then. No one could understand why he, an experienced sailor of many years, would have done such a thing unless of course it was a deliberate act to get off the ship. We did not know but if so, it was a dangerous game to play.

He had occupied a cabin on his own and upon leaving Aden, Titch my cabinmate moved into it, which gave himself and me a cabin each to ourselves. That was a big plus for us as we both liked to enjoy a little privacy. No one argued about it for Titch was a twenty odd stone man mountain, very reminiscent of Tiny who had helped me along with Colossus to keep night watch in Lagos on the 'Nacella,' and indeed I hadn't argued either when we had first met and he had claimed the lower bunk. The thought of having him in the bunk above me would I'm sure have led to many more sleepless nights.

It was early morning on the 3rd June in the relatively cool part of the day that we started back up the Red Sea heading for the Portuguese Cape Verde Islands. That meant a trip all the way around the vast bulge of North Africa as the islands were around the other side just off the West Coast of Africa.

As we progressed back through the Red Sea, the temperature touched 110 degrees Fahrenheit and the Chief Steward became a further victim of the constant incessant heat; he collapsed three days after we had left Aden. He was confined to a bed in the ship's hospital (an unoccupied cabin really, which was reserved for sick sailors), and he was still there recovering slowly four days later as the lights of Port Suez hove into view.

In the dark we could only see the silhouettes of the ships awaiting the formation of the convoy, and like everyone else we prayed that there would be no delay in getting through the canal for the only respite from the heat was what little breeze could be created by the ship's motion.

Our prayers were answered and we were called to stations soon after breakfast; we arrived in the Bitter Lakes three hours later. Unusually the southbound convoy had not cleared into the Lakes so we had to anchor to give them time to do so. Once the passage was clear, we became the fourth ship in line and immediately behind us was the '*Llandaff*.' It was a pleasant surprise to see her again but she looked a bit timeworn and travel stained with her hull streaked with rust. She looked long overdue for a refit and a touch of paint, but the probability was she had been out at sea for a long time since her last dry-docking.

We cleared Port Said by eight o'clock of the evening. Leaving the '*Llandaff*' astern, the '*Clyde Chivalry*' and her crew relished the comparative cool and balmy breezes of the Medi. Two or three hours out of Port Said, a series of loud bangs interrupted our reverie. In the alleyway right opposite my cabin was an entrance door to the engine room, and when I opened it billows of white smoke emerged followed by a flash of red flame, which shot up towards my face. I slammed the door shut and ran up the stairs to the poop deck towards my fire station fearing the worst. Fire and a full cargo of oil were not good bedmates and didn't strain the imagination as to the possible consequences.

Several of the other lads had also gathered on the deck to make towards their fire stations with no doubt the same apprehensive thoughts, but thankfully it transpired that the damage was localized and no one was hurt. Evidently a fuel valve had stuck open which had allowed excess fuel to flow.

The fault was quickly remedied and within two hours the telegraph bells for 'slow ahead' were heard. In many ways it was fortunate that the fault had occurred when it did for if it had happened during our passage through the canal, it could have caused havoc.

Heading westward along the Mediterranean was a delight, the weather got slightly cooler, although it was still hot compared to the British climate. It was 100% better than south of Suez. The engine needed constant attention requiring two further short stops on Friday 12th and Monday morning 15th June. We still left the Rock of Gibraltar astern at midday that same Monday and turned to port hugging the North African Coastline.

After yet two more minor stops, we arrived in St Vincent on Saturday 20th June and went in without delay. To test our shore legs, a few of the crew ventured ashore to what was laughingly called a bar. Ramshackle though it was, the beer was cool and as the evening progressed, the bar stools become more unbalanced, but to sailors confined in the same environment and company for quite some time, it made for a welcome change of scene.

The domestic water supply aboard ship had been a source of complaint for some time. It was apparent to the most casual observer that the brown fluid that gushed out of the showers and toilets was due to unclean tanks. Snowy, who was another AB, and I were turned to on overtime to clean out the tank. To gain access a smallish steel plate on the side of the tank had to be unbolted to allow us both to squeeze inside.

The bottom was covered in rust deposits to the depth of about four or five inches and removing it bucket by bucket took the best part of the day. Once done and dried the task was completed by an application of cement wash and when the tank was refilled with water from another tank, the problem was cured. It was nice to return to bathing in clean fresh water again.

It was only a part disposal of the cargo at St Vincent; the rest was destined for Dakar in Senegal where we arrived on Wednesday 24th June. The sickness rate onboard continued, but it was not due to the heat that time; not long after being taken alongside by the Pilot, Malcolm the deck boy, who never had to do any peggying, was rushed to hospital with acute appendicitis. One by one the dreaded lurgy was taking its toll and we all wondered who would be next.

The weather was very settled and became extremely hot again so it was with some relief that once we had discharged the rest of the cargo we headed out into the Atlantic the following night, destination unknown. Head towards the Caribbean and South America was the extent of our knowledge. That allowed the company to arrange for a further cargo for us whilst we made our way in the general direction.

The Mate, in his wisdom, decided that it was a good opportunity to clean the tanks. It was said that they had not been entered into for at least eighteen months so butterworthing alone would not do the job; it had to be a complete manual effort with shovel and bucket.

From Saturday 27th June until Wednesday 1st July all hands were employed removing eight inches of oily, rusty gunk from the bottom of thirteen of the twenty-seven tanks. The sheer amount of oily residue upheld the opinion that it had indeed collected over a period of at least eighteen months, and we cursed as we sweated cobs in the overheated, claustrophobic atmosphere.

The only consolation for my shipmates Snowy and my ex-cabinmate, the twenty odd stone man mountain Titch, and myself was most of the work for us was being done on overtime for on leaving Dakar we had been transferred from daywork into the four to eight watch. A further perk too was the tot of rum we received after finishing each day.

We flew across the Atlantic at fourteen knots with no sign of engine trouble and after a spell of cooler weather, it began to get warmer. We received orders to proceed to Cardon to take on bunkers before heading for the Maracaibo Lakes to take on a cargo of crude oil destined for Santos in Brazil. That news was not received with any enthusiasm by the lads for it had begun to look like the 'Clyde Chivalry' could be out for a long long time.

Weaving through the islands, we reached the Caribbean on the morning of Friday 3rd July and with any luck we would reach Cardon early the next day. We were not to know what the spirits of the deep had kept in store for us. I had gone to my bunk early and couldn't remember dropping off but I was in a deep sleep when the most almighty explosion literally bounced me out of my bunk.

The bangs and crashes continued for what seemed ages but probably only lasted a few seconds. The other lads, who had gathered in the alleyway, all had that apprehensive, alarmed look on their faces.

Tentatively we crept to the engine room door expecting the worst and on first examination, our fears were confirmed. The sixth cylinder of the six cylinder Doxford engine had exploded. The massive piston had gone through the cylinder casing and was stuck and bent like a crazy banana, and the casing was buckled beyond repair.

Rivets had flown, steel rods were buckled, parts of the catwalk had collapsed and two large holes had appeared in the engine casing. The scene was, I thought, reminiscent of what a ship's engine room may have looked like after being torpedoed during the war. Amidst all of the carnage, miraculously no one was hurt. "My God!" I thought, "My very first ship out of Falmouth and they are trying to blow me up." The immediate instant assessment of the damage was that it would be tugs to the rescue. "Not again please," I thought.

The engine-room staff were soon clearing away the mess so that a realistic evaluation of the damage could be made. For the next two days as we drifted, they collected bits and pieces of the broken engine and piston before a clearer idea of what could be done was reached. Eventually it was decided to make an attempt to block off the damaged cylinder and try to proceed on the remaining five. Cement boxes were made and fixed over the holes in the engine casings to seal the damage and isolate the sixth cylinder.

During the enforced four-day silent drift in the hot Caribbean sunshine, us deckhands were kept busy chipping rust and repainting various parts of the ship. In our leisure periods we reverted to our much loved pastime 'Shark fishing.' We hooked eight and landed six successfully on deck; only two got away. All were in the six-foot plus mark and the sport certainly relieved the tedium as we drifted aimlessly, thankfully well away from any shoreline.

With two mates, I sat talking in my cabin when the moment of truth arrived. The telegraph rang for standby. As one, we jumped up and headed for the door. To get three men through that door at the same time was impossible; it just wasn't wide enough, but in our anxiety to get to the poop deck, we made it in record time.

"Oh us of little faith," but if the engine was going to blow up everyone knew where they wanted to be, and it wasn't anywhere near that engine room. The crew stood by the ladder up to the boat deck with bated breath as the engine started up, first slow ahead, then half, and finally it settled into the rhythm of full ahead.

The Bosun and the dayworkers had made a buoy from an empty fifty-gallon drum for when or if we started again they had half filled it with sand and planted a yellow flag firmly into it. As soon as the engine restarted, they heaved it over the side to bob about in the water. It was to be used as a marker. We sailed away from it in a semicircle and using a sextant, the Mate took a distance reading. The time was recorded as we sailed back towards it. That gave a rough measurement of the speed that the adapted engine could achieve.

Eight knots was the estimation and we left the home made buoy floating with the knowledge that it would soon sink into the depths, and hoping that the engine would stand up we continued on with our interrupted journey pointing our bows towards Cardon. With all due credit to the skills of our engineers, it did.

* * *

There are many moments of danger and stress in a sailor's life, at least there were in mine. One thing that always surprised me was the ability that the guys who manned those ships had to put the dangers in the past the moment the crisis was over and just carry on with the job as if nothing had ever happened. I am sure that those experiences played a large part in building the character that I am today and the way I handle things and deal with problems in a way that is totally alien to the people around me here in the Midlands.

We received a change of orders shortly afterwards; they redirected us to Curacao, which was slightly nearer, and we arrived there the following afternoon. Probably due to the state of the engines, there was no delay and the Pilot took us straight in to tie up to buoys in the harbour.

In no time a Lloyd's insurance agent was onboard to assess the damage. Everyone was on tenterhooks for his decision would spell out the immediate future destination of the ship. Finally the word was passed that he had sanctioned the carriage of one more cargo provided that it was destined for the United Kingdom where the engine would then have to be repaired. Our cheers rang around the harbour, which left the Captain and the Officers in no doubt where we expected to make our next landfall, and someone else would have to pick up the Santos cargo.

Shore leave was not granted and therefore no celebrations, perhaps it was for the best for we were on our way at five o'clock the next morning, Thursday 9th July to pick up a cargo at Cardon. It was my stint at the wheel as we made our way back through the narrow channel into the open sea to arrive safely at Cardon that evening. The loading of a full cargo took two days and once again shore leave was not granted. With the crude oil safely aboard it was Land's End for orders on Saturday morning 11th July.

Still the slight possibility remained that we could be diverted to a continental port for the repairs to be done there, we made our way back up across the Caribbean and passed through the Mona Passage which separates the Dominican Republic and Puerto Rico, and entered into the Atlantic.

Eight knots did not break any speed limits, and that first evening out we stopped once again for an hour. The stoppage was evidently just for a cautionary check and with many sighs of relief the engine came back to life without any problem. The biggest problem came when for some unknown reason, the Skipper decided to check and test the emergency steering gear. That didn't please the Chief Engineer one bit; to do some of the testing, the engine would have to be stopped once more and he felt sure that stopping and starting wouldn't do the engine any good. He was of the view that testing the emergency steering gear was not something that absolutely needed to be done under those circumstances. It led to a blazing row between the two of them. But the Skipper, being the ultimate God on a ship, had his way. Perhaps he thought that if the engines did blow up again we could rig a tarpaulin up on the mast and sail home that way. Who knows?

The emergency steering gear was housed in the steerage locker in the bowels of the stern; it fell to me and Snowy to undertake the manhandling of the massive wheel that wound in the great chain connected to the rudder. It became obvious why the old windjammers needed strong men at the helm, and why Popeye had developed such muscles as we tugged and pulled to satisfy the Skipper's whim.

My personal views on the subject tended to side a little with the Chief Engineer for that was the first and only time I was ever to perform or see that particular test performed on any ship. Everything appeared to be in order to the Skipper's satisfaction and it would seem that he did know best after all as the engines restarted again without a single problem.

Fortunately old Neptune smiled upon us as we slowly made our way through the passive and sunny Atlantic at a steady eight knots. As the Azores slipped away to starboard on Monday 20th July, the Bosun appeared at my door with the news that the Mate had decided that Snowy and myself were to be put back on daywork. We were less than pleased and protested about it, but we were given no choice but to do as we were told, "What do you think this is anyway?" the Bosun asked, "Your daddy's yacht?" "Of course not" I replied, "It's bigger than this," but there was little or nothing else we could do about it.

Yet again the Bay of Biscay didn't live up to its reputation and remained calm. We received the orders to discharge the cargo in Swansea and then go on to Falmouth for repairs. Thursday 30th July saw us anchored in Swansea Bay waiting for a berth, but it was not until Saturday 1st August that we went through the lock to tie up at the standby jetty and shifted ship at six o'clock on Sunday morning to the discharging berth. Once that was done, we were given the time off until Tuesday morning.

It was the August Bank Holiday weekend and the next day was holiday Monday. It was time to renew my acquaintance with good old British ale. Despite caustic comments from some of our continental friends, there is nothing to compete with good British ale at its best. That first pint that followed a long enforced absence was something to savour when, along with Roy, another shipmate who hailed from Milford Haven, I went off to the sailors' home, which kept a good pint according to Roy.

After a couple of pints I was talked into going to the local cinema but was happy to return to the sailors' home for a few more bevvies later. Half past ten saw last orders and the towels were put on; whether it was the beer or not, Roy decided that he was going home and asked me if I would like to come with him.

Milford Haven was about sixty miles away and all public transport had been put to bed. "No problem," Roy assured me, "We will hitchhike, everyone stops to give you a lift in this part of the world," he said. With a certain misgiving I thought "Well, he is the local, who am I to disbelieve? So, what have I got to lose?" So began what turned out to be the longest march of my life, aggravated by the fact that it was the first time for a long while that I had walked further than from my cabin to the fo'c's'le head.

We left the suburbs of Swansea behind, along the hilly coastal road, the darkness hit the surrounding countryside and there was little traffic. It must have been after half an hour or so when a car stopped. "This can't be bad," I thought as I climbed into the back seat perhaps Roy is right after all. "And where are you heading at this time of night?" came the question from the driver in that quaint South West Wales accent.

"Milford Haven," we replied, "Well, I am only going for a further four miles, but maybe you could get lucky," he said in what I thought was a slightly sceptical tone. Very shortly after he dropped us off and gave a cheery wave as we began to walk again. It was edging past midnight and there was no traffic whatsoever as we trudged on and on in the darkness for what seemed an eternity. The euphoria from our bevvies had worn very thin and we welcomed the sound of an approaching car. Two young guys in a sports car who had obviously been observing the old British custom of a Saturday night bash (no breathalysers in those days) cheerily invited us to hop in, but again they could only take us a further three miles along that road. It seemed as if I had no sooner put my bum on the seat than they turned off.

I had really begun to suffer, the aches in both my feet and legs were turning into pain; the only consolation Roy could offer was the prospect of reaching Carmarthen which was roughly halfway and from there an early morning bus service would get us to Milford.

Each milestone was greeted like a lifelong friend as each painful step carried me past them. Five thirty a.m. came and still we were walking; we both knew that it was probably the wrong thing to do, but we virtually collapsed and sat on the roadside propped up against a wall for a rest. During this time our legs stiffened and set almost like concrete, but finally the pain subsided back into just a throbbing ache.

Summing up all our strength and will power after an hour's rest we forced ourselves back onto the road to be picked up by a driver from heaven. An hour later we were about three or four miles short of Carmarthen. We collapsed onto the back seat and related our night's trudge to the driver. He dropped us off in the bus station.

It was almost eight o'clock and I had trudged through some of the prettiest countryside in Wales without seeing a thing except the tarmac of the Swansea to Carmarthen road in some detail. It had taken us over nine hours to get halfway. At the bus station it was obviously not our day for our bus had just gone, and the next was not due to leave for three hours.

Roy's words of the previous night sprang back to mind, "Everybody in this part of the world will stop and pick you up," he had said. "Obviously," I thought sarcastically, "That's because the bloody public transport doesn't." It was time to mutiny, "Not one step further" was my decision. Roy accepted that as final and hobbled off to the nearest call box and rang for a taxi.

Within minutes I had sunk into the luxury of the back seat of the cab bemoaning my condition and seriously wondering if I would ever recover. As it was to prove, the human frame is a pretty resilient structure and upon arrival at Roy's home, I was well on the way to some state of normality.

It was nine o'clock and Roy's family, his girlfriend Ann and her friend Flossie made me very welcome, and my first taste of a Welsh breakfast would stay with me for many years. Roy's dad was away also at sea but locally as he was a fisherman manning a trawler out of Milford Haven. Where I found the energy from I do not know, but later in the day we all took a drive to a very beautiful, secluded, tiny, sandy beach where we all played volleyball.

It was an early start by bus the following morning to arrive back aboard by 10.30am. After taking advantage of Welsh hospitality and accepting Roy's mother's invitation to spend some time with them during our forthcoming leave, we headed back to the ship.

The call of the nectar on sale at the sailor's home proved irresistible, Roy and I slipped ashore for a couple at dinnertime. In the bar I bumped into Rusty with whom I had sailed five years previously on the *San Velino*. Rusty was the ordinary seaman who had gone on lookout wrapped in blankets and a saucepan over his head after we had spud raided that hawk, which had taken a rest on our mast.

He too was then an AB and shared my liking for the local brew; he was shipping out on a BP Tanker, the '*British Workman*' or as he termed it the British Workhouse. We reminisced and swapped yarns, but only too soon we had to wish each other good luck as we both had unfinished business elsewhere.

Later that afternoon we were Falmouth bound and it was butterworthing all the way. Snowy and I worked throughout the night tackling as many tanks as possible, which didn't do anything to ease my recovery from the long march.

For all seafarers, any time of the year is a good day to arrive back at a home port, and 5th August didn't disappoint. It was high summer and the Cornish countryside was at its best and that special charm that for me is Falmouth never failed to please. Tying up was routine and was only relieved by the arrival in port of the deep-sea tug the '*Englishman*,' the very same which had come to the aid of the '*Martagon*' in what by then seemed a previous existence and for some unfathomable reason, it felt really good to see her again.

The officials in the shipping office seemed as pleased as the crew to pay us off. There was no problem concerning changing my rail voucher to be made out to Swansea but I was told I would have to pay my own fare back from there to Wolverhampton.

Early closing day in Falmouth was Wednesdays and the need to make one or two necessary purchases found four of us heading for Truro on the first train. Once we had got our purchases we met up again with most of the rest of the crew back on the railway station. They piled on to the train the second it had stopped, while it took us four a little longer to gather our gear.

A porter then approached us and asked if we were seamen and if so the two rear coaches had been reserved for us. That was an unexpected pleasure and as none of us felt the urge to go in search of the others, we had two whole empty coaches to ourselves without the worry of being disturbed throughout the whole trip. I stretched out my still aching limbs to rest in comfort.

Changing at Swansea, Roy and I arrived in Milford Haven at midday on Thursday. To my surprise I was invited to stay with Flossie and her parents who were kindness itself and personified true Welsh hospitality. It was a pleasant, relaxing little holiday and exactly what I needed to recover from my exertions, but the weekend was to pass far too quickly. Flossie and Ann were at work on the Monday morning so were unable to come to see me off, but I said my farewells to Roy as I caught the train to Gloucester at Milford's tiny station.

That was the route I was told I would have to take and despite the beauty of the countryside, the first part of the journey proved to be endless; we never travelled at more than ten miles an hour and stopped at every wayside halt, even in the middle of fields to load milk churns. I began to despair of ever arriving in Gloucester, but for the last part it picked up speed only for me to have to wait a further two hours at Gloucester for a connection to Wolverhampton.

Late Thursday 13th August saw me catching a taxi to take me the last few miles home. It seemed a long time since I had said goodbye to the '*Clyde Chivalry*.' The journey had been long and the Welsh countryside pretty. I would long remember the hospitality I had been afforded by my newfound Welsh friends.

CHAPTER SIXTEEN

THE TREVOSE

(Of a Close Encounter with a Bucket, a Nail and a Family).

The first part of my leave spent in Milford Haven was at least novel, and certainly a change from the usual mad dash to New Street or Wolverhampton and the various means of transportation from those stations to my home.

The second part of the leave was more or less routine. I met up with Mavis and Alan at the local social club and on occasion Norman would make up a happy and friendly quartet (I did not realise at that point in time the significance that the club would have on my life and the role it would play in my entire future).

A further pleasant distraction was my habit of being lucky at bingo. The club had the normal clientele with seats that were regularly occupied each night by the same clique, and God help anyone who had the tenacity to place their backsides in those unofficial reserved seats.

It was also considered not quite the thing for someone like me to win at bingo as I was anything but a regular because I was away at sea so much. To win several times as I did while on my leaves was really too much for some so the moans and groans were quite pointed. I revelled in all of that and my apparent unconcern for their complaints only made some of the clientele even more outraged, after all it was my money that paid for my tickets.

I travelled down to Falmouth on Tuesday 18th August and after I had booked my room in Armyn House, I spent the rest of the evening strolling through the town and lazing on the beaches of which Falmouth can justifiably be proud.

I reported to the Pool the following morning and I was informed that there were no berths available with no prospect of a job until sometime the following week. I could have kicked myself for not taking the obvious opportunity to use the telephone prior to my departure from Walsall.

I took another walk and decided to catch the next train home to take advantage of my Pool contract for as I had reported back, they would pay me the basic subsistence until I was found a berth, and I thought it would be great to have an extra few days leave. My bingo winnings took care of my rail fare.

The cheerful Pool staff were only too happy to help and assured me that a telegram would be on its way as soon as a job appeared. So I went back to upsetting the regulars at the club, which I took a perverse delight in doing by winning more houses and lines at bingo. That of course was put to one side to pay for my return fare to Falmouth.

As good as their word, the Pool guys telegraphed my home on Saturday 22nd August with the request that I report to the Pool on the morning of Tuesday 25th. I travelled down on the Monday and next morning was given the '*M/V Trevose*,' a cargo boat of the Hain Steamship Company and with certain misgivings, I lugged my gear through the dock gates to the '*Trevose.*' I would have much preferred a tanker, but I didn't want to destroy the understanding that I felt I had established with the Pool guys so I had reluctantly accepted.

Most of the crew were already aboard signing articles and to see faces that I recognised from other ships was a welcome surprise. Once they had signed, most of the crew, including myself, were hustled ashore to join a coach bound for Truro hospital to get jabs against yellow fever.

Two of my shipmates from the '*Clyde Chivalry*' were sitting together close by. Jeff, who was a fireman, agreed with me that a far more reliable engine was hoped for on the '*Trevose*' than the exploding one of the '*Clyde Chivalry.*' The other guy, to my surprise, was Malcolm from the '*Clyde Chivalry*;' he was the deck boy who had been rushed to hospital in Dakar with appendicitis. He had recovered from his appendicitis operation, then had been shipped back home and had since become a JOS.

On the coach I sat next to a SOS called Pete from Plymouth with whom I eventually shared a cabin once we had returned to the ship after we had received our jabs. The cabins were twin berth, compact, comfortable and most importantly clean.

As the watches were sorted in the time-honoured fashion with the cards, it came as something of a shock to find out that all the other qualified crewmembers were EDHs and I was the only actual AB aboard. The most long-serving and senior member of the deck crew. It made me feel old.

We were called to stations at 11.00am the next day, I was in the after gang and we began to single up. With that accomplished, we awaited the final order to let go only to be told by the Bosun to hold hard. When we asked him why, the familiar words, at least to my ears, were, "They can't start the bloody engine." Inevitably we had to make fast again. "Christ!" I thought, "Here we go again; what a marvellous start" as I remembered the last trip with all its trials and tribulations.

With fingers crossed, we repeated the performance the next morning after hectic activity in the engine room; that time with success. We sailed out around Pendennis Point and came into the English Channel heading for Antwerp, Belgium, where we arrived without further delay on the morning of Saturday 29th August.

We went straight in alongside and began to load almost immediately. As we had only been signed on for a couple of days no one had any money in the ship so no one went ashore despite the attraction of those welcoming bars and good Belgium beer.

Long lengths of railway line and steel pipes about twenty-feet long were soon being stowed away in our holds. Most unusually the dockers replaced the beams and hatch boards on completion, which left only the tarpaulins for the deck crew to secure and batten down. The derricks were left topped but secured to ensure that they wouldn't swing with the ship's movement.

The weather was pleasant as we made our way back into the English Channel on our way to Dunkirk. Following the coast around it was a short trip, and we arrived at midday. Soon the hatches were stripped and the loading of more pipes and railway lines commenced. It was a week before all of the cargo was loaded, not that it took place continually for most of the time was spent waiting for different articles to arrive at the docks.

The need for the 'Jumbo,' the large heavy lifting derrick, to be rigged ready for use came as a surprise. It had to be brought into service to load a twenty-ton crane into number two hatch. As it was part of the ship's gear, breaking it out and rigging it was a job for us. It was done with great care under the supervision of the Bosun; with the lifting of such a weight everything had to be checked and double checked to make sure all the gear could take the strain. It took longer to break out, rig, check, then dismantle and secure it again than it did for the dockers to bring the crane aboard, but it was all good experience for most of us.

Towards the end of the week, we learned that all the Dunkirk parcel of cargo would be aboard and our departure was due on the Saturday. Pete and I took a small sub and went ashore to explore the port that was so important in the history of the Second World War. Naturally we inspected and sampled a couple of beers and found them to be up to the expected standard, and we quite enjoyed the variation from routine.

Still not fully loaded, we headed out into the Channel on Saturday 5th September. The same date that in 1939 the British Expeditionary Force had landed there to take on the might of Hitler's invading forces, which in turn culminated in the massive evacuation from those beaches some months later.

The lowering and securing of the derricks and covering the hatches was made more palatable by the weather that continued warm and sunny. Bayonne, close to the French / Spanish border, was to be our next port of call.

The Bay of Biscay again behaved itself, and our engines, after their initial non-start, gave no cause for concern. For most of the journey, the deck crew were kept busy painting ship, generally tidying lockers and greasing blocks and machinery. The regularity and monotony of chores on a cargo boat going in and out of ports keeps everyone busy, especially when there is little time spent at sea between ports.

When we arrived at Bayonne on Tuesday 8th September, we found it to be a small port come resort, picturesque with a very old cathedral near Pauillac where I had called when on the '*Hyala.*' Once again I marvelled at the speed of the current in that river.

Everyone had to turn to at six every morning to open the hatches to commence loading bags of sulphur on top of the railway lines. Normal day working shifts in port allowed no respite, in spite of having to turn to after tea to cover the hatches. The dockers were not as accommodating in France as their Belgian counterparts.

Pete and I went ashore several times after work to enjoy the relaxing atmosphere, the balmy weather and of course the local bars. Clouds threatened as we cast off heading for the Straits of Gibraltar and once clear of land, we stopped for forty-five minutes for the engineers to change a valve.

Once we had passed through the Straits we had Mediterranean showers, some quite heavy at times until the Rock began to fade on the horizon. Then the weather turned on its charm again as we headed for Mostaganam on the Algerian coast, but we were kept too busy to enjoy the sunshine and the twinkling blue sea.

We reached Mostaganam on Saturday 19th September and only a couple of items were taken aboard. Within a few hours we were battened down and heading for Sardinia. Although we could have done without the extra work involved with the derricks and hatches etc. during the short periods between ports, the weather was great and the prospect, as always, of visiting places not yet explored was a big plus.

It was tempting fate to even think about engine failure, but without any problem in that area, we arrived in Sant Antioco, south of the Island of Sardinia, on Tuesday 22nd September. It was a welcoming port and with the day's chores completed, Pete, an EDH called Mick from Redruth and I ventured ashore.

The islanders had a custom for the meeting of the sexes similar to the custom that I had encountered in Sagua when on the '*Granford*,' which revived memories of Chocolate and his jokes and sunny character. While the Saguan boys and girls had walked in opposite directions around the church square, in Sant Antioco they walked up and down the main street making their choices.

At around 8.30pm the boys and girls started to pair off and disappear and in a very short space of time, the main street became virtually deserted. Naturally, being full red-blooded Englishmen, we tried our hand but as in Sagua, to no avail. The girls were fully aware from where we came and that we were only ships that passed in the night so they would have no truck with us.

Rumour had it that the '*Trevose*' was probably the largest vessel that had graced the harbour for every time the tide receded the keel rested on the bottom. Remembering once being stuck on a sandbank in Singapore Harbour and the consternation that had caused, I felt a little apprehensive, but no one else seemed to worry and we came to no harm.

The word spread that our departure date was Thursday 24th September and so it was that once the incoming tide rendered us buoyant again in the late afternoon, we set sail northwards to Marseilles. Corsica, to the north of Sardinia was just a smudge on the horizon that suddenly vanished in the haze of an advancing rainstorm. It was Friday at 9.00pm when we finished tying up and the Skipper gave us our subs.

The rain was still pelting own so we didn't think it was a good idea to go searching for a bar in those conditions. A further annoyance occurred the next morning on learning that we were to depart at about teatime. I was a little annoyed because I had French francs and no opportunity to spend them.

"Could I go ashore for a couple of hours to purchase toiletries and writing paper?" I asked the Mate. "No" was the unequivocal answer.

"To hell with it," I thought, and decided to go anyway. Both Pete and Mick were of a similar mind and came ashore with me; we fully expected retribution when we returned at midday by being logged at least a day's pay for our crime.

Once we had purchased our items of need, we crept back aboard a couple of hours later. We hadn't missed dinner and no one had missed us for no one said a word. As it turned out, ironically the sailing time had been delayed until Sunday so our defiance was all to no avail and it had backfired on us in a way. We had spent all our money so we couldn't go ashore that night.

With the famous Cote d'Azur to port, we sailed along the coast leaving French territorial waters behind to arrive in Livorno (Leghorn) on Monday 28th September the next day. The port hopping in the Mediterranean was becoming very reminiscent of my passage on the 'San Velino' with us not staying anywhere for any length of time. On that occasion, in a way, it was worse being on a cargo boat, but even all the work with the derricks and hatches each time was by far and away better than having to do all that peggying.

The Mate had decided to maintain the watches so with Pete and I being on the twelve to four it gave us the morning off. The Skipper's sudden burst of generosity in giving us a sub in Marseilles was not repeated there and we were broke, but I found a thousand lira note on deck. One of the dockers must have lost it, and I presumed that should I make enquiries, every one of them would claim it as their own so I decided that perhaps it would be best to recycle it back into the Italian economy via the nearest bar.

Livorno is a place I would like to return to with a little more time to relax and explore. It seemed a lovely town and left a pleasant memory for us both, but the thousand lira note didn't go far in the bar. Again it was a quick turn around the next morning. We sailed North to Genoa, which was to be our final pickup point, arriving there the same afternoon and we anchored for a short while before going alongside the quay.

Next day we took onboard the greatest part of the cargo. Bales and boxes were stuffed into the last available spaces in the holds until each hatch was fully loaded. We then put back beams and hatch boards in place as well as securing and battening down four layers of tarpaulin. Two sizeable lorries had been lowered into number one hold followed by another six lorries as deck cargo. To my surprise and consternation boxes of mines, ammunition and explosives were lashed down onto the decks to be followed finally by two buses or touring coaches.

After four days we were fully loaded. One positive point during those four days was that we were able to go ashore in the evenings to frequent the bars and chat up the local talent. How I loved those Italian senoritas!

* * *

We were ready to sail again by Saturday 3rd October and set on a southern course all the way down the Italian coast. Monday 5th brought us below the plume of white smoke being emitted from Stromboli, which reminded us all that it still threatened; it was quite awe inspiring. We slipped through the Straits of Messina between seven and nine that same evening. No letters in jars on that occasion, and once we lost sight of the Italian coast we headed for Port Said.

There was the usual gaggle of ships of all nationalities awaiting passage through the canal when we arrived and anchored on the afternoon of Friday 9th October. It was nine o'clock that evening when the anchor was weighed for us to wend a passage through the ships and moor, stern to, onto a buoy closer to the entrance. Why the move and all the hard work that it entailed was necessary I will never know. I saw no reason why we couldn't have stayed at anchor for the next twelve hours before we started on our way through the canal.

I relieved Mick at the wheel at one o'clock; the Pilot had come onboard and cast off four hours previously. Given the presence of the Pilot I still found those stints at the wheel through the narrow confines of the canal a little scary and inspiring as we had to give total concentration to the job in hand. So I was relieved when after half hour, we turned into the cutting and tied up to allow a northbound convoy to proceed. For some unknown reason their passage north took much longer than anticipated, and it was 8.00pm that evening when we cast off to continue on our way. We cleared the southern exit in the early hours of Sunday morning. For once the gods of fortune smiled upon me as I was the 'farmer' standby throughout the watch, and I didn't have the dubious pleasure of another trick on the wheel.

As each ship cleared the canal, it resembled the start of the Grand Prix with those that could speed up doing so to head off down the Red Sea showing us their sterns, while we ambled along at a steady eleven knots amongst the stragglers. The Red Sea greeted us with its usual wall of stifling heat, and fortunately there were no 'Red Sea Tigers' amongst the crew that time.

We plodded along at our steady eleven knots, which brought us off Port Sudan in the early hours of Tuesday 13th October where we dropped anchor. Within minutes of the anchor chain coming to rest, a shore gang came out into the bay to unload the deck cargo of the boxes of mines and explosives into pontoons to be towed ashore by a tug. Was it just me who thought that they had their priorities all wrong?

When the hatches were uncovered, the cargo to be discharged was found to have been incorrectly loaded. The cargo that they needed was lying below the top layers, and the offending objects had to be lifted out onto the deck to be replaced when the appropriate cargo had been retrieved. Then to complete the discharge of the rest of the cargo destined for Sudan, the 'Trevose' went alongside the harbour proper. Pete and I could not resist stretching our legs, but only as far as the Seamen's Mission about ten minutes walk away from the docks.

Considering the mistakes in the loading, it came as no surprise to cast off only to anchor once again in the harbour for the dockers to return some boxes of explosives that they had taken that were bound for elsewhere. They then had to be stowed in the correct position and the hatches battened down. The Skipper, impatient to be away, was not best pleased with the hold up and was heard muttering a number of unrepeatable expletives.

Once again it was only a short hop down the coast to Massawa in Ethiopia where we went in alongside to tie up the following night. The lorries and the two coaches were discharged the next morning and considering the size of the vehicles, it went without a hitch and created space on the decks, which made for an easier existence.

We sailed minus two of the deckhands. They had gone ashore, and at the time of sailing, to my knowledge without even enquiring about their whereabouts or whatever, the Skipper had us cast off and we sailed without them. They could have been in clink, hospital or drunk somewhere, which appeared to give little concern to the Skipper, but there is more later about the care and consideration the Skipper afforded his crew.

It became cooler as we headed south down to the French Territories (now I believe a small country in its own right called Djibouti), arriving at the port of Djibouti early on Wednesday 21st October where more cargo was discharged, but just small amounts of boxes and bales. It took next to no time. That allowed us to sail to enjoy the cooler breezes as we crossed the Gulf of Aden on route to the Arabian Sea.

On leaving Djibouti Pete and I were changed into the eight to twelve watch. It stayed calm and the cool breeze stayed with us as we passed Ras Al Had into the Gulf of Oman on Monday 26th October. We continued on through the Strait of Hormuz and at midnight entered into the Persian Gulf. Finally on the morning of Thursday 29th October, we anchored off Bahrain.

More cargo was discharged into barges and completed that day, which allowed us to continue up the Gulf towards Kuwait the next morning. The normally placid, calm Gulf provided a surprise as a strong wind sprang up and the seas became unusually heavy.

The miniature storm blew itself out and by daybreak the Gulf was back on its best behaviour. Perhaps it was just as well for around lunchtime on the Saturday, ominous noises were heard in the engine room. Bolts had sheared in some part of the engine and soon we were drifting at the whim of the elements.

The Gulf was quite a busy stretch of water with regard to shipping but fortunately the position in which the engine failure occurred was shallow so rather than float about aimlessly it allowed us to let go both anchors. It was thought that by being held fast in one place, we constituted a far less hazard to other shipping.

Eight and a half hours later, dirty, sweaty and anything but happy, some of the engineers emerged from what must have been a hellhole down the engine room in that colossal heat. The telegraph rang "Slow ahead." From then on it took but a few hours to arrive at the next port: Mina Al Ahmadi, Kuwait where we anchored early on Sunday 1st November and went alongside at 10.00am.

A brand new seamen's canteen was the only place worthy of a visit as it dispensed cold soft drinks, which were quite palatable and tasty. Beer would have been more welcoming but unfortunately not in alcohol free Kuwait. It would be wrong to criticize the canteen for it was comfortable and welcoming, and we saw a couple of films, which provided a pleasant diversion. More bales and boxes were discharged then and for some inexplicable reason, we let go to sail out into the bay again only to anchor and discharge the rest into barges.

My gut was playing up when I awoke on Thursday morning, "It must be those ice-cold soft drinks," I thought, "alcohol free zones didn't agree with my system." But things didn't improve, even after a sharp walk around the deck and a breath of fresh air. The thought that I would work it off soon became an illusion; it got much much worse.

I decided to see the Chief Steward who was in charge of the medicine supplies. He gave me a spoonful of stomach medicine and advised me to lie down quietly for a while. He said that I had got 'Gulf tummy.' As I shuffled back towards my cabin I thought, "Gulf tummy What the hell was Gulf tummy?"

All predictions, including my own, were to be proved wrong; the pain in my stomach gradually got worse, and still worse was to come. I barely made it to the toilet and sat there, my bowels out of control and retching at the same time. I was losing fluids from both ends. The spasms got less, and after about fifteen minutes, I made my way back to the cabin. My dashes up the companionway ladder to the toilet became more frequent and the stomach pain was excruciating, but the vomiting had ceased.

By mid afternoon I was hardly able to move. I certainly couldn't make it up the ladder to the toilets anymore. I had no other choice but to grab my big galvanised bucket and place it in the middle of the cabin deck and I plonked myself upon it and doubled forward straining against the pain.

Although the Skipper had been informed that I was ill, throughout the rest of that day and all through the night I sat there totally unaware of anything other than the pain. No one at all came from amidships to see me. Friday morning arrived and I was still there, gradually getting weaker, and still my bowels were a law unto themselves. Some of the lads went to the Skipper to ask him to send for a doctor for me. He refused saying that I had only got a touch of the trots. They approached him again a couple of hours later with still the same result.

Later that afternoon, after a third delegation to the Skipper, Pete brought the good news that the Skipper had at last finally relented and agreed to send for a doctor. "Thank God," I thought, "at long last, at least I am not just going to be left here to die." However, it was not over yet. Dinnertime arrived, teatime came, then it became dark, and still there was no doctor.

I lost all track of time, but I do recall the silence being broken by first the hiss and then the rumble of the engines starting up. We were heading out to sea and still no doctor, but by then I was past caring. I was glued to the bucket throughout a further night.

Much later I was told by the man who had been on the wheel at the time that while weighing anchor, they had received on the bridge a signal from the shore stating that a doctor was on his way. The Skipper totally ignored it and sailed anyway.

The next morning, with the bucket almost completely full and implanted as an integral part of my body, I heard that for the fourth time, the lads had petitioned the Skipper, demanding that he get me a doctor at the next port of call. They had taken the unprecedented step of threatening to walk off the ship if he didn't. The fact that they were prepared to go to such lengths must at long last have made him realise the possibility that perhaps my illness was a little more than a touch of the trots, and he came to take a look for himself.

I was so ill by then that much of what happened around me was a blur. I was slipping to the very edges of consciousness. I honestly don't know if I dreamed some of it or not as it was like the occasional picture piercing my memory like the flashbacks in a film. I do recall the look of shock on the Skipper's face as he entered the cabin and saw the state that I was in; instantly he realised how ill I really was.

Only then did he begin to show any care and compassion. I can still remember the squelch of air as I was peeled off the rim of that bucket, and for some reason feeling concerned for the poor sod that had to empty it. I am sure that if it had been me, it would have gone over the side bucket and all. Which later I was told, it did.

There was still a vague recollection in my head of hands lifting me, and the heat of the sun burning into me as I was carried along the deck towards amidships. I remember the feeling of warm refreshing water from a shower and finally being covered between warm, clean sheets on a soft mattress. The Skipper reappeared later with a glass of something that put me out like a light, "Oh sweet oblivion." He later told me that the medicine had laudanum in it. I remember rousing at some point to hear the engines stopping and starting, and the clanking of anchor chains, but most of the time I was dead to the world.

Much later I was told that we had come alongside at Abadan, Persia (now Iran), and the Skipper had requested the attendance of a doctor via the charter agents. When they came onboard the Skipper asked, "Where was the doctor?" and when told that they had no idea, he exploded. "Get off the bloody ship, and don't come back without one."

That change in attitude, on reflection, was amazing, and obviously he was finally facing the fact that he had a sick man on his hands and not as I think he suspected, a malingerer. I also think he may have suddenly realised the serious position that he could have found himself in had something untoward happened to me through his neglect. He then couldn't do enough for me. It also graphically showed the power of the masters of a vessel at sea. The crew's life was essentially in their captain's hands and the whole environment was dependant on their whims and fancies.

Although I remained in constant pain, I was grateful that I had made no more mess since I had been parted from my bucket. I must admit that I found the bed in the ship's little hospital much more comfortable. It transpired that the return of the agent with no doctor promoted harsh words with the Skipper. They couldn't find a doctor willing to visit the ship. The agent had returned to escort 'Blondy,' an EDH with toothache ashore to see the dentist. The Skipper's instructions were then aimed at Blondy. "Don't come back without a doctor, bring one back at pistol point if you have to." To Blondy's great credit he arrived back onboard the ship later that evening with a doctor in tow. He had defied the agent's attempts to get him back to the ship after his own treatment and made him scour the port to find a medic willing to attend a sick sailor.

After a thorough examination, the doctor produced some evil tasting concoction plus tablets, and he gave me two injections in my backside. After forty-four hours sat glued to my bucket I didn't feel a thing; it had left me totally numb in my nether regions. Dysentery was diagnosed, but I was considered to be over the worst of it and should soon recover.

Whether it was the jabs, the tablets or the evil tasting medicine I don't know, but recover I did. After his examination, the doctor asked if he could take a look at our accommodation quarters. The Skipper refused even though they were always kept reasonably clean.

As I lay in the comparative comfort of the sickbay, a head popped through the porthole and to my surprise it was Bert, one of the two lads that we had left behind in Massawa. Both of them had been picked up and thrown into jail by the Massowa police to find that they were going to be charged with illegal entry. The bush telegraph luckily had got to the agent who had them released under some pretext and hustled them aboard a Greek ship bound for the Gulf. The voyage had taken fourteen days, at a personal cost of one pound a day each. The agent paid that and was reimbursed. Later the amount was deducted from their wages. They had docked two days before us and our arrival prevented another charge of illegal entry being brought upon them by the Iranian authorities too, which was about to happen that very afternoon.

The ship, being British territory, would shield them from that charge although the Skipper had been very reluctant to have them back onboard, but the agent persuaded him to do so as sending them home at the company's expense might well be questioned. He brought them back onboard and left them, and the Skipper then informed them that he would sign them back on only when he was good and ready.

* * *

My convalescence denied me the excitement of an action packed few days. We had anchored in the river on our arrival at Abadan and later that day, some of the locals arrived in canoes and began to shout abuse at us. 'British B*****ds,' appeared to be the most popular insult and perhaps the only English one that they knew, but it was accompanied by many Arabian insults, none of which any of our lads knew.

They had paddled back to the shore only to return with their canoes loaded full of stones and rocks which they then hurled at the ship and the crew. I was oblivious to all of it in my hospital bed. No one knew the cause of all the hostility, but the lads were not slow at replying in kind: spuds, nuts, bolts, old shackles, virtually anything that could be thrown back at them was thrown, accompanied by a range of basic English equal to anything they could conjure up. To everyone's delight the Bosun broke out the hoses and to a great deal of merriment, the crew turned them onto their attackers and soaked them until they hastily rowed their canoes out of range, defeated against the Bosun's cunning.

All those high jinks were related to me as I was not allowed from my sickbed until the afternoon of Tuesday 10th November. I took a chair from the mess that morning and sat on the poop deck with a book, sunning myself as an introduction back into the land of the living. The Skipper thought that I was fit enough to return to my cabin but not fit enough to resume my duties for a day or two.

The next day Wednesday 11th will remain in my memory as crazy Wednesday. For whatever reason the devil got into quite a lot of seamen that night. Naturally, after being laid up for so long, I felt anxious to stretch my legs and get away from the confines of the ship for a while. Pete agreed to come with me as he felt I shouldn't go alone so soon from the sickbed, and we headed for the nearby Seamen's Mission where we treated ourselves to fresh oranges. That was a treat indeed for fresh fruit as aforementioned was hardly ever seen in our mess on any ship; it was just as rare as fresh milk.

Scurvy, which ran rampant amongst the seamen of yore and was caused by the lack of fresh produce in their diet, was non-existent then, but if the voyages were still of the same duration, perhaps it still would be. Maybe the supplement of one tin of sweetened condensed milk each per week that we were issued helped to keep it at bay; I just don't know.

A second treat also lay in store for a film was showing in the institute's cinema. Alan Ladd in Hell Below Zero. Most appropriate I thought as we were in one of the hottest areas of the world. After the film Pete and I made the decision to return to the ship rather than pay a late visit to the canteen; it turned out to have been a wise one.

Be it the heat, be it the frustration caused by the lack of beer or whatever, all hell broke loose as a fight developed between the crew of a Norwegian tanker and our lot. Bert and Paddy, the two guys newly returned to us from Massawa were in the thick of it and the Skipper had still not signed them back on.

The descriptions of the melee, related by those involved, were colourful and lost nothing in the telling. By all accounts it was very similar to the barroom brawls portrayed in the old western movies. One moment everything was fine and normal, the next everyone was lashing out, throwing bottles and chairs and smashing tables. The Bosun had apparently gone to the loo with not a whiff of trouble evident so was totally ignorant of the fracas; the instant he opened the door to return he was punched on the nose and fell to the floor with a look of pain and utter astonishment on his face, Bert told me gleefully.

Our crew looked a sorry lot as they returned to the ship. Black eyes and bruised faces were everywhere you looked, but at least they were all back safely with no one thrown into the local nick. Not one of them had a clue as to what they had been fighting about or what had caused it in the first place. Then, if that wasn't enough, Paddy and his cabinmate Jack (an Ordinary Seaman) had a fight with each other. God knows what would have happened if beer or spirits had been available.

The next morning Paddy had his arm in a sling and Jack had gone missing. Where he had disappeared to was a mystery that was to be solved five days later. It was not until the following Monday when the police finally picked him up and returned him to the ship on the Tuesday that we found out he had been shacking up in a quayside shed further along the jetty. One of the young stewards had known of his whereabouts and had secretly been sneaking food to him. Fortunately there were no civil proceedings; though he was upset when the Captain logged him fifteen days pay for being absent for five. Whatever the reason was for their fight, they never said but much to everyone's amazement, they seemed to get along ever afterwards as though the incident had never happened so it must have cleared the air.

To return to that crazy Wednesday, Jeff, the fireman who was with me on the previous trip, brought me a letter that he had received from his mother. Along with it was a press cutting reporting a strange unexplainable happening that had occurred on the 'Clyde Chivalry.' It transpired that a rating had been found hung in his cabin; suicide was the implied verdict.

Later however when she had docked in Gibraltar, two members of the crew had been arrested, taken into custody and eventually sentenced to two years hard labour. For what reasons the press cutting did not state, but both Jeff and I agreed that we were well shut of the 'Clyde Chivalry.' As I discussed the strange tale with Jeff, on top of all the recent events we ourselves had been through, it suddenly occurred to me how ironic it was that the day was the 11th November. Remembrance Day.

It took nine more long days to discharge the parcel of cargo bound for Abadan, and finally with the railway lines and bags of sulphur still lying around the dock, it was 8.00am on Friday 20th November when we let go to proceed upstream. For two hours, slowly and carefully, we moved against the current to Khorramshahr. We passed ships already moored at the jetty and we let go the anchor midstream, only to find that the Pilot should have taken us straight alongside.

With much swearing from the Mate, the Chippy and the Bosun, we weighed anchors again. The ship then had to be turned around to sail down below the jetty before we edged our way alongside, in between two other ships. We came at it against the current and was gently pushed into the space by the river tugs.

The latter part of the operation for once went without a hitch (perhaps because of my absence from stations), and within minutes the hatches were off with the sulphur and railway lines soon lying deposited on the quayside. Those Khorramshahr guys worked with far more enthusiasm than their Abadan neighbours, and it was not long before a barge appeared alongside so the discharge of cargo took place on both port and to starboard.

By that time I had recovered enough to be considered fit to resume my duties and it was good to be back with my mates. Though I was a little slow at first, I was soon relishing the camaraderie and the company. That first evening, Pete and I went ashore, a little apprehensively given that there were those ashore who didn't like us and had canoed out to stone us further downstream, but we found a galaxy of eastern delight.

The bazaar was like an Aladdin's cave. Streets of bustling shops and stalls in the avenues of the marketplace full of weird and wonderful things, from strange fruit and vegetables never seen on a British market, to shops with windows full of gold ornaments and jewellery. Much of what was on display was far beyond our meagre pockets but there were a few trinkets that fell within our range and were destined to be presents for home. No one bothered us at all.

On Saturday 21st November the Arabs for some reason known only to themselves, refused to drive the winches for the 'Jumbo,' which we had to break out. The twenty-ton crane taken onboard at Dunkirk was destined to be unloaded there. So the job fell to us.

The task of breaking out the 'Jumbo,' rigging it, slowly winching the crane out of the hold, swinging it over the side, gently lowering it on to a waiting lorry, stripping and securing the 'Jumbo' back into its housing took us virtually all day, and what those local dockers were called is unrepeatable.

It was early the following week that a little good news lightened our spirits a little. The orders had been received to proceed to Western Australia to pick up a cargo of wheat for either the UK or the Continent. The mere fact that those two magic letters U and K were present within those orders was enough to lift us although there were the pessimists amongst us who bemoaned that it would be the Continent with our luck!

Bert and Paddy were not happy men. Although they had turned to for work every day since their return, the Skipper had refused to sign them on until the 23rd. They could do little until they got back into a British port, when they threatened to get the union involved if they were not paid.

The weather was good considering it was the back end of November, warm in the sun but last thing and early mornings it was a bit nippy. The dockworkers had slowed down considerably by then and there was little to note of interest until the Friday afternoon when George, a JOS, fell down a hatch and broke his ankle, and he was rushed off to Abadan hospital. It was to be hoped that he would come into better hands and doctoring than had been my experience.

The unloading continued, to be interrupted on Monday afternoon 30th November when we moved out to midstream to make way for an incoming vessel. The unloading then continued despite the heavy rain showers we were experiencing that day for within minutes barges came alongside to take the residue that was left for Khoramshahr.

The showers had cleared as we upped anchor on Tuesday December 1st and headed downstream for Bandar-e-Shahpur. As I had been sick in the ship's hospital on the way up, that was my first opportunity to see the river other than the little I could see through my porthole. It was filthy, oil spillages, the occasional dead animal carcass and other indescribable objects floated by like piles of human excrement in the middle of large leaves. Portuguese man-of-war we called them.

It was indicative of the standard of living that folk were washing their clothes in it then slapping them upon the rocks while others were often conducting their own personal ablutions allowing the river to carry it away. I felt that they must have a hard life. We had sailed without George who, as far as we knew, was still in plaster in Abadan. Probably he would be back in England long before our return.

By then fully recovered, I took the wheel that night at ten o'clock and moved to the mouth of the river; we said farewell to the Pilot and felt the first swell of the open sea. Whether the Skipper knew that there would be no berth available at Bandar-e-Shahpur till early afternoon or the fact that a heavy fog had descended upon us I don't know, but either could have been the reason for riding at anchor from about 3.00am. When the anchor was weighed, we arrived off Bandar-e-Shahpur at 11.30am but didn't go alongside until early afternoon.

Once again my duties were changed. The Mate called me over to tell me that I was to be the nightwatchman, which I welcomed for it enabled me to catch up on some of the overtime that I had lost whilst I was ill. It was also a cushy number; on that occasion, everything went smoothly, which helped me to ease back into the routine. I was also thankful for it as the empty holds had to be prepared to take aboard the cargo of grain.

Special precautions have to be taken when cargos such as wheat or grain were to be carried. To prevent the cargo moving and shifting with the rolling and lurching of the ship at sea, shifting boards have to be fitted. Failure to do so could be fatal and cause a ship to list or in the extreme to even turn turtle.

Large planks are fitted to create a structure in each hold, not unlike a gigantic beer crate; thereby preventing the wholesale movement of the grain so that its weight could not all roll to one side. That was back breaking work and I was thankful that my nightwatchman duties excluded me from it for the time being. However, my luck was not to last, but at that moment I enjoyed my night duty.

The discharging of the remaining railway lines and sulphur left in number two and four holds proceeded without interruption as the shore gangs worked day and night to finally finish during the morning of Wednesday 9th December. Meanwhile our lads had made a start on cleaning and preparing the three empty holds in readiness for the big building job.

Finally the ship was empty. It had taken three and a half months to load and discharge one cargo. Although we were on our way to Western Australia, from there we would hopefully be homeward bound. It seemed that no sooner had we cast off our shackles than we were tying up again at Bandar Mashur to take on bunkers.

It was all preparation then for the grain, and once bunkered in the early afternoon it was out into the Gulf itself. The prospect of a long period at sea heartened me. We had been far too long in those Gulf ports with the constant sounds of the winches and shouting amongst the dockers in a tongue that only they themselves could understand.

Onward down the Gulf, through the Strait of Hormuz, into the Gulf of Oman, past Ras-Al-Had the Arabian Sea and finally we came to the Indian Ocean. Mainly when on tankers in the Gulf it would be a quick turn around but for us on the 'Trevose' we had cruised around the Persian Gulf for forty-five days so I was looking forward to listening to a little English, albeit spoken in a strange, affected, long drawl from our colonial cousins down under. The term cousins in fact turned out to be uncannily true.

There was a little breakdown on the Sunday afternoon, but it was only a valve change, and within two hours we were heading again towards the land of the Southern Cross. The sea was calm, the weather was at its best: warm and sunny and it was great to be out into the vast wide-open spaces. Not another soul in the universe to disturb the peace and well-being I felt under the blue cloudless skies of the Indian Ocean that night after night displayed breathtakingly beautiful sunsets. We were all alone; we did not spot another ship for days on end. It was idyllic as we sailed on, watching the shoals of dolphins entertaining us as they dived and gambolled without a care in the world.

Flying fish scampered to get out of our way, displaying the silver of their wings framed against every shade of red known to man that was present in the sunset as they skimmed the waves for incredibly long distances.

It was worth all the trials and tribulations of those forty-five days in the Gulf. But there was a downside; the Mate decided that he needed experienced hands in the hatches where the unremitting task of fitting the shifting boards continued. The four young Ordinary Seamen were put into the watches and along with three EDHs, I was put on daywork fitting the boards.

We were forced to stop again for four hours on Thursday, but there was no lazing around to get a tan or fish for shark on that occasion as the sun didn't penetrate into the depths of the holds, and we were kept far too busy working fourteen hours a day.

As we crossed the equator on 19th December it rained heavily, but not for long and soon the balmy hot days returned. The overtime was helping to make up for my enforced rest during my sickness. We were paid on a thirty-day month basis that was all added up at the trip's end. Although those days I was off sick were not deducted, the combination of the monthly allotment I was sending home and the lack of overtime was leaving me with very little money in the ship to claim subs from so the overtime was always welcome. It was however to be short-lived; the jinx or whatever unlucky spirit it was still dogged me.

It was as we crossed the equator that the number two hold was inspected for the installation of the shifting boards. There was a lot of dunnage that had to be cleared before the main work could commence; it was scattered everywhere. I didn't notice a nail sticking up out of a plank of wood. Given my luck on that ship it was obvious that, if there was any misfortune about, I would find it. And I did. I trod on the nail; it punctured the thick rubber sole of my shoe and entered into the ball of my foot. I clambered up the ladder, leaving a trail of blood on my way to find the Chief Steward thinking that, "If he tells me it's an Indian Ocean foot, I'll deck him one."

That time however, he did show much more concern. Perhaps a lesson had been learned. He managed to staunch the bleeding, bathed it, bandaged it and gave me a shot of penicillin; I was again told to lie up for a few days. It was not until Christmas Eve that I was able to get a shoe back on and resume my stint on the shifting boards.

* * *

Compared to the Christmas Day spent the previous year on the '*Empress of Britain*,' anything would be an improvement, but other than the fact that we were allowed to buy a few cans of beer, the day passed much the same as any other at sea.

It was back to the number two hold on Boxing Day, followed by a full fourteen-hour stint the next day, Sunday. While I rested that night, my foot started to play up again. It became painful and swollen and I was unable to put on my shoe. I was laid up again. The Mate insisted that I was to keep off it until I had seen a doctor on arrival in Australia, even though the swelling and pain had disappeared after a couple of days. They were taking no more chances with me, I assumed. I had begun to believe that in my case the giant white H emblazoned on our black funnel stood not for the Hain Steamship Company but for Hospital.

Thursday, the last day of the year, brought us to Albany on the south coast of Western Australia. Early in the afternoon I was called to the Mate's cabin and he gave me the address of a local doctor. I was to make my own way to the address to see him. That unexpected, authorised trip ashore was a pleasant surprise, and after I asked directions a couple of times, I was soon ringing the doorbell of a very smart bungalow on the outskirts of town. The quiet spoken elderly man who answered, ushered me into the living room.

It didn't look like any doctor's surgery I had ever seen before but after explaining what had happened and sat in a comfortable chair, I soon had my shoe and sock off. He examined it very closely and declared that it was totally healed and that he saw no reason why I shouldn't return to work immediately.

"How long has it been since you had an anti-tetanus jab?" was his next question. "Years," I told him, "Well, better late than never," he replied. "Why does everyone want to stick needles into me?" I thought. I had had to have the yellow fever one before I joined the ship, one in the backside in Iran, now this, but what the hell, at the end of the day, what was one more? I was back at work the next morning.

There was little for the shore carpenters to do on the shifting boards as the lads had been hard at it all the way down the Indian Ocean. In a very short time the chutes were fed into the holds and within minutes we were all covered in wheat dust.

Albany was a small, very quiet place considering it is a port, and there was little to see or do. Pete and I decided to visit Middleton beach. It was our intention to spend the afternoon lazing on the beach and maybe have a swim. The latter half of those plans however, came to an abrupt end for as we stepped onto the beach a siren blared out.

On the beach were two wooden watch towers manned by beach guards who scoured the sea with binoculars, on the lookout for shark and who sounded the siren when one was spotted. Never had I seen such swimmers as they swam for the beach as if they had outboard motors strapped to their legs. No wonder the Australian swimmers always do well at the Olympic Games, they have so much practice and what better incentive could you have to learn to swim at speed than the thought of a shark snapping at your heels? The rest of the afternoon was spent lying on the beach with a fair expanse of golden sand between the lapping water and us. Not a single toe of ours went anywhere near that briny.

The following days saw the last of the good weather. High winds and rain consequently delayed the loading of the wheat. It was imperative that the wheat remained dry. Wet wheat would swell in the confined space of the ship's hold and could put a tremendous strain on the hull. Finally the weather returned to its Australian norm and loading continued until the Albany quota was aboard. Then gales and bad weather were once again forecast which delayed our departure.

The Royal Navy had been carrying out manoeuvres around the coast and, on completion of the exercises, the British ships had embarked upon a series of courtesy calls, showing the flag up and down the Australian seaboard. During our stay in Albany, two destroyers came into port. Crowds of locals lined the quayside to welcome the 'Boys in Blue,' and the local hospitality for them was lavish. The destroyers moored up directly behind the 'Trevose' so our ship's company had a grandstand view from the poop deck.

A dance was arranged in town by the local dignitaries in their honour. Any silver coin was the entrance fee. Some of our lads, Scrooges that they were, hunted round for sixpences (that being the lowest denomination silver coin that there was) to present at the door; their thinking was that it was a good opportunity to meet some of the local girls. It was all to no avail however as they were not allowed in. "We are in the wrong navy" was a moan heard in some quarters, but as I watched the ratings being paraded up and down the quay the next morning, I wasn't impressed. All that drilling and shouting was not for me.

While still very windy and with rough seas, we did manage to get away on Friday 8th January 1960. It was only a two-day journey to Freemantle where the remaining cargo was to be taken aboard. When the news of our impending visit to Western Australia had broken in the Gulf, I had written to my mother letting her know that it would be some little time before I got home again, via Australia.

On arrival in Albany a reply was waiting for me reminding me that her cousin had emigrated to Western Australia some nine years earlier and she had enclosed her address, stating that she hoped I would be able to look her up if I came within visiting distance. I thought that it was a slim chance and put it out of my mind.

We tied up in Freemantle on the Sunday afternoon, and as soon as we could Pete and I were off to the Seamen's Mission. There was not much activity going on at that moment and the excitement of a few games of table tennis soon paled. We poked our heads into a room where a dance was being held, but the patrons all looked about sixty plus and it wasn't our scene at all so we returned to the ship.

I thought then that perhaps I ought to find out where my mother's cousin lived and if it was near enough, go along and say hello. West Leederville was on the outskirts of Perth and by all accounts only half an hour by train from Freemantle. I mentioned it to Pete who volunteered to come along and we jumped onto the train to Perth.

When we arrived at Leederville station, we took a taxi to cousin Violet's home in Burgess Street. Before emigrating they had lived in Leicester and I could not recall ever having met her but when I explained to the bemused woman who answered the door who I was, we were welcomed with open arms. "You must stay for as long as you like" was her heart felt invitation, which we accepted, but we could only risk two days as they would have to be taken off without permission.

Having explained the circumstances to Violet, she introduced us to her family. Her husband Steve and their youngest son were away from home up in the north of the state and the eldest daughter Pauline who was a nurse also worked away from home. Those left were Malcolm (seventeen) Martin (fifteen) and Gillian (eleven) who all greeted us like long lost family, which in a way I suppose I was. Gillian was a charmer, always happy, smiling and joking. Both Pete and I fell in love with her instantly. The next day we were taken on a conducted tour of Perth. A bright, clean, pleasant city. "Another place I could revisit again without hesitation," I thought, should the occasion ever arise.

Like all good things, our enjoyable visit came to an end all too quickly. Gillian and Malcolm wished to have a look at the 'Trevose' so they travelled into Freemantle with us on the train only to find that we were due to sail within half an hour (how lucky could we be) so we had to pack them into a taxi, and as it pulled away Gillian sadly waved us goodbye. She had been quiet, not wanting us to leave, which perhaps was understandable after all the ice creams, milkshakes and other goodies we had plied her with.

Back onboard our shore going gear was soon stowed and it was straight to stations to let go. We couldn't believe how close we had cut it. Judging from past experiences the Skipper would certainly have gone without us. Whether he wished to keep me happy so I would not report his initial lack of care to the union while I was ill I will never know, but not a single word came down from the bridge concerning our absence. It had been a joyous diversion to find friends and be so welcomed so far from home.

The journey along the bottom of the Indian Ocean seemed a very long and lonely one. We sailed the Southern Indian Ocean like the '*Mary Celeste*,' never to make port or so it seemed.

The weather was erratic and changeable; it cut up rough for a few days then returned to warm, pleasant conditions. I noted the 1st February as the day a large bird was found on the main deck, hidden behind the winches. I had seen such birds flying high above the oceans, thousands of miles from land and have marvelled at the stamina that they have which enables them to do so.

In flight they have a long pointed tail like a marlinspike but not being a 'twitcher,' I am ignorant of birds of the feathered variety. It was big, but definitely not an albatross. No one knew its real identity but it was known to us ignorant sailors as a 'Bosun Bird.' Most bosuns carried a knife and marlinspike hanging from the rear of their waist belt; hence the nickname 'Bosun Bird' because of the long thin spike sticking out of its arse.

The bird's wingspan was so great that as we tried to corner him, they just whipped the deck; he could not get enough air beneath them to affect a take off. I suppose it was appropriate therefore that it was the Bosun who bravely caught hold of him and hoisted him into the air and without any mishap, he disappeared into the distance.

It was late one night while on lookout we were heading virtually due west when marvelling at the glory of the clear star studded night sky, which only the far reaches of the oceans can produce, I was reflecting on the bravery of my predecessors in their sailing ships who scoured the world with only those stars to go by. I was brought back to reality by a light dead ahead low on the horizon. It was a few seconds before I realised that it was not a star, but civilisation and the coast of South Africa.

We kept the coast on the starboard beam and followed it around and the anchor was finally dropped off Cape Town on Thursday 4th February and by 6.30am the 'Trevose' was tied up alongside. The Mate had decided to maintain the watches so, not having to turn to until midday, Pete and I on the twelve to four decided to go ashore. It was early and a trip on the cable car to the top of Table Top Mountain was an attractive idea, but enquiries suggested that it would take far more time than was at our disposal so we browsed around the city for a couple of hours.

As it turned out we would of had time for at midday when we returned, the Bosun greeted us with the news that the engine was in pieces and would be for two days with the shore engineers undertaking the work. "Also Kenn," said the Bosun in a parting shot, "the Mate has decided that you are to be the nightwatchman." I was at a loss to know why the Mate always seemed to think I was the best guy to do the job, unless it had something to do with me being the only fully qualified AB onboard.

The repairs however, didn't take as long as expected as the engineers worked throughout the night. There were two of our number missing yet again as we sailed late in the afternoon. One steward and Malcolm, the JOS the guy who was paid off in Dakar, Senegal with appendicitis on the 'Clyde Chivalry.' "Did that boy ever return home on the same ship he sailed away in?" I wondered. Fortunately a sister ship, the 'Trecarrol,' had called into Cape Town and both our missing friends were transported home aboard her.

With our bows heading northwards towards the equator, the temperature rose. It was hot, unbearably hot, and the discomfort was added to by the decision to paint the ship. The sweat dripped from us and mingled with the paint, which did nothing to improve the quality of the paint or our temperaments. Even during the supposed cool of the evening, we lay and slept in pools of sweat without a breath of air.

The uncertainty of our final destination didn't help either; there was no news of whether it was to be the UK or Europe. Wonderful diversions did occur however for, on Sunday 14th February a school of whales basking in the sun were within yards of us, seemingly oblivious to our presence and enjoying the cool that we all craved for.

As we rolled over the equator, a vast shoal of dolphins entertained us with their carefree gambolling and leaping, thoroughly enjoying each other's company. Obviously the dolphins and the whales we had seen were at peace with their world. No doubt there were predators who were lurking to take advantage whenever the opportunity arose but to witness such innocent pleasure and joy of life amongst what we consider to be the lesser life of animals brings into question man's supposed superiority. But such reminiscences were commonplace on the long lonely vigils on lookout, gazing out at the horizon and the heavens.

On Saturday 20th February we came abreast of the Cape Verde Islands, and three days later we stopped for four and a half hours with the engines needing further attention. Then it was onwards to pass Tenerife and Las Palmas in the Canary Islands the following day. Thankfully it had become noticeably cooler, as the Cape Verde Islands faded from sight, and so did the temper and disposition of the crew, even though our destination was still unknown.

Sunday 28th February brought a sense of reality as Finisterre signposted the entry into the Bay of Biscay. Often in my experience, the bay had not lived up to its bad reputation, but that time it did. It was rough and after the searing heat of the tropics, it felt damned cold. The only redeeming feature was a following wind and a tide that aided our progress.

Still there was no word of where the grain was to be deposited, which did nothing to calm our feelings. We were all on tenterhooks when the engines failed again on the afternoon of the 29th. It was with a great sense of relief to hear shortly after the engines came back to life that we were heading for Birkenhead.

Wednesday March 2nd saw us anchored off the Mersey Bar, and a little after midnight on the 3rd we tied up on the Birkenhead Grain Jetty where all duties then finished, I managed a few hours sleep before I packed my gear and got paid off just after midday. Along with Pete and most of the rest of the crew, we caught the ferry across to Liverpool. I was still impressed with the city's waterfront, dominated by the Liver building. We wondered around for a while and I promised to spend some time in Plymouth with Pete during my leave before we made our farewells on Lime Street Station.

Chapter Seventeen
The British Merchant / One

(Of a Quick Change of Ship, a Quick Dash and a Quick Trip).

The twenty-eight days leave ahead of me seemed to be an eternity as the Liverpool to Birmingham express carried me quickly home. I was definitely on my way to try to upset the old bingo playing fraternity and pick up again with my old friends. I had promised Pete that I would spend a couple of days with him in Plymouth, which proved to be enjoyable and interesting.

Plymouth is a place where you can't get away from the sea. It is steeped with maritime history. Be it the Royal Naval Dockyards or the land based Royal Naval Training Ship quite close to the house that I stayed in, it is not difficult to understand why seafaring folk feel at home there.

Pete and I had a few drinks; I was shown the sights, but it was over all too quickly. As well as we had got on together over the past few months, as is so often the case in the Merchant Navy where the whole world is your work place, I never saw or heard from him again and lost all touch.

Upon my return home, I met some old friends and missed others, and called house on the bingo a few times; all the moans from the other clientele fell upon deaf ears. My feet had got somewhat itchy when I received a telegram which asked me to call the Pool office in Falmouth and reverse the charges. They wanted to know if it was at all possible for me to get to Falmouth that evening.

It was April 1st so I asked if they were joking, but no they were serious. I explained that the earliest possible time of arrival there would be the following afternoon late, and that meant I would have to catch the 9.00am Cornishman Express from Wolverhampton. "Well get here as quickly as you can, he said; we have got a Shell tanker for you." Thank god, it wasn't another cargo boat. I had seen enough of derricks and hatches for the time being I thought.

I changed at Truro and the local rattler got me into Falmouth just before 6.00pm. To my utter amazement, a guy from the Pool was waiting on the platform for me. He bundled me into a car and produced the Pool forms. While I signed them, I noticed that the ship was called the 'British Merchant.' "What's happened to the Shell Tanker?" I queried. "Some bloke got paid off the BP tanker this morning and you are to replace him, but don't worry, the 'British Merchant' is a much better ship," he said. I had always suspected that the Pool office guys knew far more about the ships that they sent you to than they let on. I was also informed that she was waiting for me and was ready to sail. At that point he drove off at speed around and through the dock gates, pulled up sharply at the ship's gangway. He grabbed my suitcases and ran ahead, leaving me to follow on to the Captain's room where the articles were waiting to be signed.

With my head in a spin at the sudden speed of events, I walked aft with my gear towards the accommodation. The chap from the Pool was right in his description of the ship; the facilities were the best I had experienced to date. Everyone had a single berth with lots of space and probably the most important condition was the privacy. She was thirty-two thousand tons; by far the biggest tanker I had been on so far, and I was still coming to my senses trying to find my way around when a fireman from the 'Trevose' spotted me. While we stood there talking, it suddenly struck me that the ship had let go, and we were on our way. It had all happened so quickly. I thought that it was almost like I had been press-ganged.

The Pool's Clerk had said that she was ready to sail, but that was ridiculous. I hadn't even had time to change into my working gear let alone be called to stations, so at least I had escaped that chore. My time of arrival at the railway station was just a couple of minutes before 6.00pm, and as I headed out to sea it was still not 6.30pm.

Later in the evening I was informed by the Bosun that I would be on daywork, which gave me the chance to settle in and look around. She was a beautiful ship and for once whoever had designed her had considered the ordinary crew members needs as human beings and provided decent accommodation and comfort. A recreation and games room was well equipped with dartboard, dominoes and cards. There were plenty of comfortable chairs and tables and best of all; up on the after boat deck was a small swimming pool.

Class distinction still ruled supreme; the pool could only be used by the common herd at strictly designated times. Officers, then petty officers and engineers all had the lion's share so as not to be contaminated by those of us who shared what time remained. But that really was a minor detail. Compared to the rust buckets still afloat that had served us so well during the war, of which I had experienced my fair share, the 'British Merchant' was a palace.

Still even palaces have their problems for as we turned to early the next morning and headed down the Channel, the engines stopped. Repeated attempts to get under way failed, and it was 9.00pm before the fault was finally cured. I didn't mind one bit. It was a Sunday and I was turned to with the task of stowing the ropes, which meant that the first work I did on the ship, I was paid overtime for.

The repair finally was successful and as the Bay of Biscay was approached, the weather deteriorated. A wind got up almost to gale force and it was bitterly cold, everyone looked forward to pressing on through the Straits of Gibraltar and getting into the Medi. At 3.00am on Thursday morning 7th April, the Rock came up on the port beam. We were to be disappointed though for the improvement in the weather failed to materialize.

It was at that time that our destination became known to us. Baniyas in Syria, to pick up a cargo of crude oil was the word from the Bosun. As Malta came and went, then likewise Crete and Cyprus, still the weather remained dull and cool. We tied up to buoys a mile offshore and picked up the submerged pipeline on Thursday 14th April.

Oil gushed into our tanks at the rate of 2,500 tons an hour, which completed the allotted quota by 3.00am on Friday, then it was to stations to let go with not a second wasted. The weather improved a little on our return journey, but still the Medi didn't live up to its norm.

As we approached the Straits, something quite low in the water sped towards us. It was a submarine on the surface and at the speed that it was travelling, we could only assume that it must be one of the new atomic subs. It did not come close enough to visibly identify the nationality and in no time at all she had disappeared over the horizon.

To Land's End for orders was all we knew at that time, but as Gibraltar disappeared astern the news was passed that Fawley near Southampton was to be our destination. The Bay of Biscay again was benign and little of any consequence interrupted our steady progress up the Channel to anchor off Fawley at 6.00am on Wednesday 27th April.

For three days we lay at anchor waiting to go alongside, during which time the Cunard liner, the '*Queen Mary*' made her majestic way down, on the way to New York. Seen up close, she was indeed a magnificent vessel.

Everyone was paid off on arrival alongside and I along with most of the crew decided to sign on again, such was the satisfaction with the conditions and facilities. The Pool's Clerk had lived up to his word. I had not been disappointed.

CHAPTER EIGHTEEN
THE BRITISH MERCHANT / TWO

(Of a Family Revisited, the Death of a Cat and Utter Frustration).

Once we were tied up on Saturday morning the rest of the day was our own. Breakfast over, Mick (an EDH from Truro) came along with me to Fawley village on a shopping trip and after an early lunch back onboard, we took a launch up to Southampton. It felt good to be in England in the late spring sunshine. Another two Micks just like in my early days at sea, and I wondered where in the world the other one Bimbo was now after all those years.

A visit to the cinema occupied us for the evening; little did we realise that it would be over four and a half months before the opportunity of visiting a British cinema would arise again. It was May Day when we cast off, bound for the Gulf with a full compliment of crew; on leaving Falmouth previously the deck crew had been four or five men short, which is why I was whisked away at such speed. The shortfall however had been rectified by men from the Southampton Pool while we were tied up at Fawley. We sailed with a fully manned deck crew of eighteen men with the usual three men in each of the three watches and nine on daywork. Again my particular brand of luck sprang into action. I would have much preferred to be on one of the watches, but I drew the wrong cards and landed on daywork.

On Tuesday 3rd May, with barely a thought that it was my elder brother's 25th birthday, I sat with my fellow dayworkers as the Bosun split us into two gangs. One to work throughout the day for the duration of the time it would take to butterworth and gas free all the tanks and the other to do likewise throughout the night; thus ensuring a continuous twenty-four hour work cycle. Of course once again I would have much preferred to be in the daytime gang but need I say more. I was not the only one to moan at the prospect of having to work nights on the tanks, but the continuous workload did get the job finished far more quickly.

We passed Gibraltar again on Thursday 5th May and eventually finished all the tanks the following Sunday. The weather had improved considerably; it was quite warm with calm seas and the sense of well-being was encouraged by the living quarters, especially the modern, large recreation room with air conditioning to relax in. It was certainly the most comfortable conditions I had yet encountered, not only by me, but by most of my shipmates too. We could play darts, cards, dominoes etc. and enjoy our allowance of beer all in the air-conditioned recreation room that was an absolute godsend.

It took a week of balmy weather across the Medi. to arrive and anchor off Port Said on Thursday 12th May at 6.00am to wait our turn through the canal. The 'bumboats were soon alongside plying their wares, but it had all been seen before and what curiosity and interest that once existed had by then vanished.

We waited for four hours before we picked up anchor again to slowly nose our way in through the breakwater, only to tie up at the buoys. Again it was a mystery to me why it fell to us to do everything the hard way? Why couldn't we have just remained at anchor?

It was 11.00pm when we joined the south bound convoy and edged our way into the canal. My early excitement of journeying through the canal had paled, and as I lay in my bunk that night before I dropped off, I thought that one benefit of being on daywork was that it didn't include a stint at the wheel.

It took over six hours to reach the Bitter Lakes where we anchored until half past midday to allow the northbound convoy to clear. It was Friday 13th, and we were the thirteenth ship in the convoy. I'm not usually superstitious, but I had my fingers crossed for most of the time. Our bad luck was to come later.

We cleared Port Suez by the late afternoon, to be greeted by the heat of the Red Sea. It was remorseless and continued to be so for days. Never was the air conditioning in our cool recreation room more welcome. How we had coped without it on previous ships where such a luxury was non existent I will never know.

Aden came and was left behind as our heading changed to a more northeasterly course across the Arabian Sea. I had lost count of how many times I had crossed that particular stretch of water, but the warning of a cyclone in our path broke my reverie. Immediately preparations were made to counter such weather. We stowed away the mooring ropes, lowered the tank lids, put the watertight doors up, lashed and secured everything. In short, lots of hard work was done. All for nothing as it turned out. The cyclone blew itself out. We didn't encounter so much as a puff or even a splash of rain to cool things down a bit.

On Saturday morning the engines took a rest, but the problem was soon sorted and we were on our way again within two hours. We reached Ras-al-Had a few hours later and on into the Persian Gulf on the Sunday evening. Painful memories of my 'Gulf Tummy' flooded back and I felt a little apprehensive, but my luck held and a welcome breeze cooled us a little.

Prior to arriving in Mena-al-Ahmadi on Tuesday 24th May, as on my second trip five years earlier on the 'Llandaff,' a shoal of those black and yellow ringed snakes suddenly appeared around the ship. They swam across the surface of the water before they disappeared in our wash. I don't like snakes, especially the highly poisonous type.

Glad to feel dry land under our feet, most of the crew spent that night in the sailors' canteen getting high on the soft drinks and watching a western film called Shotgun. There were no barroom brawls that time.

Such was the efficiency of pumping oil aboard that the full cargo had been delivered into our tanks by midday the following day; we then cast off and were on our way back down the Gulf. Unbelievably we were heading for Australia, following exactly the same route that I had travelled previously on the 'Trevose,' but I was in much better spirits and much more comfortable, and far more able to enjoy and admire the spectacular sunsets.

It had been hot and humid for most of the time since we had left Suez until Sunday 29th May when a cool wind sprang up. Everyone could breathe while out on deck again. During the heat waves, the small swimming pool on the boat deck was very alluring and a luxury indeed, but in my opinion the unnecessary restrictions on the times we could use it was to me very irksome and off-putting. As previously stated, the officers, engineers and petty officers all had their own designated times, which meant that on a number of occasions it was left unused, but we were still forbidden to make use of it at those times. It was mostly in the evenings when the searing heat of the day was decreasing that we were allowed to use it for a short while.

From where on high the novel idea came was never explained, but it was suggested that as the ship carried all the gear and equipment, the crossing of the line ceremony should to take place. Six of the younger lads onboard, mostly stewards, had never crossed the equator, and the idea was welcomed by some but rejected by others. I quite saw myself as a pirate and looked forward to the fun and games but much to the relief of those young boys nothing came of it because someone would have to play the part of the Queen. No one would volunteer. It was a shame in a way as that was the one and only ship that I ever sailed on where the idea had even been mentioned.

We crossed the line on Saturday June 4th without any further ado, and the deeper south we travelled, the more the climate cooled off. It felt quite cold when on Wednesday 15th, we sighted the coast of Australia, but after the heat of the Gulf anywhere would have felt cool to us.

The only delay to going immediately alongside was the wait for the Pilot who once aboard had us tied up at Kwinana in no time. The ship had to be restocked so the rest of the day was taken up carrying food and other essentials onboard which the stewards then stored into the freezer rooms.

As stated before, fresh milk was a commodity never seen in our mess and two cartons 'somehow' took the wrong turn. They ended up being shared between four of us and was the next best thing to what I would imagine nectar to be.

Kwinana is about thirteen miles from Freemantle, and once the stores had been loaded the crew were allowed time off until Friday morning. That, I thought, was extremely generous of the Mate, it gave me the opportunity to scoot off to visit my relatives again.

Once I had showered and changed into my shore going gear, a fellow gave me a lift in his van from the refinery gate to the Freemantle bus stop from where I caught the bus into town and then the train to Perth. When I alighted at Leederville station, I took a taxi to Burgess Street to their address. As we pulled up, I could see that the house was in darkness so I asked the driver to wait while I checked. I knocked on the door and a woman I had never seen before answered. She told me my relations had moved. "Just my luck" I thought, "to have come all that way for nothing," but then she informed me that the people next door could tell me their new address, which turned out to be just a few streets away.

I was greeted like a long lost friend, all the family were home that time, with the exception of Pauline, the nurse. Gillian was extremely pleased to see me, still charming and enchanting everyone in sight. "You must stay," Violet said excitedly, "How long have you got?" "Have you eaten?" No one could have been made more welcome, and there seemed to be a genuine disappointment on being told that my visit could last only until the following evening. Gillian wanted to know where Pete was, and upon being told that he could be anywhere in the world on another ship she seemed sad that he wasn't there with us.

They told me they were planning to return to England within the next year, which surprised me a little as I had thought they all liked it out there. They intended to return to Leicester and asked me to visit them while I was on one of my leaves once they had settled in. I promised them that I would try my very best to do so.

The following evening came all to soon, and it was a tearful Gillian who waved me off, accompanied by Malcolm who saw me to the railway station. Back in Freemantle I waved down a cab and the driver was only too willing to take me to Kwinana.

"You are a Brummie aren't you?" he asked with a smile as I settled into my seat. "My God!" I said, "Is it that obvious?" He laughed and asked, "What part?" "Walsall," I replied. "Oh, I know Walsall," he said, I come from Leamore," "So do I," I replied incredulously. He had lived in Leamore Lane and had emigrated to Australia ten years previously. He was full of questions about the 'old country' as the Aussies just like the Canadians who had emigrated from the UK quaintly referred to the British Isles. "The world was shrinking by the day," I thought. It was quite a chat that we had in that thirteen-mile journey, but he still charged me full fare at the refinery gates.

371

It was a quick turnaround and as soon as we were empty, we had to return to Mina-al-Ahmadi at full speed. That made a change as fully loaded on our journey down, we had maintained an economical cruising speed of about ten or eleven knots. All the stops were then pulled out as she galloped along at a good eighteen knots.

The first couple of days proved to be troublesome; problems with the boiler it was said. Perhaps it was protesting against the extra workload, but as soon as the difficulty was put to right, we maintained the eighteen knots. Once again we undertook the butterworthing and once again I was on the night shift, and once again the job was finished within a week.

The Indian Ocean is a vast, empty space and we did not see a single ship or anything until we were well north of the equator. To help alleviate the monotony we organized a darts competition with the entrance fee of a hundred cigarettes. It was a simple knockout where the opponents' names were picked from a draw and you progressed until you lost. The matches were arranged for when the contestants were off duty, and due to different shifts and watches sometimes days could elapse between certain games. Miraculously I eventually found myself in the final. Even more miraculously, I won it. Cigarettes were not on my shopping list for almost the rest of the voyage.

Heavy winds and seas had been constantly with us as we approached the equator; they helped to keep the temperature down, but as we closed in on the Gulf, the heat started to get to us. Up through the Gulf of Oman and the Strait of Hormuz was when it really hit home as we entered the Persian Gulf itself.

Occasionally in the job of being a Merchant Seaman, a person can feel like they are trapped in some kind of time warp, transported it seems by a quantum leap. There I was that day, sailing up exactly the same stretch of water, in exactly the same weather conditions, doing exactly the same job (painting the bulkheads) in exactly the same alleyway, with exactly the same shimmering heat wave, leaving exactly the same pools of sweat on the decks where I had stood just five years earlier onboard the '*Llandaff*.' The only saving grace on that occasion was our air-conditioned recreation room. I really could not remember how we had managed to work our eight hours each day without one.

For once Mina-al-Ahmadi appeared like an oasis in the desert and on Saturday night July 2nd after our arrival, even the cold colas and lemonades served in the canteen were more than appreciated. No time was wasted and with a full cargo, we were back at sea the next day.

The Arabian Sea yet again brought back memories of the 'Llandaff' with her engine failure close to the rocks off the coast of Yemen for conditions in that part of the world can change dramatically within minutes. Brilliant sunshine one moment and into the teeth of a raging monsoon the next. A howling wind and a mountainous sea with waves crashing over the decks that would swamp a lesser vessel were our lot. The 'Llandaff' would surely have foundered on those rocks with a dead engine in such a storm that we then found ourselves in. The feel and the sight of a ship ploughing and bucking as it heads its bows into the oncoming waves never failed to fascinate me even after all my time at sea.

The conditions didn't improve until our heading changed to a northerly direction into the Red Sea. While the tempestuous seas were left astern, a strong, warm offshore wind accompanied our progress towards the Suez. It was that wind blowing from the east, off the land that brought aboard a horde of unwelcome guests. We were two days into the Red Sea when a swarm of locusts came aboard. Those horrible, giant grasshopper type creatures were like a shivering carpet on the decks everywhere. We sought brushes from all over as everyone tried to sweep them overboard.

Thousands finished up in the sea but many took to the air, only to be blown farther out to sea. Others buried themselves in any nook and cranny they could find so obviously some were not discovered. There were evidently still some hanging about for during the afternoon tea break, the ship's cat came screeching into the mess. She ran around in a frenzy, jumping, turning somersaults and generally going berserk.

Two of the lads ran to their cabins to don their thick work gloves and on their return, they managed to pin her down for a second, long enough to see that she had a locust stuck in her throat. In her torment, she wriggled free of their grasp and leapt straight through the porthole. Her momentum was such that she cleared the whole width of the alleyway outside and dropped into the sea. We ran out onto the poop deck but nothing could be done for the poor creature, and we watched in horror as she struggled in the water then disappeared in the wash from our propeller.

We lost the cat at the same time that we lost the wind, and the Red Sea returned to normal, scorching hot and out of curiosity, I checked the temperature the next day. The heat of the sun combined with the heat that reflected back up from the steel decks had reached a hundred and twenty two degrees Fahrenheit.

* * *

It was the first and only time as a sailor I received a card on the actual day of my birthday. For we reached Port Suez on Wednesday 13th July, the mail came aboard but other than the novelty of receiving the card there was little celebration.

The ever present feelings of apprehension that things could go wrong while passing through the canal were ill-founded on that occasion; we remained swinging at anchor for the whole day and entered into the canal at 5.00am on Thursday, clearing Port Said later that evening.

As always cheers echoed around the ship when we received the welcome news that Fawley was our destination. The officers packed their gear and the wages were made up to date so far, ready to be paid off. The prospect of a swift passage through the Medi. became a reality as Gibraltar was passed in what was surely record time.

As we entered Biscay, the aforementioned bad luck kicked in. All the hopes and plans were dashed when we heard the news that the National Union of Seamen had called its members out on strike and consequently we had been diverted to Dunkirk. Apparently a Norwegian tanker, which was on charter to BP slightly ahead of us was originally intended to dock at Dunkirk, had been diverted to Fawley; in other words the cargos had just been switched.

The reason was that had a British crew landed in a British port during the strike they would automatically have had to join the strike; thereby stranding another vessel in dock. Obviously the Norwegians were not governed by the rules of the British Union, but we could not come out on strike while we were still actively serving abroad, not even in a port of our nearest neighbours as it was strictly illegal and could, I believe, be considered mutiny. Only the seamen who were actually ashore in the UK at the time could participate in the strike.

It was well known from my previous experiences that on receipt of such orders the disappointment and morale of the crew on most ships reaches rock bottom and, being just two or three days from paying off coupled with the knowledge that the company could keep us out for two years should they wish to do so, did not help morale onboard.

We passed into the lock at Dunkirk on Sunday 24th July. The ship got in with just inches to spare. The '*British Merchant*' must have been one of the largest ships to be able to pass through and the discharge of the crude oil was routine. The contract engineers came aboard to tend to a boiler that had been giving trouble and they finally gave their OK on the following Thursday. It was July, but after the heat in the Red Sea, the days felt cold and it was blowing a gale. Us deckhands got soaked in the pouring rain as we let go.

The watches had been altered just prior to leaving port. I was taken off daywork and found myself in the four to eight. That went a little way to ease my frustrations but nowhere near all of them. As I stood my watch at the wheel, out of the mist came the '*Queen Mary*' on our port side and for a short while, it appeared as though it was a race between the two vessels. It was a one horse race though, we were no match for her as she cut across our bow and disappeared into the rain mist.

A good old-fashioned south westerly blew up the channel and shortly after, from the direction in which the '*Queen Mary*' had vanished, a fully rigged sailing ship appeared. Bowling along with the following wind, she looked a picture and with every piece of canvas aloft, she must have been touching well in excess of twelve knots.

The bad weather conditions continued until the Bay of Biscay was astern and the news that it was to be a repeat of the very first trip, Baniyas, then Land's End for orders cheered us up a little. We passed Gibraltar at midnight on Sunday 31st July. One of the company's latest additions to their fleet of tankers, The '*British Queen*,' a giant for that time at fifty thousand tons, passed us homeward bound from Mina-al-Ahmadi with a top up of her cargo from Baniyas.

We arrived there on Saturday August 6th and as on the previous trip, everything went like clockwork. Once fully loaded from the submerged pipeline, within twenty hours the journey back had begun. The seamen's strike was over and our spirits were rising high at the prospect of a fast run back to Fawley we hoped, but no, it was to be the Isle of Grain we were told. That did not matter, anywhere would do just so long as it was in England. Don't ever count your chickens is the phrase that springs to mind. It hit everyone like a bombshell when the word spread like wildfire that the seamen were back on strike, that time unofficially.

Immediately our orders were changed; goodbye Isle of Grain, hello Antwerp. Everyone blew their tops, even the officers who were normally very conscientious and loyal to their company, each one sent a radio message of protest to the company. All to no avail. Never had a crew been so despondent, from the Skipper down to the first trip mess boys; we were united in our antipathy of the situation. The comfortable cabins and facilities had no place in the equation anymore. Everyone wanted off. No cheery words were said as, in the reality of the situation, no one could joke about it.

On Tuesday afternoon 16th August, the Pilot came aboard to take us up to Flushing to anchor us for the night. Carrying on slowly next morning, it was 1.00pm before we passed through the lock and four o'clock before we had finished tying up.

Most of us went ashore that night with the sole intent of getting legless to drown our sorrows. I like Antwerp; I like the beer and the people and as we moved from bar to bar the cloud that had been hanging over us began to lift. For some unknown reason a crowd of us ended up in a gay bar, certainly not by design but more like we just staggered into it. The place was hilarious; full of gays, transvestites and straight people too. Some of the clientele were so obviously men masquerading in women's clothing, but it was extremely difficult to tell the difference with others.

To my surprise a number of our crewmembers, including a couple of the engineer officers and their wives who had taken the trip across the channel to be with their husbands for a few days, were also in there. No one was approached or were any suggestions made; it was like one big happy family. We got our drinks and sat down at one of the few remaining tables. A roar of laughter erupted from our table when one of the lads drew our attention to a giant jar of Vaseline standing about twelve inches tall which was placed on a shelf behind the bar with the word "STARTERS" proudly printed in black letters on the label.

After our disappointments of late it was pleasant to find ourselves in such a light and friendly atmosphere. There was even better to follow as music from a hidden gramophone filled the air. Curtains opened at the back of the room to reveal a small stage, on to which pranced a guy in full blonde wig, made up with lipstick and rouge, clad in lily-white shawls. As he glided around the stage, he slowly discarded shawl after shawl, which floated in the air around him, and one by one they fluttered gently to the ground, like the wings of a butterfly. "It's the dance of the seven veils," a voice from the audience proclaimed. Other voices then started to chorus, "Get 'em off."

To a crash of cymbals and a peel of drums, the last shawl was finally flung into the air and left to flutter gently to the ground, which left him posing like a Greek statue before us, naked except for a tiny pair of silk panties discreetly hiding vital parts.

As the music faded, there was total silence in the room for a few moments, which was suddenly broken by the gruff voice of 'Jock,' one of our ABs, proclaiming loudly in his deep, Scottish brogue, "That would look great, if it wasn't for that bloody great bulge in his knickers." The place erupted and the roars of laughter did even more to demolish our despondency. Then everyone was saying, "We WILL make it home the next time" in a far more positive attitude.

The discharge of our cargo was completed on Friday 19th August and with further repairs required to the boilers, the ship shifted to a fresh berth to make way for other ships to discharge at the terminal. I managed to get ashore again a couple of times, wandered around and bought a few toilet requirements that, after the high jinks of the Tuesday evening, was all I could afford.

There was congestion at the lock and having let go at 10.30am on Sunday 21st August, it was 11.00pm before the Pilot finally put our nose into the open sea and said his goodbyes.

If the Skipper was of the same mind as the rest of his crew, it certainly showed for it was full speed ahead down the English Channel grateful for once that it was night-time; we hugged the French coast, keeping as far away from the heartbreaking sight of those White Cliffs, which vanished into the distance again.

Not surprisingly painting the ship was the order of the day, but only places under cover as the English summer weather lived up to its reputation: cold, wet and windy. The only consolation was that heading as we were, towards the Caribbean, we would probably be seeing the other extreme shortly.

The weather continued foul until the Azores became a smudge on the horizon. As we headed on further into the Atlantic, the seas abated and it became gradually warmer. We passed between the islands of Barbados and Grenada to anchor later in a little bay ten miles down the coast from Cardon, whose refinery was clearly visible. It was Wednesday 31st August.

The people of the Caribbean Islands and surrounding mainland coasts are noted for their laid back attitude towards life and when the Pilot came aboard at 3.30pm having passed a message earlier that morning that he would arrive at midday, no one was surprised.

Although we were in port the Mate had decided to keep the watches running so still being in the four to eight watch on Saturday 3rd September, I decided a beer would be nice to wash my lunch down. There was a seamen's canteen on the jetty so that is where I spent a pleasant hour. It was fortunate that I only had two small ones for when I arrived back onboard I found that we were to sail at 3.30pm and the ship was in my hands at four o'clock to steer her most of the way down the buoyed channel and out into the open sea.

The following morning we received a hurricane warning. It forecast winds in excess of a hundred and forty miles an hour and seas to endanger all shipping. All the dayworkers and the watch on deck stowed everything securely and hammered the handles down firmly on all the storm doors. The hurricane was sweeping across the islands directly ahead of us, destroying almost all that lay in its path so the Skipper decided to take evasive action. By slowing the ship's speed, it was estimated that the weather front would pass ahead of us and the worst effects would probably be missed.

Given the speed that the ship could reach, and still in glorious sunshine, it was quite novel to be crawling along at just three or four knots. We maintained the slow pace for twenty-four hours and thankfully the ruse worked; the hurricane had crossed our path and had headed off towards Puerto Rico and the Dominican Republic.

Although we had escaped the full brunt of the storm, we still hit the tail end of it and mountainous waves pounded us, and being low in the water they came angrily crashing over our decks. It had caused untold damage to the islands it visited and reports over the radio told of fatalities and casualties throughout the area. While I was on the wheel later, the Mate came out of the chart room and told me he had estimated that our course would have put the ship right in the centre of the storm as we passed between the islands had we maintained our full speed. Not the best place to be in such conditions.

The mountainous seas stayed with us throughout Sunday, and in the early evening we sighted the island of Sombrero, the last landfall until the Azores. An American radio station reported that a light aircraft had crashed into the beacon on Sombrero during the storm, killing the occupants of the plane and destroying the tower, but as Sombrero came into our view the beacon was still in operation. It may be of course that Sombrero had more than one. Amazingly the following morning, the seas had calmed, the wind had dropped and it was hard to believe that only a few hours previously we had been in such a savage storm.

The orders to discharge the cargo at the Isle of Grain came early on Thursday 8th September whilst still in mid-Atlantic. It would be nice to think that word had got back to head office of the disquiet aboard ship and a little reassurance was needed, but maybe not. From then on, an air of apprehension began to grow amongst the crew as the weather began to cool after we left the Azores behind. There were those amongst us who, although the strike was over for the second time, were convinced that our orders would yet again be changed.

The Bay of Biscay came and went and we reached the English Channel on Thursday 15th September still the orders remained, at long last bringing a smile to our faces as we reached the Thames Estuary. It was as though fate had not yet finished for while we tied up it bucketed down and everyone got soaked to the skin, but no one really complained; we were back home. I am sure that there were some who had wished they had not re-signed for the trip in Fawley.

After getting showered and changed out of our wet clothes, we attempted to dry them before we packed them away. The tiny, hot, drying room was full to capacity. We took our last meal at 12.30pm then our suitcases were loaded into a coach on the quayside. The coach had been hired to take the crew to the station.

The Shipping Office was adjacent to the jetty and the company representatives paid everyone off. The coach again was supposed to run us only to the nearest railway station, which was Gravesend, but as was the norm after we had a whip round the driver agreed to take everyone to London.

I had forty-five minutes to wait for my train and four and a half months is a long time to go without a pint of good English ale. That was remedied before I climbed aboard the Birmingham/Wolverhampton express at Euston and thirty-two days leave.

CHAPTER NINETEEN
THE BRITISH TRADER

(Of a Merry Run Around, a Fast Run Down
the Red Sea and a Blockage).

Those thirty-two days leave flew by. I continued to upset certain bingo players but others were pleased to see me and by and large I enjoyed myself, to the extent that those thirty-two days became thirty-three. I simply stole an extra day and consequently, I was one day overdue on my arrival back in Falmouth in the normal run of things late in the afternoon of Tuesday 18th October. The sailors' home had a bed into which I was tucked after I spent the evening at the cinema.

I presented myself at the Pool office on the stroke of 9.00am the next morning, and I thought that the clerk might have had something to say about my lateness. He instead greeted me with "Ah, Mr Kenn, just the man we've been looking for. Thanks for getting here so quickly; we didn't send the telegram till yesterday. We have got a berth on the 'British Trader,' signing on Friday morning." To be given two days to further explore my favourite port was no hardship and within ten minutes I had rebooked my bed until the Friday.

Although it was mid-October, the weather remained warm and sunny, which allowed me the opportunity to once again walk the cliff top walks along the headland that led from one beach to another and laze for a while on one of those beaches.

Again I thought that it was far better than walking the streets of the city. Little did I know of the merry dance that was to ensue before the signing on procedure was completed, but it would not have spoilt the tranquil pleasure of those two days if I had.

I reported to the Pool on the Friday morning at 9.00am as requested, the clerk explained that engine repairs still had to be completed and so the deck crew would not unfortunately be signed on for at least another week, and there were no more berths available at the moment.

The clerk was, as ever, helpful and considerate when faced with the fact that as my Pool money was not available until the actual signing on, my cash flow was up against a wall, and I could not afford to stay in Falmouth for another week without pay. "Come back at eleven and I will try to fix something up for you" he said.

On my return, after I had walked aimlessly around for two hours, the clerk said, "Sorry, no luck as yet, can you give me another half an hour?" I did so by calling next door to Armyn House for a cup of tea. Upon my second return he greeted me with a written note that explained that on the BP Company's request for deck crew, the Pool had summoned me down from Walsall. As I was already travelling when they had delayed the signing, I could not be stopped in time so would it be possible to arrange for me to 'work by' aboard ship? That in fact was a request for them to sign me on immediately despite the delay. "Go and give this to the Skipper or the Mate," he said, "and see what happens."

Sod's law will always prevail; the 'British Trader' was berthed at the extreme end of the dockyard. Neither the Skipper nor the Mate were in their cabins and as I wandered around, the first fellow I bumped into was a young officer apprentice who as it turned out also came from Walsall. He offered me a smoke in his cabin but he didn't know of the Skipper's or the Mate's whereabouts.

On my return fifteen minutes later, there was still no response to my knock on the Skipper's door, but it was a relief to get a reply from the Mate. My relief was short-lived however as he read the note and said, "Sorry, this is the Skipper's responsibility, I can't help you. He is having lunch ashore at the moment, but he will be at the Federation offices at one o'clock signing on the catering staff; you will find him there," he informed me.

Back I trudged throughout the whole length of the docks, and as I came out of the dock gates, my watch told me that it was just turned

1.00pm so I walked across the road into the impressive Federation building on the corner. "You've just missed him," the guy answered to my query. "He will be back onboard ship now." By then I felt that I was going around in ever decreasing circles.

"This was ridiculous," I thought as I headed back to the ship, almost on my knees worrying about what my next move could be if the Skipper was not to be found that time, but "Come in" was the welcome response as I knocked on his door for the third time. He read the note from the Pool, gave me a hard look and said, "OK get yourself back to the Federation office and tell them to sign you on." "Thank God for that" I thought as I trudged all the way back to do his bidding and signed on the dotted line after showing my credentials to the official. Before I went to my room to collect my gear from Armyn House I sat in the canteen with another cup of tea for a well earned rest before I had to lug it all the way back to the ship.

There was only a skeleton crew aboard which consisted of one other AB who had re-signed from the previous voyage and a couple of deck boys, one of whom had been on the 'British Merchant,' and Curly, a fireman, who I struck up a friendship with and we became drinking partners.

The 'British Trader' was exactly the same tonnage as the 'British Merchant,' but built a little later. Virtually a replica with only minor modifications like a more streamlined funnel but by and large the same. The accommodation was excellent with the bulkheads panelled with light green Formica as opposed to painted steel, which made the cabin feel much warmer and homely. There was a built in wardrobe, a settee, a chest of drawers with a spacious writing top and, most importantly, a comfortable bunk.

For the next few days, there was little work to keep us two ABs and two deck boys busy. A couple of old mooring ropes were jettisoned and coiled up on the jetty to be taken away. The shore crane lifted three brand new ropes onboard, which had to have eyes spliced into each end then stowed into the rope locker. Some five-gallon drums of paint were hoisted aboard and stowed away. It could hardly be described as a hard life for those few days, and every evening Curly and I would find more than a little comfort in the harbour side taverns.

While on our way to one of those pubs one evening, Curly and I called in to Armyn House and there was a group of lads waiting to sign onto the '*British Trader*,' but they didn't know exactly when. They were all skint and there was little we could do to help as our ready cash was almost down to zero.

They finally got signed on the Thursday morning, which made me reflect on my good fortune. With the help of the Pool's Clerk and an understanding Skipper, I not only had my board and lodgings but also had a week's wages in the ship to boot.

The new crew contained several previous shipmates, two ABs and a fireman from the '*British Merchant*' and a face that I hadn't seen for five years, which belonged to an AB from the '*Llandaff*.' It was good to see old faces as it didn't happen very often. I had really begun to feel like an old salt as apart from the one eleven-month break, I had been a sailor for almost seven years.

That evening along with another AB I was detailed to stand watch as the ship underwent engine trials. As usual all we were required for was to be on hand if the mooring ropes snapped as strain would be put upon them with the propeller turning. The trial went without a hitch and we were relieved from duty by eight o'clock.

Our call to stations came on the Saturday afternoon. It was a hot afternoon for late October and with bonfire night only a few days away it was unusual to have sweat rolling off you as the numerous wires were let go and the ropes heaved inboard until we were singled up to one rope at each end. All to no avail though for at that point, it was found that a safety valve in the engine would not release itself properly. The Lloyds insurance inspector refused to sign our clearance and departure was abandoned. So we had to retie all that we had worked so hard to let go, and the faulty valve was sent ashore for repairs.

Finally the engines met with the eventual approval of the inspector at 11.00am, so on Sunday 30th October we let go again only to sail out into the bay where we anchored to pump salt water into some of the tanks for ballast.

It was during the short stoppage that we learned our destination was to be the Persian Gulf to collect a cargo of crude oil for the UK. That was the third voyage to the Gulf in a row for me, and I really did hope that we would return straight home so that perhaps I could find a ship to take me elsewhere. That certainly happened, but more of that in the next chapter.

* * *

Christmas at home was a real possibility should we return immediately and that thought heartened many of us, and in my case it would be my first Christmas at home since I had joined the Merchant Navy. The late autumn weather that I had enjoyed in Falmouth was soon forgotten as winter came to remind us that it was November. Heavy seas and torrential rain hit us well before we reached the Bay of Biscay. Sailing with ballast did help, but as well built as she was, in those seas, the '*British Trader*' bucked and rolled which indicated how important that ballast was. We were unable to open the portholes as they were constantly awash from the high rising waves, my cabin was extremely stuffy and the view from those portholes with the roll of the ship was first sky then sea repeatedly, like tock follows tick.

The Rock was in the fading distance and with the storms left astern it was full speed ahead across the Medi. on the next stage of our journey to the Gulf where Fao, we heard, was to be our loading port. Whether the hopes of getting home for Christmas had captured the Skipper's imagination I don't know, but he wasted no time to enjoy the glorious Medi. Weather; we were riding at anchor awaiting the service of the Pilot at Port Said on the morning of Monday 7th November, but again minor engine repairs delayed progress into the canal.

As we lay outside there were two noteworthy occurrences. One of the deck boys was shipped off to hospital with suspected appendicitis. History had repeated itself yet again. It did seem to me that deck boys were quite prone to accidents and illness. I must have been one of the lucky ones during my spell. The other occurrence was the liner '*Strathmere*' came through the canal, homeward bound on its regular Australian run. I later learned that she was the liner on which my relatives from Perth had returned to England.

We entered the canal at 1.30am on Wednesday 9th November and we were waiting in the Bitter Lakes for the northbound convoy to pass through by 8.00am. It was a quick, uneventful passage through for by 5.00pm, the heat of the Red Sea greeted us.

Such was the quality of the company's newer ships that before long we had overtaken all of the ships that had been ahead of us in the convoy, including the ship that had headed the south bound convoy: a German Passenger Liner called the '*Seven Seas.*' Everyone aboard got the impression that the speed of our passage didn't go down at all well with her crew.

As usual the weather was very hot and such is life at sea, one moment full of expectation and hope the next to have it all dashed by a change of orders. On Friday evening the order was received to load in the Gulf for Aden. "That is our Christmas at home gone!" was the general consensus, but it was even more worrying than that, for ships had been known to have spent months on the Gulf to Aden run, backwards and forwards, to and fro with no relief.

Aden came and went, then on into the Arabian Sea and Ras-al-Had with the unremitting heat constantly sweating pounds off us as we painted the decks. For once the Strait of Hormuz became a welcome sight; it was there that new orders were received again. Fao was out, it was Mina-al-Ahmadi we were to head for, and even the prospect of drinking just colas in the quayside canteen followed by an old B movie didn't dull our spirits; once loaded it was to be Land's End for orders.

We rounded the Strait of Hormuz into the Persian Gulf and for the third voyage in a row, on Thursday 17th November, I found myself at anchor off Mina-al-Ahmadi. Again there was no return of the Gulf Tummy, but the engine continued to need minor adjustments, which took until Friday afternoon.

During that morning a strong wind blew from the shore and delayed the tying up. We had got rid of the ballast and being light ship, the port authorities considered the ship to be in danger if caught by a sudden gust and it could also do damage to the jetty. Fortunately the storm blew itself out during the night and the docking took place on the Saturday morning.

The nightlife of Mina-al-Ahmadi was still the same. Maybe it was the incessant heat I don't know, but sometimes judging from the behaviour of some of my shipmates after partaking a few of those ice-cold soft drinks, they might just as well have been full of alcohol as they staggered and sang merrily along the quay. The film showing in the canteen was Kenneth More in 'The Sheriff of Fractured Jaw.'

With the efficiency of the loading technique in Mina, the ship was full to capacity early the next morning and we were heading out into the Gulf by 9.00am. There was still a certain air of apprehension, heightened by another report forecasting a cyclone on our heading. It proved to be as false as the report received by the 'British Merchant' on the previous trip.

We all kept our fingers crossed that our orders would not be rescinded back on to the Aden run, but the apprehension eased somewhat as Aden was left to starboard and even the heat of the Red Sea was not unwelcome as we glided nearer to the Suez.

On arrival at Port Suez, the Pilot guided us into the inner anchorage on the morning of Monday 28th November. It was obvious that there was trouble from the amount of shipping waiting to pass through the canal, at least forty vessels, and with a constant stream of new arrivals a large queue was forming.

The reason for the build up of ships was, we learned, a blockage in the canal. The story was that a tanker had leaked oil badly in the canal. It had somehow ignited and a dredger had caught fire. Dredgers were kept quite busy there helping to keep the canal clear, and the accident had blocked the canal. Also according to the grapevine, there were fatalities amongst the dredger crew, though the number was unclear.

It was two days with many more ships at anchor before the convoy formed up, and with the canal cleared, our passage through went without any further problems. Once clear at Port Said the dayworkers were called to lower the tender boats, dismantle the searchlight and do all the other work associated with the journey through the canal.

Bad weather had been forecast for the Medi. and the usual preparations were made to secure all that needed to be secured, but once again the forecast was wrong and even the Bay of Biscay was calm.

The atmosphere had lightened and the tension was gone, everyone seemed to be sure that they would be eating Christmas pudding at home. I held my breath for the fiasco on the 'British Merchant' because of the Seamen's strike was still fresh in my mind.

I need not have worried though, Cory Town, across the Thames estuary near Thames Haven became our destination (anywhere in the UK was good enough for us). The Pilot came aboard on Saturday morning 10th December. We stopped just short of our berth, and then had to wait forty-five minutes for a boat to arrive to take our ropes ashore so that we could proceed to tie up.

During the paying off process, a young guy came onboard and offered a taxi into London at a cost of four pound fifteen (£4-75) for the car. Immediately five of us clubbed together and jumped at the offer and within the hour the time table at Euston was telling me I had only half an hour to wait for my train home.

The speed of the ship may well have done us a disservice though despite all the delays. It was the 10th December and I had only ten days leave.

Chapter Twenty
The Cape Grafton

(Of Screaming Birds, Wet Mutineer's Ancestors and
an Australian Clink).

A couple of days before I was due to go back on December 20th, my stomach began to play me up. I dreaded the thought that I may be in for another bout of the dysentery that had confined me to a galvanized bucket for so long. Off I went to see the doctor who without hesitation gave me a sick note, which I immediately posted off to Falmouth.

I harboured mixed feelings throughout the Christmas period. In one way it was great at last to spend a Christmas at home with my family, the first for seven years, but it would have been much better to have been fit enough to enjoy the Christmas turkey. It was not dysentery according to the doctor, but a bug I had picked up which would work its way out of my system. Along with the stomach upset I felt low with no energy. The condition persisted for weeks. I felt as though all the strength had left my body and I couldn't seem to pull myself out of it.

The Pool regularly posted to me my Pool allowance, a small amount of money each week, but obviously that couldn't go on for ever and eventually towards the end of January 1961 they requested a further doctor's note or a clearance note. Convincing the doctor to give me a clearance note was one thing, convincing myself was something else; I knew that I was far from fit, but I thought that hanging around feeling sorry for myself was not the answer either.

I posted the clearance certificate off to Falmouth and virtually by return of post, I received the offer of a berth on the '*British Loyalty*,' That would more than likely be yet another trip to the Gulf I thought, but my body had other ideas.

My bags were packed ready to make an early dash for the Cornishman Express the next morning, but I awoke shivering and sweating alternately with an obvious bout of flu. It confined me to bed and a further doctor's note winged its way to the Pool. No doubt the condition that I had endured over the previous few weeks had lowered my immune system and made me an obvious candidate for any virus that was going around.

Mid February saw me on the mend and I notified Falmouth of my fitness to resume work. They requested my return and offered me a berth on a cargo boat, the '*Cape Grafton*' of the Lyle Shipping Company of Glasgow.

The journey down on Thursday 23rd February was horrendous, hold-ups all the way, which included a landslide over the line that had to be cleared away before the journey could continue, and I finally arrived in Falmouth four hours late. The journey, which usually took around eight hours, had taken twelve. On top of my recent illness, it made me feel extremely weary and to cap it all, it was raining cats and dogs.

A Pool Clerk greeted me on the platform and shades of the previous experience prompted thoughts of being press-ganged again. Imagine my immense relief when he told me that most of the crew had signed on already and the '*Cape Grafton*' was at anchor out in the bay so my signing on could be made in the morning. A room had been booked at the Seamen's Home, and he had a taxi booked to take me on the two-minute journey that, strange as it may sound. I was grateful for because I was exhausted.

As I entered Armyn House, I was told that they were full, but arrangements had been made to find me a room in the Penrose Hotel immediately next door. It was a guesthouse rather than a hotel and a pleasant, homely landlady showed me to my room, which was quite small but clean, cosy and comfortable. Tired as I was, I felt that it was too early to turn in and although it was still raining heavily, I thought the cinema would be much more welcoming than an empty bedroom.

Later sleep didn't come instantly as I was overtired, and as I tossed and turned, the prospect of another cargo boat didn't exactly excite me but as I had been ashore on sick leave for such a long spell, I felt that I had little choice. The next morning I couldn't even remember what film I had seen.

As previously stated, cargo boats were for me in many ways inferior to the space, privacy and comfort of the large oil tankers. With all the work and hassle that the hatch boards, beams and derricks created, and they sometimes spent days or weeks in port either loading or unloading. At least I consoled myself with the thought that there was a better chance of going somewhere other than the Gulf. Little did I know of the adventures that lay ahead or that it would be a long time before England saw me again. That was all in the future though and was not the cause of my troubled sleep.

Over breakfast the next morning in the Seamen's Home I met 'Taffy,' another AB who was also due to sign on the 'Cape Grafton' and the forms were signed at the Pool office. The doctor gave me a really good check over as he knew of my recent sickness, before he satisfied himself that I was fit enough to sign on.

At the shipping office, our orders were to be on the Custom House Quay promptly at midday where a launch would take us out to the ship. We were there dead on the dot, but it was two thirty before the launch arrived. My heart dropped as we came around the headland and saw the 'Cape Grafton' for the first time. She was an Empire Boat, like the old 'Oakhill,' 'Granford' and 'Martagon' had been. As we boarded the ship, the first person that I saw was Brian, the Second Cook from the 'British Merchant.' There was also an ordinary seaman who had been on the 'British Merchant' too.

Taffy met up with a fellow Welshman and shared his cabin, which left me with the only remaining berth. It became blatantly obvious why it was the only berth available for on opening the cabin door, it looked like a scrapyard. Wood was stacked high in one corner, rolls of leather in another with tools and metal scattered throughout.

The lockers and drawers were full to the brim of oddments and bric-a-brac and the top of the writing table had been altered to make a work bench, covered with chunks of iron and brass, at which an old fellow sat observing me apprehensively. He must have seen the look of incredibility on my face for he shrugged his shoulders and apologetically offered the explanation, "I do a lot of work." He looked so apologetic that I smiled and said, "Just give me a locker and two drawers for my gear and you can carry on with whatever it is you do." He smiled with an obvious sense of relief on his face and shook my hand. I then realised that perhaps here was a good friend in the making. Anyway, "What the hell?" I thought, "I could do all my writing in the mess." He was elderly probably in his sixties, quite old for a seafarer as it was predominantly a young man's game, and my first guess would have been of Polish origin, but Joesy as it turned out was a Latvian.

Joesy had been with the ship for a long time and considered it his home, and his apprehension of my presence led me to believe that he hadn't had to share his cabin very much, if at all up until then. It was obvious when I tried to unpack. His belongings were everywhere. He cleared one of the two lockers and two drawers, only to display more of his bits and pieces that simply added to the chaos already on show. He had for a long time laid claim to the bottom bunk so I had to take the top one, which by some miracle he had kept clear of his stuff.

At first his accent made him a little difficult to understand, especially as he chatted on at breakneck speed. His mannerisms at times appeared quite comical and his difficulty in communicating I felt had made him a lonely man who had become used to his loneliness. I think once he realised that I wasn't going to make life difficult for him in sharing his cabin, he got used to me being there and even became glad of my company and he couldn't stop talking. I also think that he may have been shunned a little by past crews and had become a little apprehensive of his fellow shipmates, but all that vanished as time went on.

Ordinarily when in the company of people with non-stop chatter, I tend to turn off after a while, but his conversation for the most part was quite interesting. I would sit and listen to him for ages, at first picking up the odd phrase or word, but eventually I got to understand him far quicker than my other shipmates.

It took them far longer to get to know him and like him, which eventually, I think most of them did. They probably had more difficulty understanding how I could share the cabin with him with the state that it was in. He was a really nice guy and would go out of his way to repay a kindness.

It transpired that Joesy had escaped from Latvia when the country was invaded during World War Two by the Soviets. He had made his way to England via America. How he had got to America from Latvia in the first place he never revealed, but he had served in the Merchant Navy since his arrival in England. His family were blacksmiths who had run a thriving business in the capital, Riga, until the arrival of the Russians who he maintained had shot his brothers for the heinous crime of being businessmen, which therefore made them capitalists.

On inspection I found the '*Cape Grafton*' to be in a far better condition than the other Empire Boats I had sailed on. Her owners and previous owners had taken good care of her and kept all but mine and Josey's cabin not only clean but also tidy.

We sailed on the evening of Saturday 25th February. Word was about that the first port of call would be in the Caribbean, but only to refuel. Rumour was that we were destined to work through the Pacific.

Leaden skies and heavy seas marred the expectations of those who had looked forward to an early escape from the damp, cold British winter. It didn't bother Joesy. In fact very little bothered Joesy as long as he could work with his chisels, files and other tools while off duty.

The weather persisted until the Azores disappeared below the horizon, but painting ship gave little time to contemplate the weather for the Mate kept the dayworkers hard at it from 7.00am till 8.30pm. That entailed three hours overtime a day with breaks only for meals and the usual fifteen-minute 'smoko' break in both the morning and afternoon. We were giving the so called 'tween decks' halfway down the holds two coats of green primer followed by a top coat of silvereen. It was hard, tiring work, and by nine o'clock most nights I was in my bunk dead to the world.

There was no let up, even on Sunday though the Mate did cut the hours on the Lord's day from 9.00am to 5.00pm as that was all overtime. The pattern continued as the days became increasingly hotter, and we finally left the Atlantic and passed between the Islands, through the Mona Passage into the Caribbean. Hurricanes were not reported or expected, but it would be foolhardy to disregard the possibility in that hot climate, thermals could gather and the whole scenario could change in a flash.

We cut southwards until the Venezuela coast was finally reached, and we put in to Caracas on the morning of Sunday March 12ᵗʰ, where the Pilot came onboard almost immediately and took us alongside ready for refuelling.

The '*Empress of Britain*' was also in dock taking on bunkers while on her way to New York. She was obviously on a cruise, taking a break from her shuttle between the UK and Canada. A couple of the lads showed an interest and decided to go across to have a look around her. "Are you coming to take a look?" I was asked. "Not bloody likely," I replied, "I sailed on her once. I've already seen all that I want to see of her." Along with Peter, an Irish EDH, I explored the sailors' canteen on the jetty instead. "A much more enjoyable excursion," I thought.

Our bunkering was soon completed, and having waved goodbye to the Pilot, it was westward for us as we followed the Venezuelan coast towards Panama and the canal, bound for the Eastern Pacific and the coast of Chile.

It was hard to believe that after eight years as a sailor, less of course the eleven months I'd had out, the Panama Canal was a new experience for me. My knowledge of the Suez coloured my expectations for when we anchored off Panama two days later on Wednesday 15ᵗʰ March, the lush greenery was another world compared to the arid, dry, barren desert of the Suez. It was a startling contrast.

Upon weighing anchor, the '*Cape Grafton*' moved gently into the canal and soon approached the concrete entrance to the first lock. Not only was the scenery entirely different to the Suez, but so was the means of passage. On our approach to the lock, six locomotives or 'Mules' as they were known, passed wire lines aboard: three each side of the ship, which we then made fast by wrapping them in figure of eights around our 'bits,' one for'ard, one amidships and one aft and, from then on, they completely controlled the motion of the ship.

As they slowly drew us into the lock, the gates closed automatically while the 'Mules' took the strain and held the ship stationary. It was a staircase lock that comprised of three lifts, and the ship was totally controlled all the way through by the 'Mules.' As the lock paddles were opened, the water gushed in and hoisted the ship to the next level in a matter of minutes. It was a fascinating experience to witness a seagoing vessel being hoisted with such ease. Once the correct level was reached the 'Mules' then pulled us into the next chamber. It took no longer to get through them than it would a little houseboat on the canals at home. A magnificent piece of engineering skill built at a great cost of human suffering and loss of life, but that is another story.

Once through those locks, it was not long before we reached the Gatun Lake. Being a fresh water lake, it gave us the opportunity to pump fresh water aboard, to top up our tanks for use in the boilers and hose the ship down from bow to stern to wash off any salt that may have accumulated on the paintwork.

The canal consists of three sets of locks and we soon reached the second one, a single drop. The 'Mules' took over and the whole exercise was completed quickly. The final lock being a double drop took a little longer, but it was still fascinating to watch the 'Mules' expertly handling the ship. After we cleared the locks, we steamed slowly along the final reaches of the canal under the guidance of the Canal Pilot, to emerge out into the Pacific at eight o'clock in the evening.

The Suez Canal had at first fascinated me, only to tire of the monotonous arid desert on consequent trips, but the continuous greenery and vegetation along the Panama Canal's banks with its ever-changing scenery was glorious and less hot; therefore far more pleasant. I didn't think I could ever tire of that.

As the Pilot's launch gathered speed to return him to his base, our heading came round to due south for the next eight days. Painting down in the holds again became the main occupation and while the weather was hot during the day, the cool evening and night breezes guaranteed a peaceful night's sleep after a long day's toil plus overtime.

* * *

Tocopilla was our orders. "Tocopilla! Never heard of it," someone said. Another voice piped in, "half of this crew has never heard of Chile." So it came as no disappointment on the morning of Thursday 23rd March to see a collection of huts and shacks at the base of an enormous line of sandy coloured cliffs as far as the eye could see.

From our anchorage in the bay a thin track could be seen, which wound its way like a snake to the top of the cliff. Other than the sea, I believe this single-track railway was the town's only link with the hinterland. "Why were we there?" "What could a place like that produce to attract the attention of a deep seagoing vessel?" Apart from the railway, the other most eye-catching feature, high up on the face of the sheer cliff were two names that stood out in a bold white. They must have been at least two-foot high for they were visible for miles. How? Whoever it was that had done it was almost as big a mystery to me as why. Whoever had taken the trouble to inscribe their names in such a place must have been either mad or drunk. Try as I may, I cannot recall exactly what those names were as for whatever reason, I failed to record them.

At dawn the next morning every member of the crew was rudely woken by the ear-piercing screeching and crying of what sounded like thousands of seabirds. The noise was deafening so I slipped into a pair of jeans and wandered out onto the poop deck where I witnessed the spectacle of literally thousands of cormorants chasing a massive shoal of fish. They flew, swam, dived and disappeared below the surface. The water was crystal clear and we could see them shooting off like mini torpedoes in all directions after the fish. There were also hundreds of pelicans, big ungainly birds that added their excited screeches to the dawn chorus. They too joined in the chase and dived from a great height, hitting the water beak first with an almighty splash. The noise from those creatures even indoors in our cabins was indescribable and seemed to magnify even more as we walked out on deck; it literally hurt the ears. I would have never thought it possible for birds to make such a racket.

Many of the hands, angry at being woken so early, shouted, waved and strove to make their voices heard above the racket, calling them as far as I could make out, noisy 'bustards.' That I must confess amused me a little, but they couldn't fool me. I knew better: they were definitely cormorants and pelicans.

In complete contrast on the other side of the ship, quite oblivious to the row being made by the birds, a number of big, brown seals floated, rolled and just lolled on the surface of the water in total tranquillity, basking in the early morning sunshine. They took absolutely no notice at all of the activities of either the birds or us. It was one of those very rare moments where one could feel totally at peace with the world, glad to be alive and privileged to see such an abundance of wild life in its natural environment.

While we rode at anchor waiting for the loading to commence, fishing became the sport of the day in our freetime. We hung a baited line over the rail and the slightest nibble could be detected with the line running over the index finger. We caught some good fish and a lot of mackerel soon found their way into the galley to be cooked and enjoyed. A rare fresh delicacy.

In such a small port, the landing jetty only accommodated small craft so we made fast out in the bay stern to onto buoys where the loading of the cargo had to be undertaken using our derricks.

The mystery of what the cargo could be was solved as one hundred weight bags of nitrate for fertiliser, lots of it, had to be shipped out in relays of barges to be transferred aboard. Eight thousand tons of the stuff was to be lowered into our holds and placed into position manually by the shore gangs. It took them fourteen days to load it all.

It had been a month since my feet had touched terra firma, and so with a couple of my mates it was time to explore the delights or otherwise of that outpost of Chile. A launch came out to take us ashore where a shock awaited us; when we reached the jetty, there was a heavy swell running, which lifted and dropped the launch at a very fast rate. One second the jetty was above us, the next we were looking down at it so the means of getting ashore was novel to say the least.

The launch was turned broadside onto the end of the jetty remaining three or four feet away, and as the swell lifted the launch, a guy on the jetty swung a rope out. To get ashore we had to catch the rope at the height of the swell then, one by one with split second timing, we had to launch ourselves ashore swinging like Tarzan.

TOCOPILLA -- (Chile)

My two shipmates made it safely, and although I was anything but happy I couldn't let them see that. I mustered up all my courage, grabbed the rope and went for it. My foot slipped on landing, which caused me to hit my shin against a board, but a guy grabbed me and hung on. After a few trips ashore, we became quite expert at it so it became fun, but for some reason we always seemed to handle it better on the return trip. Maybe the consumption of a few cold beers helped.

That first night as we walked along the dusty road that served as the town's main thoroughfare, we were delighted to find a number of bars and over the next couple of evenings, in an attempt to be fair and impartial, we sampled them all. Finally we settled on two that became our favourites. We then divided our time equally between the two bars for reasons I am about to relate.

In many parts throughout the world, in ports both large and small, there are bars with their own coterie of girls and young women. There to comfort and entertain lonely sailors or anyone else for that matter, who having been devoid of female company for many weeks, welcomed the opportunity to forgo the company of their shipmates.

There though, unlike the vast majority of places, the girls while welcoming did not harass us in any way for drinks or other pleasures. They would encourage us to sit at their tables and talk, invite us to play cards just for fun, which they were happy to do all night if that was all that was required. Of course they would graciously accept drinks once offered, but they never asked. They would also with beautiful smiling faces gently take your hand and lead you off to a bedroom within the building if you indicated your wish to do so.

All that was done so discretely and being young, free and single, and having neglected my education of late, I decided that it was time once again to resume my studies under the tutelage of Rebecca, a stunningly beautiful eighteen-year-old girl and Julie, an equally gorgeous young woman of twenty-five. Rebecca frequented one of the favoured bars and Julie the other. As we used both bars alternate nights, there was no clash of interests. That was a far cry from the classrooms of my school days.

The day off that Good Friday provided was not wasted. We spent the whole day ashore and the later part became quite hazy so which particular bar the evening was spent in is unknown. One thing that is no mystery though is the half-day's pay I was docked for not turning to on Saturday morning.

Many of us were sorry to see the last bags of nitrate loaded aboard. It had been a great fortnight, but it was time to go. The derricks were lowered and secured, the hatches battened down and everything made ready for sea. As we were letting go from the buoys, I thought how strange it was that over the two weeks we were there, we had not seen or heard a single cormorant or pelican since that very first morning.

The night of April 6th saw us bidding a sad farewell to the ladies and the end of a happy introduction to Chile and its people. As we caught the tide, it was also the start of a six thousand mile journey across the Pacific to Auckland, New Zealand. Six thousand miles is a long way, and as will be seen, there were to be happenings unforeseen that were of great interest to me: happenings which would remain with me forever.

The stay in Tocopilla had been blessed with good warm weather, in fact an unsubstantiated report stated that they hadn't had a drop of rain for two years, but we ran into dull sullen skies for the first four days into the journey. So to wake up to cloudless blue skies on the morning of the fifth day was a relief. We then basked in glorious sunshine for a whole week before we caught the odd shower.

To my surprise, the old '*Cape Grafton*' belied her age and had so far performed without a hitch. No engine failures, no false alarms, in fact much better than some of the newer tankers in which I had served, but without any hint or warning of trouble on the afternoon of Tuesday 18th April, yet again while I was at the helm, the ship suddenly swung to port. Once again I found myself on a ship travelling in a complete circle before coming to a halt.

With warning blasts from the ship's whistle and the telegraph ringing to stop engines, "Please God!" I thought, "don't say I've lost another rudder." Thankfully as it turned out I hadn't, a pin had come out in a part of the steering mechanism and thankfully yet again with no other shipping in sight. The engineers were on the ball and the fault was rectified in no time.

News travels fast anywhere, and in a closed community such as a ship, it is common knowledge in a flash. Anyone with a smattering of English naval history would know of Pitcairn Island and its significance in seafaring circles, and anyone I think would be at least a little excited at the prospect of calling at that tiny dot of land that rose from the sea miles from anywhere out of the vastness of the Pacific Ocean.

The inhabitants of Pitcairn Island monitored shipping movements by means of a radio and knew that we were quite close; hence we received a message, which requested us to call to pick up their mail. They wished it to be delivered and posted in New Zealand. So in accordance with the long held tradition of the sea it remained the Captain's decision to respond or not, but any call for help from any quarters for any reason was very rarely turned down.

Pitcairn was quite isolated at that time (1961) and had little regular service with any mainland, but was under the protection of New Zealand. Its economy was to some extent self-sufficient, helped out by the occasional supply ships. Its exportable products were a selection of beautiful hand carvings of flying fish and animals etc. and the franking of Pitcairn postage stamps. They seemed to be happy people who led busy lives.

The place excited me for it was there that Fletcher Christian and the mutineers of the '*Bounty*' ended up after setting Captain Bligh adrift in an open boat, along with those members of the crew who were loyal to him. They had searched for the isolated island little known of at the time, knowing full well the consequences that would befall them should they be apprehended by any vessel of the Royal Navy. Eventually they found the island and the mutineers made it their home in 1790, and their direct descendants still live there to this day.

Much has been written and portrayed on stage and screen concerning the mutiny on the '*Bounty*,' and also much has been made of Bligh's brutality and Fletcher Christian's compassion. But the crews of ships in those days of sail were often pressganged. Floggings and beatings were commonplace, and officers were chosen from the elite and in many cases had little consideration towards the men who manned their ships.

Contrary to the widely held belief portrayed in the stories, many historians consider Bligh to be one of the better, more enlightened officers of his day: more understanding and sympathetic of his sailors. There is one attribute that no one can take away from William Bligh though, he was unsurpassed as a navigator; not only did he steer an open boat three thousand miles to landfall, he maintained discipline with less use of the whip and the lash than most captains of his day. But all that is history and another story that has little to do with my own tale.

It was 4.00am the following day Wednesday 19th, when Pitcairn came into view. In the darkness my first impression was of a big dome that rose from the sea lush with vegetation as far as I could tell. Anchoring was impossible as the water was too deep so with the engines just ticking over, we were able to keep a very slight forward motion.

Some of the islanders came out in their boat to deliver their mail. The gangway was lowered to accommodate their access, and at the precise moment that their boat disappeared under our bow to glide along the ship's side towards the gangway, the ship veered sharply towards them despite the Helmsman's desperate attempts to counteract it. The '*Granford*' capsized them throwing both them and their mail into the water. For once thank God, that Helmsman was not me.

Fortunately we managed to fish all of the men out by pulling them one by one onto the gangway with little or no damage other than to their feelings. One guy told us later that he had found himself under the boat when it turned over and his first attempt to escape was frustrated by something which dragged him back. Fortunately his second attempt was successful. To prevent a possible second mutiny, dry clothes were found for them all and apologies were profuse.

They would try, they said, to recover what they could but unfortunately as the water was so deep they held little hope of doing so. All their goods now belonged to Neptune. But such was the sunny nature of those direct descendants of Christian, Adams and Young etc. they soon accepted our apologies and agreed that as everyone was unharmed there was at least a kind of funny side to it.

They estimated that it would be another two to three months before they would have built up enough mail to justify them calling in another ship to deliver it, to which I replied that at least by then the 'Cape Grafton' would be well away from their island. They nodded their heads in vigorous agreement.

While the engineers attended to the errant steering gear it was pleasant and interesting to talk to them and learn a little of their lonely but satisfying existence. They spoke slowly in a kind of Devonish / Cornish drawl with a smattering of the olden tongues 'Thou's' and 'Thee's.' I was amazed when they told us that not one of the one hundred and forty inhabitants at that time drank alcohol and only one person was a smoker.

At that moment in time there were little or no medical facilities, and for the moment no doctor was on the island. In cases of sickness and accident, medical assistance was summoned from New Zealand, which was still one hell of a long way away. The population was steadily declining and becoming older as the young folk left to seek their fortunes and wider aspects of life in Australia or New Zealand and even farther afield.

As dawn broke into a bright sunshiny day we could see that the island was indeed covered in lush green shrubbery and vegetation. It was approximately two miles long and two miles wide maybe slightly less, which even so is just a mere speck in the vastness of the ocean.

During the day other boats came out with their wares to sell amongst the crew. Eventually the engineers announced that the steering gear fault had been cured and presumably compensation for their loss would be argued between the islanders and the company. We waved goodbye to those seemingly happy, contented folk. The Skipper however waited until they were well clear in their boats before he gave the order to start the engines.

I had previously read a book called 'Adams of the *Bounty*' by Erle Wilson, which recorded the whole story from the very beginning when the crew first joined the ship, right through to when they were actually discovered on Pitcairn.

I had become absolutely fascinated by the whole narrative, which left me with a lifetime's interest in anything remotely relating to the mutiny and subsequent events so for me, it was like living history. I would never forget meeting the descendants of the mutinous crew of the '*Bounty*,' and I suspect that they will never forget the day when the '*Cape Grafton*' came and nearly drowned half their menfolk and lost their three months supply of mail.

As I reflected on the whole event, it struck me again how strange, inexplicable coincidences occur in life. For it was on receipt of the radio request to call at the island that the first steering failure had happened and the second time at the precise moment that their boat entered the blind spot beneath our bow that same pin had come out again.

It was for all the world as if the ship itself had decided to play a little game to amuse itself with that first time the previous day being a little dress rehearsal; not once did the steering fail again throughout the whole duration of the lengthy voyage.

* * *

The weather was quite mixed as we continued our journey across the Pacific; it was hot one day with squally, heavy rain the next. It continued along that vein until Friday 21st April when we found ourselves stationery for three hours with a minor engine fault. All the holds had been painted and were full of cargo so we were kept busy repainting the rest of the ship from bow to stern and the long balmy days just seemed to blend into each other.

Thursday 27th April brought us to the International Date Line, which meant as we were travelling East to West we jumped one complete day, i.e. we went to bed on Thursday night for a good night's sleep only to waken on Saturday morning. That pleased some of the younger crew; their reasoning was that an extra day's pay had been gained for missing the Friday. It still puzzled some though when it was pointed out that the reverse would happen on the return journey when travelling West to East, unless we came home via the Suez; thereby circumnavigating the world.

Joesy and I were used to each other by that time and got on well together. He rarely went ashore and spent practically all of his spare time working in the cabin. I found him at times fascinating to watch. He was an extremely skilled craftsman and would scrounge bits of metal and other material from the engine room or the chippie's locker, and would patiently spend hours upon end gradually, painstakingly manufacturing and shaping them into whatever he wanted them to be.

His current project was in the making of a suitcase. He first made the framework from wood before he cut and shaped the leather around it. Hinges, locks, keys, even the screws were fashioned by hand from brass and metal; it involved literally hours and hours of filing and shaping.

It took him weeks to complete it and I would sit, watch and talk as he patiently crafted the materials. Finally the suitcase was pieced together with hinges and locks that operated smoothly like the workings of a Swiss watch. I thought at that point that the suitcase was finished, but from somewhere he produced some lengths of brass piping which he cut along their lengths, opened them then flattened them into strips about an inch and a half wide. These were then highly polished and riveted around the outside of the suitcase with his handmade rivets.

He then made brass corner pieces and riveted them on to strengthen each corner and brass studs punched into the leather to make patterns all around it. He was an amazing guy with so much care and patience put into his craft, and apart from the constant chaotic mess it was an education and joy to be sharing his cabin.

The only article I ever saw him buy was a roll of patterned material, blue with Red Indians attacking a wagon train on it, which he painstakingly hand stitched to the interior of the case. It took him over six months to complete the work but the case would last until doomsday. The only fault I would find if it were mine would be its weight. It was so heavy I could hardly lift it empty, let alone full. He intended the case to be for his own use when he eventually paid off, which is just as well as although it was a work of art you would need to be a strong man to lift it, which indeed he was.

We didn't have much further to travel after we crossed the Date Line and May Day, Monday 1ˢᵗ , we sailed into Auckland Harbour, New Zealand and anchored. We were only at anchor just off the jetty for half an hour before the Docking Pilot came out to take us alongside. All the derricks had been topped and the hatches stripped on our approach in readiness to begin the discharge. Most of the crew had the same idea that first day in New Zealand, which was to get ashore.

The Pacific is a large, vast ocean and since the 'Cape Grafton' was not the fastest of ships, it had been many days since firm ground had been beneath our feet. Unfortunately just like Australia in those days, the pubs closed at six o'clock in the evening. And like Australia, it appeared from the crush in those bars that the national sport appeared to be the 'six o'clock swill,' in which most of our lads after they had finished work at 5.00pm were soon taking an active part along with the locals attempting to see how many beers they could sink before chucking out time. I, like most guys, enjoyed my pint, but being jostled amongst the crowds who were trying to get served could at times be quite amusing, but at other times quite frustrating and the logic of it failed me.

Auckland with its wonderful shopping centre was a great attraction. A clean and spacious city that I took to immediately. The price of clothing, cassette recorders, radios and suchlike I thought staggering and way above our pockets, but most other goods on display seemed reasonably priced. When we talked to the locals, it soon became apparent that New Zealand was a high wage economy, they earned money we could only dream of. Everyone seemed friendly and welcoming and told us they believed New Zealand to be the best place in the world for the ordinary working man.

Unfortunately the crew of the 'Cape Grafton' were not paid New Zealand rates. The dockworkers we came into contact with actively tried to encourage us to emigrate and take up residence there. It didn't appear to us as strangers to the place, that there was very much to do after 6.00pm except go to the cinema. As has probably become apparent I quite enjoy an evening at the cinema, and it appeared not surprisingly owing to the early closures of the shops and pubs to be popular with the locals too.

I went ashore every night with either Peter or some of the other crewmembers and on our third night, we found a small coffee bar that remained open. As we entered through the door and climbed up a flight of stairs, we emerged into a dimly lit room, which had the added attraction of a Maori group. Their guitar playing and singing was quite professional and extremely popular with the young clientele who sat at their tables swaying in rhythm to the music. Unfortunately there were no unattached young girls there, everyone seemed to be in couples but that didn't spoil our enjoyment of the music, although by one o'clock when they closed, I'd had my fill of coffee.

Only half of the cargo was destined for Auckland and the dockers completed the discharge by the Friday evening. Then for us came the usual ritual of battening down and securing the derricks that were still topped ready for departure at 2.00pm the next day Saturday 6th May.

All but three of us from the deck crew went ashore during dinner break for a final drink that Saturday morning. They must have had more than a couple because they all returned together, half an hour after what should have been our sailing time. That did not please the Skipper one bit, but he couldn't sail with that many men missing.

They returned laughing merrily and singing as they staggered along, some were holding others up as they weaved their way up the gangway. That is everyone except Peter who, for reasons known only to him, stood on the quay and refused to come aboard. Three of the others then returned ashore and tried to manhandle him aboard. Peter was having none of that and after about ten minutes struggle during which his shirt was literally ripped from his back when he fell to the ground.

All three tried to lift him to carry him onboard but he only struggled harder, trying to resist them, and all three of them together could not overpower him enough to get him up the gangway. They eventually decided to leave him and returned onboard. The Mate, who had been watching the melee from the wing of the bridge, shouted down, "OK leave him. Bring in the gangway."

Peter and I had been fairly good friends over the three months that we had been acquainted and I didn't want to leave him in that state. It was obvious that he was drunk out of his mind and didn't know what he was doing, so I decided to give it one last try to see if he would come onboard for me. As I ran down the gangway, the Mate shouted for me to come back but I pretended not to hear him and carried on. Peter watched me until I had almost reached him, then he drew his knife.

"Don't come near me," he threatened. "Don't worry," I said, "I'm not going to touch you. Stay here if you like or come back onboard. I thought we were mates," I cajoled, adding, "Why would you want to stay here anyway? The pubs close at six." Then I turned and walked back aboard and to my surprise, Peter calmly followed me up the gangway. I thought that was then the end of the matter. How wrong can one be?

The gangway was brought inboard and Peter staggered aft with the rest of the gang who were stationed aft for the purpose of letting go while I went up for'ard and we singled up. On the call to let go, the tugs came to take us away from the quay and as the gap got wider, the engines failed to start, which as it turned out was a bloody good job. We had three attempts to start our engines without success as we continually drifted away from the jetty.

A great commotion from the guys on the jetty suddenly alerted us on the bow to the fact that Peter had jumped overboard from the poop deck and was swimming back ashore so we dared not attempt to start the engines again because of the danger of swamping Peter in the wash. We could do nothing but watch as he was dragged from the dock.

Someone had alerted the police who were on the scene in double quick time and after another struggle, they overpowered and handcuffed Peter then bundled him into the police car. After previously having had his shirt ripped off, and all the rest of his gear still remained onboard, all he had was the pair of jeans he was wearing. Still that was not the end of our farewell to New Zealand; on seeing the police manhandle Peter into the car, Vic, one of the DHUs, also dived in off the poop deck. He had a much longer swim than Peter as we had drifted out farther but he made it OK only to be dealt with in a similar manner.

All of that left me feeling speechless and wishing that I hadn't bothered for having talked Peter into coming onboard, we were then two men short instead of one. "What was it that they put into the New Zealand beer?" I wondered. I had heard of men jumping ship, but not that literally. We assumed that Vic and Peter would be given a spell in jail before being shipped out back to England on the first available boat. They were lucky that our engines hadn't started as they could both have so easily been killed, Peter especially.

The tugs managed to push us slowly back towards the jetty, which allowed us to get a rope ashore and heave ourselves alongside so that the engineers could take a look at the engines. The police had taken our two errants away by the time we were back alongside.

The Skipper would not have us put out the gangway again, probably because he knew we wouldn't be there for long, but many of us assumed that it was because he didn't want the police to bring the two drunkards back again or perhaps it was to deter anyone else from joining them.

After fifteen minutes the engines sprang back into life again with no further trouble and off we went. Upon leaving the harbour with two men short I felt how lucky in a way that the engines had refused to start when they did when Peter was in the water for I may never have forgiven myself for talking him back onboard, had he come to any harm.

The Tasman Sea was unfriendly as the 'Cape Grafton' ploughed its way for two days through a gale and heavy swells towards Brisbane where a pilot was to come aboard to guide us up to Cairns, North Queensland, within the Great Barrier Reef.

Joesy secretly welcomed the rough seas, especially when the waves crashed over the decks because after every rough sea, he would comb the decks the next morning in search of flying fish that had been washed onboard by the waves and left stranded. Kissing his fingertips he would hold them up and repeat, "Very good, Very good," as he prepared them for the pan in the galley.

Bright, sunny skies greeted our arrival off Brisbane on Friday 12th May. The Pilot stayed aboard for the whole passage up the coast inside the Great Barrier Reef to Cairns. The sea inside the reef was like a vast sheet of glass with scarcely a ripple to mar its silvery blue sheen. The only disturbance was the wake of the 'Cape Grafton,' which could be seen stretching for miles to our rear.

Still it was paint ship as the multitude of islands that constituted the Barrier Reef slipped by. We arrived at Cairns late on the evening of the 14th May, and we rode at anchor till the next morning when we went alongside at seven o'clock. The dockers came aboard as soon as we were tied up to immediately begin discharging. There was by then only six hundred and fifty tons to come out.

Subs were being doled out that afternoon. "Ten Australian pounds would last me a fair while around the coast," I thought. Little did I know what was to befall my money and me. We did however hear from the ship's agent that Peter and Vic had both been sentenced to two months in jail in Auckland for entering the country illegally, after which they would be deported.

It was agreed that three of us would meet Paddy, the AB who had been with me on the 'Llandaff,' in the bar of the Royal Hotel, the nearest pub to the dock gates. He said he would follow us ashore in a short while. We sat in the bar waiting for him, but after we had bought a round each there was still no sign of him so we assumed that he had changed his mind and we went to take a look around Cairns.

After a while, bodily functions took over and I was dying to answer a call of nature. As usual everywhere closed at six so I couldn't nip into a bar to find relief. We searched and searched in vain for a public toilet but couldn't find one anywhere. When I couldn't stand it any longer, I knew desperate measures were needed.

I told my mates to carry on and that I would catch them up, and I dived up a dark and deserted alleyway to relieve myself. As I zipped myself up, my wrist was grabbed from behind and twisted up my back. I was really glad that I had finished what I was doing as it could have been embarrassing. "Right, you are coming with me" snarled the member of the law. He must have been six-foot-three if not taller, one of the biggest coppers I've ever seen in my life; he marched me through the streets of Cairns to the local nick with my arm still twisted all the way up my back.

The station cops were all of the same ilk as he handed me over to them. "I couldn't find a public toilet anywhere, and if I hadn't done it in the alleyway, I would have wet myself and most of it would have gone onto the ground anyway," I protested. Their attitude towards me I thought was disgusting; my explanation fell on totally deaf ears and was ignored. In no uncertain fashion, I was made to realise that they had got me, and they would do with me as they wished. They searched me and took everything from my pockets; they took my jacket, my belt and counted my cash, which amounted to nine pounds. They then marched me across a courtyard to a long row of cells.

What prompted the escorting officer to ask me what I had been pulled in for before I don't know? Perhaps I was a Ned Kelly lookalike, the notorious Australian outlaw or something for when I answered, "I've never been pulled in for anything." His response was, "You had better come clean for we shall find out." I told him that if he didn't believe

409

me it was his problem and that they would only be wasting their time checking. Maybe it was an attempt at a subtle deception to make me think that they didn't already know I was off the ships.

After he had unlocked a cell door he relieved me of my shoes then bundled me inside and the door clanged shut with a dull echoing thud behind me. It took some time to become accustomed to the pitch darkness, but once my eyes had adjusted I was able to take account of my surroundings. The cell was small, about eight foot square, no window, no light, no bunk, no mattress, no chair, nothing other than an evil smelling square tin standing about fourteen inches high in one corner, full to the brim with human excrement. The cell was just a concrete box with a strong steel door. There was no escape from the smell so I simply squatted on the cold floor in the corner as far away from the tin that I could get. I contemplated my ill fortune and pondered that what I had done surely didn't deserve to have put me in my present plight. I was in complete solitary confinement.

After what I judged to be about an hour had passed. The tiny flap in the door suddenly opened and a voice asked if I required a blanket. "A little compassion at last," I thought, but I should have known better. I was in shirtsleeves, it was getting chilly and the cold from the concrete had begun to make itself felt so I thought a blanket would be very welcome. Responding to my, "Yes please," a blanket was squeezed through the tiny flap. I will never know if it was indicative of Aussie humour as a whole or specific to the nature of the Cairns police that I had so far come into contact with, but the article that was pushed through bore very little resemblance to a blanket and stunk as vile as the tin in the corner.

I flung it in the general direction of the tin and retreated to squat in my corner to spend the most cold and uncomfortable night of my existence and not surprisingly, sleep just would not come. Maybe being made to stand almost naked in the icy courtyard of the training school all those years ago had stood me in good stead after all (not to mention having sat for almost two days on a galvanised bucket). Perhaps those experiences had taught me how to gain the mental strength to withstand the situation I then found myself in.

The night appeared to be a whole eternity before I heard a noise outside. I forced my stiff cold limbs into motion and painfully shuffled

410

to the door to see if I could open the little flap from the inside. It resisted a little at first but I managed to prise it open. After doing so I was able to peek out along the row of cells to see an officer releasing a prisoner.

The very first faint glimmers of light were appearing in the sky as the prisoner stepped out of his cell and spoke to the officer in a voice I recognized immediately and as the policeman lead him across the yard, "Hey Paddy," I shouted, thinking that at least he will know that I'm in here. Paddy recognized my voice and turned in surprise, and I shouted to the copper, "When do I get out of here?" "When you can afford it" came his ominous reply. My heart sank as he immediately grabbed Paddy by the arm and bundled him through the doors into the main building.

Shivering, I suddenly had a slight appreciation of the plight of all the prisoners throughout the world who were given no rights in totalitarian states. How could something like this happen in the civilized country that I had always believed Australia to be?

Paddy argued and pleaded with them for almost fifteen minutes for them to let me go. He told me later that they were very reluctant to do so but finally agreed, and it was another ten to fifteen minutes later before they came to open my door. Once outside the cell I was reunited with my shoes and frog marched across the yard with an immense feeling of relief. I was led into a little room where Paddy stood waiting for me. Two coppers flanked both sides of me glaring as the one behind the counter produced my belongings. "You came in here with nine pounds," he said, "now you have got four. You can go now." I was seething. I had been arrested for a minor offence that, I would have thought, warranted little more than a caution and those so-called protectors of the law had subjected me to almost unbearable conditions.

What horrible diseases were lurking in that tin or the blanket for that matter? On top of which, they had robbed me of five pounds. A fair sum in those days. Somehow I managed to control my temper as I realised that I was in a no win situation and that it would be prudent for me to keep silent or I may be slammed back in to that cell again for who knew how long.

Along with my depleted amount of cash and other bits of belongings back in my pocket I retreated with Paddy. The sarcastic farewell from one of the grinning coppers as we passed through the outside door was,

"Cheerio, see you again soon;" that was treated by both Paddy and I with the contempt it deserved.

Paddy told me that they had wanted to keep me in much longer but had relented when he told them that the ship would be sailing in two hours. It was then 5.30am. I couldn't thank him enough for arguing my case and I felt that I would forever be in his debt. My feelings of anger didn't abate as he too, obviously not best pleased, related his story to me on our way back to the ship. Whilst I had been arrested for a public order offence, he was arrested having committed no offence whatsoever other than that he was a sailor. It turned out that at least ten sailors from different ships had spent the night in the cells.

He had been late getting ashore and had one glass of beer in the Royal Hotel. The establishment, being a residential hotel, was allowed to serve beer till a later hour to those who would claim to be residing there. Not knowing where we had gone, he had decided to return to the ship. As he left the pub two policemen, hidden outside one on each side of the door, just grabbed an arm each and marched him off to the station where he spent the night in a cell with five other seafarers from other ships.

Later, it became known that our ship's carpenter had been a guest of the local constabulary too. He did like his booze, but claimed he was going along the street, minding his own business when two coppers bundled him into a car and locked him up until 7.00am the following morning.

On the face of it they had quite a profitable little scam going for them, I had been relieved of five pounds, the carpenter who had shared his cell with two others had been relieved of four pounds and Paddy two pounds. What they took from the other seven prisoners that we knew of is anybody's guess. Whilst Paddy and the carpenter had shared a cell with others, it was strange to me that I had been kept in solitary confinement. Yet another one of those unfathomable incidents.

It was 6.00am when we arrived back at the ship. Joesy had just completed his nightwatchman stint as we walked into the mess. He roared with laughter as we told him of our plight. "Ahhh!!! The calaboose," he chortled as he produced a very welcome cup of tea. Only then did I feel the first shivers of the cold I had inherited from the bare concrete leaving my body.

412

As usual, news travelled fast onboard the ship and word spread like wildfire that we had spent the night in the clink. Not surprisingly all the crew thought it was a great joke and throughout the day, we were ribbed mercilessly. We didn't get any sympathy from the Mate either and had to start work as usual at seven o'clock, one hour after our return. Following one of the longest, most uncomfortable nights of my life, it became one of the longest most tiring days of my life. I was dead beat and full of aches and pains. How I got through the day, I'll never know.

* * *

The dockers finished unloading and suggested to the Mate that, as they had worked over to finish it, could the crew restore the beams and batten down the hatches. That was something we did ourselves in the vast majority of ports in the world anyway, but there they considered it to be part of their job so the offer was made to pay us the Australian dockers rate for the time it took us to do the job. As it meant that the company wouldn't have to pay us overtime, the Mate readily agreed so after tea, we started work again.

It took us till 9.30pm to finish the job, and the fact that we were two hands short didn't help, plus the fact that three others had absorbed a large amount of beer and were unable to turn to, helped even less. So, we were thankful that the Skipper during the day had signed on a new member to the crew. He was a young English guy who originated from Surrey, and had been in Australia for about six years. His intention was to see a bit more of the world before he returned to England eventually. I told him that he had joined the right ship, suspecting how apt the word eventually was going to be.

With the hatches finally battened down, we were called to stations, and we let go and sailed. Because of the night I had spent and the heavy workload all day, never had those ropes been so heavy. I was literally almost on my knees and was working on automatic pilot, not really aware of my actions. It was then 10.50pm and I had worked almost non-stop for nearly sixteen hours after my sleepless, freezing night in a cell.

At long last, we were clear and I started to shuffle my way aft towards my bunk when I was beckoned by the Mate who informed me that there was a member of the eight to twelve watch flaked out drunk

413

on his bunk, dead to the world. I would have to take over his stint at the wheel at eleven o'clock till twelve. What was it that instructor had said at the Gravesend school? "It's a tough job in the Merchant Navy." He was dead right. I felt that if I had had the strength I would cheerfully have killed the Mate at that moment.

I looked at my watch. I had ten minutes, which gave me just enough time to go aft to douse myself in cold water to freshen up. It was one of the few times in my life that I had felt genuinely angry. The guy had spent hours enjoying himself into oblivion and I, after what I had just been through, was made to do his job for him and what's more, he didn't even get logged.

The Skipper and the Port Pilot were on the bridge in the wheelhouse when I took over the helm, and on my arrival the Skipper turned to the Pilot and said, "This is one of the men who spent the night in prison." "Why not get the 'sparks' to radio it to the BBC World Service?" I thought. But the Pilot seemed to be quite interested and wanted to know the details of all that had occurred so while I was at the helm I reiterated the sorry tale of the events of the previous evening and he appeared to get angry, especially when he heard about the police taking money from all of us. "They have no right to do that without even charging you," he said. "Well, I wasn't in any position to argue," I said, explaining that they were letting me go, and could so easily have chucked me back in the slammer. He nodded his understanding but remained angry.

I must admit it felt better to get it off my chest, especially to someone actually from Cairns who held a respected position who now knew what was going on in their police force with the visiting sailors. Perhaps, just maybe, something could start to be done about it. I did wonder however, if I had been deliberately chosen to do that hour at the helm in order to have that conversation with the Pilot. My relief came at midnight and ten minutes later, I was fast asleep in my warm comfortable bunk.

We made good progress down along the Great Barrier Reef. The Docking Pilot had been relieved and it was the same Pilot taking us on the return journey down the reef who had brought us up, but that time it was not quite so pleasant. It was warm with heavy swells and strong head winds at first. By the time the Reef Pilot was dropped off, the weather had picked up and so had I.

My strength on leaving Cairns behind quickly returned, with only my hurt pride and my pocket troubling me. Although to be fair, the money earned battening down on Australian dockers overtime rate had recouped my loss.

At 7.00pm that evening, after we had dropped the Pilot off, we continued on our way to Brisbane where we dropped anchor for the night before docking alongside at daybreak the next morning, which was Saturday 20th May. I had become a little wary about going ashore. We had docked about ten miles from the city near a small village which boasted of one store, one post office, a few bungalows and of course a pub. Naturally the pub attracted most of our custom.

One of the dockers gave us the wonderful information that being 'bona fide' travellers who had arrived that day, in accordance with the law, the pub could stay open beyond the six o'clock limit. Most of the crew enjoyed a great evening boozing away with the locals who joined us in a good old singsong. The fact that one of those locals enjoying himself was the very same guy who had enlightened us about the 'bona fide' travellers law, meant it didn't take a genius to work out his reasons for telling us.

The locals challenged us to a darts match, which with more to luck than skill we won, two games to one, but the promise of a free beer each from the losers was a mighty strong incentive to us sailors. It beggared belief how that happy friendly crowd who not only lived in the same country but the same state as those in Cairns could give such a different welcome to their visitors; it was truly amazing. One could have been forgiven for thinking that it was two entirely different countries. Australia was a civilized country after all.

Sunday was a totally different experience. Australia in those days died on Sundays. Nothing was open. The 'bona fide' clause was only valid on the day of arrival so could not be used as an excuse a second time. We couldn't even get a bus or any transport to go to the city.

Six of us took a stroll ashore where, after much cajoling, a storekeeper reluctantly sold us an ice cream each through a little hatch in the side of the building. It was a poor substitute for a beer, which would have quenched a thirst worthy of the wonderful hot, sunny day, but we all enjoyed a long, lazy afternoon just sat on the pleasant beach.

We sailed on the night of Monday 22nd May less than forty-eight hours later; the Pilot came aboard and took over on our arrival to pass under the magnificent Sydney Harbour Bridge. There was a breathtaking display of fireworks going off all over and as one of the guys remarked, "They must have known we were coming, but they need not have gone to so much trouble to welcome us." I believe they were celebrating Empire Day, now known as Commonwealth Day, and they were really going to town with it; the celebrations continued on late into the night.

With the daily grind finished and having collected a sub, Ken an EDH and I decided to look around the place. It was enjoyable, but Sydney like most large cities was not a cheap place. Clothes and household goods, I thought, were a bit pricey but my evening was not as expensive as my night in Cairns had been, and it was a thousand times more enjoyable.

One of the most majestic spectacles was the arrival that evening of the 'Esmeralda,' a large Chilean sailing ship. She had four masts and was a training ship. The biggest ship of sail to arrive in Sydney for fifty-two years we were informed by one of the dockers. Her masts were too tall to pass beneath the harbour bridge, so she had to anchor on the nearside, just off the point where the famous Sydney Opera House would be built later. I can only imagine what a magnificent sight she would be out to sea, fully rigged with all canvas flying.

A dockworkers dispute was in full swing so no work was performed on the Saturday, and on the Sunday absolutely nothing stirred as usual. I took a further sub and along with Paddy, we decided Taronga Park Zoo might be worth a visit. As we had both been locked up in Cairns, the thought of seeing something else behind bars was appealing. Sensibly the zoo was situated on an island in the middle of Sydney Harbour, which allowed the animals, as far as was practicable, safety and much more freedom.

Joking aside, it was a pleasure to find so few of the animals actually behind bars. They had no qualms, especially in Cairns, about putting us behind bars but had it seemed far more consideration towards the animals. The landscaping was such that the inmates were free to roam anywhere within their designated area with the more dangerous ones adequately secure. The zoo it seemed gave the animals the respect they deserved, and in some ways it appeared that they were treated better than a few ships' companies treated us.

The zoo housed the largest aquarium I had seen up to that date. Inside the building was full of strange exotic examples of marine life. They were fantastic and absorbed our attention for far longer than I would have expected. On descending some steps to a lower level of the building, we came across a pool like a giant well and on looking into it through a wire mesh, we could see two giant rays, several six-foot long sharks and other varieties of fish, the smallest of which was three or four foot in length.

Information boards detailed the various specimens on view and added the fact that it was a 'wishing well.' Coins were to be thrown in and if it landed and stayed on a ray's back whilst it completed a full circle of the pool, your wish would be granted. The cynic in me said, "Oh yeah, no thanks," as I walked away.

The weather was typically Australian: hot, which made it quite an enjoyable afternoon. The lions, tigers, bears, elephants, hippos and even the gorilla due to the freedom that the landscaping and planning afforded them did not seem discontented with their captivity. Not surprisingly, there were of course lots of kangaroos that were very friendly creatures, but everyone amongst the crowd agreed that their favourites were the timid cuddly koala bears perched amongst the trees.

It was quite an unusual but enjoyable day out for us and on catching the ferry back to the mainland it was almost dark as we stepped ashore. The ferry was dwarfed by the Chilean sailing four master. We decided to finish the day off that Saturday with a visit to the cinema and it came as quite a shock to find that there was to be no smoking in the cinema. That, in 1961, was the first time I had encountered a smoking ban in a public place.

For the crews of visiting ships who had been working seven days a week, on call twenty four hours a day, sometimes for weeks on end, Australian Sundays were a real pain with everything closed. Even during the weekdays although the bars did open during the morning, 6.00pm and most of them closed them again. When open they were little more than drinking dens with little or no comfort. They comprised of a room with a bar in the middle, no chairs, no tables, so everyone lounged against the bar or leant against a wall with their drinks. It was a moot point argued by some of the more chauvinistic types that the best thing about an Aussie bar was that apart from the occasional barmaid, there were no women allowed.

There may be something in the fact that originally Australia was a penal colony and the laws framed then were not in the interests of the common man or ex-convicts. But with the great number of immigrants that flooded into the country in the 1960s, I felt sure that the licensing laws would have to change and my little contribution to the protest started that day. I stayed onboard.

All the watches were switched around while we were in port and I found myself in my favourite, the four to eight. We sailed at 5.00pm on Monday 29th May. Since we had left Auckland we had kept the derricks topped all the while, but as we headed south then west through the Bass Strait, everything was lowered and secured because of a storm warning.

Despite the warning, the warm sunny weather continued with calm glass like seas and hardly a breath of air so everything had to be topped and rigged again ready for docking in Melbourne on Wednesday 31st May. After we picked the Pilot up at 5.00pm, he took us all the way in and we were docked by 10.00pm.

I went ashore the following evening to look around. The city itself looked very nice, but it was so big and sprawling I didn't get too adventurous for fear of getting lost. That was my one and only visit into the city itself as we were docked some distance away and I could not afford the taxi fares. Meanwhile someone had discovered where the seamen's mission was with the biggest surprise of all, "It was open on Sundays." At last!! Somewhere we could go to on the Sabbath.

Half a dozen of us invaded the place that Sunday and found that there was a dance night in progress, but we felt that we would need a few bevvies before we could join in. Unfortunately there were not any on sale so we spent the evening playing snooker instead.

We sailed again the following afternoon, Monday 5th June. I took the helm as we approached the last channel. The Pilot pointed ahead and asked me if I could see where the broken water was. I said, "Yes" to which he replied, "Well, that's a shoal of rocks and there is only a thirty foot clearance so don't let her wander or you will be spending a few more nights here." "Anything but that," I said jokingly, which was not taken as a joke by the Pilot, who became definitely sniffy. I kept her straight with no further comment from him, not even a goodbye when his launch came alongside to take him back.

On into the Great Australian Bight we went with warm sunny weather for the first couple of days, which changed suddenly into strong winds which howled through the rigging at forty miles an hour as we battled on for four days. It was very cold, uncomfortable and slowed down our progress considerably until we came north up the west coast on Sunday 11th June when it became a little warmer and more settled. As with Piraeus in my early years, Freemantle I felt was becoming my second home port, with the frequency I seemed to call there, as we went straight in to tie up alongside berth number three.

My relatives, Steve, Violet, Gillian and Co. were then back in England, but I heard on my last leave, that they were seriously thinking of returning, so there was no incentive for me to catch the train into Perth. I went ashore instead into Freemantle itself with Ken, who I teamed up with mostly by then and we spent most of our time in the seamen's mission, which was friendly and catered for most of our needs.

As I walked through the mission's door, it suddenly struck me that on all the previous occasions that I had walked through that very same threshold, I had come via the Suez Canal, but on that occasion I had come via the Panama Canal, so I had in effect circumnavigated the world, albeit in two halves, on separate occasions.

It had taken four months to load and transport one cargo and on Friday morning 16th June the dockers had finally discharged everything including the sweepings. With everything secure at 5.30am, all hands were called to stations to let go only to drop the starboard anchor out in the bay half an hour later. It was necessary to bring the port anchor inboard and detach it from its cable as the cable was to be used for mooring at the next port of call. As described before that was no simple task which required us to rig the jumbo derrick with the heavy lifting gear and needed precision manoeuvring under careful supervision, due to the colossal weight of the anchor itself.

Normally, the job was done with the Bosun in charge but as both he and the Chippy had been almost permanently under the influence of alcohol over the past few weeks, the Mate took control and it all went smoothly. We first attached the runner to the anchor before we dropped it to the seabed and dragged it along the bottom until it was plumb, then we lifted it up and onto the deck, exactly as the gentle giant of a Bosun had explained it to me on the '*San Velino*.'

Once detached the anchor was lashed and secured to the deck and by 10.00pm we headed off into the Indian Ocean bound for Christmas Island, not the one where they were experimenting with Atom Bombs in the Pacific, but the one just south of Java.

* * *

The weather deteriorated and became cold and stormy for a while, but as we edged further northward it got warmer and more pleasant. A relief from painting the ship arrived on Wednesday 21st June as we hove to off the Island and drifted gently throughout the night.

Early the next morning at 5.30am, we were called to prepare the holds to receive the next shipment, and with the derricks secured and swung out of the way, the shore gang came out in small, landing craft type pontoons to collect the anchor cable as we drifted towards the jetty. The end of the cable was taken and shackled on to a buoy. It took a further three hours for them to finish tying us up. They had brought their own mooring ropes and wires with them, and they worked hard criss-crossing the ropes and wires to their satisfaction.

With the bow shackled to a buoy by the anchor cable and the poop deck looking as if we were caught in a giant spider's web, we lay in the stranglehold position with our port beam facing the head of the jetty, which was about a hundred foot away. We would stay put whatever the tides and weather decided to do.

The conditions were extreme as we carried out the back breaking work of preparing the holds. One minute torrential rain showers soaked us to the skin and the next red-hot sunshine caused steam to rise from our bodies as well as the decks. The cycle of sun followed by showers stopped abruptly at nine o'clock and left only the stinking heat. Soon we were praying for another shower just for a welcome respite. It never happened.

It was at that point the loading began. A long chute was telescoped out, fed by a conveyor belt from a factory alongside the jetty. Once the chute was positioned over a hatch, phosphate fertiliser was soon pouring into us at a rate of knots. We were not allowed shore leave as there was no let up because, as one hatch was filled it was covered and battened down with its derricks dropped, secured and made ready for sea. Us deckhands never had a minute to catch our breath.

The phosphate was a similar colour to wall plaster in a bag but its consistency was so fine that clouds of it blew out of the holds like smoke from an explosion as it poured in and within minutes the ship was completely covered in it. You could take a handful and as tight as you could close your fist, every grain would sift through your tightly clenched fingers.

It got everywhere, in the accommodation, in our clothes, in our hair, it even clung to our eyebrows and lashes, it got into every orifice one could mention; it was vile stuff. And it kept coming. Someone said it consisted mainly of bird shit and that we were being shit upon from a great height. What a cheery thought as we were practically eating it, working with hardly a thought of the possible danger to our health, our lungs and general well-being?

We all looked like something from one of the early ghost films nevertheless, the old 'Cape Grafton' was filled to the gunnels by five o'clock in the afternoon. Eight hours to load eight thousand tons can't be bad going.

We showered and rid ourselves of the filthy dust and had our evening meal before we turned to again to batten down the last of the hatches while the shore gang dismantled their spider's web of moorings. The anchor too had to be shackled back on to its cable, lifted over the side and lowered to the bottom where it was then heaved up and housed properly.

Once that was completed, the Jumbo then had to be rehoused, stripped and all the gear stowed away before we could start on our return trip that would finally bring us to Adelaide and the delights of Australia once more. Having worked like Trojans, we were off again by eight o'clock. Fortunately during that night, we ran into heavy showers which helped to wash away much of the powdered dust that clung to the superstructure and the decks, which left us with less to clean away the following day.

The weather continued to deteriorate as we sailed south and the ship rolled heavily from side to side for days on end, and it got colder all the while. The only occurrence of any note was the delight on Joesy's face one morning when I presented him with three flying fish, each about a foot long that had been washed aboard during the night. They were delicious, he told me later.

Upon rounding the tip of South Western Australia, the Australian Bight was no more welcoming other than our arrival in Adelaide, South Australia on Tuesday 4th July. We tied up at 6.00pm just an hour after we had picked up the Pilot, which meant that we on the 'Cape Grafton' had called at every state in Australia other than the Northern Territory and Tasmania.

We lost no time in getting rid of the cargo; no sooner had we secured the ship alongside than the boards and beams came off all five hatches and the large five ton dockside grabs began to relieve us of the fertilizer. It was not pleasant for within minutes we were inches deep in the disgusting stuff again.

The general feeling was that someone up there didn't like us for the next two days it bucketed down and turned the dust into sludge. The cynics had a birthday with their quotations on the theme, "We've been shit on." It became very wearing as the stuff covered everyone from head to toe.

Port Adelaide lay fifteen miles distant from the city of Adelaide itself. A small community but big enough to have a cinema, which Ken and I visited on the Wednesday night. That was the only night we spent ashore since the discharge of cargo had been completed by the Thursday, which enabled us to let go at around five o'clock in the evening to shift ship to another berth further upstream to take on bunkers. It poured down that night as we continued to work in the phosphate sludge and muck until eleven, replacing the beams and battening down.

When one thinks of Australia, it is always the warm sunny climate that comes to mind. It was certainly not the case that night as we headed back towards the Bass Strait. The fo'c's'le head while on lookout was reminiscent of the North Sea in January. It was freezing cold. The Mate however seemed intent on warming us all up and turned everyone to including the stewards to sweep and clean up the residue of phosphate that remained in the holds. Those of us in watches did our two four-hour stints each day plus four hours overtime while off duty. The stewards, once they had finished their duties after tea, were put with the dayworkers and worked until ten o'clock at night. Empty fifty-gallon drums were lowered into the holds and the dust shovelled into them, which when full were heaved up on to the decks. You can imagine from that what a large task it was.

I was on my knees, as were the rest of us. We were so exhausted. I even had to dump a pair of my working jeans, which had become torn and clogged with gunge. We slaved away for days in those holds with clouds of phosphate dust bellowing everywhere; God knows what it was doing to our lungs as the flimsy cotton like masks we were issued with were next to useless.

The work was made harder because Saturday brought more bad weather and the conditions got worse and being empty, the ship began to pitch and roll, which made our work in the holds much more difficult. Such was the ferocity of the storm, that the Skipper sought shelter and headed in towards the coast. We dropped anchor just off the breakwater at five o'clock at a little place called Portland in Discovery Bay, and we stayed there to shelter in calmer waters for the night. Conditions improved during the night and a more favourable forecast saw us up anchoring the next morning to continue on our way through the Bass Strait, then we headed northwards.

The work in the holds continued through the weekend to reach almost pristine condition on Tuesday 11th July. That didn't mean we could sit back and rest on our laurels though; the beams then had to be taken out in preparation for the next cargo. Only two hatches were ready by knocking off time at five o'clock that evening. We were called to stations at 2.00am on Wednesday as we had arrived in Newcastle, just north of Sydney; we set to and tied up alongside immediately. Finally secure, we were stood down three hours later at 5.00am only to be called out again at 9.00am to open up the other three hatches. After all the blood, sweat and tears expended in getting those holds meticulously clean and all the overtime we had earned, it was dispiriting to think that eight thousand tons of coal was then about to be poured into them.

Due to the need to keep shifting ship back and forth along the quay to level up the conveyor belt to the appropriate hatches and to batten down each hatch as soon as it was full, the Mate introduced a two-shift system. A twelve-hour six to six shift day and night to ensure a continuous work rate. For once lady luck smiled on me, I was on the day shift.

Everyone was awarded six Australian pounds bonus for cleaning the hatches, they called it a bonus, but we found a little later that it had been paid in lieu of all the overtime, so we were no better off; in fact we all thought we had been fleeced. I felt really shattered, but it was my twenty-fifth birthday that Thursday, and shattered or not I was determined to enjoy it. Newcastle was not like Cairns and with Paddy, I went ashore to celebrate, and celebrate I did.

After he had finished the day shift on the day of our arrival, the young man we had signed on in Cairns, who wanted to see a little more of the world before eventually returning home, decided that he'd had enough so he packed his suitcase, and walked off the ship. Apparently, he had become so desperate to get away he never even tried to get his wages and we never saw him again. He had his six-pound bonus so I guess he felt that would see him through to take his chances back in Australia. He was replaced the next day by an ordinary seaman called Deacon.

The coal came along the conveyer belts and simply poured into the ship, but it was much slower than the phosphate had been, and being furnace coal, it produced only a little dust and our full compliment was loaded by 8.00am on Friday 14th July. We had taken breakfast before we battened down the last hatches and then everyone was called to stations.

The prospect of eighteen days on the open sea steaming northward across the Pacific away from the coastline was a welcome change. It was a long way to Japan, our next port of call. It would be my first time in a Japanese port and the reports that I had received from various shipmates over the years had made it a place that I longed to visit.

For the first week the weather remained great, very gradually worsening during the second week; although it remained warm we began to run into the occasional rain shower. On Saturday morning 22nd July, I observed a very unusual occurrence. It looked as though we were heading into rain clouds approaching from the north. By some freak of nature, the rain passed us by on the starboard side. It was absolutely bucketing down while we were bathed in sunshine. It was particularly unusual because at one point, the edge of the downpour seemed that close to us, I could have almost reached out to wash my hands in it, but not a drop touched the ship.

A couple of times during the next week, the engineers had to have the ship stopped in order to change fuel valves, but no other incident disturbed the ritual of painting ship. Orders had been received on our future destination so after we have got rid of the coal in Japan, we were to go back into the Pacific to Ocean Island for a further load of phosphate to be delivered to Adelaide and a quaintly named place in South Australia called Wallaroo.

Midnight on Friday 28th July saw the end of the calm weather. The northern Pacific is notorious for its typhoons, which seem to spring up from nowhere and grow out of nothing in a very short time. We ran into the tail end of one, and over the next few days we got caught up in two more, but luckily we only caught the after effects of them.

Even so the seas were mountainous; they crashed over the decks, which caused the ship to bob about like a cork. The fact that we had a good stable load helped; I would not like to have been aboard a light ship in the full grips of one of those storms. As it was for days we were extremely uncomfortable until the Sunday when we found calmer seas.

On Monday afternoon 31st July, the Japanese coast came over the horizon and we closed in and followed it for a while before we anchored in Tokyo Bay, amongst many other ships waiting just off Yokohama.

The Pilot came aboard early the next morning, Tuesday August 1st to take us up to Chiba, a two-hour journey away where we were to discharge our coal. Off in the distance gleamed the snow capped peak of Mount Fujiyama, which was a most impressive sight in the morning sunshine.

We anchored quite a distance away from the jetty on our arrival. You could take nothing for granted aboard ship. For further word went around that we would be at anchor for two days before going alongside so under the Mate's orders, everyone returned to the painting of the ship. Suddenly at four o'clock that same afternoon the Pilot came to take us alongside. It then became a mad rush. The painting was abandoned immediately for we had to top the derricks and open up the hatches ready for the dockers to start unloading as quickly as possible. That took us until eight o'clock that evening then the giant grabs wasted no time in starting to unload the coal.

425

When the day's work was finished, subs were dished out and shore passes issued, which only allowed us to go into Chiba. Most of us were too tired to go ashore after the day's gruelling work and the majority turned in. The Mate must have had a rush of blood to the head for the next day everyone was granted a half day off.

There was a limited access to the jetty as it was within a steel works and none of the ship's company was allowed to walk through the factory; hence the shore pass. Taxis were our only means of getting through the grounds. This was, I strongly suspected, just a ruse to make us spend more money.

Chiba consisted of more or less one street with a sprinkling of bars. As previously stated, I had heard so many wonderful stories about Japan being a great place, I had really been looking forward to my visit so in that respect Chiba was a little disappointing. Once ashore, as in Tocopilla, we decided to sample each bar in the small town.

When we entered each bar, we were greeted with a cheery smile and handed a very hot towel with which to wipe our hands before being served, they were so hot they almost scalded our skin. After the third bar, my hands were tingling and were the colour of ripe tomatoes. Those of the crew who had visited Japan previously, reckoned Chiba to be the worst place they had seen as far as catering to sailor's needs, and was not typical of the Japan that they knew. Maybe, perhaps, I would be lucky next time, if there were to be a next time. Who could tell?

Amazingly the Japanese with their giant grabs had shifted eight thousand ton of coal in two days. We sailed the following afternoon: Thursday August 3rd, and it was all hands working non-stop, battening down and preparing for the open sea as we sailed back down to drop anchor in the bay just off Yokohama again.

Ocean Island we learned, would require another anchor cable tie up. That meant that once again we had to rig up the 'Jumbo' to bring in the port anchor and unshackle it in the shelter of the bay before we put to sea. The weather was not kind. Rain came down as soon as the work started, and with the Bosun and Chippy pickled in alcohol as usual, shouting orders that no one could understand (the Mate was busy on that occasion), it was an unhappy crew who finally got everything prepared. It was 9.00pm. Soaked and sighing with relief, we all took showers and crawled into our bunks.

The Bosun and Chippy must have stocked up with booze in every port; they could not have got that way from the pittance of beer that we were allowed to buy onboard the ship. Their constant inebriation had not gone unnoticed though, as will soon be seen.

I awoke the next morning to the steady throb of the engines. Japan had long disappeared astern as we headed on a southerly course. For the first three days the heavens opened up, and the rain pelted down almost non-stop followed by squally, showery conditions. One minute you were soaked and the next steaming in the hot sun.

On Friday 11th August fresh orders were received, the destination for the next shipment was changed to Nauru, another small Pacific island about two hundred miles distant from Ocean Island. We arrived there at 3.00pm on Sunday 13th August. Lucky for some but not for us as it was to be a load of loose phosphate again. Nauru was only a tiny little island; a small patch of green in the middle of the vast expanse of blue Pacific Ocean. As before, we had to drift around all night as the sea was too deep to anchor and we weren't due to load until the next day.

Everyone was called at 5.00am to prepare the hatches, while the shore gang performed the tying up. I say performed, as it was exactly the same procedure as at Christmas Island, with numerous ropes and wire hawsers, which criss-crossed everywhere. They did secure the anchor cable to a buoy, which was a good job as no one would have been happy had the change of orders resulted in the cable not being used after all the hard work unshackling it in the rain.

We were soon ready to load, but whereas on Christmas Island there had been only one chute to deliver the phosphate, there there were two. Within minutes we were covered in phosphate dust again, and just six hours later a full cargo of the disgusting stuff had been taken aboard. We didn't have time to breathe, let alone take a break for those six hours. The moment the ship was ready for sea the shore gang then dismantled the spider's web of moorings.

That beggared the question why so many ropes and wires for such a short stay? But thank God it was their responsibility as none of us would have relished the job and we were busy anyway, still without a break, reshackling the anchor before we got under way at 3.30pm.

My four-hour watch began at 4.00pm, which meant that I had to take over the helm and leave everyone to hose down the decks to get rid of the dust. The island soon became a faint speck in the distance to our stern, and for the next week or so we had glorious sunny weather with calm seas; there seemed little to worry about. The typhoons were an almost forgotten memory as one day just blended into the next.

* * *

The old Empire boat, built speedily during the war to fill the gaps in the Merchant fleet created by Hitler and his 'U' boats was a remarkably sound, reliable ship. Except for the odd fuel valve change that was common to most ships, she gave little trouble, though maybe certain Pitcairn islanders may not agree, she was one of the most reliable in which I had sailed, which included the modern tankers.

On Tuesday morning 22nd August, we sighted the Australian coast and not surprisingly, it became appreciably colder. It was still midwinter in the Southern Hemisphere, and the sudden drop in temperature after such hot, lovely weather over the previous weeks found us shivering while we worked out on deck. With the heavy seas and icy winds, extra jumpers and heavy coats were the order of the day, and the general feeling was 'hurry up Wallaroo' as we followed the coast down.

We passed Newcastle and Sydney to starboard on the Wednesday morning and the next day, Thursday 24th August saw us on our new heading to take us through the Bass Strait then onward beyond Kangaroo Island into the Spencer Gulf. Eventually we arrived off Wallaroo on Sunday afternoon 27th August where with the engines stopped we just drifted for a while.

At four o'clock, I took the wheel as the Pilot came out to guide us in. As we nosed in between two jetties the Pilot decided to turn the ship around to take her in port side to the jetty. That obviously necessitated a hundred and eighty degree turn in between the two jetties with very little room to spare. First it was engines astern, helm hard to port, then engines ahead helm hard to starboard, backwards and forwards non-stop for over an hour. I was sweating cobs on the wheel responding to his orders; the muscles in my arms began to feel like Popeye's after his spinach, and I kept thinking, "Why me? Why me?"

The performance attracted quite a crowd of the local populace with amused expressions on their faces. "I hope they don't think it's my fault" was another thought that entered my head. The jetty opposite to the one we were attempting to get alongside, I noticed, had a large gap in the middle, but I was too busy to think much about it at the time. I was later told that the gap was caused by a pilot taking a ship right through it. Perhaps, I thought that the town's folk had gathered to see if he would do it again, because in my mind it was an odds on bet that it would have been down to the guy in front of me who was making me sweat so much.

We finally completed the equivalent to a three-point turn in a car, in a nine thousand ton ship, and in a relatively much smaller space. It was more like a ninety-point turn and I was practically on my knees by the time I finally brought her alongside the jetty. We reckoned we deserved a drink, although by the time we got ashore it was after six o'clock. The first pub we came to was closed and not knowing if the bona fide traveller rule applied in South Australia as it did in Queensland, we tried our luck and knocked loudly on the door. Our luck was in; to our delight the guy who answered the door let us in and never did Australian beer taste so good.

I had no plans to go ashore the next night. Ken had been ashore in the afternoon and returned just after tea. He came down to my cabin to ask me to go with him to a dance in the local town hall that evening. He spent some considerable time trying to convince me to go. I was a little puzzled as to why he was so insistent as by his own admission in the past he was not a dancing man, and he knew that I was to dancing what a hippopotamus is to ballet. I suspected an ulterior motive but he finally convinced me that even the local hop must be more interesting than watching Joesy filing a piece of metal so I gave in.

The town hall dance was obviously popular with the locals for it was well supported. Ken and I felt like a pair of bookends as we sat on the wide stairs that led down to the dance floor contenting ourselves with just watching. Suddenly I knew exactly what his ulterior motive was, and why he had been so insistent that I went ashore with him; he needed moral support. He sat watching one of two girls who were dancing together; he simply couldn't take his eyes off her. I assumed that he must have spotted her sometime during the afternoon and noticed that there was a dance on in the evening, and got me to come with him in the hope that he would see her there.

She must have become aware of his interest for soon, shy glances were being exchanged and the young lady began to blush modestly. "Go on then, ask her for a dance," I said. "What do you mean? He asked feigning ignorance, "That girl you are ogling," I said, with no little amusement. "I can't dance and you know it," was his excuse.

I was about to rib him along a little more when, just at that moment, the dancers twirled and a slight gap opened on the crowded floor. For the first time I got a clear view of the girl she was dancing with. It was then my turn to ogle. She was also gorgeous. We were both like a pair of spineless idiots, neither of us had the courage to approach them. Not even when the evening ended.

While we stood shivering at the taxi rank waiting for a cab to take us back to the ship, the two girls walked across the junction at the bottom of the street and with courage summoned up from who knows where, off shot Ken saying, "I'm going to speak to her." When he caught them up, they stopped and talked for a couple of minutes then he came running back like a two year old. He had arranged a date at another dance the following night and her friend would be there too, he told me pointedly. As he spoke, a taxi arrived and took us back to the ship.

Like the couple of idiots that we were, the following night saw us sitting in another dance hall yet again arguing as to who was to be the first to ask for a dance. I thought that as he had broken the ice by talking to them on the previous evening, Ken wouldn't hesitate, but he seemed as much lacking in the art of the ballroom as I was.

The girls kept throwing quizzical glances in our direction and before we knew it, the last waltz was called. It was a now or never situation as the girls danced past we walked onto the floor and cut in. Ken after all his claims that he couldn't dance, must have been slightly more experienced than me, for they moved off welding in with the movement of all the others on the floor. Me! I hadn't a clue, but if anything, I'm resourceful. I invented my own steps. One thing I did know about dancing the waltz was that like Ken and his newfound girl you are supposed to traverse around the whole dance floor in an orderly fashion. My steps however kept us on the same spot just revolving round and round.

As we left the dance hall, I tried to apologise stating that I was sorry, but I couldn't dance very well. A wonderful smile spread across the girl's face as she said, "I already know that." That was the icebreaker and we all started giggling and laughing. I'm sure that all four of us were thinking the same thing, "What a pair of prats Ken and I were." Despite that, they must have liked us for they took us to a little coffee bar where we sat and had a drink and a chat before we walked them home.

Her name was Raylee, which was a name totally new to me but I thought it was lovely and befitting. Her friend wished to be known as Midge, another unusual name, Madge I had heard of but not Midge. Why such a lovely girl should take on the name of a tiny irritating creature I will never know, and I wasn't about to ask. I wasn't that much of a prat.

We took them to the cinema the following night, which was also the town hall, obviously used as a multi-purpose building similar to the old Bloxwich swimming baths, which used to become a dance hall during the winter months.

During the next eight days or so we met up with them every evening and took them either to a dance or to the cinema, which appeared to be the two main leisure pastimes in the town or sometimes we simply went for a walk around, but even with the extra practice my dancing skills did not improve. They were both charming, lovely, friendly girls who made us feel very welcome and we were very glad of their company. Female company was a scarce commodity in the life of a seafarer, especially those serving on tankers or cargo boats, and it was very pleasant to return to a little normality if only for a few days. On Sunday, we took them onboard to give them a grand tour around the ship that they appeared to enjoy very much, but I suspect not as much as we enjoyed the envious glances we got from our shipmates.

The town of Wallaroo had a certain charm of its own. Small and very reminiscent of the frontier towns as portrayed in the old western movies with their dirt track streets and wooden sidewalks with a single track railway running through it. Nowhere were you far from the bush country that portrayed another kind of charm of its own.

In that pleasant way, the days simply flew by and I got to like Raylee more and more. Ken felt the same about Midge so we were really sorry when the time came for our departure. It was Wednesday afternoon 6th September, we had had ten wonderful days in Wallaroo, and after promising to correspond, it was with a wistful heart that we were on our way to get rid of the remainder of the phosphate in Port Adelaide.

We arrived there the following afternoon and all the phosphate was gone by the 8th when we shifted ship once more to the bunkering berth and sailed on Saturday morning. Ken and I managed to get ashore to telephone the girls for a last farewell chat, but then it was back to the grind of cleaning the holds. All hands worked like ants in a nest to get them spotless once again ready to accept another cargo of coal in Newcastle.

That time the Mate did dish out a bonus of five-pounds each plus the overtime, which was very welcome but only seemed to consolidate our suspicions that the six pounds we had received in lieu of overtime on the previous occasion had been a con.

Once alongside in Newcastle on Wednesday 13th September in exactly the same berth as previously, the Mate once again introduced a twelve-hour shift system to shift ship up and down the quay. That time those who were on the day shift before were put on the night shift and vice-versa that I wasn't too happy about, but it was only fair.

The following afternoon with Paddy, I went ashore to do some necessary shopping. On our return, we found that the Skipper had called the police aboard to arrest the Bosun and the Chippy for being constantly drunk and incapable of carrying out their duties. It had been a long time coming but their conduct was inexcusable and couldn't continue for, not only were they a menace to themselves, they were also a menace to the ship. I don't know exactly what laws the Skipper had used but both were given a month's hard labour. Taffy, the guy I had joined the ship with in Falmouth, was promoted to Bosun and Ken stood in as the carpenter. I then had friends in high places.

The loading of the coal went without too much trouble and we sailed again on the afternoon of Friday 15th September, and I was indeed going to get another chance to taste the delights of Japan, hoping once more to make a port much more pleasant than Chiba. Rumours spread rapidly that a period in dry dock could well be part of our stay in Japan. The weather soon began to warm up until it became unbearably hot.

During the following Thursday night and Friday morning we passed between the Solomon Islands and crossed the equator during the weekend. Although it remained hot, we began to get a few rain showers, which helped to keep it reasonable.

The bunkers taken aboard in Adelaide were causing some trouble; having stopped to change a fuel valve on the 25th September, it soon became apparent that water had mysteriously got into the fuel and had begun to slow the engines.

It was during that difficulty that the rumour was confirmed that our destination was to be Osaka, and on completion of the coal being discharged, we were to be dry-docked. That gave rise to a certain amount of speculation that perhaps the company would fly us home. I was nowhere near convinced that they would. But first we had to get there; such was the problem with the fuel, at times little more than four to five knots was being achieved.

The nearest landfall was the island of Guam, which was a large naval base in the Pacific owned by the USA and an urgent radio message was sent requesting their help. Their response was to radio back requesting information about our fuel, position and how long we could last without any. That last question was slightly puzzling, as our reasoning was that we couldn't last any time at all without any, but we assumed that they meant if we didn't have any from them.

In an effort to get rid of some of the water in the tanks, attempts had been made to syphon it away into another empty tank. In doing so much of the fuel had been syphoned away with it, and it was estimated that we had approximately three days supply of usable fuel left. That information was duly dispatched back to them. Nothing further was heard from them for over two days until Thursday 28th September. It appeared that the American Navy had to get permission from their High Command in the USA to allow us into their base; our identity would also have to be verified from the UK. No doubt the method of payment would have to be decided prior to the fuel being supplied to us; thus setting off a chain of messages across the world.

That evening around seven o'clock, the lights of the island appeared and radio messages were received saying that help was at hand, but admittance to the naval dockyard was available to us only during the hours of daylight. That left the Skipper and Chief Engineer in a dilemma. The Engineer was loath to close down the engines for the night in fear of not being able to restart them, and on the other hand with very little fuel left, would there be enough to last the night out? It was decided to just keep them ticking over.

Our luck held, and we were called at 5.30am the next morning and told that the Pilot was on his way. I had half expected an escort of battleships to surround us as we went in as the precautions that were taken were a little over the top, or so it appeared to me.

The American Navy Pilot arrived in a powerful launch took one look at the pilot ladder we had lowered over the side for him and he refused to climb it, he waved and shouted, "I will guide you in, follow my wake." We thought that was amusing, and more so as one AB remarked sarcastically in a fake American accent, "Perhaps he expected an elevator."

What all the fuss was about I will never know, as there was little or nothing to see once we were alongside. Two small rusting old naval cutters and a couple of dry docks, not at all what we had expected. My mind went back to the '*Nacella*' when we had braved the mountainous waves that crashed over the decks, trying with a small handpump to send the fuel three quarters of the length of the ship into the fuel tanks to get restarted. It was a vast improvement on that for by 11.00am, the fuel was aboard and by midday, we headed sweetly out into the Pacific again.

As I looked astern, Guam disappeared over the horizon and I thought that I had visited some historical islands in the Pacific from Pitcairn and its association with the British Royal Navy and Guam, which had its footnotes in the history of the Second World War in the Pacific. It was then 1961, sixteen years after the world hostilities had ceased and still many years later than that I believe they found a Japanese soldier who had spent all those years since 1945 alone in the jungle trying to avoid capture, not knowing that the war was over. Had they found him then, we could have taken him home.

* * *

As before, on the passage northward towards Japan, a typhoon warning was received, and shortly afterwards a distress call was picked up from a Liberian ship about four hundred miles to the north of us. She was caught in the full wrath of the storm and, such was its severity that two of her hatches had caved in. On such occasions every ship, every land station in the vicinity will relay messages and keep a listening watch. An American warship much closer to her position than us was on its way to help, but all to no avail; she couldn't be found. All ships in the area were asked to keep a lookout for her but nothing more was heard and for many hours our 'sparks' tried to contact her with no success.

We can only assume that she must have foundered, more than likely with all hands. Sometimes in life, either fate or luck takes us in hand; ironically, if water had not got into our fuel oil, it was estimated that we would have been caught up in the very same storm in almost the same spot as her last known position. We would either have been closer at hand to offer assistance or been in trouble ourselves. Luckily, by the time we arrived in that area, the typhoon had shot off in a different direction, and although a concentrated lookout was kept there was no sign of wreckage or anything.

Fate it is, for we had little or no idea what life had in store for us on our second visit to Japan; that it would be my longest stay in a foreign country and that I would leave with a far better opinion than when we left Chiba.

Thursday morning 5th October saw us anchored safely amongst forty or fifty other vessels off Osaka. It was presumed that because of the queue it would be a long wait before we would go alongside. Consequently, everything was shut down to allow maintenance work to be done on the engine.

The presumption proved wrong however, when a pilot came alongside on the Saturday morning to take us in. We should have known better as the Pilot had come out much quicker than expected the first time in Chiba when we had to abandon all the painting. As we had been given no warning, the engines were not ready and there was no steam raised, so the Pilot went away indicating that he would be back later.

Again as in Chiba we were then thrown into a frenzy of work as we had to fetch the anchor onboard to disconnect it and get all the derricks and hatches ready, jobs which by then had become almost a ritual. We worked flat out as it was a Herculean task, which was miraculously completed as the Pilot returned four hours later at ten o'clock. It was certainly better working as a team then because the Bosun and Chippy were not there to hinder us.

Again the dubiously happy experience of taking the helm fell to me, and while I hardly understood a word of command from the Pilot, we moved to weave our way through that armada of shipping to safety inside the breakwater. The anchor cable was our only mooring, shackled to a buoy under our bow to allow us to swing around the buoy with the incoming and outgoing tides.

Soon the Japanese dockers were aboard, five or six men to a hatch plus the two winch drivers. Large wicker like baskets were hooked to our runners and lowered into the holds for the coal to be loaded manually by shovel rather than with giant grabs as before. These were then lifted up, swung over the side and emptied into barges that had come alongside. "This is going to take ages" I thought, but it was amazing how quick it shifted as they all worked like Trojans and eight thousand tons were discharged in ten days.

On the afternoon after our arrival and the following afternoon, I went ashore to confirm my shipmates' opinion that Chiba was not a true picture of Japan. They were right. Osaka was a lovely, thriving community with magnificent shopping centres and everyone was polite and helpful. When we made purchases, the shopkeepers would bow and thank you for your custom and they would follow you to the shop entrance constantly bowing and offering you their gratitude. "It would be bad manners to return just one bow, then turn and walk out" or so I thought, so I walked out backwards returning each bow as I went.

The electrical goods and radio shops were fantastic. Transistor radios had not long been on the market and never had I seen such a varied and wonderful display. There were literally hundreds of them in all shapes and sizes, but it was the miniature ones that I found fascinating. I spotted one that at first glance I thought was a golf ball; it was the same size and the same colour. Wondering what it was doing amongst the vast display of radios, I took a closer look, could then see tiny minuscule nobs and buttons and realised that it actually was a radio, but priced way beyond what was left in my pocket. Everything had been so relatively cheap; I had spent my sub in no time.

The Skipper only gave out subs every Saturday. I began to call it the dearest cheap place I had ever seen, simply because there was so much you wanted to buy, money just seemed to melt away. I had to sit onboard for the rest of the week, but I looked forward to getting away from the ship for a short time each weekend; it felt good.

In the dim and distant past as it then seemed, I had bought a twenty-one piece oriental tea service in Aden while on the old 'San Velino.' It was decorated on the outside with colourful dragons and inside, on the bottom of the cups, was the face of a geisha girl. I then spotted a fifteen piece coffee set of the same design that I quickly bought to go with it.

As stated the coal was miraculously discharged in ten days, it had taken two in Chiba, which just showed what a difference those giant grabs made, but to manually shovel all eight thousand tons out in ten days is a task not to be sneered at.

The Pilot finally came onboard during the morning of Monday 16th October, and as soon as we had shackled the anchor back to its cable and rehoused it, he took us back out of the harbour into the anchorage. No one seemed to know exactly what was going to happen next. Everyone knew repairs were needed, and everyone knew we were bound for the dry dock, but no one knew where or when.

Later that day, a group of officious looking men came aboard. Armed with clipboards and pens, they scoured the ship from top to bottom, constantly making notes. Shortly after they had gone ashore, the working parties arrived and swarmed like bees around the ship. Along with them came the tools of the trade, long lengths of piping, gas bottles, burners, welding gear and large boxes of tools; soon the decks were literally strewn as the banging, tapping, knocking, burning and welding started. They were everywhere, on deck, in the accommodation, in the holds; it was impossible to move for them. Memories of the 'Granford' in Rotterdam flooded back. Nevertheless, it didn't deter the Mate; he still found plenty for us to do.

It took an hour and a half the next morning to move across the bay to Kobe. The work continued day after day; the ship became a total bedlam. Thank goodness they didn't work at night. The only happy person aboard ship was Joesy. He was in his element as he collected bits of scrap metal and other oddments which were strewn everywhere, all of which found a loving, safe home in our cabin.

One morning I rose early, not long after dawn, to take in the peace and quiet and to enjoy a nice cup of tea. I sat on one half of the bits on the poop deck before the banging started. One of the engineering officers who was taking a break from the heat of the engine room joined me, he sat on the other half of the bit. Passing the time of day he asked, "Your name is Kenn isn't it?" "Have you got a brother named Roy?" "Yes," I answered incredulously. "I sailed with him on the '*Llandaff*' he said. I couldn't believe it. It was amazing, but the thing that was even harder for me to believe, was the fact that we had both been on the ship for seven months and had only then discovered that link. The incident just confirmed that though we were all natives of a tiny mobile steel island, each department led their own lives and were small communities unto themselves. His name was Sam and he asked me to remember him to Roy the next time we met, which I duly did.

We remained at anchor off Kobe for eight days and the bedlam continued. During the evenings and weekends, most of the lads went ashore although it entailed a long boat trip. I had come down with a terrible cold which bordered on the flu and as I had no energy or zest for life, I stayed onboard so was unable to escape the mayhem with a bit of shore leave.

Finally on Monday 23rd October news came for us to move down the coast to a place called Tamano to enter dry dock. We arrived and anchored just off the docks eight hours later and could plainly see one of our company's ships, the '*Cape Wrath*' already in dry dock, and we were told that we would have to wait at anchor until she had been completely serviced.

She was the newest of the company's fleet and, although a cargo boat, she was built on the lines of a tanker with the bridge amidships, engine and funnel aft. She looked a picture as she left the dock spotless and as ready for sea as she would ever be. We talked to a couple of her crew later and they appeared to be a happier lot than us on the '*Cape Grafton.*'

We rode at anchor for the rest of the day waiting to be taken into the dock. In the afternoon, we had another crisis. The Chief Steward was mysteriously taken ill, rushed to hospital and was paid off. The Skipper gave his job to the Second Steward, which upset the Cook who thought that he had a greater claim to the Chief Steward post.

He, the Cook, was a young man with a wife and children and his comments about the Skipper and the ship were less than complimentary to say the least. He was going to get off, he told us in no uncertain manner. Later that night he proved that he meant it for he apparently

438

swallowed umpteen codeine tablets and then drank a bottle of laxative. The ship's whistle was blown to summon help from the shore to get him to hospital post-haste to have his stomach pumped out. How that could help his wife and children was beyond my powers of reasoning.

Two or three lads accompanied him in the launch and saw him safely into hospital before they returned. Within the hour news arrived that he was reacting violently and they were having difficulty in restraining him. Four men, under instructions from the Mate, were ordered ashore to help and to stay the night in the hospital with him. My cold, although slowly getting better, was still with me so I wasn't chosen I'm glad to say.

The shore gangs came aboard early the next morning and within three hours the ship was sitting high and dry in the dock. I was always amazed at how simple the dry docking operation was, and how smoothly it went.

The Cook came back during the morning looking ill and sorry for himself, saying he realised that he had made a fool of himself, but lo and behold, the idiot did the same thing again later that night. What went through the Skipper's mind is anyone's guess for the next morning he personally collected the Cook from hospital and took him by train into Kobe city for a specialist examination. He was never seen again, but it was soon known that the specialists report detailed that his mental state was exacerbated by his deep hatred of the ship, the officers and in particular of the Skipper and the Mate. That came as no surprise to us as his attitude was common knowledge. We had all known it for months, but at the end of the day, he had achieved his objective and got off the ship.

No time was wasted in returning to work on the ship once we were in dry dock. First they removed the propeller to fit a new tail shaft, the barnacles and growth were scraped from the bottom, which was repainted with red boot topping paint. Rust was chipped from the hull but only in certain places. As usual there were those amongst us who said that if they chipped away all of the rust the vessel would fall apart.

The noise each day was incessant. The electric chipping hammers on the steel were like machine gun fire except that machine guns did stop now and then. It went on all through the day each and every day.

There was no escape, we just had to grin and bear it. Perhaps the Cook had the right idea after all, but I was told that the laxative tasted vile.

Horror of horrors; holes were found in the lifeboats so they were taken ashore to have patches welded over them (thank God we hadn't been caught up in those storms). The topmast was also taken away to be worked upon and a million other jobs throughout the ship were carried out. I had always thought that the engines were fairly reliable but the Lloyds surveyor didn't think much of them at all, and he virtually condemned everything and had it torn apart, mainly to fit new bearings.

On the morning of Monday 30th October we were towed out of the dry dock, a Norwegian ship had booked in and had a prior claim; either that or we were less important. Our engine was still in its dismantled state; the tail shaft and propeller were still adrift. Once we were clear of the dock, another tug came to the aid of the one that had pulled us out and together they herded us stern first into a space between two brand new ships that were being built. We were tied up by the stern to the side of the quay with all three ships jutting out like a giant letter E and, day after day, the laborious work continued.

Soon everyone began to get on each other's nerves and we all became restless and miserable. All of us were thoroughly fed up. We were sailors, nomads of the seas, so we should be sailing out there on the ocean heading for who knows what destinations? Not stuck in one place for weeks on end. We should have been paid off and flown home ready to start anew was the general consensus of opinion.

Once I got over my cold, I went ashore for walks whenever I could, usually at weekends, just for a few drinks. Tamano itself was only a very small town, but very Japanese and I liked it.

Most but not all of the work on us came to a halt when the Norwegian tanker came into the dry dock and went. Then the order of preference to the use of the dry dock became a constant grouse; when the Norwegian tanker was refloated, another Norwegian tanker took its place, to be followed by a Greek cargo boat. Frustrations were building faster with each day, everyone began to get even more on each others nerves, tempers became more and more frayed and short.

All that while we lived amongst the constant noise and bedlam of the work that was continuing, lots of which could not be finished without the use of the dry dock so the long delays did not help. To make matters worse, the Skipper was by then only allowing enough subs to be paid out to cover just one night a week ashore, so there was little escape from the noise or each other. Why all those ships were being finished before us we never knew, and some of the crew began to complain that if we were there for much longer they could take out Japanese citizenship. The only member of the crew not to be hassled was good old Joesy, still in his element, happy as the proverbial pig in muck.

For twelve days, we were tied up waiting to return to the dry dock. I got ashore as often as possible even if it was just for a stroll. Tamano proved to be a pleasant friendly place but there were only two problems: one was making myself understood and vice versa, and the other was everywhere you went, you had to take your shoes off. Never had my socks been changed so often, just to make sure that they didn't smell.

* * *

On Monday 6th of November I was detailed for the nightwatchman duty. The Officer Cadet had carried out the task since we had arrived off Kobe and had requested a change, no one could blame him for God knows how he had got any sleep during the days with all that racket going on incessantly for weeks. Because of all the noise during the days, I wasn't very happy to be the chosen one either in that instance and wondered why the officers so often picked on me. Although the overtime would be handy, I still complained to the Mate who snapped, "Someone has to do it, and that's you. Interview terminated."

At nine o'clock on the morning of 12th November, the tugs came to take us first to an anchorage then early afternoon they pushed us back into the dry dock. It was Sunday and despite being on duty throughout the night, my presence was required on deck while those operations were taking place. It meant little sleep for me but I was used to that by then. Later that afternoon someone had arranged a slight diversion from the norm to help take our minds off our monotonous existence for a little while: A football match between our crew and a local Tamano side. We lost six two which I suppose wasn't bad, considering that none of our lads had seen a ball, never mind kicked one for months, or even years in some cases. Mind you, the Japs had played two other matches that day before taking our lot on. I was too knackered to play.

441

I was working all hours and grabbed bits of sleep whenever I could; the shore gangs slowly reassembled the engine and as the propeller was finally secured, we hoped that our frustrations and our stay in Tamano would soon be over, and it was with a great sense of relief when they refloated us. We gently became buoyant as the dock was flooded and the gates opened on Thursday 16th November.

The tugs pulled us slowly out into the harbour where we were to undergo engine trials. It was a strange but wonderful feeling to hear the steady rhythmical beat of the engines the first time they started after being silent for so long. It was like a giant animal beginning to recover from a long illness.

The trial run of the engine was probably to bed the new main bearings in. After a short while, we anchored to allow the engineers to make a few adjustments. It felt like the ship had woken from a deep coma, recovering from a long and painful operation. Finally, at two o'clock in the morning of Friday 17th November the Pilot boarded us for the twelve-hour journey to the open sea.

We weaved our way around lots of little islands and it was raining cats and dogs as we arrived at the pilot station to drop him off at 2.00pm, then we headed off into the open spaces. It was difficult to describe our feeling of relief to be once more on the move. We had been in Japan for forty-four days.

The Japanese people I had found to be polite, courteous, helpful, friendly and gentle. It was hard, almost impossible, to believe that people like them could have bombed Pearl Harbour or treated their prisoners so cruelly in the Second World War which, after all, had only been over for sixteen short years. I encountered no lingering animosity whatsoever, even after the A Bomb on Hiroshima. We simply enjoyed their hospitality.

The prospect of another load of phosphate from Christmas Island filled no one with joy, but first we were due to take on bunkers in Bornio on our way back down and the first few days were cold, damp and miserable. We sighted the Philippines on Thursday 23rd November; it was a date I well remembered for it was the date eight years earlier that I had started at the Gravesend Sea Training School.

The coastline remained within our sight as we maintained our southerly course. It had become increasingly hot and the sea was as calm as the surface of a mirror. Watches had been changed on leaving Japan and I was put into the twelve to four.

At two-thirty one morning while I was on lookout on the monkey island, I saw a dark shape on the water very close to our starboard bow, and as we got a little closer we could just make out in the darkness the silhouette of an open boat with what appeared to be a makeshift sail rigged up. I reported it to the Second Mate through the voice pipe and he ran out onto the wing of the bridge to take a better look. It carried no light, but had cut across our bow and narrowly missed a collision.

It passed down our port side so close that we could then see that it was full of people and it was very overcrowded so it couldn't have been fishermen. There was no waving or gestures from them, which gave no reason for us to think that they needed help and within minutes they had disappeared into the darkness to our stern.

It all beggared questions: Who were they? Why were they so far out to sea? Why no lights? Did they not want to be seen? Were they pirates even, looking for easier prey than us? There were many tales of such activities occurring in that part of the world. Were they refugees fleeing from some tyranny? Who knows. Sometimes strange things really do happen at sea but they were lucky, because they could so easily have been mown down (We'd had some previous practice in Pitcairn).

Considering the intensive overhaul the engine had just undergone, I was a little surprised to hear the steady beat die away on the next afternoon, but it was only for an hour or so to change a fuel valve. We left the Philippines behind, turned to starboard into the Celebes Sea and on into the Macassar Strait then anchored just off the jetties at Balikpapan in Borneo. It was 10.30am on Sunday 26th November. There was a wait of twenty-four hours before we went alongside to take on our bunkers.

The jetty we finally berthed at was number one, which happened to be exactly the same spot that we had tied up to on the 'Llandaff' six years previously. It hadn't changed a bit! It was around that time when Joesy began to complain of stomach pain and heartburn.

The estimated time for taking aboard the fuel and fresh water was approximately eight to nine hours. The Skipper had a notice posted at the top of the gangway. "No Shore Leave, no one is to go ashore without prior permission." Considering the frustrations and conditions that we had endured in Kobe and Tamano, perhaps that was a little harsh, provocative and tempting fate, so it came as no surprise when three of the lads figuratively stuck two fingers in the air and were off anyway.

When five o'clock came, the pipes were disconnected and all was made ready to cast off, there was still no sign of the wayward three, which presumably was what the Skipper had been afraid of. The Third Mate was dispatched post-haste along the track through the immediate jungle to find them and drag them back to the ship. Half an hour later, they arrived back all sprawled in a jeep. The Third Mate had found them in the first bar he had come to. "Where else?" They were practically legless so the Third Mate had persuaded a guy to drive them all back in his jeep.

We all lined up along the rails to watch with amusement as they spilled out of the jeep dressed in T shirts and shorts with a very large Mexican style straw hat each that they had picked up somewhere along the way. They staggered from the jeep giggling and carrying great bunches of bananas and pineapples over their shoulders, they swayed precariously from side to side as they painfully ascended what to them must have been like the cliff face of the gangway. By then everyone was out watching the fun as they hung onto the fruit, the rails and each other.

Deacon, the ordinary seaman who had signed on in Newcastle, was one of them. He was comical to watch at the best of times. Tall, thin, gangly and always looked as though he was off balance and in danger of slipping sideways even when sober. Escaping from his shorts were very thin, scrawny, hairy legs on the bottom of which were giant, size twelve boots with laces always undone. He was what to me was a typical couldn't care less Aussie.

They finally made it to the top of the gangway and began to stagger aft towards us. All the bunches of bananas were still very green and Deacon held on to his as if his life depended upon them. Suddenly, amongst great peals of laughter from his audience, his shorts fell down around his ankles. The look of indecision on his face was impossible to describe, as he wore no underpants. For a moment he didn't know whether to grab for his shorts or hang on to the fruit, and the drunken dance that he treated us to as he bent to reach for his shorts with one hand while holding on to the fruit with the other was hilarious. Amidst all the roars of laughter some wit shouted, "Well at least you have got one ripe one." For once we all went to stations and let go with a smile on our faces. They were logged a day's pay each.

It was scorching hot and the seas were calm with hardly a ripple, the only disturbance was caused by the wake of the '*Cape Grafton.*' Wednesday 29th November saw us sailing through the Lombok Strait. The scenery was a sight to behold as I looked across to the magnificent ten thousand foot high Bali Peak with its lush greenery, which on that particular day had a tyre of pure white cloud around its middle. It was breathtaking!

Once through the strait and out into the Indian Ocean it was a welcome relief to pick up a refreshing, cool breeze, although our cabins remained hot and sticky. The breeze stayed with us until our arrival back at Christmas Island at 2.00pm on Friday December 1st .

Our anchor had been unshackled at Balikpapan, and while waiting for another sister ship, the '*Cape York,*' to finish unloading, we drifted around throughout the night. Come daybreak the hatches were made ready while the locals tied us up to the buoy. The '*Cape York*' had sailed and was nowhere in sight.

The loading of the phosphate had been quick on the previous occasion but it was even quicker that time. Yet again we worked like mad men in a boiling sun and a choking dust. By 5.30pm the shore gang was letting go and we were on our way with everything battened down and the anchor back on its cable.

Continuing along our usual pattern our heading was southwards again for our destination was Australia. Geelong in Victoria was to be our port of call. It was warm during the days with a strong headwind but chilly at night, excellent weather compared with what was to come. On rounding the southwest tip of Australia and heading eastward across the Australian Bight, the weather took a dramatic turn for the worse. For some reason the weather gods always seemed to be angry across that particular stretch of water no matter what time of the year it was.

Over the next six days we battled on against heavy seas and a strong, gale force, freezing wind, which I was convinced came direct from the South Pole. Heavy rain showers intermittently raged across the ship and the raindrops were picked up by the strong wind and hit your face and hands. They stung as though they were little needles whenever we had reason to venture out onto the deck. I always thought that December was supposed to be the height of summer there in Aussieland but the conditions remained with us until we were well within the shelter of the coastline.

Ken and I were disappointed not to be going to Wallaroo for we had kept in touch with Raylee and Midge. However after we had tied up in Geelong on Thursday 14th December we did ring them up and have a very pleasant welcoming chat and wished them a Merry Christmas and they sounded really pleased to hear from us.

Joesy went ashore to the doctors and returned with the news that he had an ulcer. That surprised me for it was he, out of all of us, who had seemed to be by far the least stressed over the months that we had been away so far. There was no way he was going to be paid off he told me, so the doctor had given him some pills and medicine to ease his pain and discomfort until he could be treated properly. The prescription when he ran low, would have to be repeated at various ports along the way as the voyage continued.

It took six days to discharge some of the phosphate in Geelong; the rest was destined for Melbourne. It was an enjoyable six days, not for Joesy of course, and in some ways, it was an eventful six days. On the first night there, the Third Mate got tanked up ashore, returned to the ship and picked a fight with the Chief Mate and decked him one, for which he was demoted down to an AB. A dear price to pay for such a pleasure, which is what he told us it was, and it had to be said, there were those onboard who found it amusing and wished that they had the courage to have done it. The Skipper from then on took over his watch.

Where we had tied up was some distance from town. That however did not dissuade me from going ashore three or four times. It was a fair sized town with pleasant well laid out gardens. The Eastern beach was very attractive with lush green lawns that led almost down to the sea, complete with a large outdoor swimming pool and a paddling pool for the kids.

On Sunday a group of us went down to the beach. It was a glorious warm, sunny day at the height of summer. Australia at its best at last, except for the swarms of flies that just would not leave us alone as we lazed around on the grass. It was such a pity that as always on a Sunday, everything was closed.

At 10.30pm on Wednesday 20th December we let go, only to sail across Port Phillip Bay to anchor at 3.00am off Melbourne. That day marked my longest cruise, the longest I had ever been on one ship without returning to England: over nine and a half months. No cheers were heard, no applause, no bands played and I hadn't got a drink. So I climbed up onto my bunk and lay listening to Joesy snoring until we were called to stations to go alongside at seven o'clock. The grabs quickly scooped the remaining dust out of the holds and again the whole crew were soon covered in the disgusting stuff. Fortunately, the crane operatives were pretty slick and by Saturday 23rd December we were empty.

Our Chief Steward arrived back onboard; he had been flown down to rejoin us from hospital in Japan. All that trouble with the Cook had been to no avail; he would have had to revert to his old job if he had been given the promotion he thought he deserved. Codeine and laxative is not a happy cocktail. All that anguish and pain for nothing and God knows how the guy had finished up.

I managed an evening ashore before we sailed on that Saturday. Then it was back to the old routine of cleaning the phosphate remains out of the holds. As it was a slightly shorter journey from Melbourne to Newcastle than previous times, us deckhands, the stewards and even some of the engineers were pressed into service with a promise of a five-pound bonus for all, and as we would otherwise never get it done in time, we were kept at it all through the Christmas period.

The dangers of breathing in those phosphates were not known then, or at least they were not made known to us. The masks they gave us to wear while we swept up were thin cotton ones, which as I have mentioned before were not very good for the dust was so fine that some of it still filtered through. I should imagine that if that phosphate is still picked up and shipped in the same way today the protection given will be much more efficient.

There were no Christmas cards, no Father Christmas and certainly no mistletoe. Although the ex-Third Mate demoted to AB said that he would have got some if he had thought that the Chief Mate would have kissed his arse.

Everyone was plastered in the dust on Christmas Day even though on arrival off Newcastle on Christmas night, we couldn't go in for to add insult to injury once again, the whole country was closed and we steamed up and down all night. We were all tired out after cleaning the holds and all collapsed into our bunks, but there was little sleep that night for a midsummer gale blew up and being empty, we bounced and rolled throughout the night.

At six o'clock in the morning on Boxing Day, we were called to stations as we steamed into the State Dockyard. A couple of dock workers had been willing to come in to transport the ends of our mooring ropes in a boat to a buoy to tie us up, and soon we were doing just that to await a loading berth. The sarcastic amongst us were scratching their heads in bewilderment saying that they knew it was the festive season and believed that they had witnessed a miracle: two Australians working on a holiday.

By eight o'clock everything was tight and secure and the Mate announced that everyone could have the rest of the day off. Maybe that made him feel or look good in his own mind, but it was a holiday anyway; we were entitled to it off and had he worked us there would have been lots of overtime involved. There was no one at work on the launches so those who wanted to go ashore would have to swim for it. No one did for in truth, we were all exhausted and needed a rest after the recent workload. Ironically we remained tied up to that damned buoy for over seven days, until January 2nd 1962.

We knew how much the Aussies loved their holidays and weekends off, we should not have been surprised that there would be nothing done until after the break and therefore the work cleaning the hatches could have been completed in a much slower, orderly fashion, without having to work like slaves throughout Christmas.

* * *

Our immediate future was to be a cargo of coal again for Japan and we still followed the pattern of cleaning out the holds and working like slaves. This had become frustrating and monotonous, as we knew they would only be filled with coal again for us to clean the coal out ready for the phosphate. At least on that occasion we had the knowledge that we would not be spending weeks in a dry dock.

We moved into a basin for the loading to begin where a much different method of loading was adopted. Railway trucks were hoisted up by a large crane and swung over the ship till it was above the open hatch where a docker swung a maul at a release catch, which caused the floor of the truck to snap open and deposit the coal into the holds.

Only a few truckloads were done that day, probably because the dockers were still feeling sluggish on their first day back from a long holiday, but we were still called at 4.00am to shift ship to the other side of the basin from where the rest of the coal was loaded. Each truck carried around eight tons and as the loading progressed, a small caterpillar tractor was hoisted aboard and lowered into the holds to trim the cargo by pushing it into the far corners of the holds, and to keep it level as they were filled.

Paddy and I had a run ashore and bumped into the old chippy. He had been out of jail by then for quite some time and had quietened his drinking habits. He had found a good steady job ashore. If he kept his nose clean he thought his prospects were good and that the authorities might allow him to stay but like so many seafarers, his feet were beginning to itch.

The Bosun, he told us, was an AB aboard a ship called the '*Huntsfield*' and he could be anywhere. Strange as it may sound, the very next morning a rusty old tramp steamer nosed into the basin to tie up just ahead of us. As she edged past us really close we could see that it was none other than the '*Huntsfield*,' and there leaning on the rail was our ex-Bosun. Lots of waving and friendly abuse was passed to and fro, as she slowly sailed past and his comments on the characters and parentage of our Skipper and Mate made even our ears sting, but he kept well away while we were in port.

By Saturday 6th January the loading was finished and it would be seventeen days before we would possibly go ashore again as the order to let go was made. It was estimated that it would be the 23rd January when we would reach Osaka. It would I suspected be a voyage not without incident and I looked forward to returning for a further taste of Japan.

As we got into the tropics, the heat became unbearable. It became an effort to breathe let alone sleep. Again the steel angle iron of our bunks became too hot to touch for more than a split second. Never had it been so hot! How we endured it for the week that it lasted is anyone's guess, but even though it became an endeavour just to lift the roller and brush, the painting went on.

Rumour then began to circulate. We were on our way home. We dared not get our hopes up too high as it was only a rumour and easy to dismiss, especially for those of us who knew what pain and anguish there would be after all that time should the rumour turn out to be untrue.

There was an amusing distraction one afternoon while we worked outside the galley; for some inexplicable reason the funnel spouted out half a dozen perfect white smoke rings. They spun like tops as they hurtled high into the cloudless azure sky in a cluster. We called excitedly to the galley boy and mess boy to come quickly to take a look and they came running out of the galley to see what the fuss was all about. We pointed up to the rings which were still spinning fast high up in the atmosphere and we convinced them that they were flying saucers. It became even more believable to them especially as in a flash right before their eyes they suddenly disappeared. The boys were so excited, I could just imagine them writing home to tell their loved ones what they had seen.

Within days the weather had changed from unbearable heat to freezing cold. We had cleared the Solomon Islands and were out into the vastness of the Pacific, never had I known or experienced such a rapid temperature change from so hot to so cold, but it didn't stop the painting.

We arrived off Osaka on Tuesday 23rd January as estimated, but the starboard anchor held us in the bay. The next day was not a happy one for Taffy, our promoted Bosun. The port anchor once again needed to be unshackled. Under his orders we began to get on with the job by putting the heavy lifting gear on to the 'Jumbo' derrick as usual. The operation had been done so many times that it was becoming a ritual. Once the runner was shackled on to the anchor we slowly began to lower it. Then, for some reason best known to him, Taffy gave the order to heave the anchor along the side of the ship.

My mind immediately jumped back over the years to the old 'San Velino' when as a deck boy I had asked the gentle giant of a Bosun why he didn't do it that way and he had told me because it would put too much strain on the derrick. "I'm the Bosun here" Taffy snapped as I told him the anchor had to be dropped to the bottom first. I shrugged my shoulders and wondered what side of the bunk he had got out of that morning; I walked halfway down the foredeck and stood well clear.

Just then the Mate came storming up the foredeck shouting, "What the hell do you think you're doing?" he demanded. "I thought you told me to bring the anchor inboard again." Taffy said. "Well you thought wrong," shouted the Mate, "put it all back," he ordered as he turned and stormed off back towards amidships. He had not got very far when all hell broke loose. The lifting gear on the derrick snapped and the whole lot came crashing down.

When the derrick head hit the deck it bent like a banana, and the wire runner that held the weight of the anchor snapped instantly and sent the anchor plunging into the depths, which in turn made the derrick bounce up again and swing out over the rails. It buckled some of them as if they were nothing more than fuse wire. The broken runner wire shot back and buckled the head block beyond repair. At the same time, the broken lifting gear wire whipped out through the blocks at great speed, causing the snapped end to whiplash and whistle through the air in all directions like a hosepipe out of control.

Jim, the AB who was driving the winch, managed to jump clear just moments before the wire swished across where he had just been standing. He was lucky for he could have been cut in two. By some miracle, that flying wire missed everyone else too. No one had received so much as a scratch. The accident and the resulting mayhem had happened in seconds and, as everything quietened down, I looked aft towards the Mate. He was standing there open mouthed, eyes like saucers, holding his head in both hands. An utter and total picture of dejection.

The mess was cleared away, and the head of the derrick was heaved inboard by block and tackle, and by stretching safety ropes across the gap where the rails once were, everything was made as safe as it could be. Afterwards I would have loved to be a fly on the wall when Taffy was called to the Mate's cabin.

Despite the ongoing rumours that our bows would soon be heading towards the UK or maybe even because of them, one of the engineers had requested a transfer to another one of the company's ships and left the next day to fly to Australia to join her.

On Friday 26th January after we had tied up to one of the buoys, the manual discharge of the coal began. The way those Japanese kept at it, shovelling it into the wicker baskets, said a lot for their stamina. It posed the question of how long they could last. Till the ship was empty was the answer. A separate gang of men with burners also arrived to straighten out the derrick and weld a strengthening piece all around it and to replace the broken rails.

Jim and I were detailed to break out a brand new coil of three-inch circumference wire to splice an eye in each end to replace the topping lift wire, and everything was back in working order within a few days.

In mutual agreement Jim and I decided to spend a weekend ashore just for a short break away from the ship to preserve our sanity. We strolled into a bar and the proprietress was very welcoming. She spoke excellent English and joined us at our table. Laughing and joking she introduced herself as Momma San. It is a Japanese custom to add 'San' onto everyone's name, so Jim became Jima San and I was Mika San. "How that would affect guys named Phil" could be quite amusing, as on the market in those days was a pick me up medicine called Phyllosan, which was a well-known tonic for those reaching a certain age. In fact the slogan on the TV adds at that time was "Phyllosan fortifies the over forties," and was viewed by many with no small measure of amusement by us younger folk.

At one point Momma San took a single match out of a box and placed it on the table. She then gave us some chopsticks and told us that if we could pick up the match with the chopsticks and lay it on the box, she would buy us each a beer. The promise of a free beer worked like magic and guided nimble fingers, and although neither one of us had handled chopsticks before, within seconds the task was completed. Momma San was as good as her word.

We both felt that the time she had spent with us was used for an appraisal and if that were true we had met with her approval for she beckoned two girls to come and join us, then discreetly disappeared. Both girls were absolutely beautiful, oozing with Japanese charm and femininity, and after we got acquainted over another couple of drinks, we were invited to follow them. The girls themselves must have made some kind of silent agreement on the pairing as it all happened so naturally. Outside they ushered us through a doorway next to the bar.

Once inside the porch we again had to go through the ritual of removing our shoes and replace them with a pair of slippers from an alcove which housed many pigeon holes with a pair of slippers neatly placed in each. All sizes were catered for.

It soon became apparent that the removal of our shoes was only the first article of clothing to be discarded. Jim carried on down the corridor with his girl and disappeared into a room. Akimi, a beautiful name for a beautiful girl, beckoned me into the room next to it. She then disappeared, signalling that she would only be a moment. On her return, she was wearing a beautiful silk kimono and handed me one too together with a new toothbrush and paste. Without a shred of modesty, I was out of my gear and into my kimono in no time at all.

Then Akimi took my hand and led me along the corridor to another room that contained a number of small cubicles. Ceramic tiles covered the floor in the cubicles and they felt warm to the bare feet as we entered. In the middle of the cubicle was a stone bath about three feet square and two foot high, full of steaming hot water.

Removing her kimono, Akimi was soon naked and as she hung her kimono on a hook, she signalled me to do the same then, both naked, she motioned me to kneel with her on the floor by the bath facing each other. They would never actually sit in the water to bathe, as sitting in soiled water was not considered hygienic.

With soft sponges and scented soaps, she then began to bathe me and allowed me to do the same for her before we tenderly dried each other, and with a feeling of total relaxation and a satisfying glow of warmth and well-being within, she took my hand and led me back to our room. That night my education was completed.

Not until around nine o'clock the next morning did we say goodbye to our tutors as I am sure that Jim had learned a few lessons too, judging by the smile on his face. The idea then was to return to the ship and try to talk the cook into giving us some breakfast. But the ferryman refused to take us, he suggested that we try again later as a strong wind had blown up and it was a bit rough out in the bay.

As we were both starving our need to find a quick meal led us back into town and as we turned a corner, there in front of us was a sight to behold. In the middle of the busy road sat four of our shipmates obviously stoned nearly out of their minds, but still drinking more beer.

They had taken chairs from a sidewalk beer stall, and with an upturned beer crate doubling as a table, they had plonked themselves in the middle of the road singing and waving to all and sundry causing traffic chaos. Given the number of bottles on the beer crate come table and the empties on the road by their side, they were truly tanked up.

They spotted us standing on the corner and greeted us like long lost brothers shouting and cheering and beckoning for us to go and join them, but we saw a policeman approaching and the invitation was refused. Then, neither Jim or I could believe our eyes, we could only stand and gape as without a single word to the men, the policeman stood in front of them and began to direct the traffic around them.

We did not stop to see the outcome of it all and we walked a little further down the street. We came across a restaurant which was quite busy and popular with the locals so we dived in. The menu might as well have been in French, Russian or any other language as we couldn't understand a single one of those Japanese symbols. We worked on the theory that extremely hungry men have little regard for taste, Jim just pointed at something on the menu when the waiter came for our order. Within a few minutes he returned and placed a massive bowl of what appeared to be a steaming hot soup with lumps of something floating around in it before us.

For a moment my blood turned cold and a shiver ran down my back as my mind instantly jumped back five years to the '*Granford*' and I remembered those vile Hungarian Goulashes we had endured. "Nothing in the world could ever be that bad," I thought, but it smelt good and we were ravenous. Ladling it onto our plates, we attacked it with gusto as though we hadn't eaten for a week. It had been a hectic night. There was plenty of it and it tasted quite nice, although some of the lumps did taste a little rubbery. Still we did it justice and sat back with that satisfying feeling of fulfilment.

Four Japanese guys walked in and sat at the table next to us. One of them, possibly intent on practising his English, struck up a conversation with us. He seemed very interested in the fact that we worked on the ships and asked many questions about what it was like and did we visit many countries. At one point Jim picked up the menu and indicated that out of curiosity, he wanted to know what it was that we had just eaten. I immediately wished that he hadn't when we were told that it was octopus and jellyfish. We didn't quite turn green and we both managed to keep it down, but it did dampen a little our feeling of well-being. There was no sign of the drunken revellers as we returned, and

454

the ferryman was happier with the conditions so we were soon back onboard after having had a wonderful weekend. We were broke but happy.

The shore gang shovelled coal all day, every day and finished on Thursday 1st February. The orders were to return to Nauru to pick up another cargo of phosphate and it was still rumoured, then later confirmed, that the cargo was bound for Leith in Scotland. At long, long last.

The trip down to Nauru with its mixture of good and bad weather proved uneventful. The thought and the promise of a return to the UK changed the whole atmosphere, even to the extent that Taffy and the Mate were back on speaking terms.

Sunday afternoon on the 11th February found us steaming around off Nauru until six o'clock on Monday morning when we tied up to the buoy. Nauru was situated just slightly south of the equator and was almost as close to half way around the world from the UK as you could get. Speculation began as to which way the Skipper would take us home. East through the Panama or West through the Suez. Half the crew, as I did, hoped that it would be through the Suez for the simple reason that we would have circumnavigated the world on one trip. Others though preferred the Panama route. We just had to wait and see.

While in Nauru, we received onboard a lady passenger, who would be our guest on the voyage home. She was a nursing sister travelling with us first to the UK then from there home to Switzerland. Why the 'Cape Grafton' I will never know, except that the fare would be far cheaper I would imagine, but surely there were much more comfortable ways to travel.

It took approximately eight hours from tying up to letting go to take aboard a full load of phosphate, again engulfed in dust but happier knowing that it was for the last time. With the lady and her luggage safely aboard we cast off on the start of our long journey home with our bows pointing towards the Panama. It was just twelve days short of a full twelve months since we sailed out of Falmouth harbour.

We had two days of good weather then things became boisterous. With strong winds and heavy swells, the ship began to roll badly. It was hoped that our lady passenger was a good sailor for the heavy weather persisted for almost three weeks.

We crossed the International Date Line on Friday 16th February and after we had worked all day, the following morning we awoke to find that it was still Friday 16th, which dispelled all the hopes of those who had thought they had gained a day's pay for nothing on our outward journey. It had evened itself out. But it was easily the longest day in my life.

Halfway across the Pacific some financial genius let the word go round that in no way must we arrive back in Britain before the 5th April. The 5th being the end of the financial year, and as we had sailed on the 25th of February the previous year there were those of us who would have been out of the country for the whole of that financial year, therefore all income tax paid could be reclaimed.

A strange atmosphere then prevailed around the ship. On one hand, after so long away, we were all eager to get home (except perhaps Joesy who was happy with his bits and pieces). Then on the other hand, no one wanted it to be before the 5th April and we all knew that it was going to be a very close call. Some were even hoping for another engine failure to delay us. The heavy weather helped in a small way and knocked a knot or two off our speed for a while, but the days were long and monotonous. Almost a month went past since we had left Nauru without a sign of other life; not even a seabird.

Saturday March 3rd brought a change in the weather. The clouds cleared, the sea became calmer, out came the sun and the steadying of the ship was welcomed by all. During the bad weather, the painting programme had been curtailed and restricted to the sheltered places only, but then the Mate joyously exerted our energies on the more exposed areas.

Perhaps not for our lady passenger who we rarely saw, but on Friday 9th March the prayers of some were answered as the sound of our engines died into silence. The engineers gave it their full attention as we drifted around for nine hours. Some considered their prayers had only been partly answered when the engines sprang back into life again, others were thankful for small mercies.

As we drifted for those nine hours, fishing again became the number one sport for those off duty. Sharks circled the ship and within minutes, baited lines were dangled enticingly. One shark took four hunks of bait from the hook before he was finally caught. He was only five foot long but the simple act of catching him created the excitement and he was tossed back in immediately.

Monday 12th March brought further bad weather, heavy rain and strong winds, but we ran out of it the following day and in the early hours while on lookout, I spotted the lights of three ships. The first signs of other human life we had seen for twenty-eight days.

Land hove into view later that day and we arrived off the entrance of the Panama Canal within hours. There was little delay and soon the Pilot was guiding us through that fascinating waterway. When we cleared the canal, our immediate need was to take on bunkers for the last stage of the voyage so we headed southward towards Curacao and left Central America behind.

There were no delays at Curacao either and within a couple of hours we were on our way again. The Islands of the Caribbean hold their own enchantment, but all our minds were then filled with thoughts of home and there was little time to appreciate anything else. The worry of the 5th April persisted with the benign and friendly seas of the Atlantic allowing us to make good speed. That bothered some who wished for a gale or a headwind to ensure that we arrived on the 6th rather than the 5th. On we ploughed. The Azores came and went, even the Bay of Biscay was unusually calm, then finally we sighted land. After so long away, after so many adventures, that sighting was different. It was our land. Our home, not someone else's.

Up the English Channel we steamed. Never ever were the White Cliffs of Dover so welcoming. On rounding the coast we headed up the North Sea, even the friendly lights of both the English and Scottish coastal towns seemed to be saying, "Glad to see you." When the Pilot came out to take us into Leith even his Scottish brogue sounded great. We were happy. It was April 6th.

The company paid us off the next day after thirteen and a half months in foreign parts. Advice was given for us to approach the National Union of Seamen to negotiate for our Income Tax rebates for even though they would take a small percentage cut, they would be more likely to get it without too much delay.

I had no idea what Joesy's plans were. Hopefully he would seek medical attention for his ulcer. He had packed his homemade suitcase and I tried to lift it without much success, but he had no trouble at all.

457

Perhaps he planned to stay in Leith and rejoin the ship later or maybe start again on another one. Having enjoyed his company in that tiny workshop of a cabin for thirteen and a half months I wished him all the best whichever road he took.

Once we had all cleared the Customs, taxis were soon taking everyone into Edinburgh station and home. There is no better feeling than walking through the front door of your house after such a long time, to be greeted and welcomed home by your family.

CHAPTER TWENTY-ONE
THE INTERIM

(Of a Sad Time, a Happy Time and a Hard Time).

Home comforts and good English ale helped to swill away the remnants of the phosphate, coal dust and the memory of the metal workshop that had been my cabin for far too long; though the memory of Joesy lingered throughout the coming years.

As I contemplated the bottom of my current glass of beer, I felt that the last fourteen months had all helped to erode Father Neptune's spell within me a little, and the itchiness in my feet had faded somewhat. I was also probably the only one of my family, friends and acquaintances who at that moment in time had a good word to say about the taxman; I had forwarded my circumstances and appropriate documents to the tax office, which was located, strange to say, in Llandaff, Cardiff. Within days I was in receipt of a cheque for over eighty pounds as a rebate without any problem whatsoever, and without having had to pay the union or anyone else a percentage. It was quite a considerable sum of money in 1962. Riches indeed.

Never being one to look a gift horse in the mouth and feeling that if ever there was an incentive to prolong my home coming, that was it. I resumed my friendship with Mavis and Alan, picked up again on upsetting certain people in the club by winning at bingo, and I decided to stay at home.

My two-year contract with the Falmouth Pool was long since over and considering the good friendly service that they had afforded me,

I felt it only right to inform them of my decision. I wrote to them to let them know that I wouldn't be returning in the foreseeable future. I needed some normality in my life.

My friendship with Raylee by then amounted to only the occasional letter, and with little hope of our ever meeting again, they too eventually petered out.

As time passed, even the late nights and long lie-ins eventually began to lose their attraction. It was time to return to reality and find employment given the added stimulus of my ready cash diminishing quickly. So it was back to my old trade of painting and decorating, which brought in enough for me to enjoy my bachelor lifestyle. I became friendly with Gordon who not only worked for the same firm but also drank in the same club.

On Sunday dinner times we joined in with others playing card games such as brag or cribbage, which I enjoyed. It was also time then for me to become more mobile. I purchased an old Ford Thames van from Norman, Mavis's brother, in which Gordon taught me the basic elements of driving. I was not the world's brightest pupil on four wheels so he must have been a good teacher as I passed my driving test on the first attempt. That in turn gave me the confidence to buy a six-month-old Ford Cortina estate car, which I loved.

My grandmother, with whom I had a fond relationship, had never ventured beyond the shores of England in her whole eighty years. So as I had a cousin who had married a Norwegian guy and was living in Alesund in the north of Norway, one day I asked my Gran if she would like to go for a visit with me over Christmas and New Year. She, being the game old bird that she was, was absolutely delighted by the idea.

My younger brother Barry also expressed a wish to go. So it was wonderful to receive my cousin Sandra's reply to my letter stating that she would love to see all three of us as they had plenty of room. Barry was adamant that he would not be seasick, "It's all in the head," he informed us. "We shall see," I thought, and indeed we did. On the day, the North Sea was angry, and he soon found out it was his stomach that was in his head. Unfortunately Gran too was a bit under the weather so I spent a couple of hours on my own in the ferry's bar before I turned in.

Norway is magical at Christmas and we had a wonderful time. Their hospitality and friendship was second to none. Knut, Sandra's husband, was extremely fastidious about the Christmas decorations and literally spent hours doing up the tree to his satisfaction.

All the presents for the kids were placed beneath it and a member of the family, dressed as Father Christmas, visited each home of the extended families during the evening to hand them out to the kids who were delighted. Sandra told us that every family there did the same, which conjured up images in my mind of hundreds of Father Christmases running around the town in the snow.

Each home also hung up little packages of seeds or nuts outside as a present for the birds. New Year was heralded in with a bang. Spectacular fireworks lit up the sky at midnight, and with the backdrop of the snow covered trees, fields, houses and mountains it was all quite breathtaking. We did not want to leave.

On our return we found that Gran's house had been broken into and, amongst other things, a cassette was missing of our grandfather, who we had lost a couple of years earlier; the cassette contained him making a speech on their Golden Wedding. That as you can imagine, ruined everything.

Little did I know then that my prospects with the fairer sex would take a more positive step before too long. The New Year was to prove to be the most decisive year of my life, for that was when I met and wooed my future wife, Margaret.

The club where I spent most of my spare time had appointed a new steward who ran the place along with his wife. Margaret, one of their four daughters, helped by serving in the bar. My friend Gordon sensed my attraction to her and teased me unmercifully by saying, "You'll marry that girl." I always laughed at the suggestion although I did like her very much, so it was not long before I had plucked up the courage to invite her for a date. She accepted and we hit it off and got on famously. Within months we were engaged to be married.

It was at that time that my parents, with whom I still lived, moved home to Wolverhampton, which left my brother Roy, who had married and also left the Merchant Navy, to continue living in the house in which we had shared our lives since we were both toddlers.

The firm for whom I had worked for about two years, whilst decent enough employers, lost its attraction and I became disenchanted so I changed jobs. Getting a job was never a problem in those days. Gordon had also moved on to another firm and I followed him.

The new firm was OK too but after a further two years, they decided to employ me on maintaining and touching up externally on complexes of three story blocks of flats. The firm employed over one hundred men, so why they isolated me I will never know. As I worked totally alone, I soon became extremely bored with it and with the added fact that it was throughout the winter months, my loss of interest began to show. To be fair, they gave me a couple of warnings, but even those failed to lift me out of my lethargy and eventually I was fired. Strange to say, although that was the one and only time in my life I have ever been fired, it did not bother me over much as I felt that I had been freed from my shackles.

There seemed to be something in my make-up that necessitated a change every two years or so, but although I still missed the sun and the sea, I was determined to try to make a good shore life. A short distance from my new home in Wolverhampton was a depot of the Midland Counties Dairy and I applied for and landed a job as a milkman. My theory being that doing something totally different might well be the answer.

At first it appeared to work and after a couple of weeks training during which I learned all about the goods on sale, prices etc. and how to do all the bills and bookwork, I was deemed sufficiently adept to be given my own round.

Over the years, after hearing many tales of elicit goings on between sexy young wives and the milkman I was looking forward to it, but it soon became glaringly apparent that they were fairy tales. Once out on the round, to all intents and purposes you were your own gaffer and I began to enjoy it.

The work was hard, loading and unloading the crates of milk and provisions onto and off our own trucks as well as delivering it. My round took in about ten miles in a figure of eight route from the dairy and it entailed miles of walking up and down pathways and driveways to people's houses. However the wages were good, over twenty pounds a week as opposed to around fourteen pounds a week that I had earned as a painter.

It went mostly unnoticed but the British public's demand for fresh food and drink meant that a lot of people were employed seven days a week. That job was no exception and owing to a shortage of staff, I only managed to get the occasional day off.

On Sundays through to Thursdays, all the job entailed was the delivery of milk and sundries. The part of it I didn't like was the occasional drive to push our customers to buy more goods.

By starting at around 6.30am, I could be home by one or two o'clock in the afternoon but further hours were taken up on Thursday afternoons by having to work out everyone's bills. Fridays and Saturdays however, were long and tiring days for that was when the bills for the week were collected. There were over five hundred customers on my round, and just one extra minute at sixty doors was an extra hour and most of them took much longer than that to answer your knock, not to mention those who didn't answer at all.

It meant that on many occasions call backs had to be made and it could take anything upwards of twelve hours to fourteen hours to complete the round. I tried to spread the load by asking some people to pay on Thursdays, which helped a little, but few people had the cash as Friday was payday for the vast majority.

It didn't help my well-being having to travel to Walsall from Wolverhampton most nights to see Margaret. Whereas years before I had travelled from Walsall to Wolverhampton to see Sylvia, the situation had then reversed and the slightly humorous irony of that didn't escape me as it fell well within the usual patterns of my luck.

I would spend most of the evening in the club with Mavis, Alan and occasionally Norman while Marg, as she liked to be called, worked in the bar. I would then spend an hour or so with her after 11.00pm when the club was closed and cleared before I drove back home. It was in the early hours of the mornings before I got to bed and I rose again by 6.00am.

We made plans for Margaret and I to get wed in September 1966 and Marg agreed in the first instance that we would live with my parents in Wolverhampton with my explicit promise that we would have our own house in either Leamore or Bloxwich within six months.

The sudden death of Margaret's mother that August blighted the arrangements and saddened everyone, but Margaret said it would have been her mum's wish that the wedding should still go ahead, which it did on the 17th September with all our friends, cousins, aunts and uncles wishing us well in the tried and trusted fashion.

Our honeymoon was spent on my parents' old pontoon houseboat on the canal. Our plan was to go from Wolverhampton to Llangollen and back. The countryside was foreign to Marg who had until that point never ventured into it. She was delighted and fascinated with the beautiful views, also the many birds and animals which roamed free. But it was the many sights of rabbits running wild which especially delighted her.

With the September sun shining strongly every day, it was a wonderful two weeks to start our married life together and augured well for our future, despite the obvious sadness of the loss of her mother. I hoped that the little trip in the English and Welsh countryside helped her a little to come to terms with it. As always, all good things must come to an end, and our return to Wolverhampton brought us back to the true realities of life.

It was in the early months of 1967 that our quest for our first home became real. We spotted a small house in Bloxwich, in which we still live to this day and managed to arrange a mortgage. During my time at sea, the monies that I had allocated to my mother had been banked on my behalf as she would not accept board while I was not there. That money provided the deposit and we moved in at Easter. Then instead of a five-minute walk to work, I had a ten-mile drive there and back.

On Fridays and Saturdays Marg began to come to help me out, to collect in the money. Without her help, I would I think have had to give the job up sooner. Perhaps the extra journey to and from work was the straw that broke the camel's back as I gradually became more and more tired, irritable, snappy and plainly not nice to know.

Eventually, yet again after two years, something had to be done to alter the situation so I handed in my notice at the dairy and decided to try my hand as a self-employed painter and decorator. I soon found out that whilst there was plenty of work at hand, everyone wanted the jobs done for next to nothing and were not prepared to pay a decent rate for a decent job. As there was a glut of guys at that time all doing the same thing, there was always someone who would undercut your prices.

Soon I was working as hard as previously but with little reward to show for it. The bills came in thick and fast and the mortgage had to be paid. What little of the money my mother had banked for me that there was left after I had paid the deposit soon disappeared and it was hard to find money to pay for new material for forthcoming jobs. Somehow, we struggled on.

Our friends Mavis and Alan along with two more of their friends, Tom and Margaret, at that time began seriously thinking of giving up their jobs and council houses to take advantage of the ten-pound per person emigration package to Australia and they began to put pressure on Marg and I to go with them.

I could see little or no improvement of our situation in the foreseeable future and, although I had been to Australia where the pubs closed at six o'clock and the whole country shut down on Sundays, I felt sure that with the vast influx of people pouring into the country at that time, all that would have changed. Perhaps after only fourteen months of self-employment another new start was what was needed.

There were many long discussions with Marg and although she was very reluctant to leave her dad and her sisters behind, she agreed to give it a go. All six of us then went to have our X-rays taken and were given a date for our full medical.

A few days later, we all went to Australia House in Birmingham for an interview. Everything throughout the interview went extremely well with all of us agreeing that Sydney was the place we would like to settle and the guy smiled and said, "Well, providing your X-rays are OK I see no reason why you wouldn't be accepted."

"One last thing though," he said as we stood up to go, he explained to us that as Mavis and Alan had two children and Margaret and Tom had five, they would be given twelve months of accommodation in a hostel on arrival, but Marg and I with no children would have to find our own accommodation. That was like a bombshell dropping for me. I foresaw the possibility of us living in hotels for many months and all the expense that went with that. Who knew how long it could be before we could find a place of our own?

After much deliberation we decided that it would be a foolish thing to sell up our house and home on an off chance like that, and have everything we had worked for over the years going to line the pockets of hotel keepers. I pulled out.

465

Marg never said so, but I think that she was probably secretly relieved. The others were all very disappointed and, in a way, so was I. It seemed to me that everything I had tried to do had come to a sad end. We were by then really strapped for cash and the only way I could think of to turn the tide was to try to get back into the Merchant Navy, so I put the question to Marg.

Naturally, as expected, she wasn't too keen on the idea, but said if it was really what I wanted to do, then she wouldn't stand in my way as she had always nursed the feeling that I would go back to sea one day.

Harbouring a feeling of great trepidation, and remembering the run around that the Liverpool Office had given me in 1958 after a break of only eleven months, I wondered what my chances were after a break of seven years. I wrote off to the Falmouth Shipping Federation Offices and asked them if it would be possible for me to reregister.

They replied that they could see no reason why not if I could send them references from everywhere I had worked since I had been ashore. I had anticipated that from my previous experience and I subsequently did just that. Even the firm that had given me the sack gave me a surprisingly good one. Gordon provided one too, to confirm the time that I had been self-employed. I enclosed a note in the envelope with them stating that if the references were satisfactory, I was available straight away for employment. I heard nothing from them for ten days so I took the decision to ring them.

The guy, pleasant as ever, confirmed that they had received them and asked me what kind of job I wanted. That question puzzled me as they had my records and knew that I was an AB so I asked, "How do you mean?" "Well," he replied, "Do you want to go deep sea, or coaster, cargo boat, tanker or what?" "I didn't know I had that much of a choice," I said. "Oh yes, you do nowadays," he replied. "In that case I'll try a tanker." I said. "Well OK, but unfortunately there is nothing doing at the moment, we will let you know as soon as anything turns up."

That left me wondering that if I had said a cargo boat, would there have been a job for me straight away. "Was it the beginning of another run around?" Of course, I should have known different. Two hours later, the phone rang. It was Falmouth. "We have a tanker at Tilbury. The 'British Guardsman' if you are interested." I told him that I was.

He then directed me to go to the Tilbury Shipping Federation Offices on Thursday and subject to me passing a medical, Tilbury would reregister me on Falmouth's behalf. "And good luck," he said, which I really appreciated.

How different it all was to the last time I had tried to reregister at Liverpool and the months of waiting that they had put me through, even though they themselves didn't have to find me work as Falmouth had undertaken to do that.

How easy it was for one Pool to reregister people on behalf of another. Those Liverpool clerks, I had always believed, had too much power over people's livelihoods and used it when it suited. How different from them was the helpful, friendly politeness of the Falmouth guys.

I managed to find my train fare and got ready to go. "It would be odds on that Mavis, Alan, Tom and Marg and all the kids would be gone before I returned," I thought, so I said my goodbye's to them all, with the promise that if I ever got to Sydney, I would look them up.

CHAPTER TWENTY-TWO
THE BRITISH GUARDSMAN

(Of Lots of Changes, the Eye of a Storm and a Damaged Screw).

It was Thursday May 8th 1969. I had been on the beach so to speak for seven years, married for almost three years and was coming up to my thirty-third birthday. It was a tearful goodbye as Margaret waved me off from New Street Station in Birmingham; both of us were full of misgivings at the prospect of an indeterminate period of separation, the first of our marriage.

Nothing in life stands still, and little did I know of the many changes that had occurred in the seafarer's conditions since I had last signed articles. I was in an apprehensive mood and was anything but happy about our separation as I sat on the Euston bound express. It was not at all helped on my arrival at Liverpool Street Station via the underground as per my instructions, to be told that the Tilbury train left from Fenchurch Street. I finally arrived there with just minutes to spare to board the 10.05am to Tilbury.

I booked my cases into the left luggage on my arrival at Tilbury Riverside then went in search of the Shipping Federation Offices, which most conveniently were situated just a short distance along the road. "At last, something is going my way" I thought as I entered the building.

I introduced myself to the clerk and he said that they were expecting me; I was taken at once to the Seamen's Union Office where I was given the choice to either pay up the seven years arrears or rejoin for five-pounds seven shillings and six pence. As the latter was by far the cheapest route, that was the way I chose to do it.

I was left with little or nothing in my pocket, and I still had to satisfy the medical examiners of my fitness. I was not allowed to see the doctor until I had cleared my union membership. That seemed to me to be the wrong way around; if I had failed the medical, would they have immediately returned my fees? I would not have possessed my fare home had they not. Absolutely nothing it seemed could move without the union's clearance.

The doctor was extremely thorough and finally gave me his OK. That was the first medical I had undergone since I had last signed on the 'Cape Grafton' over eight years previously so my mind was eased on that score.

Once I was back at the Pool further forms had to be signed, and the clerk explained some of the many changes which had taken place during my absence, the rest I would have to pick up as I went along. I could hardly believe the ease in which I was re-registered after seven years absence in Tilbury on behalf of Falmouth on the other side of the country.

The friendly attitude of the Pool staff compared to the downright obstructionism of the Liverpool lot when I had last attempted to re-register was a revelation. They then allotted me a berth on the 'British Guardsman.' A further pleasant surprise was the increased amount then paid to ABs and indeed all other ratings too, half as much again than it was when I left. Yet again, I was amazed when I was reimbursed for my rail fare and told to go next door to the canteen for some lunch and return to the desk at 2.00pm.

The food was good and cheap, and the men for the crew of the 'British Guardsman' had begun to assemble. I then walked back to the station to collect my suitcases from the left luggage office, and I returned with them to the Pool. They were quite heavy, and I was a little out of breath by the time I got back. As it turned out it was a mistake; no sooner had I dumped them on the floor of the Pool office, the clerk came and in a cheery voice said, "OK follow me." He marched us back to the station then told us to wait a few minutes for him outside the left luggage office!

On his return, he led us through the station and on down to the riverside. The ferry that would take us across the river to Gravesend was just docking, and a coach was waiting to take us to the ship. We formed a human chain and passed the quite considerable amount of luggage along to load onto the deck of the ferry. We did the same at the other end, off the boat and into the coach; the driver commented that he had never been loaded so quick.

It was over fifteen years since I had completed my period at the training school, and there was little of the town that my faded memory could recognise as we sped quickly through and onwards to the Isle of Grain where the 'British Guardsman' was berthed.

Half an hour later we turned into the gates of the oil refinery. The driver got the coach as near to the ship as possible, which still left quite a long trudge along a large jetty where the ship was moored. Of course she was right at the very far end of it. Where else would she be? I was joining her.

The signing on took place in the crew's mess, and it soon became glaringly apparent that things had changed aboard ship too. Tankers had always been my preference as far as comfort and accommodation were concerned, and that ship was no exception. Everything was shiny new, and my cabin was a single berth with a large bunk and ample cupboard space in which to stow my belongings. Even after all my worldly goods were unpacked and put away, there was still space to spare.

The cabin contained a combined dressing and writing table, a bench settee that ran along the length of the bulkhead and a spacious built-in wardrobe, but the icing on the cake was the whole ship was air-conditioned. When I recalled the hovel that I had shared with Joesy for fourteen months, that cabin by comparison was sheer luxury. A whole different world.

The 'British Guardsman' was fifty-two thousand tons of the newer design that had been introduced around the early sixties when I had left the sea. The bridge housing and accommodation was all aft. Gone was the centre castle that left one long foredeck free from clutter, which allowed for ease of access and a safer working environment.

It would appear that 'hopefully,' the days of the 'Rust Buckets' and the scant regard for the personal comforts of the crews were gone. Also, it seemed, so were the totally dry ships, for a Pig was provided as in Pig

471

and Whistle. It was of course the crew's recreation room but complete with a bar where if you had the wherewithal, there was as much cold beer as you could afford to buy.

Also situated in the alleyway was an iced water drinking fountain, which proved to be worth far more than its weight in gold in the blazing hot climes. One thing prevailed: the total segregation between the officers and men. They of course still had their own separate accommodation, even far more luxurious and upmarket than the crews', which thereby preserved the great divide.

We were not called to turn to until mid morning the next day, which was probably a good thing given the state of most of my new shipmates who had been taking advantage of the delights in the Pig. The first task, for those of us who were in any condition to work, was to separate the port anchor from the cable, a job that I had done on many previous occasions.

That time however, the practice of heaving the anchor itself inboard had been discarded. Intertwining a wire several times around our bits and through one of the links of the cable to keep the anchor in its place, we were able then to coil the cable along the deck as it came off the windlass, and separate it at the first shackle to leave the anchor hanging on the wire. That I thought was a far more intelligent and simpler method of achieving our aim.

Unfortunately, the passage of time and the innovation of new ideas, still did not prevent accidents from happening; as we were using a wire runner to help us pull the cable along the deck, it snapped and whipped back, and the very tip of the broken edge caught one of the lads on his ankle. He was left with a nasty gash and consequently a scar that he would probably have with him for the rest of his life. He was lucky in as much as had he been standing just a few short inches nearer or the wire had parted a little farther along, it could have taken his foot off.

Later that afternoon we shifted ship from the jetty and moved out into the river where we tied up with the anchor cable to the buoys. The following morning, one end of a rope was passed beneath the cable then lowered in a large U shape over the bow and dragged aft under the ship. With the ends on each side of the ship, when a certain position was reached both ends were then made fast.

I remembered my fascination about the times of the tall ships and the men who sailed in them, I asked the Bosun who he intended to 'keelhaul.' "You, if you are not careful" was his instant reply with a grin. So, early in the relationship, it was good to find my first-line supervisor had a ready sense of humour.

Evidently one of the intakes was faulty, and the rope was to enable a diver to hold on under the ship to work on the fault. He had several attempts to cure the problem but to no avail; it would have to be a dry dock job. Was my jinx clicking in again after seven years? It took quite some time to find and locate a dry dock, which could take us on such a short notice as normally they had to be booked well in advance.

Eventually we let go on Wednesday 14th May and sailed out into the estuary and south to the English Channel bound for Falmouth of all places. We arrived there the next day and anchored in the bay then on into the dry dock the very next morning. The whole operation was completed by 10.00am.

I had been detailed to the eight to twelve watch on our way round and expected to be working while the trouble with the intake was being sorted. But I was amazed to find that I could sub two-pounds, and we were given the rest of the day off. I couldn't believe it. In the past in my own personal experience on most ships, we would have had to work the full eight hours. It was nice to see a little consideration being shown at last.

Along with Tony, a DHU who was embarking on his very first trip, I went ashore and had a couple of drinks in the Admiral Nelson pub just outside the dock gates, after which Tony returned aboard, but I was not going to miss the unexpected chance to renew my acquaintance with my beloved Falmouth.

As I walked along Castle Drive, I peeped through the rail over the wall to see the '*British Guardsman*' nestling in the dry dock below. The weather was perfect, a lovely

sunny day. I carried on walking round the headland and onto the beach where I spent the rest of the afternoon on the sands sat with my back against the sea wall to soak up the sunshine and watch the sea gently lapping in.

Later, as the gentle waves darted forward to lick at my shoes, I was reluctantly forced to move, and took a steady stroll into town. Once in the town centre it was amazing how little had changed, except that one of the two cinemas had been converted into a Bingo Hall. Back onboard, I took an early night.

The problem with the intake was soon cleared and during the night, the dock was flooded. We sailed at seven o'clock that morning, Saturday 17th May, bound for Mina-al-Ahmadi, "Back to Gulf tummy land," I remembered with a wry smile.

Due to some technical problem, the Suez Canal was temporarily closed, which meant that our route was the long way round, down the West African coast and around the Cape. I'm not sure whether the ship was too big to go through anyway.

Once out into the open spaces of the Atlantic, the ship was put on to automatic pilot, known to us as the 'Iron Mike.' Once the ship was steering itself, it allowed for only one man in each watch to standby on the wing of the bridge or monkey island and double up as lookout during the hours of darkness.

A rota system was in operation with one man initially doing a three-week spell in each of the watches whilst the rest of the crew were on daywork, with an all change at the end of those three weeks, or when the Mate remembered to do it. I remained for that first period in the eight to twelve.

The 'Iron Mike' was not the only innovation new to me. Back in my early days on the twelve thousand ton 'San Velino,' the number of crew from Master down totalled between sixty and seventy men, but by 1969 the 'British Guardsman' at fifty-two thousand ton had a full compliment of around a mere thirty.

The weather improved and soon became warmer. As we proceeded south, the temperature rose up into the eighties by the 22nd and 23rd May. The humidity and stillness with no breeze made for a sweaty hell out on the open decks, but the accommodation was cool and comfortable with the blessed air conditioning. How had we ever existed without it?

It was on the Saturday morning when I took up my watch, I remarked to the Third Mate that we could do with a drop of rain to clear the air. No sooner had the words been uttered than a huge dark cloud appeared over the horizon and headed towards us at a terrific rate. "A drop of rain!" I must have been joking. One moment we were bathed in sunshine and the next, a solid wall of water hit us. Visibility was virtually nil. In an instant we were hardly able to make out the deck stretching out in front of us. Lightning flashed and thunder exploded around us as if we were under a mortar attack. I can't ever remember seeing a rainstorm of such magnitude as that. We had to slow our speed right down and sound the ship's whistle every few seconds to alert any ships that may be around of our presence.

Suddenly the torrential rain stopped although the lightening and thunder continued to display their anger around the enclosed horizon that encircled us. Everything became quite eerie as if we were inside a bubble or travelling in a time capsule. The very air we breathed was warm and tasted slightly acrid then, for the second time, the downpour hit us and shortly after that, as if coming through an open door, we sailed out into blazing sunshine again. I can only assume that we had sailed right through the eye of the storm, which was a very strange experience.

For forty minutes or there about, the storm had raged around us and as the tempest disappeared to our rear, the Third Mate came out and suggested that something nasty might happen if I ever mentioned rain to him again. "It was alright for him," I thought as he had been inside the shelter of the wheelhouse, while I had been on the wing of the bridge with the impossible task of trying to keep a look out, huddled up in what meagre shelter there was up against the wheelhouse bulkhead. I was like a drowned rat, but as he had said it with a smile, I saw the funny side of it.

* * *

Once we were beyond the Canary Islands, the weather returned to its balmy warmth with a little breeze to make it more bearable for a few days. From then on the days remained warm and the breeze gathered in the warmth, which remained with us for the rest of the journey down the coast; it cooled a little as we approached the Cape where once again a new innovation was witnessed.

Heavy showers and a mist obscured the coastline as we came abreast of Cape Town at 8.00am on Monday 2nd June. Just as I went on to the wing of the bridge for standby at the beginning of my watch, out of the mist appeared a helicopter to deliver fresh food and durables to us, which had been ordered by radio. The lads had painted two six-foot white squares on the deck to indicate the dropping area.

Hovering above, the helicopter crew lowered large nets that contained all the goods including a change of films. Our lads who were of course standing on the steel decks had to wear rubber gloves to unhook the nets for fear of static electricity. Once emptied, the nets were bundled together and were hauled back up. Then the Pilot waved us goodbye and disappeared into the mist and showers.

We had taken stores onboard without even stopping, we hadn't even had to slow down. It was another novel experience, and although I once again got soaked, I had a grandstand view from the wing of the bridge of the whole operation, which took less than ten minutes. In the old days, it would have meant calling in to Cape Town to take on stores with the consequent loss of time. There had been no change of course and no slacking of speed as we maintained our sixteen knots, it was an extremely slick operation and the novelty was added to when Geoff, a young shipmate who hailed from Halesowen delivered to me from the newly arrived mail bag, a letter from Margaret. "That really was what you would call air mail," I thought.

The receipt of that letter really did help to lift my spirits somewhat as that was my first trip away from home as a married man and I sorely missed Margaret and all my home comforts not to mention the constant question nagging away in my mind: was I doing the right thing?

Two hours later as we altered course to round the Cape we left the showery weather behind and it became lovely, clear and sunny. Within a couple of days, we sailed up the East coast of Africa between Mozambique and Madagascar. Suddenly, as we approached the equator, the temperature increased to blazing hot. Each day that passed, our day's work was spent chipping the old paint and what nodules of rust there were off the steel decks in preparation for repainting them.

One morning as the blazing sun rose higher in the sky, and the heat reflected upwards from the steel of the decks, the temperature approached 118ºF. Obviously the job, in that heat, literally sweated pounds off us. Never was the sheer joy of a refreshing cold shower at the day's end, then a cold beer while we sat in the benefit of the air conditioning so much appreciated.

We received orders on the evening before we arrived off Ras-al-Had, to proceed to a place called Umm Said in Qatar to take on a part load before we proceeded to Das Island to top up and take on bunkers. The full cargo was then to be delivered to Lavara in the South of France.

Ever onwards into the Strait of Hormuz we went, and the heat was relentless as we sailed into the Persian Gulf on Saturday night 14th June. The next morning as I was enjoying a cup of tea before I started work, I sat in the shade of the starboard alleyway when suddenly, I heard a loud clank like two pieces of metal banging together. The stern of the ship rose up in the air and sank back down again into the calm water like a speeding car over a hump back bridge.

The stern of the ship then began to wobble from side to side similar to a dogs wagging tail. Obviously the propeller had struck some unknown submerged object. I jumped up immediately to peer over the side and the stern but there was nothing to be seen. A reduction in knots was necessary to reduce the vibrations, and we proceeded at the much slower speed of six to seven knots.

Upon our arrival off Umm Said in the early afternoon, the Pilot came aboard to guide us in through the buoyed channel. It took about half an hour before we were in position to tie up at the mooring buoys about half a mile off shore. The loading began almost immediately via the submarine pipeline, and the task was made more pleasant by a cool offshore breeze, which was a little unusual in that part of the world at that time of year.

Following the evening meal, the poop deck was occupied by those keen fishermen amongst us, and I tried my hand with one unattended line. Within minutes I landed a horrible looking sucker fish about eighteen inches long that I hastily threw back. Suddenly a boat with an outboard motor appeared out of nowhere right under the stern, there was much annoyance as it snagged and broke three of the lines.

One of the Ordinary Seamen, in very profound and colourful language, shouted verbal abuse down at them thinking that the occupants of the boat were locals; they were all fatherless misbegotten so-and-so's. Boy was his face red when he saw the faces of the Skipper, Chief Mate and the Chief Engineer glaring back up at him. He was quite lucky because they took no action against him.

We never knew what the object was that we hit, but they were trying to assess what damage had been done to the propeller. Soon word was passed that about a three foot chunk had been broken off the end of one of the blades, but we would be able to continue the voyage albeit at a much reduced speed.

Just across the bay lay a beached, burnt out hulk. It was a company vessel, the 'British Crown,' which two years earlier had exploded whilst loading a cargo there. Evidently there was a terrific explosion during the night, and within minutes the ship was a blazing inferno. Those who could jumped for their lives, but I was told that about nineteen hands had perished. It was said that once she had been pulled clear of all the pipeline connections and such, she was just allowed to burn herself out as the heat was too strong; it took three months for the flames to finally die.

Our Second Engineer must have had mixed emotions at the sight of her, for he was a member of her crew when the incident happened and was one of the lucky ones who escaped the inferno. I believe that he was given an award for bravery, but he could not be drawn to speak on the subject.

I wouldn't have thought it was very pleasant for him to look across at her again with all the memories she must have invoked. She stood beached as both a salutary and sinister reminder of one of the many dangers that faced all of those who go to the sea in ships. Yet another reminder to spare a thought the next time the car tank is filled. By then, with the propeller broken, I was convinced that my jinx had kicked back in again, but I had never been on a ship so unlucky as that Second Engineer had.

While the process of loading was being carried out, the Mate increased the watch to three men per watch so my duty was from eight to twelve that night, checking the input to the tanks, turning valves and diverting the flow into other tanks once one was full. Such was the change of duty during my seven years absence, that task was previously performed by the pumpman, a further indication of the multi-duty trends that were being introduced into the workplace in the name of productivity.

In the early hours of Monday 16th June, during the twelve to four watch, a tank overflowed and spilled oil out all over the decks due to someone's inattention. Finally the loading was completed that morning with just three tanks remaining empty.

Still our departure was delayed due to an AB who had slipped on a patch of oil while we were still at the buoys in the Isle of Grain. He had badly cut his wrist and there was the possibility of a fracture. The doctor ashore had put stitches in it, and he had sailed with us with his arm in plaster and a sling. Why he had insisted on sailing with us instead of being paid off, and why the Skipper had allowed him to I'll never know.

He had gone ashore to have the plaster taken off and the stitches taken out. On his return he informed us that the doctor on examination had told him to report to his own doctor as soon as possible because there was a strong possibility that he could lose the use of his middle finger.

* * *

The journey to Das Island was a short one, and we were at anchor by ten o'clock that same night. We tied up to the loading buoys at lunchtime the next day. I was really pleased about the timing of that because I was in the eight to twelve watch; I escaped being involved in the final topping up of the last three tanks, especially as they managed to spill quite a lot of crude oil over the part of the deck that had just recently been chipped and repainted.

There was by then quite a strong breeze blowing but it was still hot and sticky. I hate to think what it would have been like without that breeze. It was my watch when we finally let go at nine o'clock that night. A further problem added to our difficulties: a fan in the boiler had failed and it was beyond the capabilities of our engineers to mend it. It further reduced our speed, but with the load we were much deeper in the water, and that reduced the tendency to sway from side to side because of the broken propeller blade. The result was more of a rhythmic little jerk that we soon got used to, and shortly it became virtually unnoticed.

The first two days were spent cleaning the spilt oil from the deck as we returned through the Strait of Hormuz on the afternoon of Wednesday 18th June. Once out of the Gulf of Oman and into the open sea a strong wind blew up; we welcomed it at first, but it resulted eventually into a rough sea with salty spray that covered the housing and the waves came rolling over the decks. For me it felt good to feel once again like a normal being, free from the constant sweat with a cool breeze on my face.

For ten days the seas and the wind made our passage difficult, and reduced our already slow speed even further, but we plodded on. Eventually the seas began to calm and the long rolling waves stopped cascading over the decks, the sun also eventually came out so it was then time to start painting the ship.

The company in their wisdom, had decided to change the colour scheme of their ships. The whole complex of stanchions that supported the Flying Bridge, which ran up the centre of the whole of the deck from the housing to the fo'c's'le head, was the first attack, and given its awkward angles and height, it could only be tackled in the calmer seas.

The Flying Bridge at that time was painted a light grey, but it had to be repainted green. It was a daunting task even in a calm sea, and even though the temperature was dropping as we headed south at a very sedate pace, it was still great to get into a shower and the comfort of my cabin at the end of a long day.

It was slow, it was tedious and so it was good to sight the Comoros Islands and find ourselves steaming through the Mozambique Channel. Orders were received on Thursday 3rd July to deliver the faulty fan motor into Durban to be repaired, after which we were to pick it up again in Cape Town.

The crane in the engine room was rigged up and topped, and the offending machine was hoisted up through the skylights then landed and secured on deck. It weighed around about one ton. It was also a hot, sweaty job as we had the colossal heat rising from the engine room through the skylights to contend with.

We anchored in Durban Harbour at midday the following day, Friday, and considering no one's feet had touched dry land since we had left Falmouth two months earlier, the sight of Durban's skyline and its golden beaches was temptation personified; a temptation that unfortunately no one could take advantage of; before too long, a boat came alongside and the fan motor was lowered and taken away.

Immediately it was up anchor and we were away. As we rounded the Cape, it became very cold and we arrived in a very chilly Cape Town at 7.00am on Tuesday 8th July. Once again the buildings were tantalisingly close, nestling under the foot of Table Top Mountain and once again, all we could do was look, but as we steamed dead slow ahead, a boat came alongside and while keeping pace with us, it delivered the repaired fan motor along with a few more provisions and mail.

Yet again it was a pretty slick operation lifting that thing aboard and lowering it into position back down the engine room while we were still on the move. Our engineers had it fitted by the next morning so it was a relief to then be travelling at a more normal speed of fourteen knots albeit still with that slight rhythmic sideways little jerk.

The cold, dull and showery weather persisted, but we were heading northwards towards the Equator and the sunshine. Just south of the equator we ran into a fog bank as thick as pea soup, for twelve hours our speed was reduced yet again to dead slow ahead, and we had to continually blow the ship's whistle.

I had been on daywork since we left Cape Town, and once we cleared the Equator and headed up towards the Canary Islands, we cruised along in beautiful sunshine with long, sunny days and hardly a cloud in the sky or a ripple on the water. The temperature was a balmy 86ºF.

Once we passed the Canaries, with no explanation from the Bosun other than "because the Mate said so," I was put back on watch again, that time the twelve to four. It pleased me a lot, as I much preferred to be on a watch rather than on daywork. We set course for the Straits of Gibraltar and ever onwards, we passed through at 5.30am on the morning of Friday 25th July.

The weather was good, sunny and remained in the eighties, which made for quite a pleasant existence and we anchored off Lavara at midday on Saturday 26th July. Those of us who were already on watch were kept on our respective watches to keep an anchor watch.

Again we were allowed to draw subs, and despite the fact that no one had been able to leave the ship since we had sailed from Falmouth, we still couldn't get ashore as no shore boat had been laid on for us. Except that is, for two of the firemen.

A lot of us were taking air on the poop deck that evening, and in the fading light, a man in a small boat came within hailing distance. He heeded to a call from the two firemen and came under our stern. The end of a mooring rope was then dangled over, they both shimmied down it into his boat and they were taken ashore.

They returned the same way at 11.30pm and a rope ladder was lowered for them to climb aboard. Several large bottles of French wine accompanied them, which attracted immense instant attention and were empty before you could say the word 'corkscrew'.

The next morning while we were still at anchor, I witnessed a further instance of the changes that had taken place in the service during my absence, at least within the BP Company: the Skipper, the Third Mate and one or two of the engineers were all relieved of duty and flown home as they had been on the ship for six months. We had not yet got six months in, but that would not have mattered as no such rule applied to us. The crews would have to stick it out until a homeport was made.

From our anchorage we could see many tankers at their berths discharging their cargos. Beyond was a canal cutting, which I suddenly recognised was the entrance into Lake Berre that I had visited so many times when a boy on the old 'San Velino' so many years earlier.

At that moment in time, little did I realise that I was in for a very hectic twenty-four hours. At midnight I started my anchor watch until 4.00am. At 5.00am I was called to stations as we went alongside to tie up. That task took us up to 6.45am and we soon began to discharge. Then as we were all safely tied up in port we were put onto daywork that started at 7.00am.

The shift for me seemed endless, with only very short meal breaks and continuous valve turning we worked on through the next twelve hours and finished at 7.00pm that evening. I had still not set foot on dry land so far on the voyage so although absolutely shattered, I realised that if I didn't get ashore for a break that evening, it was unlikely that I would have another chance for some time.

Once showered and cleaned up, I walked alone along to the brand new Seamen's Home just outside the dock gates. I felt that I had earned a couple of cool beers on the balcony to relax on a deck chair and soak in the warm, balmy, evening air. Then it was back to my much-neglected bunk.

I was put on day watch again the next morning. It was strange that I seemed to be picked out for all those unusual watches. Possibly, perhaps the Chief Mate had thought that I was probably the most sober of a pretty boisterous lot, who after having been cooped up on the ship for a total of seventy-three days, had been given all day Monday and most of Tuesday off. They went on a bender, and who in a way could blame them. Every single one of them got plastered and some found trouble.

One of the young stewards, while he staggered back to the ship that night in a drunken state, stole a car and gave his mates a lift back to the ship from the Seamen's Home, which was only a few minutes walk anyway, then he went for a joy ride. He was as drunk as a skunk so the police promptly arrested him, and he spent the night in the slammer. Unbelievably they let him go the next day. Perhaps as the car was returned to its rightful owner completely undamaged he had decided not to press charges.

Others journeyed to the nearby village of Martigues where two of them managed to pick a fight with two Frenchmen: one AB ended up with a split lip and the other with a split eyelid that required stitches. He was lucky he didn't lose his eye.

We let go at six o'clock that Tuesday night, I don't know how we managed as I think that I was the only one in the deck department who was sober. Once we were back at sea, everything gradually settled down into its normal routine.

We set a course for Tripoli in the Lebanon, the weather was warm and the sea almost like a sheet of glass, as we were light ship again that little sideways jerk had worsened. Nevertheless we arrived off Tripoli on Sunday the 3rd August. The Pilot came out and took us right in to the buoys about a quarter of a mile from shore where we tied up. Again a submarine pipeline was lifted onboard, connected up and the loading commenced immediately.

Later that afternoon the bumboats arrived and spread their wares in our recreation room. There were transistor radios, tape recorders, watches and numerous other items on display. I thought that a lot of the stuff was quite expensive, but I bought a couple of items as presents for Margaret. Many of the guys bought quite a lot and in that one night they took over four hundred and twenty pounds before they left, after a very profitable evening.

The good news that we were loading for home lightened the atmosphere as it always did, and with the prospect of being home within a couple of weeks, we set sail on Monday 4th August with happy hearts and headed across the whole length of the Medi. towards the Straits of Gibraltar. It was 98° Fahrenheit for almost all of the journey back across the Medi. and it was good to work in the sunshine with the knowledge that a nice cool beer could be enjoyed at the day's end.

However all good things come to an end. As soon as we passed under the Rock, we encountered what was to us freezing weather; winds and heavy seas blew up as is to be expected in the Bay of Biscay. On beyond Ushant and Finisterre into the English Channel we sailed and sighted Dungeness at four o'clock on Friday morning 15th August.

The Pilot came aboard and the tricky part of the journey began; it was crucial that the timing of our arrival at the Isle of Grain was at the very peak of high tide for there would be only inches clearance between the river bed and the bottom of the ship.

Slowly we came around the coast and up the Thames Estuary. Once again I caught for the helm as we approached our berth, which was a gap between two vessels that were already moored there. As we very slowly edged our nose into the gap, it soon became glaringly obvious that we were getting ominously close to the stern of the ship moored ahead of us.

Even with five tugs in attendance, the Pilot telegraphed full astern and ordered me to hold the helm hard over to port to bring our bow away from the other ship. All that was to no avail as the 'British Guardsman' stubbornly refused to stop; slowly she continued to cut forward through the water inch by inch.

Whether the damage to the propeller played any part in the failure to reverse the forward motion I don't know, but from the wheelhouse, at the point of impact, there seemed to be hardly any motion at all other than a sudden slight jerk. Even so, the solid steel plates of the apron on our bow ripped asunder as if made of cardboard. The crew on the fo'c's'le head scattered.

What the personnel onboard the other ship had thought was happening at that moment, I dread to think, but looking on the bright side, it had served its purpose. We had stopped. So without any more hassle, she was drawn alongside and safely tied up. Fortunately, no one was hurt.

The pipe connections and the discharging of the cargo had to start immediately to lighten the ship in conjunction with the tide receding, and to ensure our continued buoyancy. The deckhands had finished, got showered, changed and packed our gear, but then we were kept hanging around until eight o'clock in the evening before we were finally paid off.

Then as on a previous occasion, a bus was provided to take us to Tilbury and after having a whip round for him, the driver agreed to drop us off at our appropriate stations in London. Geoff and I caught the Birmingham train at Euston, which got into Birmingham New Street just after midnight. After saying our goodbyes, I left him to continue the last lap of his journey to Halesowen.

I on the other hand, found that there were no trains or buses to Walsall for a few hours so I caught a taxi and arrived home at 12.45am. It was Saturday. I let myself in and frightened the life out of Margaret, who was asleep in bed until she realised it was that sailor home from the sea.

Margaret loved her little presents and after having got over her fright thinking that someone had broken in, she forgave me and welcomed me home. I had been away for three months and it felt great to come home to her and my own house.

I had a little time then to reflect on my first voyage for seven years, and I concluded that one thing hadn't changed: given the blocked intakes, the broken propeller and the collision, I knew. The jinx was definitely still with me.

CHAPTER TWENTY-THREE

THE LANCASTRIAN PRINCE / ONE

(Of a Wonderful Holiday, a Long Wait for a Berth and a Jolly Crew).

My thirteen days leave was wonderful but over all too soon. As I had predicted, Mavis and Alan along with Tom, Marg and all the kids were in Sydney, Australia, and they had asked Margaret to remind me of my promise to look them up should I ever make port there.

Marg had never been to Falmouth, and since I was due back on Thursday 28th August, I longed to show her the town I had come to love so we decided to make a small holiday while I waited for my next berth. The Penrose Hotel next door to Armyn House, where I had stayed the time Armyn House had been fully booked, had a vacancy so we booked a room in advance by phone and travelled down on Saturday 23rd August, five days prior to the end of my leave.

Margaret was really thrilled with every aspect of Falmouth, as I had felt sure she would be, with the character of the town and the activity in the harbour with the coming and goings of the many vessels of all shapes, sizes and nationalities. She didn't want to miss a thing.

As it was holiday time and there was only one guy on duty when I called into the Pool on the Monday morning, four days early, which was definitely a first for me. I just wanted to get some idea of what berths were due to be coming up. He told me that if I had been five minutes earlier I could have sailed on the 'Octavia Bridge,' a large Iron Ore carrier.

We had stood and watched her leave the dry dock on the evening before and I thought, "Thank god I was five minutes late, especially as I was back early from my leave and wanted to spend at least a couple of days more with Marg before I set sail again." "Try again in the morning" was his advice, "there may be something coming up for you."

Come the morrow I was informed that there would be two jobs coming up towards the end of the week. One was the 'British Statesman,' the other was the 'Lancastrian Prince,' which I had noticed in the dockyard. She was a small cargo/passenger boat, similar in build and size to the 'Albemarle,' she looked OK and belonged to the Furness Withy Company. As I had only just returned from the Gulf on a British tanker, the strong prospect of a repeated voyage loomed large, so my preference for the tankers took second place in that instance, and I accepted the 'Lancastrian Prince.'

The conditions of contracting to the Pool had also been altered. In the past the commitment was for two years; it had been changed so that you could then sign for a continuous period of time but with a three-month notice option either way. That sounded a much fairer system to me, so I saw the doctor, passed my medical and signed.

With all the business over, along with Margaret I then walked up to the Labour Exchange (Job Centre), and I signed on the dole as I was not gainfully employed while I was waiting to sign articles. There was nothing else to do then except to enjoy Falmouth and what time we had together, which is exactly what we did. The weather was beautiful every day and we walked for miles along the cliff tops and beaches. It was a really wonderful time.

On the Thursday, I called into the Pool again to be told that neither ship was signing till late the following week. Other ships were on offer at various ports around the country but I felt that as I had already travelled miles to be in Falmouth, I would hang on for the '*Lancastrian Prince*.' The Pool Clerk suggested that I go onboard to ask if I could possibly 'work by' until the actual signing on, which I did, but the Mate wouldn't hear of it. He told me I would have to wait until Friday.

Our ready cash had run dangerously low and we could not afford for both of us to remain so, after discussing it with Marg, it was with great reluctance that I waved goodbye to her at Falmouth station. She had enjoyed every moment of her first visit and, like me, fell in love with the place. As she left for home I found myself at a complete loss, I wandered around aimlessly and spent one of the loneliest long weekends I can remember.

On the Monday morning, I went onboard the '*British Statesman*' and found that they would commence signing on in two days time. The lightness of my pocket made me consider changing my mind and take her instead until I took a look at the crew's accommodation, which was filthy and disgusting, and I instantly changed my mind back again.

I called into the Pool the next morning to see if there had been any change to the '*Lancastrian Prince's*' signing date; there was none. Then I stayed well clear on Wednesday because I feared that I might be coerced into accepting the '*British Statesman*.' However, as I walked through the town that evening, I bumped into one of the Pool clerks, "Ah! Mr Kenn." he called, "come in and see us first thing in the morning."

I feared the worst, which was that they hadn't got a full crew for the '*British Statesman*,' but I was told instead that the '*Lancastrian Prince*' was signing on at two o'clock that afternoon. All my forms were then processed and I received a payment of ten-pound Pool pay as I had signed their contract, which was a godsend, and I made my way to sign off the dole.

I was to be disappointed for I was informed that I didn't qualify for any payment as over the past six months, I had only four months stamps

489

as an employee; the other two months I had been self-employed. The payment of the stamps during the period of my self-employment, which were compulsory apparently did not count. Angrily I asked, "What was the point of me having to pay those stamps if I could not receive any benefit from them?" There was no joy to be had there and as I left, I failed to catch the clerk's final comment, but I was past caring.

At two o'clock that day, Thursday 11th September, after I had signed articles onboard, I went aft to find a cabin. I was not surprised to find that being so small a vessel, they too were a little small and cramped, especially with three men sharing. Nevertheless I stowed my gear and began to write a letter home when suddenly the door burst open and a suitcase was thrown onto the deck and a guy said, "Hi, I'm Terry," and he vanished in an instant.

He was there and gone so fast I was left sitting there wondering if I had had some kind of a brainstorm, but the suitcase standing there reassured me that I hadn't. He didn't show up again until the next day when I met the rest of my new shipmates, all young guys and full of fun. That augured well for the future I thought.

Midday Saturday 13th September found us heading up the English Channel bound for the great German port of Hamburg then on to Antwerp. After all the hanging around I had endured waiting for the berth, we were only going to the continent then back to London.

As we passed the Isle of Wight, we ran into a bank of mist, which reduced our speed. It persisted until the Pilot came aboard to take us up the river Elbe. It was Monday 15th September, and once again I was at the helm as we came up to the mooring buoys in the middle of the river. On approaching them, the helm had to be swung hard over so that we did a one hundred and eighty degree turn and slid up to them by going astern and we were soon safely tied up facing the way we had come.

We had been signed on for less than a week and everyone had very little money in the ship so unfortunately we were all trapped onboard, that however did not seem to dampen the spirits of the young crew as they laughed and joked all day long.

My thoughts were with Margaret as Wednesday 17th September was our third wedding anniversary, which I celebrated by starting to load fifty tons of steel brought out by barges. That was soon accomplished, and we cast off in the late afternoon for Antwerp. The fog had cleared completely, the Pilot came aboard off Antwerp, Belgium the next morning, and we continued straight on to our berth.

Once again no one went ashore and the loading of a further hundred ton of steel began as soon as we were tied up. That was completed the next morning, which allowed us to sail heading for London docks on the Friday afternoon.

The trip back across the English Channel was non-eventful, and we were tied up and secure by ten o'clock the following morning. It had only been a short trip, just a week or so but they were the most happy-go-lucky, fun loving group I had ever sailed with, always laughing with endless jokes and camaraderie.

I had enjoyed it so much with them that when the whole crew were asked if they wished to remain with the ship for the next trip and they had said yes, I had no hesitation in saying yes too. There were other reasons too why I agreed, but I thought that it would be great to continue the happy relationship with those guys.

In addition there was also the possibility that I could wangle an extra two days leave over and above the two that I was already due; each day spent with loved ones was special for a sailor. Thirdly, the next trip was to Central America, which I hadn't seen a great deal of, and the icing on the cake was we were told that we would be home by Christmas.

A fellow named Chris and I decided to leave our gear onboard rather than lug it home and back again. Although everyone had signed on in Falmouth, strangely most of the crew were Londoners.

That time, the owner of a minibus came onboard and offered those of us who needed it to take us to our stations for a nominal fee, and within minutes of arriving at Euston I was on a train heading for Birmingham. I hoped that Margaret had received the letter I had posted in Antwerp so that on that occasion, she would know that I was coming.

CHAPTER TWENTY-FOUR
THE LANCASTRIAN PRINCE / TWO
(Of a Disappointment, a Stable Job and a Mine).

The weekend, as usual, passed far too quickly, and on Tuesday I was notified that I was to rejoin the ship the next day so Margaret waved me goodbye from the station platform at New Street and I caught the early morning train.

On my arrival at Euston, for convenience sake, I took a taxi and was back onboard by midday, only to be told that they had mistakenly called me back too early and they wouldn't be signing on till the next morning. As it was their fault, the Mate gave me my cabin key, along with some bedlinen from the Chief Steward. I trudged aft to my cabin and I silently cursed them under my breath as I settled back in. All my gear was just where I had left it, and I idled the rest of the afternoon away.

The loading was going ahead. It was all general cargo, a myriad of different items such as clothes, toys, perfumes, glasses and what appeared to be Christmas present type items. There were also thousands of cases of whiskey. There was no sign whatsoever of any of my shipmates. In fact, as I signed on the following morning Thursday 25th September, I made sure that it was backdated to the previous day. Not one of the old crew had returned, and a fresh crew from the London Pool was signed.

I felt really disappointed; they had been a wonderful bunch of guys and I had been looking forward so much to sailing with them, but such is life, and there were other reasons for my return. Chris, the other guy who had left his gear onboard, did not reappear either and my curiosity about his failure to return was settled when the message came through that he was in hospital; he had been involved in an accident, so his gear had to be listed by the Bosun and I and put ashore. The Bosun and I were the only ones of the deck crew who were onboard. I hadn't yet met any of the new ones as they had come onboard, signed on and disappeared, most of them were local lads I guessed. We finally met when they all returned on Friday morning.

Our schedule was to sail that night but during the afternoon, the dockers had decided that they couldn't possibly complete the loading by knocking off time, and as there was an overtime ban on or some such dispute, it would have to be concluded on Monday. As soon as that became general knowledge, as quick as a flash, all the deck department vanished again. I cursed as I had little money, otherwise I would have vanished too, an extra weekend at home would have been very welcome, but all I could do was hang around.

That afternoon the Bosun came to my cabin with the news that five horses would be coming aboard to be shipped to Venezuela, and he would need a man to help him tend to their needs during the voyage. I told him that I knew absolutely nothing about horses other than that they had a leg on each corner and a tail at one end. I also recalled from an early age being sent by my father complete with bucket and shovel to follow the milkman and the baker's horses and carts delivering their wares around the streets. According to him the manure they deposited produced excellent fertilizer for the garden. "Not to worry" the Bosun said, "there is a list of do's and don'ts and there will be an extra twenty-five pounds in it for you over and above your normal wages." That settled it in my mind so I told him I would give it a go. The remainder of the weekend was quiet with nothing to do so Monday couldn't come quick enough for me. I was glad when the rest of the crew returned and the dockers completed the loading.

All the derricks were then lowered and the hatches battened down as each one was filled, and everything was secured ready for the voyage. Lastly, the horses arrived and were hoisted aboard in their individual wooden crates or makeshift stables, which were lashed securely in a row along the port side of the main deck, then we started on our way down river just before tea.

Our instructions for looking after the horses were written on a card that the Bosun and I were given, and they were comprehensive and explicit. Little did I know that it would be virtually a full-time job, and neither did I realise that horses needed so much attention.

Almost immediately after we had let go, we had to feed them with a mixture of bran and oats. Later, at about 7.00pm, we gave them some water and bedded them down for the night. I soon realised that looking after them was going to be a lot harder work than I had thought. Our daily routine started by rising at 5.30am to grab a quick cup of tea, and on the stroke of 6.00am, each horse was given a bucket of water and their mixture of bran and oats, which was fed into a trough hooked onto the horsebox door.

They could then be left unattended until we had taken our breakfast at 8.00am. After which, the mucking out started. The Bosun held the horses' heads and I, under his instructions, had to enter each stable in turn to shovel out the muck and straw bedding. "Oh for the privilege of rank," I thought.

I had to move them to one side to first clean the empty space and then move them over to complete the cleaning up from where they had been standing. Quite often, one or other of the horses would refuse to budge and it was sometimes difficult to get them to do so. Initially the muck and straw was shovelled out onto the deck and I would accidentally on purpose make sure some of it would land or spatter onto the Bosun's shoes. "That will teach him to pull rank and give himself the best job," I thought as I smirked behind his back. He never once realised that it was done deliberately, or at least he never let on that he did.

Upon completion of all five boxes, I was shattered, literally on my knees. I was certainly earning my twenty-five quid. Fresh straw, which was piled high on the top of number four hatch had to be laid, and occasionally the floors of the stables had to be hosed down too. Their hay bags had to be kept full at all times and they were given another bucket of water. Grooming and brushing each one individually took a considerable amount of time, and I was lucky if I was finished by lunchtime when they had to be fed and watered again.

The afternoons were less hectic as we only needed to ensure that they had water and hay before we fed them at five o'clock, and we closed them up for the night at 7.00pm. Each horse had its own quirks, temperament and character; of course, I had my favourite.

It did not take them long to become aware of who it was that was caring for them, and they also seemed able to be aware of time, especially in the early morning. If the clock ticked past the six o'clock mark and their morning feed and watering was overdue by so much as a minute, they would nudge their empty buckets with their noses and make them rattle against the door to indicate their impatience until we responded. That was repeated every day of the week with no respite.

They were five lovely racehorses to whom I became quite fond and attached, despite the hard work and time that their care demanded. They all had a different temperament and personality. There was no information as to why they were being shipped out to Venezuela. Maybe to race or even for stud purposes. I never knew.

Four of them were colts; the other, a filly called 'Luli Belle' was brown, quiet and even-tempered. Next in line was 'Silver Spray,' also brown with a white blaze down his nose. There is always one and he was it, he had to be watched for he was not averse to taking a crafty nip out of you if you were unaware and not paying attention.

When we were only a few days out, he developed colic; it was distressing to see the obvious pain he was in as he kept turning and writhing on the floor of his box and rolling from side to side. As he thrashed in agony, he banged his head, which raised a bump just above his eye; he also scratched a large patch on his flank against the sides of the stable. The whole episode was extremely upsetting. It almost broke my heart to see him suffer so much.

I thanked God the instructions had anticipated such an occurrence and detailed how to deal with the problem. Epsom salt was put into his drinking water with a dosage of Colicure. He took the Epsom salt OK, but we had difficulties getting him to take the Colicure, which he didn't like one bit. After a couple of days, the treatment began to work and he started to improve. Shortly afterwards he was as right as rain. It was great to see him back to normal.

'Aquit,' a great big black horse, was my favourite. He would obligingly lift his legs up out of the way one at a time as I mucked him out. That made it so much easier to shovel everything out from under him and he always gave a little whinny when his food was delivered as though to say "Thank you."

Next to 'Aquit,' was the Bosun's favourite, 'Motet,' another black horse, but not as big as 'Aquit.' He was a character, full of life and mischievously unpredictable. He also had to be watched. With his body, he would quite deliberately try to pin me up against the side of the stall and press into me. I could never tell what he was likely to do next, and for that reason, I always felt a little uneasy when I was inside the stall with him, and perhaps he knew it.

He was his own worst enemy because before we had even reached the river estuary, he had ripped all the padding off the walls of his stall that was there to lessen any possible injuries, and he would kick all the straw into one corner so that he stood on the bare wooden floor. On occasions, he would put his head under his trough and lift it to spill out all its contents; he once bit through the rope from which his bucket hung and soaked the lower half of his legs.

A further endearing trick that caused much merriment and was, I'm sure, the reason he was the Bosun's favourite, was that he would deliberately poke his head out of the top half of his stable door every time the Bosun walked past. He would grab the peak of his cap between his teeth, yank it off his head and fling it to one side. The Bosun's language was colourful to say the least, but it was all friendly abuse as he enjoyed the funny side of it and on many occasions would deliberately walk past the box when he didn't need to just to make it happen for a laugh.

Lastly came 'Floretti,' a very similar horse both in appearance and temperament to 'Luli Belle' who would on most occasions, respond willingly to our wishes. While it was quite time consuming and hard work, I came to enjoy it.

The weather had been chilly for the first few days of the trip as we progressed down the channel. On leaving Land's End behind on Tuesday afternoon, I happened to look up from what I was doing and spotted a black, round, spiky object in the water about thirty foot away from the starboard side, "God! It's a mine." I fled up to the bridge and the Second Mate got his binoculars, as it was by then some little distance astern. "Jesus! It does look like a mine. This will have to be reported. I'll get the sparks to deal with it," he said.

As it happened, there were two minesweepers some distance ahead of us. Perhaps it had already been reported and they were looking for it. I went back to work and heard nothing more about the incident. If it actually had been a mine, broken loose from its rusted anchorage bobbing about amongst those busy shipping lanes, it was disconcerting to say the least, to think about how close we had passed it by.

* * *

The weather remained chilly until we passed the Azores on Saturday 4th October, then the change was remarkable. As each day passed, the temperature rose, and soon the dress order of the day was shorts. The heat then got to the horses who began to sweat a lot, which created the need for further attention from the Bosun and I to do whatever we could to make them more comfortable.

On beyond the Windward Islands we sailed, into the Caribbean and the Pilot came aboard as we arrived off La Guaira, Caracas, Venezuela on Sunday afternoon 12th October. The shoreline was imposing with a high ridge. On the side of the ridge were little wooden shacks of different colours scattered at random wherever a space could be found to build. The town itself was just around a corner of the coastline, and as it was a pretty long walk from where we were moored, I didn't bother to go ashore.

As we came alongside, I heard a shout from the quay, and when I looked down, low and behold, there stood Terry, my shipmate on the previous trip across to the Continent. He came onboard as soon as the gangway was lowered. He was very surprised to learn that I was the only one of the original deck crew who had returned.

He had arrived just ahead of us on a ship called the '*Lombardy*' of the Royal Mail Line. He told me that he had fully intended to come back and had even been given a rail voucher to return to the '*Lancastrian Prince*.' He had then been persuaded to take the '*Lombardy*,' which had called in to Falmouth, because someone had jumped ship and a replacement was urgently required. He was also full of woe.

No wonder the guy had jumped ship if the conditions he described were to be believed. "It was," he said "a terrible ship. Bad accommodation with little or no overtime." He also said the food was lousy so everyone was starving to death." I could empathize with him on that score as I too had been there.

The dockers came bright and early the next morning, and their first task was to immediately unload the horses. I had mixed feelings, as in one way, I was sorry to see them go because we'd had some laughs with them, and I had grown quite fond of them in the short time that they had been with us. On the other hand I wouldn't miss the work that they entailed and 'terra firma' was the right place for them to be, where they could be looked after properly and given the exercise they needed after being cooped up in those boxes for two weeks.

True to his word, the Bosun turned up later that day with twenty-five pounds worth of American dollars, which I welcomed as a currency valid and accepted anywhere, and it meant I didn't have to put in for any subs. He said that the owners of the horses were also very happy and pleased with their condition and congratulated us on a job well done.

The designated cargo was quickly discharged, and early on Tuesday morning 14th October we cast off bound for Puerto Cabello just a few miles up the coast. The '*Lombardy*' had already gone. On our arrival later that same afternoon, the '*Lombardy*' was there ahead of us and Terry, once again, came onboard for a chat. I think he was glad of the chance to get off his ship even for a little while.

That was to be the pattern of our visitation to Central and South America. Short trips to ports up and down the coast to receive and deliver cargos of every description, and to witness squalor and poverty that no human being should have to endure.

The dockers worked hard throughout the night, which enabled our departure for Curacao the next afternoon. In the early hours of Thursday, the Pilot came aboard and took us through the narrow passage and beyond the pontoon bridge to Willemstad, which even after my long absence, felt almost like a home port as I had lost count of the amount of times that I had visited there.

We were then left alone to catch up on a little sleep until 8.00am when many boxes of motor oil were loaded into number four hatch and lots of forty-five gallon drums of oil came aboard and were lashed to the decks, which made for even more cramped conditions than the horses stables had left us. We could only just manage to squeeze past.

Little time was lost once it was all aboard, and we cast off in the early hours of Friday 17th October. Daylight revealed a jungle: green, dense and foreboding. The water of the river Magdalina was thick, brown and disgustingly muddy, full of massive tree trunks and other jungle foliage. Not a river to swim in.

Fortunately our passage along it was short, and we were tied up to the quay by eight o'clock. From our berth, we could look over the rooftop of the warehouse, across a piece of wasteland and a valley to the buildings and churches of the city of Barranquilla. We were in Columbia. Unbelievably, there once again was the '*Lombardy*' and Terry.

They were bound for Cristobal, Panama with no orders thereafter he told us, but rumour had it that they would be heading for Vietnam. He really was not a very happy young man. They sailed the next day and that was our last sighting of them, but I silently wished him good luck.

Along with an Ordinary Seaman, I was detailed the job of nightwatchman by the Chief Mate and was specially warned to keep watch for thieves and outlaws who came alongside the ships in the dead of night to climb aboard to steal and plunder. "Déjà vu," I thought again as my mind went straight back to the '*Nacella*' in Lagos, some twelve years earlier where I was taken ashore by the police to give a statement after the same sort of incident. I definitely did not want to go through something like that again, even though I still had fond memories of Tiny and Colossus. I had been forewarned. So, I resolved to keep a very sharp vigilance.

The temperature even at around two o'clock in the morning was very warm and the Ordinary Seaman and I were sitting on the bits on the poop deck, enjoying a chat and a cup of tea when we heard a slight bump on the side of the hull. We looked over the ship's rail and there below us we saw two guys in a canoe holding on to the ship's side. As we both shouted at them, they looked up at us startled and let go, drifted off and disappeared into the darkness.

As they disappeared, an outboard motor was heard to start for the first time and off they went. Apparently, they had drifted silently downstream from the jungle on the tide to arrive quietly and unannounced. Obviously a practice that was quite common in those parts.

About an hour later from the bridge as we were doing the rounds, very faintly in the gloom, we spotted the shadow of a canoe alongside the vessel moored ahead of us. They had silently returned. I called the Third Mate (who was on cargo watch) to the bridge; he had brought an Aldis lamp with him and he shone it straight on to them just as the Mate on the '*Nacella*' had done. Unlike the '*Nacella*' though, the light attracted attention from some of the crew, which caused the canoeists to steal away for a second time.

Once again, an engine was heard to start and the Third Mate found them with the lamp as they headed back upstream and, in the dazzling beam of light, we saw the man in the front of the canoe angrily shaking his fist at us before they disappeared into the dark cover of the jungle. They didn't return that night. For once, our vigil had paid off.

All hands were called at five o'clock to batten down the hatches and secure the derricks. We let go just after six o'clock to move a short distance along the coast to Cartagena where we arrived mid afternoon on Sunday 19th October. We went straight in, tied up and took on just bits and bobs of cargo. We were on our way again within a couple of hours

Like the '*Lombardy*' we too were bound for Cristobal, Panama, and after another short run we arrived there the following afternoon, Monday 20th October. All the time the weather had been stifling hot with just the occasional rain shower to freshen up the atmosphere a little, which was most welcome.

It was all go for a while; the ship was really earning its keep. Part of the cargo, including the oil drums from the deck was discharged only to be replaced with lorries and cars. Deck cargo seemed to be the order of the day with the '*Lancastrian Prince.*' Firstly horses, then oil drums, then road vehicles that had to be lashed down.

At lunchtime the next day, the Mate gave permission for the crew to take the afternoon off to allow a little time ashore for shopping. Everyone with the exception of myself and Paddy, another AB, scooted ashore like a flash. At one o'clock, the Bosun came to turn us to. "We have got the afternoon off," we cried. "Oh no, only those who wanted to do some shopping," he said. "That is exactly what we are about to do then," we told him and walked down the gangway.

The way into town was via a narrow track through a vast area of wasteland of high bracken. We strolled along merrily discussing the cheek of the Bosun trying to set us to work, when we suddenly both froze solid in mid-stride for there, about ten yards in front of us totally blocking the pathway, stood a giant lizard.

We both stood there, rooted to the spot. He was the ugliest, most frightening creature I had ever seen in my life; he stood about two-foot high and around six-foot in length from his head to the tip of his tail; his big round eyes fixed upon us intensely and glared at us ominously. We were both completely paralysed, unable to move, galvanised to the spot for what seemed like a lifetime as we faced each other out.

The hairs on the back of our necks prickled with fear as he slowly took a few steps towards us. We were both certain that he was about to attack, so imagine our relief when he veered off into the bracken, ran around us and disappeared. Then and only then did my mind go back to the time in 1957 on the '*Granford*' when I had sat painting the bow on the stages, and a hammerhead shark surfaced just inches beneath my feet, I then thought it strange how, in one lifetime, one man can find two different instant cures for constipation! The creature, I found out later, was a giant green iguana and was a vegetarian so we were safe from being his dinner. If only we had known that at the time.

Once in town, Paddy went into a bank to change some Columbian notes and came out with the princely sum of seventy-two cents. We wandered around seeing the sights, not that there was much to see, we were both in need of a stiff drink after our encounter with that blown up gecko.

Suddenly everything went dark and it rained. No, it didn't rain, it was a cloud burst with spots as big as half crowns or today's fifty pence pieces. That gave us the extra excuse, that we didn't need, to dive into the nearest bar. Paddy's seventy two cents and more went on the first round. Fortunately I still had the American dollars that were more than willingly accepted for the rain did not cease until 6.30pm. When we made our way back to the ship, we kept a very sharp lookout for any giant lizards.

All the casting off and tying up had become tedious, and I longed for the vast expanse of the ocean reaches, but it wasn't too bad as we headed into the Panama Canal, which was always a thrill to go through. All went well without incident, and we cleared the other end and spilled out into the Gulf of Panama just before midnight.

After following the coastline to our starboard all the way round, we eventually turned northward and arrived off Puntarenas in Costa Rica the following day and anchored there to take our place in the queue of ships waiting to go alongside. One solitary jetty jutted out from the beach and consequently only two vessels one on each side could load or discharge at a time, which left us to be at anchor for five days until Tuesday 28th October. When we eventually went alongside, we found that we were riding a terrific swell and from the deck at any given moment, you would be looking down on to the jetty and the next the jetty would be way above you. Once at the top of the rise the ship appeared to plummet down towards the jetty again.

Riding the waves out on the open oceans obviously becomes second nature to a sailor, but that visible fast rise and fall against the man-made structure of the jetty sent my head spinning, and I had to look away from it. That was the nearest I had come to feeling seasickness for years since my very first trip.

For once I was glad our visitation was of short duration and was more than pleased to get out to sea again, even if it was for only about twelve hours to anchor at our next port of call, San Juan del Sur across the border in Nicaragua. An extremely strong tide was running; twice during the night, the anchor dragged and the ship had to be moved further out to sea away from the rocks, which in the darkness seemed to surround us. For a third time, the sound of the engines being started aroused me from my slumber, and believing we were dragging anchor again I turned over and went back to sleep.

Dawn found us in a U shaped harbour surrounded by high, jungle covered hills with a few small buildings scattered along the shoreline. The local dockers rowed out to us in small boats towing barges behind them, into which their quota of the cargo was lowered. That took no time at all and it was up, off and away again later that same evening.

Arriving at Corinto still in Nicaragua, we docked alongside as soon as the Pilot was aboard. "The jungle heat must be sending a rush of blood to the Mate's head." I thought as he gave us the afternoon off for which we were very grateful and most of the crew were ashore in a trice. I followed on my own just a little later as I preferred a more leisurely pace.

After about twenty minutes by following a dirt road paved through the jungle and vegetation I came into Corinto. It could only be described as a shantytown. Rows and rows of small wooden shacks. There were little children running naked in and out of them, urinating where they stood. Other dirt roads criss-crossed the place, which were no more than tracks really. There had been a heavy shower just prior to me going ashore, which had turned parts of the tracks into mud and puddles. With the hot sun burning down, steam was rising from the ground creating an acrid stench of muck and piddle.

Cats and dogs chased each other about and fat sows waddled in the mud of the streets accompanied by their litters of piglets. Thin, scraggly chickens squawked their protest as they scurried out of my path, and great hulking oxen roamed freely amongst the buildings, wallowing in the slime.

Happy voices in a tongue I recognised drew me into a bar where most of my shipmates were indulging in one of their favourite pastimes. It was an open sided shack, the wooden floor of which was raised a little clear of the mud, which was hardening in the hot sun. Tables and chairs were scattered around haphazardly in front of the bar.

I bought a couple of cans of beer and I was surprised to find that they were cold. "Lo and behold! They had a fridge," Thank God! While I sat swapping yarns with a group of the lads, our talk was disturbed by three great big oxen, covered in mud and brown smelly stuff caked all over their backsides, they had decided to take a short cut through the bar.

They meandered their way between the tables with heavy hooves reverberating on the wooden floor and went out the other side, which left us with no doubts in our minds who they thought had the greatest right to be there; it obviously was a common occurrence for no one apart from us took any notice of them whatsoever.

After another couple of beers, I made my way back to the ship. For some reason I felt quite amused by the afternoon's events, but also saddened by the obvious squalor and poverty that those people lived in.

* * *

On Saturday evening 1st November, we set sail again and steamed up the coast at half speed as no one would be available to tie us up in Cutuco, still in Nicaragua, until daybreak Sunday morning. As it was, we still arrived too early and had to continue to steam up and down offshore. There, once again, the discharge took only a few short hours.

All the places began to look the same to us. Little, tiny, out of the way places surrounded by jungle and rich vegetation. Cutuco was nothing but a small wharf in the middle of nowhere. Again we were only there for a few hours and sailed in the afternoon of the same day. On up the Pacific seaboard we went and arrived at La Libertad in El Salvador the next morning, which was Monday 3rd November. It was another anchorage port where they unloaded into barges and once again, we were on our way before the day was out.

By then we felt more like a floating bus than a ship. Each time we arrived or left port we had to tie up, let go, put out the gangway, take it in again or do the same with the accommodation ladder if we anchored. We also had to break out or secure the derricks and lift or batten down the hatches as well as doing our watches. We worked all sorts of crazy hours.

From there however, we began to head back down the coast and anchored off Amapala in Honduras on Tuesday 4th November. Out came the barges again and took the last of our cargo before we sailed the next day. Our next port of call was San Lorenzo also in Honduras where they loaded timber into some of our holds. I had been told that Honduras only had ten miles of coastline on the Pacific side so I knew that we hadn't got far to go.

We moved along the coast for a little while then turned into an opening in the jungle and continued for a short distance till we slid into another cutting just off the opening and dropped anchor. From where we were it looked for all the world as if we had been dropped in the middle of an inland lake with the jungle completely surrounding us. We couldn't even make out the entrance where we had come in, and there wasn't a single wooden shack in sight. We were well and truly up the creek.

After a while a small boat emerged from the jungle towing a large barge behind it, which was loaded down with great chunks of timber. They proceeded to load it into our holds using our derricks, which took four terribly long, boring days to complete. Finally during the afternoon of Sunday 9th November, we heaved up anchor and somehow managed to find our way back out to sea again. We carried on down the coast only to find ourselves anchored off Puerto Samosa in Nicaragua the next day.

That proved to be our final destination on the Pacific side. Out came the big barges again loaded with large sacks full of cottonseed. They threw those into cargo nets a dozen or so at a time, and using our derricks, we lifted them up, over and down into our holds on to our 'tween decks. Once there a couple of men would take the bags from the nets open them up and allow the contents to fall to the bottom of the holds making sure that whatever timber was due to come out first was well clear.

That appeared to be a long winded way of loading to me; surely it would be quicker and easier for the bags to go directly to the bottom to be opened there, but perhaps they had their reasons. Cottonseed! "They could have fooled me." It looked just like topsoil to me. Evidently it was to be compressed and treated to make cattle feed.

Although it was back breaking work for them, it was amazing how quick they loaded it. That time when they had finished loading, instead of just securing the derricks we had to lower them properly for it was then that the joyous news was received. It was back through the canal into the Atlantic bound for Santa Cruz in Tenerife. So it was that on Tuesday 11th November, we started on our way again.

Everyone was really pleased; although we had only been around the Central American coasts for a couple of weeks, because of all the whistle-stop ports, it had somehow seemed more like a couple of months; it was good to arrive off Panama City even at two o'clock in the morning on Friday 14th November. To everyone's surprise, the Pilot came straight out and boarded us from his boat without slacking speed and immediately he took us in.

I was by then on the twelve to four watch and was second wheelman from 2.00am till 4.00am so I took over the helm and under the Pilot's instructions I guided her into the canal and continued up to the first lock where at four o'clock I was relieved and glad to seek the comfort of my bunk.

When I awoke, we were anchored in Gatun Lake, only to be on our way again at midday. After being the second wheelman the previous night, I was supposed to be the 'farmer' on standby, but the Skipper would not allow the Ordinary Seamen to take over the helm in such a narrow waterway so it fell to me again to take her through the rest of the way out.

Upon reaching Cristobal, we swung around to starboard, slid alongside and tied up for bunkers. There was no shore leave allowed as the bunkering was completed by 6.00pm so thankfully there were no more encounters with monster lizards, and then we headed out into the Caribbean and beyond the Islands into the Atlantic.

Despite the heavy swell, which rolled along for four days, it was great to be back on the open sea and into our normal routines. The weather calmed and there was a nip in the air, but after the heat of the Pacific, we noticed any slight drop in the temperature. Had we been outward bound, coming from cooler climbs, we would have thought that it was hot.

Thursday 27th November brought my first sighting of Santa Cruz, a much bigger and grander place than I had somehow expected. As was the norm for that voyage, it took a very short time to unload their quota of the timber and by midday on Friday, we sailed across to Las Palmas where we arrived shortly before midnight. The lights of a bar only a couple of hundred yards from where we were berthed, beckoned and the temptation was too great so, despite the lateness of the hour, Barry, an EDH and I slipped into a clean pair of jeans once we had finished mooring up and nipped ashore for a nightcap.

Saturday was taken up repainting the bow, so there was no afternoon off, but in the evening Barry and I, along with an Ordinary Seaman, went off to see the sights. The shops along the magnificent promenade on the seafront were full of expensive luxurious goods such as beautiful Spanish dolls, music boxes and myriads of different souvenirs. They were geared heavily towards the imagined needs of the hordes of visitors and holiday makers that the place attracted. Although then, in late November, there were not as many people around as I would imagine there to be in the height of summer.

As we walked back along that magnificent promenade we came upon a small crowd that had gathered on the beach; they were watching the antics of two young guys (they had to be seamen) obviously drunk, prancing around on the sand. They had stripped off down to their underpants before they ran into the sea. A big burly policeman was shouting at them to come out, throwing his arms around with angry gestures, but to no avail. Of course, when they finally did emerge from the water, their white underpants were soaking wet and had become transparent, leaving absolutely nothing to the imagination, much to the delight of the young girls in their early teens who were gathered within the crowd. They broke into helpless giggles, and who could blame them! By then police reinforcements had arrived and the show was over; they were soon bundled into a paddy waggon.

Why Las Palmas had become a popular holiday rendezvous was obvious, with such a good climate and posh hotels and restaurants it was extremely attractive, and a complete contrast from the Latin Americas we had recently left behind.

After a further discharge of timber, we cast off on Sunday afternoon, heading for Vigo in Northern Spain where we arrived on Thursday 4th December. There was no delay going alongside to discharge more of the timber. It looked a nice place with all its high-rise buildings and skyscrapers. After nature's green jungle, that by contrast was a jungle made of concrete, bustling with the activities of immense trade and commerce. Its inhabitants drove their cars enjoying the comparative wealth it brings like in most of our westernized countries.

It was in complete contrast to the inhabitants of the jungles of Central America who picked out a meagre living however and whenever they could, and whose children ran naked in the mud and stench. It was as though over the last few weeks we had visited two entirely different planets. We sailed the next day.

The Bay of Biscay behaved itself, which was not bad for the time of the year, but the cold increased. On into the English Channel we glided heading for Rotterdam in Holland with the cottonseed. "Here we go again," I thought, as the White Cliffs of Dover came up on our port side. I began to have misgivings that, if we picked up another cargo in Rotterdam and were sent out again, as had happened on more than one occasion in the past, that could be as close as I would get to England and home, and being home for Christmas would be another false promise.

My fears, as it turned out, were unfounded as on arrival, everyone was given a choice. Upon the discharge of the cottonseed, a cargo for the UK was to be loaded and we could re-sign to do the home trade run or we could be paid off and flown home to London. That was further proof of the immense changes that had taken place during my absence. In those earlier years, we never had that option.

I was undecided for a while as, what little leave I had would end just a few days before Christmas. On the other hand, there was no guarantee that the next cargo would be loaded in time to get us home for the festivities. Finally, I decided to pay off as I would then have more control over my own destiny.

The Pilot guided us up the river Maas where we were swallowed up in the vast complex network of docks that makes Rotterdam one of the busiest ports in Europe, and we finished tying up at 9.00pm. The Skipper then requested a list of names of all those who wished to pay off, and later the following day everyone, with the exception of Paddy who had decided to stay aboard, received their payslips. The bus arrived early afternoon to transport us to the airport where our luggage was seen to by the airport staff.

Once we had received our tickets and passed through the customs, it was time then for a couple of beers in the lounge. They were needed, as I was about to add another experience to my list. It was to be my first flight and I had been looking forward to it with a certain amount of trepidation and apprehension so those couple of beers were most welcome.

At 3.30pm we boarded the plane, which had been chartered from British Air Ferries and I was determined to grab a window seat. I held my breath as we taxied to the end of the runway where the air hostess went through the ritual safety regulations, which I found to be somewhat amusing.

We were held at the end of the runway for several minutes until within seconds, with the engines on full power, we hurtled along ever faster and faster and suddenly we were airborne. The ground fell away, and with my nose pressed flat against the window, I looked down to see the pattern of the fields become criss-crossed, so too did the roads with miniature cars, which crawled along at what appeared to be almost a snail's pace.

After we crossed the coastline, I could see the sea below us with tiny ships trailing a silver wake. I found that it was extremely enjoyable until we flew into a cloudbank in which we remained until the seat belt sign was illuminated and my ears began to pop as we descended through the cloud.

As we emerged once again into daylight, there below us was the English coastline with a river that cut its way through the land like a giant snake into the distance. There was little or no sensation of descending other than the trees and houses getting bigger, and before we knew it, we were taxiing along the runway at Southend airport just one hour after taking off.

In reception, a company rep was there to pay us off. We picked up our cases and one by one, we passed through customs. Putting the cases onto a trolley, we made our way to the car park where there was a bus waiting to take everyone to London to be dropped at our various stations.

I was lucky again; the Birmingham train at Euston was about to depart as I arrived. That was in the days when trains ran on time and it was the second time in my career that I had been paid off on the 10th December with just ten days leave, the other being on my return from the 'British Trader' some nine years earlier. I took a taxi from New Street station and was home by 9.00pm, determined to stay at home over the Christmas holiday.

CHAPTER TWENTY-FIVE

THE WESTBURY / ONE

(Of a New Friend, the End of a War and a Heart Breaking Show).

During my leave, both Margaret and I caught the Asian flu and I finally went to the doctor on Wednesday 17th December. He gave me a doctor's note that I sent down to Falmouth. We both felt quite ill so we spent a quiet Christmas together and hardly moved out of the house. It was not the happy Christmas I had been looking forward to. The flu took a lot of shaking off but by Wednesday 31st, New Year's Eve, I felt well enough to write to Falmouth to let them know that I was fit for work.

On Monday 5th January 1970, I received a telephone call from Falmouth, which asked me if I was interested in a job on the '*British Beech*' in Swansea. Although I favoured tankers, I thought I might get a couple of extra days at home by replying that on that occasion I would prefer a cargo boat.

The clerk said that he would keep me in mind and the following day he rang back to see if I would like the '*Westbury*,' one of the Holder Brothers ships, which was moored in Tilbury. I felt that I couldn't refuse again, and as I was familiar with the journey down and the Pool at Tilbury where I had re-registered, I accepted and was told to report to Tilbury on Thursday 8th January.

That Thursday morning Margaret again came with me as far as Birmingham New Street to see me off. It was freezing cold and there was no heating in the carriage so I sat and shivered all the way to Euston. On our arrival, I found that I had been sitting in the only carriage on the train that had no heating. "How bloody typical," I thought.

Once at Euston, I got a taxi to Fenchurch Street; finances by then were a little easier. I had to wait twenty minutes for my connection to Tilbury, and I arrived there at the Tilbury Pool at 10.45am. At the desk I introduced myself and said that I had been sent from Falmouth for the '*Westbury*.' The clerk said, "Oh, there are two more of your lads here," and pointed out two guys who stood further up the counter. We introduced ourselves. One was a chap named Terry from Falmouth, and the other was named Bent, a Danish chap who was married to a Cornish girl and lived in Polruan. We called him Ben.

As usual, I had to go to pay my union dues before I returned for my medical. After I had passed that, I received my Pool forms etc, my Pool pay and rail fare from Falmouth. As I had only travelled from Birmingham, I didn't complain. A taxi was ordered and paid for by the Pool to take us to the ship. On our arrival at the docks, the driver actually dropped us off at the foot of the gangway to the ship. We went onboard to find our accommodation, and I had a quick look at her, she looked really nice.

Our quarters were all amidships, which made a nice change from the rather cramped quarters that I had always been used to right down aft on all the other cargo boats I had previously been on. What's more, all the cabins were single berths with Formica bulkheads and thick lino on the decks. It looked by far the most comfortable cargo boat that I had ever been on; only the large tankers' accommodation came anywhere near.

After we had chosen our cabins, we made our way along the passageway and into the large crew's recreation room where we signed on. I then had to go up top, to one of the officers' cabins where I saw another doctor who gave me a yellow fever inoculation, which didn't please me much at all. I then got settled into my cabin.

After tea, the three of us went ashore to the seamen's mission for a drink, a game of snooker and to watch television before we returned to the ship. We were turned to at nine o'clock the next morning to get the ship ready for sea.

The loading had been finished and the hatches were already battened down. The derricks had been lowered but we had to stow the gear away while the dockers used the shore cranes to load the deck cargo, which consisted of half a dozen big lorries, some giant breakdown trucks and one large petrol tanker. There was hardly any room at all to walk by the time they were finished.

We were told that we were going down the west coast of Africa. Lagos was one of the ports that I felt apprehensive about as the Biafran war was still going on. One of the lads said that we would be on double pay for the whole time we were in the war zone. Even if that were true, I felt that it could compensate for nothing after I had seen the pictures of starving children on the television.

It was midday on Saturday 10th January when we set sail, and it rained all the time we negotiated the lock to enter the river. At three o'clock we had to anchor in the river while some minor adjustments were made to the engines, and we didn't get mobile again till 7.30pm that evening when we carried on down the river and dropped the Pilot off at midnight. It was still raining as we made our way down towards the English Channel.

While I chatted with Terry the next day, he told me that his last ship had been the '*British Statesman*.' He had signed on her in Falmouth the day before I had signed on the '*Lancastrian Prince*.' I learned from him that they had paid off in Antwerp on December 20th, and the reason that they had signed off was because they had been in a collision in the river, which involved a number of ships, and the '*British Statesman*,' had come out of it with a big hole in her side. I was so glad that I had changed my mind about going on her.

We passed Ushant at 11.00pm on Sunday 11th and immediately ran into a gale in the Bay of Biscay. That meant that we had to live with an uncomfortable roll of the ship for the next few days and regularly had to check the lashings that held the lorries down to the decks to make sure that they were secure.

Forever onwards we sailed, and passed the Canary Islands at 8.00am on Friday 16th January. It was then we heard that the hostilities had ceased in Nigeria, which for us was good news although there was the occasional rumbling from the odd quarter about losing double pay. The seas calmed down, the weather got warmer and it was a lovely, clear day when we arrived in Dakar, Senegal, on Sunday evening.

There was no delay going alongside and the shore gangs came onboard as soon as we put the gangway out. We were then kept busy well into the night, setting the derricks into position, closing the hatches as they finished and making everything ready for sea.

We let go at 3.30am the next morning. The weather had become very hot and we followed the coast round for the next few days until we arrived off Tema close to Accra in Ghana at 3.00am on Friday 23rd January. We stayed at anchor till six o'clock before we went alongside. We were not given a sub at that time so I didn't go ashore at all.

The shore gangs finished unloading their share of the cargo on Sunday afternoon and we started to let go. We had singled up to one rope and a back spring at each end when, out of nowhere, a strong wind came up and within minutes a tropical storm was raging. The wind became a real problem, and it was really pelting down with rain so we had to tie up again.

It was another half an hour before we could start on our way again, and it was still raining quite heavily. Fortunately, as soon as we were out to sea, the bad weather passed over and we were in hot sunshine again.

Lagos was our next port of call, and we arrived there at 9.30am the next morning and dropped anchor. Our hearts faltered when we realised there were at least a dozen ships already there at anchor waiting to go in all loaded with essential aid for the war ravaged people. "It could be a long time, possibly weeks, before our turn to go in came around," we thought, but it turned out to be only six long, motionless days when the Pilot came out to take us alongside; thereby jumping the queue in front of many of the ships that were there before us. The reason for that soon became apparent.

As we went in on Sunday morning the 1st February, there was a continuous line of ships along the jetty at Apapa, which was opposite Lagos in the river, and we went into a space left by a ship that had just sailed. When I looked across the river, I could see the row of buoys to which we had been moored on the 'Nacella' when we had all the paint stolen and I wondered what had become of Tiny and Colossus.

The shore gangs came onboard and immediately began to unload the armoured cars out of one of the holds. It appeared that they were still a priority even though the war had finished. We were told that we may have to go out and anchor again once the armoured cars and the lorries had been discharged, but luckily for us they kept finding room on the already congested quay to stack some of our cargo.

At four o'clock in the afternoon of Monday 2nd February, we shifted ship to a place further down the quay, beyond two ships that lay astern of us. We managed to slide out into the river with no problem before we went astern till we were in position. We then eased the bow into the quay and that's where we stayed for the next half an hour, with our nose touching the quay and our stern sticking out into the river, until a tug finally arrived and pushed us alongside. It took an hour and a half to complete the move from start to finish.

Due to some strange regulations, we couldn't post any letters. The ship's agent wouldn't accept them neither would the staff at the seamen's mission. They told us that there was a law forbidding them to accept the money for the stamps so they didn't dare take the risk.

We couldn't even take the money from our own mates to post their letters for them, it all had to be done personally. Whether that was some strange anomaly resulting from the war, I do not know. We had to ask the Mate for the afternoon off on Wednesday so that we could walk the two miles to the post office to post them ourselves.

515

We set out for the post office and as we walked along the jetty a vast area of the ground was covered with one-inch long cockroaches that scurried in every direction; they were a seething mass like a moving carpet. There was no way of avoiding them and we could hear them cracking and scrunching under our feet as we walked through them.

The long days passed slowly, stinking hot with hardly a breath of air anywhere. Although there was a bar in our recreation room where we could buy as much beer as we could afford, Ben and I would sometimes walk to the seamen's mission. Once there, we would have a couple of beers and watch the open air movies that were shown every night except Tuesdays. It all helped to break the monotony but only slightly.

On Sunday 8th February, we had to shift ship again just fifty feet astern. Two days later on Tuesday, the Bosun collapsed in our recreation room. He was suffering from heatstroke, and although we tried to cool him down by rubbing ice on to him, he gradually seemed to get worse and became delirious. An ambulance was called for immediately but it didn't arrive so after half an hour of waiting, we had to take action ourselves.

We put him in a straight jacket to carry him down the gangway as he was thrashing around. It gave me yet another feeling of 'déjà vu' as we had done exactly the same thing to our Bosun on the 'Nacella,' moored to the buoys just a short distance away in that very river there in Lagos, when he had collapsed with a slipped disc.

Once on the quayside, we put him into a dockyard van and he was rushed to hospital. We later heard that the ambulance had broken down on the way but no one had bothered to let us know or call another one. The Bosun had begun to come round when they got him to the hospital but they kept him in for a few hours for observation, after which he returned to the ship. He had to return to the hospital the following day for vitamin injections but he was fine after that.

For a couple of weeks the rest of the crew seemed to take it in turns to go down with upset stomachs and a lot of them had the trots, but like the Asian Flu on that other previous occasion in Lagos, it missed me altogether thank goodness. Two of the engineers also came down with heatstroke but not nearly as severely as the Bosun, and they soon recovered.

On our outward journey one of the EDHs had his leg cut open on a piece of wire and the Skipper himself had put six stitches in it so he was laid up for a while. He recovered enough to turn to while we were alongside, and after a couple of days, while lifting off a ventilator; he dropped it on his foot. That broke his big toe and laid him up for the rest of the trip. It put me in mind of the torrid trip that I had had on the '*Trevose*.' On the one hand, I felt sorry for him but on the other, I was glad in one way that it was at long last, someone else's turn.

Finally at 6.00am on Sunday 15th February, after being alongside for over two weeks, we began to shift ship across to Lagos. It took us till 9.15am to tie up again. At midday we shifted again farther up the jetty and yet again it took till seven o'clock that evening before they were satisfied that we were securely moored.

The following Wednesday night, all the cargo was finally discharged and we sailed at 6.00am the next morning, Thursday 19th February. It felt great to be on the move again, but it was not for long as we only went a little further along the coast. We arrived off the bar of the river Niger at four o'clock that afternoon. We nosed our way slowly through the buoyed channel till we came to the entrance of the river and the pilotage.

A large number of natives came out to us in dug out canoes and began shouting up to the ship at the same time. I couldn't tell what they were shouting, but it appeared that they were each after the job to pilot us up the creeks. Amid cries of disappointment from the others, the Skipper picked out one canoe, and the chap came onboard along with two boys whose job it was to take over the steering of the ship up the river under his guidance. That pleased me no end as one of the two-hour stints at the wheel would have been mine.

We all thought that the Biafran war had been over for more than two weeks, but before we knew what was happening, some jungle soldiers came onboard, they all carried rifles over their shoulders and silently searched all our cabins. They didn't ask permission to do it but just took it for granted that no one would challenge them and as they looked extremely menacing with their guns, no one did. It was so unexpected it took us all by surprise and we never did learn what or who they were looking for. After they had gone, we moved about a mile up the river to where it began to narrow, and there we anchored for the night.

Soon there were dozens of natives who seemed to appear out of nowhere to arrive at the ship's side in little boats. A few of the crew, for some strange reason began to throw old rubbish into the water, things like empty tin cans, old rags etc. The natives dived in and jumped all over each other as they pushed, shouted and splashed around in a frantic scramble to retrieve them.

They gave proof to the old adage that 'One man's rubbish is another man's treasure.' The war perhaps had robbed them of everything they had, as little as that probably was in the first place, and those items of rubbish seemed to have great value to them. They did seem to have some kind of a gentleman's agreement between them that the first person to get hold of any item had the right to claim it as his own, and the others would climb back into their boats and wait for something else to be thrown down.

Unfortunately that agreement broke down when one of the engineers threw an old woollen pullover down into the water, it immediately became water logged and swiftly began to sink. When they saw what it was, there were shouts, screams and cries of expectation, then began a frantic scramble as they all went into the water to retrieve it.

Two of the boys appeared to grab a different sleeve at the same time, and that began an almighty tug of war. Neither would give in to the other as they pulled and tugged at it in the water. They both somehow managed to get back into their respective canoes still holding on to a sleeve each, and the battle continued like a tug of war contest. They shouted abuse at each other, they even tried to throw punches at each other without letting go of it. That went on for a good half hour until one of them finally managed to pull it away from the other. It was by then twice as big as it was originally, and I thought the loser was going to jump from one canoe to the other to get at the winners throat, but some of the others restrained him and managed to calm him down.

I personally felt that I had witnessed a terrible, heart-rending, spectacle. For people to become so poverty stricken and desperate that an empty tin can or an old jumper were prize possessions to be fought over was very sad indeed. There but for the grace of God go I.

* * *

At daybreak we set sail and started up the river. I'm sure that at some point, we must have left the main river and entered into some creeks as the waterway got very narrow, and we had to manoeuvre round some very sharp U bends. There was thick jungle on both sides, and on some of the bends we had to put the bow of the ship right up to the banks and slide round, breaking branches off the trees as we went. I'm glad it was those native boys at the wheel and not me.

We had all been warned to watch out for mango flies and other creepy-crawlies as some of them could lay their eggs under your skin, but although there were plenty of them about, no one got bitten.

In isolated spots along the banks, there were occasional little clearings where a couple of mud huts with thatched, vegetation roofs had been built. There were usually a handful of natives hanging around, some in canoes; both men and women with nothing on except for a cloth, more like a rag really, around their middles. They too were waiting I supposed for anything that may be thrown down from the ship.

Finally we came to a large clearing that looked full of dirt and mud with hundreds of little wooden shacks sprawled about everywhere. It looked like one huge 'tat' yard, but in fact it was the town of Sapele. By contrast, just a little further on along the banks of the creek, we could see the great big houses and luxury bungalows with big gardens and lush green lawns that rolled down to the water's edge where we assumed the European bosses of the timber factory lived.

We turned off into a cutting where there were massive rafts of logs floating around. There were also hundreds of single ones floating around too, one of which we hit with our propeller. Fortunately no damage was done.

It was just before one o'clock that afternoon when we tied up to the wharf by the side of the timber mill. For the whole duration of our stay so far, up the creeks and in the middle of the jungle, the temperature never dropped below 102° Fahrenheit. Indeed, sometimes it was as high as 110°, add to that the humidity and it was murder; We could hardly breathe it was so hot.

We were given salt tablets daily to prevent dehydration and replace the body salts we lost every minute of the day as we sweated profusely. I couldn't ever remember being so hot and uncomfortable in my entire life, even up the Persian Gulf. It was the steamy humidity of the surrounding jungle that did it; it drained every last ounce of energy from our bodies so that it became an effort just to move. How we got through our work every day I just don't know; the iced water machine in the alleyway had never been so totally overworked.

The local workers started loading some dressed timber from the quayside into both number one and five holds. In numbers two, three and four holds they began to load giant logs, which in reality were portions of huge tree trunks. They were loaded from our outboard side, and as they were floated along they were tied together with a wire stapled to each one. They looked like massive rafts, sometimes two or three hundred feet long.

The workers lowered the wire runner from our derricks, down to where others were standing on the logs in the water. They then passed a wire strop under and around each log then shackled our runner to it. When the derrick tightened up just enough to take the weight, the staple was hammered out and one by one the logs were lifted up over the side of the ship and down into the holds. The days passed slowly like that and, despite the incessant heat, we still worked, either painting or rigging up some gear for the dockers when and where they wanted it.

Each day was as hot and humid as the last; there was no respite. At night our cabins were so hot we were lucky if we managed to get a couple of hours sleep. We all felt completely drained and exhausted as we continued each day to work for eight to ten hours. The strength just ebbed away from our bodies with rivers of sweat running down to the decks, only to evaporate on the heat of the steel. We couldn't even break the monotony by going ashore. There was nowhere to go so the company got large chunks of our wages back from the amount of beer that was sold in our recreation room when the day's work was complete.

A large number of the logs had been in the water for so long they had become waterlogged and sunk to the bottom, possibly due to delays that the war would have imposed. One day we had to rig one of the derricks up with the doubling up gear so that it could lift twice the weight.

A diver went down to the riverbed, and the runner was lowered down to him. He somehow managed to shackle the logs on to it so that one by one, they were lifted out of the water and loaded on to the ship. Some of the logs were a good eight-foot in diameter and had been sawn off in sections of about eight-foot, and each one weighed in excess of ten tons. At long last, at three o'clock on Wednesday afternoon 25th February, we finally let go and moved till we were just out of the cutting and tied up to some buoys in the main stream.

It wasn't any cooler, but the very fact that we had made a move made us feel a little better; at least it had broken the pattern of those long days. Only five days in all, but in that unbearable heat and humidity, it had seemed more like five weeks.

The loading continued until the early hours of Saturday 28th February when the last log came onboard. We secured everything ready for sea and finally sailed at 9.00am that morning. It was the same performance again going down the river as we nosed up to the banks and slid round the hairpin bends. Finally we arrived safely at the river bar at 4.00pm and anchored for a while to allow the tide to come in to give us enough depth in the water to get out. We were there all night, but that time there were no natives in their canoes waiting to dive in after tin cans.

It was ten o'clock the next morning before we set sail: the date was Sunday 1st March. It was still very hot but it felt so good to be out into the open sea once more. It felt as if we had been holding our breath for days in the heat and humidity of the jungle, and we could at last fill our lungs with fresh air again.

That night I went to call the Second Mate at 11.40pm to get ready for his midnight watch, and I found him lying on the deck in his cabin looking very ill. I thought it was ironic that he had endured all that time up the creeks with no ill effect only to come down with heat exhaustion as soon as we were clear. No one knew how long he had lain there like that. I went to inform the Chief Steward who came to look at him. The Skipper had to do his watch for him, but within a couple of days he had fully recovered.

Two days later at 3.00am on Tuesday 3rd March, we arrived and anchored off Abidjan on the Ivory Coast (Côte D' Ivoire). We remained at anchor all day, going in and tying up to some buoys at 5.30pm that afternoon. More logs were then floated down for us to load.

We were at the buoys till 8.30am on Friday 6th March when we let go to shift ship alongside the jetty. The jetty had a long line of ships all along it except for one space in the middle where we were to go. We sailed slowly past it and then tried to turn inwards towards the gap. The idea was that we should turn completely round to go alongside with our starboard side to the jetty.

I don't know if the Pilot misjudged it or what but it was soon pretty obvious to those of us who were standing at stations on the bow that we were not going to make our complete turn as our bow headed straight towards one of the ships. We were moving pretty fast, and I thought we were going to hit her right amidships. I remembered how easily the steel apron had seemed to rip on the bow of the 'British Guardsman' in a similar situation, so I stood well back. They put the engines in reverse and gave them as much power as they possibly could get until the whole ship was vibrating violently. We finally stopped about three feet away from her and gradually began to back away.

There was a man on a paint stage, painting the side of his ship, who seemed so engrossed in his work that he was totally oblivious to what was happening right over his shoulder. The Mate shouted down to him and when he turned and saw how close we were to him, a look of complete horror and amazement spread over his face. He must have had the fright of his life. I can imagine how he felt painting merrily away, and suddenly turning round to see the bow of a ship just a couple of feet away from the back of his neck.

He tried frantically to untie his lifeline, but he was so panicked he couldn't; he must have been so relieved when we began to slide away from him. Finally he got loose and scrambled up his rope ladder like a spider in his web. I remembered vividly how I had felt with my encounters with both the hammerhead shark and the giant lizard, and I felt for certain that he was at that moment searching for some paper. We eventually completed our turn and went alongside with no further mishaps.

The following day, Saturday 7th March, we shifted ship at midday as another ship had moved out. We moved just seventy feet up the jetty. As the dockers finished topping off the holds that evening, we battened them down.

Throughout the night the loading continued with more logs being placed on our decks; they left just enough room between them and the hatch to be able to walk through. Finally we were finished in the early hours of Sunday morning, 8th March, and we were all called to let go at 5.30am. We moved off the jetty out into the bay and tied up to a buoy with a couple of ropes from our bow so that we were just swinging from it.

We then had all sixteen derricks to lower and secure, and all the logs had to be lashed down with chains and bottle screws before we could venture out to sea. The Mate said he didn't care how long it took, but the sooner it was all done the sooner we could be on our way home.

It was 2.30pm when we sailed, and although it was still hot for the first two or three days, there was a most welcome light breeze blowing. As we got further north, it gradually began to cool down. We continued northwards and arrived off Las Palmas at 7.30pm Saturday 14th March.

The Pilot came out and we went in through the breakwater and slid alongside the first jetty for bunkers. The bumboats arrived and the Bosun bought a load of dolls while the lads got a supply of Bacardi rum in. No one went ashore and as soon as both the ship and crew had taken bunkers, we were on our way again. It was 2.30am on the morning of Sunday 15th March.

All the way home we had the big job of painting and cleaning everything so that the ship would look nice and clean on arrival back in Tilbury. Soon after leaving Las Palmas, we ran into a heavy swell and began to roll a little so we had to constantly check the chains holding the logs to make sure they were taking the strain, although what we could have done if one had broken loose I don't know.

Surprisingly once we got into the Bay of Biscay, the swell calmed down a little and we passed Ushant at 1.30pm on the afternoon of Thursday 19th March and continued into the English Channel. A cold wind was blowing, but the sun was shining and it was quite warm when we were sheltered from the wind. As we got nearer to Dover, we ran into a thick bank of fog that forced us to reduce speed, and we began to blow our whistle.

After a little while we began to get an answering whistle from astern of us and it was coming closer all the time. Suddenly a large tanker loomed up out of the fog and sped past us on our port side much too close for comfort and travelling at full speed. Within minutes it had disappeared into the fog ahead of us. We continued at slow speed until the fog cleared.

The Pilot was picked up at Folkestone and as we got into the Thames Estuary, we could see the tanker stuck at anchor so all his speeding through the fog hadn't done him much good. Fortunately for us, we didn't have to anchor and we carried on up the river to Tilbury where we turned off into the lock. Once through, the tugs helped us round to our berth and we tied up alongside. That was us finished. It was 11.45pm on Friday 20th March.

We all showered and turned in for the night and next morning, dressed in our best gear, we packed our belongings and waited for pay off. The officers informed us that the next voyage was to New Zealand and back and that the ship would be away for four and a half months. The sailing date was April 16th and we were all asked if we wanted to come back to sign on for that trip. A quick calculation worked out that it was only March 21st, and I had ten days leave so, by agreeing to return, I could possibly have an extra couple of weeks at home so I agreed and everyone else did too.

We were paid off just after 10.00am, and we all piled into taxis that were waiting for us. I was dropped off at Euston station where, unbelievably, again I walked right onto my train and was soon on my way back home to enjoy my leave. Margaret was delighted that I had some extra time at home.

CHAPTER TWENTY-SIX
THE WESTBURY / TWO
(Of an Ill Friend's Return, a Return to Pitcairn and
a Lot of Girls).

As always, the time passed so quickly and just before we were due to go back, Ben rang me from Cornwall to find out if I had heard anything from the company yet. I told him that I hadn't so he volunteered to ring the company in London the following day to ask them what was happening.

I was pleased to know that he was taking such an interest in returning to the ship, especially after my experience on the '*Lancastrian Prince*' when everyone had said they would return but no one did. Ben had so badly wanted to learn how to play cribbage, and he used to come into my cabin almost every spare minute to play a few hands.

I rang him back the next day and he said that he had been told not to worry as they hadn't forgotten us, and indeed they hadn't. On Monday 13th April, I received two telegrams at the same time. The one told me to report to the ship in the Royal Albert Dock in London on Thursday 16th April, and the other said that the signing on was delayed twenty-four hours and I was to report on Friday 17th April.

Margaret came to see me off at Walsall station and once again I was on my way. I changed trains at Birmingham then travelled on to Euston where I got a taxi back to the ship. I arrived just after eleven and was the last of the deck crew to sign on, which I did right away and settled back into my cabin. Only two of the original seven had not returned so we had two new ABs and an extra deck boy.

The company paid us all our travel expenses, for which I was very grateful, and I wasn't too surprised to discover that the cargo was still being loaded. It was mainly engines and spare parts for cars and other machinery.

A small piece of information that went around the ship at the time was that those giant segments of tree trunks that had been discharged at Tilbury, particularly the waterlogged ones, would have to be stored in the timber yard to dry out and season for anything up to a hundred years before the timber could be used. Who on earth would buy timber that could not be used for a hundred years? This was the question that came to my mind so how much truth there was in that tale I don't know.

The loading wasn't completed till the following Tuesday 21st April, which I wasn't best pleased about, as I could quite easily have had an extra weekend at home. The last two things to come onboard were, believe it or not, two racehorses. They were both brown and were named Colours Flying and Eden Valley. It wasn't my job to look after them on that occasion as that had been delegated to the two officer cadets. I felt really sorry for those horses as they were going all the way to New Zealand and would be cooped up for five weeks.

We sailed later that night and the following day as we travelled down the English Channel, Ben began to complain of a stiff neck. We all assumed it was nothing more than the usual bit of stiffness that would right itself in a day or so, but it didn't. It continued to get worse until he could hardly move his neck at all, and by the time we were out into the Atlantic Ocean, he was in terrible pain. None of the pills or drugs that he was given seemed to have any effect on him so eventually the Skipper got in touch with the radio doctor who, after hearing the symptoms, diagnosed possible mastoids and recommended that he should receive immediate treatment.

The company were then contacted by radio to gain permission to divert to the Azores to enable Ben to get the treatment he needed. The company made all the arrangements with a hospital in the Azores so that Ben was expected. The Skipper came down to Ben's cabin to reassure him that he would be looked after till he was well enough to work again, which I thought was nice.

His wife was also contacted and given the full facts to alleviate any concerns she might have. "How things had changed" was my immediate thought. The Skipper told Ben that if he was well enough in time, he could be flown from the Azores to New York and from there to the Panama to rejoin the ship when we arrived, or alternatively he could be flown home. Ben agreed that he would like to rejoin the ship if that was at all possible.

I thought what a good company Holder Brothers were. I couldn't help but compare the treatment Ben had received to how I was treated when I had dysentery. I helped him pack his gear so that he was ready to leave when we arrived off Delgada, on the Island of San Miguel, on the afternoon of Sunday 26th April.

After we eased our way in towards the port, the Pilot came out and guided us in just a little nearer to the breakwater where we anchored. The boat didn't come out till just after tea. Ben only took the gear with him that he thought he would need and left the rest in his cabin. I told him that if he didn't return to the ship I would look after his belongings and take it down to Polruan when we returned to England. I wished him luck as he struggled down the gangway into the boat and headed off towards the shore.

We weighed anchor and continued on our way. As the days passed it got really hot, the horses began to sweat a little, and the two lads had to work really hard to care for them. We were kept busy too, taking the blocks from the derricks. We had to take them apart, clean, oil and grease them before putting them back together and shackling them back on to the derricks. We also had to overhaul all the ship's working gear that badly needed doing. I was in the eight to twelve watch and worked twelve hours a day, seven days a week.

Finally we passed through the islands and into the Caribbean, arriving in Curacao just before midnight on Monday May 4th. I had to take the wheel when the Pilot came aboard and we went in alongside a tanker jetty for bunkers.

The ship's agent came onboard with our letters and seemed surprised when he was asked what was going to happen to the one hundred and five mailbags that we had in number four hold which were destined for the island. He said he didn't know anything about them and had to dash ashore to rouse the postal authorities out of their beds who then had to send a lorry to us. As there were no dockers available at that time of night we had to discharge them ourselves before we could turn in.

Our heads had hardly touched our pillows before we were called again to let go and set sail. It was four o'clock in the morning on Tuesday 5th May. At seven we carried on overhauling more blocks all day and I still had my eight to twelve watch to do that night.

Upon our arrival off Cristobal, Panama, just after midday on Thursday 7th May, we anchored and I was pleased to see Ben's smiling face as he came back onboard later that afternoon. He told us that he'd had an inflamed muscle in his neck, which had needed fast treatment. If he hadn't had the treatment when he did, it could have affected his nervous system and could have eventually caused paralysis in part of his body. It was good to know that he was OK again. The company had paid all his medical expenses and for his flight to return to the ship.

He said that the American authorities in New York didn't know how to deal with him and scratched their heads in confusion. They couldn't seem to understand how a Dane could have a British Seamen's documents, and they didn't know how to fill in their forms. They wouldn't allow him out of the airport and it was twenty-six hours before he got his connection to Panama. On his arrival, they had put him up in an old building which he had felt sure was an old prison of some kind. The rooms were cold and dank with water running down the walls. He had to wait there for three days until we arrived. As usual, there were those amongst us who couldn't understand it when he said that he was glad to be back even though most of them had recently resigned themselves.

We picked up some mail and some fifty-gallon drums of kerosine for Pitcairn Island of all places. Immediately my memory jumped back nine years to when I had called there on the 'Cape Grafton' for their mail and had spilled both the islanders and their mail into the drink. All those years later, I was going to reverse the reason for calling by taking their mail to them.

Just after five o'clock, we weighed anchor and slowly headed into the canal. Naturally, when it came to my turn at the wheel we were in the narrowest part. A little while later we began to develop engine trouble.

It would sometimes take three or four attempts before it would start when the Pilot wanted to manoeuvre the ship.

He wouldn't risk going through the last lock so we tied up alongside on the approach to it to enable our engineers to sort out the problem. It didn't take them long and we were soon on our way again, through the last lock and out into the Pacific by 2.30am on the morning of Friday 8th May.

* * *

At first the weather seemed to cool down a little, then it rallied in an attempt to pick up, then it finally gave up and cooled down for good. After ten days of being completely alone on the ocean, a tiny speck of land appeared on the horizon ahead of us. That I imagined would be just how those mutineers on the 'Bounty' all those years ago would have first sighted it after months of searching.

Just a couple of hours later we arrived off Pitcairn. We went in till we were about three quarters of a mile off Adamstown, the only town on the island and we hove to as before since the water was too deep to anchor. The island itself, as far as I could remember, hadn't altered much in the past nine years. It was a little after 4.00pm on Monday 18th May and it was full daylight so we had no problem seeing them as they came out to us in their boats. There would have been no excuse if anything had gone wrong that time.

The islanders clambered onboard carrying their large baskets of fruit and bananas with them. They also still had postcards of the island and postage stamps, which they franked for you if you purchased them, as well as all sorts of little knick-knacks and wooden carvings that they still sold as souvenirs. Indeed nothing had changed.

Apart from the mail and the kerosine, we had four boxes in our cargo for them, but I had no idea what they contained. As soon as the islanders were ready for them, we lowered them down into their boats and we took on their mail (safely this time), which we were to take on to New Zealand. We also picked up five passengers, a man named Purvis Young, his wife, and their two children. They were a boy aged about fourteen and a girl around ten years old. The other passenger was the wife's grandfather.

As soon as they were all onboard, the Skipper blew the whistle for everyone else to get off, which they did by climbing back down into their boats. They only went a short distance away and formed a little ark on our port side. Then they all began to sing a song dedicated, I imagine, to the old man. That was immediately followed by another song, which, although I couldn't quite make out the words, I felt they were singing a song of goodbye to the ship.

The old man stood motionless at the rail of the ship silently listening to them with a tear in his eye, and as the last strains of their voices fell away, he lifted both arms up into the air in a salute to them and they all cheered him like mad. It was a heart-rending, emotional moment. They must have thought the world of him as he was at that moment in time the oldest inhabitant on the island and the nearest link to their history. His name was Parkin Christian, and he was a direct descendant of Fletcher Christian of the 'Bounty' and the mutineers. Parkin was the grandson of a number of generations.

As the engines started and we began to move, I saw him turn away with sadness in his eyes. I wondered if he thought he might never see his beloved island or its people again as he was going to hospital in New Zealand. He had an ulcerated leg and there were fears that it may have to be amputated. He spent most of the journey in the little hospital cabin up on the bridge.

The island soon disappeared from sight, and in the days that followed, Purvis and sometimes his wife, came down to our recreation room in the evenings for a chat. He told us quite a lot about their life on the island at that time. He told us that he was the magistrate for the island, but he didn't have much to do in that respect except settle the occasional petty squabble that arose from time to time. He had six months leave due to him, which he was going to spend in New Zealand with his family.

The islanders he said, generally rose around 5.00am and turned in about midnight. When asked what they did with themselves all day he replied that they tended to their gardens, grew vegetables and fruit for their own use as well as for export. Also, there was a high demand for their little wooden carvings of flying fish so that too kept them busy. They built and maintained their own houses and the number of ships that called in had increased dramatically over the recent years so that at that present time, one called in on average once a week. "There is always plenty to do," he said.

In the early nineteen sixties there were around one hundred and forty inhabitants on the island but ten years on it had fallen to just over eighty. That was mainly due to the young people who, when they came of age, wanted to go out and explore the wider world and so drifted off, mostly to Australia or New Zealand as soon as they could.

All meetings were then held in a large communal hall that was also used for film shows and games etc. There were no animals native to the island, although some years previously someone had imported some goats, but they were then running wild so they didn't attempt to harvest their milk.

There wasn't enough water to keep sheep or cattle, but there was a regular supply of fresh milk and meat shipped in from New Zealand. That was stored in large, communal fridges until it was needed. The same ships also brought their films. They had a large diesel generator that supplied power for the radios and their electricity but it was closed down at night, and then they used the kerosine lamps.

The olden time English they sometimes spoke had almost vanished as they had built a school for their children. The teacher came from New Zealand on a two-year contract after which he was relieved. They also had a State Registered Nurse so, although the outward appearance of the island hadn't changed much, the life style of the inhabitants had altered immensely, and for the better in his view.

They didn't have chickens for they had found it very difficult to keep them; every year they caught some kind of disease and died. There were also a lot of turtles and sharks, which they would catch. The islanders owned two tractors and two small jeeps.

Pitcairn he told us, was approximately two miles long and around a mile and a half wide, and is over several hundred miles from the nearest inhabited islands. It rises to a height of a thousand feet and the people have built a little road winding round up to the top. It was he informed us, the only road on the island and is just two miles long. Purvis also told us that quite a lot of the people were the proud owners of small Honda motorcycles, in fact his wife had owned one for two years and it already had six thousand miles on the clock. I guess she must have been up and down that road a few times.

I found all of that very fascinating and asked him if there were many outsiders on the island. He said there were nine at that moment in time, mostly Americans. "That figures," I thought, "They seemed to get everywhere." On impulse, I asked him "If, when I left the Merchant Navy, could I bring my wife and come and live on his island?" He told me we would be welcome, but I guess I knew what Margaret would think of that idea.

One night I asked him if he remembered the incident about nine years earlier when a ship called into Pitcairn and capsized one of their boats. His eyes widened in surprise as he looked at me. His wife immediately broke in saying "Yes! The 'Cape Grafton.'" Purvis then said that he remembered it well. Not quite sure what his reaction would be, I told him that I was on that ship, "and I was on that boat," he retorted.

As I had thought at the time, the incident would be the main topic of conversation on the island for a long time and he confirmed it. "It wasn't a very pleasant experience for us, but we could laugh about it afterwards," he informed me.

I told them that this was the first time I had been back to Pitcairn since then and I wasn't sure if I would be welcome. They laughed at that and Purvis explained how they had managed to save the boat by towing it upside down in the water, round to the leeward side of the island where they hauled it up onto the shore. They mended it, cleaned it and made it seaworthy again.

Astonishingly enough, considering the depth of the water, they had also managed to retrieve some of the mailbags by dragging hooks on the end of extremely long ropes along the bottom, but the seawater had destroyed their letters and most of their contents. Some of the items lost were of value and the company had to compensate them for it. I was pleased to have experienced the sequel to that little story and to have learned the outcome of that incident of so long ago.

Again days followed days. Purvis's son came out most days to work on deck, and he took to it as if he had been doing it all his life, not surprising for a boy with his family history. First we had a spell where a cold wind blew, then it got a little warmer for a while, then the biting cold wind came back, which built up to almost gale force. The seas developed heavy swells and brought our speed down to fourteen knots. I was glad that the weather had, for the most part, remained cool for the horses' sake. I don't know how they would have fared, being cooped up like they were for such a long spell if the weather had been sweltering hot.

At midnight on Monday 25th May, we crossed the International Date Line so our time moved forward twenty-four hours, which made the next day Wednesday 27th May. I felt sorry for Purvis and his wife as Tuesday 26th May was their fifteenth wedding anniversary, and they missed it.

The weather and seas calmed down a little for the last couple of days so we were able to put the ship on maximum revs, and soon we were doing sixteen knots. Finally we arrived at the Wellington pilot station on Friday morning where we had to hang around a little while for the Pilot. When he arrived, he took us in through the entrance and alongside our berth. It was my turn at the wheel, and I was kept up there till we were all tied up and the gangway was put out.

The Third Mate came running into the wheelhouse from the wing of the bridge and exclaimed "Captain, there's a load of girls just come onboard!" The Skipper looked at him for a moment then just said," Well, if the girls are onboard, I know where the men will be when I want them.

I had finished my eight to twelve watch and still had to work through the afternoon. I had also been informed that I was nightwatchman for the first week, which meant that yet again, I had to be on duty from 8.00am one day through to 7.00am the next; I was really shattered.

Some of the girls came onboard just to party and have a good time and went home each night. Others stayed and were all paired off by the time I was finished. Just as well really as I was a happily married man.

* * *

A gang of dockers arrived almost immediately to take off the horses and some of the deck cargo. There was a lot of noise being generated from their activities, and despite having been on duty for twenty-three hours, I was frequently disturbed and woken up. I gave up trying to sleep and got up at twelve, had lunch and decided to go for a walk ashore to stretch my legs after being stuck onboard for over five weeks. It was an odds on bet, under sod's law, that the noisy dockers would knock off before I went, and they did. I walked all the way around town even though there was hardly anything open, and I got back onboard just after four. That gave me chance to grab another couple of hours sleep before it was time to go on watch again.

The dockers didn't work on Sundays and as Monday was an official holiday on shore, all the docks were quiet again. Along the same quay to which we were berthed, there were two German ships and a Japanese; they all observed the holiday. We were the only ones working, which was ironic really and says something about our British working mentality. The holiday was in celebration of our Queen's Coronation Day.

At 5.30am on Tuesday 2nd June, I had to call all hands to shift ship further up the quayside. The dockers held a meeting during the morning, and it was well into the afternoon before they began work. The bottom step on our gangway was broken so they refused to come up it until it was mended. All that posturing meant that they only did about an hour's work before knocking off time.

That evening it started to rain. It poured down all through the night and all next day. The dockers didn't work in the rain; they said they needed protective clothing, so a makeshift shelter was put up on the quay in which were hung a number of oilskin coats, but they then said they would get wet going to fetch them so nothing was done till the rain stopped.

It finally stopped at 5.00am on Thursday so at last they managed to discharge something. I got up at midday and went ashore again. Everything was open and in full swing that time, and I quite enjoyed myself just browsing around.

That night it started to rain again and from then on, whenever it rained during the day, the dockers knocked off and sheltered in our communal accommodation; sometimes they only worked for an hour here or a couple of hours there between the showers.

As we were due to return to Wellington before we were to begin the journey home, we all clubbed together to hire a television set to take around the coast; it was installed in our recreation room. Thursday night was my last night as nightwatchman and it felt good to get back to normal again.

The dockers not only stopped work in the rain but also held lots of meetings that lasted for hours. They were in dispute with the Harbour Authorities who, they claimed, owed them thirteen months back pay. We never knew the actual facts on how the phenomenon had occurred. They had taken the authorities to court over it and were waiting to hear the outcome before they decided what further action to take. Despite all of that, the work gradually moved ahead until Saturday 13th June when the discharge of Wellington's share of the cargo was completed during the afternoon.

We put to sea at four o'clock after we had made everything secure. It had taken sixteen days in Wellington, during which time two of our engineers had got engaged. The girls were going to come to England when we arrived home, but I don't know if they ever did. We also sailed without our Second Cook. No one knew where he had got to.

At the speed we travelled, we were due to arrive off Lyttelton, South Island at 4.30am the following morning, but we received a message on the VHF that they didn't want us there before 8.30am. Consequently we reduced speed and just cruised along slowly, allowing the Pilot onboard at 8.45am. I took over the wheel to take her in alongside, and we tied up at the jetty that was farthest from town.

We were in a lovely little bay with the town to our stern and were surrounded by beautiful, green hills and meadows with houses of various colours dotted here and there. It was really quite pleasant. I imagine it would be wonderful in the summer. Most of the girls had travelled down to rejoin the ship on its arrival.

The dockers there were much more business like. They came onboard at 7.00am on Monday 15th June, and worked right through till 6.00pm with only an hour for their dinner break. I nipped ashore that evening with Ben to post some letters and buy postcards. The town of Lyttelton itself was only a tiny place: one blink and you could have missed it type of town, but it was very pleasant.

A tunnel had been built through the mountain so that people could travel by road to the city of Christchurch, built on the Canterbury plains, seven miles away on the other side. There was also a rail link through the tunnel. We were happy enough to stay in Lyttelton so after shopping and a couple of lazy beers, we returned to the ship.

After they had discharged their share of the cargo, the dockers began loading between six and seven hundred ton of cargo into the ship. It consisted of beans, hides, wool etc. destined for the UK. It was good to see its destination written on it as it meant the company was true to its word and the trip would be, "Out to New Zealand and back again," although it was to be quite a while before we were homeward bound.

At 7.00am the next day, the work began again and as always as each hatch was finished, we had to secure everything. We were all squared up by 5.30pm and sailed at 6.00pm heading south again only to pick up the Pilot at 7.30am the next morning, Wednesday 17th June in the Otago Peninsula. We were just into the estuary at eight o'clock when I had to go up to take over the wheel.

Then followed an hour and a half of pretty tricky steering. I took my orders from the Pilot and had to guide the ship up a very narrow, winding channel right up past Port Charmers and through an extremely narrow passage between two small islands. We continued to follow the channel all around the right hand bank, and as before we had to turn the ship around, almost in its own full length until we faced back downstream and were finally able to slip alongside with the help of the tugs. It was just on 9.30am when the Pilot said "That will be it for the wheel," and I was able to go down to help my shipmates finish tying up. The girls were all already down on the quay waiting for us to put the gangway out.

The dockers didn't come onboard till 3.30pm and only worked for two hours. I took a walk ashore again that evening with Ben. Dunedin, for that is where we were, looked a really nice place, spotlessly clean as were all the places we visited in New Zealand. The main road, which cut right through the middle of the town, seemed to be one big, fantastic shopping centre with shops and supermarkets of all shapes, sizes and descriptions, which stretched along on both sides for what seemed like miles.

There were also numerous streets that cut off the main one. After a while it started to rain so we headed back to the ship. The next day we were given half a day off so I went ashore again in the afternoon to buy some toiletries and to catch the post office as I always tried to write home as much as I could to both Margaret and my parents.

As usual we squared up the derricks as each one was finished with, and the following day, Saturday 20th June, we were completed by 4.30pm; we sailed at 5.30pm. I was thankful that it wasn't my turn for the wheel that time so I didn't have to take her back down that channel. We were out into the open sea and on automatic steering by eight o'clock when I had to go up to the wheelhouse, so all I had to do was keep a lookout on the wing of the bridge.

We were headed northwards and the following afternoon saw us going through the Cook Strait, between the two islands. It was a healthy crisp, cool day, nice, bright and bracing. We could look across the clear, smooth, blue water on our port side and see the coastline of high, snow-capped mountains. Wonderful. That evening there was a beautiful bright orange and red sunset all along and above the rugged snow capped skyline of the dark mountains. A magnificent view that almost took your breath away.

We dropped anchor just after midnight in Golden Bay, right on the northeast tip of South Island, to wait for news of a berth in our next port of call. We remained there until eight o'clock on the night of Tuesday 23rd June when we heaved up anchor and continued northwards again and arrived off New Plymouth at daybreak the next morning.

As soon as the Pilot was onboard, we went in alongside where we were in for a new experience as we had to heave up great big, heavy chains almost like anchor chains from the quay and tie up with those. Only the port authorities knew the reason for that.

It was back breaking work and as soon as we were finished, one of the men on the quay shouted up, "How long are you in for?" "About six months from the look of those chains," I shouted back. He replied, "I shouldn't joke about it if I were you." "You might very well be," "Okay," I thought, "I'll keep my mouth shut in future."

There too the town was tucked away on the curve of the shoreline with little wooden bungalows and houses dotted around the surrounding green hills. Just beyond those hills were the white, snow-covered slopes of Mount Egmont that reached high into the sky. It was indeed a beautiful sight.

The loading began immediately, mostly bales of wool but there were also some large boxes of machinery destined for Cork in the Irish Republic. One box that came onboard measured about twenty-foot in height, fourteen-foot wide and eighteen-foot long. It weighed almost eight tons and we had to rig up the heavy lifting gear on hatch number two derricks, like we had in Sapele, to enable them to lift it onboard and lower it into the hold. It was a plant for a casing factory in Ireland and, I believe, that it was the first ever single export order of that size to be shipped out of New Plymouth.

We were all ready to sail again at five o'clock the next evening so we let them have their chains back and set off. We came back down through the Cook Strait during the night and into Wellington Harbour before breakfast the next morning. It was Friday 26th June.

The Pilot came out and took us directly alongside, port side to, on Aotea Quay, in exactly the same spot that we had first tied up in and we were made to triple the mooring ropes up. It seemed like a lot of hard work for nothing as the ship just sat there all day in idleness, just waiting.

Surely it would have made more sense to leave us anchored in the harbour until our loading berth was ready. We had to let go at 7.00pm that evening, turn around and go further down the harbour only to tie up all over again on the Glasgow Wharf. That time we were starboard side to, so we had to change the gangway over as well as everything else. It was nine-thirty when we were finished, and it was my turn to be the nightwatchman again.

The rest of the night passed quietly enough and the next morning two gangs of dockers came onboard to begin loading. It soon became apparent, at least to me, that they hadn't yet resolved their dispute with the harbour authorities.

When they went down the hatches to the 'tween decks and checked the wool that had been loaded previously, they declared that it was stored incorrectly and claimed that it was supposed to be three-feet away from the opening of the lower holds all the way around. After they had measured it they found some of the bales were only two-foot eight inches away from the edge in places and refused to load any more cargo until they had been moved back.

It took them all morning to complete the task, and then they knocked off for the weekend. I wasn't sure whether they were playing games or taking the mickey. The rains came again on Monday and they only loaded small amounts between showers. It remained dry on Tuesday 30th June, and they were all finished by seven o'clock that evening.

We secured the remaining derricks for sea and let go at 8.00pm. Once again, I had to take the wheel, and as all the electrical system for the automatic steering and gyrocompass had broken down, we had to revert to the old magnetic compass and remain on hand steering all the way. It reminded me of the early years when we had no choice in the matter and had to hand steer all the while before all the modern systems made it so easy. With all the manoeuvres I had to do while under the pilotage I was glad when my first hour was over, and by the time I went back up to do my ten till eleven stint, we were out to sea so it wasn't quite so bad.

We headed northwards again, arriving at Napier at noon the next day, Wednesday 1st July. We went right in alongside and tied up; we felt very small beneath the towering cliffs. As I wasn't due on nightwatchman duty again until 7.00pm. I took a walk ashore alone and was really struck by the beauty of the place.

It was a lovely sunny day even though it was midwinter, a fact that may account for the reason that everything was so quiet. I walked practically the whole length of Marine Parade with its parks, gardens, swimming pools and water fountains. There was even a dolphin pool with the dolphins showing off their tricks. I much prefer to see them in their natural habitat, but I guess I was luckier than most to be able to do that. The surf was roaring in all along the length of the black shale beach, and I thought it must be a great place to come for a holiday during the summer when everything was in full swing.

From what I was told, it appeared that in 1931 there was an earthquake that caused the British ships to slip their moorings, leave the harbour and ride out the waves at sea. When the situation calmed down they came back into the harbour, sheltered and fed the people.

To show their appreciation, the inhabitants of Napier donated the money to have a clubhouse and mission built in the town for all British seamen. It's a lovely place that stands in its own little gardens.

* * *

When I returned to the ship I found that the dockers hadn't come onboard till 4.00pm, and as they had just finished on one ship they didn't much like the idea of starting on another one at that time of day. They appeared to deliberately set out to make as big a nuisance of themselves as they could by claiming that none of the ship's loading gear was any good, and they made lots of demands that sent our lads scurrying all over the ship searching for extra gear.

One example was a request by them for five-ton shackles for a derrick that was only built to lift two tons, and then they used their own strops that wouldn't lift even half a ton to bring the bales of wool onboard. They also wanted the safety rails put up in the 'tween decks, which was fair enough, but as soon as the lads had erected them the dockers took them down again claiming that they were in the way. And so it went on. The Bosun was fuming.

I don't know what their problem was, but the dockers there appeared to be even worse than those in Wellington. The next day they brought their union representative with them to check all the gear, but as it had all been tested and passed when we first arrived in Wellington, it got them nowhere.

If they had come onboard and just got on with the job instead of messing about, they would have finished quite early, but as it was they were still at it at two o'clock on Saturday afternoon, when it began to pour down with rain. That caused them to knock off again, and the Skipper finally had his fill of the dockers delaying tactics and gave orders to sail at five o'clock, leaving about three hundred bales of wool behind.

The Skipper had sent back to England for some spare parts for the gyro and electrical steering gear when it had broken, and while in Napier we heard that they had been sent to Auckland, which meant that we still had to spend our watches standing at the wheel. After we crossed the Bay of Plenty, we picked up the Pilot off Auckland at nine o'clock the following night, Sunday 5th July. He guided us in until we were just off our berth where he anchored us for the night, and we tied up at seven o'clock the next morning.

The dockers began to load the ship at 8.00am but didn't do much because of heavy rain showers. The next day was the same but Wednesday was nice, warm and sunny, so they didn't do so badly; the only interruption was when we had to shift ship at lunchtime to about two hundred foot astern. The work of loading the last of our cargo seemed agonisingly slow due, no doubt, to the fact that it was our last port of call before we headed home.

On Saturday lunchtime word came from the Shaw Saville offices for the dockers to knock off. No one could understand why as the dockers themselves said that they could have finished that afternoon. As rumour had it Shaw Saville were the people who were chartering the ship for nine hundred and sixty pounds a day so the dockers had to down tools. It meant that we were there until Monday 13th July, which was my thirty-fourth birthday. The dockers came onboard in the morning and worked quite slowly, seemingly intent on making a full day out of it instead of half a day.

We were kept busy as usual, lowering and securing the derricks and hatches. As each one was finished, as well as securing everything for the long journey home. All the girls had to go ashore and the TV was collected by the same firm that we had rented it from in Wellington. The coterie of girls had followed us all the way around the coast, and had come onboard in every port. It must have cost them a fortune in travel expenses. Various relationships had been formed, but the time had come for most of them to end.

The dockers finally finished loading just before tea, after which it absolutely poured down with rain. We got soaked through as we finished securing the last of the derricks, and we had to lash down some cargo that had been stacked on top of number four hatch. The next task was to take in the gangway then we immediately went to our stations to let go.

It was by then seven o'clock, and once we were clear of the berth and on our way, we had to stow away all the ropes and wires. I was still in the eight to twelve watch with Ben for that night, and we had to be well clear of land before the repaired automatic steering could be turned on and Ben left the watch to go on daywork. That meant I had worked from 7.00am almost non-stop through to midnight. It was the busiest, wettest birthday I had ever spent in my life, and I warned everyone not to wish me many happy returns.

As before on the '*Cape Grafton*' when we set sail for home from Nauru I would have liked to have circumnavigated the world by coming home through the Suez Canal, but once again the Skipper decided to go home the way we had come, across the Pacific. Despite the behaviour of the dockers in some of the ports, and all that rain, I came away liking what I had seen of New Zealand. Some of the scenery was spectacular, the places so clean and the inhabitants generally friendly, especially the girls!

One of the ABs who had been an extremely heavy drinker from day one of joining the ship in London went on an alcoholic binge for the whole of the six weeks that we had been round the coast of New Zealand. Shortly after we sailed he seemed to lose his mind completely. For four days and nights, he wandered around the ship in some sort of trance with a chipping hammer in his hand, hitting anything that took his fancy.

He kept asking for a phone and talked to imaginary people, he dressed up to go ashore even though we were well out to sea. He didn't recognize anyone and kept asking where all his friends were who had come onboard with him. He would also go down into the engine room and try to turn on all different valves even though he knew nothing about them. Because of the obvious danger of allowing it to continue, he was locked up in the ship's cabin hospital, but he managed to climb out of the porthole that was then sealed before he was locked in again. Then he broke the lock off the door.

A two-man watch was put on him for twenty-four hours a day to try to keep him in good humour and follow him wherever he went. They were to make sure he didn't do anything that could endanger the ship or try to jump over the side when he took it in his mind to go ashore.

They also had to watch that he didn't become aggressive, especially as he occasionally shouted that he was going to kill someone.

For most of the trip I had been in the eight to twelve watch while he had been in the twelve to four, and on a number of occasions he had failed to relieve me at midnight, so he and I had been known to have a few run-ins. On one occasion the Third Mate reported him for failing to come on watch on time so he had been logged a day's pay, for which he mistakenly blamed me. Obviously when he started threatening to kill someone, I was taking no chances.

It was an unwritten code in the Merchant Navy that no one locked their cabin doors while at sea as it could be looked upon as a slur on your shipmates integrity, but I locked mine for those few nights and slept very lightly. Although he was given enough drugs and tranquillizers to knock out a horse, they seemed to have no effect on him whatsoever.

I refused point blank to take part in the rota system of two men watching him because of the way I knew he felt about me and it could well trigger his aggression. That plus the fact that his problems were self-inflicted, were the reasons I gave the Mate for my refusal. Thankfully, he accepted my reasoning.

During that time, while on watch one night, the Skipper came out onto the wing of the bridge where I was keeping lookout and began talking to me about him. He had been looking up the symptoms in his medical book and it said that after about four days, the AB would either go to sleep or go into a coma. Whatever happened even though we were homeward bound, the Skipper told me he was going to put him ashore in Panama.

As the book had said, he did go to sleep after four days, and when he finally woke up, he seemed OK although he was very quiet from then on. I think everyone was glad, not only for his sake but for the relief from the strain we had been living under because of him.

While all that was happening we had made our way far out into the Pacific where we encountered some pretty heavy seas, but the waves were rolling with the ship which helped her along a little. The clocks were altered for the Date Line on Wednesday 15th July so when we got up next morning it was still Wednesday 15th.

I was sorry in a way that we hadn't sailed on the Saturday, as that would have meant we would have crossed the Date Line on Monday.

I would then have had a birthday that would have lasted for two days, and that would have been much better than the one I did have in all that rain despite the problems with the AB.

After seven days of heavy weather, the seas did a complete turn round so that instead of helping us along, the waves were pushing against us. Once more, we were kept busy repainting as much of the ship as we could. Ben took over the eight to twelve watch from me again, and I went on daywork.

After we passed Pitcairn Island on the night of Tuesday 21st July, we turned into a slightly more northeasterly direction, at which point it gradually began to get warmer. We had to stop for about an hour on Thursday morning with engine trouble, which occurred again the next day.

On Tuesday 28th July, we passed another ship going in the opposite direction. It was the first sign of other human life we had seen for sixteen days. After that we began to sight other ships fairly regularly, which confirmed that we were getting closer to the canal and, sure enough at 12.30pm on Sunday afternoon 2nd August, we dropped anchor among other ships to await news of our passage through. Our long haul across the Pacific was over. Counting the two days in one that we had when we crossed the Date Line, it had taken us twenty-one days to cross the Pacific with not even a stop in Pitcairn to break the monotony.

The Skipper was true to his word and paid off the AB in Panama. We then received another piece of good news. We were supposed to start our transit through the canal at 1.30am the following morning but at 6.30pm that same evening, the Pilot came onboard to take us through. He was due to have taken another ship through, but when he got onboard, he found that they had broken down and couldn't heave up their anchor. When he reported it to his headquarters over the walkie-talkie, instead of giving him the night off, they told him to take us through instead.

As two men were needed in the watches while we were under the Pilot, I went back on the eight to twelve watch with Ben for a while. He went up on the wheel at 8.00pm for the first hour and took us through the first lock before I took over at 9.00pm, just in time to take her through most of the narrow cutting. We were almost out of it by 10.00pm when Ben relieved me for his second hour. By 11.00pm, we were in the wide channel so I didn't mind that so much. We anchored shortly afterwards in the lake before going through the other locks so I had a fairly easy second hour.

When the new twelve to four man relieved me, I went down to my cabin and turned in. By the time I got up the next morning, we were well clear and were suddenly in sweltering hot weather, working in just our shorts. Two days later on Wednesday 5th August we arrived off Curacao.

The Pilot took us in through the narrow entrance, and I tried to remember how many times I had been there, but I had to give it up as a bad job. I thought over the years it must have been dozens of times. Ironically that was to be my very last visit. We turned completely round once inside the bay, then nosed back into the channel again and tied up alongside, starboard side to, just on the inside of the old pontoon bridge.

I noticed that a proper road bridge was being built across the channel and thought it would be a pity if they did away with the old pontoon bridge altogether after it had served them so well for so many years. For me it was part and parcel of the charm of the place.

The pipeline was put onboard and we started to take on our bunkers. While we were there we received warning of a hurricane in the Caribbean so when we sailed at one o'clock, we took a more southerly course than intended in order to avoid it.

As soon as we were clear of Curacao, we ran into a strong wind again, but it was a really warm wind. It sometimes made you feel hot and sticky yet at times it was so strong you could hardly walk against it. It gave us a lot of problems in getting the ship painted for the next couple of days as the hot, salt spray blew everywhere.

On Friday morning 7th August, we passed through the islands between Martinique and Dominica, instead of Guadeloupe and Antigua as originally planned, and headed out into the Atlantic. On Sunday night, the wind finally died down, and we began to enjoy a spell of decent weather for a change.

On Monday afternoon, we again were forced to stop with a touch of engine trouble. It couldn't have been too serious though as we were on our way again within half an hour. The days became long and really warm and sunny. There was hardly a ripple on the water, which was a lovely deep blue colour and reflected the sun, making the surface shine like glass.

On Friday morning 14th August, we passed the Azores, and a few days later we entered the English Channel and turned northwards once we had passed Dover. On our way up the east coast, the Royal Yacht Brittania passed quite close to us, on her way back down to London I presumed, so we gave her a salute on our ship's whistle.

We arrived off Hull on the evening of Wednesday 19th August, and the Pilot came out to take us in. He told us we were lucky as, very occasionally the water level in the harbour was the same as the level in the river, and when that happened they left the lock gates open. It was one of those times so ships were able to go straight through without stopping. Sod's law then intervened to make sure that it, of course, would not apply to us; we had to stop.

As we approached the lock, we could see another ship on the other side heading towards the exit. They appeared to be trying to make a race of it. Our pilot carried on making a race of it too. We both entered the lock almost simultaneously from opposite directions. The other ship beat us by getting her nose in a few seconds before we did so we had to back out again and move out of the way to let her pass.

Before she was clear of us another ship entered the lock behind her so we had to wait for them to come out and get clear too, which meant that we had been kept waiting for almost an hour. We finally managed to get through and the tugs swung us around and slowly helped us alongside our berth. We were finished tying up by 9.30pm.

There was a phone box down on the quay so I rang Margaret to let her know that we were in safely. The company informed us that we would be paid off the next morning. They also said that the ship was going from Hull to Cork before coming back across to Liverpool to finish discharging. She was then going to Hamburg, Rotterdam, Marseilles and Genoa to load her next cargo, which was then bound for Australia.

We were told that the ship was chartered for one cargo only and at the moment there was no cargo to bring home, but the company was trying for a full cargo of sugar to bring back. The trip was expected to take four to five months again.

We had sixteen days official leave, but the Skipper said that if we wanted to return to the ship we would have three to four weeks leave prior to rejoining the ship in Rotterdam. I remembered the promise that I had made to Mavis, Alan, Tom and Marg as well as all the kids before they emigrated, that I would look them up if I ever got the chance so I asked the Mate if Sydney was to be one of the ports of call. He didn't know but said it stood every chance. That possibility, coupled with the chance of extra leave, I agreed to do another trip in her as did six of the other eight in the deck crew.

It was 11.30am the following morning before we were paid off, and Ben and I took a taxi to the station. There was a little time to wait for our train so we had a pint first. Once back on the platform we met up with another couple of the lads who also had to catch the same train south so for a change, I had company all the way to Birmingham, and I arrived home early that evening.

CHAPTER TWENTY-SEVEN
THE WESTBURY / THREE
(Of a Quick Dash Back, a Welcome Reunion, and an End).

As usual I spent the first few days at home meeting up with old friends and relatives, but for the second week Marg and I had booked a holiday in Falmouth. While there we travelled up to Fowey then took the ferry, which was little more than a rowing boat really, across to Polruan to visit Ben and his wife Jean. They lived at the top of a really steep hill, and it nearly killed us getting up to their house. A festival was taking place in the small town with lots of dancing in the streets and lots of drinking too so once we had got our breath back we had a really good time.

Margaret seemed to like Cornwall as much as I did, and we quite enjoyed the holiday, but unfortunately all good things come to an end, and our enjoyment was brought to a sudden halt. We had left a contact number with Margaret's sister and at 9.30pm on Thursday night, she phoned us at the Penrose Hotel, and said that a letter had arrived from Holder Brothers.

They wanted me to rejoin the ship the following day, the 4th September, at 2.00pm in Liverpool. The plans had changed and it had been decided that we would be recalled to Liverpool instead of Rotterdam. "So much for three to four weeks leave," I thought. The last train to leave Falmouth that night had already gone so it was impossible for me to get home the next day, pack my gear then get to Liverpool for two o'clock.

I rang Ben but his wife told us that he had already left. So, I asked her if she would ring up the company the next morning on my behalf and explain to them that I personally could not ring them as we would be travelling all day from Falmouth back to Walsall and could she explain the situation to them. I would then ring the company myself as soon as I got home. There were no such things as mobile phones in 1970.

Neither Margaret nor I were impressed at being called back at such short notice but my original sixteen days leave would have been up on the Friday anyway. If I didn't go back on the '*Westbury*,' I would have to get another ship right away, and I thought it was better the devil you knew than the one you don't.

I rang them as soon as we arrived home shortly after 5.00pm on Friday evening, but the person I spoke to didn't seem to know much about anything. He said that he would ring me back the next morning to let me know if a full crew had already been signed on or not. Then I rang Jean to thank her and she told me that the person she had spoken to had said it would be all right for me to join the ship on Saturday. There was nothing I could do then but pack my gear and wait.

The call came at 9.05am the next morning and the clerk said that it would be OK for me to rejoin the ship if I could promise him faithfully that I would be onboard no later than midday on Monday. I told him that I would. "You won't let me down will you?" he asked. I assured him that I wouldn't as I smiled to myself at the thought that, at least, I had an extra weekend at home.

Margaret drove me to Wolverhampton station on Monday morning, the 7th. I kissed her goodbye and told her that I would see her in four and a half months. She asked me to give everyone her love if I managed to get to Sydney. I then caught the train and arrived in Lime Street station in Liverpool at 10.40am.

I was completely taken aback as I walked out of the station. So many alterations had taken place over the ten years since Liverpool and I had parted company and gone our separate ways. Great, high buildings and office blocks had sprung up all over the place. The roads seemed much wider, with flyovers and all sorts of things. I could hardly recognise anything of the old Liverpool that I had known.

I got a taxi right away and arrived back onboard just after 11.00am. Ben was glad that I had made it. There were two new crewmembers onboard and one of them had taken my old cabin so I had to take another one. As I had only just painted the deckhead in the other one during the homeward voyage on the last trip, I was a bit miffed, not enough to make a song and dance about it, but I decided that the deckhead in the new one would stay as it was.

Although I had to promise faithfully to be back onboard the ship before midday, I wasn't signed on until four o'clock. The set of officers who had taken the ship around the coast were still onboard and we were told that our own officers wouldn't be back until Rotterdam. That is probably the reason why our Skipper told us on the previous pay off day that we would rejoin in Rotterdam too.

We let go just before 7.00pm and came out into a basin, swung right around into the lock then emerged into the river. I was in the eight to twelve watch again but was the second wheelman so by the time I went up at nine o'clock we had dropped the Pilot off and were out to sea. Then we continued on our way down the coast, into the English Channel, on up past Dover and into the North Sea.

During the afternoon of Thursday 10th September, we picked up the Pilot who took us straight up the river and we tied up alongside in Hamburg. As it happened we were directly opposite the spot where I had been almost twelve months before on the 'Lancastrian Prince.' When we had finished mooring up, we had to top all the derricks ready for the next day. We finished that at 8.00pm and knocked off for the night.

The dockers arrived the next morning and began to load the cargo, which consisted mainly of boxes of spare parts for cars again and machinery etc. While we were there, we were informed that as there was a docker's dispute in Rotterdam, we would most likely go straight to Marseilles where our regular officers would rejoin us.

On Sunday night we sailed with no further information about what was to happen. We headed out into the North Sea and cruised along in a large U shaped course. We and ran into a couple of mist patches on the way, but we arrived safely at the mouth of the river Maas where a pilot took us up to Rotterdam late on Monday night.

As usual us crewmembers seemed to be kept totally in the dark about what was happening. First, we were told we were heading for Rotterdam, then we were to bypass that and go straight to Marseilles, then we sailed and ended up in Rotterdam after all. I had long since stopped being surprised at anything that happened in the Merchant Navy. There was one piece of good news for me though; it had been confirmed that Sydney was to be one of our ports of call in Australia.

By the time we had finished tying up it was two o'clock in the morning and we all had to get up again at 5.30am to top the derricks. More cargo was then loaded, and we continued working throughout the day. All hands were called at 5.30am again the next morning to shift ship from one side of the dock to the other.

By Friday night the loading was almost complete, and as soon as the quota from Rotterdam was in a couple of the hatches we had to start work: lowering and securing those derricks that were no longer required. We didn't finish until midnight and the loading was completed totally just after that so we had to begin lowering and securing the rest of the derricks again at 2.00am on Saturday 19th September. We then had to let go and finally finished at 5.00pm so I went and got my head down on my settee. It was not worth turning in properly for I was to be called at 7.30pm for my eight to twelve watch.

There was no sign of the return of our officers and the current ones somehow seemed very curt and abrupt in comparison. The atmosphere on the ship was already heading downhill fast. I also felt that I couldn't settle down into the trip at all. I felt restless and short tempered for no apparent reason, unless I was reacting to the new officers' attitudes. We also had a new Bosun, an elderly chap from Liverpool, who I didn't get on with very well. None of that helped and I felt most uncomfortable.

As we sailed back down the English Channel and into the Bay of Biscay, we ran into thick fog patches, which only lifted for a couple of hours occasionally, then they would settle again as bad as ever.

One morning as I was about to start my watch, I noticed the Bosun hobbling along the alleyway holding his hip. He told me that he had slipped in the alleyway the previous night and that he was going to see a doctor in Marseilles. I remembered all the previous accident-prone Bosuns that I had sailed with; I thought it must be an extremely dangerous job for them especially if I with all my jinxes was a member of the crew.

The foggy weather continued and it was really thick the morning we passed through the Straits of Gibraltar. I only got a small glimpse of the very top of the rock as it popped out above the fog for a few moments before it was swallowed up again. The fog stayed with us for the rest of the day before it finally cleared in the evening. Then we headed at full speed to Marseilles, where we arrived on Friday 25th September and we were taken right in to our berth without delay.

Our original set of officers came back onboard later. At least they'd had a nice long leave. All the temporary officers, except one who was to do the trip in the '*Westbury*,' were flown home and, amongst all the confusion of the handover, the Bosun never got word about when he could go to see a doctor.

There wasn't much cargo left to be loaded so we were secure and ready for sea again the next day and we sailed just after lunch. We were in a basin, and as the tugs pulled us out stern first, we hit the corner arm of a jetty amidships. The ship gave a little shake then moved off again and we got out to sea with no further mishaps.

We followed the coastline around until we arrived off Genoa in Italy the next morning, Sunday 27th September. Again, there was no one waiting to go in so as soon as the Pilot was onboard, we went alongside. The next day the ship that was moored ahead of us sailed, and we had to shift ship two hundred feet up the jetty into her position.

Our next task was to rig up a stage over the side so that a surveyor could go down to check what damage had been caused when we had hit the jetty. There was a large dent in the side of the ship and a couple of rivets had sprung slightly, but he said that there was nothing to worry about.

On Tuesday the Bosun finally got ashore to see a doctor, who discovered that he had fractured a bone in his back. Although the doctor wanted him to go to hospital, he preferred to pay off and have his treatment at home. He was the third Bosun that I had sailed with throughout my career who had damaged their back in one way or another, and he was flown home on Friday night. The job was offered to Paddy, an AB who was on contract with the company and had been a Bosun before. He readily accepted the job so another AB was flown out from England to take his place.

That was our last loading port but somehow, it seemed to be a very slow process as the hatches were filled up with still more boxes of all shapes and sizes. Quite a lot of booze came onboard too, all for Christmas down under I assumed.

Finally at 5.30am on Saturday 3rd October, we were called to shift ship back along the jetty to our original mooring. Another ship came in and took the place ahead of us that we had just left. Why we were the ones subjected to all the hard back breaking work that the juggling around entailed I shall never know, but it always seemed to be that way. It took only a few hours more to finish loading the remainder of the cargo then we got everything ready for sea and sailed early that afternoon.

Following the departure of the Bosun, who I felt quite sorry for at the end, and the arrival of our original officers with their much friendlier attitude, together with the knowledge that we were finally starting properly on our journey to Australia, the atmosphere became much better. The funny, strained atmosphere completely vanished and everyone settled down again.

If the ambience aboard ship as I had always thought, really was down to the attitude of the officers towards their men, then that went a long way to prove it. The ship suddenly seemed much more like the 'Westbury' of the two previous voyages.

Upon our departure from Genoa with us being already in the Medi., I fully expected to head toward the Suez Canal but for some inexplicable reason, that I never got to the bottom of, our bow was pointed to the Straits of Gibraltar. We were going the long way round.

The weather was lovely and calm when I went on watch that night at eight o'clock, but by ten there was a fair wind blowing. The Skipper walked onto the wing of the bridge where I was keeping lookout and I commented that the wind seemed to be getting up a bit. He replied, "Yes, the weather forecast says there's a force nine storm ahead of us." "That's all we need," I thought, and by morning we were well and truly in it.

The wind whipped up the waves like mountains, and the ship began to roll and toss violently. On one occasion she gave a sudden lurch and I heard the clatter of crockery falling and breaking somewhere in the direction of the galley. "It will be scrambled eggs for breakfast," I thought.

She then rolled again quite violently; the drawers under my bunk shot out of their runners, flew across the cabin and crashed against the door. I retrieved them but had to wedge them in. God! I hoped that the surveyor in Genoa was right and that the damage caused to the ship's side on leaving Marseilles wasn't anything to worry about. We battled with the storm all day but ran out of it later that night. "Oh sleep, lovely sleep."

We came out past Gibraltar at one o'clock in the morning of Tuesday 6th October. The loading had taken one month, and we were only then starting on our way. Already we were beginning to suspect that the journey may be much longer than the four to five month trip that we had been told it would be; on the last trip we were actually in New Zealand after one month.

As we turned to port and began to follow the African coast down, we were kept busy overhauling all the ship's gear again and then repainting everything. The days became warm with a soft wind that kept it bearable as we travelled on. Sliding through the water, we first passed the Canaries then the Cape Verde Islands, and we crossed the Equator on the night of Tuesday 13th October. After a while the soft winds turned into a cool breeze, and it began to get quite chilly.

A week later, on Tuesday 20th October, we ran into a thick bank of fog so we had to ease down our speed quite considerably. That night while I was on watch, the radar picked up the echo of another ship coming towards us. We kept track of it until it was just two miles away off our starboard bow. The Skipper altered course so that we would pass about a mile away from each other. Suddenly the radar broke so he switched to the back up one, which worked for about three minutes then that broke too.

We had no way of knowing where the other ship was, or what it was doing so the Skipper turned our ship around until we were travelling in the same direction that she had been heading the last time we saw her on the radar screen. We then went dead slow ahead for a little while before we came to a complete stop.

The fog had become really thick and all we could do was sit there waiting and listening. It was all very eerie, stuck inside what seemed to be a dense, grey bubble, in total silence except for the gentle lapping of the water against the side of the ship. We broke the silence regularly with an ear-shattering blast on our whistle, but we didn't see or hear anything in return from the other ship.

The Skipper waited a while until he felt absolutely certain that she had gone past us before he started the engines again and had me bring her round again on to our original course. We carried on our way very cautiously and slowly without any radar.

It was dinnertime the next day before the fog cleared, and then it was full speed ahead again. The fog came down yet again that evening but cleared away in the early hours, which allowed us to arrive safely off Cape Town at two o'clock that afternoon. It was Thursday 22nd October. We went straight in and tied up for bunkers.

We received our mail, and an engineer came onboard to repair both the radars then, at eight o'clock that night, we sailed again. We were by then beginning to get a little restless, having spent eighteen days at sea only to be alongside for just six hours. We weren't allowed shore leave and we were off again for another nineteen days or so.

During those endless days and nights out on the vast open ocean, I spent many long lonely hours on lookout, either on the wing of the bridge or the monkey island, feeling the warm breeze on my face and marvelling at the thousands of bright twinkling stars that shone in the cloudless sky.

That was the part of the job that I loved but, still the feeling of restlessness persisted, my mind would begin to wander and ask the same questions over and over again. Particularly, what was I doing there, facing the dangers of the fogs and the storms, when I could be at home in my own little house with the woman I loved? I was missing her.

* * *

As we continued to travel due east, we immediately ran into a very strong wind which stayed with us for six days. It was quite chilly and the ship developed a steady roll again. On Wednesday 28th October, the wind died down to a gentle breeze, and later that same day we had to stop with a bit of engine trouble, but only for an hour and a half. Despite all that, we had long since finished overhauling the ship's gear, we were all out day after day, on overtime painting her up, and the 'Westbury' began to look spotless.

The further east we went towards where the sun was supposed to be, the colder it got. Some nights were so cold I had to borrow Ben's big, fur lined anorak to wear while on lookout. Ben could play cribbage quite skilfully by then, and in a recent knockout competition, in which each crewmember that took part put cigarettes into the kitty for the winner, Ben and I were both in the final. I managed to beat him, but only by the skin of my teeth, and I didn't have to buy any cigarettes for weeks.

Apart from that minor diversion, the days were long and uneventful; they followed slowly one after another. It became a conscious effort to keep track of them otherwise; they just rolled on and merged into each other. Finally at 8.45pm on the night of Friday 6th November, while on lookout, I picked up a flashing light on the horizon. Land at last.

We had reached the south coast of Western Australia. The land was in view to us all through the following morning until we started to cross the Australian Bight. I had hoped that the weather would calm down a little as we neared the coast, but there was no such luck. It stayed with us up until we hove to off Adelaide on Wednesday 11th November and waited for the Pilot. He came onboard almost immediately and took us up the channel where we at last had a bit of calm. We were all tied up and finished by 8.00pm.

They had told us at the start that we would be away for four and a half months, and already just over two months of that had gone. Much to my amazement, the dockers came onboard and began work that same night. They operated in gangs that worked in shifts around the clock. They were full of praise for the condition of the ship, saying that it was the cleanest British ship that had ever been in there.

Next morning customs came onboard for a look around. One of them came into my cabin, but I only had to show him my camera. He stood there shaking his head repeating, "It's a lovely ship, it's a lovely ship" as though he just couldn't believe it. I jokingly told him that he could have my job on her if he wanted to, but he gave me a funny look and walked out.

Thursday and Friday were nice sunny days, but I didn't go ashore, as I wanted to save as much money as I could for Sydney. We sailed again on the evening of Friday 13th November. It was a beautiful, clear, warm night, which was really pleasant as I had forgotten what it was like to be on watch without a coat on. It was a short-lived respite; when I got up the next morning, it was belting down with rain that didn't stop all day or throughout the night. It was still raining at eight o'clock on Sunday morning when I went up on watch.

We were heading to Melbourne, and the rain only stopped when we were close in to the coast. We picked up the Pilot just after 9.00am and he took us up the river where we docked just after dinner. As in Adelaide, we seemed to be miles away from the main town. A gang of dockers came onboard and began work that evening. The days passed slowly as Melbourne's share of the cargo was unloaded throughout the following week.

Two of the hatches were finished on Saturday 21st November, and we secured those derricks ready for sea. The remainder of the hatches were finished the next day so once everything was ready, we let go, went back down the river and headed out into the open sea.

We then followed the coast up towards Sydney and arrived there during the morning of Tuesday 24th November. Once the Pilot was onboard, we went alongside at Wooloomaloo, just before the bridge. We were all tied up before eleven o'clock. It was exactly what I had been waiting and hoping for, to see if I could fulfil my promise to our friends. I went straight up to see the Mate to ask him if I could have a couple of days off.

Perhaps he remembered me asking him at the end of the previous trip if Sydney would be one of our ports of call and had guessed the reason why because he agreed without any problem and told me that I could go there and then and return on Thursday night. I didn't need to be told twice so I immediately took a shower and got changed. I had the addresses of both families, one in Fairfield and one in St. Mary's. One of the dockers told me that they were both about thirty miles away in the suburbs. "Just my luck," I thought.

When I was in Melbourne, I had received a letter from Tom, which let me know that everyone knew I was coming, and they were looking forward to us all meeting up again. He had given me his work's phone number and asked me to ring him when I got in so that he could tell me where and when he could pick me up.

I got my sub and hung around till two o'clock in the hope that they would put a phone onboard. That had been one of the first things done in the other Australian ports, but there was no sign of it, so I decided to try and make my own way.

Being crafty, I thought that I would try to find my way to Tom's place in Fairfield first because I knew that he had a car and would take me on to see the others. I then set off down the gangway, along the quay and out through the gate. It was fine and sunny as I stood there, trying to flag down a taxi, but they just looked at me and passed me by. I then walked along for about half a mile; still I had no luck. Then suddenly everything turned dark and lightening flashed all over the place; astonishingly, I had never witnessed such a dramatic instant change in the weather anywhere I had travelled so far.

I began to walk back to the ship expecting to get drenched, and indeed just before I reached the gate it started to rain, then a taxi came along. I half-heartedly lifted up my arm and much to my amazement he stopped. I asked him if he could take me to Fairfield. He gave me a funny look and said that he would take me to one of the city stations from where I could take a train. "Charming," I thought, but realised I had no choice so that would have to do.

A few minutes later, he pulled up outside a large arcade type of place in the middle of the city. He pointed to where I was to walk through to come to the station. I thanked him as I paid, then did as he said. I bought my ticket and went through the gate, where I asked the man punching tickets which platform I needed. He directed me up the steps to platform three.

When I got there a large crowd of people were standing around and almost immediately a train came in. Although there was no announcement as to the destination quite a few people got on. I noticed a big board above my head with a long list of place names on it.

As one train left the platform, another one would follow it in succession. As each train came in, little lights came on in front of some of the place names and went off again when the train moved. As each train arrived, different places were lit up and more people got on.

I could have stood there all day watching the trains come, go and get nowhere fast. So I assumed that the lights only came on in front of the stations that the particular train standing at the platform would be stopping at, so when a train arrived and the little light came on in front of Fairfield, I decided to check my theory. I asked a man standing next to me if that particular train stopped at Fairfield, "Most probably," he said, looking down his nose at me. "Welcome to Australia," I thought as I decided to risk it and jumped on the train anyway.

We stopped every few minutes at small stations and got further and further away from the city. After a while I began to get worried, thinking to myself that it would look well if I ended up in Perth or somewhere on the opposite side of the country. I carried on for another couple of stations and began to think that I should get off the train soon and retrace my steps when there it was. At the next stop, I looked through the window and heaved a sigh of relief as I saw the name Fairfield. I got up very quickly as the trains only stopped for a couple of minutes at each station.

No one asked for my ticket as I walked from the station into the street where I was lucky enough to get a taxi straight away. I jumped in and gave the driver Tom and Marg's address. It only took him minutes to get there. I thanked him as I paid and off he went.

Julie, the youngest in the family when they left England, was playing in the front garden when I arrived, so I walked up to her and said "Hello Julie, I bet you don't remember me do you?" She looked at me with puzzlement on her face and said "No." How soon young minds can forget faces.

Marg came to the door with the rest of the kids and welcomed me in. Then the penny dropped and Julie suddenly remembered who I was. The kids had grown a lot in the two years since I had seen them and they bombarded me with questions, all on the same theme. "Are you staying for good?" "Is Auntie Marg with you?" "Why not?" "Is she going to come?" and so on. I was then introduced to the newest member of the family, little Mark, who was only a few months old. The first true Aussie of the clan.

The house was a private, rented one as Tom for some reason didn't want to buy. It was very comfortable and they seemed to manage quite well. It was in pleasant surroundings in a quiet street where every house had open lawns and grass verges. The only thing that spoilt it was the lack of sewers. All the houses had to use their dry toilets in small sheds in the back gardens.

I was warned to make sure that there were no spiders in it before I used it, as some of them were likely to give a nasty, poisonous nip in embarrassing places. Men who came during the night emptied the toilets twice a week. What a job.

When Tom came home later, he said that he would ring his employers and take the next day off. Of course, when they heard that, the kids all chorused that they wanted the day off from school as well. They all moaned when Tom wouldn't allow it, except for Yvonne who had a broken finger.

Tom told me that they were hoping to get a commissioned house next year. That is a council house with all amenities with cheaper rent. Marg said she would never come back to live in England as she was really happy there. We spent the rest of the evening talking, watching the TV and generally catching up with everything.

Next day when the kids had all gone off to school, still protesting, Tom, Marg, Yvonne, baby Mark and myself all piled into the car and they took me to Warragamba Dam. It was a fantastic feat of engineering and an impressive sight, built across the river to hold back and harness enough water for the whole of the Sydney area, and I really enjoyed it.

The day was really bright and sunny but was slightly spoiled for me because I was wearing a white shirt that seemed to attract hundreds of flies. At times, I seemed to be covered in them so in one way I was glad to get back in the car to get rid of them. We got back to the house shortly before the kids returned from school, then we had tea before we piled back into the car to go to Mavis and Alan's house in St. Mary's, another brand new township, which had recently sprung up in the Sydney suburbs.

With three adults and six kids in the car, I began to think I preferred the flies. I couldn't believe it when I saw Mavis and Alan's house. It was a lovely, brand new bungalow standing in between two others. One of those was empty, but the other was owned by an Australian couple named Brian and yet another Marg. They along with Mavis and Alan, were the only people living in the street at that time as all the other houses were still under construction. The area to the rear of the houses was open fields and bush land, which I couldn't help but think how great it was.

Mavis and Alan's two children, Karen and Catherine, hadn't changed too much, except that Karen had put on a little weight. Catherine, who had a broken arm, was still as moody as ever, but they were all pleased to see me. Mavis and Alan had become close friends with their Australian neighbours, and when I was introduced, they welcomed me like a long lost brother. They all spent ages begging me to come to live out there. Brian and Marg seemed to be more vocal and persistent than the others, even though we had only just met.

The empty, brand new bungalow next door was for sale and they kept pressing me to put down ten australian dollars, the currency having been changed from australian pounds to dollars long since, and they said that the builder would hold it for me for as long as I wanted.

Ten dollars was worth about five english pounds at that time. I must confess to feeling a little sceptical that any builder would put a sale on hold for as long as I would have needed for such a small sum of money, but they assured me that they would. They said that I could chose any house that I wanted as there were lots of others being built locally, or I could have one built to my own specification if I couldn't see anything that I liked.

I told them that I no longer had any emigration plans, and even if I had, I wouldn't commit myself to anything like that without first thoroughly talking it through with Margaret, as it would be as much her decision as mine. They all said that they would write to her to try to persuade her to come, but they never did.

There seemed to be kids everywhere as Brian and Marg also had two little girls, and later that evening all of them were piled together into Brian's house and a nearby neighbour from another street was called and asked to babysit. She agreed, though why anyone in their right mind would want to baby sit for ten of them was beyond me; it was more like a school classroom. Using Brian and Tom's cars, all seven of us went to a club called Rooty Hill. not too far away,

It was one of those must wear a tie places, which I wasn't too happy about as I hate anything tight around my neck. When we arrived we had to walk through a large room where crowds of people were playing on hundreds of one-armed bandit machines. That room alone was as big as most of the clubs in total at home and Brian told me that they were thinking of building another club because that one wasn't big enough. I thought back a few years to my previous visits to Australia and couldn't help but compare that to those little drinking bars that were standing room only with no women allowed and closed at 6.00pm.

We walked on through a massive concert room, which was also very crowded, but Brian somehow managed to find us some seats. At one end of the room was a large stage with an equally large dance floor. It was waiter/waitress service only, even for the beer, but crowded and busy as it was, we hardly had to wait at all to be served. There was a large menu of food available as well if required, and all in all we had a wonderful time.

The band played almost non-stop throughout the night, and occasionally a girl singer went on stage and sang quite a few numbers. They played a lot of slow, ballad type songs, and I think there must have been something in the Australian beer because Mavis actually got me up for a couple of dances. We left the club at about eleven o'clock as Tom and Marg had to collect their kids and drive back to Fairfield. Tom had an early start for work the next day. Mavis and Alan kept me up until 2.30am, and we caught up with all the gossip.

When we got up the next morning, Alan rang in to work and told them he wouldn't be in. Brian hadn't been to work for about eight weeks as he had fallen off his motorbike and hurt his leg.

After a little breakfast Brian, Alan and I got into Brian's car and spent the rest of the morning and early afternoon driving around to different garages to try to find a new tyre for his car, as one of them was completely bald. The cost varied greatly, and we called at numerous places before he was offered one that suited his pocket.

On our return to town we had to go to a motor vehicle licensing office as Alan, despite the fact that he had a full English driving licence, needed a permit to drive as well as displaying L plates until he passed an Australian test. Our next port of call was Parramatta for Brian to pay some money off his car, and of course we took in a visit to a pub on the way back. The first words out of Mavis's mouth when we got back were "Don't blame me if your dinners are spoiled." It was nice to have a little taste of normality in my life again.

Later that afternoon we went to fetch Brian's wife Marg from work, and I was amazed to learn that women could earn up to sixty dollars a week. That was over thirty pounds, "Excellent money," I thought, as women in England would be lucky to be on ten to twelve pounds doing a similar type of job. I only got slightly over twice that amount for a month's wage.

They told me that the shop prices in the city were very expensive, but out there in the provinces, it was no more expensive than at home, and because of the long days and warmer weather, their utility bills were nowhere near what they had paid at home. The warmer climate and long hot summers also meant that clothing didn't knock such a dent in their money. They were certainly trying to paint a wonderful, possibly irresistible, picture for me.

Tom brought the family out to us that evening, and we all sat and talked until it was time for me to begin the long drive to return to the ship. Neighbour Marg stayed at home to put her two little girls to bed, but everyone else piled into the two cars to escort me.

Karen and Pam almost pulled me apart as one hung on to my right arm while the other hung on to my left. They both tugged at me begging me to travel in their car. It was a choice I could not make, as I couldn't please one without upsetting the other. Tom finally settled it by telling Pam to shut up and get into the car. Alan drove Brian's car while Brian navigated. I wasn't sure if that was wise or not, but I kept those thoughts to myself, and we finally got to the docks just before 11.00pm.

Everyone got out of the cars as they wanted to take a look at the 'Westbury,' and she was out of sight behind a wharf shed. As there didn't seem to be anyone around, I took them all through the gate to stand at the corner of the quay from where they could see her.

A man who, I assumed, should have been on the gate walked towards us. I thought that he was going to kick us all off so I explained that I was a crewmember from the 'Westbury.' After hearing that the people were all my friends from England who now resided in Australia, he allowed us all to walk along the dock for a closer look at the ship as long as we kept the kids away from the edge.

I took them all onboard once we reached her and they all crowded into my cabin. I fetched drinks from the bar for all of us, and it was well after midnight when they left the ship. I walked with them to their cars and kissed the kids goodbye before I returned to my cabin and crashed on my bunk.

* * *

The next morning, I went to the Chief Mate and asked when we would be sailing. He told me that it would not be until Tuesday. That surprised me as I had expected we would be gone over the weekend. As it was then only Friday I asked him if it was all right for me to leave again to which he replied, "Alright, get lost, but be back here on Monday morning." Based on my years of experience with uncompromising officers, I couldn't believe how generous he was being, but they were the best set of officers I had ever sailed with.

A phone had been installed onboard in my absence so I called Tom at work and he told me to catch the train to the town of Lidcome, another suburban township and he would pick me up there at 4.15pm. After I had got ready, I hung around for a while as I didn't want to get there too early.

I had just stepped off the gangway when the port supervisor pulled up in his big, posh, American car. He asked me if I was going into town, to which I replied, "Yes, I need to get to Lidcome." He told me that he just wanted a word with the Skipper and would only be a few minutes and added that he would drop me off at one of the stations if I wanted to sit in his car and wait for him. In my best Aussie accent, I said, "Good on yer mate" and went to the car.

Some of the lads were down on the quay, painting the side of the ship with rollers attached to long bamboo canes. It felt really good sat there in the luxury of the car watching them get on with it. The Mate came down to check on them and looked in amazement when he saw me sitting there like a lord. I nearly gave him the royal wave but thought I hadn't better, especially as he had given me all the time off.

The port supervisor was true to his word, and a few minutes later he returned to his car. He dropped me off at a different station to the previous one, but I had learned the system, and I caught the train with no problems. I arrived at Lidcome at 3.30pm and as I had a little time to kill, I took a stroll down the main street to look at the shops. It seemed to me that all the new towns had a kind of sameness about them, but there was an ambience in the air, an atmosphere of hope around them, and I felt that people had a sense of looking forward to a great future. Tom was waiting when I returned to the station and he drove me back to his home. As before, they were all glad to see me and we spent the evening relaxing and watching TV.

The next day they took me into Fairfield to do some Christmas shopping for the kids. We went into a huge superstore that seemed to sell everything you could possibly want, but all I wanted to do was to get out. They seemed to take forever picking and choosing, and boy was I relieved when we finally found an exit and escaped.

Later that afternoon we drove to St. Mary's again. They weren't expecting me as Alan had read in the newspaper that we were to sail on Sunday. I didn't know what to do then, but they persuaded me to stay the night and made plans for the next day. The idea was for all of us to get up early and set out for the ship at 7.00am to make sure that she wasn't sailing. It was necessary to do that because, in my usual brilliance, I hadn't made a note of the ship's phone number. If we were not sailing, they said we would all go off and spend the day on one of the beaches.

Brian said that if the ship had already sailed, I wasn't to worry as he would drive me up to Brisbane, which was our next port of call, to rejoin her. His wife Marg said that I could always stay and they would hide me. Marg and Tom had to leave to take their lads to a football presentation at their school so after they had gone, the rest of us went to the Rooty Hill club again.

Marg, Tom and their six kids arrived spot on seven o'clock the next morning. How did they do that? It was testament to the kind of guy that Tom was, if he told you that he would do something that is exactly what he would do. None of us were up, so it was about 9.30am when we finally started out. There were seventeen of us in two cars! Fortunately most of them were kids. We called first at a place where Brian had to pay an instalment off his mortgage, and when they came out, he said that he had asked about the house next door to Mavis, but it had been sold.

He had been told that there were plenty more to go up yet, and if I was interested I could put ten dollars deposit for one to be held for me. Even then, after it had been confirmed, I still found it difficult to believe that a house could be held for an indefinite period for such a small sum. Also what was beyond my understanding was why they, my friends, refused to accept the fact that we may not go out there to live?

We carried on down to the docks to find the ship was still there so I went onboard to see the Mate. He confirmed that we were still sailing on Tuesday so I went down to my cabin to put my swimming trunks on under my trousers before I went back to the cars to tell them that all was fine. I expected to go straight to the beach, but we stopped outside a house and I had to go in to meet Brian's mom and dad. We stayed there for a little while before we headed for the beach.

I was a little disappointed that we didn't go to Bondai beach as I, like most people, had heard so much about it, but they said that it was no good and it was dirty. They claimed Coogee beach was much better so that's where we went. On arrival we all took off our shoes and socks to walk on to the beach.

It created really strange sensations as I walked; the sand felt quite hot but it was so fine and silky that, with each step, it seemed to slowly roll away beneath my feet, and I didn't quite know where they would end up. As we got closer to the water within the tide line, the sand became firmer so we all sat and took advantage of the sun while the kids went off to play. There were lots of people on the beach but still plenty of space.

After a while without a word, Tom jumped up and ran into the sea. Although I had had my trunks for years, they had never been wet, so it was with certain reluctance that I decided to christen them. Not being the hero that Tom was, I slowly inched my way up to my knees. Maybe because of the sun and sand being really hot, the water felt freezing. Suddenly a great swell came in and the water instantly rose till it was over my shoulders. I gasped, but at least my trunks were wet at last. After the initial shock it felt fine, and I enjoyed myself for quite a while by standing with my back to the incoming waves; I dived into them as they came level with me and let them carry me ashore.

After a while we rested on the beach and ate a few sandwiches. I was the only one who didn't get sore with the rays of the sun, which surprised me a little as they lived in it permanently. I could only assume that they didn't sunbathe very often. We packed everything up at about 2.30pm and drove off again.

We didn't seem to be heading for anywhere in particular and appeared to be going all over the place before we finally pulled up somewhere that Tom recognised and from where he knew the way home to Fairfield. I kissed all their kids goodbye for the second time, thanked Tom and Marg for everything and off they went.

We travelled back to Brian's parents house where I had a shower and a shave before we sat down to a salad tea while watching the Aussie versus England test match on the TV. Brian said we could go to the Apia club later where he worked as a waiter a few nights a week when he was fit.

Someone named Sandy Scott was going to be on that night, and when I asked who he was, Marg looked at me in disgust. Apparently he was fast becoming a top-line artist out there, crooning many love songs and ballads, always on TV and Marg was really gone on him. Mavis said to me, "Wait till you see him. He looks just like your Barry," my younger brother.

We left Brian's mom and dad to look after the kids while the five of us went to the club. I thought Rooty Hill was posh, but that was even more so. Not only did you have to wear a tie, but also we had to keep our jackets on at all times. I wasn't sure if I would ever understand those kinds of rules! The place had a massive entrance hall with extra large glass doors, and just inside was a life-sized bronze statue of a naked man throwing a discus.

Mavis, who hadn't been there before, just stood there with her eyes glued to one particular point of his anatomy. I told her that if such a small thing was all that you needed to throw a discus then I could be a champion, and I rushed up the stairs before she could ask me to prove it.

There was no entrance fee so we walked directly into a large foyer, similar to a cinema foyer where you wait for the film to end before going in for your showing. That one though was carpeted and furnished in a much grander style. Brian asked us to wait while he saw the manager to get us a good table, and it worked; he gave us one right next to the stage.

The room we were in was massive. Any of the concert rooms in the clubs in Walsall would look the size of a postage stamp in comparison. The stage was large with a beautiful dance floor immediately in front of it, and there must have been hundreds of tables in the area at the back and alongside the dance floor. The whole of that area was fitted with thick pile carpet.

The waiter arrived at the table and we ordered a round of beers, 'middies,' which was about half a pint. As soon as he brought them to the table Brian ordered another round. He said that it was necessary to do so because sometimes the waiters could be a long time getting back to you. I could well believe that as within half an hour of our arrival, there wasn't an empty seat in the place. He also said that meals were served there too and they were fantastic. They cost a fortune but you wouldn't want to eat again for a week they were so big.

As usual, there was a band with a female singer so I just sat there and enjoyed myself as I drank, talked, listened to the music and watched the dancers on the floor. I was totally disinterested in all the miniskirts on display of course! Marg acted as if she was sitting on a hedgehog or something, constantly asking, "When is Sandy Scott coming on?"

At about 9.30pm, I thought that I had had one beer too many as the stage seemed to be moving. I soon realised that the front part was in fact sliding out onto the dance floor; thus extending the stage further out. A bloke jumped up grabbed the mike and said "Cabaret time at the Apia Club." He went on to introduce four female dancers who came on and did a couple of routines. We were probably too near the stage, and the sliding extension had made it so we looked sideways on so we did not get the proper effect. I was relieved when they had finished.

The fellow on the mike then introduced Sandy Scott. Marg was halfway out of her seat and all glassy eyed when he ran out onto the stage, then she sank back into her seat saying, "Ohhhh, I could lick him from the bottom of his feet to the top of his head." Mavis had told me that he looked like my brother Barry, and for one moment I thought it was him. I told Marg that the likeness really was incredible, to which she replied, "Well, bring him out here with you as well."

As he sang, he held the audience spellbound and he was quite good. There wasn't a murmur out of the hundreds of people in the room while he sang, but the applause was deafening and people shouted for more every time he finished a song. He was on stage for over an hour then the female dancers performed for a few minutes before the band returned to play dance music for us. We stayed on only a little while longer before we called it a night, and they drove me back to the ship. Marg had one last attempt to try to get me to stay, but I told her that I couldn't and sadly waved goodbye as they drove off.

* * *

We didn't actually sail until lunchtime on Wednesday 2nd December, but I didn't go ashore or get in touch with them again as I felt that I couldn't keep saying goodbye to them. On our way up the coast to Brisbane we ran into more showers and arrived off the pilotage during the morning of Friday 4th December. We picked up the Pilot who then guided us the fifty or so miles up to our berth, and we docked at dinner time.

The heavens opened up at that moment, and it poured down solidly for the next five days. I asked one of the dockers what it was like in the rainy season if this was the summer. He just walked off muttering something about Pommies. I got the impression that I hadn't made a friend somehow.

Much to my amazement the rain didn't stop the dockers working, and we were unloaded by the following day. A gang of men were then sent onboard to clean out the holds. They hosed them down from top to bottom, but I personally thought that the rain could have done the job for them if they had simply left the hatches open.

They then had big problems to get the water out, as the bilge pumps kept getting blocked up. As I had experienced a similar problem in the past I was glad it was their problem that time, not mine. They did eventually manage to get them dry.

It was then that depression returned and swept through the ship. There had been no further mention of a cargo of sugar for home, and we received our new orders. We were to sail southwards to a place called Ardrossen to pick up a cargo of grain bound for Biera in Mozambique, East Africa.

Once the holds were dry, a gang of carpenters arrived onboard to build the shifting boards. They say every cloud has a silver lining. "It was a much better idea than us having to do it," I thought, as my mind went back to the 'Trevose' when I had stepped on a nail while doing the same job.

Up until then there had always been a slight ray of hope that we would receive that cargo of sugar for home, but it was glaringly obvious to us all by then, that the trip was going to be much longer than the four to five months that we had been told originally. We had already been out for three months.

It was at that point I decided that it was going to be my last trip. I had had enough. Now that I was married, I missed Marg too much so however long the trip turned out to be, that was going to be it. No longer would we be oceans apart. I posted a letter to the Pool at Falmouth to tell them of my decision and gave them my three months notice.

Considering all the problems that I felt I had had over the years with all the authorities and officers' attitudes, it was ironic that I chose the one ship whose whole compliment of officers had treated us with respect to be my very last voyage.

The work took the carpenters until Tuesday 8th December, and we sailed just after tea. Finally we sailed out of the rain on Wednesday. After those five days of constant rain, the weather became warm and sunny again. It took us just over a week to get to Ardrossen, arriving early on Wednesday morning, 16th December where we anchored. From where we were, all we could see was what appeared to be a vast, golden, sandy desert, but it was actually fields of grain. There was a large mill on the shoreline with a little cluster of houses off to the one side of it.

There was only one jetty that was just big enough for one ship. The place was totally isolated and desolate, and one could only hope, for the inhabitants sake, that their namesake, Ardrossen in Scotland, was better than that. One ship was already alongside being loaded, and as we were the only one at anchor, we assumed that we wouldn't have long to wait.

Later that morning some officials came onboard. We expected them to tell us when we could go in, but instead they went down the hatches, and despite the clean up by the gang at Brisbane, they decided that they were not clean enough. I must say that the decision surprised me, as the holds of the 'Westbury' were spotless in comparison to every other ship that I had ever sailed on. We had to work on the holds till midnight; they even called the stewards out to help us.

As it turned out there was no need for any of the rush because during the night, a Japanese ship came in and anchored. We strongly suspected that the order to clean our holds had been delaying tactics from the port authorities. That seemed to be even more evident the next morning when they began to play chess with us. The ship that was being loaded was finished and she sailed. Then the Japanese ship went alongside, but the next morning she had to come out to anchor again to allow an Australian ship to steam in and go immediately alongside. It seemed to us that their cargos obviously took priority over ours. We always seemed to catch the wrong end of the stick as those decisions resulted in lots of hard work and lost sleep for us.

The Australian ship sailed later that same afternoon, and the Japanese ship then went back in to finish loading. We finally went alongside on Saturday night. The grain was transported along the jetty by a long, covered conveyer belt that led from the mill. It then flowed down a chute into our holds. The ship had to be loaded in such a way to enable us to keep her on an even keel, which meant that we had to keep shifting ship up and down the quay whenever the chute had to be lined up with another hatch.

Again it was hard work for us but gradually, bit by bit, the grain was poured in. It was just like loading that phosphate on the '*Cape Grafton.*' The only difference was that it was clouds of golden grain dust bellowing out that covered everything. The whole ship was soon carpeted in it, and just like the phosphate dust, it got in our hair, our clothes, our cabins and even in our food. We began to feel that we were almost choking on it. It all helped to deepen the depression that was settling around us at the time.

Although I would have loved to escape from under the golden fog of grain dust, there was no point in going ashore as there didn't seem to be anywhere to go so I didn't bother, and the loading continued until Tuesday 22nd December.

During the evening, when the ship's keel was just three feet off the seabed, we sailed. There was by then another British ship waiting to follow us in, and she was going to load a cargo of grain to bring home. That piece of news was like a hammer blow to our already low spirits. Although we were supposed to go to Port Lincoln almost on the tip of the Eyre Peninsula in the Spencer Gulf, South Australia, we went instead to Port Giles, just fifty miles down the coast to finish loading.

It was only a short distance and dark, but we had to make sure all the hatches were battened down properly, to make certain no water could get in if a wave came over the deck. Once we had finished battening down, we only had time to wash a little bit of the dust from the decks as it only took just over three hours to get to Port Giles where we anchored for the rest of the night.

We went alongside the next morning to discover that the place was even bleaker than Ardrossen. There was only one jetty with a silo at the end of it, and there was hardly another building in sight all along the coast. What a place to spend Christmas! At least there were five chutes there, one for each hold so we didn't have the job of shifting ship every few hours. The holds just needed to be topped up, and we were assured that if it were possible, we would be away before Christmas, but the next day, Christmas Eve, everyone stopped work at lunchtime and vanished.

To add to our problems we got the news that after Beira, we were to go down to Durban, South Africa to load a cargo of anthracite (furnace coal) for Tasmania. That really did hammer the final nail in our Christmas coffin. Everyone was then at rock bottom, we thought that we were never going to get home, and a thoroughly miserable Christmas was had by all.

The dockers returned on Boxing Day and took just two hours to finish the job, but it was four o'clock before we got everything squared up and sailed, with eight and a half thousand tons of grain onboard. The rumour around the ship was that the Australian nation had gifted fifty thousand tons of grain to the people of Mozambique. It would apparently take six ships to transport it, and we were one of them.

After all the muck and dust, not to mention the heat, in our last two ports it was good to be out on the open sea again with the fresh breezes. The next few days were spent giving the ship a thorough wash down from the top of the masts right down to the decks, before we could settle back into our routines. The mood began to lighten, and everyone cheered up as we convinced ourselves, as sailors always seemed to do, that our next orders from Tasmania would be for home.

On New Year's Day everyone, except those on watch, were given the day off. As I was still on the eight to twelve watch I still had to do my four hours in the morning and four hours again at night, as did the guys in the other two watches. I booked my eight hours in as overtime but was told a few days later that I wasn't entitled to it.

I saw red and, most unlike me to my everlasting shame, I had a real bust up with the Mate. Many things had changed during my years ashore, but I couldn't believe the union, any union, would agree to a man working eight hours on a Bank Holiday and get paid exactly the same for it as those who had the day off doing nothing. The unfairness seemed ludicrous to me. I wrote to the union headquarters to ask for clarification. Later when my anger had settled I felt guilty that I had been very unfair to the Mate, especially after he had given me all that time off in Sydney with me still being paid the same as those who had worked.

A few weeks later, I received a reply from the union, which supported the Mate, stating that he was perfectly correct. The new agreement superseded the rules when I was last in the Merchant Navy. Overtime had always been paid for working on Bank Holidays in the past, and that was the first time I had encountered the eventuality since my return. That ruling plus the fact that a day's leave was no longer given for spending a Sunday at sea, in return for a small pay rise and a few extra days annual leave, made me think that much more had been lost than gained following the strike that they had held during my time ashore.

However, I apologized to the Mate the next time I saw him. He accepted my apology gracefully. Perhaps he too believed I had been totally unreasonable, and the strained atmosphere that had risen between us disappeared immediately. I hoped that he harboured at least a little gratitude for me being big enough to apologize.

The temperature rose up into the eighties and a string of long, sunny days followed one after the other, so it was somewhat of a shock when a gale sprang up out of nowhere. It was during the early hours of the morning of Margaret's birthday, 11th January 1971. Again, the ship developed a nasty roll and we relied on the shifting boards to do their job by stopping the grain from rolling too.

We spent an uncomfortable twenty-four hours before it calmed down and returned to the warmer weather. Shortly afterwards we sighted land and rounded the south coast of Madagascar, then headed in a more northwesterly course towards Beira.

After Rhodesia had declared a unilateral independence from Britain, trade sanctions had been imposed so we were not allowed to trade with them. Mozambique had a long borderline with Rhodesia and the word was that Beira was suspected of being one of the ports where supplies were being shipped in.

There was a British warship patrolling around the approaches to the harbour, I assume in an attempt to stop or intercept any ship they suspected of breaking the sanctions. We could see her a short distance away as we arrived. Whether it was because we were a British ship or had been cleared by radio I have no idea, but we were allowed to sail right in, and we dropped our hook in the sea anchorage about five miles from the shoreline.

It was teatime on Wednesday 13th January, and we were told, via the ship-to-shore radio, that we would be at anchor for eleven days. That was yet another blow to the morale of the crew and to make matters worse, there was absolutely no sign of our mail.

It was two days later that they radioed us during the evening and said that there was some mail for us in the launch, which they couldn't bring out to us that night as we were anchored too far away. They would only bring it out the next day if we would give them some bread. The Skipper agreed so they brought it next morning. They took quite a lot of loaves of bread and off they went, but still refused to take our mail with them to post ashore.

The Pilot came out at 6.00am on Sunday 17th January much earlier than expected, he came to take us in through the sandbanks and we tied up alongside. "At last," we thought, something was going our way. Only four days at anchor instead of eleven.

Onboard came a gang of four or five men to each hatch, supervised by another local with a rifle who stood watch over them as they worked. They had to shovel like mad, without a moment's respite. At the slightest sign of anyone slowing down or to catch a breath the gunman on top would turn the rifle towards the guilty man and threaten him. The only time they could straighten their backs was when the crane had lifted the scoop to empty it into the trucks, which had Rhodesian Railways written all over them, but that only took a matter of seconds.

For two days they worked day and night to unload a large portion of the cargo. We were then told that they had run out of trucks so at 6.00am on Tuesday 19th January, we had to come off the jetty and anchor again. It was pure speculation on my part, but my guess was that we would have to wait for the train to return from its questionable destination. Rhodesia did eventually gain its independence and changed its name to Zimbabwe.

The whole harbour seemed to be overrun with sharks. Every time a few scraps went over the side, shoals of them came up to the surface after them. They were amongst the largest I had ever seen. Even the smallest were eight to ten feet long; they were much too strong and powerful for us to try to catch.

I didn't draw any money as I wasn't interested in going ashore, but Ben did and rang his wife. I wished that I had thought of that and done the same, especially as Margaret had written that her dad had suffered a heart attack and was very ill in hospital. She had said that she was very worried and I felt so helpless being so far away. I don't know what I hoped to achieve but I went to see the Skipper and he was no help at all, he just told me to try not to worry about it. When Ben came back, he said that Jean was going to give Margaret a call to bring her up to date.

One of the letters I received was from the Pool at Falmouth, they had accepted my notice, but they wanted to know if I wished to continue my seagoing service as an unestablished seaman not on contract to them. That meant I had to write to them again to tell them that it was my intention to leave the sea altogether, but I had to wait till we reached Durban before I could post it.

We went back alongside on Friday morning 22nd January and again they started to shovel away like mad. The opportunity for another sub was offered so I withdrew eight pounds to make sure that I had enough to ring home, only then to learn that the post office strike at home was affecting the phone lines. So I ended up with eight pounds worth of Mozambique money and nothing to spend it on.

The method of unloading the grain with shovels meant that there was very little grain dust around so I was given a pot of white gloss and a paintbrush and sent up onto the fo'c's'le head to do some painting. One morning as I walked along the foredeck to start work, I heard one of the local workers who was standing by the rail, shout something down to one of the gunmen on the quay.

I haven't got a clue what he had said, but the gunman's response was immediate: he turned swiftly, ran along the quay, bound up the gangway, along the deck and hit the worker across the jaw with the butt of his riffle. It all happened so fast I simply could not believe what I had just witnessed. There were numerous people on and around the deck and not one so much as batted an eyelid. He, the worker, was carried away unconscious.

576

That same dinnertime, when I returned along the alleyway amidships from painting the rails on the fo'c's'le head, as I walked towards our mess carrying my pot of white gloss, one of the native workers was skulking in a doorway. He appeared to be hiding from God knows what, and as I walked past him, he whispered, "You paint me white mista?" I stopped in my tracks and looked at him.

I saw the pain and suffering in his eyes and my heart went out to him. All I could say was, "I only wish I could, so believe me I would." For just an instant, I thought I saw the slightest glimmer of light return to those almost lifeless eyes and the faintest of smiles flicker across his lips as he whispered, "Thank you" as he skulked back into the depths of the corridor.

We finally sailed on Saturday 30th January and headed south towards Durban. Time was then spent working day and night to clean up the hatches as best we could. We breathed in those clouds of grain dust again, and the routine continued until the early hours of Tuesday morning when we arrived off Durban where we dropped anchor.

During that time, one of the stewards became ill and no one knew what was wrong with him. When we finally went alongside on Friday 5th February, a doctor came onboard to examine him and diagnosed scarlet fever. He said that we were lucky that it had been caught in time before it got a real hold over him, as the whole ship would then have had to go in quarantine for two weeks if it had gone unchecked for much longer. The steward was taken to hospital where he only had to stay for a couple of days before he returned to the ship.

As we had come alongside, a series of events turned the whole thing into a farce. The first event was, as we moved towards the bunker berth to refuel, we ran directly over a buoy and broke it off its anchor. We carried it for about one hundred yards, attached to our propeller before it luckily managed to free itself. The second event happened as we came alongside: we hit the jetty and put another big dent in the side. Once again, a Lloyds surveyor came to take a look and he found that we had sprung a small leak so they had to weld another steel plate over it.

As we shifted ship to our loading berth the next morning, we managed to snap one of our forward mooring wires. I bet some of those people in Durban were wondering what kind of ship we were. Just like the '*Nacella*.' Despite everything over the weekend, eight hundred tons

577

of anthracite was loaded before we battened down and sailed in the evening of Monday 8th February.

We ran into heavy seas almost immediately and ploughed along for five days. A cyclone warning was then received, so we spent time waiting and listening to the weather reports in the hope that it would alter direction. Despite many twists and turns it remained heading in our general direction. The Skipper seemed to know exactly where it was at all times and kept track of it until it was only a few hours ahead of us. He then decided that it was our turn to do the dodging and showed us what he was worth.

For three full days as the cyclone changed direction, time and again he took us all over the ocean, changing direction with it, and the storm completely missed us. To make matters worse, during all of that manoeuvring, our iron mike packed up again so it was back to steering by hand. Despite that, it was nice to be clear of the storm and on course again.

The feeling was short-lived however as there was another cyclone warning a few hours later. Luckily for us it veered off to the north. Over the radio, we heard that it was a particularly vicious storm that caused mountainous seas, and we picked up an SOS from a Greek ship caught in its clutches.

They were about a thousand miles north of us, and there were fears that their ship was going to break up. It would have taken us five days to reach them but a German deep-sea tug responded to their appeal and they were much closer to them and far better equipped to deal with the situation than us. We never did learn the fate of the stricken ship.

* * *

Yet a third cyclone sprang up shortly afterwards; it too was travelling towards us. Although it veered back and forth slightly, it kept its general direction heading towards us. It seemed determined to do battle with us, but yet again the Skipper edged away from it, and we gradually slipped further and further south until we were down into the roaring forties with strong winds. At least it was not as bad as the cyclone would have been.

By the time the cyclone reached the latitude that we were at when we heard the warning, we had slipped out from under it. The Skipper had again shown his skills at missing the storms so I nicknamed him the artful dodger. Not to his face of course.

Eventually by Friday 19th February the weather changed; it became nice and warm. We passed another ship on Sunday, which was the first we had seen for eleven days. We had expected to hear where we were going to after Hobart while we were still in Durban, but we were by then more than half way across the Indian Ocean with still no news. You could cut the atmosphere onboard with a knife, and everyone was on edge waiting to hear if we were going home. Not a morning passed without someone saying "We should get our orders today," but still there was nothing but silence from the company.

The weather turned again on Thursday 25th February. Not cyclones but strong winds and heavy seas, which we ploughed through for the next two days before they died down. We sighted land on Tuesday afternoon 2nd March and arrived safely at 4.30am the following morning. We went in without delay and tied up immediately seventeen miles south of Hobart, right in the wilds of Tasmania, in what appeared to be a kind of lake with only two very narrow entrances into it from the sea.

There were green hills all around us, very similar to those at Falmouth but spoilt by a horrible scar, caused by a foundry belching out smoke and fumes twenty-four hours a day. It produced carbide for batteries or something, and it was a real eyesore in the beauty of the surrounding countryside. We were tied up at a little jetty at the edge of the factory grounds. The coal was for their furnace, and they had one shipload delivered every ten months. I hoped we weren't going to be the ones that brought them their next shipment.

As no one else was interested, I volunteered for the nightwatchman's post so after a good morning's sleep, I spent a few afternoons doing a spot of fishing; I caught quite a lot of fish of different varieties and sizes at all different depths. It was extremely deep where we were, but one day I dropped my bait right down to the bottom. After a while, I felt a strong pull on the line and immediately began to bring it in.

Whatever I was bringing up from the depths felt quite heavy and, as I swung it over the rail and landed it on the deck, I saw that it was a great big, horrible squid. The hook had caught in one of his tentacles, and there was no way that I was going anywhere near it.

As luck would have it, one of the dockers walked along the alley on his way to the poop deck. He stopped in his stride when he saw it and said, "Wow! What a beaut." I told him if he could take my hook out, he could have it. "Are you sure?" he asked. "I'm certain," I replied. He immediately took out his knife, cut off the tentacle just above the hook, and threw my line over the side again. "There you go, and you've still got some bait to carry on fishing with," he said, before he picked up the squid and walked off down the alley saying, "This is my tea for tonight."

The postal strike at home had only finished a week earlier so still no one had any mail except for Ben. His wife had been across to the continent and posted some to him while she was there. Everyone envied him as nothing lifts your spirits like a letter from home, especially as our spirits then took another severe blow. We received orders to return to Sydney to load over eleven thousand tons of flour, all in bags, bound for somewhere in Ceylon, now Sri Lanka.

The morale of the crew hit an all time low. We were already two months beyond the original estimate of our journey time, and there was still no sign of a cargo for home. Added to those feelings was the gargantuan task of cleaning the holds again especially as we were about to carry flour, immediately after a cargo of coal. Like me some of the guys had been through it all a number of times in the past so they just stuck their heads down and got on with it.

As each hold was emptied, everyone had to go down, sweep up and shovel all the coal dust out before it was hosed down from top to bottom. They worked like Trojans, and the sweat dripped from them all day long. They emerged in the evenings covered from head to toe in black coal dust, conjuring up memories for me from long ago as on the 'Oakhill.'

As fast as one hold was cleaned up, another had been emptied and was ready for them to start all over again. The process was repeated until all five were finished. Personally, I didn't mind one little bit. I was nightwatchman and, not for the first time, I was glad that I had volunteered, as I didn't have to do a thing. The unloading was completed on Saturday evening 13th March, but we stayed alongside while the lads finished cleaning the last hold. That allowed us to sail at 3.30pm on Sunday afternoon.

While we were in port, the iron mike had been mended so we were back on automatic steering as soon as we were out into the open sea. It was only for a couple of days though, as we picked up the Pilot for Sydney at 9.30pm on Tuesday night. He took us straight in and by eleven o'clock, we were safely moored up at Glebe Island. I had come on the trip in the hope that I would be able to visit my friends, little did I know then that I would get the chance twice.

The first day after we had arrived in Hobart, the Mate had given everyone the day off but as I was nightwatchman, I didn't get it. So as we were then in Sydney, I asked him if I could have Friday off to make up for it and have a long weekend. He agreed so on Thursday I rang Tom at work. He was surprised to hear that I was back. He asked me if I had been home yet and when I told him no, he replied, "That's a bit hard on Marg isn't it?" I couldn't have agreed more and told him that it was definitely my very last trip.

After I explained to him that when I finished work at 5.00pm, I was free for the weekend, he arranged for me to catch the train to a place called Cabramatta where he would meet me. I was by then getting good at that. I may not have seen a great deal of the city, but I certainly got around the suburbs.

When I arrived at Cabramatta station Tom was waiting in the car with Yvonne, Julie, Paul and David. Pamela and baby Mark had stayed at home with Marg. Julie told me that Pam had started to cry when she heard that I was visiting again, and I hoped that it was because she was pleased about it, as the rest of them seemed to be. Even little Mark greeted me with a smile when we arrived at the house, although it could have been wind I suppose, but he really started to chuckle when he saw me light my pipe and puff great clouds of smoke out. He seemed to think it was the funniest thing in the world.

We spent a quiet evening watching TV and chatting. At one point a squabble broke out over something between Paul and David, which resulted in them lashing out at each other. Tom was out of his chair like a shot, he pushed all the furniture towards the walls, even with the rest of us sitting on it. He shouted, "Stand there" to the two boys, pointing to the space he had created. He then disappeared from the room but reappeared within seconds with two pairs of boxing gloves.

With him as the referee and advice giver, he made them both put on the gloves and start to box each other until they were both exhausted. I just sat there in amazement. I couldn't believe what I was seeing, but Tom said if they were going to fight they must learn to fight and defend themselves properly, and they were soon the best of friends again afterwards.

As Tom had the following day off, I went into Fairfield with him and Marg to help shop for their groceries and to post a letter home. The ship was going to be in Sydney for three weeks so Tom said I should stay with them for that weekend and with Mavis and Alan the following one. He drove me over to St Mary's later that afternoon to let them know that I was there again. Mavis was really surprised and pleased to see me again stating that, of course, I could come and stay the following weekend. Alan was still at work so we didn't stay long as Tom wanted to get home for tea.

When we arrived, Marg told me she had been to see one of her neighbours who had kindly said that I could use her phone to call Margaret back home. I went straight over and put in a call through the operator expecting to wait a while for it to come through. To my surprise, I was put through almost immediately.

Margaret sounded flabbergasted to hear from me, as she was just about to go out to work. It was really wonderful to hear her voice again after such a long time, I felt quite excited and relieved to learn that she was OK, and her Dad was well on the way to recovery. It lifted a great weight off my mind but our time was short as I was only allowed three minutes on the line, and Tom's Marg also wanted to say hallo.

After I hung up, I had to ring the operator to find out the cost of the call so I could pay the neighbour for letting me use her phone. It cost just over seven pounds for those three minutes, but I felt it was worth every penny. In comparison to telephone charges thirty years later the cost would seem to be prohibitive, but at that time there was no choice. I thanked the lady very much for the use of her phone as I handed her the money.

Since my last visit, Marg's brother John and his wife (yet another Marg) had come out to Australia and were living two doors away from Tom and Marg, who seemed really happy and settled now that they were there. That evening John, Tom and myself went to the Fairfield Hotel for a couple of drinks.

During the course of conversation, it came out that John knew both my wife and Eric, my father in law, from the Working Men's Club where Eric used to be steward. John said he used to work for a while on the elevator lorry that was used for mending the trolleybus wires, before they discontinued trolleybuses.

Margaret had a job as a lollipop lady for a while not far from our home in Bloxwich, and they would shout friendly banter at her as they went past. I thought to myself that it was strange that I had come ten thousand miles to find that out. I don't know what they used to shout to her but, knowing my Margaret, I'm sure that they got just as good back as they gave. Like everyone else, he said that he and his family absolutely loved it out there.

The next morning, I went with Tom to watch David and Paul play football for their school. Every form year in every school had their own football team, and they played matches against neighbouring schools. That particular week they were playing on a large, open area of playing fields and we drove right into it and parked. It was a really hot, sweltering day, so we sat on the grass at the side of the pitches.

Kids of all sizes were everywhere and lots of parents too, but the thing that really struck me more than anything was the amount of teachers there. Tom said that they regularly gave up their Saturday mornings to supervise the kids and organise their games.

The first match was Fairfield against another school. It was fifteen minutes each way for those under eights, and I've never enjoyed a football match so much in all my life. It was played on a full sized pitch, and the two little goalkeepers looked completely lost in their goalmouths; it almost strained your eyes to see them.

When the game started, apart from those goalkeepers standing alone between the posts, the rest of the players, all twenty of them from both sides, surrounded the ball using their little legs to run and kick out towards the ball whenever it came anywhere near them. It was like a swarm of bees to-ing and fro-ing all over the pitch.

At one point, they were all in Fairfield's penalty area, and it resembled a rugby scrum until suddenly the ball broke loose out of the pack. One little chap saw it quicker than anyone else and belted it into the net. The only trouble was that it was his own goal. Fairfield finally lost 7-0.

David's team played in the next match, which was half an hour each half. Tom said that he would give him twenty cents (about two shillings then) for every goal he scored. David asked me how much I would give him and Tom said I need have no fear about paying him, as he hadn't scored a goal in two years. I didn't have time to answer him as he was called onto the field while Tom was talking. Within five minutes of kick off Fairfield was a goal down. Tom shouted to David to "Get stuck in," at which David ran at the lad who had got the ball and deliberately kicked his legs from under him.

Tom stood there, stunned for a moment, then ran on to the pitch, grabbed David and shook him by the shoulders. "Don't you ever let me see you do anything like that again, if you are going to play, you play fair," he shouted. The referee then came up and told David that if he did it again he would be sent off.

A few minutes later David got hold of the ball and struck a beauty, putting it in the back of the net from about ten yards. Tom was shouting and cheering, "Good old Dave," just as if he were at Wembley. Fairfield soon scored another one that made it 2-1 at half-time, and as soon as David came off the pitch, he reminded his dad that he owed him twenty cents.

About twenty minutes into the second half David scored another beauty. Tom said, "Christ, that's forty cents I owe him now," and from then on, every time a Fairfield player got the ball Tom shouted, "Don't pass it to David." "I hope he breaks his leg," he said turning to me, but it was only in jest, you could tell that he was proud of him. Fairfield won 4-1.

Paul's team played in the next match, but he was a defender not a striker so Tom didn't have the same dilemma. It was a fairly tame match after the fun and excitement of the other two, and unfortunately Paul's team lost 5-0.

Upon our return home, we watched sport on the TV. Most of the kids were playing outside, but after a little while Yvonne came running in. She was crying and claimed that another girl, who lived further up the road, was hitting her with a stick. Once again, Tom reverted to his unique brand of parenting; he jumped out of his chair, ran into the kitchen and grabbed hold of the sweeping brush. He knocked the head off it, handed the handle to Yvonne and said, "You've got a stick now," and sent her out to play again.

That evening Tom, Marg, John, Marg and me, without my Marg, went to a brand new pub that had only been open for a couple of months close to where they lived. I never did get the name of it but it was a really posh place, built and decorated in the Spanish style. We had a pleasant evening partaking of a few bottles of ice-cold beer.

It was red-hot again the next day, and in the morning we went over to a different playing field for a game of cricket. Altogether there were three adults, Tom, John and myself, with about ten kids. Some of Tom's own, plus others from the neighbourhood. We split into two teams with me and Tom as captains and my team won, mainly because I won the toss and got to choose first for my team, and I chose John. I was really shattered by the time it was all over.

A young couple named Sue and Pete, who had come out from St. Helens in Lancashire with their two little boys, drove Mavis and Alan and their two girls out to Fairfield to see us during the afternoon and we spent a lazy, pleasant few hours just sitting around and chatting. Alan gave me his work's phone number and I said I would ring him to let him know about the following weekend.

After everyone left, we sat and watched TV till well after midnight. Tom called me up at 5.30am on Monday 22nd March, and we left the house at 6.00am. He dropped me off at Lidcome station, near his work, from where I caught the train back to Central station, and then I hailed a taxi to take me back to the ship.

I was back onboard by 7.30am ready to start work at eight o'clock. By the time it came to knocking off at five o'clock I felt really shattered so I had a quick shower and right after tea I lay on my bunk. I intended to have five minutes rest before I started a letter for home but when I woke up it was 10.30pm and I still felt really done in so I turned in properly and slept right through till seven o'clock the next morning.

After work was finished that day, I went ashore with Ben and we sat in the posh lounge of one of the nearby pubs for a quiet drink and a chat. It was a far cry from those 'men only' drinking dens of my earlier visits to Australia. For the first time in months I got a little drunk, I think it must have been a reaction to the relief I felt at hearing Margaret's voice over the phone and learning that everything was all right at home and with her dad. I felt that I should have been with her in her time of need. After weeks of silence caused by the postal strike, I got a little tipsy. It did me the world of good.

* * *

The loading of the bags of flour seemed to go very slowly, so we carried on painting wherever and whenever we could. On Thursday 25th March, I phoned Alan at work, which was an ice cream making place somewhere in the city, and we arranged to meet at Central station at 4.30pm on Friday afternoon. That meant that I was going to have to finish work early; next morning I told the Bosun that I was going to knock off at 3.30pm in a tone of voice that suggested that I would, whether he liked it or not. Not for one moment did I think it would work, but to my amazement he said that I could knock off at 3.00pm if I wanted to, so I did.

I took my time to have a shower and get changed, and then I walked out of the docks and onto the main road. It took me about fifteen minutes to flag down a taxi, but I was still a little early arriving at the station so I bought my ticket and waited for Alan.

He arrived shortly after I did and, as we were still early, we decided to have a quick drink. We didn't have to leave the station as there was an open beer store inside, so we had a glass each then went onto the platform for our train. The rush hour out of the city on those trains had to be seen to be believed.

The carriages were double-decked, but people were still packed like cattle in trucks with not a spare inch of space in them. People literally hung out of the windows. Thankfully each little stop at different townships saw a few more people get off than got on, but we still couldn't manage to find a seat until we had almost arrived at St. Mary's. The thought of having to do that journey every day, squashed in with all those people, in that heat, would have driven me crazy.

As soon as we got off the train, we popped into the lounge garden of another pub for a welcome cold beer before we caught the bus to Alan's house. Mavis was next door when we arrived so we nipped in to say hello to Brian and Marg, but Brian was not at home. His wife Marg was chomping at the bit and was furious with him. It was their wedding anniversary and Brian had gone out early that morning to celebrate, and hadn't returned. Needless to say that, due to Marg's mood, we didn't stop long. He didn't actually return until teatime the following day.

After tea we spent time watching TV and chatting. Alan told me that he had passed his Australian driving test the previous Tuesday. He only had to demonstrate the basic skills to them as he had a full British driving licence and he was thinking of getting a car.

That evening more visitors arrived; they were friends of Mavis and Alan whose names were George and Lil (thank God it wasn't yet another Marg). They had with them their two daughters: one was twenty years old and about to get married, and the other one was twelve. They had come to Australia from London two years previously and George spoke with a pure cockney accent. After a while, George drove Alan and I into town to pick up some beers and, of course, we had to have one while we were waiting to be served, which was our excuse.

George was quite chatty and told me that he had started work almost as soon as they had arrived in Australia as a self-employed bricklayer. He subcontracted work from larger building firms, and he already had five men working for him. He believed that if I were to come out there as a painter and decorator I would make a fortune. I thought, "Here we go again," so I said that I might bring my wife out on a two year working holiday to see how it goes. No more was said on the subject after that.

It was after 11.30pm before they went home, and as Alan went into work on overtime the next morning, I went into town with Mavis and the kids to do some shopping. Our first port of call was the post office so that I could send a letter home. Fifteen minutes later, Mavis and the kids were in a shop further down the high street while I waited outside. Two young women came up and asked if I knew where the post office was. As I had only just come from there, I had no hesitation in giving them directions. I felt quite good as I thought to myself that they probably believed that I was a local. They thanked me and moved on.

It was well after midday when we returned to the house, and I spent an idle afternoon relaxing until Alan came home in time for tea. Marg from next door came round to tell us that Brian had finally returned and that he was in the doghouse. She had taken his club card and badge so that he couldn't get into the club, and she had told him that he could stay in and watch the kids for a change while she went out. She asked us to go with her.

We all got ready, caught the bus into town then got a taxi to the Rooty Hill club. As before there was a band and dancing so Mavis again tried to get me onto the floor, but I didn't fancy it that time. I probably hadn't had enough to drink. We had a good time and were finally kicked out at midnight. We took a taxi back to Marg's house and went in for a cup of coffee before we turned in. All the kids were in bed and Brian was fast asleep on the chair. If looks could kill, the look that Marg shot at him would have meant instant death.

Next day Alan and I took a Sunday morning stroll to a car showroom. There was nothing there that he fancied so we came straight back. After lunch, Sue and Pete came to visit with their two little lads, and a little later George and Lil came again. George told Alan that he would take us to a car showroom in Parramatta, where he had bought his car from a few months earlier if Alan was interested. He was of course, so we all piled into George's car and set off followed by Sue and Pete. It was a huge car sales place, and there were some beauties in there. George went inside and came out with the salesman. Alan said he wanted to buy a car and was told to take his pick.

The salesman pointed to a couple of cars that I thought were a bit expensive for Alan who started to hedge a bit. The bloke then said, "I think I know exactly what you are looking for" and took us to a little Volkswagon, not a Beetle but a nice little family saloon. As soon as Alan saw it, he liked it, so the salesman told him to take it out for a short trial run if he wanted to.

While Alan was away, the salesman asked me if I was interested in buying a car. I told him no and explained that I was just a visitor off the ships. He then asked me if I was coming out to stay, a question everyone seemed ask, so I told him that I was thinking about it. "You come on out, we need you," he said. Which I thought was rather nice. Mavis of course heard what he had said and took to him right away.

When Alan returned a few minutes later, he told the salesman that he was pleased with the car, to which the salesman replied, "Well, before you make up your mind why not take the wife out for a run and see what she thinks?" Mavis asked me to come along as well, so we all piled in and off we went.

We hadn't gone far when Alan realised that he was lost, and it took us nearly half an hour to find our way back to the car sales garage. The bloke didn't say anything, but he must have started to worry. He did smile though when they told him that they had decided to buy the car.

Sue and Pete had traded in their old car for a lovely Hillman Hunter while we were away so we all waited outside while Mavis and Alan went into the office to talk about terms. It took about ten minutes, during which time a girl came out and gave us all a cup of coffee. Alan had the car keys in his hand and a voucher that entitled him to fill up with petrol, free of charge to him, at a petrol station down the road. The car was his to drive away.

Sue and Pete drove off in their new car after they had arranged to meet us back at Mave's house. We all got into the VW, and Alan drove off to the petrol station. George waited while we filled up so that we could follow him back to St. Mary's, as Alan wasn't quite sure of the way.

Once on the way Alan started to tell me how easy it had been to buy the car. All he had to do was give the salesman the name of any finance company that he was already in debt with so that the new loan could be arranged. It was almost impossible to get a loan if you were not already in debt with proof that you paid back regularly. You were considered a bad risk if you owed nothing to anyone, and as Alan already had a mortgage, he was considered a good risk. All that seemed crazy to me.

After a little haggling the salesman had knocked two hundred dollars off the price of the car, given Alan a twelve-month guarantee and the petrol voucher. The repayments would be eight dollars a week. There was a deposit of one hundred dollars required, but Alan had six months in which to pay it.

That meant he had the keys, the car and the petrol plus six months in which to to pay the deposit without a penny changing hands. I for one had never heard of a deal so good before or since. By the time he had finished telling me all of that, he suddenly realised that George was nowhere in sight and again we were well and truly lost. We then embarked upon what appeared to be a zigzag tour of New South Wales, and Alan got more and more frustrated; the giggles from Mavis in the back didn't help either. We finally got to a spot that Alan recognised, so from there we headed home.

When we got there, everyone was waiting and demanded to know where the hell we had been. "Almost down to Melbourne," I told them. Alan wasn't amused but it set Mavis off giggling again. We stood chatting for a while till they all left, and we went round the corner to see some more friends of Mavis named Brian and Sylvia. That couple had emigrated to Sydney a couple of months after Mavis and Alan. There had been a few days difference between vacating their house and their sailing date. It had been arranged with my Margaret that they would stay at our house just as Margaret had played host to Tom and Marg.

I had never met them as I was away at sea at the time, but they wanted to meet me and thank me for letting them stay, even though I had had nothing to do with it. They seemed pleased to meet me and asked how Margaret was. We chatted for a while before we drove back. It was one o'clock before we went to bed. I had planned to get up at 5.30am to catch the train back to the city with Alan, but I changed my mind as after the late night I didn't fancy it. I told them that I was going to pinch a day off so they let me sleep in.

I got up just after 9.00am and had the place to myself. As it was Monday, Alan was at work, the kids were at school and Mavis had gone to start a new job at a place a few streets away. She was spot welding or something like that for forty dollars a week. That worked out to be nearly as much as I was on. "Was my wage really worth all the trials and tribulations that I experienced?" I thought to myself as I relaxed and enjoyed the comfort of Mave and Alan's home for the day.

During the weekend, the two little girls, lovely as they were, had almost driven me round the bend with their constant noise. I wasn't used to it and it was made worse because they had acquired a three-month-old boxer puppy named Bengo, which was teased and plagued by the girls. It was so lovely for me to have that day of peace and quiet that was such a change from shipboard life. After having a bite of toast and a cup of tea I spent the rest of the day very lazily and just pottered around then watched TV till mid afternoon when they all returned home.

After tea we all set off in the car to visit yet more friends. They were out so Alan took us to the immigration hostel that they had stayed in when they first arrived in Australia. Parts of it were old army huts that I didn't like the look of, but there were also several little flatlets that

590

looked comfortable enough. They pointed out the one that they had stayed in for just under twelve months and told me that it was a little cramped for the four of them, but for the most part it was an enjoyable stay as they had made many friends among the other new immigrants from all over the UK. We drove back to St. Mary's and didn't get lost once.

Later that evening George called around, he had returned to the car sales garage in Parramatta and wanted to show off his new car, so we all rushed outside to see it. It was a beautiful, big, metallic blue Ford Falcon automatic. It was a really lovely car, and it was obvious that he was proud of it. After we had all inspected it and sung its praises to George, we stood around it chatting.

Alan and George stood with their backsides against the wing while I leaned on the driver's door as George told us about the deal that he had made. He had been down to Parramatta car sales that day and, apart from all the usual deals and the trade in for his old car, he had been offered forty dollars each as extra allowances for the two new customers that he had brought in the previous day, namely Alan and Pete. He felt that he had done quite well out of it overall.

Just then, I caught a slight movement out of the corner of my eye so I turned slightly to see what it was and instantly froze. My blood turned to ice, as it had on two previous occasions in my life, on encountering a certain hammerhead shark and a giant green lizard. There, slowly crawling up the bonnet towards the windscreen was a great, big, hairy tarantula spider.

"L-l-l-l-look out," I managed to splutter, and they both turned round to see what the problem was. I was mesmerised, but George cooly took off one of his shoes and with one mighty 'Thwack,' splattered it against the bonnet. How ignorant we were about such creatures in those days. He put his shoe back on then nonchalantly asked if we wanted to take a ride round the block. Believe me, it was the last thing that I felt like doing, but there was no way I could let them see that so I gingerly climbed into the back seat.

I had no idea where the giant spider could have come from. I could only assume that it must have found a comfortable spot somewhere in the engine compartment. It could have been there for months for all any of us knew. It only took a few minutes to drive around the block, but it was one of the most uncomfortable few minutes of my life. Not because the car wasn't comfortable as the seats were luxury itself, but my eyes were searching every nook and cranny to make sure that there were no more hairy monsters coming out of them. I'm not normally afraid of spiders, but that one was the limit and I can't tell you how glad I was to get out of the car and into the house again.

Once my blood pressure had returned to normal, I reflected upon those afore mentioned encounters with the shark and the lizard where there had been little or no fast escape route. The encounter with the spider on the other hand did not quite qualify for a third instant cure for constipation as I had the whole of Australia in which to escape, but it still left me with a severe bowel complaint.

I was up with Alan at 5.30am Tuesday 30th March. Brian was also back at work (but still not quite out of the doghouse) so all three of us caught the bus back to the station and then the train back to Sydney. Again, as before, it was standing room only right into Central Station where we all went off in different directions. I hailed a taxi and was back onboard at 7.20am. The Chief Mate stood and watched me walk up the gangway but never said a word about me having had Monday off. He was probably as fed up as everyone else about the way the trip had gone. No one would have minded quite so much perhaps if the promise of a short trip of four to five months hadn't been made at the start of the trip.

* * *

We had been away by then for just a few days short of seven months with still no sign of when we could point our bows towards home. I went to my cabin, changed into my working gear and spent the day doing as little as possible. All of the five holds were over half full with the bags of flour so I didn't think I would be lucky enough to get another weekend. However, the dockers stopped work later that same day as they had loaded all that they had got, and we had to wait three days for more to arrive.

I met Alan again on the following weekend, Friday afternoon 2nd April, after I had spent the rest of the week performing normal, menial tasks around the ship. We had both arrived at Central Station a little earlier than the previous time so instead of having a quick beer, we decided to catch an earlier train that would take us up to a place called Blacktown, about four stops down from St. Mary's. As we were that little earlier, we both managed to get a seat all the way.

I asked Alan why he hadn't commuted in his new car and he replied that he didn't feel confident enough to drive around the city yet. I nearly asked if it was because he might get lost, but thought that I hadn't better. In any case, I thought that it was a wise decision of his, considering some of the driving I had seen in the city in the brief spaces of time that I had been in it.

The St. Mary's train came in at Blacktown almost immediately after ours, and as usual it was packed, so we had to stand the rest of the way. It was better than having to stand for the whole journey though. We again called into the pub for a quick, cold beer to put us right for the bus ride home. Mavis had our tea ready for us when we arrived, and I tucked in with relish to a lovely, big, juicy T-bone steak. I certainly did it justice.

A little later, just as it began to get dark, we all got into the car and went to a drive-in movie. I had always wanted to go to one just to see what it was like. It was a big area of open land with a giant screen at one end. We paid at the entrance gate and drove through. It was like a large car park with spaces laid out in front of the screen. As we pulled into one of the spaces Alan wound down his window, reached out for a microphone, that was hanging on a stump, through which we could listen to the soundtrack; he hooked it onto his window and turned it on.

The films being shown were Clint Eastwood in 'Hang 'em High' and 'Play Dirty' with Michael Caine. I didn't think that they were too bad but Mavis and the girls didn't seem too impressed as they fell asleep in the back of the car. It was a new experience for me, and I thoroughly enjoyed it. The films finished about midnight so we then went home and turned in.

The next morning Alan went to work so Mavis and I went into town to do some shopping. We had planned to walk it but hadn't got far when the man who had bought the bungalow next door, which Mavis had so desperately wanted me to have, pulled up and offered us a lift in his car. While driving, he told us that he and his wife had only been in Australia for six months. He used to be a Second Engineer in the Merchant Navy and both he and his wife liked it out there so far.

By that time, we had arrived in town so we didn't have much time to continue the conversation. He dropped us off at the post office and continued on his way. I posted some letters then followed Mavis around the shops until she had got all she wanted. We then went to the pub that Alan and I had called into a couple of times straight off the train. It was a stinking hot day and a refreshing glass of cold beer seemed to be called for. I went up to the bar and ordered two beers that disappeared fairly quickly, so I got two more.

Directly opposite where we were sitting was a door marked 'Gentlemen' in large letters. As we sat there, a man came out of the door carrying two glasses of beer. At least we assumed it was beer, but knowing Mavis's sense of humour and seeing the look on her face, I knew exactly what she thought was in those glasses. We looked at each other and said, "The mind boggles" and both burst out laughing. After that Mavis sat with her eyes glued to the door and practically everyone that came out was carrying something, which caused fresh bursts of laughter from our table. There was of course a corridor leading through from another bar, off which the toilets led, but we enjoyed the funny side of it before we finished our beers and walked home, where we watched TV until Alan returned from work and we had our tea.

That evening we got into the VW again and Alan took us all to Fairfield. Tom, John and the two Margs had already gone out so we left Karen and Catherine with the other kids and their minder and went to the Spanish style pub that they had taken me to when I had stayed with them. They were all sat there drinking so we joined them and had quite an enjoyable night until we were kicked out at closing time.

We went back to Tom's to pick up the two girls and to say my goodbyes to all of them again as I felt sure that I would be gone before the next weekend, and that I wouldn't see them again. We then drove back to St. Mary's and bed.

It was early to rise on Sunday, and after a little breakfast Mavis made up a large picnic hamper. When everything was ready, we set off again. Alan drove us about fifty miles to a place called Katoomba up in the Blue Mountains. It was a lovely little place and the ride to get there was very pleasant. We parked the car and went into a cafe for a cup of tea.

Behind the cafe was a proper picnic area with tables and benches set among the trees, so we sat down at one of them and attacked Mave's hamper. In a matter of minutes there wasn't so much as a crumb left.

We decided to take a stroll and came to a kind of observation platform where I could look down over the rail to see a sheer drop below my feet into the valley. We were so high that the trees below only looked about half an inch tall, so it was quite a drop. As I lifted my eyes across the expanse of the valley to the opposite side, I could see a wall of mountains rising from the green-carpeted forest floor, shimmering in a haze of blue. The whole spectacle was breathtakingly beautiful.

Just a little further on from the observation platform, we came to a spot where a small forest of trees was growing from a high plateau. The tops of all the trees were more or less level with our eyes, and flitting about among the branches was a large flock of multicoloured wild parrots. It was fascinating to watch them with their vivid reds, blues and greens; sometimes they came so close I could almost reach out and touch them.

We carried on along a narrow pathway, round the edge of the mountain until we could go no further as the path came to an end and was railed off. From there we overlooked a mountain rock that rose up from the valley with three high, narrow peaks like church spires. They were called the three sisters. Just to our left were some steep steps that went down the cliff face, to give people a view of the peaks from a different angle I presumed. I didn't know how far down they went and wasn't tempted to find out, as I thought I had a perfectly good view from where I was. Those that did go down came back up puffing and panting with red faces, so that may also have influenced my decision.

As we looked across, we could see a small group of people on the three sisters rock and could make out the small figure of a man halfway up one of the peaks. As we watched, he inched his way slowly to the top. When he finally made it and stood on the highest peak, a man standing next to me said indignantly, "So what did that prove?" I replied, "Maybe he got a rise out of it," to which he just snorted, shot me a funny look and walked off. Yet another person who didn't seem to approve of my sense of humour.

We followed him back along the path and came across a little park where the kids were allowed to play for the next twenty minutes. Alan then said that we should go to visit the lion park on our way back; that sounded like a good idea so we returned to the car and drove back through the little town of Katoomba, out on to the Great Western Highway.

After we had driven along the highway for about half an hour, Alan suddenly noticed a sign for Sydney that was pointing back the way that we had just come. He was of course going the wrong way so we had to turn around and go all the way back through Katoomba again. That caused another bout of the giggles again from Mavis. After that it was a straight road towards Sydney. We passed through lots of townships and suburbs on the way.

The traffic ground to a halt just outside a little place called Falconbridge. There was a long queue ahead of us, as far as the eye could see, and within minutes it was exactly the same behind us. The other side of the road was perfectly clear and after a while a police car came along. One of the policemen inside it was talking through a loudspeaker to let everyone know that there was an accident about a mile ahead. I thought, "What a good idea. It must eliminate a lot of frustration amongst all the drivers in the queue to at least know what the cause of the hold up was and how far away from it they were."

We all kept edging along a few feet at a time, and it took us ages to reach the scene of the accident. The two cars involved had obviously had a head on collision and judging by the way they were concertinaed up, I wouldn't have given much for the chances of anyone in them. We never did find out any more about it. Once we were clear of the accident scene we picked up speed again, drove up to Penrith where Brian and Sylvia lived, but instead of visiting them, we cut off to the right and across the countryside; eventually we came out at the Warragamba Dam.

As we drove towards the entrance of the African Safari Lion Park, we saw a sign on a tree in the thicket along either side of the road that said, "Drive through, but keep your windows closed." I supposed there must be some people around that needed telling! A little farther on we saw some signs stating that the park was closed, so we turned round and drove back through the countryside towards Penrith.

As soon as we hit the main road we found ourselves in another traffic jam, and from then on we literally crawled all the way back to St. Mary's. We finally arrived back home late in the afternoon, and we spent the rest of the evening watching TV, or rather the kids and I did, Mave and Alan fell asleep in their chairs.

At 5.30am the next morning, Alan and I rose from our beds, had breakfast and were soon ready to go. It was Monday 5th April. Mavis threw her arms around me and gave me a hug. They all had visible tears in their eyes as Mavis told the two little girls to "give Uncle Mick a kiss because you might never see him again." I replied that, "you never know, maybe one day we will come out for a holiday," then Alan and I set out on the by then familiar route of bus into town then train into Sydney.

Once back on Central Station Alan reiterated that if ever I wanted to bring Margaret out to live we would be welcome to stay with them until we could get settled in a place of our own. I thanked him, shook his hand and wished him good luck before he went off to work while I got a taxi back to the ship. I had thoroughly enjoyed the time spent with my friends away from the ship; I believe it helped to strengthen my resolve to leave the Merchant Navy.

I was heading towards my thirty-fifth birthday and thought that a normal life with my wife and a comfortable home was where my future lay. I had already written to Marg to tell her of my decision, and I felt sure that it would please her.

The next two days were spent battening down the hatches as each hold was completed. They were filled to the top with the bags of flour and, little by little, we got everything ready for sea. The last hold was finished at midday on Thursday 8th April and we sailed shortly afterwards. It had been confirmed that we were to go to Columbo in Ceylon (Sri Lanka), but there was no news as to where our destination was after that, so the crew's morale began to sink yet again.

* * *

Once clear of the Sydney Harbour entrance and out to sea again, we turned south for a little while, then later headed west around the tip of Southern Australia and on across the Australian Bight. Halfway across we hit some bad weather. It first became extremely cold then whipped up into gale force winds, the mountainous seas built up and crashed over the decks. There was also lots of rain day after day, but we continued to plough on through it as the ship rolled and bounced all over the place. There was very little sleep for any of us for the next five days.

As we gradually approached the coast of Western Australia, the storm slowly abated and the weather improved little by little. By the time we passed Albany we had started to see a little bit of sunshine occasionally. I was then on the twelve to four watch, and one night I saw something that I had never seen before: climbing up from the horizon, a white streak appeared just off our starboard bow.

As I watched fascinated, its edge began to travel across the sky in a large arc before it dropped back towards the horizon off our port bow. It formed a perfect, pearly white arc right in front of us, and the bow of the ship appeared to be heading right through the centre of it. The Second Mate came out and said that it looked just like Sydney Harbour Bridge. I commented that I hoped it wasn't an omen that the gods were telling us we were going to return there after Ceylon, even though I did have many friends there.

I don't think I deserved the look he gave me as he replied, "Well, if it is the gods, they are about the only ones sending us any orders." I took that as verbal confirmation that the officers were getting just as fed up as we were. I assumed that the beautiful, pearly white arc was some kind of albino rainbow without its colours; perhaps as it was night, it remained a pearly white with no sunlight to reflect off it.

The promise of a four to five month trip was by then a real fallacy, as we had been away for almost eight months and we still hadn't reached Columbo. On Thursday evening 15th April, we turned the corner of South Western Australia and headed in a more northwesterly direction out into the Indian Ocean up towards Ceylon. At that point the storms died down altogether. Each day got warmer and warmer until Tuesday 20th April, when we ran into some monsoons with tropical rain showers that came down in sheets like I had rarely seen before. They sprang up without any warning and stopped as instantly as they began.

We bathed in sunshine for a little while before the next one would hit us, and we were in amongst them for twenty-four hours, one after another, until they finally cleared away about midday on Wednesday. From then on, it became stinking hot.

We crossed the equator during the evening of Saturday 24th April, arriving and anchoring off Columbo on the following Monday afternoon. We topped all the derricks and did as much as we could in preparation for the discharging of the flour. As it turned out, there was no rush as we didn't go in until five o'clock the next afternoon, then we only tied up to buoys both fore and aft in the harbour, taking our place in a line of ships that were moored in the same way.

The dockers were expected to come out the next day and make a start but they didn't as there had been some trouble ashore and a curfew had been imposed. A few dockers had come onboard and slept wherever they could. One of them told us that anyone seen on the streets after 8.00pm would be shot without questions, so they couldn't go home. They were all right as long as they stayed within the dock area.

At 7.30pm that same evening, Wednesday 28th April, it began to rain heavily and gusts of wind hit us. We were suddenly in a violent thunderstorm. The ship astern of us broke away from her after moorings and as she was held on by her for'ard moorings to the buoy, the wind and rain caused her to swing around towards us.

She was frantically blowing her whistle that alerted one of the harbour tugs that was on standby close at hand. The tug's crew were well on the ball and they managed to insert the tug, with fenders all around her, into the rapidly decreasing gap between us, but they needed full power to push the ship away from us.

We later found out that the ship was fully loaded with high explosives. Sometimes, when those events happen, it's lucky you don't know the full extent of the danger you are really in. The tug eventually got her back into position and her crew tied her up again.

The following evening at 5.30pm we experienced another thunder storm, but it was not quite so severe as the previous one so there were no further incidents to cause excitement.

Next day one barge was brought out and was loaded with flour before it left again. From then on that's how it seemed to go, the odd barge coming out occasionally for a load. It began to look as though we could be there for weeks, and there was still no word from the company about further orders. That all resulted in the already low morale descending into a deep despondency amongst the crew again.

One day, to our surprise, the Bosun walked into our mess while we were eating our meal. He waved a piece of paper in the air and said, "Will those of you who wish to fly home please write their names on this?" For a moment there was a stunned silence before someone said, "You're joking?" "No I'm not" he said, "we have just received a message from the company that said that they thought eight months was long enough, and that any crewmember who wished to go home could fly home and a replacement would be flown out all at the company's expense," he replied.

Suddenly, the realisation that he was speaking the truth sank into all of us simultaneously, and a huge cheer resounded around the mess; the Bosun was almost flattened in the rush. He told us that it would take a few days to arrange it all especially as I don't think there was a single crewmember that didn't sign.

The days that followed saw a different atmosphere on the ship. It completely turned around. Everyone was happy, smiling and we were all mates again. On the morning of Friday 7th May, we all woke up to the news that the relief crew had arrived in Columbo during the early hours of the morning. They were currently at a hotel at the airport so they would be coming out to the ship later that day. The cheers rang out again.

Most of us had packed our cases days before, except for the clothes we needed to work in, and after breakfast we all set to work cleaning our cabins and the accommodation in general, then we showered and dressed in our best gear. We completed the last bits of packing and piled our cases in the recreation room. There was to be no more work for us, just anxious hours of waiting.

The day passed excruciatingly slowly, and it was after tea before a launch brought the new crew out. Most of them had obviously spent the day imbibing at the hotel bar or some similar oasis. They climbed up the gangway shouting, whistling and they had great difficulty in balancing. They pushed each other up with howls of merriment.

As soon as they were aboard most of them disappeared into various cabins and we didn't see them again so it was safe to assume that they simply crashed out into their bunks. We on the other hand, had to hang around for another hour before we were called into the officers' recreation room to have our discharges stamped into our books and receive our payslips.

We all took our luggage and climbed down into the launch, which took us ashore once we were all onboard. As I stepped onto dry land

I turned to look back at the '*Westbury*,' which had been my home for sixteen months over the three voyages since I had first joined her in Tilbury on the 8th January 1970, and I waved her goodbye. Then we all piled into a waiting bus with our luggage, which took us a short journey through the streets of Columbo and deposited us outside the doors of a hotel.

It was 7.45pm when we all traipsed into the reception where we were told that we must stay inside the hotel till morning. The curfew was still in force, and under no circumstances were we allowed out after 8.00pm. We were also informed that the bus would pick us up at midday the next day to take us to the airport, which was just over an hour's drive away.

After being given our keys to a room each, we all went in search of them. Mine was only two floors up and I was pleasantly surprised at how luxurious it was, and how spotlessly clean. Cynic that I am, I had assumed that we would have been put somewhere a little less posh. Maybe memories of the way we were treated on our journey home from Greece after my first trip influenced my train of thought in that, and I did not take into account how much things had moved on since those years I don't know, but I did know I wasn't going to knock the comfort I then found myself in.

The room was fitted with wall-to-wall thick pile carpet and had a large bed. Along one wall were a wardrobe and a chest of drawers; along another were three large, comfortable chairs. There was also a TV. The bathroom was situated behind a large screen and was bigger than I had expected.

Inside was a huge bath, separate shower, washbasin, toilet and bidet, the first I had ever seen in my life. I had no money to go down to the bar for a drink so I sat and watched TV for a while before I settled down for an early night. The next morning I made my way down to the dining room for breakfast. I chose a full English breakfast, but the portions were very small.

As it was quite early, most of the lads were still in bed, but there were a couple at the breakfast tables so I joined them. When we finished, we decided to take a short stroll around the local area to stretch our legs. It was safe to do so as it was then daylight. As we left the hotel with its air conditioning, the heat of the streets made us catch our breath even

601

though it was not yet eight o'clock, but we quite enjoyed walking up and down a couple of the little streets next to the hotel.

We turned one corner and saw a group of people waving their arms, shouting and haggling, so we decided to go to see what was happening. As we edged our way into the crowd, we could see a row of crudely built tables. They appeared to have been put together from anything and everything that had come to hand.

At first all we could see on the tables was a shimmering blanket of black flies. Only when some of them were disturbed by a hand waving them off could you see, for a brief moment before the flies landed again, that the vendors were selling fish. There was no mistaking the excitement of the customers who handed over their coins, but the smell and the sight of those flies to us were so vile that we moved away in haste and quickly returned to the hotel.

We hung around all morning thinking that the bus would pick us up at midday but it didn't arrive. At 12.30pm we were told to go into the dining room for lunch that looked like some sort of alien concoction and was inedible; the memory of all those flies on the fish outside didn't help my appetite.

All afternoon we waited in the hotel lounge and still the bus didn't arrive. At five o'clock we were all ushered in for tea. I never have been a great lover of seafood, in fact I can't stand the stuff, so I was disappointed to see crabs, prawns and the like as the only dish on offer. I know I had eaten octopus and jellyfish in a certain Japanese cafe once, but I hadn't known at the time of eating it what it was. That time I was in no doubt, but as I had not eaten lunch, I was by then starving. I also remembered the hunger pangs I had experienced on my journey home from abroad on my first trip and I didn't want a repeat performance on my last so, one by one, I put them into my mouth, closed my eyes and swallowed, and I promised myself that I would never again eat the vile creatures.

All of us by then had got a little worried as we had been told that it was over an hour's drive to the airport, and the bus still hadn't arrived by 6.45pm. We had visions of still being out in the streets after the curfew deadline of eight o'clock, so when the bus finally did arrive, we lost no time at all scrambling onto it.

Once out of the main city and into the outskirts, we could see small clusters of little huts through the windows of the bus as we passed. They were huddled together and seemed to be built out of literally anything that had come to hand. The immediate area surrounding the huts was a quagmire of mud with sad faced people dressed in rags and almost naked children wallowing around in it. The poverty was amongst the worst I had ever seen during all of my extensive travels.

It was exactly eight o'clock when we turned into the relative safety of the airport. Our Third Mate and some of our junior engineering officers were travelling with us but the Skipper and senior officers remained onboard the ship. They had to wait for their relief officers so that they could hand over before being flown home later. The Third Mate was in charge of all the tickets and documents. Once we were all off the bus, we carried our luggage into the terminal where we had to hang around again for a while.

A couple of the engineers disappeared for a time; they were probably the only ones with any money in their pockets and had wandered off to find a beer oasis. When they returned, we were hustled along to collect our luggage and get it checked in as quickly as possible. As it disappeared along a conveyor belt, we went through to wait in the departure lounge for about ten minutes before we boarded the plane that belonged to the Dutch Airways.

The plane was by no means full. There were plenty of empty seats and I was glad to have a window seat. I thought that at least I might have something to look at for part of the journey. We took off at about nine o'clock, and as I was not used to flying, my heart went walk about down into my stomach for a while as we climbed into the sky. It soon settled back into its rightful place once we levelled out.

At first I could see lots of lights down below, but it soon went totally black so I assumed that we were flying over the sea. The flight crew then served us with a hot prepacked lunch that wasn't too bad, although, just like the hotel, there wasn't much of it. We washed it down with a couple of small cans of beer and there was definitely nowhere near enough of that for most of us. We spent the next two hours or so dozing or talking, and I spent a lot of time just sitting and feeling the vibrations of the plane as I stared out of the window into the darkness. I was hoping to spot something just as if I was on lookout.

It was midnight when we landed at Bombay (Mumbai) and we were told to disembark. As soon as we walked out of the plane, the heat hit us hard. We had to climb down the gangway and take a short walk across the tarmac to the transit lounge. There had obviously just been a downpour as the heat was causing great clouds of steam to rise up from the ground. It was as if we were walking through a large sauna, and although we were just in our shirtsleeves, we all felt hot and sticky in the few minutes it took us to walk to the comparative coolness of the lounge.

Once inside we found that it was quite a large room, and we took the opportunity to stretch our legs a little and walked around. On one wall there was a small screen with rows of chairs in front of it so after a while most of us sat down as a film was shown.

I thought it might have helped to pass the time, but as I have no grasp of the Indian language, I soon lost interest. Perhaps because we were then on terra firma, I fell asleep in the chair and the next thing I knew, Ben was shaking me awake and everyone was walking out towards the plane ready to board again.

I had only slept for about an hour and we were all back in our seats by 1.30am. It was Sunday 9th May and we took off at 2.00am. I felt a little apprehensive as we began the ascent but was soon OK again once on level keel. More passengers had joined us onboard and the plane was nearly full. We were then fed again, and once everything was cleared away, they informed us that it was an eight-hour flight to Athens and suggested that we all try to get some sleep and they turned out the lights.

As tired as I felt, I was unable to sleep again perhaps due to being in the air I don't know, so I spent the rest of the night staring out into the darkness again, twisting and turning in my seat in a desperate attempt to get comfortable, but I was unsuccessful. All the different tones and notes of the various snoring didn't help one bit so it was with a feeling of great relief when I saw the first glimmers of light through the window. I sat there watching the new day being born and I hoped that the letter I had sent home to let Marg know I was coming would arrive before I did. As I looked down out of my window, I could see that we were flying in a patch of sky above a vast sea of cloud. The other passengers gradually began to wake up and at eight o'clock we ate again.

We landed at Athens airport at 9.30am where again we had to disembark, but that time we were collected by buses that came out to transport us to the transit lounge about half a mile away. That lounge was much more comfortable than the one in Bombay, and I was not the only one glad of the chance to walk about and stretch my legs for a while before I settled down in a comfortable chair. I think I must have gone past the sleep barrier as despite being awake all night, I just couldn't nod off, even though I was comfortable. I sat there talking to Ben for most of the time.

After two hours the buses came to take us back to the plane, and we took off at about midday. I had got used to the take off and landings by then and in a strange way I had begun to enjoy them.

By mid-afternoon we were flying over the Alps. There was no cloud around anywhere and the views below were really stark and foreboding, but at the same time, absolutely breathtakingly beautiful. As far as the eye could see was a vista of barren, angry looking peaks and valleys. I could see icy glaciers dotted about, and here and there were some snow-covered mountain peaks, like the fingers of a giant hand reaching out towards us as if trying to pluck us out of the sky. It was a frightening thought that if anything happened right there and then, we wouldn't stand a chance.

My mind also went back to my very first trip all those years ago on the 'Oakhill' in 1954, when we had paid off in Greece. That time we had travelled through the Alps by train and an extremely kind Arab gentleman with his packet of chocolate biscuits saved my life. I thought that it was somehow fitting that that was on my first trip, and this time I was flying over the Alps going home on my very last trip.

Just under two hours later, we landed at Frankfurt. A few of the passengers disembarked but the rest of us had to remain onboard to continue our journey about an hour later. I sat and looked down from my little window and picked out the lights of various towns and villages where they were starting to glimmer in the growing darkness again. We were then given another meal.

Upon landing at Amsterdam at around 7.00pm, we had to disembark once more. We all milled around the transit lounge while the Third Mate and a couple of the engineers went off to sort out our connecting flight to Heathrow. When they returned the news was not good. The connecting plane had already left. I had thought that it was all going too smoothly. The three of them vanished again to try to sort something out and were gone for over two hours; it all seemed very familiar to me.

When they came running back, they told us that our luggage was already being loaded on to a plane and that we had to board immediately. We did a quick check to make sure everyone was there, and fortunately we had all stayed together so we were ushered straight through to the plane. The flight was an American Pan Am plane, which was travelling from Amsterdam to London practically empty, presumably to pick up most of its passengers at Heathrow for the journey home to the States.

In comparison to the previous plane on which we had spent so many hours, the American one was very spacious and comfortable with plenty of legroom. The stewardesses were very nice too. I imagine that Pan Am were glad to find a group like us to fill some of the empty seats. The question of payment for those seats would be settled between the shipping company and the airline later I assumed, after our return home, if indeed, it hadn't been already. We were certainly lucky to find a flight for the whole group of us.

There was hardly time for us to settle in our seats before we took off. It was ten o'clock and we landed at Heathrow just an hour later. At last we were back in good old England, just a little over thirty hours since we had left the hotel in Columbo. As we walked through the arrivals gate, we were met by a representative of the company who ushered us into a room where three other company men were sat at a table ready to pay us off.

As they gave us our money (all of it, not just ten pounds as had happened to me on the other occasions that I had been paid off abroad), they let us know that one of the company's ships, the 'Royston Grange,' would be signing on about the time that our leave was up. They said that they would let us know when and give us first chance of signing on if we wished to. I told them not to bother with me as I had decided that it was my last voyage. They said that they would let me know anyway in case I changed my mind.

We were told that a bus was waiting to take us into London so we went to collect our luggage and none was missing. There was no delay through customs, so we were soon on the bus and on our way. I said my goodbyes to Ben and the others as they were dropped off at Paddington while I went on to Euston. Yet again I was lucky enough to find my train standing at the platform and in no time at all I was on my way home.

Once at Birmingham New Street, I had no problem in getting a taxi to Bloxwich and he dropped me off outside my house just after 1.30am on Monday 10th May. Margaret had received my letter so she was expecting me at any time, but due to the lateness of the hour I still let myself in quietly and crept up the stairs to let her know I was home, frightening the life out of her again. She soon forgave me and got up to cook me a big fry up. I was home for good.

EPILOGUE

At the end of my allotted leave I received a letter from the company that asked me if I wanted to go back. I had not changed my mind so I just ignored it. Some decisions you make can have a profound effect in life and that turned out to be one of them. I would have loved to have sailed on more trips with Ben, and I felt certain in my mind that he would have sailed on the '*Royston Grange.*' Imagine my horror a few weeks later to hear on the news that the '*Royston Grange*' had been in a collision with another ship in the River Plate and had been engulfed in a ball of flames. All hands had died.

Although I had Ben's phone number, I was afraid to use it in case it confirmed my worst fears. For whatever reason, I felt that it was better not to know. I don't know how many of my ex-shipmates from the '*Westbury*' had sailed on her and I don't suppose I shall ever find out.

It was more than twenty years later when we (Margaret and I) were having a big clear out, that we came across the piece of paper with Ben's phone number on it. Without telling me, Margaret rang them and Jean answered. After finding out what had happened to Ben, she came running to tell me that Ben was fine and was right there in the room with Jean at home. That was really good news and we had a good chat.

While holidaying in Falmouth the following year, we went to Polruan and knocked on their door. They made us very welcome and we had a great reunion. I believed that fate had dealt me a really good hand when I made the decision not to return to sea, and my jinx was over for good as I feel sure that I would have been on the 'Royston Grange' and as it turned out, Ben wouldn't have sailed with me.

He had been called back for the 'Royston Grange' and had already left the house when Jean received a telephone call from the company: they wanted Ben to join another ship. Jean rushed out and just managed to catch him in time at the railway station. Fate had been even more kind to him that day.

When I was a youth
I travelled the world
Each day that I lived
A new adventure unfurled.

For I was a sailor
In love with the sea
She was my mistress
Who meant so much to me.

I was young and single
And so full of life
The seas and the oceans
They were my wife.

I then met a girl
Sent from heaven above
A human being
I could cherish and love.

My love grew so strong
It was apparent to me
That true love was for her
And not for the sea.

But I was a nomad
Who was given to roam
Not to stay put
And build up a home.

How would I cope?
So far away from the sea?
That was a problem
Which so bothered me.

But that was made easy
The adjustment in life
By the wonderful girl
Who was now my new wife.

When I walked ashore
She held my hand
Which made me believe
I could live on this land.

The waves in her hair
Were the waves of the ocean
That captivated me
And all my devotion.

When I looked in her eyes
I firstly hadn't a clue
But then suddenly realised
They were the oceans so blue.

Her smile was the sun
Which kept me so warm
And gave me more happiness
Since the day I was born.

So yes, my first love
Was the oceans and sea
And a place in my heart
There always will be.

But my love for this girl
And her love for me
Is what gave me the strength
to give up the sea.

Printed in Great Britain
by Amazon

43480729R00354